Advance praise for
A BOUNTIFUL HARVEST

"These letters between two old friends, each a master of his craft, are a delight. They are full of wit and high spirits, and shot through with Rabelaisian humor. Along the way, we learn a good deal about architecture and enjoy a feast of literary gossip, as well as recondite bits of lore. Such gifts for a reader are rare."

ELEANOR COOK, UNIVERSITY OF TORONTO
author of *Elizabeth Bishop at Work*, and *A Reader's Guide to Wallace Stevens*

"In their rapid shifts between intimacy, reflection, verbal wit, playful impersonations, and satirical sketches, their moving acts of memory and sharp notes on human foibles, these letters offer a fascinating map of two minds, one a great American poet and the other an important scholar of ancient architecture. Along with a sense of beauty, a strong, often dark sense of history, a vital sense of inherited culture, marks both writers, and it's perhaps no accident that thoughts of Rome, city of ruins and reconstructions, so often link the two in their letters."

KENNETH GROSS, UNIVERSITY OF ROCHESTER
author of *The Dream of the Moving Statue*, and *Shakespeare's Noise*

"In the elegance, gravity, and genius of Anthony Hecht's poetry, we sometimes catch a spirit of repartee – the same spirit that animates so much of the correspondence in this volume. In each letter Hecht exchanged with the Roman architectural historian William L. MacDonald, we follow the chase of wit from salutation to subscription. Philip Hoy's graceful and discerning practice as editor achieves his sought-after 'Accuracy / Relevance / Concision / Interest,' illuminating their minds at work and play on the page."

SASKIA HAMILTON, BARNARD COLLEGE
editor of *The Letters of Robert Lowell,* and co-editor (with Thomas Travisano) of
Words in Air: The Complete Correspondence Between Elizabeth Bishop and Robert Lowell

"Reading the correspondence of poet Anthony Hecht and architectural historian William L. MacDonald is like listening in on an extended, intimate, learned, and always entertaining conversation between two extraordinary men – witty raconteurs, brilliant intellectuals and incisive wordsmiths – as they explore their interior lives, comment on friends and events, and return, again and again, to the tribulations and joys of their creative work."

JOHN PINTO, PRINCETON UNIVERSITY
author of *The Trevi Fountain*, and co-author (with Elisabeth Kieven) of *Pietro Bracci and
Eighteenth-Century Rome: Drawings for Architecture and Sculpture in the Canadian Centre for
Architecture and Other Collections*

Advance praise for
A Bountiful Harvest

"It is rare to find a pair of writers with such exhilarating flair for the epistolary sport as Hecht and MacDonald. Still rarer is it for letters to find so judicious and resourceful an editor as Philip Hoy. I am reminded of a great Wimbledon final: the players have all the shots, and the umpire never misses a call."

Jonathan Post, University of California, Los Angeles
author of *A Thickness of Particulars: The Poetry of Anthony Hecht*,
and editor of *The Selected Letters of Anthony Hecht*

"Robert Frost said he entertained ideas only to see if they entertained him. Hecht and MacDonald devote all their energies to entertaining each other. They sign off letters by the likes of Sir Cairo Portcullis, or Eddie Puss, or Timon of Akron, or Engle & Bert Humperdinck. They revel in shared feelings of contempt for a mutually disliked colleague, 'The great arch-fool and world's leading nitwit.' Hecht offers to provide 'filthy pictures' for MacDonald's book on Russian cities and does so under the name Jeremy Bentham. For these two close friends, every letter was a chance to perform in strikingly amusing ways. Now we can share in these entertaining performances."

William Pritchard, Amherst College
author of *Updike: America's Man of Letters*, and *Frost: A Literary Life Reconsidered*

"This is a unique and exhilarating yield indeed, a decades-long epistolary exchange between two of late twentieth-century America's wittiest and most creative minds, inventing as they go a parlance (mostly English, with much exotic admixture) at once deeply learned and wickedly ribald, parodically arch and touchingly percipient. More often than not the points of departure are the visual arts, architecture, and literature, and other subjects include extravagant 'lagniappes of culture,' while in counterpoint we have Philip Hoy's energetic, resourceful exactitude. His curiosity shines its light into every nook and cranny – crook and nanny, as one under the pertinent influence might say – and indeed there are moments at which the reader suspects the editor is participating in the game he broadcasts. His scrupulous notes about their stationery dovetail with the correspondents' ingenious allonyms, and his carefully chosen photos and other visual aids provide welcome context.

"Turn to this book at any point for spiritual stimulation – as inspiration for an essay on the classical, the romantic, or the baroque, as an antidote to academic ennui, as a *livre de chevet* – and be gratified and thankful."

Stephen Yenser, University of California, Los Angeles
author of *The Consuming Myth: The Work of James Merrill*
and co-editor of the *Selected Letters of James Merrill*

A Bountiful Harvest

A Bountiful Harvest

THE CORRESPONDENCE OF

Anthony Hecht

AND

William L. MacDonald

EDITED BY PHILIP HOY

WAYWISER

First published in 2018 by

THE WAYWISER PRESS

Christmas Cottage, Church Enstone, Chipping Norton, Oxfordshire, OX7 4NN, UK
P. O. Box 6205, Baltimore, MD 21206, USA
https://waywiser-press.com

Editor-in-Chief
Philip Hoy

Senior American Editor
Joseph Harrison

Associate Editors
Eric McHenry | Dora Malech | V. Penelope Pelizzon | Clive Watkins
Greg Williamson | Matthew Yorke

Anthony Hecht's correspondence copyright © 2018 by The Estate of Anthony Hecht
William L. MacDonald's correspondence copyright © 2018 by The Estate of William L. MacDonald
Editorial matter copyright © 2018 by Philip Hoy

The right of Philip Hoy to be identified as the editor of this work
has been asserted by him in accordance with section 77 of the
Copyright, Designs and Patents Act of 1988.

All rights reserved. No part of this publication may be reproduced, stored in a
retrieval system, or transmitted in any form or by any means, electronic, mechanical,
photocopying, recording, or otherwise, without the prior permission of both the
copyright owner and the above publisher of this book.

9 7 5 3 1 2 4 6 8

A CIP catalogue record for this book is available from the British Library

ISBN 978-1-904130-90-1

Printed and bound by
T. J. International Ltd., Padstow, Cornwall, PL28 8RW, UK

To J. D. McClatchy

*... for in companions
That do converse and waste the time together,
Whose souls do bear an equal yoke of love,
There must be needs a like proportion
Of lineaments, of manners, and of spirit ...*

Contents

Introduction 11

A Note on the Text 21

1. 1957–1968 27

2. 1969–1980 47

3. 1981–1992 277

Afterword 459

Chronology 467

Glossary of Names 479

Acknowledgments 511

Index 517

Principal Publications

Anthony Hecht

A Summoning of Stones
The Hard Hours
Jiggery-Pokery: A Compendium of Double Dactyls
edited by AH and John Hollander, with illustrations by Milton Glaser
Aeschylus: Seven Against Thebes
translated by AH and Helen Bacon
Millions of Strange Shadows
The Venetian Vespers
Obbligati: Essays in Criticism
The Essential Herbert
edited and with an introduction by AH
Collected Earlier Poems
The Transparent Man
The Hidden Law: The Poetry of W. H. Auden
On the Laws of the Poetic Art: The A. W. Mellon Lectures in the Fine Arts, 1992
Flight Among the Tombs
The Darkness and the Light
Melodies Unheard: Essays on the Mysteries of Poetry
Collected Later Poems
Anthony Hecht: Selected Poems
edited by J. D. McClatchy
Interior Skies: Late Poems from Liguria
with engravings by Abigail Rorer, and a foreword by Philip Hoy

William L. MacDonald

Early Christian & Byzantine Architecture
The Architecture of the Roman Empire, Vol. I: An Introductory Study
Northampton, Massachusetts: Architecture & Buildings
The Pantheon: Design, Meaning, and Progeny
Piranesi's Carceri: Sources of Invention
Columns in the Collection of the Cooper-Hewitt Museum
The Architecture of the Roman Empire, Vol. II: An Urban Appraisal
Hadrian's Villa and Its Legacy
with John Pinto

Introduction

Anthony Hecht and William L. MacDonald met for the first time in the fall of 1954, shortly after each had arrived in Rome, Hecht on a Guggenheim Fellowship, MacDonald on a Rome Fellowship at the American Academy.

Hecht was 31 years old, and MacDonald 33; both were recently married; and each was on his way to making a name for himself, Hecht as one of the era's most esteemed poets, and MacDonald as one of its most accomplished architectural historians.

Though neither man could have realized it at the time, this was to be the start of a friendship which would endure for the better part of four decades, a friendship that would generate a large body of correspondence – a total of 440 letters and postcards have come down to us – the character of which is likely to come as a surprise to anyone who knew the men only from their published works.

The Background

Anthony Evan Hecht was born in New York City on January 16th, 1923, the first son of Melvyn Hahlo Hecht and Dorothea Grace Hecht (née Holzman). Hecht Sr., had been a student at Harvard, but left before graduating after his father went blind and he was obliged take over his father's business, The New England Enamel Company.

After schooling in Manhattan, Hecht entered Bard College, an experimental adjunct of Columbia University situated in Annandale-on-Hudson, upstate New York, in 1940, and it was there that he discovered his passion for poetry. His studies were interrupted when, in 1943, he joined the U.S. Army's Enlisted Reserve Corps. After training he was assigned to the 97th Infantry Division, and shipped to Europe, where he saw action on the German front, amongst other things taking part in the liberation of Flossenbürg concentration camp. Before his discharge in the spring of 1946, he also spent several months on occupation duty in Japan.

Hecht was awarded his B.A. *in absentia*, and on returning to civilian life enrolled as a non-matriculating student at Kenyon College in Ohio. There he was taught by John Crowe Ransom and Charles Coffin, but he also encountered Allen Tate, who was to play an important part in his life. Hecht began his teaching career at Kenyon, and had his first poems published in *The Kenyon Review*. Late in 1947, however, while working as a graduate teaching assistant at the State University of Iowa, he had a nervous breakdown, suffering from what would nowadays be called Post-Traumatic Stress Syndrome.

After leaving the New York hospital where he was treated, he remained in the city, undergoing psychoanalysis, but he also persuaded Allen Tate, then lecturing at New York University, to see him for private tuition. When, not much later, Tate accepted an appointment at the University of Minnesota, he made his high opinion of the twenty-five year old clear by recommending that he take over his teaching at NYU, something Hecht was very happy to do.

Hecht enrolled for an M.A. at Columbia University in the fall of 1949, and graduated in 1950 with a dissertation entitled "Poetry as a Form of Knowledge." After this, using money left over from his army discharge, he went back to Europe, staying for a time in Amsterdam, and then heading south to the island of Ischia, some twenty miles off the coast of Naples. There he met W. H. Auden, who had been summering on the island since 1949, and who proved to be very encouraging of his work. Still on Ischia in May 1951, he learnt that the American Academy of Arts and Letters had awarded him the first ever Rome Fellowship in Literature, an honor which would allow him to spend a whole year at the American Academy in Rome.

Hecht arrived at the Academy's Villa Aurelia, a magnificent 17th Century building perched on top of Rome's second highest hill, the Janiculum, in October, and embarked on what he later told me was "one of the most satisfactory experiences of my life ... Rome to me was a revelation: exciting, beautiful, full of infinite complexity. One of the great luxuries of a year at the [AAR] was the opportunity to spend that time in the august company of classicists, archaeologists, art and architectural historians, who were brilliantly illuminating to listen to about every aspect of the city ..."[1]

The year in Rome was a very productive one: not only did he write most of the poems that went into his first collection, he also found time to collaborate with the composers Lukas Foss and Leo Smit, producing translations of Rilke for the former and a cycle of his own poems for the latter.

After his Fellowship in Rome came to an end, in September 1952, Hecht returned to the States and within days was teaching at his alma mater, Bard College, where he had been offered an instructorship. At Bard he got to know Saul Bellow, Irma Brandeis, Heinrich Blücher, and, through Blücher, Blücher's wife, Hannah Arendt. He also started to encounter some of the contemporary poets he would most come to admire, amongst them Mona Van Duyn, Robert Fitzgerald, John Hollander, Richard Howard, W. S. Merwin, Howard Moss, Howard Nemerov, Mark Strand, and Richard Wilbur.

In early 1954, Hecht married Patricia Harris, an aspiring model. He also celebrated the publication of *A Summoning of Stones*, his first collection of poems, which attracted a small number of mostly positive notices. Joseph Bennett, writing for *The Hudson Review*, described it as "a first volume of sustained charm and elegance," and

---

1 *Anthony Hecht in Conversation with Philip Hoy* (London: Between The Lines, 1999), p. 38.

praised Hecht's "most individual style, a sort of reflective effervescence set in variable mood-keys." Arthur Mizener, writing for *The Kenyon Review*, also praised the collection, but with some caveats: "*A Summoning of Stones* ... shows [Mr Hecht] to be a poet of great charm, possibly even too great charm, for when these poems fall below [his] highest standard, as of course they occasionally do, it is always because his witty fancy gets out of control."[1] Striking a not dissimilar note in the *New Yorker*, Louise Bogan wrote, "If Hecht, often disturbed by disorder and death, is drawn to ideal proportion, elegance and color ... he is yielding to promptings that at his age only a fanatically serious spectator would deny him."[2]

In 1954, Hecht was also awarded a Guggenheim Fellowship, a grant which enabled him to finance another year's stay in Rome. He and Pat arrived there in late September or early October and took up temporary residence at the Villa Aurelia while they looked around for an apartment they could rent for the rest of their stay. Hecht's first impressions on his return to Rome were unfavorable. Writing to his parents on October 3rd, he said: "We met [Laurance] Roberts and his wife as soon as we arrived; they were cordial and friendly, as usual. I saw Frank Brown for just a moment before he left for England and America, and there are two people back again (as I am) who were here when I was here. They were not particularly close friends of mine, and on the whole the group here now is a lot more solemn and less lively than the one I knew before."[3] Not even the news that Richard Wilbur was at the Academy that year – they had already met at a cocktail party in New York, and were admirers of each other's work – was enough to lift his spirits. Although he didn't rule out the possibility that things would improve once people got to know each other, he told his parents he didn't think it likely.

Personal problems were almost certainly coloring Hecht's judgment of the situation. He and Pat had only been married for seven months, but they were already experiencing difficulties. Perhaps not coincidentally, Hecht was also having trouble with his work, there being little or nothing to show for the five or six months he had already spent on the Guggenheim Fellowship. The situation was made no easier by the discovery – made shortly after Hecht had sent that letter to his parents – that Pat was pregnant. Late in November, however, she miscarried. There was talk of her returning to the States as soon as she had recovered, and of his following her once she had settled in and found work; but the miscarriage seems to have brought the couple closer together again, and plans for an early return were put on hold.

However difficult things were for the couple during those early months in Rome, it is clear that Hecht changed his mind about the people he was mixing with at the Academy. These included the sculptor Dimitri Hadzi, the architect Robert Venturi, the composer Yehudi Wyner, and the artist Jack Zajac, each of whom he came to admire and befriend. The group also included William L. MacDonald, who was embarking on a two-year Fellowship in Classics and Archaeology. MacDonald had

---

1 Arthur Mizener, *The Kenyon Review*, 16:3 (Summer, 1954), pp. 473-481.
2 Louise Bogan, *The New Yorker*, June 5th, 1954, p. 134.
3 *The Selected Letters of Anthony Hecht*, p. 106.

arrived at the Academy at the same time as Hecht, after first crossing the Atlantic on board the SS Liberté, spending some time touring the English home counties, and then driving down through France, Germany, Austria, and northern Italy. He brought with him his own recently-married wife, Dale (née Ely).

William Lloyd MacDonald, Jr., to give him his full name, was born in Putnam, Connecticut on July 12th, 1921, the second son of William Lloyd MacDonald, Sr., and Susan MacDonald (née Elrod). MacDonald Sr., a graduate of Brown University, had started out as a school teacher, but by the time of his second son's birth had a successful career in banking. After schooling in Byfield, Massachusetts, and Sanford, Maine, MacDonald Jr. had entered the University of New Hampshire, but he withdrew after just one term, finding it a bad fit. The year after that, he moved to Boston, where he found employment in the ticket office of American Airlines, and started dating Betsey Adams Schadt. The very next year, he and Betsey moved to Bangor, Maine, and there they got married.

MacDonald served in the United States Army Air Corps during the war, being trained as a Bombardier/Navigator but serving as an Air Instructor and as a Bombardier Instructor, first at Kirtland Field in Albuquerque, New Mexico, then at Smyrna Air Base near Nashville, Tennessee, and finally at Santa Ana Air Base in Costa Mesa, California, where he rose to the rank of First Lieutenant.

After the war, he and Betsey divorced, and he entered Harvard, where he studied with Kenneth John Conant and Robert Pierpoint Blake, and encountered a number of people who would become lifelong friends, amongst them Arthur Trottenberg and Gerry Gillerman (who nicknamed him MacDonaldstein).

MacDonald obtained his B.A. in 1949, but stayed on at Harvard, first as a candidate for the M.A., which was conferred in 1953, and then as a candidate for the Ph.D. Between 1950 and 1954, he lectured in the history of architecture at the Architectural Center in Boston, Massachusetts, and, between 1953 and 1954, he also taught classics at Wheaton College in Norton, Massachusetts.

It was in 1952, at a party in Cambridge, Massachusetts, that he first met Dale Ely, a graduate of Wells College in Aurora, New York, who, during the three years after the war, worked as a model in France – where she was pursued by the republic's future President, Valéry Giscard d'Estaing – then worked as a stewardess for Pan American Airways, and by the time of their meeting was working as a junior editor at Little Brown. The couple were married the following year, and shortly after that MacDonald was awarded the Rome Prize, which enabled him to quit teaching and move with Dale to Rome, where he continued working on his doctoral dissertation.

MacDonald was new not just to the Academy but to Rome itself, and a journal he and Dale kept at this time makes it clear just how wholeheartedly the couple embraced their new circumstances. His (mostly handwritten) and her (mostly typed) entries tell of just how excited they both were. "The setup couldn't be better – for the work we want to do, and for wonderful living," wrote Dale, drafting out a letter to friends back home. "[T]his atmosphere of intelligent people will spoil me completely should we end up sometime in an average neighborhood – that sounds very snobbish, but these people have, most of them, a genuine curiosity in knowing what the world's about, and a number of them have a few of the answers."[1]

How quickly Hecht started to reassess the people he was getting to know during his second sojourn in Rome isn't entirely clear, but it seems to have been within a matter of weeks. The MacDonalds' journal gives an almost daily account of the people they were spending time with, the places they were visiting, and the things they were doing. The first mention of the Hechts occurs on October 24th, three and a half weeks after their arrival, when we learn that they went to the beach with Yehudi Wyner's wife Nancy and "Pat and Tony Hecht."[2] The next reference to the couple is in a more interesting entry for October 30th: "We are having Wyners, Zajac, Hechts, and [the sculptor Ira] Matteson in for martinis before dinner, then on to the Wyners' bemasked and bepunched Halloween blast."[3] This was almost certainly the evening MacDonald recollected in a letter he sent to Hecht two and a half decades later: "Off to The Hub to see D'Oyly Carte's Iolanthe. Was it not the patter song therefrom that brought us together in Yehudi [Wyner]'s studio that night in '54?"[4]

Interesting though they are, the MacDonalds' journals rarely do more than catalogue their daily activities. We know whom they met, where they went, and what they did, but only occasionally does one or other of them say what they thought about these things, and when they do, it is usually to extol the beauty of their surroundings. As a result we can only guess how the friendship developed which started that evening in Yehudi Wyner's studio – with Hecht and MacDonald doubtless taking it in turns to recite verses from Gilbert & Sullivan's so-called "Nightmare Song." Overlapping interests will have played a big part – Hecht's in architecture and MacDonald's in literature – but it's not until we read their later correspondence that we can begin to appreciate how many things they had in common.

MacDonald finished work on his doctoral dissertation in the spring of 1955, and a journal entry for March 17th tells us that Dale was hard at work typing it for him. There is then a longish gap, with the next entry in this journal not being made till May 29th. In the intervening weeks, the couple made what MacDonald later called "the trip of a lifetime," driving all the way to Israel and back, going through Greece, Turkey, Syria, and Lebanon on the way out and through the former Yugoslavia on the way back.[5] According to the May 29th entry which records their return to the AAR, they had covered 8,000 miles in nine and a half weeks – an average of 120 miles a day.

Disappointing news awaited them: MacDonald's dissertation had been rejected by the two examiners to whom his supervisor had submitted it. His response to this was surprisingly stoical: "They're undoubtedly right, but the system got gummed

---

1 Journal entry for October 3rd, 1954, p. 3.

2 Journal entry for October 24th, 1954, p. 10.

3 Journal entry for October 30th, 1954, p. 10.

4 See letter #208, dated August 19th, 1978.

5 The longish gap mentioned in the previous sentence was only a longish gap in this particular journal; the MacDonalds kept a separate journal for their trip.

up somewhere."[1] At least he wasn't being refused the chance to re-submit, and over the summer he went to work on a new dissertation, this one devoted to the hippodrome structure in Byzantium. A rough draft of this was seen and approved by the examiners – not, as MacDonald observed, without one of them appending some "acid comments" – as early as the following October,[2] and although more work had to be done, he was awarded the Ph.D in time for his return to the States in the summer of 1956.

An entry in the MacDonalds' journal for June 9th, 1955 reads as follows: "Gil Franklin gave a party in the Villino in honor of the departing – Pat Hecht, the Whites [Bobby and Claire], & Wilburs [Dick and Charlee]."[3] The plan for Pat's return to the States had been revived, but she was to return without Hecht, who would not follow for several months. He travelled with her to Naples, and on June 13th saw her aboard the SS Cristoforo Columbo, which was sailing for New York. Instead of going straight back to Rome, however, Hecht took a ferry to Ischia, where he had spent so many enjoyable months on his previous stay in Italy. Two days later, on the 15th, he wrote to his father, letting him know that Pat was on her way back, and expressing the hope that the break would be good for him and for his work. "This would have been a very difficult letter to write if I had written it when I first intended," he explained, "but I am feeling a good deal better now, and I have some friends from the Academy staying here with me, and am settling down to a calmer view of things."[4] The unnamed friends were almost certainly the MacDonalds, whose journal entry for July 28th looks back on what they had been doing since the middle of June, and notes: "Went to Ischia for 5 days with Tony …"[5] Again, unfortunately, no more is said.

When Hecht returned to Rome towards the end of the summer, he moved into an apartment belonging to the poet, actress, and former artists' model, Iris Tree, whom he'd met while on Ischia, and who had offered him the use of her place while she was away in London. Not until he arrived there did he understand quite how generous this offer had been: "Her apartment was at the top of the building right next to the Keats house, and one storey higher, so that it looked out over the Keats house at the Spanish Steps and the Piazza di Spagna, across the city to St. Peter's in the west, and just about everywhere else. Moreover, very neat and small as the apartment was, it boasted a very large terrace with plants and flowering oleander – just the place for cocktail parties, which, trust me, I gave for my Roman friends."[6] The MacDonalds record one such party in their journal, a party which was attended by the Irish actress Constance Smith, amongst others: "Full moon, or nearly full, over the Trinità dei Monti. The

---

1 Journal entry for May 29th, 1955, p. 28.

2 Journal entry for October 31st, 1955, p. 36.

3 Journal entry for June 9th, 1955, p. 31.

4 Letter, AH to Melvyn Hecht, June 15th, 1955, *The Selected Letters of Anthony Hecht*, p. 110.

5 Journal entry for July 28th, 1955, p. 32.

6 Letter, AH to B. H. Fairchild, July 25th, 1998, *The Selected Letters of Anthony Hecht*, p. 296. The apartment is well described in Daphne Fielding's biography of Tree, *The Rainbow Picnic* (London: Eyre Methuen, 1974), pp.121–122.

cloisters of that church were one pale gold color in the sunset and the Medici Palace was a richer orange, both facing down over Rome, lovely. This dusk and moonrise had that quickened knife-sharp light that would make any party magic."[1]

Early in December 1955 MacDonald noted in his journal: "Dale to MD: 95% Yes." Dale was pregnant with their first child, and even though they hadn't yet spoken to their own families about it, that same evening they made a point of telling Hecht: "Tony came up after dinner, and we heaved the news at him."[2] We might ponder the odd choice of words here. Why would this piece of news have to be heaved at Hecht rather than simply given to him? One possible explanation is that the MacDonalds weren't entirely overjoyed at the news themselves, if only because of its timing. MacDonald had been sending off numerous job applications, and none of them had come to anything, so that he and Dale were facing a somewhat uncertain future. A more likely explanation is that they knew all about the Hechts' marital problems, and were aware that the couple's six-month separation, which Hecht had hoped would free him to write poems, had done nothing to help. This had left Hecht deeply dejected, as we can see from a letter he sent his parents in early November, by which time he was once again staying at the Academy:

"I have been back from my trip for some time, and should have written before but didn't, and for reasons that I shall try to explain. For one thing, I wanted very much to get back to work, and didn't want any excuse for not working to get in the way of it. But the work has been going forward with the greatest difficulty, chiefly because I cannot concentrate. I have no feeling about whether what I am writing is good or bad, and the whole business is totally without excitement and pleasure for me. And I am sure I know the reason. It's that I can't stand leaving unresolved my situation with Pat. I hear from her fairly frequently, asking when I plan to come back, and she knows that I am supposed to appear at the poetry reading in the middle of January. It is not mainly loneliness I feel, though I feel it; but I have been lonely before. It is quite frankly the fact that nothing is really settled between us, and that in the mean time I worry about how things are going to work out. This has made my work more difficult than it has ever been before. And there has been no lack of encouragement. I don't know whether I told you, but there was a quite talented and successful young German composer [Hans Werner Henze] down in Ischia who has been commissioned to write five songs for Benjamin Britten and Peter Pears, and which they will take on a world tour of recitals, and the composer wants me to do the texts. I have only been able to turn out one short one so far, and he needs them soon, and not being able to work panics me and makes writing even more difficult. And there have been other requests for work.

1 Journal entry for September 6th, 1955, p. 35
2 Journal entry for December 2nd, 1955, p. 49.

Introduction | 19

Anyway, the point is that I am feeling very tense and uncomfortable here and am not really having a good time, and am not getting much work done, and since the chance to work was the original excuse for staying here, it seems to me pointless now. So I plan to go down today or tomorrow and pick up reservations on a ship coming back. There's one that sails from here on the 11th of Dec. and gets in in time for Christmas, and I'll try to get on that. Unless you have any reason to suppose that this is a bad idea, I should like to try to get back as soon as possible. If you have reasons to recommend to the contrary, please let me know. But be assured that I am not doing this merely because I have been getting a lot of affectionate letters from Pat. The effect would have been the same, perhaps even more violent, if she had never written at all."[1]

Hecht left Rome on December 10th, and sailed for America, as planned, on the 11th. In the run-up to his departure, no fewer than three parties were given in his honor, the last of them at the Wyners' apartment, where MacDonald records that Hecht "told his finest stories" and played recordings of "various poems, and of Joyce." It would seem that Hecht also read at least one of his own poems, for after jotting down two lines from Wallace Stevens's "Sunday Morning" – presumably one of the poems the guests heard a recording of – MacDonald then did the same with the opening sentence of Hecht's "Roman Holiday,"[2] though without identifying it as such.[3] In the company of his friends, it seems, he had still been able to enjoy himself, at least on occasions.

MacDonald and his wife stayed on at the Academy till the middle of August 1956, and they appear to have relished every moment. Almost thirty years later, MacDonald reminisced about his two-year fellowship in terms not very different from those we have already seen Hecht use to describe his first sojourn there: "Being at the Academy," he wrote, "was a very great experience … In a way I've been living off the capital acquired during that experience … ever since."[4]

When the time came to leave, the couple – whose first child, Noel, had arrived just three weeks earlier – no longer faced so uncertain a future, since the search for an academic post had finally come to an end with the offer of an instructorship in the Department of Art History at Yale.

By this time, Hecht had also found himself an instructorship, and was teaching freshman English at Smith College. Despite their ongoing difficulties, he and Pat were also expecting a baby: Jason was born in early November, in fact. These parallel developments will surely have helped cement the friendship that had first blossomed in the fall of 1954, and they weren't to be the last.

---

1 Letter, AH to Melvyn and Dorothea Hecht, November 9th, 1955, *The Selected Letters of Anthony Hecht*, p. 112.
2 "A Roman Holiday" had been published in AH's first collection, *A Summoning of Stones*.
3 Journal entry for December 9th, 1955, p. 52.
4 Letter #353, August 29th, 1984.

A Note on the Text

Most of the correspondence between Hecht and MacDonald was typewritten, and because both men were efficient typists, transcription rarely presented a problem. The smaller number of handwritten exchanges did throw up some puzzles, but only a handful resisted solution, and these are indicated with the square-bracketed word "illegible."

Neither man had any problem with spelling, punctuation, or grammar. Where, very occasionally, one of them slipped up, the error has therefore been corrected silently.

Where either man used an abbreviation – BCRO, for example – and its significance is not immediately clear, I have spelt out in full what was meant, using square brackets to indicate what I have interpolated, thus: B[oylston] C[hair] of R[hetoric] & O[ratory].

Where a person is referred to by one name only, or by a nickname, and their identity is otherwise unclear, I have supplied the missing information, either in the form of a square-bracketed interpolation or else in the form of a footnote.

Both men were occasionally inconsistent in their styling of titles, here using underlining for a book title, and there using inverted commas. So as to avoid confusion, I have silently regularized everything, using underlining for all book titles, and inverted commas for the titles of articles, poems, lectures, etc.

All but one of the items in this volume reached me in the form of a photocopy prepared by the Manuscript and Rare Book Library (MARBL) of the Woodruff Library at Emory University in Atlanta, Georgia, where Hecht's papers are archived. The exception was letter #113, dated March 10th, 1976, a scanned copy of which was forwarded to me by Nicholas MacDonald after he found the original tucked inside one of his late father's books.[1] The transcriptions prepared from Emory's photocopies were cross-checked against the original documents on two separate weeklong visits to the university.

Some of the correspondence was undated, and where no envelopes survived, or the date stamps on them could not be deciphered, working out where an item belonged in the sequence had to be done using internal or contextual evidence, some of it short of conclusive. Any uncertainty about a date is indicated with a square-bracketed "???" or a square-bracketed "Probably."

As has already been noted, there are 440 items in all, only 403 of which were

---

1 A copy of this was subsequently deposited in the Hecht archive.

thought worth including here, the remainder being omitted on the grounds that they were too ephemeral, too close in content to something which had already been selected for inclusion, or, in a very small number of cases, out of concern for the sensitivities of the still living. The same considerations led me to make a small number of cuts to the included items as well. Where such cuts have been made, they have been indicated with a square-bracketed three-point ellipsis.

To obtain a text that is as clear as possible, the layout of each item has been standardized. Top left comes the item's number in the sequence, thus: **[12]**. Then, on the right, come the bracketed initials of the author – [AH] for Hecht and [WLM] for MacDonald. Beneath the initials comes the date, always given in this general form: January 21st, 1985. Beneath the date comes the address of the sender. Beneath these things, and centered on the page, comes a square-bracketed and italicized headnote stating whether the item is a letter or a postcard, whether it was typed or handwritten, what stationery was used, how it was addressed, and whether it contained any enclosures. For example:

[Letter, typed on a Hôtel de Crillon, 10, Plaçe de la Concorde, Paris, France, letterhead, posted in a Gramercy Park Hotel envelope, addressed to Field Marshal Dr. (h.c.) Anthony Hecht, The Poetry Office, The Library of Congress, Washington, D.C. 20540, with enclosure].[1]

After this, the body of the item is laid out in regularized fashion, except in a handful of instances where I judged that the original should be reproduced or its layout emulated. The body of the text is then followed by the valediction and sign-off, where these are present, again laid out in regularized fashion, except where I once more judged that the original should be reproduced or its layout emulated. Very occasionally, an item has no valediction or sign-off; their absence is indicated by a square-bracketed "unsigned."

I have divided the correspondence into three numbered sections. Section 1 contains everything sent between 1957 and 1968; section 2 contains everything sent between 1969 and 1980; and section 3 contains everything sent between 1981 and 1992. The division into twelve-year blocks is not entirely arbitrary but roughly coincides with significant developments in the friends' lives, and also with changes in their writing habits.

Each of the book's three numbered sections has its own introduction, the aim of which is to say something about what was going on in the two men's lives during the relevant period, filling in gaps left by the correspondence itself.

A Chronology is supplied, the purpose of which is to help readers orient themselves more or less at a glance. Because it lists events which occurred after the correspondence came to an end, it will also help to satisfy those left curious about the

---

1 Lest the decision to include such a detailed description be thought excessive, I should explain that one of the delights of reading this correspondence is seeing how resourceful the friends were when it came to their choice of stationery, how playful they could be in their addressings, and how often they sought to amuse each other with a cutting, announcement, or other communication that had tickled their fancy.

last few years of the two mens' lives.

The volume comes with a Glossary of Names, which gives basic information about most of the many hundreds of people who get referred to in these pages. Though this is as comprehensive as I have been able to make it, there are gaps. Where I could discover nothing about an individual, save for what could be gleaned from the correspondence – as in the case of Nancy L. Stark, for example, whom MacDonald dated in the late 1960s and early 1970s – no entry is given.

I have tried not to encumber the volume with too many footnotes. Anne Olivier Bell, who edited *The Diary of Virginia Woolf*, found the job of annotating its five volumes the most difficult of her many tasks, and sought to avoid clutter by attending to a notice she'd pinned above her desk: "Accuracy / Relevance / Concision / Interest."[1] Since the readership for *A Bountiful Harvest* is likely to be made up of people who know something about Hecht and poetry but little or nothing about MacDonald and architectural history, or something about MacDonald and architectural history but little or nothing about Hecht and poetry, the chances are that I have failed to achieve the last of Bell's objectives as often as I might have hoped, but I console myself with the thought that footnotes can be looked at or ignored, just as a reader sees fit.

The last of the book's three numbered sections is followed by an Afterword, in which I seek to explain what brought the correspondence to an end.

---

1 *Editing Virginia Woolf's Diary* (London: The Bloomsbury Workshop, 1990), p. 22.

1. 1957–1968

The earliest item in this gathering is a postcard from Hecht to MacDonald which, although undated, was probably sent in June 1957, at a time when both men were still on the first rung of their university careers. The postcard's content, as well as its tone and its sign-off, strongly suggest that this was not the earliest of their written communications, merely the earliest to survive. As a matter of fact, we know that it wasn't the earliest. That distinction goes to a postcard or letter Hecht sent MacDonald three months earlier, something we are only aware of because MacDonald mentioned it in a journal entry for March 15th, 1957 which reads as follows:

"AEH writes:

There once was a man named King Henery
Who was given to licence and venery
He drank and he ate
At a frightening rate
And his sexual sessions were plenary."[1]

Between 1957 and 1968, we know of just sixteen more items, all of which are included here. Three of these date from 1960, four from 1961, two from 1962, one each from 1964, 1965, and 1967, and the last four from 1968. It is a striking fact that only four of these are by Hecht, but it would be wrong to draw any conclusions from this – most obviously, that Hecht was the less enthusiastic correspondent – because, as its fitful and disjointed nature makes clear, this early correspondence is some way short of being complete.

Exactly how much has been lost is unclear, but we shouldn't suppose that it amounted to a great deal. I say this because, after they settled back in America – Hecht in 1955 and MacDonald in 1956 – and for as long as they were living within a two-hour drive of each other, it is clear that the two men were getting together on a frequent basis, making correspondence less important than it would later become.

1 Journal entry for March 15th, 1957, p. 90. The archive does contain one still earlier item, a postcard written by Dale to AH and PH on August 7th, 1956, while she and MacDonald were still in Rome, but not posted until September 3rd, when they were back in the US. The postcard announces the arrival of their son Noel, and looks forward to the couples being reunited in the fall.

29

Not three weeks after they flew out of Rome, the MacDonalds enjoyed "4 glorious days" with the Hechts at the home they were then renting in Florence, Massachusetts, a ten-minute drive from the Smith campus.[1] Three weeks after that, they visited the Hechts again, this time "on the spur of the moment," and were treated to dinner with one of Hecht's academic colleagues, the distinguished literary critic, Newton Arvin.[2] A little over two weeks after that, the Hechts spent a weekend with the MacDonalds, a "good weekend of scotch and talk."[3] And so it continued, certainly for the next two years, and, it seems reasonable to suppose, right the way through till 1967, when Hecht moved to Rochester, almost tripling the distance between them.[4] As well as the visits, there were plenty of phone-calls. The MacDonalds were amongst the first to hear about Jason Hecht's birth On November 4th, 1956, and two years later, on October 26th, 1958, they were amongst the first to hear of Adam Hecht's as well.

The frequency of their get-togethers and telephone calls helps to explain why the two men – busy as they were with their teaching, their families and their work – found less time for writing each other than they would in later years. It also helps to resolve a puzzle thrown up by the correspondence, which is the almost complete absence from it of all but the most oblique references to the life-changing events with which these twelve years were filled.

What was going on in the two men's lives that is not addressed – except in one or two instances obliquely – in these early postcards and letters?

For one thing, the MacDonalds suffered the loss of a child, their second son, Darius, being born in December 1957, and dying just a few weeks later.

More happily, each couple went on to have another son, Adam (as has already been said) being born to the Hechts in 1958, and Nicholas to the MacDonalds in 1959.

There was also good news on the career front. Hecht was promoted to Assistant Professor at Smith in 1958, and left there to become Associate Professor at Bard in 1962; and MacDonald was promoted to Assistant Professor at Yale in 1959, and to Associate Professor there in 1963.

We have already seen that the Hechts' marriage had been in trouble almost from the start. The births of Jason and Adam did nothing to alleviate the situation, and things finally came to a head in 1959. The couple's separation that year was followed by divorce in 1961, and the divorce was followed in 1962 by Pat's marriage to Baron Philippe Lambert, a banker, and the removal, not long after that, of Pat, Jason, and Adam to Lambert's native Belgium. Hecht later told J. D. McClatchy that it was Pat who wanted the divorce, not him, and that the breakdown of their marriage "deliv-

---

1 Journal entry for September 17th, 1956, p. 58.

2 Journal entry for October 6th, 1956, p. 62.

3 Journal entry for October 21st, 1956, p. 64.

4 In December 1958, MacDonald chose to give up keeping a journal for anything but recording his travels, and in the absence of his testimony we cannot be absolutely sure that the visits continued to be as frequent, but everything tells in its favour.

ered a terrible blow to [his] self-esteem."[1] But the resultant separation from his sons caused Hecht a great deal of suffering – so much suffering, indeed, that he wound up spending three months in New York's Gracie Square Hospital, being treated for depression.[2]

1962 saw yet more significant developments in MacDonald's career. To begin with, his first book, *Early Christian and Byzantine Architecture*, was published by Braziller as one of its The Great Ages of World Architecture Series, a series whose other contributors included already established scholars such as Frank E. Brown, Henry A. Millon, and Vincent Scully. But although the series as a whole was well-received – Walter L. Creese, writing in *Art Journal*, described it as "a bold venture in publishing … deserv[ing] considerable recognition"[3] – MacDonald's own contribution garnered only one notice, and that a somewhat grudging one. Glanville Downey, writing in *Archaeology*, began by commending the book for its production values, but then, in each of its remaining paragraphs, struck a critical note: "Dr. MacDonald has not always made the best use of his material," "The reader is disappointed to find …," "Some readers may find the introduction less rewarding," "the reader might have expected a little more detail …"[4] Helping to offset any disappointment MacDonald might have felt, Yale awarded him one of its prestigious Morse Fellowships, the proceeds from which enabled him to return for a third year to the American Academy in Rome, this time taking the whole family with him. There, undeterred by the chilly reception of *Early Christian and Byzantine Architecture*, he was able to do solid work on his next book, a book that was to be much more ambitious in its scope.

On his return to the States in 1963, MacDonald took another step up the academic ladder, being promoted to Associate Professor. And just two years later Yale University Press published his second book, *The Architecture of the Roman Empire*, this time to reviews both numerous and enthusiastic. Kjeld de Fine Licht, writing in the *Journal of Architectural Historians*, said of the book that it "marks an important advance in the examination of the Roman architecture belonging to the formative period in the decades before and after AD 100," and that it "provides a welcome contribution to the knowledge and evaluation of the architecture of the Romans."[5] And Mark P. O. Morford, writing for *The Classical Journal*, declared it a "splendid book," one which gave readers cause to "look forward eagerly to MacDonald's subse-

---

1 "[W]hile the marriage had been an unhappy one … its failure was a terrible blow to my self-esteem, and it was not I who sought to terminate it." Letter to J. D. McClatchy, dated December 26th, 1984, *The Selected Letters of Anthony Hecht*, p. 218.

2 Just how close Hecht had become to the MacDonalds by this time can be judged from the fact that after being discharged from the hospital, he spent time recuperating with them at their home in Guilford, Connecticut. Nicholas, just six years old at the time, has vivid memories of sitting around and watching TV with their chain-smoking guest.

3 Walter L. Creese, *Art Journal*, 22:3 (Spring, 1963), p. 192.

4 Glanville Downey, *Archaeology*, 16:2 (June, 1963), pp. 147-148.

5 Kjeld de Fine Licht, *Journal of the Society of Architectural Historians*, 25:3, (October, 1966), pp. 221-222.

quent volumes."¹ After this, MacDonald had every reason to expect that Yale would grant him tenure, but when he and two of his talented younger colleagues had their applications turned down, what one commentator has called "a bitter bloodbath" occurred,² with all three resigning and accepting tenured positions elsewhere – William Crelly at Emory, Spiro Kostof at Berkeley, and MacDonald at Hecht's former perch, Smith.

While all of this was unfolding, Hecht returned to his teaching at Bard, and in 1966, four years after his hospitalization, was promoted to full professor. Bard was not to be his home for much longer, however. The very next year, in fact, and not long after appearing on the same London stage as Yehuda Amichai, W. H. Auden, John Berryman, Yves Bonnefoy, William Empson, Allen Ginsberg, Hugh MacDiarmid, Pablo Neruda, Ann Sexton, Giuseppe Ungaretti, Andrei Voznesensky, and Yevgeny Yevtushenko,³ he left there to take up a professorship at the University of Rochester in upstate New York. Within weeks of the move, Atheneum published his long-awaited second collection, *The Hard Hours*, a development which was to make an even bigger difference to his career than publication of *The Architecture of the Roman Empire* had made to MacDonald's. Allen Tate and Ted Hughes had both written glowing endorsements for the book, Tate declaring that "[W]hoever else may be at the top, Hecht is there too; for there is nobody better," and Hughes calling him "a poet with an immense burden of something to say ... an inspired artist," someone whose poems were amongst "the most powerful and unforgettable ... at present being written in America." Positive notices soon followed. Richard A. Johnson wrote as follows: "Hecht works against the grain, but so smoothly that we almost fail to notice. He gives us valved emotion; rather than direct expression of feeling, he presents, in magnificent variety of forms, the artifices we construct in the face of our historical and biological condition. Thus we get both formal brilliance and intense, often bitter, irony – and, more difficult to trace, a humane and kindly sympathy for man, inadequate as he struggles against destruction."⁴ In the spring of 1968, Hecht was rewarded with that most coveted of literary prizes, the Pulitzer, and not just that but the Russell Loines Award, the Miles Poetry Prize, and an Academy of American Poets' Honorary Fellow grant as well. The acclaim secured him something else besides, in the shape of a named chair – the John H. Deane Professor of Rhetoric and Poetry – at the University of Rochester.

1967 saw publication by Atheneum not just of *The Hard Hours* but also of *Jiggery-Pokery: A Compendium of Double Dactyls*, a volume Hecht had co-edited with John Hollander. This too had its admirers. One unnamed reviewer, writing in

---

1 Mark P. O. Morford. *The Classical Journal*, 63:1 (October, 1967), pp. 40-42.

2 Elizabeth Sears, "The Art-Historical Work of Walter Cahn," published in *Romanesque Art and Thought in the Twelfth Century: Essays in Honor of Walter Cahn*, edited by Colum Hourihane (University Park, PA: Pennsylvania State Press, 2008, p. 21, note 42).

3 This was the four-day Poetry International, held at the Queen Elizabeth Hall and the Purcell Room on the South Bank between July 12th and 16th, an event which was directed that year by Ted Hughes and Patrick Garland.

4 Richard A. Johnson, *The Sewanee Review*, 76:4 (Autumn, 1968), p. 685.

Prairie Schooner, described the volume as a gathering of "nimble light-verse offerings all cast in a rollicking form," and went on to say that "after reading the clever pieces in the 'canon,' many of which are written by editors Hecht and Hollander, one is tempted to try the form. But it's harder than it looks ..."[1] How high Hecht's star had risen by this time may be gauged from the fact that, in late 1968, even though he had only recently been appointed to the named chair at Rochester, he was granted a year's leave of absence, returning for a third time to the American Academy in Rome, there to work with the classicist Helen Bacon on a translation of Aeschylus's *Seven Against Thebes*.

If none of these important developments gets any direct mention in the handful of letters and cards that have come down to us from this period, the exchanges nevertheless make for entertaining reading, and in their heady mix of low and high, playful and serious, fanciful and down-to-earth, they go some way to preparing us for the bountiful harvest that follows.

---

1 *Prairie Schooner*, 41:1 (Spring, 1967), pp. 92-93.

[1]

[AH]
[Probably June, 1957]
Smith College, Northampton, Massachusetts, Department of English

[Letter, typed on a Smith College letterhead]

Things are looking better than you would have guessed from your visit here. In token of which joyful tidings, I enclose the following epic:

> His Highness, the Bey of Baldeen,
> Has invented a fucking machine
> Which has fittings of brass
> And is powered by gas
> And accounts for his title, "Serene."

Two more like this, and my book will be finished.
Henri, duc d'Orléans et de South Bend

[2]

[WLM]
[Probably June, 1960]
[21 George Street, Guilford, Connecticut]

[Letter, typed]

Mon 20th

Dear Antonius,
  What time is your reading Sunday? & in what building? Send a card, just in case we're back from Peterborough. In a while our lives will uncomplicate, and we can profligate, mate.
  Neither of the 2 Herodians were alive in Valerian's reign, nor of course was Cassius Dio. That leaves the *Historia Augusta*.[1] and some bits and pieces (most imp.) in Zosimas [Historicus], [Johannes] Zonaras, and Aurelius, V[ictor]. Oxford Classical Dictionary[2] has it thus: "... Valerian attempted to relieve Bithynia (from Gothic attack – WM), but was recalled to the Front by a new Persian attack. Owing to plague in his army, he attempted negotiations, but by a perfidious ruse was arrested by King Sapor and carried off to die in captivity (260)." " ... yet Valerian was neither a fool nor a knave, and in a more peaceful age might have governed with

---

1 The title given by Isaac Casaubon to a collection of biographies of Roman Emperors and Caesars written by divers hands between AD 117 and 284.

2 *Oxford Classical Dictionary*, edited by Max Cary with the assistance of H. J. Rose, H. P. Harvey, and A. Souter (New York: Oxford University Press, 1949).

unoffending moderation."

And, after all, he was the father of the truly great Gallienus.

<u>Cambridge Ancient History</u> XII (pp. 135ff) says: Zosimus represents the capture as a "treacherous breach of faith on the part of Shapur," but "others would place it after a battle" in which the emperor had insufficient forces to manage victory over the superior Persian army; still others, and the mod. author refutes, or rather discards, this idea, say that Valerian fled from Edessa to the arms of Shahanshah.

I recommend <u>CAH</u> XII as the best place to go; there is so little mention of the Hist. Aug. in my secondary works that as usual one infers that mod. scholarship places little reliance on that strange, fascinating collection; and, of course, the chapters we have of the life of V. are only fragments and there is little in them. <u>CAH</u> XII is it, and good, I thought.

Would go further, but I am so damned far behind, having missed work for about 4 weeks, that I must pull myself together for a lecture on the meaning of Pompeian painting. But let's chase Publius Licinius Valerianus further. I like him. Try the new 2nd ed. of H. M. D. Parker's <u>The Roman World from 138 to 337</u>,[1] also.[2]

Keep in touch,
Vale,
Alexamenos

[3]

[WLM]
August 6th, [1960]
21 George Street, Guilford, Connecticut

[Letter, typed, addressed to Anthony Hecht, Esquire, 415 East 80th Street, New York, N.Y.]

Dear Tony,

I don't know how, or when, this will reach you, but I hope it does, because I want to tell you that we feel very badly about not accepting your invitation for next week-end.

The situation is that I have two deadlines to meet, one (the TV shows) for money, which I need badly, being really strapped. Then we are going to Peterborough [New Hampshire] the following Tuesday or Wednesday for my father's birthday; all the clan is to gather.

We talked and talked about coming down, and reluctantly decided that we shouldn't try it. Please come and see us, with or without boy or boys, when your Fire Islanding is finished ... All this is not to plead poverty and overwork in order to fill

---

1 H. M. D. Parker, *A History of the Roman World from* A.D. *138 to 337*, Second Edition (New York: Macmillan, 1958).

2 Though the letter to which WLM is responding here is missing, it seems safe to assume that AH was doing background research for "Behold the Lilies of the Field," which was first published in the Fall 1961 issue of *The Hudson Review*, and was subsequently included in his second collection, *The Hard Hours*.

your eyes with sweet tears, but rather because we really do want to see you, and gave the idea up with a great deal of reluctance.

No news here, really. I don't know where Frank & Jackie [Brown] are, other than the fact that they reached Rome safely, in June. My book is coming along slowly, but I am more or less satisfied with it and have a really terrific draughtsman doing some difficult drawings for me. The Yale Press hasn't committed itself yet, but is sniffing. I want to have it done by the day classes start.[1]

Didst see the review of Al Kernan's book on satire (The Cankered Muse)[2] in the Times Literary Supplement?[3] Al: "At last – I know I can get a job."

Dale, Noel, Nick thrive … There is still a drink or two in the bottle of Cutty Sark you left here when you and Jason were up.

      Best always from us all,
      Louise Phillipe

[4]

[AH]
[November 30th, 1960]
Smith College, Northampton, Massachusetts, Department of English

[Smith College, Department of English, postcard, typed, addressed to Professor and Lady Wm. MacDonald, 21 George St. Guilford, Conn]

  My heart, a mere handful of dust,
  Is yet stirred by the thrust of a bust;
   For all tottering clay
   Is constrained to obey
  Kant's bold Categorical Must.

  A metaphysician named Smith
  Put his inklings with vigor and pith:
   "What seemeth pure light
   To the ignorant wight,
  Not cloudily seemeth – it ith."

     Love,
     Smith

---

1 WLM was working on his first book, *Early Christian & Byzantine Architecture*.
2 Alvin B. Kernan, *The Cankered Muse* (New Haven, CT: Yale University Press, 1959).
3 Unsigned review by Agnes Latham, "The Savage Eye," *Times Literary Supplement*, July 8th, 1960.

[5]

[WLM]
January 9th, 1961
[Boston, Massachusetts]

[Postcard, with a photograph showing a panoramic view of Palermo, addressed to Mr Anthony Hecht M.A., 415 East 80th Street, New York, N.Y.]

Tonino –
    Pretty cramped over here but just wished to say how much we enjoyed having you and the boys & hope you'll be up again soon. Dale's V[irgin] I[sland] trip with Peg. M. seems in danger of falling through; Fyre Eyeland[1] sounds good. Kernan book on the way to you.

Yrs.
Antoninus Pius
Cos.Tert. Fecit

[6]

[WLM]
July 16th, 1961
21 George Street, Guilford, Connecticut

[Blank postcard, typed, addressed to Mr A. Hecht, 415 East 80th St., New York, N.Y.]

Tonino-issimo,
    I hope you notice the "1" this machine has – not at all like the "1" most machines slide over to you … Book 1, for Braziller, finished; will appear in February 1962. #2 will be done by Labor Day, health and age permitting. I am utterly underground, except for a few trips to Peterborough. Sorry I can't come to the Island – would love to, but I am caught up in this thing and enjoying it. Wilburs said they [have] seen you. <u>Times</u> reviewer obviously hadn't read [Robert] Graves' "Sgt Lamb" books,[2] or is a knurd anyway … Paul Weiss, reputedly a philosopher, says F[rank] E. B[rown] is a pagan, that there are very few but Frank is the real thing, and this explains why he is devoid of Christian sentiment, love, forgiveness, and is so cosmopolitan and learned all the same. See you, I hope, for a good long visit in Sept. Best from

Guglielmo-issimo

---

1 AH spent many of his summers in a rented house on Fire Island, one of the outer barrier islands to the south shore of Long Island, New York.

2 Graves wrote three such stories: *Sergeant Lamb of the Ninth* (London: Methuem, 1940), *Proceed, Sergeant Lamb* (New York: Random House, 1941), and *Sergeant Lamb's America* (New York: Random House, 1940).

[7]

[WLM]
September 5th, 1961
[Yale Art Gallery 402, New Haven, Connecticut, U.S.A]

[Blank postcard, typed, addressed to Anthony Hecht, Esq., 415 East 80th St, New York, NY]

Antoninus L.F. Imp. Caes. Cos. Tert.

All through last month in the 100% humidity I thought jealously of you on the beach. Come & see us when you can. Tied up Sept 16th weekend, and one other (date not set yet) afterwards; otherwise free; want to see you. 2nd book[1] almost done … We are all well. Nick's talking (I think you could call it that), and Noel starts school tomorrow. Can you plan your life so as to be in Europe next year? We could make many gastronomic tours, wagering on the authorships of Talmudic glosses and the names of distant stars.

Yours,
Had

[8]

[AH]
September 20th 1961
415 East 80th, NYC

[Blank postcard, typed and handwritten, addressed to MacDonald, 21 George St., Guilford, Conn]

Walpurgisnacht, 1532

A fruity young Yale art historian
Declared, with the charm of a saurian,
    "These plans from the pen
    Of Sir Christopher Wren
Seem pale to a robust Victorian."

How are you fixed for entertaining a wizened old man and two appealing young boys? These are part of a small troupe of itinerant actors who have toured Paraguay in "The Wild Duck" and have turned to me for help. Their tastes are modest, but they snore in Norwegian.

Grimaldi[2]

---

1 *The Architecture of the Roman Empire: An Introductory Study.*
2 The person whose name AH tries on here is presumably Agostino Grimaldi, Regent of Monaco, Bishop of Grasse and Abbot of Lérins. Born in 1482, he died in 1532, but on April 14th, a little over two weeks before the spurious Walpurgisnacht date given by AH at the head of this postcard.

[9]

[WLM]
January 5th [1962]
Yale Art Gallery 402, New Haven, Conn, U.S.A.

[Blank postcard, typed, addressed to Anthony Hecht, 415 East 80th St, New York, NY]

Hope you will join up after the lecture, which is on Roman architecture, and not that ladies' crap. Have an invite after for drinks at a nice young couple's place, and have said you might be along. Dale, alas, can't get down this time, but we are both coming down in Feb. Cheers, & please come up when you feel like it. Am out of circulation only weekend of Jan 27th ...

[Unsigned]

[10]

[WLM]
March 17th [1962]
Tunis [Tunisia]

[Postcard, with a photograph of an ancient head of Pan, from the collection of the Bardo National Museum in Tunis, handwritten, addressed to Anthony Hecht, 415 E. 80th St., New York N.Y., Etats-Unis]

Tony –
 How are you? A line would be <u>very</u> welcome. Tunisia is magnificent. To Roma tomorrow.

Bill

[11]

[AH]
November 23rd, 1964
[240 East 82nd Street, New York, N.Y.]

[Letter, typed]

Dear Bill,
 A late epic, which is all yours.

> A crusty old scholar from Leeds
> Remarked of Caligula's deeds,
> "The effect of his horse
> On the consular force
> Would cause you to shit in your tweeds."

Thanks for a fine time.

P. Ovidius Naso

[12]

[WLM]
[September 9th, 1965]
409 Prospect Street, Northampton, Massachusetts 01060

[Letter, typed on reverse side of Yale University, Department of the History of Art, letterhead, addressed to Professor Anthony Hecht, 240 East 82nd Street, New York, NY, with enclosure]

If you think me prolific from the last communiqué, wait til you read the enclosed.

Glad to see Gowers hasn't taken the article Out-Herod from Fowler. Be a terrible thing if he had.[1]

Can't wait for you to see the house. And have you seen my cigarette lighter, shaped like W. C. Fields' head, with a red nose you press in order to light up the top of his battered top hat? Well, if you haven't, come <u>soon</u>.

The quality of these deathless lines is to be judged only after being informed that I am reading Index proof, and checking each entry (13 double col pp) in the page proofs for accuracy. I am going out of my cotton-picking mind. Al Kernan is now Associate Provost Yale.

I have to come to New Haven from time to time; could pick you up there.

What set me off was a crate shaped like none I had ever seen before. When I saw it, I knew I had the 4th lecture title; much better, it seems to me, than "Great Hats I have Worn." I think we ought to prepare a sober flyer, listing this series in all seriousness, have it mimeographed, and send it to all our friends in the Academic racket. What I enclose is miserable, debasing, hardly the pullulating parousia I had hoped for, but I send it along anyway in the hope that it will awaken in you something of the tremulous opportunity we have. It ain't camp, it ain't been done in our time, and it COULD be just the greatest.

Along these lines I'm working (in my mind) on my monograph on Santa Messalina in Flagrante. Don't spread the word. It will have plans and elevations, murky photos, a text on archit., reliques, history, textual sources, etc. I hope that you will contribute either a preface, or a fine olde poem that can be discovered in an English pilgrim's crypte. If I can do it well enough I'll get someone to print it up for private circ.

Serious about all this, you know. And again seriously, the Colorado lecture,[2] which

---

1 Sir Ernest Gowers, editor, *H. W. Fowler: A Dictionary of Modern English Usage*, Second Edition (New York: Oxford University Press, 1965).

It seems likely that WLM had seen a draft of the poem by AH which takes the Shakespearian line "It Out-Herods Herod. Pray You, Avoid It" as its title, and which was included in his second collection, *The Hard Hours*.

2 It has not been possible to identify this lecture with any certainty, but it is quite possibly "On the

I have studied carefully, is splendid. Christ but you're intelligent. I wish I could think clearly.

       Fervid Fosdick

[Enclosure]

       A n n o u n c i n g

A Course of Lectures, Illusrated by Deed and By Magic Lantern

         GIVEN BY

    Professor Anthony Hecht, Bard, Bard, and

    Professor William MacDonald, Smith, Smith

  f a m o u s   r i v a l s   i n s p e a k i n g   a n d t a l k

Messrs Hecht & MacDonald, having long prepared this extraordinary series, now feel ready to offer it th a discriminating Public. This very unusual and extremely stimulating series is presented in four parts.

  I   <u>Famous Streetcar Accidents</u>   (Professor Hecht)

  II   <u>LITTLE Women</u> (Professor MacDonald)

  III   <u>Great Literary</u> ~~Famous~~ <u>Non-Swimmers</u> (Professor Hecht)

  IV   Different-shaped Crates (Professor MacDonald)

It is possible to have all four lectures in one day, indeed even in one evening, though the recommended pace is one each day.

Particular suitable for Clubs, Elks, Lions, and Unicorns. The Fee, plus all expenses, is $2000 for the series. Contact either of the two speaks for further information.

  A N   U N E Q U A L L E D   O P P O R T U N I T Y   ! ! !

Methods and Ambitions of Poetry," which was published in the winter 1965-66 issue of *The Hudson Review*.

[13]

[WLM]
December 26th, 1967
[409 Prospect Street, Northampton, Massachusetts 01060]

[Italian postcard, with a photograph of the view from the terrace of the Grand Hotel dei Cappuccini, Amalfi, typed, addressed to A. E. Hecht, 440 East 82nd St., New York, N.Y.]

Tonino –
 Dale gave me an American Academy of Rome baldric for Christmas and I am most anxious that you be the first to have the great news.[1] Will you come up, wearing yours, so that we can compare and fondle them? Do they have any fine uses other than processional? Naturally I look to you for advice and counsel in this.
– Benito

[14]

[WLM]
[March 9th, 1968]

[Blank postcard, with the sender's address given as Admiral T., The CIA, Somewhere 00000, addressed to General-Oberst Antonio von Hecht, (Eisenkreuz mit Diamanten), 19 East Boulevard, Rochester, NY 14610]

vii ante Ides Marti, MCMLXVIII
Dear Dr Iyedjhe,
 I address you thus because I believe, with all the faithful, that you are Dr I. J., the Mental Fox.[2] Well, to the questions. 1) Do you not think that Mr Tito uses Grecian Formula no. 55? Or maybe 45, in honour of his victory? But Much More Important, 2) Will you join in my Great Discovery, that the Dulleses and the Barrymores are one and the same, shuttling coast to coast? Ethel, sublime, all from above, is Eleanor.

---

1 The baldric is given to winners of the American Academy in Rome's Rome Prize, which is awarded on an annual basis to fifteen emerging artists (people working in the fields of architecture, landscape architecture, design, historic preservation and conservation, literature, musical composition, or the visual arts) and to fifteen scholars (people working in the fields of ancient, medieval, renaissance and early modern, or modern Italian studies). Rome Prize winners receive a stipend, room and board, and are also given an individual work space at the AAR's eleven-acre campus on the Janiculum. There they are encouraged to refine and enlarge their artistic or scholarly skills, drawing on their fellow prize winners' erudition and experience.

2 Dr I. J., the Mental Fox, was a character invented by the humorist and radio broadcaster Henry Morgan, and used by him to lampoon radio game shows. Himself a game-show host, Dr I. J. always managed to avoid being parted from the silver dollars he jingled in front of the contestants. Thus: MORGAN: "Sixteen silver dollars to this lady if she can answer this question correctly. I will give you a list of words. You are to tell me which one does not belong. 'Elk, moose, lion, Herman!'" WOMAN: "Herman!" MORGAN: "Oh, I'm sorry … But if you inquire you will find that Herman does belong to the Elks, the Moose and the Lions."

John, waxer of wimmin, is Allen. And Lionel – ah, how he fooled us – Lionel is Foster ... When you think on it, it all becomes clear. First the Bs established themselves in our hearts, and then - ah, how insidious – they changed a bit, and became – the Dulleses! Reflect. It's true. Three only, and we thought they were six!

Jimmy

[15]

[WLM]
[March 21st, 1968]
[409 Prospect Street, Northampton, Massachusetts 01060]

[Letter, typed]

Jesú,

I Your agentes in rebus stationed within Atheneum are correct: I <u>have</u> been dilatory; I am impenitent; the book proceedeth and is <u>almost</u> finished (it is <u>always</u> <u>almost</u> finished).

II You have made grievous errors, and divers, in your exposition of the matter of Caesar, fair Kleopatra, and the monuments of Rome. Exemplum: you say that Kleopatra hath her finger up Caesar's ass; not so, she hath her great stone finger up his <u>ash</u>. A good deal of trouble has been caused in Europe and roundabout by this kind of error. Ashes incorrectly for asses; apse for apes; and the like. So Beware! You say your Easter sermon "is capable of great extrapolation." Now I would say to the contrary, that it is chiefly and largely capable of intrapolation, a form of crapolation, a matter insufficiently studied. My feeling is that the sermon could be delivered with a great and seemly brevity; in fact, in one word, a Great Word which my own purity and modesty forbiddeth me to issue. I think you should keep the hell out of mixed media.

III When in hell's name do you go to Rome? We thought you were there arredy. I go to Iran on May 14th; expect to be able to entertain you in my suite at the Hilton by June 2nd or thereabouts. Are you game? Are you even ripe?

IV Never, <u>never</u>, mistake asthma for passion.

Dad

VI post Id. Martii
MCMLXVIII

16]

[WLM]
[April 19th, 1968]
Smith College, Northampton, Massachusetts, Department of Art

[Letter, typed, addressed to Anthony E. Hecht, Guildenstern Professor of Rosencranz, Department of English, The University of Rochester, Rochester, N.Y., 14627]

1 Q: What do you call a fifteen year-old Polack in the fourth grade? A: Gifted.
2 In some Rochester Hospital there is a nurse whose first name is Hilary and my bet is that she's a splendid fuck. I'm sorry I don't know her last name or the name of the hospital, but knowing your devotion to research, not to mention Waylanding,[1] I send this bit of information gratis.
3 I will be in New York next weekend and will call a], to see if you are there, and b] to see if you want to down a few Sprites, or Frescas.
4 Between Rochester and the Island, you will be in New York City?
5 I <u>would</u> like a part as a cell in your new <u>Carmen</u>. Perhaps you can use one of my songes, a] Euthanasia, or My Childhood in Siberia, or b] Give My Heart a Break.
6 Meanwhile,

[Unsigned]

[17]

[WLM]
July 23rd, 1968
Fogg Museum, Harvard University, Cambridge, Massachusetts

[Blank postcard, addressed to Anthony Hecht Esq, 240 East 82nd St., New York, N.Y.]

Tonino –
  Roma was raining but fun. You need an armoured car to get in città; the traffic is incredible. Frank [Brown] ages but talks as always.
  Being a Harvard Prof. is fun but taxing.
  Hope to get to NY in August or Sept so let me have your dates of leaving 1) Fire Is[land], 2) USA, OK? Address over.

Best
Simon + Garfunkel

---

1 This appears to be a reference to the redoubtable Wayland Young, the 2nd Baron Kennet. Young was a writer, politician, and journalist, and in 1954, when AH and WLM were first getting to know each other, he was working as Rome correspondent for *The Observer*. Young and his no less redoubtable wife, Elizabeth, who was a writer, researcher, poet, artist, and political campaigner, were regulars at the AAR, and became good friends with Richard and Charlee Wilbur.

2. 1969–1980

If we have been left with just seventeen items from the years 1957–1968, the years 1969–1980 were to be very different, yielding a crop of two hundred and seventy-eight items.[1] While not everything of importance in the friends' lives finds its way into these letters and postcards, and some of those that do are dealt with only glancingly, a biographer would find these exchanges a lot more informative than the seventeen that went before, and this despite the fact that even here quite a few items have been lost.[2]

What could account for the dramatic increase in the amount of correspondence the two men exchanged during these years? The most important factor is one I mentioned in my introduction to the previous section. For as long as Hecht was at Smith or Bard while MacDonald was at Yale, or Hecht was at Bard while MacDonald was at Smith, the two men were never living more than a two-hour drive from each other, so that visiting was relatively easy. But after Hecht moved to Rochester in 1967 they were living a five-hour drive from each other, and opportunities for "scotch and talk" were inevitably less frequent.

I suspect that a number of other factors were also at work. To begin with, each man had at last found a measure of job security, Hecht having been given a full professorship at the University of Rochester, and MacDonald the same at Smith. Then again, both men were enjoying vocational as well as academic success, their second books having been very well-received, and their reputations considerably enhanced. Both men were still extremely busy, of course, and neither was resting on his laurels, but freed of some of the uncertainties they had been living with since 1957, they will surely have found it more of a pleasure and less of a distraction to sit down and write letters.[3]

1 Not all of the two hundred and seventy-eight are included here. Twenty-six have been excluded, for the reasons given on p. 24, i.e., because they are too ephemeral, too close in content to something which had already been selected for inclusion, or, in a very small number of cases, out of concern for the still living.

2 In the very first item, for example, we find Hecht writing from Rome, thanking MacDonald for news of a visit MacDonald hopes to make in the spring, and responding positively to the suggestion that they undertake a trip together, but the last surviving communication from MacDonald to Hecht is a postcard sent some six months earlier, and this makes no mention of a visit or a trip. In case it be thought possible that Hecht was responding to a phone-call rather than a piece of correspondence, it should be pointed out that the tenor of Hecht's response makes it perfectly clear that he is not returning to matters already discussed but is addressing them for the very first time.

3 This was certainly true for Hecht, more than eight hundred of whose letters and postcards survive from the years 1968-1982. See *The Selected Letters of Anthony Hecht*, p. 133. Whether there was a similar

Another thing which might have contributed to the increased flow of correspondence was the breakdown of the MacDonalds' marriage, which occurred in the summer of 1969. MacDonald writes to Hecht in July, and very much in passing tells him that he and Dale are discussing separation. Though nothing in the earlier exchanges has prepared *us* for this, it won't have come as a surprise to *Hecht*, as we can tell from the fact that MacDonald says "nothing new" accounts for this turn of events.[1] We don't know when MacDonald first discussed his marital problems with Hecht, but it is quite possible that Hecht heard about them in the first instance not from him but from Dale, and as early as the summer of 1966, when the MacDonalds were Hecht's guests on Fire Island.[2] Hecht had taken the breakdown of his own marriage very badly, as we have seen, and in the letter to J. D. McClatchy from which I quoted earlier he makes it clear that the unhappiness set in straight away, not just after the boys had been taken off to Belgium: "I invested all my frustrated familial feelings on the two boys whom I saw, like most divorced fathers, on weekends, making those days unhealthily emotional, and completely without any ease or naturalness." As we shall see, MacDonald was not one to wear his heart on his sleeve, but the evidence of his correspondence suggests that he did not suffer in anything like the same way, perhaps because his situation in 1969 – he had weathered one broken marriage already, could see his sons whenever he wished to,[3] and was now enjoying the added security of a full professorship – was significantly different from the one Hecht had found himself in ten years earlier. Whatever the explanation, it seems that MacDonald resumed the life of the bachelor scholar with some gusto.

While leaving married life behind him seems to have helped turn MacDonald into a more frequent correspondent, the very same effect seems to have been produced on Hecht by a move in the opposite direction. In March of 1971, while attending the National Book Awards ceremony in New York,[4] Hecht ran into Helen D'Alessandro, who had been a student of his at Smith, and was now working as an editor for the New York publishing house, Walker & Co. Four days after this encounter, Hecht asked her out for a date; six days after that they were engaged; and not three months after that they were married. The marriage brought Hecht great joy, and, as Jonathan Post has observed, it also brought him emotional stability – the sort of stability he needed for his writing, whether of poetry or prose, whether of

---

increase in the amount of correspondence MacDonald had with others is unclear, his papers never having been archived like Hecht's.

1 See letter #20, July 1st, 1969.

2 In a letter Dale sent Hecht on August 21st, 1966, she talks at length about the gulf that has opened up between her and her husband, but two-thirds of the way through interjects the following remark: "[W]e did enjoy ourselves on Fire Island, many thanks. It was particularly good to talk to you – life seems less kooky now with someone close to us … knowing that charade we play is not for real." (Anthony Hecht Papers, Box 46, file 4.)

3 Despite MacDonald's changes of address and Dale's, they were not to live more than a few miles apart for the next three years.

4 Where he saw his old friends Mona Van Duyn and Saul Bellow receive that year's awards for poetry and fiction, respectively,

things intended for publication or things intended only for private consumption.

Another factor which might have spurred the two friends to correspond more frequently was a growing competitiveness. We have already seen the two men horsing around with their salutations and signings-off – "Tonino-issomo," and "Grimaldi," are just two of the ones we have already encountered – but as time goes by we see them not only continuing in this vein, but becoming ever more resourceful. In the 440 letters and postcards that have come down to us, Hecht only salutes MacDonald using his real name on 23 occasions, and only signs off using his own on 14, while MacDonald only salutes Hecht using his real name on 24 occasions, and only signs off using his own on 21. Had I chosen to include it, the index of aliases, allonyms, cognomens, handles, monikers, nicknames, pseudonyms and soubriquets used in the salutations, signings-off and addressings would have contained no less than 697 items.

The urge to compete began to take another form as well, as we can see from a tongue-in-cheek letter Hecht sent his UK editor some years later:

> Dear Jon,
>
> It occurs to me that in the murky future, when it has been at length determined that I am a poet of sufficient interest to merit the publication of a volume of <u>Selected Letters</u>, the editor of the book will be at a loss to convey what may, in the last analysis, be the most sprightly, various, and original part of my correspondence: my letter paper. Indeed, I am engaged in a serious rivalry with a good friend of mine, one William MacDonald ... and our duel consists of trying to outdo each other in exotic letter paper. Since his profession calls for a good deal of travel, he has been able to pick up dandy stationery from hotels in Petra and Abydos and Mogador. I have not his same advantages, but I have my spies and wily ways, and was able to send him, at one point, a rather intimate and sinister memo from Spiro Agnew to Richard Nixon, on White House stationery. I dare say you can appreciate how the rich, full flavor of this will be lost to future readers. Ah, well.
> [...]
>
> Tony[1]

Initially, the stationery the two men used came from the institutions and organizations for which they worked or which they visited, but this was obviously too restrictive, and in next to no time they were using stationery lifted – sometimes, as Hecht admitted, by friends – from hotels, guest-houses, publishers, magazines, embassies, museums, and galleries. Anything would do, and the more exotic the better. In a still later letter, sent to an old friend of MacDonald's, Hecht joked: "My current notion of real exclusiveness would be the paper of the Warden of the Regina Coeli

---

1 Letter to Jon Stallworthy, December 22nd, 1976. *The Selected Letters of Anthony Hecht*, p. 160. (The memo Hecht refers to in the penultimate sentence has unfortunately been lost.)

Prison in Rome. Neither of us has come up with this as yet, though we've both made noble tries."[1] Over the years, Hecht amassed a veritable arsenal of these letterheads, with items from as far afield as Amman, Buenos Aires, Dubrovnik, Jerusalem, Kathmandu, Kyoto, Papeete, and Shanghai, not to mention several places in the UK and all points in the United States.

One last thing should be mentioned at this point. This has to do, not so much with the quantity of correspondence being *exchanged* as with the quantity which has *survived* from this period. In August of 1969, Hecht writes to MacDonald as follows:

> Dear Dodge Owner,
> I hope, fer Cry Sakes, that you have kept my entire correspondence on file so that in due course you can make a mint of money by publishing my letters, you lucky bastard. I will even give you a few hints and guidelines for the introduction, which, I think, might begin somewhat along these lines: "When I first knew Anthony Hecht he had not yet attained to the world-wide celebrity that was later to be his; he was a simple, charming, and modest young man – and all these qualities (except, possibly, his youth) he maintained throughout his career and despite his eminence." Something along that line, if you see what I mean. A few cheerful anecdotes to illustrate my natural wit and good nature might not be out of place, if judiciously chosen. But I suggest that if you must err, it be on the side of brevity, and that you let the letters speak for themselves.
> […][2]

In December of the following year, Hecht adds a postscript to a letter he has signed "Marcus Aurelius, Imp.": "Some day you may be able to sell my letters at auction, purely for their signatures. A Marcus Aurelius is very rare, and should fetch a good price."[3] A few days later, MacDonald responds to this with a postcard saying "And I hope you're keeping my letters, too."[4] Although these remarks are undoubtedly sportive, I think it fair to say that both men were now alert – as previously they had not been – to the possibility that their correspondence merited preservation, and shouldn't be discarded.[5]

The years 1969–1980 were to be no less eventful than the years 1957–1968. I

---

1 Letter to Judith Testa, March 30th, 1983. *The Selected Letters of Anthony Hecht*, p. 207.

2 Letter #21, August 7th, 1969.

3 Letter #53, December 21st, 1970.

4 Postcard #55, January 4th, 1971.

5 Eleven years later, WLM would send AH a jesting reassurance: "Your letters, complete with envelopes, are filed in my correspondence drawers between Harvard and History, and that ought to make you feel good. Grand, inclusive headings, eh?" Letter #254, January 23rd, 1980.

have already mentioned MacDonald's second divorce and Hecht's second marriage, but the period was memorable for much else besides.

Hecht was to be honored in many ways: in 1969, he was elected a Fellow of the Academy of American Poets; in 1970, he was awarded an honorary degree by Bard, and became a member of the National Institute of Arts and Letters; in 1972, he was invited to represent the USA at an international literary conference in São Paulo, Brazil; and in 1975, he was elected a Fellow of the American Academy of Arts and Sciences. He also enjoyed spells as a visiting professor, at Washington University in St. Louis Missouri in 1971, at Harvard in 1973, and at Yale in 1977.

Though MacDonald was in a much better position than he had been before becoming a full professor, he still felt less than entirely secure, and in the years leading up to 1974, when Smith offered him a named chair, making him the Alice Pratt Brown Professor of History of Art, he seems to have welcomed overtures made by several other institutions, amongst them Hecht's own university, Rochester. Nothing came of these overtures, however, and he remained at Smith until his retirement, enjoying the freedom it allowed him to accept visiting positions around the country, giving lectures at Berkeley, Cornell, Harvard, MIT, New York University, Princeton, and elsewhere.

Both men were busy on the vocational as well as the academic fronts. Hecht and Bacon's translation of *Seven Against Thebes*, which they had embarked on in 1968, was published by Oxford University Press in 1973, and attracted a number of admiring reviews. H. D. Cameron said of the pair that they had "produced a translation of the *Seven* which makes exciting reading in its own right as English dramatic poetry,"[1] and George P. Elliott called it a "splendid restitution … due to the working together of a scholar … who had the intimate knowledge, and a poet … who had the full, strong, supple language to imagine this play out from its obscurity."[2] The translation didn't go altogether uncriticized, however: P. T. Stevens drew attention to a number of "deviations" and "additions" he regarded as unjustified, and complained about a number of "coinages" he regarded as infelicitous, but he nevertheless commended the work as "forceful, idiomatic and also surprisingly close to the original." Hecht himself came to think the translation of *Seven Against Thebes* unsuccessful,[3] but his disappointment with it didn't prevent him from agreeing to tackle a second classic, Sophocles's *Oedipus at Colonos*, this time working with another classicist from Smith, George Dimock. The collaboration did not work out, however, and all that survives of it is "Praise for Kolonos," this being one of the previously unpublished poems which were included in *Millions of Strange Shadows*.[4]

MacDonald's next two books appeared in quick succession, *Northampton Massa-*

1 *The Classical World*, 69:3 (November, 1975), pp. 205-206.

2 *The American Poetry Review*, 3:1 (January-February, 1974),

3 For more on this, see See *Anthony Hecht in Conversation with Philip Hoy*, p. 62.

4 Hecht made a second attempt on the play slightly later on, this time working with William Arrowsmith, who was General Editor of *The Greek Tragedy in New Translations* series, for which the collaboration with Dimock was intended, and to which *Seven Against Thebes* belonged. There will be more about this second attempt in the sequel.

chusetts: *Architecture & Buildings* being published by the Northampton Bicentennial Committee in 1975 and *The Pantheon: Design, Meaning, and Progeny* being published by Harvard University Press (in the States) and by Penguin Books (in the UK) in 1976. At over 180 pages, and packed with hundreds of photographs, most of which had been taken by MacDonald himself, *Northampton Massachusetts* was intended, so its introduction makes clear, as "a close, affectionate look at [Northampton's] gallery of buildings, good and not so good alike, [using] them to make a modest excursion into the nature and meaning of American architecture." While calling it a "congenially written, well-illustrated essay … essentially an informal guide to stylistic shifts in American architecture as exemplified in the rich variety of Northampton, Massachusetts," Roger B. Stein still thought it appropriate to chide MacDonald for not having written a very different kind of book. *Northampton, Massachusetts*, he said, was "one more example of a species of book which stands between the scholarly architectural monograph and the new local history," and then opined that "its very success at its limited task may discourage the undertaking of more precise, historically and aesthetically more valuable studies."[1]

The Pantheon: Design, Meaning, and Progeny was also intended for a wide readership. Carl Condit, though he found things to admire in the book, voiced feelings not dissimilar to Stein's: "The work before us … hardly offers a proper introduction to the author's abilities, although this is not to imply any failure on his part. The little volume was written as one of a series presumably on great buildings of the past, but neither the author nor the editors have seen fit to tell us anything about its aim or character. All I can infer from the text is that it was intended for readers who used to be called 'educated laymen' and who were regarded as willing to read serious books as long as their minds were not taxed by difficult technical detail."[2] John J. Bishop was much less grudging: "This slender volume is both an expansion and condensation of the author's earlier *The Architecture of the Roman Empire*, a work which was geared principally for the scholar. We have here perhaps something written more for the layman and general student of classical art. Considering its size and the brevity of each section, the text is profusely illustrated and well-documented. While no radically new interpretations are advanced here, and the majority of those opinions offered are orthodox, we are to congratulate Professor MacDonald for presenting the history and significance of such an important building as the Pantheon in a clear and judicious fashion."[3]

1976 saw publication of yet another book in whose genesis MacDonald had played a serious part. This was *The Princeton Encyclopedia of Classical Sites*, for which he was an associate editor, and to which he had made numerous contributions. Running to more than 1,000 pages, this was a hugely ambitious volume, and one that was generally very well received. "This book brings to fruition a project vast in concept, international in scope," wrote Paul MacKendrick. "It covers, and pinpoints

---

1 *The Journal of American History*, 63:3 (December, 1976), pp. 708-709.
2 *Technology and Culture*, 18:2 (April. 1977), p. 243.
3 *Art Journal*, 37:1 (Autumn, 1977), p. 92.

on twenty maps, nearly 3,000 sites, dating from 750 BC to AD 365, described by 398 contributors from 17 countries. Nearly all the important sites are described by their excavators, or by persons of recognized expertise."[1] Another reviewer, William M. Calder III, could barely contain his enthusiasm: "Already I cannot imagine life without this wonderful book. I have consulted and cited it again and again ... [This is] a much needed, permanent work of reference."[2]

MacDonald produced one more book during the period under consideration. In the summer of 1978, he was asked by Smith College to give the annual Katherine Asher Engel lecture. The lectureship had been established in 1958, and under the terms of its endowment the honoree had to be a member of the Smith College faculty "who has made an outstanding contribution to knowledge in his or her field." MacDonald chose to talk about the sources of Piranesi's architectural imagery. The lecture, entitled "Piranesi's Carceri: Sources of Invention," was given that November, and Smith published it as a 32-page booklet the following year.

Thanks in no small measure to the success of *The Hard Hours*, Hecht's poems were in great demand throughout this period. Of the thirty-one he included in his 1977 collection, *Millions of Strange Shadows*, twenty-six had already appeared in print, and in as many as fourteen different journals, amongst them the *New Yorker*, *Encounter*, *Harper's*, *The American Scholar*, *Antaeus*, the *Hudson Review*, *Ploughshares*, and the UK's *New Statesman* and *Times Literary Supplement*. Another of the thirty-one had been published in a limited edition by the prestigious Penmaen Press, and two more had been given as Phi Beta Kappa poems, the first at Swarthmore College and the second at Harvard.

After *Millions of Strange Shadows* was published – by Atheneum in the States and by Oxford University Press in the UK – it received a great many laudatory reviews. Richard Howard, in a lengthy piece which got to the latest collection only after reflecting on its predecessors, spoke of the new poems' "magnificence."[3] And Harold Bloom, in a piece surveying what he called "the middle generation of American poets," wrote as follows: "Emotional intensity and formal power were combined in Hecht from his beginnings ... The 30 poems in Hecht's new book are fully *written*, but several truly are the best he has published and are very likely to endure."[4] A dissenting opinion was voiced by Denis Donoghue, however. "Emily Dickinson said of poetry: 'If I read a book and it makes my whole body so cold no fire can ever warm me, I know that is poetry. If I feel physically as if the top of my head were taken off, I know that is poetry.' By this criterion Mr. Hecht's poems are seldom poetry: it is easy to admire them but hard to keep the admiration from being frigid."[5] On the same day this review appeared, Hecht wrote about it to Harry Ford, his editor

---

1 *Classical Philology*, 74:1 (January 1979), p. 78.

2 *The Classical Journal*, 73:4 (April–May, 1978), pp. 359-360.

3 *Poetry*, 131:2 (November, 1977), p. 105.

4 *The New Republic* (November 26th, 1977), pp. 24-25.

5 *The New York Times*, March 27th, 1977, p. 266. The review can be read online at http://www.nytimes.com/1977/03/27/archives/millions-of-strange-shadows.html

at Atheneum: "We have just returned from a spring vacation in Florida ... and I breezed into the Yale Co-op [Hecht was a visiting professor at Yale at this time] to see how things were doing, and one of the young men who works there and knows me asked if I had yet seen The New York Times Book Review of my book. As he fished about for it he told me it was by Denis Donoghue, and I remarked that he was a critic I admired. And then I read the review as the young man stood there and watched. It was a little bit like being publicly disemboweled."[1]

Only two years after Atheneum and OUP released their US and UK editions of *Millions of Strange Shadows*, the same two publishers released their editions of Hecht's fourth collection, *The Venetian Vespers*. This time, Hecht could take pleasure in what the *New York Times*'s reviewer had to say: "In its clear-eyed mercy towards human weakness, Anthony Hecht's poetry goes from strength to strength. *The Venetian Vespers* is at once an intense corroboration and an ample extension of his subtle, supple talents. Nothing human is alien to him ... Hecht [is] a poet of the widest apprehensions and comprehension, and this without the gigantism that so haunts American poetic ambition."[2] Another admiring notice appeared in the UK's *Literary Review*: "*The Venetian Vespers* places [Hecht] firmly in the forefront of contemporary poetry. With a vocabulary as rich and strange as Hart Crane's, and an imagination and intelligence well beyond the scope of that writer, he has produced a narrative poem of thirty pages (the title-work of this volume) which is virtually unique among contemporary long poems, in that at it never sags or diffuses into ponderous rumination, but consistently impels the reader forward with a force that is part rhetorical, and part the urgency of a man who has found, in his response to Venice, access to the thing that affects him most vitally; a sense of the world as at once grotesque and beautiful."[3] The collection won the UK's Poetry Book Society Recommendation.

I have said something about developments on the academic and vocational fronts. I now need to say something more about developments on the personal fronts.

After his marriage to Helen D'Alessandro, the next big occurrence in Hecht's private life was the arrival of their son, who was born in the spring of 1972. Scattered

---

[1] When David Mason reviewed *The Selected Letters of Anthony Hecht*, he described Donoghue's *New York Times* notice as "scathing." Donoghue denied the charge: "I am afraid David Mason has read my prose with a carelessness it does not deserve ... Any careful reader would see that the review, far from being scathing, is reverent, as in the presence of a master of a certain style, a poet sensitive to the cost of achieving such a style." Mason responded by quoting from Hecht's letter to Ford (see *The Selected Letters of Anthony Hecht*, p. 161), and from another letter Hecht sent on the same day to W. D. Snodgrass (see *The Selected Letters of Anthony Hecht*, p. 162), saying that Donoghue had "clobbered" him. Hecht's own reading of Donoghue's piece is undeniably significant, but I think it would have been more effective if Mason had also quoted Donoghue's own words, since there is no getting round their critical purport. Mason's review appeared in *The New Criterion*, 31:8 (April, 2013), p. 33, and Donoghue's rebutting letter together with Mason's response to it appeared in *The New Criterion*, 32:1 (September, 2013), p. 80.

[2] Christopher Ricks, "Poets Who Have Learned Their Trade," *New York Times Book Review* (December 2nd, 1979), p. 1. The full review can be read online at: http://www.nytimes.com/1979/12/02/archives/poets-who-have-learned-their-trade-the-venetian-vespers.html?_r=0

[3] James Lasdun, "Spiced and Curious," *Literary Review* (July, 1980).

throughout the correspondence thereafter are fond references to the boy's progress, the earliest of which, written just a few weeks later, records that "Evan Alexander, ever on the move, has advanced from colic to constipation," and welcomes this as making for "liveliness and variety."[1]

Less welcome events occurred later on. In 1977, in the very same week that *Millions of Strange Shadows* received its hammering in the *New York Times*, Hecht's father attempted suicide. The attempt was unsuccessful, but there can be little doubt about the distress it caused, not least because of its effects on his mother and brother. In September of 1978, Hecht Sr. finally passed away, to be followed, in February, 1979, by Hecht's mother. None of these developments is mentioned in the extant correspondence, which, given that 1977, 1978, and 1979, were the three years in which that correspondence was at its peak, may seem a little surprising, unless we suppose that Hecht didn't wish to burden MacDonald with bad news.

Earlier on, I ventured to suggest that MacDonald, so far from being troubled by the break-up of his marriage to Dale, might actually have welcomed it. I did not mean to suggest that he welcomed every aspect of it, naturally. For one thing, he and Dale found they could not agree on how their assets were to be divided, and lawyers had to be brought in, as he explains in a letter sent to Hecht early in 1970:

> Life here is chaotic. Dale's lawyers have at last presented my lawyer with demands as to money & property settlements, and they are preposterous. But as Dale is suing me, and this is an adversary action, I may just have to sit still and be skinned alive. It galls me, but I don't know what else to do. And then of course I'm having a little woman trouble – not too serious, but as always more diverting that one would wish. I'm not very bright about such things.[2]

But for another thing, the easy access to his sons that MacDonald had been enjoying was not to last. In May of 1973, he writes to Hecht as follows:

> Did I tell you that [Dale and the boys] are moving to Oregon about July first? Big Thing, not clear why Dale wants to do it; but she's sold her Amherst house and that's that. I shall miss them a great deal, but it is likely that Noel will go to College in the East, so that will help somewhat. Life is mystifying.[3]

By this time, though, MacDonald was embarked on a new relationship. A certain Nancy Stark had already come and gone, but since her departure MacDonald had been dating Barbara E. Satz, a reporter working for the *Holyoke Daily Transcript-Telegram*. Her presence in his life doubtless helped him to adjust to the changing

---

1 Letter #80, May 15th, 1972.
2 Letter #44, February 11th, 1970.
3 Letter #93, [May] 15th, 1973.

circumstances, and it is clear that, even though they never lived together (though they did talk about doing so at one point), and the relationship wasn't always easy, she was for several years a supportive and resourceful companion.[1]

Three other developments in MacDonald's personal life are worth noting here. Early in June 1977, just as the Hechts were about to depart for Salzburg, they learned that MacDonald had been hospitalized, though they didn't know why. A little under two weeks later, the patient was able to put their minds at rest:

> I'd time only to alert Nick & Noel, Barbara, & my brother John. A nightmare. I'm home now, and recovering slowly but well, though I've no staying power. Whole thing clears the mind marvelously, to invent a phrase. No cancer. Going to be all right.[2]

While reassuring the Hechts that he does not have cancer, and is going to be "all right," he neglects to tell them what it was that he had had to be treated for, which was a potentially life-threatening intestinal blockage. (His casualness about this is reminiscent of his casualness a few months earlier, when, barely a month after moving out of the family home, he had dropped this bit of news into a letter: "Have just had pneumonia but am over it now."[3])

Only four months after MacDonald tells the Hechts that he doesn't have cancer and is going to be all right, he has to write to them with news about Dale:

> I talked with Dale's surgeon Wednesday, I think it was, + the prognosis is not good. She begins radiation therapy today as the cancer is inoperable.[4]

There is something a little shocking about what MacDonald goes on to say immediately after this, and in closing:

> I enclose a lady for Evan, in the hope that she will guide him toward a fine taste in such matters.[5]

What the now missing enclosure was we have no way of knowing – a newspaper cutting, perhaps, or a postcard – and in its absence we cannot guess what MacDonald

---

1 On page v of his 1975 book, *Northampton Massachusetts: Architecture and Buildings,* MacDonald credits Satz with a critical reading of the book and thanks her for help with the photography. On page 9 of his 1976 book, *The Pantheon: Design, Meaning, and Progeny,* he writes: "Barbara Satz read the manuscript with painstaking care, exposing vague and infelicitous passages, and I want to thank her for her patient, productive help." And on [the unnumbered] page 5 of his 1979 book, *Piranesi's Carceri: Sources of Invention,* he once again thanks her for her "suggestions and criticisms."

2 Postcard #139, June 20th, 1977.

3 Letter #31, September 28th, 1969.

4 Letter #181, October 27th, 1977.

5 Ibid.

means to be saying about it, but the light-hearted note is unmistakable, and jarring. Dale was the mother of his two sons, after all, and someone Hecht had known and liked. To close a letter this grave on a note so light surely argues unusual insensitivity? I think what the letter actually shows is not insensitivity but awkwardness, the awkwardness of a bewildered man who is uncomfortable with displays of emotion, and who seeks to avoid any such display by availing himself of yet another amusing enclosure – these having become a stock item in the two men's correspondence.

A little later, MacDonald does say something about his feelings concerning Dale's illness: "I don't exactly know how I feel, other than sorrow and indeed a kind of pity …"[1] His awkwardness is manifest even here, however, the statement being tucked away in the second of two postscripts to a longish and otherwise typical letter, one which comes complete with jokey salutation ("My dear Lord Byron) and sign-off ("Orville Wright"). Hecht's response to this letter repays close consideration:

> As I feel sure you have divined, I have found it forbiddingly difficult to write you about Dale, about all the horror she is now going through, and all the horror you and your sons are imaginatively going through with her. There is nothing to say except to acknowledge the terrible facts, and it would be a heartless impertinence to cast about for cheap consolations or edifying maxims. I send, in their place, my love.[2]

Would Hecht have found it so forbiddingly difficult to write about Dale's plight if he had taken at face value MacDonald's claim not to know how he himself felt about it? And why would he have spoken about the horror that both MacDonald and his sons would be "imaginatively going through," when all that MacDonald had admitted to feeling was "sorrow and indeed a kind of pity"? Hecht, I'm sure, was not merely being polite; he believed that his friend was suffering, even if his friend found it hard to acknowledge.

Dale died on May 27th, 1978, and MacDonald, writing to inform the Hechts, concludes his brief note saying, "I'm all right, but if it weren't for Noel and Nicholas I'd be worse off."[3] Ten days later, he writes again, chiefly to thank Hecht for his touching response to the news of Dale's death, but also to share yet more bad news. He is about to fly to California to visit someone else who is dying of cancer, this time his oldest friend, Lanny Larson. Some months go by, and then, in early December, he mentions Larson once more:

> The boys are fine. My work goes well. My old friend Lanny Larson, with whom I flew in the war, died of cancer the day before Thanksgiving.

1 Letter #169, January 11th, 1978.

2 Letter #171, January 17th, 1978. The day before he sent this letter, AH had sent WLM a light-hearted postcard, deploring the fact that he had just turned 55. I think it clear that he had not received letter #169 by this time. That letter, though it was written on the 11th, wasn't posted until the 12th, and we can be reasonably sure that it did not reach him until after the weekend of the 14th and 15th.

3 Postcard #194, May 28th, 1978.

All had been waiting for it. I didn't go out, as there was no service; I'd seen him a couple of times during the summer.[1]

Once again, the bad news is tucked into the last lines of an otherwise cheerful-sounding letter.

If MacDonald's side of the correspondence isn't much given to emotional display, it is only fair to say that neither is Hecht's. From quite early on, the friends seem to have found their natural element in the light-hearted, the playful, and the bantering – in a word, in *badinage*. Both men were perfectly capable of turning serious, of course – when talking about their own work, for example, or each other's, or their families, or their colleagues, or their travels, or their wartime experiences, or their health – but such turnings were understood to be departures from the norm, a norm typically returned to within the space of a paragraph or two, or, just occasionally, a letter or two.[2]

One further development in MacDonald's life needs to be mentioned here – a development which cannot be described as academic, or vocational, or personal, because it encompassed all three. Early in 1980, fifteen years after moving to Northampton, MacDonald gave Smith College notice. He would quit his chair at the end of the academic year, so as to devote himself more fully to his writing while continuing to accept visiting lectureships around the country. He would also be looking for somewhere else to live. "Don't know where I'll move to eventually; things will be so much different in five or so years that it strikes me the only thing to do is to keep on writing, and let the future, for the nonce (what the hell is a nonce?) look after itself."[3]

---

1 Letter #222, 1st December, 1978.

2 This may help to explain another noteworthy feature of the Hecht-MacDonald correspondence, which is its avoidance of all but an occasional and passing reference to events in the wider world, except where these can be harnessed for comic or satirical purposes. One can read one's way through the letters and postcards they sent each other between 1969 and 1980, for example, without encountering any substantial reference to the Vietnam war, the Pentagon Papers, the Watergate scandal, the OPEC-sponsored oil crisis, President Nixon's resignation, the ascendancy of Gerald Ford, the ending of the war, the inauguration of President Carter, the signing of the Camp David Accords, the Three Mile Island accident, or the Iran hostage crisis (to mention only some of the most significant events of the period).

3 Letter #257, [February 15th, 1980].

[18]

[AH]
January 20th, 1969
American Academy in Rome, Via Angelo Masina, 5 (Porta S. Pancrazio), 00153, Rome

[Letter, typed on an American Academy in Rome letterhead]

Dear Sir John,

There is an air of quiet but distinct rejoicing in Vatican circles these days, prompted by the news of the conversion of Tennessee Williams.[1] Barely in modern times has the church received such an opportunity for the widest and most popular sort of propagation of the faith. It is rumored that the playwright will shortly undertake the rewriting of the Oberammergau Passion Play. In the new version, Christ, a well hung, clean limbed, thick chested, blond headed, blue eyed, young sexual athlete, clad only in a thick leather belt and one earring, summons his disciples to The Last Supper; but when he offers them the wine and the bread, saying, "This is my blood, and this is my body," they refuse to accept any cheap substitutes; and, leaping upon him with all the old familiar cannibalistic enthusiasm we all came to love so much in early works like "Suddenly Last Summer," they dismember him, and have a really hearty, bang-up meal in place of the thin fare he was offering. Mr. Williams is known to have felt that the original version of the play was much too long. "Compression," he has remarked, "is the essence of art." We must look forward with delighted anticipation to the opening, which, by special arrangement with the town council of Oberammergau, will take place at Lincoln Center in New York. And we may be certain beforehand of the emphatic endorsement of the work by Brooks Atkinson.

Your news is cheery, and I look forward to your visit, and have already mentioned to some here (F[rank] E. B[rown] & Helen Bacon) your primavera advent, accompanied, I should hope, by Flora and a scattering of nymphs. And good to hear was the news that Learned Buskin[2] has authored another young gent. Pass on to him and the family my warm good wishes.

I am in the winter doldrums with my own work, damn it, but have the translation[3] to keep me steadily occupied, which is a good thing. But itching steadily away at the back of my mind is the knowledge that, despite friends here and much good company, I am lonely and hard up. I'm only half complaining; there are all the compensations of even being here at all – and almost under the best circumstances. Today a gaggle of Roman tree surgeons cut down some dead timber obstructing the view from my living room window, and I can now see perfectly clearly what Frank Brown properly calls the ugliest dome in Rome: the big Synagogue across the Tiber.

1 Williams had converted to Roman Catholicism in 1968.
2 The artist Leonard Baskin, who was a colleague of WLM's at Smith College.
3 AH was collaborating with the classicist Helen Bacon on a translation of Aeschylus's *Seven Against Thebes*.

The trip you suggest sounds great, and I hope both our schedules work out to allow it. I must come back to Rochester for a few days in May to find a house for next fall. On my return I will stop off along the French Riviera to find a place to take the children during the month of June or thereabouts. Let me know your plans when they clarify.

Love,
Prince Hal

WEIGHED AND FOUND
WANTING

[19]

[WLM]
May 8th, 1969
409 Prospect Street, Northampton, Massachusetts 01060

[Blank note, typed, addressed to Professor Anthony HECHT,
Accademia Americana, Via A. Masina, 5, 00153 <u>ROMA</u>, Italia]

There is a nice, 30-ish, woman at Mount Holyoke who has had or is about to get an offer from the Art Dept at the University of Rochester. She is hesitating, not having any idea of what kind of a place R. is to live in and, more importantly, because she seems to read into the administration-Department relationships the potential for trouble. I know that this is vague, but do you have any gen on this? Dale & I are fond of her and thought we would drop you this line to see if you have any scoop; all scoop kept anonymous.

PTO →→

I bet you don't have an arrow like that!

I saw in Harvard Square the other day a sign saying that a store carried a rubber stamp which prints "BULLSHIT." Admiring as I do your W. & Found Wanting, I went in to get a B. for you, but they were sold out. I just wanted you to know that I'm thinking of you ... Talked to [Dimitri] Hadzi on the phone the other day, but didn't get a chance to see him. We're off to Ireland in 2 weeks. Please reply instantly.

Vegetius Rector
8v69 (drives my colleagues wild)

[...]

[20]

[WLM]
July 1st, 1969
409 Prospect Street, Northampton, Mass 01060

[Letter, typed, addressed to Professor Anthony HECHT, Accademia Americana, Via A. Masina, 5, 00153 ROMA, Italia]

Dear Tony,

[…]

Do you like Offenbach? Just bought the Urania recording of "La Grande Duchesse de Gerolstein." Great.

Seneca, Burrus, and Petronius were trying to get up something really good for Nero's birthday. Finally they hit upon the crucifixion of a hundred Christians along the Appian way. When Nero came up from Antium for his birthday celebration and saw this, he was immensely pleased. He slowed his chariot and looked at each dead face. But at the end there was a live one, far gone, to be sure, but alive. The man seemed to be gesturing, so Nero dismounted and walked up to this last cross. "Whatever is this one doing?" he asked; but at that moment the man fixed the emperor's eye, fluttered a ghastly little gesture with one hand, and slowly croaked, "Happy Birthday, Nero."

Dale and I are discussing separation. Nothing new, don't know how it will come out … I'll be here all summer & will hope to visit Fire Island if I'm invited. Saltaire, 11706? … Ireland wet, rocky, alcoholic. Liked it. Then to walk Hadrian's wall, and a week or ten days in London town. I'd forgotten how much I like London; it was just great.

Trying to finish the Atheneum book![1] Only four years, four months overdue, which isn't too bad.

Give my love to Frank and Jackie [Brown]; and give a call when you have a minute after you get back. Many things to discuss.

> Veuillez, agréer, Monsieur, mes
> salutations distinguées; et
> croyez a l'expression de mes
> sentiments les meilleurs.[2]

[Signature illegible]

---

1 Even before he had completed work on *The Architecture of the Roman Empire: An Introductory Study*, which he did during 1962-63, WLM had embarked on something he called its "sequel." Although the first book was published by Yale University Press, the second was under contract to Atheneum. It seems not to have had a proper title at this time, hence his references to it, here and subsequently, as "the Atheneum book," "the Cities book," and "the Atheneum / Cities book."

2 A formal valediction of the kind once popular with the French, which can be literally rendered along the lines of: "Please accept, Sir, my distinguished salutations; and believe in the expression of my best wishes."

[21]

[AH]
August 7th, 1969
Saltaire, Fire Island, New York 11706

[Letter, typed on a The University of Rochester, College of Arts and Science, River Campus Station, Rochester, New York 14627, Department of English, letterhead]

Dear Dodge Owner,

I hope, fer Cry Sakes, that you have kept my entire correspondence on file so that in due course you can make a mint of money by publishing my letters, you lucky bastard. I will even give you a few hints and guide-lines for the introduction, which, I think, might begin somewhat along these lines: "When I first knew Anthony Hecht he had not yet attained to the world-wide celebrity that was later to be his; he was a simple, charming, and modest young man – and all these qualities (except, possibly, his youth) he maintained throughout his career and despite his eminence." Something along that line, if you see what I mean. A few cheerful anecdotes to illustrate my natural wit and good nature might not be out of place, if judiciously chosen. But I suggest that if you must err, it be on the side of brevity, and that you let the letters speak for themselves.

I have just completed a poem on a touching, religious theme, which I send you forthwith:

> Said Mary to Gabriel, "Oi!
> Well, at least I am glad it's a boy.
> But what should I say
> When my waistline gives way?
> That I'm filled with elation and goy?"

I have an idea for some really filthy pictures for your book on Roman cities; I'm sure Mike Bessie will approve.[1] After all, it will really sell the book.

Forever,
Jeremy Bentham

---

1 Mike Bessie was Atheneum's president.

[22]

[AH]
[August 11th, 1969]
[Saltaire, Fire Island, New York 11706]

[Letter, typed on a The University of Rochester, College of Arts and Science, River Campus Station, Rochester, New York 14627, Department of English, letterhead]

Dear Mr. Answer-Man,
   Is it true that in the name of the Vice-President of the United States, Spiro stands for spirochete? My father says, yes, but my mother says, oh shit, Sam, what'r ye telling the boy?[1]

Sincerely,
Sam, Jr. (10 years old)

We must be in touch by phone so that I can tell you about ferry schedules. How are you planning to come?

[23]

[WLM]
August 21st, 1969
409 Prospect Street, Northampton, Massachusetts 01060

[Draft flier, addressed to A.E. Hecht Esq., Saltaire, L.I., N.Y., 11706, Fire Island]

A New Concept in Lecturing! Two Distinguished
writer-scholars offer five very unusual, indeed numinous,
lectures designed for today's modern needs! There is
nothing like this
anywhere!

The lecturers:

Anthony Hecht, BA, DHL promised, FAAR, etc, etc, author of numerous well-thought-of poems; speaker, raconteur, traveler; co-inventor of the murderously difficult double dactyl form; presently ABC Prof of XYZ at the UnivRoch

---

1 Spiro T. Agnew, Vice-President under Richard Nixon, and the only person so far to have resigned that office as a result of facing criminal proceedings. In the summer of 1973 – four years after AH's letter was written – Agnew was under investigation by the United States Attorney's office for the District of Maryland on charges of extortion, tax fraud, bribery, and conspiracy. That October, he was charged with having accepted bribes totaling more than $100,000 while holding office as Baltimore County Executive, Governor of Maryland, and Vice President of the United States. He was allowed to plead no contest to a single charge that he had failed to report $29,500 of income received in 1967, but only on condition that he resign the office of Vice President, which he did.

William L. MacDonald, A.B., A.M., Ph.D, F.A.A.R.; author of numerous well-thought-of articles and books; speaker, raconteur, traveler; presently Sophia Smith Professor of Art and the History of Architecture at Smith College.

The lectures:

There are five listed below. This is a package deal, all must be taken. For highly sophisticated audiences one of the lectures will, on request, be given <u>by the two lecturers together</u>, achieving an effect so splendid as to defy description.

Lecture number 1 (Hecht) <u>Famous Streetcar Accidents</u>. This extraordinary and learned discourse probes matters of which few educators and students have ever dreamed. Perhaps if Melanchthon's great recipe for gooseberry pie is invoked here, some sense of this marvelous talk will be suggested.

Lecture number 2 (MacDonald) <u>"Little" Women</u>. There is nothing prurient in this talk, though it is illustrated by color slides (2×2," one projector, powerful) taken by the speaker in out-of-the-way parts of the world. Charts will be displayed. For General audiences (G).

Lecture number 3 (Hecht). <u>Little-Known Facts in the Sex Life of Harriet Beecher Stowe</u>. This <u>is</u> a little prurient, but no slides will be shown <u>at all</u>. Suggested for (M) mature audiences. Mrs Stowe will surprise you.

Lecture number 4 (MacDonald) <u>Great Hats I Have Worn</u>. Basically, this lecture is as serious as the others. The speaker concerns himself with matters of style, and tends to dispute Mark Twain's famous dictum.[1] Interesting, tendentious dicta follow. Anyone can come, and not be concerned.

Lecture number 5 (Hecht, or for the more sophisticated, Hecht and MacDonald; tricky). <u>The Phlogiston Theory: Will It Make a Comeback?</u> Here the two cultures, made famous by Snow White, are imploded against each other. A pyrotechnical display of erudition. The dual performance is recommended, even though there is a surcharge (see below).

The normal spacing of these lectures is two on a Saturday afternoon, two that evening, and the great no. 5 on Sunday morning, rather early.

Fees: high to very high, but negotiable.

Contact

[1] It is difficult to be sure, but the dictum referred to here may well be this: "Clothes make the man. Naked people have little or no influence on society." The only source for the attribution to Twain is *More Maxims of Mark*, edited and privately published by Merle Johnson (1927).

AEH　　　　　WLM
Roch　　or　　Smith

[Unsigned][1]

[24]

[AH]
August 25th, 1969
Saltaire, Fire Island, New York 11706

[Letter, typed on an Adam International Review, 28 Emperor's Gate, London, S.W. 7, England, *letterhead]*

Dear Comrade,

    Your outline of the lecture series is fine; we should be inundated with invitations. We must formulate some discreet way of indicating that the fees include the provision of beautiful chicks for the night. Indeed, as I think about it, I come more and more to feel that no invitation ought seriously to be considered unless it included large, glossy photographs of the two young ladies, clad, if at all, in nothing more than bikinis; as well as affectionate personal notes from them, urging us to come, in every sense. My <u>Webster's New World Dictionary</u>,[2] which is anything but a blameless volume, offers as its third definition of "enharmonic," this: "relating to tones nearly identical in pitch, as E-flat and D-sharp, produced by the same key on a keyed instrument;…" Would you be so good as to explain the meaning of "nearly"?

    Tom and Emily Schumacher were out, Emily for almost a week, and Tom for this past weekend. I made a great curry of lamb, which turned out fine. According to Tom and Emily, everyone at Cornell believed and continues to believe that the reason the appointment was not offered to you was because Steve Jacobs would not have it, and scotched the whole thing. Tom said everyone there was enormously enthusiastic about your lecture, and that this story about Jacobs was not wild academic surmise but "known facts" supplied by "informed persons." They were both rather surprised, therefore, to hear the story as you told it to me.

    Hope the baths[3] are going well,

                  A. N. Whitehead

---

1 As the reader will have gathered, the lecture series proposed here was not intended seriously, though as we shall see in the sequel, AH did once deliver a lecture he had entitled "Little Known Facts in the Sex-Life of Harriet Beecher Stowe."

2 *Webster's New World Dictionary of the American Language*, College Edition, edited by David B. Guralnik (Cleveland, OH and New York: World Publishing Company), 1969.

3 WLM was writing an article about the so-called "small baths" at the great villa constructed by Emperor Hadrian near Tivoli.

[25]

[WLM]
August 26th, 1969
409 Prospect Street, Northampton, Massachusetts 01060

[Letter, typed, addressed to A E Hecht, Saltaire, Long Island NY 11706]

like the 26th

Tovarich,

Wish I'd been there for the curry. Can see Tom S. clearly in my mind; can't recover Emily. Is she a dish? Where will they be this coming year?

The Cornell thing bothers me a little. I've written to Jacobs without mentioning any names or circumstances, saying that I went in good faith at the request of the student lecture committee, and was not looking for a place. I emphasized to him that no one at all ever told me I was being "looked over" and closed by saying that it was probably the usual academic fog, & that I wanted the air clear between us. But it's nice to know they liked my lecture; as a matter of fact they were right to react that way; it's very good.

I do agree about the pix & notes from chicks at places where we might perform; it's a nice touch. Shows we're serious, normal, expect a lot. I find that people like it if you expect a lot. Non-expectancy, that's the world's problem. I could go on …

I am working on the enharmonic "nearly." It's a doozer. It may be that in their usual muddled way, Webster's have mixed this word up with enhamonic, the condition induced by eating pork insufficiently cooked, that is,   ,[1] (I can't remember the name of the disease, which rather weakens my point), pork. When that happens, one is as "nearly" as one can get, if you get my point. For further muddling, see "median"; Issus / Ipsus[2] (which they mix up and which no amount of letter writing or threats moves them*). Why can't they adopt the leisurely ways of the Encyclopedia Britannica which, under "Phoenix," says that the p. seen in 36 BC in the Campus Martius "was generally thought to be spurious"?

*truly, I have been at war with them for over 20 yrs about this; they cite things like the Encyclopedia Britannica! Also, try "Theodoric" in their dirty companion book, Webster's Biographical Dictionary.[3]

Baths march
Sir Cairo Portcullis, Bt.

---

1 WLM subsequently remembered the word and hand-wrote it in the blank space: "trichinosis."

2 WLM is complaining about the confusion of two battles, the Battle of Issus, which took place near the southern Anatolian town of that name in BC 333 and the Battle of Ipsus, which took place near the village of that name in Phrygia in BC 301.

3 *Webster's Biographical Dictionary* (Springfield, MA: G & C Merriam Co.,1969.

[26]

[AH]
August 28th [1969]
Saltaire, etc.

[Letter, typed on a The Hudson Review, *65 East 55th Street, New York, NY 10022, letterhead]*

Dear fellow-citizen,

    It is merely a feeble and boneless sentimentality that accounts for your attachment to the Encyclopedia Britannica. Please to remember in your weaker moments of Anglophilia, that the bloody thing is published in Chicago, and probably written in large part by Mayor Daley's publicity staff under the sharp-eyed and merciless supervision of Mortimer Adler. I am glad, however, to see that we both agree about Webster's, and at your suggestion I did look up "median," which I had always thought to be the language of the ancient Medes. You are quite right; they are poor on the subject. What charms me most about my volume (it is the New World Dictionary of the American Language) is the patent and explicit nepotism of the editorial board, Etymological and Linguistics Editor: Harold E. Whitehall. Asst. Editor: Laura Robinson Whitehall. Also on the staff: Bryant M. & Dorothee French; Herman & Orah C. Briscoe; James Holly & Ursula Hanford; Goldie & Oscar Rimson; Josephine McCarter & Hugo Gunther; Horace & Jane G. Hilb.[1] Now figure to yourself, as the Frogs say, the giddy domestic wrangles that went into the making of this volume. Among other things, it is remarkably prudish. "Cunt" does not appear, and "prick" only in its innocent meanings. Whose "American" language is this, For Crying Out Loud? The Browning Society's, I suppose; and not Robert but Elizabeth Barrett. It is a sad fall for poor James Holly Hanford, who has been, among other things, an excellent editor of Milton. It would be pleasant to know how many of these great minds went into the making of the third definition of "enharmonic."

    I'm surprised that you do not recall Emily S. for she is, as you say, a dish. A slender, Limoges sort of dish, to be sure, but very pretty. They will be in New York more or less indefinitely, since Tom is working for I. M. Pei. They're a nice couple.

    Be out here about a week more, then total confusion till I arrive in Rochester. Good luck with the baths.

                            Dicky Mountbatten

---

1 AH might also have remarked on the presence of a third Whitehall on the editorial board, namely Alice Whitehall, who is identified in the book's front matter as one of the dictionary's "Special and Contributing Editors." Whether any of these Whitehalls were related remains unclear, however. Harold E. was married twice and had one child, a daughter, but none of these three women was called Laura or Alice.

[27]

[WLM]
August 29th, 1969
[409 Prospect Street, Northampton, Massachusetts 01060]

[Letter, typed on a The Byzantine Institute Inc. letterhead, addressed to Anthony Hecht, Laureate,[1] Saltaire, Long Island, New York, 11706]

Northampton indeed

Dear Mortimer Adler,

I didn't mean that Abomination, the EB14 and its 57 varieties; I meant the EB, 11th ed., lovable, friendly, often wrong, but like the (old) Fowler, nifty. 14 has no good Phoenix spirit; for that sort of thing you need 9 or 11. By the way, when you have nothing else to do, which I suppose is most of the time, try the article "Wines" in 11.

When you get settled in Rochester or wherever it is, and send me your address, I will send you a large copy of the baths plan. Properly colored it ought to make a swell wall decoration. You'll love it. It's big.

G. Frances Perkins of the State Department, that shining example of Amurkan Purity, has removed the can't-go-to-Syria stamp in my passport, so maybe I'll get to the Damascus archaeological conference in October after all. Program says Frank [Brown] is to be one of the speakers. Thought I'd stop off in London Town for a few days on the way back. Care to join?

My quite nice apartment is ready for me and I am starting to take boxes of stuff over. I can't recall if I've signalled you (Australian admiral aboard Melbourne?), but the new genn is:

12 Bedford Terrace, Northampton 01060
413.584.3284
After Sept. 3rd.

I look forward to classes. I always do at this time of year. I dig in, get started, and the next thing I know the term is more than half over. Don't bother to explain this ...

Frederick Morgan[2]

---

1 WLM hereby anticipates by thirteen years AH's 1982-84 appointment as Consultant in Poetry to the Library of Congress, a position which was renamed in 1986 as Poet Laureate Consultant in Poetry to the Library in Congress.

2 The name being tried on here is likely to be that of AH's friend and almost exact contemporary, the poet and founding editor of *The Hudson Review*.

[28]

[AH]
[August 30th, 1969]
[Probably Saltaire, Fire Island, New York 11706]

[Letter, typed on a The Hudson Review *letterhead]*

like the 30th

Dear bird-lover,

The grosbeak (or, grosbeak) though it gathers weeds, twigs, and bits of string for its nest, gathers no moss, and is therefore frequently mistaken for a rolling stone. This is unfortunate, but serves to explain the general fear of avalanches by uninformed people in the mid-west.

We hope you will want to contribute to our fund, which is concerned in part with the better education of mid-western people all over the world, and which is ultimately dedicated to restoring the name of the grosbeak (or, grosbeak) to the dignity which it formerly enjoyed.

fraternally,
Buckminster Fuller

P.S. I have just been asked to give the inaugural convocation address at the University of Rochester on Sept. 21. I wish I had "Famous Streetcar Accidents" ready for the occasion.

[29]

[WLM]
September 8th, 1969
12 Bedford Terrace, Northampton, Massachusetts, 01060

[Letter, typed on a Massachusetts Institute of Technology memorandum slip, addressed to Adjunct Professor Anthony Hecht, Dept. of English, University of Rochester, Rochester, NY., with enclosure]

There was a young lady named Colehill
Who sat down one day on a molehill
    The resident mole
    Stuck his nose up her hole
Miss Colehill's O.K., but the mole's ill

Not original,[1] but rather dainty, don't you think?

---

1 The original appears to date from 1951 and goes as follows: "There was a young lady of Wohl's Hill / Who sat down one day on a mole's hill. / The resident mole / stuck his nose up her hole – The lady's alright, but the mole's ill." Cited in *The Limerick: 1700 Examples, with Notes, Variants and Index*, edited by G. Legman (New York: Bell Publishing Company, 1969).

I. Lessin Gaza

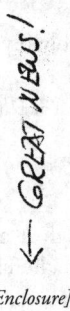

[Enclosure]

[30]

[AH]
[September 24th, 1969]
[The University of Rochester, College of Arts and Science, River Campus Station, Rochester, New York 14627, Department of English]

[Letter, typed on a Smith College memorandum slip]

Kind Sir:

I should very much like to have your mural-sized drawing of the small baths in Hadrian's Villa. I have a small bath of my own, and it would be interesting to compare them. I may add that I quite like the air of abandon with which you suggest taking off to hear Frank Brown in some remote part of the world in mid-October. I'm not sure, however, that I could quite explain that to my colleagues. You will be cheered to know that I addressed the opening convocation of the university this past Sunday. I was introduced by the president, who announced the title of my discourse: "The Phlogiston Theory: Is It Making a Comeback?" I may say that it went very well.

Love
Benedetto Croce

[31]

[WLM]
September 28th, 1969
[12 Bedford Terrace, Northampton, Massachusetts, 01060]

[Letter, typed on a Donald L. Ferguson Cruise: Voyage into Antiquity letterhead]

Hecht:

I worked like hell on your Convocation speech but couldn't reach you by 'phone to read it to you. The Rochester information operators have an Abraham Hecht over on South Gully, but they've never heard of you. In case you get another request to make a speech and I have to go through that again, I enclose a self-addressed, stamped card on which you are to enter various numbers …

Webster's has a dandy tautology under "fugacious": "Fleeing away"! How's that? You can tell anyone you like.

Basking[1] given message, viz.: "What the hell did you do with that poem Tony sent you last February?" The result of this was that Basking smiled, slightly, & looked owlish & mystical, and walked off. Really.

Living alone has its compensations. So far I don't seem to be lonely, but then I can see the boys almost anytime. Have just had pneumonia but am over it now.

I recall the Saltaire weekend with great pleasure. I particularly liked your friends' friend – the Teutonic male. I know now he was just acting a part that he expected we expected of him.

Cheers,
Andrew the Fool
For Christ's Sake

[32]

[WLM]
October 5th, 1969
[12 Bedford Terrace, Northampton, Massachusetts, 01060]

[Letter, typed on a Society of Architectural Historians letterhead, posted in a Society of Architectural Historians' envelope, addressed to A. Hecht, Dep't. of English, Univ. of Rochester, Rochester, N.Y.]

Major Assbum:

It is said that Lord Brougham, summoned to the palace, could find nowhere to leave his carriage. Instructing his driver, then, just to leave it in the courtyard, he stepped out, only to hear Queen Victoria, who was leaning from one of the façade windows, say: "Kindly park elsewhere, Lord Brougham; we are not a mews."

(Gleaned from the Spectator …)

1 Leonard Baskin.

Well I wish I could have heard "Flo Giston Theory." After all, that was Our Beginning. Was it taped? Was it written out? It must be preserved.

Off Friday for the wild and mysterious East. See you some time in November.

Cheers,
General Disorder

[33]

[WLM]
October 29th, 1969
[12 Bedford Terrace, Northampton, Massachusetts, 01060]

[Letter, typed on a New Omayad Hotel, Damas, Republique Arabe Syrienne, letterhead, posted in the same hotel's airmail envelope, addressed to Anthony HECHT, Department of English, University of Rochester, Rochester, N.Y.]

Dear Miss Taylor,

A group of tourists, travelling in northern Wales, were taken to an imposing cenotaph. They gathered round, and the tour guide read the simple inscription:

"Here lies Jacob Rothenstein, Unknown Soldier & Merchant"

"But how," enquired a lively tourist, "could he have been an unknown soldier and a merchant?" "As a soldier," the tour guide replied,"he <u>was</u> unknown; but as a merchant he was famous." Joke.

I have reserved a double at the Commander off the Square for the night of the 14th for both of us, they have your name, we can extend it to Sat. night if we wish, I have influence, or clout, as Trottenberg would say. I have invited about eight or ten people for drinks, including some very juicy broads, for the evening of the 14th. I don't know who will be busy, who can or can't come, &c., or even where we'll have this party (secretly hoping that my pathetic reference to having no place, in my invitations, will ensure that some nice girl will offer her apartment). In any event, things are in train.

Yours,
Mason Hammond

[34]

[WLM]
November 24th, 1969
12 Bedford Terrace, Northampton, Massachusetts 01060

[Letter, typed on a Smith College letterhead, with a now missing enclosure]

Dear Tony,
 How's this for an exotic letterhead? Better than the New Omayad in Damascus, what?
 & here is the photo I spoke of.
 Howard Merritt called to say that only the 19th of December would work as far as the UnivRoch authorities' available time goes. So the 19th it is. I will either fly in on the 18th in the evening or early the next morning; it depends on the flights available. I realise that this is at the beginning of Christmas vacation & that you may well plan to be in NYCity by then. But apparently there are no alternatives to scheduling so I'll come out whether you are there or not. I'll leave your plan with Merritt.
 It was good to see you in Cambridge; I'm sorry the party at Métraux' was a flop. The luncheon with the Kaplans was very enjoyable. Things here are quiet. Nancy and I continue to see each other but that matter is I think under control. I lecture at Columbia after thanksgiving and must get at it.

    Best & goodth,
    Marta Thatcher

[35]

[AH]
[November 27th, 1969]
[315 Rockingham Street, Rochester, New York 14620]

[Letter, typed on a The University of Rochester, Department of English, letterhead, with a now missing enclosure]

WEIGHED AND FOUND WANTING

Thanksgiving, 1969

Dear Bill,
 I didn't realise till a few days ago, when Howard Merritt or somebody let the information slide out smoothly, that you are being considered as a possible chairman. In view of that, there is an awful lot about the department you ought to know, and much of which I can't tell you because I don't know it myself. But at least I can tell you that they've already had some guy from Yale with a German name up here for

a visit in connection with the same job; and having looked the place over, he told the provost in a very straightforward way that he wouldn't consider the chairmanship unless they strengthened the department by at least two or three full-time staff. I don't remember exactly what his stipulations were (there are people here who can tell you) but they apparently seemed excessive to the provost, and I guess the offer was not made – which is why you are coming out. It may be that you know someone at Yale in art history with a German name and can find out more about it from him. In any case, I've been thinking about what the whole thing might mean to you, and three possibilities have occurred to me. (l) You might find that you liked the place, the terms, and, with only minor quibbling, the staff. (2) You might feel, as the Yale guy did, that the staff needs strengthening, but might also find the offer sufficiently attractive to take the job in the hope of enlarging your operations after you've settled in and without any firm commitments from the provost. (3) You might take the Yale man's line, and, with sufficient skill, win over the provost, or at least get him into a bargaining position that was reasonably satisfactory. And now it occurs to me that what I'm really leading up to is a fourth possibility. (4) You may decide very quickly that you want no part of the job; but if you should, you could still do something to help strengthen the department whether you come here eventually or not; and you could do this by pointing out explicitly and in detail to the provost the weaknesses you find in the present department. I may say that there are one or two people here who hope you will do that. They feel that if the provost hears the same message loud and clear several times from distinguished candidates whom the university finds itself unable to secure, he may wise up and fork out. Please don't understand by this last passage, which is not well put, that anyone here is hoping you'll turn the job down. Rather, I have been emphasizing the attractiveness of your present situation, and the convenience of being able to give graduate courses at Harvard or Yale or even New York, so that people here are not altogether hopeful of your accepting. In this mood, therefore, they are hoping that at least some good will come of your visit in the form of wising up the provost.

Have you heard of my recent good fortune? I have just been named a Fellow of the Academy of American Poets, chosen by their Board of Chancellors, which consists of: W. H. Auden, John Berryman, Elizabeth Bishop, Louise Bogan, Robert Fitzgerald, Robert Lowell, William Meredith, Norman Holmes Pearson, Frederick A. Pottle, Allen Tate, John Hall Wheelock, and Richard Wilbur. The fellowship carries with it an award of $10,000. People up here are in something of a tizzy about it (I was invited to dinner by the president, but can't make it because I'll be touring the Tennessee Poetry Circuit this coming week.) Anyway, I am in the process of negotiating another leave, and it looks very much as if I shall be given the spring and fall semesters of '71. I shall probably spend them in my New York apt.

And one further surprise. My children are now attending an American school. Pat arrived with them only a few days ago, and the boys are going to a school near her Long Island house.[1] Needless to say, she did not bother to tell me any of this; I found it out

---

1 Patricia Harris, to whom AH was married between 1954 and 1961, had taken their two sons, Jason and Adam, to Belgium with her soon after her 1962 marriage to Philippe Lambert.

last night through a phone call from my mother. I spoke to Jason on the phone this morning. The rest of them were out; he sounded fine.

I look forward to your visit on the 19th, and hope you will find you can get in on the previous evening. But in any case it will be good to see you and have a chance to booze and chat.

Best
Erwin Panofsky

P.S. Many thanks for the photograph.

[36]

[WLM]
December 1st, 1969
12 Bedford Terrace, Northampton, Massachusetts 01060

[Letter, typed, addressed to Professor Anthony E. Hecht, 315 Rockingham Street, Rochester, N.Y. 14620]

Dear Tony,

What wonderful news about your new Fellowship! It is really great. One's friends' successes are the most marvelous lifter-uppers, too. But it really is great, and all congratulations.

I can see from your long and very useful letter – many, many thanks for taking the time with it – that Rochester without knowing me much is in a marriageable state. I don't know who the Yale man you mention might be – perhaps Walter Cahn, whom I do not know personally. I am most grateful for all the information you give. As I told Merritt with some care, I am just coming out for a look-see, but I get the impression that they have hot pants. Well, we'll see; I've been as diffident, indeed almost as disinterested, as I can be, and have given no encouragements whatsoever to them. Along that line it was most useful for you to have stressed the good sides of my job here … In short, I thought that my forthcoming visit would be very much of a preliminary one, but from your letter it sounds as if they might make an offer. I just can't tell from here what my reaction might be …

My plan is to fly out from Bradley on Thursday the 18th and return on the late afternoon or early evening of the next day. If you're free, we could spend the evening of the 18th together; I will look forward very much to that … I find I'm due in at Rochester airport at 8:39 p.m. on Mohawk 183 on the 18th.

Things here are quiet. Nancy and I see each other about once a week and have quite good, and surprisingly quiet, times. You're right, she's a flirt, but she's also good company, and I can't live without women.

Delighted to hear that your boys are close; probably you'll see them soon.

Cheers,
Arnold Gingrich

[37]

[AH]
[December 1969]
[315 Rockingham Street, Rochester, New York 14620]

[Letter, typed on a The University of Rochester, Intramural Correspondence, letterhead, with enclosure]

Dear Sir,

We are grateful to you for sending us your dossier, which our staffing committee has examined with great care. Indeed, it has persuaded us to examine our own present staff in the light of the particular strengths and qualifications you could bring to it; and this examination, we think, has proved extremely fruitful. It has raised issues we had not properly considered before, and seems likely to foreshadow a very serious reassessment of our future policy of appointments.

With this in mind, we address ourselves first of all to your case. We are obliged to confess, with some embarrassment, that we already have too many Capricorns on the department staff, and of these, a very large majority are of tenured rank, and consequently likely to be with us for some time to come. We are aware, moreover, of an injudiciously large number of Capricorns at the junior level; and we shall probably have to make some abrupt and surgical changes there.

It should consequently be clear to you, from the situation as outlined above, that we do not see our way to offering you an appointment in the near future. What we really need at present is a nice Gemini and a couple of Scorpios. The department is notably deficient in these areas, though we hope to remedy this as soon as possible.

Given the present configuration of departmental horoscopes, it may be said that you would not fit in well here. Aside from the many Capricorns, and a certain widespread and unfortunate tendency to "cuspiness," we have a disproportionately large number of Pisces ("small fry" as we like to call them here) all of them very shy and diffident people, who would undoubtedly be scared to death by anyone like yourself, who "readily harbors grudges" and does "not forget slights or injuries." We regard the potential explosiveness of such a mixture with the greatest alarm. We have, in fact, taken the precaution of consulting the Dean's medium, and she has largely confirmed our anxieties on precisely this point.

At the same time, we are confident that, gifted as you are with "mastery over your emotions" and "an indomitable perseverance which is backed up by will power and strength," you will be able to accept our decision with appropriate fortitude, and will in due course pursue your destiny with undoubted success at some other institution of learning.

Astrophel
Acting Chairman
Department of English

ASTROFLASH   HOROSCOPE 24693   ESTABLISHED ON OCTOBER 20-1969   PAGE C

TAKING THE POSITION OF THE SUN AND THE ASCENDANT INTO CONSIDERATION, WHAT FOLLOWS REPRESENTS THE BASIC ELEMENTS OF YOUR PERSONALITY AND THE CHARACTER TRAITS WHICH FORM THE BACKGROUND OF YOUR EXISTENCE.

SUBJECT'S SIGN OF BIRTH= CAPRICORN
SIGN OF HIS ASCENDANT= CANCER

DEEP WITHIN YOU ENJOY A FORTUNATE BALANCE DUE TO YOUR DELIBERATE MASTERY OVER YOUR EMOTIONS AND THE STRICTNESS OF YOUR CHARACTER. YOUR PERSONALITY IS CONCENTRATED AND AMBITIOUS - YOU'RE DETERMINED TO GET AHEAD. YET THERE IS ANOTHER SECTOR OF YOUR NATURE, AN EMOTIONAL AND SENTIMENTAL TEMPERAMENT WHICH LOOKS BACK TENDERLY ON THE PAST. CONSEQUENTLY, YOU MAY OSCILLATE BETWEEN SERIOUSNESS AND CAPRICE, RUTHLESSNESS AND SOFT-HEARTEDNESS.

LUCKILY, THE TWO SIGNS INFLUENCING YOU HAVE A COMMON TRAIT WHICH RECONCILES THIS CONTRADICTION. THE TRAIT IS AN INDOMITABLE PERSEVERENCE WHICH IS BACKED UP BY WILL-POWER AND STRENGTH. YOUR AMBITION IS SERVED BY A CLEAR MIND, AND YOUR DETERMINATION IS MODERATED BY A CERTAIN SLOWNESS IN DECIDING TO ACT. TO SOME, YOU MAY APPEAR SLUGGISH AND OVER-CAUTIOUS, BUT ACTUALLY YOU ARE QUITE FIRM AND DETERMINED ONCE YOUR PLANS ARE MADE. IT TAKES ONLY A STRONG GUST OF FEELING TO SET IN MOTION THE SCHEME YOU'VE BEEN SLOWLY TURNING OVER IN YOUR MIND.

BECAUSE OF YOUR PRE-MEDITATION AND WELL STOCKED MEMORY, YOU CAN READILY HARBOR GRUDGES. YOU NEVER FORGET SLIGHTS OR INJURIES, PARTICULARLY IF THEY THREATEN THE COMFORTABLE SURROUNDINGS WHICH YOU SEEK TO CREATE FOR YOURSELF. SIMILARLY, YOU ARE ADAMENTLY UNFORGIVING ABOUT ANY ATTACK ON THOSE CLOSE TO YOU, FOR THOUGH YOU MAY APPEAR EGOISTIC, AT HEART YOU HAVE DEEP CLAN FEELINGS. YOU ARE LOYAL TO YOUR FRIENDS, CONSTANT IN YOUR CHOICES AND STUBBORN IN YOUR VOCATION.

YOUR ASSETS=
- YOUR INNER STRENGTH AND COOL COLLECTED MIND, IN A WORD YOUR SOLIDITY.
- YOUR IMPERVIOUSNESS TO PASSION WHICH ENABLES YOU TO KEEP YOUR HEAD AND JUDGE THINGS IMPARTIALLY.
- YOUR FAITHFUL ADHERENCE TO YOUR PRINCIPLES AND VALUES, YOUR RARE HONOR WHICH IS HIGHLY APPRECIATED IN THE BUSINESS WORLD AS WELL AS ELSEWHERE.

[38]

[AH]
December 12th, 1969
[315 Rockingham Street, Rochester, New York 14620]

[Postcard, with a photograph of The Read House and Motor Inn in Chattanooga, Tennessee, handwritten, addressed to Wm. MacDonald, 12 Bedford Terrace, Northampton, Mass. 01060]

My liege –

For some reason Howard Merritt wants to pick you up at the airport, though I had planned to. He will feed you if you're not fed, and otherwise fill you in with poop – and them deliver you to my place. I look forward to your visit.

Edgar Wind

[39]

[AH]
December 19th, 1969
[315 Rockingham Street, Rochester, New York 14620]

[Letter, handwritten on a The Read House and Motor Inn, Chattanooga, Tennessee, letterhead]

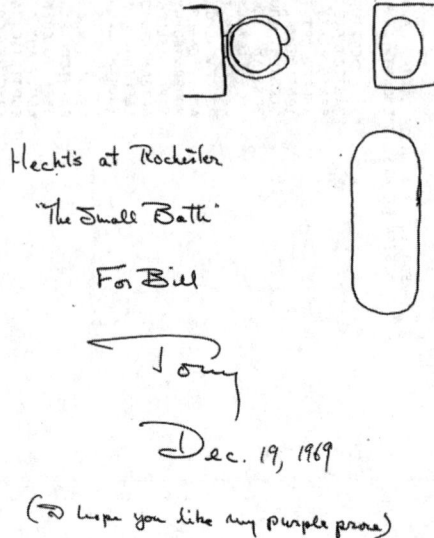

Hecht's at Rochester
"The Small Bath"
For Bill
Tony
Dec. 19, 1969
(→ hope you like my purple prose)[1]

---

1 This letter was written in purple ink.

[40]

[AH]
January 9th, 1970
[The University of Rochester, College of Arts and Science, River Campus Station,
Rochester, New York 14627, Department of English]

[Letter, typed on a The University of Rochester, Department of English, letterhead]

Dear whatsizname?

I just remembered what it was I wanted to tell you when you phoned a couple of days ago, but couldn't think of at the time. I discovered over the holidays that the great arch-fool and world's leading nitwit, Robert T. Petersson, has had a book accepted by – with due horror I say it – our own publisher, Atheneum. I suppose he's probably already told you this. The book seems to be on St. Thérèse, as she appears in her own works and in those of Bernini and Crashaw as well. Harry Ford, who told me all this, also said that P. showed his ms. to Irving Lavin, who did a thorough job of revising and suggesting, and the book has been sent to a number of art historians (some of them indeed rather distinguished) for appraisal, and it has been well spoken of by them. Hard to believe, what? Maybe Suzie [Petersson] wrote it. I can't think of a thoughtful word coming out of old Ho-ho-ho Bob.

What cha gonna do? Has the Provost made his offer to you? Is it attractive? Will you take the job?

You will be interested to know that at long last I have found a bird. Further details must wait upon more intimate circumstances.

Vale,
F. Villon

WEIGHED AND FOUND WANTING

[41]

[WLM]
January 13th, 1970
12 Bedford Terrace, Northampton, Massachusetts 01060

*[Letter, handwritten on a Smith College, Department of Art, letterhead, addressed to
Prof. A · E · Hecht, Dept of English, Univ. Rochester, Rochester, N.Y., 14627]*

Tonino:

The Peterssen thing is a Great Mystery – a case of Immaculate Conception?

No message / offer from Clark-Sproull, tho' Merritt calls frequently. No offer, so no response from me. But I understand they are to make an offer. I've no idea, now, how I'll decide … Great news about the bird. I have one too, not the Nancy you met. Life is not too bad.

Cheers,
<u>The</u> Dickens

[42]

[AH]
January 16th, 1970
[315 Rockingham Street, Rochester, NY 14620]

[Letter, typed on a The University of Rochester, Department of English, letterhead]

You lucky bastard,

You are about to be treated to one of my latest and hottest works. Your thanks are bound to be inadequate, so don't bother. Here it is.

> There was a young Gaul from the Somme
> Whom sexual ennui made glum.
>   At such moments he'd sigh
>   With a tear in his eye,
> "Il n'y a que des femmes et des hommes."[1]

One of the things that may be delaying Sproull from writing to you is that he's only just learning. His capitals are good, though it's hard to tell his Ms from his Ws, and after about four lines it looks as if he's writing Arabic. We are working with him patiently in our remedial program, and if you can just hold on for a few years you may get something legible and intelligible from him yet. Part of our problem centers around the fact that there is a segment of opinion which maintains that he really is writing Arabic, and choice Arabic at that; filled with lusty expletives and delicious fulminations. Until this matter is settled, our progress is likely to be slow.

Pax,
J.S.B.

---

1 French = "There are only women and men."

[43]

[WLM]
January 20th, 1970
[12 Bedford Terrace, Northampton, Massachusetts 01060]

[Letter, handwritten on a Smith College memorandum slip]

Univ Roch Bullshit

After much fucking about, Merritt called last night to say there were certain snags, + to ask what salary range I would find suitable. All this, + more, has cooled me off, + I am to call him tomorrow night to say I'll stay in the race or get out; I've about decided to get out. No offer, no decision possible. <u>Now</u> Merritt tells me I should have met <u>all</u> the dept – Christ, academia! Meanwhile I've turned up a <u>possible</u>, for Fall '71, in the Boston area ——

[Unsigned]

[44]

[WLM]
February 11th, 1970
[12 Bedford Terrace, Northampton, Massachusetts 01060]

[Letter, typed]

Dear Brother in Christ,

Well man the Rochester types played it pretty badly. Not Howard [Merritt] & Archie [Miller], who couldn't have been nicer. But as time passed & more & more questions came about how much does Smith pay me and all that I realised that I didn't want a job based upon the idea that I was going to fight with Sproull and Clark for a Department obviously not very high on their list, indeed one close to the bottom. No offer ever did come through, and it turned out that after caucusing on me the Department decided not everyone had met me … hardly my fault. My only regret is that had I come we could have had many a yak and wassail (can one wassail at other than the Saturnalia … ?)

Life here is chaotic. Dale's lawyers have at last presented <u>my</u> lawyer with demands as to money & property settlements, and they are preposterous. But as Dale is suing me, and this is an adversary action, I may just have to sit still and be skinned alive. It galls me, but I don't know what else to do. And then of course I'm having a little woman trouble – not too serious, but as always more diverting that one would wish. I'm not very bright about such things.

But in other ways things move along fairly well. I'm getting some, not much, work done. Bob Peterssen is auditing my Baroque architecture course and as you'll so readily realise, <u>that's</u> a thrill.

Do write when you have the time. Tell me about your bird, and consider the possibility of a trip here when the layers of ice slide into the Connecticut.
                Love,
              Clovis Sangrail

[45]

[WLM]
February 25th, 1970
12 Bedford Terrace, Northampton, Massachusetts 01060]

[Blank postcard, typed, addressed to A E Hecht, 315 Rockingham Street, Rochester, NY 14620]

My dear Sir,
    The Smith student art festival committee wants one more of our Pop Lectures for their festival in April, the date to be something like the 21st. They're serious. Are you game? I think I am. Do let me know if you are interested.
    Things here are hectic as I try and make good on promises for written material foolishly given aeons ago. Hope all's well with you.
                Servus,
              Caligula

[46]

[AH]
February 28th, 1970
[315 Rockingham Street, Rochester, NY 14620]

[Letter, typed on a The University of Rochester, Department of English, letterhead]

Dear Imperator,
    The odd thing is that I will actually be up in your neck of the woods around April 21st. I have contracted to spend a whole week, beginning April 20th, at Trinity College in Hartford; I will be giving two poetry readings and a lecture while there, and of course hope to barge in on you and make a general nuisance of myself around Northampton during whatever intervals I have. And it is not that I am chickening out about the pop lecture, but the truth is that I don't really have time to prepare one. My lecture for Trinity is, thank God, already written; but I have to give a talk a week before that which I have yet before me to write. Actually, this year I've had to give more damn speeches than I've given in all the rest of my life. Composing them is time-consuming; pleasant, of course, if you have nothing else to do, but … So I will come up and sit in the audience and applaud your speech with vigor.
    By the time you get this you should also have gotten a chain letter from me. I've never been in one of these things before, and have no idea whether they work,

but it only costs a buck, and the prospect of getting all that moola has its singular appeal, which I thought you, too, might find attractive. I believe, incidentally, that it's against the law: being an unrecorded form of income. But there is also a certain lure in the idea of cheating the government. Especially our government. In fact, if one thinks about all that money NOT going into missiles or the C.I.A. one can get a positive moral orgasm out of it. I observe, incidentally, that you are on Trinity's summer staff in Rome. Rather dandy. I have some good news: as you may have heard from my lord Baskin, I've been elected to the National Institute of Arts & Letters. And when, by the way, is my lord Baskin going to finish the fucking broadside of the poem I sent him a year ago?

Love,
Julius Caesar Scaliger

[47]

[AH]
March 7th, 1970
[315 Rockingham Street, Rochester, NY 14620]]

Letter, typed on a The University of Rochester, Department of English, letterhead]

Dear Vitruvius,

Don't laugh. Don't gnash your teeth, either. Howard Merritt stopped me on campus yesterday, and asked me to sound you out about whether you would be willing to revisit the university next fall, with an eye to accepting a genuine offer of chairmanship. He was somewhat flustered when he said this. I have tried to find out what really happened, and I think it goes something like this. The administration, having other, more pressing concerns, were probably willing to let the art department slide along for one more year without a permanent chairman. But their way of doing this (and I assume their reasons were purely budgetary) was to observe that, strictly according to the book, Merritt had failed to present you to every fucking member of the department, (which is in truth, the normal procedure) and therefore was not in a position to say that you were the unanimous choice of the department. It is purely a technicality, and part of the ritual mating dance of the provost. This, in any case, is my guess. If I'm right, it may be sufficiently discouraging to you. And of course you may have other and better offers. But I think poor Merritt was too embarrassed to be able to write you about this himself. Anyway, I may be quite wrong in my interpretation of what happened. Everybody seems to be trying to cover for everyone else. I suggest, therefore, that if you're even the teeniest bit interested, if only in finding out what the fuck happened, that you write to Merritt, saying that I have passed the word along to you about a revisit next year, and that you would like to find out just what happened this year, and receive some assurance that it wouldn't happen again.

Augustus, Imp.

[48]

[WLM]
March 13th, 1970
12 Bedford Terrace, Northampton, Massachusetts 01060

[Letter, typed, addressed to Anthony Hecht, scrivener, 315 Rockingham Street, Rochester N Y 14620]

Friday the 13th

Dear Spartianus,

You shure did a lousy job with Hadrian's biography. Can't wait to see what you'll do with Antoninus Pius.

Re Rochester art dept.: Many thanks for the very informative letter. It was never clear to me just what happened, other than that my visit and the approaches to me were handled awkwardly to say the least. I know this was not Howard's fault, but rather that of the clout boys.

I really don't think I'm interested. The urge to leave Smith (this for your eyes only) has subsided somewhat, though I confess that a Boston area offer of any quality would cause me to sit up and chirp a bit. The divorce has finally been decreed and I feel freer and less constricted. Of course Smith's position is somewhat precarious, though I'm happy to say far less so than schools like Mount Holyoke, and the future is difficult in the extreme to discern, and if you can get through this sentence you'll realise that I'm saying that I'm not sure what's going to happen. Meanwhile, I think that the condition of art history at Rochester requires radical or near-radical surgery, and I wouldn't, honestly, be any good at that at all.

Our girls are much disappointed that you can't make it for the Arts Festival. I of course expect you for a week or two. We do have a lot of drinking and talking to do.

How's your love life? Nancy (the flirt) and I have settled down to a rather comfortable once-a-week-drinks-and-dinner; we're not sleeping together; curiously, I like her quite a lot. My sex life isn't much, but there is a little of it; just enough, apparently. I look forward to hearing about your friend. I find the forties really wonderful in many ways, but I haven't solved the woman problem. We must devote several sessions to it when you come next month. I'm off for the west coast for a couple of weeks.

Lectured at Trinity / Hartford last night. Good crowd, responsive. "Rome Unseen: Under the Seven Hills." How's that? When you go you'll meet a nice, rather lightweight, old friend of mine, John Dando, Prof. English; he's alright; harmless. Kaplans told me that time we had lunch with them last Nov. that they were to be here at Smith last Wed. 11th, but I couldn't discover them.

Love,
Hosius, B[isho]p of Cordova

[49]

[AH]
circa March 15th, 1970
[315 Rockingham Street, Rochester, NY 14620]

[Letter, typed on a The University of Rochester, Department of English, letterhead]

Ides of March, or thereabouts

My dear son,

We read in one of Wind's footnotes that "Caesar's ashes were supposed to be enclosed in the sphere on the top of the Vatican obelisk ..."[1] By this the holy church betokeneth divers things; but chiefly that Caesar is shafted by his ambitions to worldly glory; and that Cleopatra, whose person and whose nation he violated, hath in the end made her requital, and with this her great stone finger given it him in the ass even before the fact of St. Peter. So that all men may read therein the true sense of the words, "Render unto Caesar those things which are Caesar's ..."

By this means doth the church at once display and conceal a great truth, Viz., that worldly vanity is buggery, and vice versa. And thus are the words recalled, "Vanity of vanities, saith the preacher; all is buggery." For, my son, what doth it mean that one attain to fame in this world but that another hath been cast down and buggered thereby? And for such buggery how shall he be requited but to be buggered in his turn? These be the fixed laws of this vain world, whose justice without truth the sphere and obelisk doth present. And by this sign you may know that it's not worth farting around trying to be a good art historian.

This is the kernel of my Easter sermon, which I am sending on ahead of time for your comment and approval. As you can see at once, it is susceptible of great elaboration and extrapolation: all the ups and downs of this world, who's on top, etc., as contrasted with the bringing low of Christ and his resurrection in aeternam. A few passages from <u>The Naked Lunch</u> and one or two choice color slides that I don't

---

1 Edgar Wind, *Pagan Mysteries of the Renaissance,* second revised edition (New York: W. W. Norton, 1968), p. 38.

think you've seen yet, might make it really a quite stirring thing. The congregation has become restless during the past few months, and it has been increasingly difficult to cope. Several of them have declared that they find bingo a bit tame; and the cake sale was, I must mournfully confess, a real flop. But I am not disheartened; rather I rejoice in knowing that these tribulations are but signs of a chastening love; and that when I have put my soul in order, bingo will come back.

I remain, my son, your ghostly daddy-o,
Jonathan Edwards

[50]

[WLM]
July 8th, 1970
[American Academy in Rome, Via Angelo Masina, 5 (Porta S. Pancrazio), 00153, Rome]

[Italian postcard, with a photograph of the Canopus in Hadrian's Villa, Rome, handwritten, addressed to Anthony E. Hecht, 315 Rockingham St., Rochester N.Y., 14620, Stati Uniti]

Dear Tony,

Hope this gets forwarded properly. Rome is so noisy, crowded, + seductive as ever. I'm having a good time; lectures going well – almost completed – plus an elaborate photographic campaign. Next week the students go home, hope to hit the Cities[1] hard … Everyone of course is here, except you and [Jack] Zajac, and there have been a couple of good parties. Do write me at the Academy if you have the time.

Love,
Ossian

[51]

[WLM]
August 5th, 1970
[American Academy in Rome, Via Angelo Masina, 5 (Porta S. Pancrazio), 00153, Rome]

[Letter, handwritten on an American Academy in Rome, Via Angelo Masina, 5 (Porta SS. Pancrazio), 00153, Rome, letterhead, addressed to Anthony Hecht, Saltaire, Fire Island, N.Y. 11706, Stati Uniti]

O Poet,

When in 1799 Desaix' French army came to the plain of Thebes in Egypt, strewn with colossal ruins, the soldiers, without command, halted as a man and presented arms!

---

1 WLM is referring to the sequel to his *The Architecture of the Roman Empire: An Introductory Study*.

The functionary in the Colosseum who used his triple-pronged staff to prod the Christians toward the lions was known as a martyr-forker.

There, that'll keep you in dining-out shape. Hot as hell here; writing moving along, a nice lady to screw, and all in all a good summer, except for missing my boys so much. Your news of a new poem that you feel is as good as anything you've done is very exciting.[1] I can't say the same for what I'm doing, but I think it's OK; i.e. 6.7 or 6.8 on a scale of 1.0 to 10.0 ———

The CCNY thing might suit you down to the ground? Just had an informal feeler from Berkeley myself – answered with mild interest, like HOW MUCH MONEY? etc. Pretty good place in my field. Will relay your Dimock message; haven't seen them yet. [Henry] Weinberg is about, and so are a host of other Old Codgers; Frank [Brown] seems fine; and life is tolerable to good.

Yours in Satan,
Marta Thatcher

One man's Mead is another's McKim ———[2]
I look forward very much to post-Feb. NY visits

[52]

[WLM]
October 1st, 1970
12 Bedford Terrace, Northampton, Massachusetts 01060

[Letter, typed on a New Omayad Hotel letterhead, addressed to Mr Anthony Hecht, rhymer, Dept of English, Rochester University, Rochester NY, ZIP = 14627!]

Dear Ali,

Loved your White House Missle. You know Vonnegut's story[3] about selling storm windows to Mr Rumfoord, who lived across from the Kennedy Compound at Hyannis Port? Pretty good. I would kick Leonard Baskino in the balls, as you requested, but I can't. He is, if you read <u>Newsweek</u>, the "god-like poet laureate of art," and I really can't, with my formal upbringing, kick a laureate, I just might kick him in the head, but in his wreathèd balls, never.

Actually I haven't seen him, but when I do I'll enquire about your enquiry. Do you have another house? Where do we stay in New York until your flat comes back? Is there a good, cheap, hotel?

1 The poem was almost certainly "Green: An Epistle," which first appeared in the May 22nd, 1971 issue of *The New Yorker*, and was later included in *Millions of Strange Shadows*.

2 A reference to the architects William Rutherford Mead and Charles Follen McKim. In the late 1870s, McKim had formed a partnership, first with Mead and then with Mead and Stanford White. All three men played a significant part in the establishment of the American Academy in Rome.

3 Kurt Vonnegut, "Welcome to the Monkey House," in *Welcome to the Monkey House: Stories* (New York: Dell, 1970).

The book moves, and I am happy.
Love to all 69, Baba

[53]

[AH]
December 21st, 1970
[315 Rockingham Street, Rochester, New York 14620]

[Letter, typed on a The University of Rochester, Department of English, letterhead]

Dear Sir,

I'm sure you must be as distressed as I am about what the Church has done to St. Ursula. They have de-canonized her; scratched her from the calendar, broken her halo, plucked off her wings, and tossed her harp into the discard. And all this simply because some recent investigation suggests (merely <u>suggests</u>, mind you) that those eleven thousand virgins were not precisely virgins. In fact, it now appears that Ursula was making a pretty penny in the white slave racket, and headed an organization that might easily rival the PLAYBOY empire. Personally, I think this is altogether to her credit, and represents all the high and virtuous things that Hugh Heffner stands for: industry, managerial ability, a capacity to deal with the rough and tumble of this world – in fact, the very virtues that were most praised in St. Teresa and St. Catherine of Siena.

It is, in fact, altogether possible that Heffner got his idea in the first place from his studies in hagiography, undertaken in the seventh grade of Mrs. Fiske's School for Boys. It seems that Ursula's girls did not dress as bunnies but as mink – or, minx, in the plural. They had these cute little tails, and there was a medieval saying about mink that was highly suggestive. You will no doubt have come across it in your readings of bestiaries. Anyway, in her privately circulated autobiography and memoirs, "Like A Mink," Ursula speaks of her success with remarkable modesty – a part of the text which Heffner presumably ignored.

I felt sure you would want me to share these Christmas thoughts with you, and you are welcome to share them, in turn, with your students if you find they are properly edifying and in the spirit of the season.

On a somewhat more comic note, you will be interested to know that Pat is leaving Philippe, and plans to settle either in London or on Long Island at Southampton.

Marcus Aurelius, Imp.

P.S.: Some day you may be able to sell my letters at auction, purely for their signatures. A Marcus Aurelius is very rare, and should fetch a good price.

[54]

[WLM]
[December 27th, 1970]
12 Bedford Terrace, Northampton, Massachusetts 01060

*[Letter, typed, addressed to Prof. Anthony HECHT, Department of English,
The University of Rochester, Rochester, N. Y. 14627]*

My dear Hecht,

Your hard-won but ill-digested learning about S. Ursula demands comment, for you have left out the most significant part of the story. I've been thinking about you, and about Ursula, though not at the same time, and I have decided that it will be alright for you to know this: In the ninth century of Our Redeemer she was, effectively, known as 'Urse,' the medieval mind being given much to verbal transmogrification. This of course – have you guessed it? – is the origin of the phrase, so often so fondly used, "to get, to have, or to promote, a piece of Urse." Naturally the years have fucked up the spelling and pronunciation, but you now have revealed for you the <u>reason</u> why those 11,000 broads danced attendance on her. She <u>knew</u>!

Mink, of course, is a red herring.

Yes, you did tell me Pat is leaving Philippe. I hope your boys will live reasonably near you.

A good evening with Baskin recently. He was in top form & we had a good three-hour session, knocking each other out. He had three cokes and a bottle of beer! Lisa is really something, I think.

Berkeley threatened a professorship; the department voted it; the dean refused them (money). Just as glad. Am to be in <u>Who's Who</u>, a fact that affects me no wise; am to be in the <u>Dictionary of International Biography</u>; ditto.

Christmas with the Trottenbergs in their huge shingle-style house in Pelham. When do you move to the City? What will your 'phone number be? What will your attitude be toward paying guests? Non-paying guests?

Giving eight lectures at Harvard in the Spring for 3500 clams, am to be Kea Dist. Prof, lecturer at the Univ. of Maryland, 4 lectures, fewer clams pro rata.

      Yours in the arms of Isis,

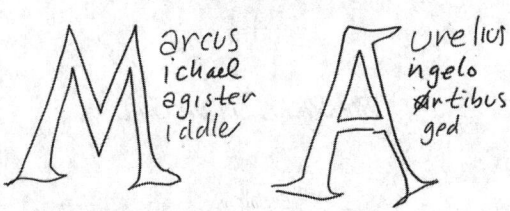

Given at the Saturnalia, in the consulship of Puella otia and Corborunda vagina.

[55]

[WLM]
January 4th, 1971
[12 Bedford Terrace, Northampton, Massachusetts 01060]

[French postcard, with reproduction of Benjamin Constant's Portrait of a Young Man, *handwritten, addressed to Anthony Hecht, Dep't English, Univ. Rochester, Rochester, N.Y.]*

And I hope you're keeping <u>my</u> letters, too!
                      Constant (Benj.)

[56]

[WLM]
[January 6th, 1971]
[12 Bedford Terrace, Northampton, Massachusetts 01060]

[Postcard, addressed to A · Hecht, Dep't English, Univ. Rochester, Rochester, N.Y., with enclosure]

THE SHAKE 'EM UP GIRL

[Enclosure]

[57]

[WLM]
[January, 1971?]
[12 Bedford Terrace, Northampton, Massachusetts 01060]

[Postcard, handwritten, addressed to A · E · Hecht, yes, 240 East 82nd St., New York, N.Y., 10028]

Odorono:

    P. + P. under control – the difference between them, I mean[1] ... Will the Bullocks give you another 10,000 clams?[2] Or a bullock?

              Mann wer mit Fräulein pennt
              Gegen wegen Establishment[3]

    Hope to be in NYC late Feb or early March for much heavy talk + drink.
        – The Venerable Bead

---

1 "P. + P." would seem to be a reference to Pat and Philippe.

2 Marie Bullock and her husband Hugh had founded the Academy of American Poets, which in 1968-69 had given AH the Honorary Fellow grant. (In the spring of 1971, he would be appointed a Chancellor to that same institution.)

3 The couplet is in poor German, though it is just about construable as meaning "The man who sleeps with a young woman / Goes against the Establishment." WLM seems to be making play with a saying that was popular in counter-cultural Germany in the late 1960s: "Wer zwei mal mit derselben pennt / gehört schon zum Establishment," which can be translated as follows: "Whoever sleeps with the same person twice / Already belongs to the Establishment."

[58]

[WLM]
[February 4th, 1971]
[12 Bedford Terrace, Northampton, Massachusetts 01060]

[French postcard, with a photograph of Place du Marche Neuf in Evreux, France, handwritten, addressed to ANTHONY HECHT, 240 E. 82nd St., N.Y., N.Y.]

Tonino:
    Nice of Bullocks to ask me; can't; have a 9 a.m. class + a big Tuesday. All good things always.

Laurence Pee Roberts

[59]

[AH]
February 6th, 1971
240 East 82nd St., NYC 10028

[Letter, typed on a The University of Rochester, Intramural Correspondence, letterhead]

Dear pal,
    So you have a 9 a.m. class, eh? Pretty cagey of you; get hold of those young girls when they're too groggy and muddle-headed to tell a penis from a pendentive. But then, as I remember, Smith girls are not required to know the difference. I'm sorry that your early morning schedule (accompanied, I trust, by Mozart's "Eine Kleine Morgen Krankheit") prohibits a visit just now. Ah, well. I was finally reduced to phoning Baskin. He and Lisa both had the flu at the time. But he sounded cheerful and friendly, and was not at all disturbed about being deluged by me with letters that he never answered. Anyway, greet them for me when they're up and about; and the Dimocks, too. (I let it be known to one of the gang at Atheneum that you were making progress on your book; they didn't bat an eye.) Curious news from Belgium, requiring much talk over a couple of good, strong pepsis.

Yrs.
John Wilmot, Earl of Rochester

[60]

[WLM]
[February 10th, 1971]
[12 Bedford Terrace, Northampton, Massachusetts 01060]

[Letter, posted in a New Omayad Hotel's airmail envelope, addressed to Prof. Anthony Hecht, 240 East 82nd Street, New York NY]

New Omayad Hotel
DAMAS
REPUBLIQUE ARABE SYRIENNE
☎ 17700 - 4 Lignes
Telegr. : NEWOMAYAR

```
                                    7 Obsidian
                                    Hergira 881

midear Mr Essht,

    We are taking pleasure. in sending you
swatches our high-cless febriks.

    You pik febrik, our derwishes making.
you suitings incroiable (Syrie once French
mandrake).

    Sometimes Chinese taylor 'ere too, speak
Duck

    Your orders qikly processed woth ample
akkursy.
          Remaining.  yr servants,


                         Omar Farouk & Sue'rs.
                         per


    Pee Ess; ball-rpom our specialité.you need
         "        "    we supplie
```

[61]

[WLM]
[February 18th, 1971]
[12 Bedford Terrace, Northampton, Massachusetts 01060]

[Letter, typed on a Charing Cross Hotel, Strand, London, WC2, letterhead, with enclosure]

like 18 Feb 217 BC

Hey there Bud,

I thought the enclosed would give you a couple of days' laughs. It's genuine! Hold on to it until I see you, for I may have it framed. Since it arrived, I have been trying hard to emulate the man.

Finally found the Noel Coward album[1] that you have, and have been knocking myself out with "Piccola Marina," and "Alice is at it again"… the man's a minor genius {or is that like being a huge midget?} How do you like my { }s?[2] Not everyone has them, you know.

Baskin looks a little poorly. At a recent high-temperature session he charged in like an old fire horse who has just heard the bell. I like him, & we have some fun, but he is unbearably rude and boorish when he is telling everybody off.

I find I have some Univ. Md. lectures in March, one on Mon. 22. How would it be iffn I came to New York the day before & had a 7-Up or 2 with you?* How is your sex life? Mine is modest indeed these days.

Berkeley professorship evaporated, as I may have told you they haven't any cash money! And that after the Dept voted me a place. How odd …

My boys are huge & fine. We go to Boston this morning and have a liddle fun. They are on vacation for some reason or other. Noel (IX grade) got 5 straight A's at mid-year(!)

I don't care for pot.

Do write when the spirit moves you.

I know some strange women in New York.

I told the oom-ta-ra-ra story in good company the other night and, if I do say so, and I do, I told it rather well.[3] The other poets round about then quit, saying they couldn't follow <u>that</u>. So … one of your pupils has arrived, if only in Hampshire county.

Love,
Maffeo Barberini

---

1 *Noel Coward at Las Vegas* (Columbia Records, 1955).

2 The brackets WLM is inviting AH to admire at this point are in fact square; to avoid confusion with editorial insertions, these have been replaced with braces.

3 This might be a reference to the story told about the great pianist Paderewski, who is supposed to have visited a nightclub in St Louis in the 1890s and so enjoyed the performance of a singer of bawdy songs called Mary Lou that he sat at the piano and had her teach him the "Ta-ra-ra-boom-de-ay" song, a song later described by R. H. Gretton in his *A Modern History of the English People* (London, 1912) as a "tasteless and irrepressible air" and "a universal annoyance."

* = 14-Up

[Enclosure]

[Letter, typed on Professor [...]'s letterhead]

February 1st, 1971

Dear Sir:

It gives me great pleasure to write you this letter. I am a young [...] historian and I am enclosing herewith my Resume for your perusal.

My educational background includes [...] doctoral level degrees [...]: I have traveled world-wide, have worked at [...] in a significant administrative capacity and I have taught [...] for nearly [...] years. I have been associated with [...] colleges as a professor – at the first two I was nominated by my colleagues for Distinguished Professorships and at the College where I am now teaching I was, just last week, chosen for the annual Faculty Award. I am also a qualified [...], [...], [...], [...] and published poet and author (my writings have been admired by men like [...], [...] and [...]). I have always believed that an artist looks ahead into the future and makes it seen. I have never subscribed to the notion that artists are those superfluous creatures in a society who are good for nothing except to paint pretty pictures. I endorse Henry James when he says: "Art lives upon discussion, upon experiment, upon curiosity, upon variety of attempt, upon exchange of views and the comparison of standpoints."

As an artist I have never appealed to anyone except to the finest and in the finest fashion. [...] once dedicated a lecture at [...]: "To [...], who has [...]." True, I have exhibited in some of the most significant expositions of modern art (and [...] won the [...] Award and the great admiration of [...]) and the finest collections have bought my work, but unfortunately, quality and quantity have not met yet, in my case. I am not a commercial success and am seldom mentioned in tabloid-type career-engineering situations (here I confess that [...] magazine once wrote me off as a "young virtuoso"). However, Dr. [...] of [...], is writing a book "<u>The Art of [...]</u>," to be published by [...] [...] and I am mentioned in all notable who's whos. There are some thirty earned initials after my name, yet I consider myself a self-educated man and have never felt the need to think that I know everything. In fact, I consider my students as my colleagues, involved in the learning process. I have now come to the United States as an immigrant (because I came to the sad conclusion that I could not, in spite of a fabulous affluence, continue in a military dictatorship prevailing in [...]; besides, as far as my art is concerned, practically all of my audience is in the United States) and so I am an American artist by choice.

I have wondered if you could consider me for a visiting professorship in art. Ideally I wish to be associated again in the realm of studio-related concerns. However, I am willing to organize and conduct seminars in art history – […] and […], are my specialities in this connection. I will consider it a privilege to be working under you. However, if there are no vacancies in the art department, then could you please forward a copy of my letter and resume to the President of your institution so that he may consider me for a Visiting Professorship in Humanities. I can furnish the highest references from […], […] and […] professors. Incidentally, I shall be pleased to come for a lecture or as a visiting critic for two or three days (and for this I desire no fee) and I am also interested in the possibility of an exhibition of my work at your college. I shall look forward to hearing from you soon. With sincere regards.

Respectfully,
[Signature illegible]

[62]

[AH]
February 23rd, 1971
[240 East 82nd Street, New York, N.Y. 10028]

[Letter, typed on a The University of Rochester, Department of English, letterhead]

Yer Wholliness,
    Here are some moving verses by one James Smith (circa 1840).

> Virgil, whose epic song enthralls,
> (And who in song is greater?)
> Throughout, his Trojan hero calls
> Now "pious" and now "pater."
>
> But when, the worst intent to brave,
> With sentiments that pain us,
> Queen Dido meets him in the cave,
> He dubs him "Dux Trojanus."
>
> And well he alters there the word,
> For, in this station, sure,

> "Pious" Aeneas were absurd,
> And "pater" premature.[1]

Your timing is poor; as it happens, a colleague from Rochester will be visiting just the weekend you have set aside for your Maryland lecture. I wish I could say the colleague was a gorgeous blonde, but it is a rather portly man. You are not to infer anything from this about my tastes. I shall save the letter from Prof. [...] for some other visit of yours. It is such a splendid amalgam of servility and arrogance that it would be hard to match. I was a little surprised to see Jim Ackerman cited as an admirer. I am off to read at Wesleyan University tomorrow, and then, thank God, no more readings till April – I think. Best to Dimocks & Dan Aaron. And tell Baskin that Ted Hughes and his wife [Carol] will be staying with me when they come to NY in mid-March.

McGeorge

[63]

[WLM]
[May 12th, 1971]
[12 Bedford Terrace, Northampton, Massachusetts 01060]

[Postcard identical to the one shown at Letter 66 above, handwritten, addressed to A. E. Hecht, 240 East 82nd, St., New York, N.Y.]

Just can't tell now about the 27th.[2] May I play it by ear, + call later? (Papers, exams).
Cheers,
Clavico Odorono

Petersson panned and how in <u>New York Review of Books</u>! Whee!!! Justice!![3]

---

1 James Smith, "Pius Virgil," included in Volume 1 of *Memoirs, Letters, and Comic Miscellanies of the Late James Smith, Esq.*, edited by his brother, Horace Smith (London: Henry Colburn, 1840).

2 AH had met Helen D'Alessandro, a former student of his, that March, and had proposed to her shortly afterwards. Susan Halpern (a Smith College classmate of Helen's), and her then-husband John were to host an engagement party for the couple at their apartment in New York, and this is WLM's response to the invitation.

3 Robert M. Adams, "The High Wire of Faith," a review of Robert T. Petersson's *The Art of Ecstasy* in the May 20th, 1971 issue of *New York Review of Books*. An excerpt will suffice to give the flavour: "Mr Petersson is a serious and well-informed author; he has made every effort to ground his cross-disciplinary comparisons responsibly in detailed perception and analysis of the objects before him. Atheneum has contributed a well-designed and handsomely produced volume. The omens are all good; what can go wrong? As it happens, only one thing, the importance of which every reader must estimate for himself. The author cannot write, either forcefully or imaginatively or correctly."

[64]

[AH]
May 18th, 1971
[240 East 82nd Street, New York, N.Y. 10028]

[Letter, typed on a The Dana-Palmer House, Cambridge, letterhead]

Dear old Centurion,

Just back from a little jaunt to a place where they make up my letterpaper for me. As a matter of fact, there seems to be a good chance that Harvard will invite me to be a visiting prof. for a semester some time in the future. Having just seen it in blossom, as it were, with the lilacs and the dogwood and the bosoms all out and abundant, I feel inclined to accept. I hope you decide to accept the invitation to the bash on the 27th.

Your Emperor, Irving

[65]

[WLM]
July 17th, 1971
25 Henshaw Avenue, Northampton, Massachusetts 01060

[Letter, typed on a University of Maryland, University College, Center of Adult Education, College Park, Maryland 20740 letterhead, addressed to Mr and Mrs A. E. Hecht, yes, Saltaire, Fire Island, L. I., N.Y. 11706]

Dear Pave:

"The male inflorescence forms a panicle; the flowers consist or a small greenish five-parted perianth enclosing five stamens, whose anthers open by terminal slits. The female inflorescence is less conspicuous in the young state. The catkin or strobile consists of a number of small acute bracts, with two sessile ovaries at their base, each subtended by a rounded bractlet …forming, when fully grown, the membranous scales of the strobile, known as "petals" by hop growers … The perianth is short, cup-shaped, undivided … In the young strobile the two purple hairy styles of each ovary project beyond the bracts … The light dusty pollen is carried by the wind from the male to the female flowers."

Isn't that poetic? Isn't that beautiful? Imagine the courage it took to write it, for the <u>Encyclopedia Britannica</u> in 1929! I have of course edited the passage slightly, for your young and young-ish ears, as my ellipses indicate. But I knew you'd want to read it, even Bowdlerized. It's particularly fine read aloud, or allowed; slowly …

But what I find particularly telling is the fact that the hop growers, bless them, had the unvarnished guts to call those membranous scales of the strobiles "petals." That gives one confidence, doesn't it?

Love,
Wittig the Unwilling

[66]

[AH]
July 22nd, 1971
Saltaire, Fire Island, New York 11706

[Letter, typed on a The University of Rochester, Intramural Correspondence letterhead]

Like July 22, 1971

Hail to thee, blithe spirit:

Bird thou obviously never wert. Fish, yes. Reptile, yes. Ape, in the great phylogenic sequence, of course. But bird, never. You have a right to feel cheated and disadvantaged. A rotten and deprived childhood. Brings to mind the later work of Dickens. But you've borne up under the handicap pretty well, and seem to bear no resentment for the deprivations you suffered in the womb. I have it in mind to send you some birdseed as a sort of consolation. And you might enjoy whistling now and then.

You certainly read dirty books. I got an erection just skimming that passage about stamens and anthers and terminal slits. Helen was embarrassed, and we had to sneak hastily into the bedroom, me swathed in a beach towel to conceal my swelling organ from the children's view. She has suggested to me that I might do well to browse through the passage every night before retiring. She's a rather libidinous type, which is what I suppose is meant by Women's Lib, and being the sensitive, cultivated guy I am, I don't know how much of this depravity I can take.

Charles the Fat*

*as distinguished from Charles I, Charles II, Charlie Chan, Ray Charles, etc.

[67]

[AH]
[October or November, 1971]
[Washington University in St. Louis, Missouri]

[Letter, typed, with enclosure]

Dear Guru,

I hope you will note with approval the lecture topic I am offering here on Nov. 3rd, which is intended to keep me in the mainstream of the American cultural tradition.[1]

Things here are truly dandy, the temperature being in the seventies every day, the faculty genial, indeed generous, the students friendly and no dumber than usual. But what most astonishes is the price of houses and real estate: You can find splendid, brick-built Victorian mansions of fifteen rooms with tiffany windows and much wood panelling, surrounded by large and spacious grounds, for about half what they would

---

1 AH was Visiting Fannie Hurst Lecturer at the University.

cost anywhere in the east. The meanest member of the faculty could live well here (though food prices are about the same) and a top-ranking man could find himself a place like Mendenhall's[1] with no trouble at all, and not too much outlay. In a word, we like it. But we are taking off at the end of the week for a killing reading tour of Oregon and Washington. Sixteen performances at as many places. I hope Helen can take it.[2] We have arranged with the Dimocks to spend some part of the Thanksgiving holidays with them in Northampton, during which time I want very much to introduce you to Helen. We shall arrive at Bradley Field on the eve of the 23rd, and will stay on (always assuming the Dimocks can cope with us) till the afternoon of the 26th. I expect you will be busy both with family and chairman-like duties, still, I hope we can see as much of you as you can spare time for.

Warmest greetings,
Ringo Starr

[Enclosure: flier]

Please post
Please announce to your classes

ANTHONY HECHT
Visiting Hurst Professor, Department of English

will give two programs:

WEDNESDAY, NOVEMBER 3: A lecture entitled "Little-Known Facts in the Sex Life of Harriet Beecher Stowe"[3]

January 110 (formerly Law School court room)
4:10 p.m.

FRIDAY, NOVEMBER 5: A Poetry Reading

Women's Building Lounge
8:30 p.m.

1 Thomas Mendenhall was the president of Smith College.

2 AH had married Helen D'Alessandro on June 12th, and she was by now three or four months pregnant.

3 The reader will recall that WLM and AH had talked about including a lecture entitled "Little-Known Facts in the Life of Harriet Beecher Stowe" in the series of "pop" lectures they had joked about presenting at least since 1969 (see letter #23, August 21st, 1969). Lest it be thought that Hecht is simply keeping the joke alive here, it should be pointed out that he did indeed give a lecture with this title while visiting Washington University. One wonders what his audience made of it when, after a few prefatory remarks, he came clean, saying: "… I shall have to begin by candidly confessing that my title does not truly indicate the nature of my subject, and was merely a Barnum-like pretext to draw you here." (Anthony Hecht Papers, Box 109, File 44.)

[68]

[WLM]
December 6th, [1971]
[25 Henshaw Avenue, Northampton, Massachusetts 01060]

Postcard, addressed Mr & Mrs Anthony Hecht, 240 East 82nd St., New York, NY, 10028]"

Dear Helen + Tony –

Wonderful to see /meet you. And the Column of Trajan poem[1] is great. I have slides somewhere of couples on Vespas rounding the Col. by Santa Maria di Loreto, + once from atop the Col. I saw a 2-Vespa crash. Learned, experienced.

See you soon.

Love, Wm.

[69]

[WLM]
[December] 31st, [1971]
[25 Henshaw Avenue, Northampton, Massachusetts 01060]

[Postcard, with a photograph of the Musée des Beaux Arts in Brussels, handwritten, addressed to Mr & Mrs A·E· Hecht, 240 East 82nd Street, New York, N.Y. 10028]

Dear Helen and Tony,

The Mother Goose book is marvelous. How intricately clever the man is! And

---

1 WLM is referring to "The Cost," which was first published in the July 1971 issue of *Encounter*, and was later included in AH's 1977 collection, *Millions of Strange Shadows*.

the illustrations are splendid.¹

All thanks; + see you on the 15th.

Love,
Evinrude the Messy

[70]

[WLM]
February 16th, 1972
25 Henshaw Avenue, Northampton, Massachusetts 01060

[Blank postcard, addressed to Professor & Mrs Anthony HECHT, yes, Dept of English, University of Rochester, Rochester NY 14627]

Dear Helen & Tony,

How was it? Can't wait to hear. My seismograph didn't record any particularly Brazilian disturbances, so I guess it all went off smoothly.²

When you have a home address, do send it along. I have at last a wedding present for you, which of course you'll love forever. Here work goes along fairly well, and each day I thank Saint Bernard (Berenson) for not having to go into the Dept. Did you know that Darwin hired a trombonist to play three hours a day to a row of string beans? Jesus!

PICK ONE → Howard / Henry- Russell / Hughes / Hitchcock [handwritten]

[71]

[WLM]
March 1st, 1972
25 Henshaw Avenue, Northampton, Massachusetts 01060

[Blank postcard, addressed to → → → Helen und Anthony Hecht, 45 Knollwood Drive, Rochester NY 14618]

→ I am in love with Nancy L. Stark. Don't tell me – I know she's gorgeous, intelligent, rich, & sexy. But <u>where</u> is she?

→ A package wingeth its way en route (that's French) to you.

→ Once upon a time there was a great chief, who dwelt in a mansion of grass. His

1 *Rimes de la Mère Oie: Mother Goose Rhymes*, translated into French by Ormonde de Kay Jr., with illustrations by Seymour Chwast, Milton Glaser and Barry Zaid (Boston, MA: Little Brown, 1971).

2 AH had been awarded a lectureship in American literature by the U.S. State Department and had represented the United States at an international literary conference held in São Paolo. He was accompanied by his wife Helen, who was now in an advanced state of pregnancy.

nation so loved him they gave him a great throne. But he awreddy had a throne, so he put the new one in the attic. Soon however the new throne came crashing down, crashing down through the floor, killing the chief.

→ The moral of this is, People who live in grass houses shouldn't stow thrones.

Alas; love,

→ Are you on the telephone?
→ Baby coming to Roch. or NYC?

Amadeus, leader of the Wolfgang

[72]

[AH]
March 11th, 1972
45 Knollwood Drive, Rochester, New York 14618

*[Letter, typed, addressed to Prof. Wm. MacDonald (Hot Dog!),
25 Henshaw Ave, Northampton, Mass 01060, with enclosure]*

Dear Sir or Madam,

Did you know that Guido d'Arezzo is generally credited with the introduction of the F clef in musical notation? This useful fact, as well as others too numerous to mention, is at my instant disposal by virtue of the arrival of twenty-four – count 'em – twenty-four volumes of the Fourteenth fucking edition of the <u>Encyclopaedia Britannica</u>, and for the last few days I have been gibbering with delight. I seem to find as much pleasure browsing among the illustrious names of the contributors as I do in picking up hot tips on Canon Law and surface tension. It is a splendid – nay, a spectacular gift – and I assume, on the basis of what is after all pretty flimsy evidence, that it comes from you. The flimsy evidence was a highly suggestive postcard you sent us, employing a lewd French phrase (<u>en route</u>, I think it was) and the fact that the books arrived in two cartons from some outfit in Springfield. Helen and I have consulted our Ouija board, but have only been able to get in touch with one Henrik Steffens (1773–1845), a choleric German who refuses to cooperate, and claims, moreover, that he's never heard of you. You may imagine our frustration. But the books console us, and will keep us happy and occupied till we find out if our message of gratitude is directed to the right party. Helen insists on inserting a message of her own.

Rudolph of Saxony

At present I find it difficult to say which is my favorite volume. There is much to be said, for example, in behalf of ANNU to BALT; but RAYN to SARR is catchy in its own way, and has a lot of terrific characters in it.[1]

---

1 This P.S. is typed on the back of the envelope.

[Handwritten enclosure]

Dear Bill,

What a fabulous gift. We love it; it is the best gift we have or shall receive. That is, I am fairly sure I love it, having had thus far little opportunity to browse through many volumes. Tony cleverly monopolizes the whole thing at once, and I have seen little of him the past few days. He staggers to bed bleary-eyed at shocking hours, muttering about Chinese wall hangings, German composers and rare gems. Occasionally, on the pretext of offering a meal, I am able to separate him from uninterrupted perusal of the new encyc. (His classes, of course, have been forgotten, and he rarely shaves anymore.)

Love,
Helen

P.S. Foetus also thanks you, considering it a monumental boon toward future scholastic achievement. (He and I are also partial to the pictures.)

[73]

[WLM]
March 18th, 1972
25 Henshaw Avenue, Northampton, Massachusetts 01060

[Blank postcard, typed, addressed to Mr and Mrs Anthony Hecht, 45 Knollwood Drive, Rochester NY 14618]

RAYN-SARR is all very well in its own way, but for me it's LIBI-MARY all the way, Feminine, sexy. I haven't liked a volume so much since the old Compton's CRA-FRO (which, it turns out, was Dick Wilbur's favorite tool back in '29; notice the economy of letters, as befitted an encyclopedia running to a mere nine volumes).[1] Another thing, the pictures: zeppelins, gems, flags, medals, lighthouses ... my, and to think you Didn't Have a 14th <u>Encyclopedia Britannica</u> ... The other day I was reading Dams (not too bad if you're not constipated), which sent me for some reason, to Quebec, and that to ... a clear case of <u>EB</u>14-itis? to bed, head in a swirl, but happy, caring ...

Love to all 2 & 8/9ths,
Gascoyne Gascoyne

'phone?

---

1 *Compton's Pictured Encyclopedia*, founded by Frank E. Compton in 1922, subsequently acquired by Encyclopedia Britannica, Inc., renamed *Compton's Encyclopedia and Fact-Index*, and presently sold as *Compton's by Britannica*.

[74]

[AH]
April 2nd, 1972
45 Knollwood Dr., Rochester, New York 14618

[Letter, typed on a The University of Rochester, Department of English, letterhead]

like April 2, 1972

Dear friend,

Are you aware that, according to the latest theories, the much admired archaic smiles of Etruscan funerary sculpture are thought to be due largely to gas? Lying down like that, propped on one elbow is not good for digestion; and though the Etruscans may have known a lot about building and painting and things like that, they were, on the whole, a flatulent people.

The Dr. has postponed our due date till April 10th or so; consequently there are still only the two of us.[1] But we have been impulsive and rash, and are planning to buy a house. It is a big thing. Seven bathrooms. And one extra John in the cellar. Thirteen rooms, as I recall. The bank will let us know this coming week whether they will let us have the sort of mortgage we want. If so, we will occupy in middle or late June. We shall also have more than enough beds, so if you care to visit, we can take care of you in lumpy style. Our present phone number, which you have been bugging us about, is (716) 381-1260.

Louvre
E. H. Gombrich

---

1 Evan Hecht arrived, ahead of schedule, on April 5th.

[75]

[WLM]
[April 12th, 1972]
[25 Henshaw Avenue, Northampton, Massachusetts 01060]

[Letter, typed on Royal Hibernian Hotel Ltd, Dublin 2, letterhead, posted in the same hotel's envelope, addressed to A. E. Hecht, Esq., 45 Knollwood Drive, Rochester NY 14618]

> Things in Dublin are Pretty Good. People are asking me things, and I'm telling them....
>
> And of course you are mistaken about the Etruscan smile. It comes from the assistants of the Greek sculptors, who, in aiding their maîtres (that's French), said Μαθιvo to their sitters, meaning, roughly, Stillstand! But the word you will know is extremely close the the Etruscan 田乩|+己, meaning, as perhaps you may not know, it will be all right, it won't hurt, just for Christ's sakes endure, or some such. That is why the Etruscan statue is so enduring, or endearing (Etruscology is not a precise thing).
>
> All hail all Hechts! I am fine. I will hope, for nefarious purposes, to use your NY apt soon. Will call & make demands.
>
> au fait,
> Vögelsanger

[76]

[WLM]
[April 13th, 1972]
25 Henshaw Ave., Northampton, Massachusetts 01060

[Letter, typed on a University College, Center of Adult Education, letterhead, addressed to Feldwebel Antonio von hecht, 45 Knollwood Drive, Rochester NY 14618]

> Forgot to say that anastasomasy means
>
> Raymond Massey playing Anastasia as a Trans-Siberian transvestite …

---

1 The first two handwritten expressions in this letter – the one seeming to be Greek, the other Etruscan – are in fact meaningless. The allonym, Vögelsanger, with which WLM signs off is a not uncommon German name.

That's an <u>awfully</u> pedestrian zip code you've got – no character at <u>all</u> – as I keep telling you –

[Unsigned]

[77]

[AH]
April 19th, 1972

The University of Rochester, Rochester, New York 14627, Department of English

[Letter, typed on a The University of Rochester, Department of English, letterhead, addressed to Prof. Wm. MacDonald (hotsy-totsy), 25 Henshaw Ave., Northampton, Mass. 01060]

Peasant!

    Your snide and uneducated comments on our zip code betray the taste (if I may extend that term somewhat) of a parvenu (French) in these matters. You are obviously the sort who would be impressed by cheap, rhinestone-like zips like 84507 or 93159. It takes a person of rather more cultivation than you apparently can command to see the rather subtle strengths, the traditional, unostentatious values embodied in our zip. It should immediately declare to anyone of discernment something of the principles of the founding fathers, the signature of John Hancock (to whom, as new home-owners, we are deeply in debt) and a number of other things that bring a catch to the throat and a rise to the gorge. I do not want to appear to boast. It would probably fail to impress someone with your vulgar tastes in any case.

Thine,
Emma Bovary

[78]

[WLM]
[25 Henshaw Avenue, Northampton, Massachusetts 01060]
May 4th, 1972

[Blank postcard, typed, with enclosure]

Kind sir,

    Glad to have the picture of the Konservatorium in your new house. I enclose a shot of my new bowling alley, which as you'll probably notice was finished off in a nice, comfy blue.

    ¶ Did you know that the Baroness Kalipzo van Hallendstadt-Mundtmordt was convicted of <u>emmisio fractabilé</u>?*

¶ Some damned fool told me that after reading Saint-Simon I'd never be the same. Well, I've read him, and I'm exactly the same …

Love,
Conrad Count Cunt

*maybe that should read <u>spectabile</u>?

[Enclosure: card, typed]

April 24th, 1972

MS. Civale,

I have received a quote on the out of print book you requested, ROMAN ARCHITECTURE. I have only received one quote. A description follows. ROMAN ARCHITECTURE, by MacDonald, Yale U. Press, 1965, Mint condition at $42.50*. Please let me know if you would like this. It is still possible that we will receive other quotes on the book, but it is now more than a month since the book was advertised. My number is 941-5899.

Thanks,
John Crutcher

One of my students handed me this the day after your appearance here.

*Immortality? Stupidity?

[79]

[WLM]
[Undated, but written some time between May 4th and 15th, 1972]]
[25 Henshaw Avenue, Northampton, Massachusetts 01060]

[Library accession card, typed]

Dear Helen,

Are you tired of Tony yet? If not, why not? Well, I just wanted to say that if you are, and I could understand it if you were, as Alice would say, I'd be more than glad to waltz over every other Sunday and have breakfast with you and keep your spirits up; after all, it can't be easy for you, with Him around all the time. I've tried to help a little by promoting him from Feldwebel to Viscount; but, on 2nd think, they ain't so good, those Viscounts, and it may go to his head and make him all the worse. In any event, if you need Help, Holler.

Love,
Willyum

[80]

[AH]
May 15th, 1972
[45 Knollwood Dr., Rochester, New York 14618]

[Letter, typed on a The University of Rochester, Department of English, letterhead, with handwritten note by Helen Hecht appended]

Comrade,

My wife is tantalized by your kind offer of sexual license and abandon, but is in some doubt about whether your license may not have expired. Out here in the Midwest we are very touchy about seeing that all the formalities are observed. And the sheriffs are really tough if they catch you with an expired license; they're not pigs, exactly; more like wart-hogs. There used to be a wart-hog in the Bronx Zoo that looked exactly like H. L. Mencken. Now they are both dead, gone to some better, statelier and more pearly-gated zoo where, over steins of Pilsner, they will affectionately recall the good old days.

We both liked your blue bowling alley. Are the pins set electrically, or do you have frock-coated and bewigged pin-boys?

Evan Alexander, ever on the move, has advanced from colic to constipation. It makes for liveliness and variety. Yesterday, Mother's Day, I took out my old lady (Helen) and got her sloshed. She's still hung over, but is making brownies out of gratitude. She may wish to append a note.

Groucho

Dearest William,

Yes. I accept. Thank you. (Tony's fears about the sheriff are absolutely unfounded. You see, he comes every second and fourth Sunday. Now if you were to come on first and third Sundays ...)

Prospectively yrs,
H.

[81]

[WLM]
July 27th, 1972
[25 Henshaw Avenue, Northampton, Massachusetts 01060]

[Letter, typed on a Fogg Art Museum, memorandum slip]

VI kal. Aug. MCMLXXII

Hello there humble folk:
I wear my Baldric as I write.
Etymologeez for humble folk:

Today's word is – you've guessed –

BUMWAD

Bumwad is not an easily understood matter at all at all. Ektually, it comes from an igorant British Civil Cervant sent into that part of Africa now known (or know nown) as Ruinpranda. The local chief, then, imported tons of toilet paper stamped with his name, or with his name best as the Liverpool shippers could handle it. His ektual name was Bu M'Wad. You've probably guessed the rest … and indeed you may be thankful that I'm not carrying this any further.

Do you have { }s?[1]

All the best,
as they say,
Marmaduke Poindexter

[82]

[AH]
[August 21st, 1972]
19 East Boulevard, Rochester, New York 14610

[Blank postcard, typed, addressed to Wm. MacDonald, 45 [sic]
Henshaw Ave., Northampton, Mass. 01060]

There's a minority group that neither the Republicans nor Democrats are doing anything about: left-handed foot-fetishists of Peruvian ancestry. And it's a crying shame. The very fact that the group is really small, with no real political voice, means that we must all be vigilant to see that their rights are safeguarded. Not one of them has ever been elected to the Senate or the judiciary. Talk about prejudice.

I feel certain that you will be willing to subscribe your name to a letter I am preparing for the <u>New York Times</u> in their behalf, and will be happy to send me, as treasurer of the organization to defend their cause a generous contribution. Here on East Boulevard we try to make Democracy work. You may make the check payable to me personally to expedite this great crusade.

Federigo da Montefeltro

---

1 Once again, braces have been substituted for WLM's square brackets, so as to avoid confusion with editorial insertions.

[83]

[AH]
[August 31st, 1972]
[19 East Boulevard, Rochester, New York 14610]

[Blank postcard, typed, addressed to Wm. MacDonald,
45 [sic] Henshaw Avenue, Northampton, Mass. 01060]

I'm sending this to you now because postal rates are likely to go up next year. As I told you on the phone, Helen and I have worried about your personal appearance, especially your casual – not to say slovenly – dress when lecturing and on other formal academic occasions. We are therefore planning to beat the post office to the draw by sending you your Christmas present early – if we can ever get around to it. We have selected an elegant garment with a blazonment indicative of your professional status, such as would not dishonor you when accepting honorary degrees. No doubt you will have trouble finding adequate words with which to thank us. Work on it.
      Desiderius

[84]

[WLM]
[Early September, 1972]
[25 Henshaw Avenue, Northampton, Massachusetts 01060]

[Letter, typed on a The Byzantine Institute Inc., letterhead, with a now missing enclosure]

    Every Day is Labor Day at the Boston Lying-In ......

Dear Sir or Madam, as the Case May Be,
 Fully supportive of the left-handed foot-fetishists of Peruvian ancestry, I enclose my donation as requested. I understand that these two Iron men will buy a lot of foot support; might I recommend my ole pal Dr Scholl? Or has he taken a powder?
 As to the blazoned academic garment, I can't wait. You are sure you don't mean varmint? For if you do, don't bother; there are plenty here.
      Yours in the horn of plenty,
      With affectation,
      Eddie Puss

[85]

[WLM]
October [23rd], 1972
[25 Henshaw Avenue, Northampton, Massachusetts 01060]

[Letter, typed on a Hotel Eva, Faro, Algarve, Portugal, letterhead, posted in an Air Mail envelope, addressed to Anthony Hecht, 19, East Boulevard, ROCHESTER, New York, 14610]

Gentlemen,
    Again I write with my baldric nearby.
    You can't, you really can't, ask for more than that.
    I write to say that WHENEVER YOU CAN, you should take umbrage. By no means is enough umbrage taken.
    As you bucket about, take it. In my own travels, I am taking it increasingly.
    The matter is so serious that I am forming the Committee for Umbrage Not Taken, that is, C.U.N.T. We're going to soak it up [… illegible …]
    Joining is neither tedious nor expensive. Write for further details.
                                Yours,
                        [Signature illegible]

[86]

[WLM]
[November 3rd, 1972]
25 Henshaw Avenue, Northampton, Massachusetts 01060

*[Blank postcard, typed and handwritten, addressed to H A & E Hecht,
19 East Boulevard, Rochester NY 14610]*

Memories of Dr Fell ——

Read down Col. I   Col. II
         ↓   ↓

I cannot hear   It is because
The roses grow   there are no laws
Upon your garden lawn;   against your hunting-horn.

I do not care   Do blow it please
if squirrels play   with greater ease
about your iron faun.   and mostly in the day;

114 | *A Bountiful Harvest*

Read down Col. I ↓	Col. II ↓
And if I slight	And pray you, knight,
throughout the night	desist at night
gazebos all forlorn	from winding roundelay.

[1]

[87]

[WLM]
[Early November, 1972]
25 Henshaw Avenue, Northampton, Massachusetts 01060

[Letter, typed]

Saturday

Dear Helen & Tony,

I feel very badly about it, but I just can't make it next week. It's not only that I am swamped with work and departmental duties, but that I broke my nose and though I'm all right I want to stay home and watch after it. After all, it isn't every day that you get an opportunity to nose-watch.

I had worked late at night and, early the next morning, I was shuffling about in my kitchen when I reached high on a shelf for something or other. A quart bottle of Schweppes Soda water, annoyed by this, attacked me from above, neatly doing the job. I'll <u>never</u> buy Schweppes again! After passing through several sets of hands and some fancy machinery, everyone decided I <u>had</u> broken it, and that I should go home. I did. The best moment was perhaps when an officious nurse asked me if I had The Insurance. I gave her my Hertz card.

    Love to all, and deep regrets.
      Bill

[88]

[AH]
[November, 1972]
[19 East Boulevard, Rochester, New York 14610]

[Letter, typed on a Ludicrous House – Publishers letterhead]

Dear Old MacDonald,

How's yer farm? We hear that, you're a writer-fellow, and that you write books.

---

1 This appears to be WLM's response to the well-known nursery rhyme, "I do not like thee, Dr. Fell," which, after 1926, thanks to Robert Graves, had regularly been included in Mother Goose anthologies.

We here at LUDICROUS HOUSE would mightily like to publish a book of yours. There doesn't have to be too much writing in it, long as there's pictures. Worth a thousand words, a picture is. What we have in mind is dirty pictures of late Roman Emperors You know what we mean. Something to cheer the spirits of old ladies, at Christmas, a coffee-table book. If you could dig up some nice pictures of Hadrian and Antinous[1] doing it together, that would really turn on the public. We hear you have a lot of slides of that sort. Contract terms can be worked out later. Let us, know, also, what you have on Augustus and his mommy.

> In going from room to room in the dark,
> I reached out blindly to save my face,
> but neglected, however lightly, to lace
> My fingers and close my arms in an arc.
> A slim door got in past my guard,
> And hit me a blow in the head so hard
> I had my native simile jarred.
> So people and things don't pair any more
> with what they used to pair with before.
>
> R. Frost[2]

I trust this didn't happen to you in your encounter with the bottle. But what a reputation to have earned: MacDonald, distinguished bon vivant & celebrated tipster of Northampton, smashes nose on bottle. For sheer eagerness and gusto, nothing can match it. Take care of your prow.
Luca della Robbia

[89]

[WLM]
November 16th, 1972
[25 Henshaw Avenue, Northampton, Massachusetts, 01060]

[Letter, typed on a The Westbury Hotel, Madison Avenue at 69th Street, New York, NY 10021, letterhead, with now missing enclosures]

My dear General,
This is as close as I can come. The Mérida joint[3] is filled with juicy shots of

---

1 Antinous (AD 111–130), Bithynian Greek, and the favorite – perhaps also the lover – of the Emperor Hadrian, who had him deified after his untimely death.

2 Robert Frost, "The Door in the Dark," from Frost's *West-Running Brook* (New York: Henry Holt, 1928).

3 Mérida is the capital of the autonomous community of Extremadura in western Spain. Originally known as Emerita Augusta, it was founded by Octavius Augustus in BC 25, going on to become one of

Augustus Imp. & his mom, whereas the Capela dos Ossos[1] is given over, as you might guess, to Hadrian and Tinou,[2] as we used ta call him; H. has a hard on, thus the Ossos. (No relation to Aristotle An-Ossos.)

I throw in the Museu Militar[3] for like free.

Hope your ulcer is better. The thought of you not drinking is somehow unassimilable. But it will be good to have you all in Cantabrigia,[4] & perhaps then we can get you back on the sauce.

Disrespectfully,
Joan Perón

[90]

[WLM]
December 10th, 1972
25 Henshaw Avenue, Northampton, Massachusetts 01060

[Letter, handwritten, addressed to A · HECHT, yup!, 19 E. Boulevard, Rochester N.Y., 14610]

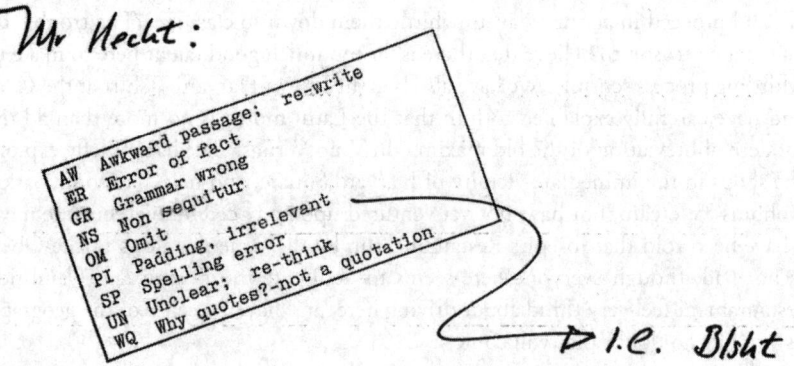

Rekanizing you're poor teaching – I hear a lot about it here – I let you in without charge into my NEW INVENSHUN, above. Great, huh? Saves time, assuming the student can read. Just stamp his / her paper, + AW / WQ /PI away. It's fun. Build your own!
Roscoe Pound

the most important cities in the Roman Empire. Since 1993 it has been a UNESCO World Heritage site.

1 The Capela dos Ossos is in Évora, Portugal. Its walls are decorated with the bones of thousands of Franciscan monks.

2 Antinous.

3 The Museu Nacional Militar, in Lisbon, Portugal, is a military museum, and is said to house the most extensive display of guns and swords anywhere in the world.

4 AH had been invited to lecture at Harvard in Cambridge, Massachusetts.

[91]

[AH]
February 6th, 1973
F111, Leverett House, Harvard University, Cambridge, Massachusetts

[Letter, typed on a Leverett House, Harvard University, letterhead]

Dear Pearl Buck,

From our infinitely desirable eleventh-floor apartment, with tinted picture windows and extra bed for distinguished visitors, we look out upon a prospect of the Charlie River, the domes (green) of Eliot House and (blue) of Lowell House, and the stunning old Romanesque church of St. George in Debt. There are certain undeniable attractive qualities to Harvard, not the least of them being the weather. It has been sunny and temperate since we arrived on the third. The lazy interval since then has provided a few diversions: I met my first classes yesterday, and they scared the shit out of me – for the following plausible reasons. I am teaching two courses, one in fiction writing and the other in the writing of poetry. Over 50 students showed up for the poetry course, and about 30 for the prose. The ideal number would be 10 or 12 for poetry and about 8 for prose. Tomorrow I get mss. from them all, and proceed in about a day, to whittle them down to class size. The trouble is, I have much reason to believe that there is far too much good talent here to make the whittling process sensible. We have also bought Evan a Harvard T-shirt at the Coop, and have carefully explained to him that the Latin motto is no more than a brisk, modern abbreviation of the old maxim, "In Vino Veritas." We have briefly explored the shops in the immediate vicinity of Harvard Square, and have had some Baskin-Robbins ice-cream, but have not yet ventured upon any ceremonial, outside meals. I have been told that Joseph's Restaurant, run by the same people as Locke-Ober's, is not bad; though everyone here seems to denigrate the Boston and Cambridge restaurants. I feel very timid about driving here, and have no sense of the geography as yet, but no doubt that will come.

When you toss in your chairman's towel let us know and come for a visit. Our phone is 498-2778. We hope to hear that as a final gesture of your chairman's authority you have fired all the non-tenured members by way of letting in a little fresh air. Keep things moving, that's what I say.

Yours,
M. P.
Marcel Proust

P.S.: Today Evan said, "Gorki," which rather surprised us, since, up to this time his interests have been confined to cheap and highly questionable French literature.

[92]

[WLM]
[February 16th or 17th, 1973]
[25 Henshaw Avenue, Northampton, Massachusetts 01060]

[Letter, typed, posted in Royal Hibernian Hotel, Dublin 2, Ireland, envelope, addressed to Professeur Antonie HECHT, Leverett House F111, Harvard the University, Cambridge Mass. 02138, with enclosure]

Ides Feb. + 4, MCMLXXIII; AUC 2726[1]

My dear Coperinicus,

Even (Evan?) a sun who claims to say "Gorki" cannot be in the middle of everything. Soviet law prohibits.

The raisins you have so many in your séances (that's FRENCH) is be-cause I spread the word that you had pornographs that you would bring to class. So ……

I am a little bombed, as They Say, filled to the perixial lompt with the Chairmanship. I am taking your sage advice, & firing Everyone. Four weeks to go.

Interim (THAT'S Latin), I am providing an Irish stamp, above, so you can mail this to some unsuspecting enemy and confuse the Hell out of him …… In Any Event, I note your 'phone no. & address, and that you and your Lady are Available, and I will Be In Soon, to explain things to you …

Galley-Layo

[93]

[WLM]
[May] 15th, [1973]
[25 Henshaw Avenue, Northampton, Massachusetts 01060]

[Letter, typed on a Hotel Eva letterhead, addressed to Professor & Mrs Anthony Evan HECHT & son, Leverett House F entry, Harvard University, Cambridge Massachusetts 02138, with enclosure]

the 15th of the month …

Dear Helen, Tony, & Evan,

I feel just awful about not coming in to see you. It is on my mind a great deal; every week I say to myself that I will come but I never do it. I've not been to Cambridge / Boston since last November, when I gave a lecture at the MIT School of Architecture, and I've only been out of here once this term, to go to Ohio a week

---

1 WLM's Roman calendar datings are sometimes less than straightforward. Here, he departs from his usual practise of giving the year its AD styling, instead employing the AUC styling (Anno Urbis Conditae [from the founding of the City {Rome}]). As well, the "Ides Feb. + 4" construction is WLM's own, and leaves it unclear whether he meant February 16th or 17th, which would more properly be rendered as XIV. Kal. Mar and XIII. Kal. Mar, respectively.

or two ago for the same purpose.

I don't know just what the reasons are, other than that it has nothing to do with any failure to want to see you. I am rather tied down – the Departmental chairmanship until the end of April, and now of course grattecieli of term papers and exams – but those aren't the reasons, really. I used fairly to commute to the Square, and maybe I've been too often. But when I get right down to it, it may be just the calendar and a smooth and nice affair that I'm involved in. I have the boys every other week, and on the alternate weekends Barbara [E. Satz] (she's a reporter for a Holyoke paper, and we've been together for six or eight months now; very young) is here; and weekdays are not good for trips. Finally, I don't enjoy driving much any more …

All this to say that I miss you, and that when I found you were to be next door, so to speak, in Cambridge, I was very happy, envisioning regular meetings and much talk & coca-cola … but it hasn't worked out that way. Sorry.

When do you leave Cambridge?

I am at work, having finished some stuff, and I plan to stay right here for the summer and try to keep it up. Bessie quite properly withdrew his contract with me and I paid back the advance, but other houses Love Me. I take the boys to Gloucester on June 16th for a week or so. Did I tell you that they are moving to Oregon about July first? Big Thing, not clear why Dale wants to do it; but she's sold her Amherst house and that's that. I shall miss them a great deal, but it is likely that Noel will go to College in the East, so that will help somewhat. Life is mystifying.

But let none of this cause you to light candles and offer up prayers. I am fine, and although you will not credit it, I will shortly be on the Ameche[1] to make a date.

    Much love,
    Frobenius Jr.

---

1 A slang expression for the telephone, deriving from the actor Don Ameche's starring role in the film *The Story of Alexander Graham Bell*.

[Enclosure: flier]

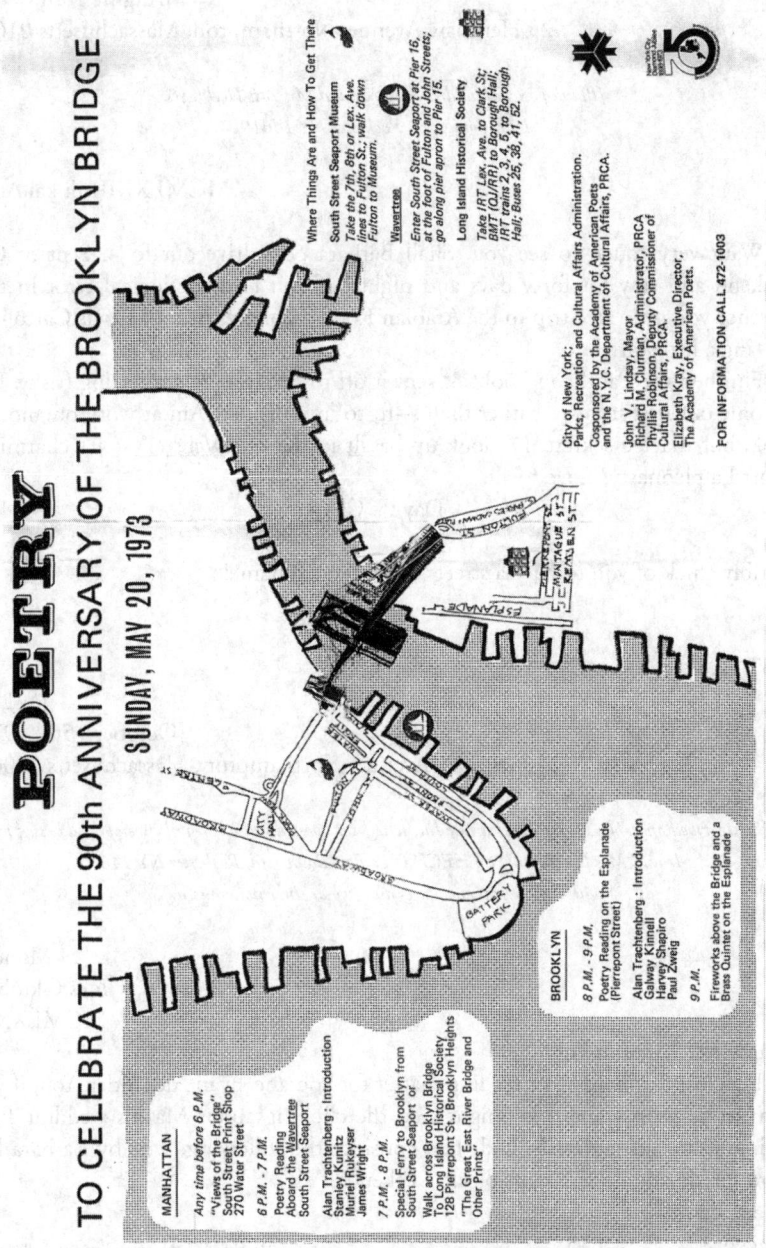

[94]

[WLM]
[August 18th, 1973]
25 Henshaw Avenue, Northampton, Massachusetts 01060

[Blank postcard, addressed to Mr and Mrs A E Hecht, yes,
19 E Boulevard, Rochester NY 14610]

MCMLXXIII iii kal.Aug.[1]

Yes:

Want very much to see you. Shall Barbara & I drive out for a Sept or Oct weekend and stay for forty days and nights? If you find the logical error in that sentence you get a free trip to the Arabian Roc <u>or</u> a plaster bust of Lewis Carroll ph ----- ing a little girl.

Finished the Pantheon book[2] & sent it off to Penguin & am feeling frisky. It is to come out first in h--rd rather than s--ft, to my surprise. Am at work on another book, but that's a sekrett. Do look up <u>basalt</u> in the big <u>Webster's</u> – it's charming. Aren't I a pleonasty? Love to all.

Day C. Chayne

Terribly chick of you to have a street with a French name!

[95]

[WLM]
[October 15th, 1973]
[25 Henshaw Avenue, Northampton, Massachusetts 01060]

[Letter, typed on a The Byzantine Institute Inc. letterhead, posted in an airmail envelope, addressed to
Mr and Mrs Lin Yutang, c/o HECHT, 19 East Boulevard, Rochester NY 14610,
with two present enclosures and two or three now missing]

Monday
Ides Oktobrii,
MCMLXXIII

Dear Mr & Mrs Lin Yutang,

I enclose a good deal of reading matter for you and Evan Alexander. You, if you want to be proper about it, might read the clipping about Mazie's wedding first, noting all the little details, and then consider the following, writ by Barbara but forgotten during the Delights of the weekend:

---

1 WLM's Roman calendar dating seems to have gone awry here, III.Kal.Aug being July 30th, while the postcard was posted on August 18th.
2 *The Pantheon: Design, Meaning, and Progeny.*

> Friggery Pokery
> Mazie, a Smith A.B.
> Gave up her Cox to become a fall bride
> Enthusiastically
> Lying in wait to see*
> One prick turn into a Thorne in her side

Then there is Modine Gunch, Hoving's jug, and so on.[1]
Please fill in the enclosed card and mail right away if not sooner.
We had a marvelous time. There's no sense denying it. It was moving to see you both so happy, and we were strengthened by your happiness.
> Much love,
> Nate + Natalie

*There are those who want "bed" for "wait." A personal choice is necessary.

[Enclosure 1: clipping]

Tradition is thrown to the winds at Mazie Cox, Brink Thorne Wedding

Westhampton Beach, L.I., Sept. 9 – Miss Mary Ann Livingston Delafield Cox and Brinkley Stimson Thorne were married here today at Sunswyck, the country home of Mr. and Mrs. Howard Ellis Cox, parents of the bride. The bridegroom is a son of Mr. and Mrs. Edwin Thorne of Greenwich, Conn.

Off in a Puff of Smoke

As soon as the ceremony was over, the couple, throwing tradition to the winds, changed into bathing suits and joined their guests in the informal "celebration" that replaced the usual reception.

Guests helped themselves to an alfresco luncheon of shrimp, green salad, fruit salad, sandwiches, cheese, bread and white wine; swam in the pool, and played volley ball or croquet as the mood took them. The afternoon's proceedings wound up with a show by George Ross, a magician hired from a theatrical agency in New York. For the finale, he caused the bride and bridegroom to disappear in a puff of smoke. "I love magic," confessed Mazie Cox.

---

1 Modine Gunch had won the little-known Miss Vacant Lot of the World contest in 1973, and was doubtless the subject of one of the now missing enclosures. "Hoving's Jug" was almost certainly the subject of another of the now missing enclosures, but was known to the world at large as the Euphronios Krater, a Greek vase created around BC 515 which Thomas Hoving, then Director of the Metropolitan Museum of Art, had recently purchased for the museum at a cost of $1m.

Dispensing with attendants, she chose her mother as her witness, and the bridegroom had his father as his witness.

Also among the guests were the bride's brothers, Howard E. Cox Jr. and Edward Finch Cox, with their wives, Julia Dempsey Cox and Tricia Nixon Cox, as well as the bridegroom's brothers – Edwin Thorne Jr., and his wife, Missie Gary Thorne, Gordon Grand Thorne, with his wife, Lee Ammidon Thorne, and Peter A. Thorne, who is a freshman at Yale.

The bride, a graduate of the Chapin School, Smith College, class of '67, and the Yale School of Architecture, class of '71, teaches architectural design at Smith and is a consultant to the First Woman's Bank and Trust Company in New York.

Mr Thorne, who is known as Brink, was graduated from St. Paul's School in Concord, N.H. and in 1968 from Yale College, having taken a year off to study piano in Paris. He received his architecture degree from Yale in 1972 and plans to practice architecture in Amherst, Mass., while researching alternative sources of energy. His father is a private investor and chairman of the Advance Investors Corporation. The bride's father is a member of the New York law firm of Cox, Treanor & Shaughnessy.[1]

[Enclosure 2: clipping]

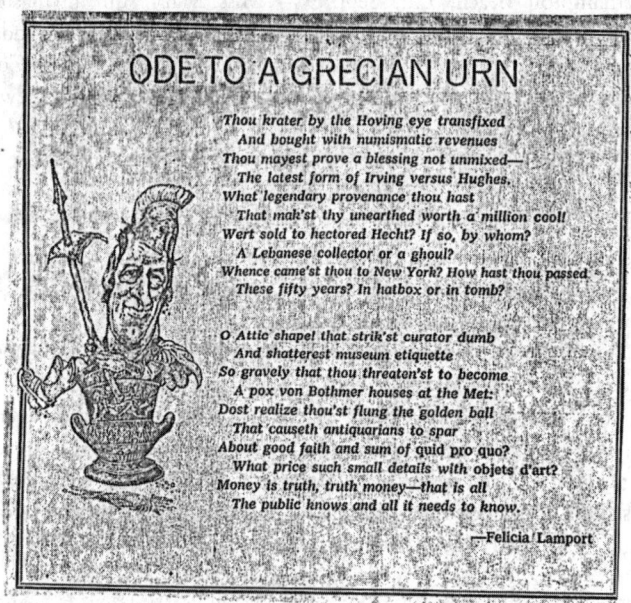

1 *New York Times*, September 10th, 1973.
2 *New York Times*, March 11th, 1973.

[96]

[AH]
October 19th, 1973
[University of Rochester, Rochester, New York 14627, Department of English]

[Letter, typed on a Hotel Lenox, Buffalo, New York, letterhead, posted in a Dana-Palmer House, Harvard University envelope, addressed to Professor Wm. MacDonald (hotsy-totsy), Hagia Sophia Smith Professor of Byzantine Art History in the first forty-five minutes of the reign of Justinian, 25 Henshaw Ave, Northampton, Mass. 01060]

Dear Bill,

I had a brief, informal chat with Dean Kenneth Clark about the Art Department Chairmanship here. In sum, he said that a short note from you to him, expressing even a mild interest in the job, would place you among the candidates, and would result in your being invited back for serious talk about it.

I found this odd, but said nothing. I'm not sure I understand why the initiative, however mild, should now come from you; or even what more they want to learn from you that they didn't learn last time. It sounds like administrative evasiveness to me; and my private guess is that there may be some plan to shake up the present department a good deal more by acts of pointed discouragement before getting in a new broom. But maybe I've been watching too much Watergate.

Still, I hope you won't let this half-assed procedural business prevent you from sending a note of "mild interest" to Clark. I told him, by the way, that you had just relinquished the chairmanship at Smith, and were delighted to be quit of it. But I hope you will let them try to tempt you. Selfishly, Helen and I would both delight in having you here.

She has just written you a note herself, telling you how happy we both were to have you and Barbara here, and inviting you both back for Thanksgiving. Unless your boys come to see you, or you go to see them, we hope you'll come here.

Tony

[97]

[WLM]
[November 4th, 1973]
25 Henshaw Avenue, Northampton, Massachusetts 01060

[Blank postcard, addressed to The Hechts (Aaaah), 19, E Boulevard, Rochester NY 14610]

Barbara and I yesterday, with the help of a fairly good Montbazillac '69, produced

> Pompey's striker, polishing brass
> Said "The Old Man's lacking in class.

> Though a feminine charmer,
> He's happiest in a cuirass."

Get it? Get it?

iv. xi. MCMLXXIII

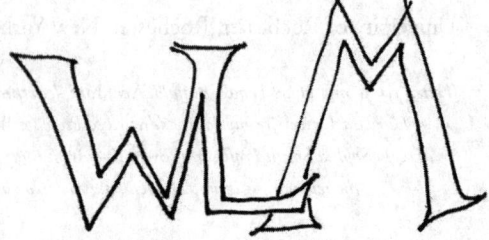

[98]

[WLM]
December 17th, 1973
[25 Henshaw Avenue, Northampton, Massachusetts 01060]

[Letter, typed on a Hotel Eva letterhead]

My dear Colonel Featherstonehaugh,

I am much of mixture of mind about the University of Rochester Art Department job. One moment I reach for quill and parchment to address Dean Clark, another I say Oh No, I shouldn't suggest that I'll come out if I'm not really going to follow through on it.

One thing that is on my mind is the attitude of the Department, I wouldn't want to appear as if I was putting my oar into what I gather may be a slightly sticky internal affair. On the other hand I wouldn't want to pass up something potentially good, especially in these days of Smith's financially questionable future (I serve as an elected faculty member on the College Planning and Resources Committee, and though it's an awful bore in some ways, I am in a fashion an expert on the College's finances).

So: what can you tell me about the Situation there in the Art Department? Do you advise, in that respect, my going ahead with a note to Lord Clark?[1] And would you be so kind as to ask one of your secretaries to send me a current catalogue, so that I can gain some idea of the flavour and textour of the Dept? All thanks.

Read, but not dictated, by
Garnet Woolsey, Bt.

Love and Greetings to you both, to Evan, + to the cat. (If you don't have a cat, put a plain, pressure-sensitive label over the words ",+ to the cat.") (Or, go out and get a

---

1 WLM is playing on Clark's name, which he shared with the British art historian, Sir Kenneth M. Clark.

126 | *A Bountiful Harvest*

cat, + let the remark stand).

[99]

[AH]
[January 4th, 1974]
[19 East Boulevard, Rochester, New York 14610]

[Postcard, addressed to Prof. W. MacDonald, 25 Henshaw, Northampton, Mass. 01060]

Dear Bill,
    This is my worst student. As you can see, she is trying to improve her grade by sitting on my wall. She will fail. It takes more than sitting on a wall to sway me. Let Nixon take notice that there is some integrity left in the country.
                                      Erwin Panofsky

[100]

[WLM]
[January 7th, 1974]
[25 Henshaw Avenue, Northampton, Massachusetts 01060]

[Postcard, addressed to Prof. A&E Hecht, 19, East Boulevard, ROCHESTER NY 14610]

Early Jan.
Friend:
    Yeah, well, there's <u>no</u> integrity here at all. <u>This</u> is a student of mine, equipped as you can see to get over any wall. I am deeply involved with her ... Will fly out on the 22nd, and see you that nite [...] .... Meanwhile, man your walls!
    J. J. Winckelman

[101]

[WLM]
[Some time between January 20th and 28th, 1974]
[25 Henshaw Avenue, Northampton, Massachusetts 01060]

[The following letter, typed on an Amherst College, Department of Fine Arts, letterhead, was sent to WLM by someone signing off merely as Chandler. This was almost certainly W. Chandler Kirwin, then an Assistant Professor in the department. WLM typed a message at the foot of his letter, and forwarded it to AH]

19 gennaio, 1974

Salve Bill!
Ne siamo sicurissimi: ci saranno dei fuochi artificiali ...[1]
Ciao –
Chandler

What in hell do you suppose HE wants?
Ha! → → I think I know! Anyway:

There was a Young Man, name of Rex
With extremely small organs of sex,
When accused of exposure
He replied with composure:
"De minimis non curat lex."[2]

[102]

[WLM]
[January 28th, 1974]
[25 Henshaw Avenue, Northampton, Massachusetts 01060]

[Blank postcard, typed, addressed to The Hechts, 19 East Boulevard, Rochester, NY 14610]

Or –

Constantine's architect, Paul,
Said "You're all in the emperor's thrall.
This jerry-built apse
Will surely collapse
If you bastards don't get on the ball."

[Unsigned]

---

1 Italian = "Hi Bill! We are sure: there will be fireworks ..."
2 Latin = "The law does not concern itself with trifles."

[103]

[AH]
February 13th, 1974
[25 Henshaw Avenue, Northampton, Massachusetts 01060]

[French postcard with an reproduction of an engraving of the Duc D'Angoulème, typed, addressed to A E HECHT, 19, E. Boulevard, Rochester NY, 14610]

My dear Sir, or Madame,
    I hope you will find it convenient to look up "umbel" in <u>Webster's 2nd Intl</u>; it's pretty damn exciting … Can't recall if KClark said anything about When; I think he didn't. If I don't hear in a while, I'll tickle him.
                  Love to all.
                   Pry Mary

[104]

WLM
[March 8th, 1974]
[Massachusetts]

[Blank postcard, addressed to Mr and Mrs Anthony Evan HECHT and Off-Spring, 19, East Boulevard, Rochester NY 14610]

I've not heard a word from Ken Clark
He's keeping me much in the dark
    He should be a fair man
    And pick out a chairman
And not treat the job as a lark.

But it <u>could</u> be his name, that is, Clark,
Is actually not Clark but Snark,
    And the Beaver and Banker
    And Bellman all hanker
To keep the affair in the dark.

But I'm sure that you both will agree
That preserving the department's ésprit
    Requires they park
    To one side the vile Snark
And take on a good man, like me.

[105]

[WLM]
[April 16th, 1974]
25 Henshaw Avenue, Northampton, Massachusetts 01060

[Blank postcard, addressed to H, A, & E Hecht, 19, E Boulevard, Rochester NY 14610, with two enclosed newspaper clippings]

[Enclosure 1]

Bishop Sheen and Cardinal Spellman are holding a service in St Patrick's Cathedral when they notice that Christ and Moses are in the congregation:

> SHEEN: They're standing in the back – don't look now, you idiot! They can see us.
> SPELLMAN: Which ones are they?
> SHEEN: The ones that are glowing. *Hoo! Glowing!* Terrible.
> SPELLMAN: Are you sure it's them?
> SHEEN: I've just seen 'em in pictures, but I'm pretty sure – Moses is a ringer for Charlton Heston.
> SPELLMAN: Are they armed?
> SHEEN: I dunno.
> SPELLMAN: Poor box locked?

[Enclosure 2]

By the way, have you heard the one about the man who dropped a piece of bread on the floor and it fell butter side up? He rushed straight round to the Rabbi. "Rabbi," he said, "I dropped a piece of bread on the floor already, and it fell butter side up." "Come, Hymie," said the Rabbi, "Who are you trying to fool?" Hymie persisted in his story and finally managed to convince the Rabbi, who thought he should consult a higher authority about an occurrence which was clearly in defiance of one of the basic principles of the universe. He sent the problem to the Chief Rabbi. After months of meditation this wise man came up with the answer. "The bread must have been buttered on the wrong side."

I've made quite a fine, elaborating story out of this.

[Unsigned]

[106]

[WLM]
[May, 1974]
25 Henshaw Avenue, Northampton, Massachusetts 01060

[Blank postcard, addressed to All the Hechts, 19, East Boulevard, Rochester NY 14610, with the sender's address given as MacDee / 01060]

A prize-winning rhymer named Hecht
Married Beautiful Helen – nicht schlecht![1]
Now they have Evan
And sing "My Blue Heaven."
And that's all there is to this limerick,
Actually.

[Unsigned]

[107]

[WLM]
[June 13th, 1974]
[25 Henshaw Avenue, Northampton, Massachusetts 01060]

[Letter, typed on a Society of Architectural Historians letterhead]

Ides Junii MCMLXXIV

Folks,

All of us Walnuts here want to wish you a Very Happy Flag Day, The Zinnias are coming up, Zeugmas are rife, and with any luck will be able to send you a Zeppelin kit soon. Zs are nice, little sung. Qs are good, and they were one of the most satisfactory aspects of living in Albuquerque NM.

Meanwhile, like life isn't too bad. Teaching at Harvard Summer School, beginning July 1st (!) – or, better, [!] – to get up some → bread for Noel's tuition bills. He arrives here any day now, after driving his ancient VW van across the country, and will spend the summer with me; he starts in the fall at something called Windham College, in Putney VT., the place he wants …

No word, from K. Clark Hero of the Rochester University Flag Day kids. No, no word.

Went to California to lecture at Berkeley – wow'd 'em – and spent a weekend with Noel & Nick in Eureka! California. Nice. Drank a lot of beer in an expensive hotel suite, something I'd not done for a long time but which is a Good Thing … I see by the papers that the Harvards gave Ole Ralphie an hon. degree.[2]

---

1 German = Not bad!

2 Ralph Ellison was awarded an honorary doctorate by Harvard on the day this letter was written (along-

Princeton is making mild wooing sounds, but it seems to me that it is unlikely that (how do you like this sentence?) anything will come of it. Barbara is fine, giving 'em hell in Holyoke, sends her love, as does

>Your hmbl obt svt,
>Inept P. Nippleman

[108]

[WLM]
June 23rd, 1974
[25 Henshaw Avenue, Northampton, Massachusetts 01060]

[Norwegian postcard, with a photograph of a mocked-up room in the Norsk Folkemuseum in Oslo, handwritten, addressed to A · E · HECHT, 19, E. Boulevard, Rochester N.Y., 14610]

Antonio mio:

Just had my aptmt. redecorated, as you can see / Letter from Clark, saying the search has been discontinued, + that probably when they resume it they will look for a younger person. Too bad in that if it had worked we would have been all nearby.

>Hi Helen! W^m

side MIT President Jerome B. Wiesner, cellist Mstislav Rostropovich and opera singer Beverly Sills).

[109]

[WLM]
[September 26th, 1974]
[25 Henshaw Avenue, Northampton, Massachusetts 01060]

[A cutting from The Student Newspaper of Case Western Reserve University, *Cleveland, Ohio, dated September 17th, 1974, beneath which is a typed note signed R.S.B., and to the side of which WLM has appended his own typed comment]*

Dr. Love pleads innocent in bizarre slaying

by Herman Chiu

Dr. David Love, who is an assistant professor of anatomy at the Case Western Reserve School of Medicine, pleaded innocent to a charge of involuntary manslaughter during the committing of a felonious assault. Love, 42, was indicted by the Cuyahoga County Grand Jury following the June 22 death of his wife, Virginia, also 42, and released on personal bond by Common Pleas Court Judge Frank Gorman.

County Prosecutor said the indictment charges that Love suspended his wife, who was nude, from a third-floor window of their home at 2972 Meadowbrook Boulevard in Cleveland Heights by a rope tied around her ankle in order to perform a sex act. The rope slipped from Love's hand, and Mrs. Love fell, after which Love removed the rope and called the police, Corrigan said.

Love was charged with involuntary manslaughter after the newspaper boy on his street reported that he had seen the Loves perform the act twice before. The charge carries a minimum sentence of between four and seven years, and a maximum of twenty-five years.

According to J. A. McKee, the university attorney, a member of the faculty could be terminated from the university for grave misconduct if he were tried and convicted, even if tenured. However, Dr. Marcus Singer said that although Love is not tenured, the matter was still unclear, as tenure policies have not been well-defined. Singer further stated that any decision concerning Love's status has to come from the university, which he hoped would allow Love to make his own decision concerning his status while his case is being adjudicated.

Singer said that there had been precedents in the past in which the university had taken an enlightened stand in permitting employees who had been convicted on political charges to return to work.

Although Mr. Richard Baznik, the Director of Communications at the university, said that Love is currently teaching, Singer added that although Love's teaching plans for the year were indefinite, he hoped that Love would be able to continue his scientific work in the

future.
  Sources at the Cuyahoga County Prosecutor's Office said that if the trial would be held …

Yale University
Higher Education and Law
(Spring, 1975)

  A retrospective problem: What difference does it make, if any, whether Professor Love is
  (A) tenured?
  (B) non-tenured?
  Would it be proper for the university to suspend <u>him</u>?
R.S.B.

My dear Professor Ekutuh,
  I suppose any comment by me would be superfluous, but I do wonder if the Loves had in mind some Act of Congress?
        Yours,
        O. W. Holmes

[110]

[WLM]
March 25th, 1975
[25 Henshaw Avenue, Northampton, Massachusetts 01060]

[Letter, typed on a Hotel Santa Catalina, Lasa Palmas, Gran Canaria, letterhead, addressed to Mr + Mrs Anthony Evan Hecht, 19, East Boulevard, Rochester, N.Y., 14610]

Hello There!
  I am in the business of distributing off-color [by that I mean badly-printed] art reproductions. I have one of Winckelmann entreating Dora Panofsky not to dance with Walter Friedlander. Would you be interested? Or perhaps you'd like the one of Ruskin trying to wrassle the Vatican pine-cone into the oculus of the Pantheon, in order to stop the rain from coming down on Queen Christina?[1] (A choice one, that, as the Queen is wearing a heliotrope wimple.)
  As you can tell, we didn't get to New York because of this thriving business.
  Ektuahlly, I've been in California, where the University of California at Santa Barbara is very interested in me & is about to make an offer. I've half a mind – no

---

1 Queen Christina of Sweden – the former Queen Christina, that is, for she had abdicated the throne in 1654 and moved to Rome 28 years before her death – had wanted to be buried in the Pantheon, but the Pope denied the request and had her interred in St. Peter's Basilica instead.

comments, please – to go, but not until '76. Saw Nick; 5' 9." coming out of the awful age. Noel is around a lot, spent summer & winter vacs with me, is fine. Dale <u>still</u> has no job, & I pay & pay, and wish to get out of it but can't quite bring myself to do it – that is, stop sending all that alimony.

Whoever taught Gielgud to say reh VEN yoo for revenue was on the right track. It's nice that way, isn't it?

Little book on Northampton buildings for Bicentennial, is in page proof, will send a copy along in May. Pantheon book still languishes in London, very discouraging. Every two or three months a letter comes saying that I will soon have a tentative production schedule … but so far, nothing.

Love to all,
Wm + Barbara (who flourishes, prob. because I'm such a Great Guy)

[111]

[WLM]
July 13th, 1975
[25 Henshaw Avenue, Northampton, Massachusetts 01060]

[Italian postcard, with a photograph of the Palazzo Pitti in Florence, addressed to
Mr + Mrs A. E. Hecht, 19, East Boulevard, Rochester NY, 14610]

Dear Hechts,

Glad you like the Northampton book[1] – it was fun + easy to do. <u>Pantheon</u> at long last being set, galleys soon, out next winter (2½ years late!). Meanwhile am at it solidly, with the fall term off. Barbara + I are talking living together / marriage but no decision yet. She really needs to be in the City + I'm so comfortable here … California waning but also not settled.

Love,
W^m (author)

Would love to visit – fall?

[112]

[WLM]
January 14th, 1976
[25 Henshaw Avenue, Northampton, Massachusetts 01060]

[Letter, typed on a Santa Barbara Biltmore Hotel and Cottages, Montecito, California, letterhead]

Dear Madame or Sir (We are an Equal Oppertunity,* Affirmative Ekshun, 1/2 vermouth

---

1 *Northampton, Massachusetts: Architecture and Buildings.*

1/2 gin emploer, and will not be underequalled by no one):

A poem, and a very fine one. The setting is the "phoney war" of 1940, when everyone in Great Britain was trying to get at the enemy, and all sorts of hair-brained schemes abounded:

BAKU, or The Map Game

It's jolly to look at the map
And finish the foe in a day.
It's not easy to get at the chap?
Those neutrals are so in the way.
But if you say "What would <u>you</u> do
To fill the aggressor with gloom?"
Well, we might drop a bomb on Baku,
Or, what about bombs on Batum?[1]

Refrain:

I'm all for some bombs on Baku
And, of course, a few bombs on Batum.

You can set it to music, if you want. In any event, I'd have Evan memorize it. When I come to visit you we can check him and, if you've the music ready, we can sing it, a lot.
Love,
A. P. Herbert

* Meaning we spell as we like.

[113]

[AH]
March 10th, 1976
[19 East Boulevard, Rochester, New York 14610]

[Letter, typed on a Harvard University, Department of English, letterhead]

Dear Sir,

Thought you might like to have a little verse to cheer your bleak hours in the slide catalogue.

---

1 The poem of which this is the first verse is by A. P. Herbert, and comes from his *Siren Song* (New York: Doubleday, Doran and Company, Inc., 1941).

Goliardic Song

In classical environs
    Deity misbehaves:
There nereids and sirens
    Bucket the whomping waves.
As tritons sound their conches
    With fat, distended cheeks,
Welded are buxom haunches
    To muscular physiques.

Out of that frothy pageant
    Venus Pandemos rose,
Great genetrix and regent
    Of human unrepose.
Not age nor custom cripples
    Her heavenly commands,
Imperative of nipples
    And tyrannous of glands.

We who have been her students,
    Matriculated clerks
In scholia of imprudence
    And vast, venereal Works,
Taken and passed our orals,
    Salute her classic poise:
Ur-Satirist of Morals
    And Mother of our joys.

[1]

We send you our pornographic love, and look forward to your visit, with Barbara, who is a syllogism of the first figure.
    Phil Brunelleschi

---

1 This poem was included in AH's next collection, *Millions of Strange Shadows*.

[114]

[AH]
March 22nd, 1976
[19, East Boulevard Rochester, New York 14610]

[Letter, typed on a Campus Inn, Ann Arbor, Michigan, letterhead, addressed to William MacDonald, Burgermeister, 25 Henshaw Ave., Northampton, Mass. 01060]

Yr Eminence,

I understand you are a collector of last words. Your own recent find, "It serves me right," is an admirable item, and ought to go for a handsome sum on the current market. There are two I could let you consider on a speculative basis. One is from Henry James, who, in his final, completely conscious moments, and knowing he was about to die, remarked, "Ah, the Distinguished Thing Itself." The other is Sir Thomas More's. Being brought to the scaffold where he was to be beheaded, and being extremely feeble from long imprisonment in the Tower, he asked assistance of a sergeant-at-arms in getting up the steps, remarking, "As for getting down, I can shift for myself." Some people, like Socrates, for example, talk too much; they seem to lack a sense of the pithy, the really quotable utterance.

We all rejoiced in the Wiley Post poem. Life here is pleasant and genial except for the wind-chill factor. And taxes. And prices.

There is a neighborhood fracas going on about the Frank Lloyd Wright house across the street, which the owners want to turn into a "residential museum," – which means that they would continue to live in it, but open it up to the public on a payment basis, with scheduled hours for visits, etc.; and all this in order to restore and maintain the house and property - which, if it were properly to be done, would be far beyond their private resources. As you can guess, I am all in favor. But many of our neighbors are not. Under the pretense of objecting that the traffic of visitors would be too heavy and inconvenient, I think that most of them are jealously worried that the house might be made tax-exempt, and that the owners would end up with a handsome income merely from the receipts at the gate. Their own homes, of course, are not Wright houses, or indeed landmarks of any sort. Louis Clark, the Wright house owner, now wants to establish a board of trustees, who will appreciate the artistic value of the place and the need to restore and preserve it according to impeccable standards. I have suggested your name to him.[1]

X   Newton, his mark

---

1 The proposal seems to have failed, and the Edward E. Boynton House at 16 East Boulevard, Rochester, though it was once owned by The Landmark Society, was subsequently sold again, with covenants, and remains in private hands and closed to the general public.

[115]

[AH]
May 11th, 1976
[19 East Boulevard, Rochester, New York 14610]

[Letter, typed on a The Stanhope Hotel, Fifth Avenue at 81st Street, New York 10028, letterhead]

Dear Bill,

I am delighted beyond clear expression at receiving our copy of <u>The Pantheon</u>.[1] It is sumptuous and handsome, and remarkably generous in photographic citations. Given the fact that it retails for ten pounds, I can understand why a larger format with colored pictures must have been ruled out as ludicrously impractical; and yet I guess I had envisioned something the size and majestic shape of your Roman Architecture book. Still, with the assistance of a lens I thought I was able to make out, in the concluding picture, the lineaments of the author, his then wife, and a genial poetic type named Wilbur. So that rather adroitly, in the manner of Alfred Hitchcock (not Henry-Russell) you have contrived to insinuate yourself into your own work in an unexpected way.[2]

Some things rather surprised me. For example, while in your notes you make mention of the Guggenheim, and compare its volume to the Pantheon's, it is not cited as among the Pantheon's progeny. And then, of course, while you do venture to quote descriptive appraisals of the Pantheon by Shelley, Frank Brown, etc., there is a conspicuous omission of any quotations by me. I can assure you that I have made many comments on the Pantheon, from the terse and pithy, "Gee Whiz," to rather extended reveries and meditations.

Will the book be distributed in this country, or will it have an American publisher?[3] How can copies be secured? I really would like to know.

We all send you our love, our congratulations, and our admiration.

Tony

---

1 *The Pantheon: Design, Meaning, Progeny.*
2 The photograph is reproduced at the top of page 232 *vii*
3 The American edition, published by Harvard University Press, also appeared in 1976.

[116]

[WLM]
May 28th, 1976
[25 Henshaw Avenue, Northampton, Massachusetts 01060]

[Swiss postcard, with a photograph of a detail from the Reformation Wall in Geneva, Switzerland, handwritten, addressed to A. E. HECHTE, 19, East Boulevard, Rochester NY, 14610]

My dear Sir,
 In reading a book call'd <u>The Art of Ecstasy</u>[1] I find, on folio 52, the following: "the <u>concetto</u> served to center the meaning of the subject ... and it was 'literary' in the sense that it can be formulated in words." <The IIe set of italicks have been added.> I hope, sirrah, that you find this sublimely funnye; if not, sende for our Survival Kitte: "Howe to lauggh." I am sirre,
 G. Jaeger

[117]

[AH]
June 10th, 1976
19 East Boulevard, Rochester, New York 14610.

[Letter, typed on a Leverett House, Harvard University, letterhead]

Dear Cardinal,
 We delight in the prospect of a visit from you and Miss Barbara, and suggest the 26th or any time thereafter as being uncommitted and eminently suitable to us. Helen has checked dates, and it seems that on the 24th we are signed up for an especially stuffy dinner party. Anyway, choose ad libitum from the 26th on.
 We have just returned from a visit to Atlanta, which has more interesting modern architecture – much of it by local talent – than most American cities can boast of. Fellow named John Portman (?)[2] did two admirable buildings we considerably admired.
 To my suprise, I am within a stone's throw of finishing a book of poems.[3] If nothing holds me up, I should have it ready before school begins again. But even if that should not work out, my teaching schedule at Yale is so light and so compactly fitted into Monday and Tuesday afternoons, that I should be able to do my own work without much trouble.

1 The book is by Robert T. Petersson and was first mentioned by AH in Letter #40 of January 9th, 1970, and by WLM in postcard #63 of May 12th, 1971. WLM will mention it again in letter #273 of February 20th, 1981.

2 John Calvin Portman, Jr., responsible for Atlanta's Peachtree Center complex, and the city's Hyatt, Westin and Marriott hotels.

3 *Millions of Strange Shadows*, published by Atheneum the following year.

Let us know when you plan to come.
                                    Eric, the Pink

[118]

[WLM]
June 17th, 1976
25 Henshaw Avenue, Northampton, Massachusetts 01060

Letter, typed, addressed to A. Hecht, 19 E Boulevard, Rochester N.Y., 14610, sender's address given as Me, 25 H, 01060]

Tony,

When I wrote you about coming out Barbara and I had patched things up and I thought we would be together. But now it is clear that that is not the case, and because of the circumstances I don't feel I can make any plans now. We've been on-and-off for a while, and now it clearly is best that we go our separate ways. A little like a soap opera in some senses, but four years is a long time. So much as I would love to see you I can't manage it now.

Your old 1755 house[1] is – brace yourself – now being wedded to a Mini-Market-Basket, or some such thing, built right up against it. One of the workmen said to me (for I am famous and well known around here): "Don't worry, it'll match the house front." So ....

                            Love to you all,
                            Skiapod Sam

[119]

[AH]
June 18th, 1976
19 East Boulevard, Rochester, New York 14610.

[Letter, typed on a The University of Rochester, College of Arts and Science, River Campus Station, Rochester, New York 14627, Department of English, letterhead]

Dear Bill,

Helen and I are both distressed by the latest turn of events in your life, and while we're eager to respect your desire for privacy, we hold out some hope that a little affectionate company might do you good. Which is to say, while not in the least doubting that you know your own mind, I'm writing in the hope of persuading you to change it, and to come alone for a visit of a few days. We could promise you,

---

1 WLM appears to be referring to 41 W. Main Street, Northampton, Massachusetts, where AH lived while teaching at Smith College between 1956 and 1959.

besides the customary high standards of booze and food, some felicitous architectural experiences. Our neighbors in the Frank Lloyd Wright house across the street have told us to bring you over for drinks and a tour of their place. The university has just opened a very handsome new building by I. M. Pei,[1] which will be virtually copied (by Pei himself) as a new addition to the National Gallery in Washington. And the city boasts a rather celebrated Unitarian Church by Louis Kahn.[2] But both Helen and I suspect that a change of scene might be soothing and pleasant; and you might want to bring some work with you, for which we could supply you with quiet, time, typewriter, etc. Think on it. It might be tonic and salubrious, possibly even fun.

You will be amused to know that a friend of ours here, an Episcopal priest,[3] is moving himself and his family to New York City where, this fall, he will be inducted as rector of St. James' Church at 71st St. & Madison Avenue – one of the most posh of New York churches; and desiring to purchase a coop apartment, he asked me to write a letter to serve as a character reference.

Please reconsider visiting us; it's been too long since we've seen you.
      Simone Martini
      With olive

[120]

[WLM]
June 22nd, 1976
[25 Henshaw Avenue, Northampton, Massachusetts 01060]

[Letter, typed]

Dear Tony,

Thanks ever so much for your thoughtful letter. I would love to come out, and hope to do so this summer. But first Barbara and I have to get sorted out – we are in good shape, she is job-hunting in the Boston-Cambridge publishing sector and has no place to go until something comes through for her, and I am as a result tied down here. Then I simply must finish a manuscript I have in hand, before classes start. When Barbara is more or less settled, and my work seems to be well along, I'll call and see when you are free, for I would very much like to see you all.

The news that you have another book of poems all but finished is wonderful indeed. And that you will soon be in New Haven is equally good news from my point of view.

Did I tell you §1 that I've applied for an National Endowment for the Humanities Fellowship for 1977-79? Might get it; hot ziggety – 15 months to write. §2 Oxford

---

1 The Wilson Commons Building, a center for student activity on the university's River Campus.

2 The First Unitarian Church of Rochester, work on which had been completed in 1962.

3 The priest referred to here was Hays Rockwell, to whom AH's poem "Gladness of the Best" (which was to be included in *Millions of Strange Shadows*) is dedicated.

(NY) wants me to consider a <u>Companion to Architecture</u>, and I am, scheming away. It would give me a chance to §a (I love that §) say things I've always wanted to say on the subject – it should be "tart & witty" – that's me, isn't it?; §b if a success would get me out of teaching all that sooner. However, if you think I wouldn't make a good Companion (Bath? Garter? B.E.?), write Mr Oxford & let him know.

But seriously, that was an awfully nice letter to get, and all I can do in return is send my love to all of you. The corpus proper will come later.

Thine,
Uriah, all in a Heap

[121]

[AH]
August 3rd, 1976
[19 East Boulevard, Rochester, New York 14610]

[Letter, typed on a Faculty Club, Harvard University, letterhead]

Dear Consumer,

Although it was not widely reported at the time, the reason that Poland did not field a water-polo team at the recent Olympics is that their horses drowned.

> Here lies Priapus Jones who, in his day,
> Impartial to his partners' gender, lay
> With buxom girls and rangy boys whom he
> Deflowered passionately, Ovidly.

When are you coming to visit us? I have a new book of poems almost done; there remains only a translation to do – with help – from the Russian.[1] I think it will be a good book.

Arthur Treacher

---

1 The new collection was *Millions of Strange Shadows*, which does not contain any poems translated from the Russian. It seems safe to assume that the poem he mentions here is one of the two – "Cape Cod Lullaby" and "Lagoon" – which he included in his next-but-one collection, *The Venetian Vespers*.

[122]

[AH]
August 28th, 1976
19 East Boulevard, Rochester, New York 14610

*[Letter, typed on a The Stanhope Hotel, New York, letterhead,
posted in an airmail envelope, addressed to The Illustrious Wm. MacDonald,
25 Henshaw Avenue, Northampton, Mass. 01060]*

MacDonald, you exceptionally lucky bastard,

It's not too late to change your mind and come visit us. And there are special reasons to celebrate, which I'm sure you would not want to miss out on. Let me point out that classes here don't begin till Wednesday, Sept. 8th, and that all of this coming week – Aug. 30 to Sept. 5 – looks clear and free from here. Jason will come to visit some time during that week, when and for how long we don't know, but that should not deter you. The cause for celebration is that a week ago yesterday I finished a book. It was called "Tom Brown's School Days," and I loved it. My reading is really improving. More seriously, I sent it off, this book of my poems, to my editor at Atheneum on Monday, he got to read it on Tuesday and on Wednesday phoned to tell me that he hoped to have it in print by January or February. He is asking Baskin to do a jacket design or frontispiece, and the format, typeface, etc. will match <u>The Hard Hours</u>. One of the facets of all this that most pleases and amuses Helen and me is that the book will appear shortly after I begin teaching at Yale, a fact which will greatly annoy and disturb my chairman and dean. May all manner of good come from their agitation.

If it is any inducement, know that Helen has made and frozen away a great supply of <u>pesto</u>, concocted from our own basil plants, and that we also have on hand a supply of home-made Tarama Salata. If that doesn't fetch you, you must have a heart of stone.

Mike Psellus

[123]

[WLM]
October 5th, 1976
[25 Henshaw Avenue, Northampton, Massachusetts 01060]

[Letter, typed on a Hotel Ritz, Madrid, Spain, letterhead, addressed to Professor Anthony E. Hecht, 19, East Boulevard, Rochester NY 14610, with two enclosures, one of which is now missing]

Mountain Day[1]

This, my dear Sir,

    is a very serious letter. I have come across something of the highest significance, something that proves absolutely, and even to those who read no poetry, that you are a Very Great Artist. What is even more important is the fact that my discovery (for I pride myself on the obvious conclusion that no one has ever noticed this before) links you with the Great Ages of the past, and establishes your genealogy forty times further back than ever has been established, up to now.

    If you will go to your local Biblioteca and there procure a copy of James Breckenridge's book, <u>Likeness</u>, and turn to p. 188, you will see what a fabulous breakthrough I have made.[2] For there is a portrait of Virgil and, as you will instantly perceive, it

LOOKS LIKE YOU!!

3

You will notice that I do not say you look like it, or Virgil, but that it looks like you.

---

1 A Smith College tradition since 1877, Mountain Day is a surprise break from classes. The president chooses a beautiful fall day and announces the holiday by ringing the college bells.

2 James D. Breckenridge, *Likeness: A Conceptual History of Ancient Portraiture* (Evanston, IL: Northwestern University Press, 1968).

3 The photograph, which is missing from the letter, is reproduced here from Breckenridge's book.

I am a Modern, Sir, and much as I appreciate the past, I am not one of those who goes slanting about the Coffee Houses saying all Antiquitie is perfect; no, Modern, sir, is It; and thus I can say that You Look Like Virgil, because I am Educated; put things in their proper way, I do, and thus prefer to say that Virgil Looks Like You.

Knowing your modesty, you'll say you look like him. But never mind. What I hope is a) that this will inspire you, and b) that your publishers will print on the jacket of your next book both your picture and Virgil's; better than any puff from Rod McKuen, eh?

With respect, O Poet; and
Hail, Rochester, Mother of Men!
Saturn's Land! And all that stuff.
Palladius
(a pseudonym)

[Enclosure 2: a handwritten transcription of the caption accompanying the photograph]

Breckenridge, p 188:
"– the recent identification of this image as that of Virgil. Although this attribution remains tentative, there can be little doubt that we are in the presence of a psychological masterpiece in the portrayal of <u>a sensitive yet tough-minded man of culture</u>."

<italics [i.e. underlined] added>

[124]

[AH]
[October 9th, 1976]
19 East Boulevard, Rochester, New York 14610

[Letter, typed on a Colgate Inn, Hamilton, New York, letterhead, addressed to Prof. Wm. L. MacDonald (Hotsy-totsy!), 25 Henshaw Avenue., Northampton, Mass. 01060]

My dear young man,

It is, I think, salubrious and worthwhile for us all to meditate, from time to time, on the great theme of mutability and transience to mortify our overweening vanity, and to say with the preacher, "What profit hath a man of all his labour ..." and so forth. What, after all, is Fame? And what, Celebrity? Fleeting evanescences, mere toys and illusions. I know you will think this simple modesty in me, and dismiss it with a casual wave of the hand. But when you attain to my age and gravity you will know that some of those goals which in your youth seemed the only possible or valuable target upon which attention could seriously be fixed turn out in the end to be gossamer-frail or utterly illusory. What are we, after all, but a handful of dust, if I may thus express myself? I know you too well to doubt that you will protest, and point to the value of scholarship and the arts as in themselves conferring a sort of immortality. Ah, but we must chasten our hopes with a little dose of Sir Thomas Browne and Marcus Aurelius and Epictetus. Let me offer a salutary instance.

Remaindered books have their own humbling effect, of course, and no doubt this is truly beneficial to us all, but my instance only begins with that given datum. Browsing, as was my wont, in the university bookstore, I came upon a volume called Ancient Rome: From Romulus to Remus, by Georgina Masson, originally published in England under the title A Concise History of Republican Rome, and now (in a rough sense of that word) published in this country by Viking Press at $13.95, but reduced, when I encountered it in a sort of feverish clearance sale, to $3.48.[1] You may not believe it, but I sighed the sigh of Heraclitean Flux, and a tear from the depths of some divine despair, of which Tennyson speaks, rose to my eye. But I bought it, and took it home. It is an interesting book, and perhaps it deserves its swift slippage toward oblivion, since it offers no acknowledgement to any other scholar in the field. Poetic justice, you may say; the cold, retributive force called up by vanity. But even this is not my instance. In the back of the book is what is called there a "Select bibliography." Not "selected" in the unpretentious sense merely of "chosen" or "picked out," but "Select" in the snobbish, patrician sense of the term. It must be admitted that some of the names that appear there are reasonably distinguished: Lanciani, Boethius, Rostovtzeff, L. R. Taylor. But, and here at last is my instance, one of the cited volumes was The Architecture of the Roman Empire, Vol. I New Haven, 1965 by one L. Macdonald. These are the things, as I say, that instruct us.

St. Pelagia, The Harlot

[125]

[AH]
November 8th, 1976
19 East Boulevard, Rochester, New York 14610

[Letter, typed on a The Stanhope Hotel, New York, letterhead,

Dear old archimandrite,

I have constantly in mind the plight you face in trying to keep your students and other audiences awake during lectures on Carolingian brickwork, Etrurian plinths, and deconsecrated apses. I know you try your best, and of course color slides are a help up to a point. But the fact must be faced that one's enthusiasm for bricks, howsoever beautifully projected on a large screen, howsoever eloquently characterized in artful prose, will go only just so far and not a bit further, after the manner of Balaam's ass. Without intending any slight whatever, without prejudice either to the wit and style of your lecture or the artistry of those long-dead masons, people incline to drift off to sleep and begin to snore rather loudly, don't they? It's

---

1 Georgina Masson, *Ancient Rome: From Romulus to Remus* (New York: Viking, 1974).

distressing, I know; I am full of sympathy. I am sure, moreover, that you have tried many cunning devices – spot quizzes, dropping your pointer with a loud clatter on the classroom floor, snappy architectural jokes – but without much effect. The torpor that seems to seize people in the presence of bricks is profound if inexplicable. And so I offer you, and enclose here, as a sort of Christmas bonus, a couple of slides you might insinuate into your course. They will liven things up, suggest a good many architectural metaphors, and generally focus the wandering attention of those disposed to slumber. Don't try to thank me. It is enough to know in my heart how much good I have done.

It now looks as if we will be occupying an apartment in Morse College, starting in early January. The book should be out in February.
Sam Gregorovius

[126]

[WLM]
November 18th, 1976
[25 Henshaw Avenue, Northampton, Massachusetts 01060]

[Letter, typed on a The Michigan League letterhead, posted in a The Michigan League envelope, addressed to Mr Anthony Hecht, Al Chemist, 19, East Boulevard, Rochester, New York 14610]

My dear Doctor Sam,

Taking your advice (I always do) I put the slides in my famous lecture on What the Triton in the Piazza Barberini is Really Doing. The effect, as you predicted, was spectacular, though not, as you will see, for the reasons you had thought.

The first one to appear, just as I had the audience worked up into visions of some hidden kind of maritime hanky-panky, was the lady in the white blouse. Aha, I could feel the audience thinking, he's done some investigative reporting on the Triton's sidelines. But this impression was fleeting, for in the first balcony a rather plain girl sobbed "That's my mother!" Really, you shouldn't have put me in that position.

But that was nothing, nothing at all, compared with the effect the next slide had. People had quieted the first-balcony girl down successfully – I noticed she didn't leave – and things had more or less gotten back to normal (that is, several hundred people were quiet as a mess of pins, hanging on my every authoritative word). Well, sir, the second slide, of the lady with the D. Lamour swept-back hair, came on and two young persons shouted simultaneously "That's my father!" Can you envision the scene? I know your audiences are much smaller, but perhaps you can think of a revival meeting, with two people shouting their conviction to the crowd, rising as it were to testify to something deliciously horrifying.

I stopped the lecture, asked questions, and found that both people – one male and one uncertain – were the offspring of some kind of athlete; a tennis player? When I got back to the Triton everyone was very receptive, because as you see the

Triton and the Sea Monster, well ...... Play it again,
Yours in Newtonian Complications,
E. Llipsis

[127]

[WLM]
January 3rd, 1977
[25 Henshaw Avenue, Northampton, Massachusetts 01060]

[Postcard, addressed to Prof. A. E. Hecht, 19, E. Boulevard, Rochester N.Y., 14610]

It was just a hardened old fossil –
As a find, nothing colossal –
But the Vatican thought, from
The wonders it wrought,
'Twas the peter of Paul, the Apostle.

15th: YES: send details by next courier, or whatever.
BES und WLM

150 | *A Bountiful Harvest*

[128]

[AH]
January 26th, 1977
3357 Morse College, Yale University, New Haven, Connecticut 06520[1]

[Letter, typed on a Yale University, New Haven, Connecticut 06520, Department of English, letterhead]

Dear chap,

Thank you for your sinister OPEC propaganda (I got it, I got it) and perhaps you can help me out in a (racially) related matter. I've been going nuts trying to remember the name of the third Magus, along with Melchior and Balthazar. I'm sure it's going to turn out to be something obvious, like Irving, but it has eluded me for a week or so, and I am becoming very peevish and difficult to live with. So if you wish, after the fashion of the nation's founders, to ensure domestic tranquility, please let me know.

And I hope, in due course, you can also send that particularly notable issue of the TLS.[2]

We have begun to meet a few people around here, and while they lack both the distinction and the charm of the people at Harvard, they are pleasant and interesting in their own inferior ways. Though perhaps this is a hasty judgment of unmerited indulgence, brought on by the fatigue of a day's hard work.

Next week we go to NY because production of the book will be completed: publication date to be a month later. I'm going in to inscribe complimentary copies to friends, and to have a bash of sorts.

Love to you and Barbara,
Frobenius

[129]

[AH]
February 1st, 1977
3357 Morse College, Yale University, New Haven, Connecticut 06520

[Letter, typed on a Yale University, Department of English, letterhead]

From Publius Ovidius Naso to Sam Goody, Greeting:

What has struck us with special delight is the charm and architectural variety of the churches in and about New Haven. Even to such amateur enthusiasts as we are, very

---

1 AH had been appointed visiting professor at Yale.

2 It would seem that WLM had told AH about the January 21st issue of the *Times Literary Supplement*, which featured an article – "Reputations Revisited" – in which leading literary figures listed some of the writers they thought over- and some they thought under-rated. D. J. Enright, a poet, essayist and anthologist AH greatly respected, had named him as one of the people he thought underrated.

modestly traveled, they offer a spectrum of styles not everywhere to be encountered. I scarcely need to commend to anyone so knowledgeable as you the unusual, perhaps unique, character of St. George the Barfly, with its genial services (from 5 to 7 p.m.) locally known as "the happy hour," its free lunch in the west transept, and its handsome, period spittoons along the altar rail. And before coming here we had of course heard of St. Hilda in Perplexity, with its pure interior of white bathroom tile, its charming little pay-booths which the Supreme Court has just declared unconstitutional. It may be that only in Rome itself, in the Piazza del Popolo, can two such perfectly twinned churches be found as St. Paul in the Soup and St. Philip in the Red. These are not nearly so well known as they ought to be, and one can only admire the courage of the Church in commissioning Rauschenberg[1] to be their architect. We have yet before us a number of gems to explore, and we especially look forward to visiting the little chapel in the Stamford railroad station dedicated to St. Christopher the Commuter. The services there, we have been told, are interminable.

So it appears that New Haven is not altogether without culture, as so many people suppose. For the spring we are outlining to ourselves a tour of the most important parking areas – one cannot hope to do them all – and perhaps to prepare a little catalogue raisonné as a tribute to the best of them. I'm sure this will seem wildly impulsive to you, but I think there is an undeniable gap that could be filled with such a monograph as we have in mind, and, even taking into account the great expense of the pictures – without which the very idea of such a work would be ludicrous – I think the whole thing might be published at Antwerp for a comparatively modest sum. Toward this end we are taking up a collection from among those of our friends who are likely to be in sympathy with such a project, and of course we instantly thought of you.

We salute you with the motto of this place, "<u>Luxe</u> et <u>Vanitas</u>."

[Unsigned]

[130]

[AH]
February 2nd, 1977
3357 Morse College, Yale University, New Haven, Connecticut 06520

[Letter, typed on a Yale University, Department of English, letterhead]

That naughty old Sappho of Greece
Said, "What I prefer to a piece
   Is to have my pudenda
   Rubbed hard by the enda
The little pink nose of my niece."

---

1 Presumably a tongue-in-cheek reference to the abstract expressionist painter Robert Rauschenberg rather than the German architect Friedrich Wilhelm Rauschenberg, who seems never to have worked outside Germany.

A scandal involving an oyster
Sent the Countess of Clewes to a cloister.
    She preferred it in bed
    To the Count, so she said,
Being longer and stronger and moister.

"Far dearer to me than my treasure,"
An heiress declared, "is my leisure.
    For then I can screw
    The whole Harvard crew –
They're slow, but that lengthens the pleasure.'

There was a young student of Trinity
Who shattered his sister's virginity.
    He buggered his brother,
    Had twins by his mother,
And still took a first in Divinity.

There was a young lady named Gloria
Who was had by Sir Gerald Du Maurier.
    And then by six men,
    Sir Gerald again,
And the band at the Waldorf Astoria.

As you can see, there's a good deal of culture down here at New Haven.
    Timon of Brooklyn

[131]

[AH]
February 3rd, 1977
3357 Morse College, Yale University, New Haven, Connecticut 06520

[Letter, typed on a Yale University, Department of English, letterhead]

I don't know where things went awry but the TLS never appeared. Was it included in the same envelope with the pamphlet on The Dome of the Rock? If so, I found only the pamphlet, and must have thrown away the clipping with the envelope. If it was sent under separate cover it never reached me. Sorry.

    We are off momentarily – within the next 10 minutes – to New York, where I will inscribe copies of the new book and we will comport ourselves in the proper spirit of debauchery, while Evan will be "sat" for us by Helen's mother, who will join us especially to provide her unpaid services. We'll return on Sunday, and shortly you should have a copy of Millions of Strange Shadows. It has already received a favorable review from Kirkus [Review] Service, though pub date is not till late February.[1]

Hope you like the limericks.

Antiochus of Hoboken

[132]

[WLM]
[February 5th, 1977]
[Massachusetts]

[Letter, typed on a Fogg Art Museum letterhead, posted in a Hotel Ritz, Madrid, envelope, addressed to Professor A. & E. Hecht (Rye-master), 3357 Morse College, Yale University, New Haven, Conn. 06520

TO Timon von Brooklyn
FROM S. Messalina in Flagrante
DATE V.ii.MCMLXXVII

Plenty cultchuh up here, too, Mac. Anyway, I've got that book you cribbed from. Try:

> Erat olim puella Romana
> Quae munera omnibus danda
>   Putabat et dedit –
>   Penes etiam editit –
> Nunc medicis illa curanda.[2]

We here realise that a translation would be a mere superfluity. Phelps Hall, top floors, is the place though to go in an emergency of ignorance. Or try this:

---

1 AH must have received advance notice of *Kirkus*'s review, since it wasn't published until February 21st. "Here is God's plenty," the reviewer wrote. "Hecht's style has smoothed out since his first collection was published in 1954, grown more elegant but not less sharp. Verse, at his hand, is a well-honed instrument of various uses. He can write a sestina on the unpromising topic of Rochester, New York, and make it sing. He can devise rhyme schemes that never appear in works on prosody – so lightly that one hardly notices. He can write a Cowleyan ode about a Broadway production of *The Tempest* (with the title 'Peripeteia') and make it interesting enough to keep children from their games. And he can paraphrase Voltaire in couplets Alexander Pope might have envied. It is easy to like his light verse, presented mostly in the early pages of this volume, but the complacent reader will be startled by 'The Feast of Stephen' locker-room morality woven up with a martyrdom, and stopped in his tracks by the terrible 'Apprehensions,' where a thunderstorm turns into the holocaust." The whole review can be read online at https://www.kirkusreviews.com/book-reviews/anthony-hecht-3/millions-of-strange-shadows/

2 Latin = A Lady of Rome thought it dandy / to bestow all her charms on the randy; / her mouth gulped each prick, / which made her quite sick, / So her doctor now plies her with brandy. For this loose but compelling gloss I am indebted to Dr. Richard Gordon, Honorary Professor of Ancient Religions, and Fellow at the Max Weber center at Universität Erfurt.

There was a young lady named Colehill
Who sat one fine day on a molehill.
   The resident mole
   Stuck his nose up her hole –
Miss Colehill's O.K., but the mole's ill.

And, because all of us here love you, we send:

There once was a young man from York
Who, when feeling bemused or euphor'c,
   Could produce, for inspection,
   Three kinds of erection:
Corinthian, Ionic, or Dor'c.

Please don't read these to just anyone. At Yale not many people laugh, for fear they'll be thought in competition with Us. It is wise to test your hearers with a mild joke about BullDogs, to see what humorousness you can expect (I don't mean from the BullDogs; I've actually never seen one laugh; take their work seriously, they do …).
                              Mr. Elliot

[A note handwritten directly above the Hotel Ritz's crest on the back of the envelope in which this was posted reads: "doubt you can match this:"]

[133]

[WLM]
[March 8th, 1977]
[25 Henshaw Avenue, Northampton, Massachusetts, 01060]

[Letter, typed on a Carpenter Center for the Visual Arts, Harvard University, letterhead, with a now missing enclosure]

to: You
from: Me
date: viii a.d Id. Martii MCMLXXVII

Dear Friend,
    You of course know me as too modest to fill out the enclosed; perhaps you will do it for me. I hadn't realised that my fine poems had travelled all the way to the Other Cambridge; I guess I'll just have to accept Fame.
    Don't forget to include particulars on my masterwork, "The Ballad of Piano-Legs Frohoawk," last sung at the West Over-Shoe Writers and Scribblers Workshop in 1937.
                          Yours in East Rhyme,

Faithfully,
Al Tenny's Son

[…]

[134]

[WLM]
May 9th, 1977
25 Henshaw Avenue, Northampton, Massachusetts 01060

[Blank postcard, addressed to A. E. Hecht & Co., 19, East Boulevard, Rochester NY 14610]

My dear Doctor,

I think it is fitting, indeed nice, that we share the current <u>TLS</u>.[1] At last The World will recognize our worth. I don't know who the hell all those other people are in that issue, but We Two stand out … You were more fortunate in your reviewer than I was, but considering that John Ward-Perkins dislikes most people and, for quite a while, me in particular, I came out of it quite well.[2]

Many regrets that you were not longer in New Haven, a fact we failed to grasp sufficiently early. We went to Philadelphia and had a marvelous 3 days recently, partly with the Venturis, who are splendid people.

Love to all,
HAD · IMP[3]

---

1 In one and the same issue of the *Times Literary Supplement* for May 6th, 1977, George P. Elliott reviewed AH's *Millions of Strange Shadows* ("The Freshness of the Text") and John Ward-Perkins reviewed WLM's *The Pantheon: Design, Meaning and Progeny* ("Rome's Rotunda").

2 Elliott was unstinting in his praise: "Hecht's voice is his own, but his language, more amply than that of any other living poet writing in English, derives from, adds to, is part of the great tradition." Ward-Perkins, having begun by praising WLM for "a concise, well-illustrated general account of the [Pantheon], its history and its meaning," went on to register his dissatisfaction with the chapter in which he sought to explain the building's meaning, quoting WLM as saying "The Pantheon rotunda is a metaphor in architecture for the ecumenical pretensions of the Roman Empire, the girdling cornices a statement in architectural form of the nine-thousand-mile boundary that surrounded the later Greco-Roman world" and denouncing the passage in no uncertain terms: "There is a certain type of architectural criticism where such rhetoric is in place and may even have a meaning. In a work of popularizing scholarship it rings a discordant note." Towards the end of his review, Ward-Perkins returns with more praise, describing *The Pantheon* as "pleasantly and thoughtfully produced" and calling its documentation "ample without being obtrusive," but his last words on the subject are hardly a ringing endorsement: "It fills a gap."

3 Emperor Hadrian.

[135]

[AH]
May 20th, 1977
[19 East Boulevard, Rochester, New York 14610]

[Letter, typed on a The University of Rochester, Department of English, letterhead, with now missing enclosures]

Dear Bill,

I was rather shocked at the cool condescension of the Ward-Perkins review of your Pantheon book, the more so since I was, apparently wrongly, under the impression that he was a pal of yours from Roman days. Was he not for a while the director of the British Academy there? Did you not see something of him then? But after all, that review had its marked resemblance to the New York Times review of my poems by Denis Donoghue[1] – wearily patient in its fault-finding. As for my TLS review, I confess with an awkward smile that it was done by a good friend who lives "just down the road" in Syracuse.

Tell me, am I right in thinking that the Hotel Inghilterra is near the Via Frattina and the Piazza di Spagna? If that's the place I'm thinking of I hope to put us all up there when we go abroad this summer. The Academy found itself unable to supply us with any accommodations whatever.

I've just finished book reviews of Wilbur and Elizabeth Bishop for TLS, and an article on Auden, which I have not decided where to send.[2] Most luxuriously of all, I now begin a sabbatical.

I enclose an important clipping.[3]

Sejanus

---

1 Denis Donoghue, "Millions of Strange Shadows," *New York Times Book Review*, March 27th, 1977, p. 266. The review can be read online at http://www.nytimes.com/1977/03/27/archives/millions-of-strange-shadows.html

2 "The Motions of the Mind," AH's review of Wilbur's *The Mind Reader*, appeared on page 602 of the May 20th, 1977 issue of the *Times Literary Supplement*; "Awful But Cheerful," his review of Bishop's *Geography III*, appeared on page 1024 of the August 26th, 1977 issue of the same journal. Both pieces – re-titled "Richard Wilbur" and "Elizabeth Bishop" respectively, were reprinted in AH's *Obbligati: Essays in Criticism*, as was the third essay mentioned here, "On W. H. Auden's 'In Praise of Limestone,'" about which more will be said in the sequel.

3 It seems likely that as well as the now missing clipping, AH enclosed a draft of his review of Richard Wilbur.

[136]

[WLM]
May 25th, 1977
[25 Henshaw Avenue, Northampton, Massachusetts, 01060]

[Letter, typed on a The Dunfey Family's Parker House, Boston, Massachusetts 02107 letterhead, with a now missing enclosure]

Antoninus:

First I want to say how good and sensitive and, it seems to my ear, accurate your essay on Wilbur is. I learned from it; it is very well written; and there seems to be no excess anywhere.

I had refrained from mentioning the ghastly NYTimes review you got. We were badly put out by it, but the TLS review seems to make up for it extremely well.

Yes, Ward Perkins (sometimes referred to as Weird Porkins) is a man I've known for almost thirty years. We travelled together in the Near East in 1955. He seems to have gotten a Thing about me when my 1965 book came out, a Thing I tried to exorcize in 1975 when I was in Rome, with some success. He felt, I gather, that I had encroached on his territory. So when I saw his name atop the TLS column I feared the worst, but when I read it through I realised that all in all I had come out of it fairly well. The condescension you mention is his normal tone; he is something of a misanthrope; he knows his material very well but is distrustful of analyses of meaning and of any imagination unchecked by those facts he requires for intellectual comfort. He never sees any poetry in buildings at all …

The Inghilterra is at no. 14, Via Bocca di Leone and thus, as you intimate, close by the di Spagna. Can't imagine why the Academy is filled up. Lucky you all. I've a sabbatical in the Spring of '79 and am thinking of taking a term off without pay to extend it to a year off. Small Baths[1] about to go off; Cities book within striking distance I hope; Nick arrives about 1 July and will also be at University of Massachusetts] next fall; Pantheon already being reprinted so yippee! I want you both to study the enclosed with care. Perhaps you can work a seminar around it when you come back to duty.

Love to you all,
Aetherius

---

1 Collaborating with Bernard Michael Boyle, WLM had written an article entitled "The Small Baths at Hadrian's Villa." The article was published in the *Journal of the Society of Architectural Historians*, 39:1 (1980).

[137]

[AH]
June 8th, 1977
19 East Boulevard, Rochester, N. Y. 14610

[Letter, typed on a Yale University, Department of English, letterhead]

Dear Bill,

We leave in roughly half an hour for Salzburg,[1] but Charlee Wilbur just phoned to tell us where you were, and we are as alarmed and disheartened and concerned as the Wilburs obviously are.[2] I have just tried to phone you, and have been told by the authorities that you "are not accepting any calls." It was Helen to whom Charlee spoke, so I have such medical knowledge of you as I have at about fifth or sixth hand. But it sounds serious. I wish there were something we could do, yet I suspect that even postcards from Yurp Nittly will not be soothing. We will be in Salzburg till the 2nd of July, and I would be very grateful to hear some reassuring news of your recovery. If you can, and feel up to it, please write us at: Salzburg Seminar, Schloss Leopoldskron, Box 129, A-5010 Salzburg, Austria.

We send you our love, and our hopes for a thorough recovery as soon as possible.

Tony

---

1 AH had accepted appointment to the faculty of the Salzburg Seminar in American Studies, which was convened between June 12th and July 2nd. The other faculty members that year included Christopher Bigsby, Winfried Fluck, Brigitte Scheer-Schazler, John Ehle, John Gardner and Reynolds Price.

2 WLM had been taken ill, and rushed to the Cooley Dickinson Hospital in Northampton, after suffering an intestinal blockage.

[138]

[AH]
June 19th, 1977
Schloss Leopoldskron, Box 129, A-5010, Salzburg, Austria

[Postcard, with a photograph of the Schloss Leopoldskron and its lake, addressed to Prof. Wm. MacDonald, 25 Henshaw Ave, Northampton, Mass 01060, U.S.A.]

Dear Bill,

This is where we are staying, in baroque grandeur. It was built by an 18 cent. archbishop for his mistress and himself. She was northern Italian and missed the lakes – hence the artificial lake here. It was later owned and restored by Max Reinhardt. There are about 60 Fellows from all over Eastern and Western Europe, and a faculty of 5. The session (on contemporary lit) lasts 3 weeks, the first just finished. May this find you utterly recovered. We both send you our love.

Tony

[139]

[WLM]
June 20th, 1977
25 Henshaw Avenue, Northampton, Massachusetts 01060

[Blank postcard, typed, addressed to Prof. & Mrs. Anthony HECHT, Salzburg Seminar, Schloss Leopoldskron, Box 129, A-5010 <u>SALZBURG</u> Austria / Oesterreich]

Dear Helen & Tony,

Thanks for your note. I'd time only to alert Nick & Noel, Barbara, & my brother John. A nightmare. I'm home now, and recovering slowly but well, though I've no staying power. Whole things clears the mind marvelously, to invent a phrase. No cancer. Going to be all right.

Reading Literary Anecdotes[1] systematically, & so far my favourite is "Another damned thick quarto, eh Mr. Gibbon? Scribble, scribble, scribble, eh Mr. Gibbon?"

Love,
Bill

[140]

[AH]
July 5th, 1977
Venice, Italy

[Postcard, with a reproduction of Gentile Bellini's Procession in the Piazza San Marco, Venice, *handwritten, addressed to Wm. MacDonald, 25 Henshaw Ave, Northampton, Mass, 01060, U.S.A]*

We rejoice in your restoration and have arranged a celebratory procession in the style of the one in verso. Venice is hot and very crowded. But the food, especially after a starchy Austrian diet, is superb, and all the important things are here: pictures, buildings, booze, etc. The Robertses have skipped town,[2] but we are blissfully pleased to be back.

Love,
Helen + Tony

---

1 *The Oxford Book of Literary Anecdotes*, edited by James Sutherland (New York: Oxford University Press, 1975).

2 Laurance and Isabel Roberts had settled in Venice after he retired from the Directorship of the AAR.

[141]

[AH]
[July 1977]
Venice, Italy

*[Postcard, handwritten, addressed to Prof. Wm. MacDonald,
25 Henshaw Ave, Northampton, Mass 01060, U.S.A]*

This is Helen feeding the pigeons in the piazzetta. As you can surmise, her fashionable dress is covered with pigeon shit. You will also observe that the crowd is keeping a sensible distance. We plan visits to Padua, Vicenza and Verona, and all is well to date. Our hotel is on a blind canal corner, so the gondoliers, to warn of their arrival, have a sort of Jewish cry of "Oi!" We seem to hear it all night, and it has a poignant religious tone to it.

[Unsigned]

[142]

[AH]
July 23rd, 1977
19 East Boulevard, Rochester, N. Y. 14610

[Letter, typed on a Salzburg Seminar in American Studies, Schloss Leopoldskron, A-5010 Salzburg, Box 129, Austria, letterhead, with two enclosures, one now missing]

Dear Imperator,

You may not actually have noticed this, but the fact is that one of the chief skills of an Italian waiter is concerned with the delicate matter of preparing the "conto," and there is reason to believe – for example, I believe it implicitly myself – that as much care and training goes into this as goes into the preparation of food on the part of the chef. And the core, the central genius of the waiter's technique, is directed towards making the price of items more and more obscure, increasingly illegible and unintelligible as the list advances through pastas to meats, from salads to terrifying and undecipherable "dolces." I enclose a modest instance for your consideration. The intention, clearly, is to suggest that the waiter has been so overcome with horror at the choices you – a vulgar foreigner, a very barbarian – have made for your repast that in the very course of totalling it up he has been seized by a kind of convulsion, not unlike Parkinson's Disease, from which, perhaps, a sufficiently generous tip might restore him. This "degenerative calligraphy," this lapsing into helpless squiggles, is a very considerable art in itself, having the double effect of, first, baffling the tourist, and then rendering him too embarrassed to raise any inquiry lest it should seem that he is questioning the waiter's honesty or his capacity to add. I also enclose a valuable coupon which, together with hard cash, can get you almost anything.

We were in Rome a week; it was hot and sunny throughout. Wretched Italian hippies vending home-made belts and necklaces on the Spanish Steps. Saw Jack & Corda Zajac (both in fine shape and high spirits) the night before they left for a year or two in Santa Cruz, Cal. Saw Irving and Marilyn Lavin briefly; he is now at the Princeton Institute for Advanced Studies. But most important and cheering of all, saw, had lunch at the Academy with, Jackie and Frank Brown. Frank has grown a leonine head of white hair – very handsome – and while I know you will regard it as improbable, I've taken some pictures for proof, and will send you a copy in due course.[1] We all spoke of you affectionately. Frank will be teaching at Austin, Texas, in the spring term of '78, and is preparing the Jerome Lectures on Cosa for publication by Michigan.[2] He was, as always, the soul of charm and warmth, perhaps a bit mellower but with all his marbles intact. Jackie told me a lovely story at lunch. We were all discussing [Bernard] Berenson, and Jackie said she was once summoned to sit beside him, and he immediately asked, "Tell me, why did you remarry Frank?" To

---

1 Ever since AH and WLM had first got to know Frank Brown, he had been without any hair. What AH had discovered was that Brown wasn't naturally bald but shaven-headed.

2 The Thomas Spencer Jerome Lectures delivered by Brown were published in 1980 as *Cosa: The Making of a Roman Town*.

which, she said, she responded, "Because I never met anyone I admired more." I was very touched and honored by such candor, for the intervals between our meetings are enormous, and the meetings always brief. Anyway, we took young Evan through St. Peter's and the Vatican Gallery and Museum, and the Borghese Gallery, and the Pantheon, and the Borromini church at Quattro Fontane, and the Bernini church of St. Andrea – and he professed to like them all. We are now back, and while wishing we could have stayed longer, are not dissatisfied to be home. We send you our love, and hope you are feeling fit again.

Come see us.

Signorelli

[Enclosure]

[143]

[WLM]
August 4th, 1977
25 Henshaw Avenue, Northampton, Massachusetts, 01060

[Letter, typed]

Dear President Arthur,

As you may know, the Minneapolis City Zoo acquired a few months past a fine, rare example of the female baboon known as <u>babuina hypermammifera</u>. The authorities at the Zoo have sent round about for a male, for purposes of p_____n. Unable to find one, and much exercised at the thought of not being able to m__e their lady, they have been very unhappy, indeed despondent. They had thought of very great fame …

When recently I was in the Twin Cities (as we call them), I met with the Zoo people and suggested that they hire a young man for the job. At first astonished and a little upset, they came under the force of my ingenious presentation gradually to agree, and the next morning placed a discreet advertisement in the Minneapolis papers. Only one young man applied, a certain Stash Mzganowski. I think it may be good for western civilisation, but in any event, only one applied for the post.

The Zoo people explained his duties to him, saying that there was a fee of $2,500 involved. Stash replied that he would think it over, and return on the morrow (I'm from New England, and we talk that way here). When he came back he said he'd given the matter a lot of thought, and had decided to take them up on their, uh, er, proposition.

But, says Stash, "I've three points I want to make."

"Shoot," says the Zoo Boss. He meant it figuratively.

"Well," says Stash, "if they's any kids they gotta be brought up Catholic."

"Done," they say.

"An' I don't have to kiss her?"

"No," say the Zoo-ers, "What else?"

"Well," says Stash, with some reserve, "I have to say that it's gonna take me a few days to raise the twenty-five hundred."

And that, Mr President, is your Polish joke for the day.

With best regards to Mrs Arthur, inter alia, and

Yours sincerely,
James G. Blaine

[144]

[AH]
[August 6th, 1977]
19 East Boulevard, Rochester, New York 14610

[French postcard, with a photograph of the Royal Chateau de Blois, France, typed, addressed to Prof. Wm. MacDonald, 25 Henshaw Avenue, Northampton, Mass. 01060]

My Shorter OED has Faux Pas – a slip, a trip; esp. a woman's lapse from virtue. (1676) That should cheer you with a true sense of moral liberation. F[rank] Brown says Weird Porkins' Guide to Roman Sites[1] is full of grotesque typos, a scandal at publication.

Tasso

---

1 WLM is referring to John Ward-Perkins's recently published book, *Roman Architecture* (New York: H. N. Abrams, 1977).

[145]

[WLM]
[August 10th, 1977]
[25 Henshaw Avenue, Northampton, Massachusetts, 01060]

[Postcard, typed, addressed to A. & E. & H. Hecht, 19 East Boulevard, Rochester NY, 14610]

Dear Dr Dynamo,
   You've the <u>shorter</u> <u>OED</u>? You may have the shortest; not all the data are in yet. Mine is 4' 7" and growing. I water it with essence de mot (Benjamin, if I can get him). You'd better measure yours and send the information to

   Central OED Measurements, Inc.
   National Endowment for Word Height
   Library of Congress
   Washington, D.C.

   I'm not <u>positive</u>, mind, but I <u>think</u> there's a prize for the person with the shortest one. My Arab correspondents think I'm measuring oueds (A. for river), & I'm having a little trouble; after all, what is a dry <u>OED</u>? In '? And one female thinks I'm to OED her ... aha, ha, aha, ha, ha ...
   Patty O'Furniture

[146]

[AH]
August 19th, 1977
19 East Boulevard, Rochester, New York 14610

[Letter, typed on a The University of Rochester, Department of English, letterhead]

Eminence:
   It occurred to me that nothing would interest you more than a representative sample of the correspondence I conducted in 1972 with the then chairman of the faculty club of the university, and so, with no further barricades to your impatience, I quote forthwith.

   Dear Bernard:
      I write, however tardily, to congratulate you upon your reinstallation as <u>primum inter pares</u> of the Board of Directors of the Faculty Club. I have read, with enthusiasm and complete assent, your outline of future policy; but I had no idea that imaginative innovations would so quickly go into effect. I refer particularly to the delicacy we are to be offered on the 16th, 17th and 18th of November, which is called

(and I quote exactly from the Faculty Club list of Spécialités) "Mixed Grilled On A Wooden Plank Esterházy." This is an old favorite of mine, which I am happy to see return to the regular repertory, and though it is widely known, not everyone is familiar with its origin.

The young Count Antal Esterházy (1676-1722) was an energetic and accomplished huntsman. One day when he and his retinue were out for wild boar, a rather churlish member of the group was heard to remark that the Count "couldn't hit the side of a barn door," or Hungarian words to that effect. The Count, whose sporting blood was up, immediately proposed a wager, which he proceeded to win with skill and ease, to the delight and acclaim of his friends; and the barn door was brought back to the castle in triumph, garnished with a sprig of thyme (optional) and served. This charming little incident was the basis and origin of what we have all come to know and love as "Wooden Plank Esterházy."

In gastronomic fraternity, etc.

Ektually, I'm writing to ask a serious question. I'm at work on what looks as if it will turn out to be a quite long poem, which is set in Venice, and which is the as yet unripened fruit of our recent visit abroad. What I want to know is: is there a Pantokrator figure in the mosaic work inside St. Mark's? I can't myself remember, and seem to have no guide books at hand that would help.

Yours,
Sergius & Bacchus, Attorneys

[147]

[WLM]
[September 1st, 1977
[25 Henshaw Avenue, Northampton, Massachusetts, 01060]

[Blank postcard, typed, addressed to Antonio von Hecht, 19 East Boulevard, Rochester, N.Y. 14610]

Etymologies for Humble Folk, XVI:
"Itsa," as in "Itsa nice day," derives, obviously, from the Aztec, such as say Chicken Itsa. But how many know that "Itll," as in "It'll be all right," is Mayan? "Itll" means mountain, as is obvious from "Pocacapititll," or "Macramalatitll." My big discovery is of the Aztec linguistic phononymic migration to Mayan territory which, when I expound it at the next meeting of the MLA, will astound all and make me Peribleptos, as we say in Constantinople. The crux of my argument is of course (you've guessed, I'm sure) Chicken Itll, later corrupted in the War of '47 by the gringoes (which, incidentally, comes from the Mexican interpretation of the troops' great song, "Green Grow the Rashes Oh") into Chicken Little.

C. T. Onions

[148]

[AH]
September 9th, 1977
[19 East Boulevard, Rochester, New York 14610]

[Letter, typed on a The University of Rochester, Department of English, letterhead]

Dear Bill,

I suppose it was simple envy of the quality of your Polish joke that kept me from telling you in a straightforward way how splendid it is – surely the best I've ever encountered – and not only how splendid it is but the hysterical effect it continued to have on Helen and me for most of the day it arrived. Periodically we would lapse, without uttering a word, without reference to anything, into convulsions of laughter, like blithering idiots. I wish I could hope to match it, but one of the things that seems to characterize the impoverished culture of Rochester is 1) the absence of good restaurants, and 2) the absence of fresh jokes. Even in Iowa City (God help us) I heard more and better jokes in a few months than I have heard here in ten years.

With regard to St. Mark's, I've been reading Ruskin, as of course I should have done right away. After getting our eyes used to the underwater dimness of the interior he remarks, "It is the Cross that is first seen, and always, burning in the center of the temple; and every dome and hollow of its roof has the figure of Christ in the utmost height of it, raised in power, or returning in judgment." (Without meaning to quibble, I am absolutely certain that one of the domes, I think the west, or entrance, one has the dove of the Holy Spirit, not Christ, at its center.) It is true, in any case, which is Ruskin's main point, that while much attention is paid by inscription and design to the Virgin, Christ is in fact the presiding figure. But if he is here presented, as he is, whether in the domes or elsewhere, as "raised in power, or returning in judgment," may he not be called Pantokrator? What are the special conditions that permit the use of that term? Must it be confined to buildings or images to the east of a certain meridian? I hope I don't seem to be nagging about a small point.

Ruskin is absolutely astonishing; I never read him before with any care. He has his moments of exhortation and rank evangelism, a sort of shrill and even hectoring high moral tone, reminding one uncomfortably that his father was a clergyman (I think) and suggesting that he is being weakly filial. But I find it easy enough to put those moments aside in the name of the vast variety of things that are brilliant and good and sane about him. Not least of these is that sound moral sense which condemns that aesthetic and moralistic purist who, finding an unsullied spiritual simplicity in Fra Angelico, is unable to stomach the worldly exuberance and vigor of, in his example, Rubens. (See appendix 15 of the First Book.) But even this sound, well-founded amplitude and catholicity of taste, is not in itself what impresses. What I find so striking on virtually every page is a vast knowledge – including the geological and topographical conditions that antedate all building – together with a deeply felt (I suppose there is no other word for it) "Moral" sense of the ways we live, or ought to live, or have failed to live, and the ways that these modes of living, healthy and unhealthy, worldly and spiritual, exalted or debauched, reflect themselves in works of art, and especially of architecture. There is no question but that he does exactly what Ward Perkins reprehended you for doing: interpreting architecture as an experience comparable to other forms of human experience. This seems to me, indeed, what all the best art historians are concerned to do; though perhaps I may confide a heresy to you. I suppose Panofsky and Wind are among the Dominations and Powers of art criticism in this century, and I admit to reading them both with fascination and delight, and of course with improvement. But their notion of iconography is essentially literary, and their approach to art is often a narrowly literary one. It may be an irony that I should be one to complain of this, and I don't mean really to complain. But reading their work has about it the kind of pleasure I get from detective fiction, in which the brilliance of the deducer or his fund of arcane knowledge is carefully and slowly played out like fishing line, and hauled in with the catch of a revelation at the end. Ruskin is simply far more philosophic, immediate, and direct, risking more and not showing off as much. Perhaps I'm just carried away by a current enthusiasm.

 May all things go well with you. I hope I can make my pome justify all the ruminative pleasure I am taking in reading about Venice.
Unicus Aretinus

[149]
[AH]
September 11th, 1977
[19 East Boulevard, Rochester, New York 14610]

*[Postcard, with a photograph of the Schloss Leopoldskron and its lake,
addressed to Wm. MacDonald, 25 Henshaw Ave, Northampton, Mass 01060]*

I thought you'd be pleased to know that the splendid <u>Britannica</u> you gave us says this of Bertrand Russell: "His admirable and lucid English style may be attributed to the fact that he did not undergo a classical education at a public school; …" It may be said that not all biographies are as lively and candid as this.
Snug, the Joiner

[150]

[AH]
[September 12th, 1977]
[19 East Boulevard, Rochester, New York 14610]

[Postcard, with a reproduction of Dürer's portrait of Wilibald Perkheimer, addressed to Wm. MacDonald (hic, haec, hoc), 25 Henshaw, Northampton, Mass. 01060]

Didja hear about the guy who joined the armed forces because he read that they were "all spit and polish"?

W. W. Skeat

[151]

[WLM]
[September 12th or 13th, 1977]
[25 Henshaw Avenue, Northampton, Massachusetts, 01060]

[Postcard, with an illustration of the Seacroft Guest House and Cottages at Niles Beach, Gloucester, Massachusetts, addressed to HECHT, (Skiapod), 19, E. Boulevard, Rochester NY, 14610]

That's quite delicious about Bert Russell. In the 11th ed. Of the <u>Encyclopedia Britannica</u> is an entry s.v. Phoenix, that I've always been fond of, and I pass it along as it seems to have been extirpated from the 14th: (the Phoenix appeared at various times) "and again in AD 34, after an interval so short that its genuineness was suspected. The phoenix that was shown in Rome in the year of the secular games, AD 47, was universally admitted to be an imposture." Nice?

ii id. Sept. MCMLXXVII[1]
Salvianus cos. III ord.

[152]

[WLM]
September 14th, 1977
[25 Henshaw Avenue, Northampton, Massachusetts, 01060]

[Letter, typed on a Waldorf-Astoria Hotel, New York, letterhead]

General-Oberst!

Just got in from Venice, where I flew over for a couple of days to check out the information you require. Met a dwarf Patagonian contortionist ... but's that's

---

1 This card is a reply to postcard #149 and was almost certainly written on September 12th or 13th, in which case the Roman date should have been shown as pridie Id. Sept. or Id. Sept, respectively.

another story.

Proceeding from the general to the particular: you <u>could</u> say that the medallion bust of Jesus Christ in the sanctuary of S. Marco, the Immanuel cupola, is a Pantókrator, but strictly speaking I think that would be wrong. A Pantókrator ought to be shown alone, as in the dome of Daphni, outside Athens, or at Cefalù on the north coast of Sicily, and at a great scale relevant to the surface upon which he is mosaicked and to the building in which he is placed. Now the S. Marco Immanuel cupola medallion is of a Byzantine style, of the XIII century, and in <u>form</u> suits the kind of image one describes as a Pantókrator. But, as it is associated with the Virgin and Isaiah and Daniel, and eleven other characters, it isn't a P., which must be seen, as the word clearly says, as All-Ruler. So, though you might get away with it, I wouldn't try were I a prize-winning, winsome, winterized poet …

It is even clearer that the other Christs hanging around in domes in S. Marco can't qualify: the one in the Ascension cupola, at the crossing, for example. ~~If you need a P, switch churches~~ Oh – none in Venice.

The reasoning behind all this is that in the western "colonial," provincial churches an Ascension scene was kept on, but the received Byzantine tradition didn't allow both Ascensions and Pantókrators. See Otto Demus, <u>Byzantine Mosaic Decoration</u>,[1] pp. 19 etc. In sum, though there are several Christs at S. Marco, none of them properly can take the appellation Pantókrator.

I've not read Ruskin for many years. I used I think to find him wearying and precious, coming up now and again with a fine idea or observation. His much-praised style, though, I need to be re-acquainted with, and your letter may get me started if I ever get caught up with my pre-illness plans. I have finished a long article, though, and the re-printing of the <u>Pantheon</u> has been a fine boost (though I can't seem to get any royalties out of the publisher!).

I am to lecture at Syracuse University in the College of Architecture on Wednesday October 26th. I'm not sure if it is an afternoon or evening lecture, but I've the thought I ought to come to Rochester the day before, or the day after, depending on the lecture hour, and take you out to dinner. Howzat?

      Love to all,
      Athemius von Tralles

Appendix I. Yes, not all domes at S. Marco have Christs in them; the Pentecost cupola is the major example.

Appendix II. I am something of an outsider in my insistence on <u>experiencing</u> architecture, on the emotional content of it. Ward Perkins, as you observe, doesn't like this, and he is not alone. It's not "scholarly." But just the other day, in a fine review of the <u>Pantheon</u>, a leading historian, Carl Condit,[2] said I was right to do so

---

1 Otto Demus, *Byzantine Mosaic Decoration: Aspects of Monumental Art in Byzantium* (New Rochelle, NY: Caratzas Brothers, 1976).

2 Carl W. Condit, review of William L. MacDonald's *The Pantheon*, in *Technology and Culture*, 18:2, (April 1977), pp. 241-243.

because I combined such expositions with factual data, history, and the like. He even went on to say that I am one of the best architectural historians because of this ... so perhaps matters are changing a bit. In any event, I will go right on explaining why I think great buildings have powerful messages in them, and why lesser buildings partake, in their stylistic and emotional connexions with their prototypes, of those messages ... but at this point the Sermon will have to end, as I've a class. These are matters that deserve more talk. Maybe I'll have read some Ruskin before we see each other again, again ......

[153]

[AH]
[September 17th, 1977]
[19 East Boulevard, Rochester, New York 14610]

[Postcard, with a photograph of The Stanhope Hotel, New York, typed, addressed to William MacDonald, 25 Henshaw Ave., Northampton, Mass. 01060]

By all means come before, after, or during your Syracuse lecture. The visit is overdue. I take your word on the absence of a Pantokrator in S. Mark's, though there is a solitary judicial Jesus Christ in the apse behind the altar. But clearly there are at least three (Jesus Christ, Blessed Virgin Mary & Mark) regnant figures in that cathedral.
Geoffrey Hartman,
Geoffrey Hartman

P.S. Is John Van Doren in the history dept. there? Used to be. I knew him and his wife, Mira.

[154]

[AH]
[September 21st, 1977]
[19 East Boulevard, Rochester, New York 14610]

[Italian postcard, with an engraving of a street scene by Cristoforo Dall'Acqua, typed, addressed to Prof. Wm. MacDonald, 25 Henshaw Ave., Northampton, Mass. 01060]

"In an average first-class restaurant a reasonably accurate rule is a minimum tip of 25c, whether for one person or two, for a bill that totals less than $2; 35c for $2[1] to $3; 40c for $3 to $4; and a minimum of 20c per person for a lunch or dinner party." Thus Emily Post in her Etiquette book with 1945 copyright,[2] which I am reading

1 AH had slipped and typed 1 instead of 2 here.
2 Emily Post, *Etiquette: The Blue Book of Social Usage* (New York: Funk and Wagnalls, 1945).

avidly in behalf of the same poem for which I read Ruskin.[1] The note about the doubtful phoenix was great. I believe Pliny the Elder claims to have seen a real one, though in the state of ashes. I assume you are seeing something of Dick Wilbur now that school has begun.

Hans Arp

[155]

[WLM]
September 21st, 1977
[25 Henshaw Avenue, Northampton, Massachusetts, 01060]

[Postcard, with an illustration of the Seacroft Guest House and Cottages at Niles Beach, Gloucester, Massachusetts, addressed to Mme. + M. A · E · Hecht, 19, E · Boulevard, ROCHESTER NY, 14610]

Hŏkay! Arrive Rochester Thurs. 27 Oct. on Al-Egainy's #105, 10:38 a.m.; don't bother meet. Leave crack of dawn next day; don't bother take. Can't find a picture anywhere of Marco's apsidal Christ!

Love, J. J. Winckelmann

P.S. Pls make resrnt reserves 27th …

(no Van Dor)

[156]

[AH]
[September 26th, 1977]
[19 East Boulevard, Rochester, New York 14610]

[French postcard, with a reproduction of Le Douanier Rousseau's Football Players, *typed and handwritten, addressed to Wm. MacDonald, 25 Henshaw Ave., Northampton, Mass. 01060]*

How about bringing Barbara along? We got lots of room, and we'd be glad to see her. Let us know.

Helen will not hear of any restaurant plans, and has it firmly in mind to cook you a home dinner. As for the apsidal Christ, I have a picture here I can show you. I have finished the S. Marco part of the poem, and have kept the Pantókrator out of it. I am pleased with my description of the place and look forward to showing it to you. We will meet you, or both of you, despite your protest, at 10:38 on Thursday, Oct. 27.

Sidney Smith

---

1 The poem he was working on, and in which Emily Post's book on etiquette was indeed to figure, was "The Venetian Vespers."

The rain it raineth every day
Upon the just and unjust fella
But more upon the just, because
The unjust hath the just's umbrella.¹

[157]

[WLM]
September 29th, 1977
[25 Henshaw Avenue, Northampton, Massachusetts, 01060]

[Dutch postcard, with a photograph of three young girls in traditional Dutch costume, handwritten, addressed to A · E · Hecht, 19, E. Boulevard, Rochester N.Y., 14610]

Sir, –

Barbara can't come because of her job – she'd like to, but can't. Haven't seen Wilbur at all. Trying to figure out how to retire early, + whether or not to sign up with Oxford for a huge Companion to Architecture.

See you soon –

Engle + Bert Humperdinck

A knight with an ebony pie-pan
Rode by on a quizzical mare
And said, "The flora on Saipan
Are waving at José Ferrer."

[158]

[AH]
[October 3rd, 1977]
[19 East Boulevard, Rochester, New York 14610]

[French postcard, with a reproduction of Ingres's The Valpinçon Bather, *typed, addressed to Wm. MacDonald, 25 Henshaw Ave., Northampton, Mass 01060]*

Scout's honor, this is a blurb on a book I just received. The commender is Moshe Greenberg, Prof. of Bible, Hebrew U. of Jerusalem. He writes: "Marcia Falk's translation of the Song of Songs is a very affecting and successful set of lyrics whose effect on me not once was to uncover new possibilities in the original Hebrew."²

---

1 This poem is attributed to Charles Bowen, and takes its opening line from the refrain to "When that I was and a tiny little boy," Feste's song in Act 5, Scene 1 of Shakespeare's *Twelfth Night*.

2 The book AH had been sent was Marcia Falk's *The Song of Songs: Love Lyrics from the Bible* (New York: Harcourt Brace Jovanovich, 1977). Later editions corrected the error thus: "A very affecting and successful set of lyrics whose effect on me more than once was to uncover new possibilities in the original

Louisa May Woolcott

[159]

[WLM]
October 13th, 1977
[25 Henshaw Avenue, Northampton, Massachusetts, 01060]

[Postcard, with a photograph of the Ruskin monument, Friars Crag, Derwentwater, Lake District, handwritten, addressed to A.E. Hecht, 19 E. Boulevard, Rochester N.Y., 14610]

Dear Mr Hecht –
I've heard you are reading me. Is it loud and clear? Have you met my kid Dean Rusk, an academic?

Yours,
Ruskie

Hebrew." Eleven years after sending WLM this postcard, AH received one from Richard Wilbur: "Dear Tony, Today's Times book review contains something similar to Prof. Greenberg's unintentionally crushing praise of Marcia Falk. Bryan Forbes, reviewing Anthony Holden's biography of Laurence Olivier, says 'At the height of his powers he had only to step on the stage for brightness to fall from the air.'" (Postcard dated October 23rd, 1988 [Anthony Hecht papers, Box 74, Folder 41].)

[160]

[WLM]
October 27th, 1977
[25 Henshaw Avenue, Northampton, Massachusetts, 01060]

[Letter, handwritten, with a now missing enclosure]

Dear Helen + Tony –

Many regrets for not showing up. The situation is better here, as Nick has managed to look at things quite maturely. I talked with Dale's surgeon Wednesday, I think it was, + the prognosis is not good. She begins radiation therapy today as the cancer is inoperable.

I enclose a lady for Evan, in the hope that she will guide him toward a fine taste in such matters.

Love to all,
Bill

[161]

[WLM]
November 11th, 1977
[25 Henshaw Avenue, Northampton, Massachusetts, 01060]

[Swiss postcard, with a photograph of a detail from the Reformation Wall in Geneva, typed, addressed to Anthony Hecht, umm!\ 19, East Boulevard, Rochester NY, 14610]

Barbara, to me, on a card written after your reading last Tuesday[1]: "If A.E.H. is not the most accomplished and gifted and sensitive poet living, then I can't imagine who is. Even canvassing beyond the realm of the living calls forth few names to match his richness and elegance of diction." (You may, I think, use this for blurbs {do you know Fowler's "slaver, slobber, slubber"?[2]}, for a fee.)

Love to you all,
William the Archivolt

---

1 AH had been invited by Dimitri Hadzi to read at Harvard's Carpenter Center for the Visual Arts.

2 Fowler's definition reads, in part, as follows: "The base meaning [of all three words] is to run at the mouth (1), with kissing (2), licking (3), fulsome flattery (4), emotional gush (5), & superficial smoothing over or mere tinkering (6), as developments." *H. W. Fowler: A Dictionary of Modern English Usage*, edited by Sir Ernest Gowers, Second Edition (New York: Oxford University Press, 1965), p. 540.

[162]

[AH]
November 21st, 1977
[19 East Boulevard, Rochester, New York 14610]

[Letter, typed on a The University of Rochester, Department of English, letterhead, enclosing a 29-page typed and hand-corrected draft of AH's poem "The Venetian Vespers"]

Dear Bill,

I should have written earlier to acknowledge with gratitude your postcard with Barbara's message of high praise. But I thought that if I were able to delay just long enough to risk being insulting or ungrateful I would have the whole Venice poem finished (if not done with) and would be able to send you the thing I've been working on with such enthusiasm since we came back this summer. And here it is. Which is not to say that I have finished tinkering with it, or that I'm complacently satisfied. Still, I am pleased, and I hope you will be too.

Our twenty-four hours at Harvard could scarcely have been better. All manner of old friends seemed suddenly to have appeared in Cambridge just this term. My undergraduate room-mate from Bard College (who is now a dean and shrink at MIT) was there; a poet of sorts who was at Kenyon College when I was there; a former colleague and good friend (in Chemistry) from my teaching years at Bard; Dan & Janet Aaron; Robert Fitzgerald; and of course Dimitri [Hadzi]– who took several of us out to dinner at the Parthenon on Massachusetts Avenue after the reading. The weather was atrocious, and poor Dimitri very reasonably feared that I would get no more than 15 or 20 for an audience – in spite of the fact that there had been a good deal of publicity, and many enormous and handsome posters. But for all the impetuosity of the rain, the posters must have worked, for I must have had between 100 and 150 in the audience, and they were warmly and emphatically enthusiastic. I read Section III of the Venice poem – a section that can endure excerption, as not all of them can. After the reading Barbara very hastily and shyly came up to shake hands, but disappeared almost immediately. Thank her for me, and also for Helen, for those enthusiastic words of hers.

                We both send our love,
                Tony

[Enclosure - Page 1]

The Venetian Vespers

"..where's that palace whereinto foul things
Sometimes intrude not? Who has a breast so
                                          pure
But some uncleanly apprehensions
Keep leets and law days, and in session sit
With meditations lawful?"
                    Othello: III, iii, 136-41

"We cannot all have our gardens now, nor our
   pleasant fields to meditate in at eventide."
              Ruskin: The Stones of Venice,
                             Bk. I, Ch. XXX.

I

       What's merciful is not knowing where you are,
What time it is, even your name or age,
But merely a clean coolness at the temple —
That, says the spirit softly, is enough
For the mind to adventure on its half-hidden path
Like starlight interrupted by dense trees
Journeying backwards on a winter trip
While you are going, as you fancy, forwards,
And the stars are keeping pace with everything.
Where to begin? With the white, wrinkled membrane,
The disgusting skin that gathers on hot milk?
Or narrow slabs of jasper light at sundown
That fit themselves softly around the legs
Of chairs, and entertain a drift of motes,
A tide of sadness, a failing, a dying fall?
Or the glass jar, like a dry cell battery,
Full of electric coils and boiling resins,
Its tin Pinnochio nose with one small nostril,
And both of us under a tent of towels
Like child conspirators, the tin nose breathing
Health at me steadily, like the insufflation of God?
Yes, but also the sight, on a gray morning,
Beneath the crossbar of an iron railing

[1]

---

[1] This is page 1 of the 29-page typescript AH sent WLM.

[163]

[WLM]
November 22nd, 1977
[25 Henshaw Avenue, Northampton, Massachusetts, 01060]

[Blank postcard, typed, with sender's name and address given as J. J. Homonym, Cadastral,, Minn., addressed to Mr and Mrs A E Hecht, 19 East Boulevard, Rochester NY 14610]

Queries. 1) "like a sitting duck." I've been checking on a mess of ducks and find that they walk, swim, waddle, etc., but have not caught one actually sitting. One of them said he "wouldn't be caught dead sitting down." 2) "like shooting fish in a barrel." Well, I got a barrel, filled it up with water, and rented a mess of fish from the five & dime. Borrowed a rifle, stood on a chair, and let go. Missed all the fish but put a big hole in the barrel and all the water ran right out. I think there's something missing in that Olde Sayinghe. You do get a lot of fish, assuming you have properly stocked your barrel … If there's anything else you really need to know, write.
"J. J."

[164]

[AH]
[November 28th, 1977]
[19 East Boulevard, Rochester, New York 14610]

[Letter, typed on a The Dana Palmer House, Cambridge, letterhead, posted in an envelope with the sender's address given as Secretary to the Corporation, Harvard University, Cambridge, Massachusetts 02138, addressed to William MacDonald, 25 Henshaw Avenue, Northampton, Mass. 01060]

Dear friend,
I am currently at work on a new poem which rises, I think, to a clarion pitch and culmination in the following lines:

> And laying his finger inside of his nose,
> With a wink of his eye, up the chimney he rose;
> And I heard him declare, as he rose out of sight,
> "Merry Christmas to all, and to all a fat lip."

It may still need a little polishing, but the main thrust of it is powerful and effective. In fact, I've tried it out on local members of the family, and they assure me, in the most soothing terms, that this is a really effective item, and suited to trends of the season. Once you've seen the whole thing I'm sure you'll agree. It has an interesting plot to it, involving this broken-down drunk in red flannels whose hang-up is buggering reindeer, and to soothe his conscience he goes on a binge of philanthropy once a year.

Love,
Richard the Pigeon-Livered

[165]

[WLM]
November 29th, 1977
[25 Henshaw Avenue, Northampton, Massachusetts, 01060]

[British postcard, with a photograph of the gardens in St. John's College, Oxford, handwritten, addressed to A.E. Hecht, 19 E. Boulevard, Rochester N.Y., 14610]

Dear Tony –
A line to say your wonderful poem has come – more later. Caught up in Harvard lectures etc. Dale in a kind of stasis – boys just back – we wait – still in hospital, having radiation therapy.

Best to you all,
Bill

[166]

[WLM]
December 30th, 1977
[25 Henshaw Avenue, Northampton, Massachusetts, 01060]

[Letter, typewritten]

Dear Tony,
    Can you forgive me for not writing sooner about your wonderful poem? I hope so. I can only plead the usual – stacks of blue books and term papers, holidays, and so on, I read the poem right off when it came, and since then I've studied it and thought about it a good deal, so perhaps the delay is, after all, in some ways not a bad thing.
    Where shall I begin? That it is a wonderful poem, with an extraordinary transparency, solid, yet somehow gossamer, suspended from your extraordinary mind? That it weaves from Vision to Concrete in the most satisfying, complete way? That it makes Time viable? I don't know; I don't have the words. It is beautiful, and it is I think complete.
    I see I repeat complete. That is right now my deepest feeling about it. The first four pages are no less marvelous than the rest, but the way the lines bring one into your view of this world <u>is</u> marvelous. That Venice can be used like a painter's concetto to sum up a life is so striking as to be all but perfect; no, that's not what I want to say, I want to say that making Venice the counterpoint to the narrator's life is inspired, and creates resonances of the most powerful kind, for me on second and

third readings more than at first. And my own childhood ... SALADA ... uncles ... my!

The cinema sequence is also inspired; the line "We never heard from him again" jolted me as an electric shock, a strong one, would. And lines like "My whole life was changed ..." and "Blessed be the ..." are equally inspired. In fact, though there are a number of words I don't know and will in due time look up, I do know that the use of "meringues," "isometric," "divan," "ochre pastes," "crumbs," "enamelled," "Allagashes," and many more is perfect, only perfect. "Dentures" is lovely, as is "Corpus Iuris." And the juxtaposition, actual or implied, with the sacred and the profane is extremely telling: soul/midriff, and the like. The Emily Post-man is splendid.

The only word I'd take out is louche, and I say that probably because it's so In, spread all over the TLS and such watering holes. Is "presumeably" correct? And may I deferentially ask why "the incontinent" is in inverted commas? I'm missing something there I'm sure ... Finally, as far as my inability to understand this and that goes, why didn't the uncle(s), otherwise so kind, respond to the Toledo letters? Again, I probably missed something, even after re-readings.

The great Church comes through exactly right. The words for colors and surfaces and light, all through the poem, are themselves luminescent. Baudelaire would be jealous of that.

Love to you all,
Bill

[167]

[AH]
January 4th, 1978
19 East Boulevard, Rochester, New York 14610

[Letter, typed on a The University of Rochester, College of Arts and Science,
River Campus Station, Rochester, New York 14627, Department of English, letterhead]

Dear Bill,

I can't tell you how gratified, how truly delighted, how reassured I am by your reaction to "The Venetian Vespers." I wasn't the least disconcerted by the thoroughly understandable pause before your long letter: after all, you had sent an enthusiastic postcard, and I know how crammed exam time and the holidays can be, and for you this year there has been a special anxiety and concern that might well have excluded anything else whatever from your attention. I knew all that, so the extended care with which you read the poem and wrote about it touches me all the more. All your fine comments make me extremely happy. So I'm all the more eager to satisfy you in those matters in which the poem gives rise to doubt or uncertainty. I have in fact been fiddling with it since completing the draft I sent you, and I've introduced about eleven new lines into the poem, about half in the first part of the poem, the rest in the last, which are intended not quite to clarify everything (since one of the points of the poem is that, for the narrator at least, some things will never be completely clear – and it may be that this is one of the conditions of life for all of us) but at least to point the reader in the right direction. What I want to do in this letter is to quote the Part I insertions, along with the lines that immediately precede and follow them, so that you can scribble them into your copy, and I enclose the last two pages revised (since I happen to have copies of them on hand.) These constitute, along with the correction of a grammatical blemish on page 7 (For "They are swept up and gathered with their makers" read "A wealth swept up and gathered with its makers") what I hope may be the final revisions in the poem. So here goes. On page 3, near the bottom: "The heatless burnings of the elderly / In memorized, imaginary lusts, / Visions of noontide infidelities, / Crude hallway gropings, cruel lubricities, / A fire as cold and slow as rusting metal." And on page 4, near the top, "With head and feet tucked under, playing possum. / A meat-hooked ham, hung like a traitor's head / For the public's notice in a butcher shop, / Faintly resembling the gartered thigh / Of an acrobatic, overweight soubrette. / And a scaled, crusted animal whose head /…" These, along with the five and a half lines inserted in the last pages, ought, I hope, to be enough, not quite to tell you why the narrator's father was left to rot in Toledo, but rather what the narrator suspects – but can never know – the reason may have been.

Having just said I hoped all necessary changes have now been made, I returned to your letter, and see that there are several points that need still to be considered. You may be quite right about "louche" being fashionable cant; I want to think about that. As for "presumeably," it's a word that Helen questioned, too. I put it in because the impression I want to give here is of the narrator speaking inventively (as he supposes), giving what he thinks of as imaginative instances of "hellishness," whereas in fact at least a few, key images are not the product of his "poetic invention" but fished up from a deep and troubled memory of his past. The abandoned box-car, for example, is like the one that brought his father home. That the row of houses are also abandoned continues the theme of abandonment, which was his father's fate. As it was his father's fate to be "condemned." But the narrator is not aware at this point that he is speaking so intimately; he supposes that he is merely supplying symbols or emblems, freely and randomly chosen, to represent or concretize his frame of mind. So that for him, the word "presumeably" is a way of indicating that these are not "real" houses, or remembered ones, but simply the fruit of his imagination, some details of which (like whether or not they've been condemned) he has not bothered to specify, since it's not relevant to his purposes. Something of the same sort is intended by the quotation marks around "the incontinent." It has to do with the twinned conscious and unconscious meanings of the speaker. Old people who cannot contain their urine are of course referred to as incontinent, and there's no special need to supply emphasis to the word by putting it in quotes or italics. But for a reason central to the speaker's mental state, incontinent is a word that makes him very self-conscious. There are many forms of incontinence, and urinating is only one, and to the speaker, by no means the most important of them.

With visible distortions. Among the stones
Of the railbed, fragments of shattered amber
That held a pint of rye. The carapace
Of a dried beetle. A broken orange crate
Streaked with tobacco stains at the nailheads
In the gray, fractured slats. And over all
A dust of oblivion finer than milled flour
Where chips of brick, clinkers and old iron
Burn in their slow, invisible decay.
Or else it is late afternoon in autumn,
The sunlight rusting on the western fronts
Of a long block of Victorian brick houses,
Untenanted, presumeably condemned,
Their brownstone grapes, their grand entablatures,
Their straining caryatid muscle-men
Rendered at once ridiculous and sad
By the black scars of zigzag fire escapes
That double themselves in isometric shadows.
And all their vacancy is given voice
By the endless flapping of one window-shade.
And then there is the rank, familiar smell
Of underpasses, the dark piers of bridges,
Where old men, "the incontinent," urinate.
The acid small of poverty, the jest
Of adolescent boys exchanging quips
About bedpans, the motorman's comfort,
A hospital world of syphons and thick tubes
That they know nothing of. Nor do they know
The heatless burnings of the elderly
In memorized, imaginary lusts,
A fire as cold and slow as rusting metal.
It's but a child's step, it's but an old man's totter
From this to the appalling world of dreams.

In memorized, imaginary lusts,
Visions of noontide infidelities,
Crude hallway gropings, cruel lubricities,

---

1 This page and the two that follow show, respectively, pages 3, 4, and 7 of the typescript AH sent WLM, with the revisions AH called for in letter #167 of January 4th, 1978 handwritten by WLM. (The other handwritten corrections on page 4 had already been made by AH himself.)

A meat-hooked ham, hung like a traitor's head
For the public's notice in a butcher shop,
Family resembling a gartered thigh
Of an acrobatic, overweight soubrette.
Gray bottled babies in formaldehyde
As in their primal amneotic bath.
Pale dowagers hiding their liver-spots
In a fine chalk, confectionery dust.
And then the unbearable close-up of a wart
With a tough bristle of hair, like a small beast
With head and feet tucked under, playing possum.
And a scaled, crusted animal whose head
Fits in a Nazi helmet, whose webbed feet
Are cold upon the white flanks of dreaming lovers,
While thorned and furry legs embrace each other
As black mandibles tick. Immature girls,
Naked but for the stockings they stretch tight
To tempt the mucid glitter of an eye.
And the truncated snout of a small bat,
Like one whose nose, undermined by the pox,
Falls back to the skull's socket. Deepest of all,
Like the converging lines in diagrams
Of vanishing points, those underwater blades,
Those quills or sunburst spokes of marine light,
Flutings and gilded shafts in which one sees
In the drowned star of intersecting beams
Just at that final moment of suffocation
The terrifying and unmeaning rictus
Of the sand shark's stretched, involuntary grin.
In the upstairs room, when somebody had died,
There were flowers, there were underwater globes,
Mercury seedpearls. It was my mother died.
After a long illness and long ago.

    San Pantaleone, heavenly buffoon,
Patron of dotards and of gondolas,
Forgive us the obsessional daydream

7

The ochre pastes and puddings of dogshit
Keep us earthbound in half a dozen ways,
Curbing the spirit's tendency to pride.
The palaces decay. Venice is rich
Chiefly in the deposits of her dogs.
A wealth
~~They are~~ swept up and gathered with ~~their~~ its makers.
Canaries, mutts, love-birds and alley cats
Are sacked away like so many Monte Cristos,
There being neither lawns, meadows nor hill sides
To fertilize or to be buried in.
For them the glass is broken in the dark
As a rememberance by the garbage men.
I am their mourner at collection time
With an invented litany of my own.
Wagner died here, Stravinsky's buried here,
They say that Cimarosa's enemies
Poisoned him here. The mind at four A. M.
Is a poor, blotched, vermiculated thing.
I've seen it spilled like sweetbreads, and I've dreamed
Of Byron writing, "Many a fine day
I should have blown my brains out but for the thought
Of the pleasure it would give my mother-in-law."
Thus virtues, it is said, are forced upon us
By our own impudent crimes. I think of him
With his consorts of whores and countesses
Smelling of animal musk, lilac and garlic,
A ménage that was in fact a menagerie,
A fox, a wolf, a mastiff, birds and monkeys,
Corbaccios and corvinos, spintriae,
The lees of the Venetian underworld,
A plague of iridescent flies. Spilled out.
O lights and livers. Deader than dead weight.
In a casket lined with tufted tea-rose silk.
O that the soul should tie its shoes, the mind

His feelings about that word may perhaps be clarified by the new lines that come to you with this letter. Perhaps these "defenses" of "presumeably" and "incontinent" are altogether too fancy, intricate, remote and Byzantine to be operative in the reading of the poem, and I am flattering myself by indulging in subtleties that I alone will ever relish. I'd like your serious opinion on this.[1]

Meanwhile I am warmed and exhilarated by your attentive scrutiny of the poem, and your detailed appreciation of it. I hope you will approve what I send here.

Your postcard mentioned Harvard lectures without further specifics. What of them? When / on what? Let us know.

Love,
Tony

[168]

[AH]
January 7th, 1978
[19 East Boulevard, Rochester, New York 14610]

[Letter, typed on a The University of Rochester, Department of English, letterhead, addressed to Wm. MacDonald, (The American Vitruvius), 25 Henshaw Avenue, Northampton, Mass. 01060, with a now missing enclosure]

Dear Bill,

Here is the picture I promised you so long ago. In the cortile of the Academy, from left to right: Frank [Brown], Jackie [Brown], and Marilyn Lavin. Is not that leonine head impressive? Einsteinian? He is in the States right now, I think. He is lecturing this term in Texas. (Did I ever write you that General Sherman said that if he owned both Hell and Texas he'd move to Hell and rent out Texas?)

I still sit around, relishing your letter of praise. I hope the emendations I sent will clear up major problems in the poem.

When are you going to come visit us? I realise you have a teaching schedule while I haven't, and I take it from an obscure reference in a postcard that you have some teaching obligations at Harvard this term. I know you can't just shove all that aside and drive off into blizzards and closed thruways. But come spring perhaps you can wangle a trip. I have been dropping your name like a ton of bricks on the sensitive feet of a very nice lady here who works at the Memorial Art Gallery and for the landmark Preservation Board, and who is rather knowledgeable about architecture. We have spoken of bringing you here to lecture FOR A FEE! She said she'd be in touch with me about it. What she wants is a talk on some aspect – any aspect – of American Architecture.

1 In the published version of the poem, AH retained the word "louche" but substituted "presumably" for "presumeably" and removed the inverted commas around "the incontinent." A handful of other changes not discussed in this letter were also incorporated, the biggest of which involved the cutting of what would have been section V's thirty-fifth line – "In a set of Diabolico Variations."

Love,
Richard The Pussy-Footed

[169]

[WLM]
January 11th, 1978
[25 Henshaw Avenue, Northampton, Massachusetts, 01060]

[Letter, typed on a Waldorf-Astoria Hotel, New York, letterhead, posted in a Northern Illinois University envelope, with the sender's address given as Vice Chancellor, Northern Illinois University, Dekalb, Illinois 60115, and addressed to Anthony Hecht, Worthy, 19 East Boulevard, Rochester NY 14610, with a now missing enclosure]

My dear Lord Byron,
    Not to be outdone, I send you a photograph as well: Uncle Misha and Uncle Saul just before they realised that the young man coming toward them is Raskolnikov (he's only pretending to give them the right-of-way). All part of my copyrighted Real Live Action Photo Service prints; send for the brochure … I've a friend, a novelist, who lives nearby; he's about our age, more or less, and has, like us, many a fine story (for example, on coming out of a low bar in Dar--es-Salaam he called to Malcolm X, who had now passed a little down the block, "Call me Friday," whereupon Malcolm called back, "Only if you call <u>me</u> Robinson Crusoe!"). Anyway, this friend of mine, the novelist, said that many a year ago when he was in his teens his father sat down at the piano, at home in Plainfield, Massachusetts, and played quite wonderfully; my friend had never once heard him play. Do you think that Frank let his hair grow out for some like reason? It has occurred to me that he had planned to do so for say forty years, and that after some myriads (you notice I use the word correctly) of people had come on four continents to know him as we did, he let it grow out. It would rather be like him, I think. I envy that kind of waiting-power.
    (I have to interrupt this to point out to you that I know the proper sequence of page use when employing a four-fold of note paper? my mother taught me, about 1929. A lot of people are ignorant of this correct usage. By the way, do either you or Helen, or, indeed both of you, speaking of such things, know what it means to leave your card with the upper left-hand corner turned down? Advise.)
    Texas. Yes. I had a marvelous note from him some months back, saying that although the Austin functionaries had agreed to his visit, letters of recommendation were needed, and would I write a fulsome one? After I got over laughing – <u>me</u> writing for <u>Frank</u> – I actually wrote for him. A rather choice letter if I do say so; god knows what they thought of it, but it has had some circulation because a young friend who called me on another matter mentioned it. In order to clear

matters up, in the fashion of Benchley's stupendous Treasurer's Report,[1] I'll come right out and say that the friend was calling from Austin. I hope that clears that up. I am to venture down there to lecture in April; and there is a move afoot to get Frank up here at some point.

Harvard. Gave two lectures there in November at the Graduate School of Design. They were good lectures, but the class was shifty and sleazy and had little if any idea of what I was talking about. Not entirely their fault (its fault?), because the High Mucker made a course out of visiting lecturers, which simply can't be done, and the kids were confused ...

I have a whole slew of wonderful lectures (that's right, this is the next page) on American architecture, and would only need say a couple of thousand as a Fee (I'm typing down here because I don't want to type over the embossed heraldry). Seriously, I'd love to come out, lecture or no.

I've not yet had the time to conflate lines in the poem, but will do so shortly. Thanks for the various explanations. If after I read the Revised Standard Version I have more to say, you can be sure I will.

Meanwhile, love to all. Don't forget, though, the photograph is copyrighted. You can't just show it around will-he nil-he.

Orville Wright

Frank looks enormously different. I've spent a lot of time looking at the photo, for which many thanks, and am somewhat puzzled by the extraordinary change in his appearance ... Did I tell you that I go on half time, beginning next Fall? Teach only Spring Terms? Aaahhh ......

Dale starts chemotherapy about now. How awful. The boys seem to be taking it well, but it is too early to take an accurate reading there. I don't exactly know how I feel, other than sorrow and indeed a kind of pity ...

[170]

[AH]
January 16th, 1978
[19 East Boulevard, Rochester, New York 14610]

[French postcard, with a reproduction of a Japanese scroll painting featuring the young Buddhist monk Kobo Daishi, handwritten, addressed to Prof. Wm. MacDonald, Defender of the Faith, 25 Henshaw Ave, Northampton, Mass. 01060]

Excellency –
Have you heard about the Pole who flung himself to the ground – and missed?

---

1 Robert Benchley's *The Treasurer's Report* was a comedy sketch, made into a short film, and portrays the assistant treasurer of an organization struggling to present its annual report.

Today, God save us, I am 55; it would give one pause if there were time for such frivolities.

Love
T

[171]

[AH]
January 17th, 1978
[19 East Boulevard, Rochester, New York 14610]

[Letter, typed on an Ocean Manor Resort Hotel, Fort Lauderdale, Florida, letterhead]

Dear old Tetrarch,

Of course we knew about folding over the upper left-hand corner of calling cards. Who do you think we are, parvenus, arrivistes, the great unwashed, the many-headed throng? It indicates that a call has been made at a house, but that it need not be acknowledged. Are you, on the other hand, aware of what is conveyed by the turning down of the <u>lower</u> left-hand corner of the calling card? It is a sentiment of roughly the following order: "While in our all too mechanized, liberated and jet-propelled times the patient discriminations and nice qualifications of an earlier, more leisurely and old-fashioned age may be blurred and perhaps altogether lost sight of, I for one know you to be a contemptible bugger of eight-year-old, left-handed, cross-eyed boys, which your friends proclaim a highly cultivated taste, but which I recognize for the peculiar perversion that it is."

I am currently serving on a damned literary jury – it seems I always am – but there are some advantages to this particular one – the literary jury of The American Academy and Institute of Arts & Letters.[1] They don't pay any fee for your services, but they fly you into NY for jury meetings (three or four of these a year) and pay all expenses, including overnight stays at good hotels. But as opposed to most other juries I've served on, in which you have to read, say, all the poetry published in a given year, for this jury – which awards prizes in <u>all</u> fields of writing, poetry, fiction, and all branches of non-fiction – one reads only work that has already been highly commended. This of course comes to a great deal of reading. But the good part of it is that you discover things you might never otherwise have known about. All this is prefatory to commending to your attention a book of stories by one Leslie Epstein, called "The Steinway Quintet, Plus Four," published by Little, Brown.[2] The whole book is fine, but there is a story I think you may particularly like, called, "The Disciple of Bacon," about a community of rationalist, Enlightenment-minded Jews of Bucharest, and of one young man in their midst who has dedicated himself to

---

1 The American Academy and Institute of Arts and Letters was the previous name of the American Academy of Arts and Letters. The change of name dates from 1992. The jury was chaired by Dwight MacDonald and also included Gwendolyn Brooks, John Cheever and Elizabeth Hardwick.

2 Leslie Epstein, *The Steinway Quintet: Plus Four* (Boston: Little Brown, 1976).

proving that Mozart was a Jew.[1]

As I feel sure you have divined, I have found it forbiddingly difficult to write you about Dale, about all the horror she is now going through, and all the horror you and your sons are imaginatively going through with her. There is nothing to say except to acknowledge the terrible facts, and it would be a heartless impertinence to cast about for cheap consolations or edifying maxims. I send, in their place, my love.

Tony

[172]

[WLM]
January 21st, 1978
[25 Henshaw Avenue, Northampton, Massachusetts, 01060]

[Letter, typed on a Gramercy Park Hotel, Two Lexington Avenue at 21st Street, New York 10010-212, letterhead, posted in a The Michigan League envelope with sender's name given as Toussaint L'Envoi, and addressed to A E Hecht, Bitlis Professor of Bituminous Studies, 19 East Boulevard, Rochester, NY 14610]

Dear Tony,

I assume you are all as snowed in, under, as we are. I took Nick to the airport Thursday night and got chased up 1-91 by the storm on the way home about midnight. Made it, though, as Nick made his plane to Denver. Have you noticed that we always make it? Surviving types, we are.

Dale has started chemotherapy and her morale is apparently fairly good. Nick and Noel are taking it well on the whole. We have tried to bring it out in the open now and again, but there's really little you can do but wait. I'll know more about the details when Nick comes back next Friday, but of course such knowledge really furthers nothing. Noel is a little hard to read, and he has his law School applications (did I tell you he scored in the 97th percentile on his Law School Aptitude Test?) and his marriage in June to occupy his mind in any event. Nick is apprehensive in the long run but in good shape at present. He will inevitably be drawn into the never-ending squabbles among Dale, her sister, and their brother, but he knows what he is getting into. Even the present situation doesn't seem to have any effect on that relationship. As for myself, I don't exactly know what I feel.

Of course most of my apprehensions concern the boys. But they are now in many senses men, thank god, and have at least some of the means of living through all this. As for Dale, I am sorry, and it is much on my mind, but beyond that I'm not sure how I feel. I don't seem to feel guilty. Several people I have known well have died of cancer, one a very close friend, and the cumulative effect of all such is, or can be, devastating when one is not immersed in work or love, or late at night. You are no stranger to suffering, and I appreciate your words in

---

1 It was Epstein's book which won the American Academy and Institute of Arts and Letters' Arts and Letters Award that year.

your last letter a great deal. One lives through it, I guess. A weak sort of statement, but what else is there? On balance, I'm glad to be able to say, we all seem to be all right as of now. We know no more about timing than we did in October, when her surgeon said she would live from three to nine months. A few people have told me that this particular kind of cancer has now and again been cured, but none of those people have been the professionals I've talked to.

I will look in the Epstein book as you suggest. I've been reading, in addition to my usual diet of odds and ends, [André] Malraux's <u>Anti-Memoirs</u>,[1] which has been hanging about here for several years now and which I find very good on the whole. He strikes what is to me a fraudulent note now and then, but Jesus, he's been a lot of places and had a lot of really quite refreshing and evocative thoughts.

Love to you all, & a belated Happy Birthday. We thought of you on the day.
William the Orange

[173]

[AH]
[? January 27th, 1978]
[19 East Boulevard, Rochester, New York 14610]

[Postcard, with a photograph of a couple standing in front of the entrance to the Gotham Hotel, New York, handwritten, addressed to Prof. Wm. MacDonald, 25 Henshaw Ave, Northampton, Mass 01060]

1 André Malraux, *Anti-Memoirs* (New York: Bantam, 1967).

This is me picking up a pro (-phylactic in brief-case) in Sin City. Note dog, which serves as a trade-mark for this merchandise.
Arturo Sclerosis

P.S. Where did the story of the Rvd. Elisha Fawcett, circa 1817 come from?

[174]

[WLM]
[Late January / Early February, 1978]
[25 Henshaw Avenue, Northampton, Massachusetts 01060]

[Postcard, with a photograph of Kevin Delaney's Pontiac dealership in Dorchester, Massachusetts, with storage tanks behind it, addressed to A. von Hecht, 19. E. Boulevard, Rochester NY 14610

The Fawcett q. is beyond me: don't know him <u>or</u> the story! 1/2 time because I want as little to do w/academic life as possible, & want to write more. Mrs [Jean] France & I haven't yet found a date (I'm booked, or she is, on the dates available) but I think we will find one & I look forward v. much to seeing you all.
Pierre Louis

Tank in background filled w/air from Committee meetings!

[175]

[WLM]
February 4th, 1978
25 Henshaw Avenue, Northampton, Massachusetts 01060

[Blank postcard, typed, addressed to Anthony Evan Hecht, Esq., (A Great Man if There Ever Was One), 19 East Boulevard, Rochester NY 14610, posted in an envelope with the sender's address given as Oxford Companion to Architecture, William L. MacDonald, 25 Henshaw Avenue, Northampton, Mass. 01060]

Tonino,

A hasty line to say that thanks to your kind efforts. I've a lecture in Rochester April 28th in the morning, and will plan to come in the day before. Mrs [Jean] France couldn't have been nicer in working out a date to our mutual satisfaction. I'm lecturing all over the map this spring, and I think that she had to do a fair amount of swishing about to make room for me, and I am very appreciative. I plan to knock 'em into the aisles with: "The Roof is NOT the Place You Start," or maybe, with apologies to T. H. White, "Everything in Architecture that is Not Forbidden is Compulsory."[1]

1 The novelist T. H. White had once proposed "Everything which is not forbidden is compulsory" as the

Love to all,
Frank Borromini

[176]

[AH]
February 7th, 1978
19 East Boulevard, Rochester, New York 14610

[Letter, typed on a The University of Rochester, Department of English, letterhead, addressed to William MacDonald, (Auf Erd Ist nicht sein Gleichen[1]), 25 Henshaw Avenue, Northampton, Mass. 01060]

(midblizzard)

Your Reverence,

    Delighted by the establishment of the 28 of April as your lecture date here, and of your arrival the 27th. Your titles sound lovely, and could inaugurate a series that might contain "The Stones of Hoboken," "Distinctive Washroom Porcelains," "Great Hotel Fire-Escapes," and "A Brief Survey of Central Heating in Mohawk and Algonquin Teepees."

    It astonishes me that you should fail to recognize the name of the Revd. Fawcett, and claim never to have heard of him, since it was from you that I learned the following moving facts: "The Revd Elisha Fawcett, circa 1817, a Manchester Evangelist who devoted his life to teaching the natives of the Admiralty Islands the Commandments of God and the Laws of Cricket. Too poor to purchase a monument to this good man, his parishioners erected his wooden leg upon his grave. In that fertile climate it miraculously took root and for many years provided a bountiful harvest of bats."[2]

    It is ridiculous to be sitting here writing to you when the Rochester postal service has frankly abandoned all pretense to keeping to its motto about "faithful couriers"

---

principle of totalitarianism. See *The Sword in the Stone*, Book 1 of his novel, *The Once and Future King* (New York: G. P. Putnam's Sons, 1939).

1 German = "On earth he has no equal." This is a line from a psalm attributed to Martin Luther, "Ein feste Burg ist unser Gott" (= "A Mighty Fortress is Our God"). It is sometimes referred to as "The Battle Hymn of the Reformation."

2 An undated scrap of paper exists in the Hecht archive in Emory University's Woodruff Library (Box 110, Folder 10) on which AH had typed out this passage about the Reverend Fawcett, giving it the heading "Memo from Bill MacDonald." It would seem that after WLM denied being the source, AH concluded that it must have come from another old friend, and he drew a line through WLM's name and replaced it with that of Hays Rockwell. According to Helen Hecht, however, Hays Rockwell also denied knowing anything about the story, and AH never did find out who had sent it to him. The ultimate source appears to have been J. L. Carr's *Carr's Dictionary of Extra-ordinary English Cricketers* (Kettering, Northamptonshire: The Quince Tree Press, 1977), which reproduces the passage quoted here more or less word for word.

    The story's significance lies in the fact that it became the inspiration for AH's poem "A Bountiful Harvest," which he included in his fifth collection, *The Transparent Man*. AH was to send WLM a draft of it four years later (see Letter #297, July 10th, 1982), when the passage quoted here, only very slightly modified, appeared as its epigraph.

and their "appointed rounds." Postmen here have become a cynical lot; they sit around the post office, examining with candid envy the posted lists of wanted criminals, and quoting Seneca to the effect that the vices of one generation have become the habits of another. Fortunately, we are well-stocked with food, booze and fuel, so though you may not get this till the spring thaw be assured that we are all well.

       Timon of South Bend

[177]

[WLM]
February 10th, 1978
25 Henshaw Avenue, Northampton, Massachusetts 01060

[Blank postcard, typed, addressed to Professor and Mrs Anthony Evan Hecht, (A Fine Couple Indeed), 19 East Boulevard, Rochester NY 14610]

Dear Helen and Tony,

 The faithful Feds brang, as Pogo[1] used to say, a package from you this noon & I rush to the machine to send thanks for the wonderful Piranesi/Levit book[2] it enclosed (the package, not the machine). Do I detect some Evanesque lettering? I am most grateful. I'd not seen it. It's great. Many, many thanks. You may know that I'm in a small way becoming a Piranesi student, & have been able to acquire two or three more prints in recent years, one very fine, a small view of the early Vedute di Roma series, of the flank of the Aventine, where he was in time to place his only building, the great Santa Maria del Priorato. So the book, if possible, is even more welcome than it might otherwise have been. Swamped: guess who's Chair of the Lehmann[3] replacement committee; & who takes on 9 Spring lectures becz he likes the applause ...

       Love, Bill

---

1 A character in the long-running (1948-1975) newspaper comic strip of the same name created by the former Disney animator Walt Kelly.

2 *Views of Rome: Then and Now*, with illustrations by Giovanni Battista Piranesi and text by Herschel Levit (New York: Dover Publications Inc: 1976).

3 Phyllis Williams Lehmann, a classical archaeologist, had been a member of the Smith College faculty from 1946 until her retirement in 1978.

[178]

[WLM]
February 18th, 1978
25 Henshaw Avenue, Northampton, Massachusetts 01060

[Letter, typed on a Gramercy Park Hotel, New York, letterhead, with a now missing enclosure]

Y'Eminence,

In Pynchon's <u>The Crying of Lot 49</u>[1] there is as you probably know a poem of such splendor, of such a grand sweep, as to demand the close attention of us all. I quote what is probably the finest stanza from that masterpiece, "Baby Igor's Song" (You'll recall that Baby Igor, his father, and his dog are cruising off Gallipoli in the Dardanelles, in a midget submarine during 1915):

> 'Gainst the Hun and the Turk never once do we shirk
>   My daddy, my doggie, and me.
> Through the perilous years, like the Three Musketeers
>   We will stick just as close as can be.
> Soon our sub's periscope'll sight Constantinople,
>   As again we set hopeful to sea;
> Once more into the breach for those boys upon the beach,
>   Just my daddy, my doggie, and me.

I'm told you have some knowledge of poetry. If that is so, you will have felt your heart leap with joy at the effect, the sheer luminous beauty, of the great periscope line.

Well, my purpose is to ask you to set this to music, so that when I come to Rochester next month but one we will be able to sing it, adding, as it were, another dimension to this great work of art. Something in three parts, perhaps, the third for a schnauzer, or perhaps an Anatolian wolf-hound. But I leave that all up to you. I'm sure that you are the kind of person who can rise to a situation like this. Think of it as a commission if you like, from the Discalzed and Disgraced Order of Santa Fidgeta.

Do set to it right away. There's not all that much time.

            Yours in harmony,
            Father Messalina in Flagrante
            · O · OB · OBE · OBER · OBERST ·

P.S. Nick <u>may</u> come with me in April. OK?

P.P.S. I enclose a little something to stimulate your imagination. That's me at the furthest left, in disguise.

---

[1] Thomas Pynchon, *The Crying of Lot 49* (New York: Harper & Row, 1965).

[179]

[WLM]
February 27th, 1978
[25 Henshaw Avenue, Northampton, Massachusetts 01060]

[Italian postcard, with a photograph of the graves of John Keats and Joseph Severn in the Protestant Cemetery in Rome, handwritten, addressed to A · E · van Hecht, 19 E · Boulevard, Rochester · NY · 14610]

O Seer!

We here are unable to trace the source of "Millions of Strange Shadows" – Your own? The competition's? Do advise at leisure.

All's well,

James Auto-Bahn

[180]

[AH]
March 2nd, 1978
19 East Boulevard, Rochester, NY 14610

[Letter, typed, posted in a The University of Rochester envelope, addressed to William MacDonald, (Raconteur, Fox-trotter and Ornament of Society), 25 Henshaw Ave., Northampton, Mass. 01060]

Esteemed Greatness,

Let me answer some of your piled-up questions. It is, of course, fine with us if you bring Nick along. Barbara, too, for that matter. And we hope that you will plan to stay for the weekend. Is there anyone here you'd especially like to meet? Or would you prefer a private debauch?

"Millions of strange shadows" comes from the competition: Shakespeare's 53rd sonnet, the first two lines of which I quote in "A Birthday Poem."

I've started another long poem, but herewith I send a brief lyric.

> Who are the wise? Those first Athenian sages,
> Keen to resolve The Many and The One?
> Those who admonished from the earliest ages
> That there is no new thing under the sun?
>
> The Stoic of determined resignation
> Whose solitary goal is to endure?
> Erasmian Fools, pronounced "your only nation,"
> Their minds as simple as their hearts are pure?

> All such as suffered meekly in their time
> That they might persevere in History's books?
> Those who aspired to the high sublime,
> Or we, who are the husbands of great cooks?[1]
>
> Douglas Bush

[181]

[WLM]
March 3rd, 1978
[25 Henshaw Avenue, Northampton, Massachusetts 01060]

[Letter, typed on a Harvard Club of Boston, 374 Commonwealth Avenue, Boston, Massachusetts 02215, letterhead, with a now missing enclosure]

Dear Colonel,

Did you hear about the Englishman, the German, and the Pole who, upon arriving at the Olympic Games, found there were no seats to be had at any price? You haven't? Well, they were in despair, milling about and smacking their foreheads (each his own forehead), when the Englishman noted a length of pipe lying on the ground at a construction site. He stripped off his outer clothing in a flash of inspiration and, grabbing the pipe, sprinted through the contestants' gate in his shorts, shouting "England! Javelin! Smith-Waterford!"

The German quickly picked up a big stone, stripped to his shorts, and ran along behind, shouting "Schott-Putt! Germany! Hoffmann!" Both men were admitted without a murmur.

The Pole, grasping the point with admirable speed, quickly removed all his clothes except his underwear, speedily wrapped himself in the construction site's barbed wire, and tottered through the gate, yelling "Poland! Grabowski! Fencing!"

I enclose a picture of the family out shopping; they all send greetings.

With respect, and a few giggles,
Lucian K. Truscott V
Commanding

---

1 This poem remained uncollected.

[182]

[WLM]
March 8th, 1978
[25 Henshaw Avenue, Northampton, Massachusetts 01060]

[French postcard, with a photograph of the tympanum over the western porch of the Saint Julian Cathedral in Le Mans, showing Christ in the centre, and on either side of him the symbols of the four Evangelists, handwritten, addressed to A. E. Hecht, 19 E. Boulevard, Rochester, NY, 14610]

Dear Merlin:

    That's me in the center, flanked by jealous faculty members; students below, in their places ... Barbara would like to come, not sure about time away; advise later. We expect to drive out Thurs. 27, back Sat. (mountains of work). 3's a lot – motel for B. + me? Looking forward to it muchly. Can't think of any invitees.

Yrs, Arthur

[183]

[WLM]
March 14th, 1978
25 Henshaw Avenue, Northampton, Massachusetts 01060

[Blank postcard, typed, with the sender's address given as Karl Ph. Emm. Bloch, 25 H / 01060, addressed to Ill. no. Prof. Anthony Hecht, 19 East Boulevard, Rochester NY, 14610]

Poet:

    Did you know that Elbert Hubbard's <u>Message to Garcia</u>, which sold some fifty million copies, was once distributed to the <u>entire</u> Japanese army? I lie about thinking about this. It is probably the single most staggering fact I've ever possessed. Let me have your reactions to it.[1]

Me

[184]

[AH]
March 21st, 1978
[19 East Boulevard, Rochester, NY 14610]

[Letter, typed on a The University of Rochester, Department of English, letterhead, with a now missing enclosure]

Offendi (Arabic parlance)

Thought you might he innerrested in the enclosed which appeared in the March issue of the <u>Bulletin</u> of the American Academy of Arts & Sciences. Have they polled you about translation needs? The project seems innerresting to me, and think of what would be involved if they expanded from architectural history to plain old art history. That could go on for ever.

We seem to be thawing out over here. Temperatures in the unheard-of 50's.

Where did you get all those pictures of your Slavic relatives?

Winifred of South Bend

[185]

[AH]
March 22nd, 1978
19 East Boulevard, Rochester, NY 14610

[Letter, typed on a The University of Rochester, Department of English, letterhead, addressed to William MacDonald (author of this and that), 25 Henshaw Avenue, Northampton, Mass. 01060]

> Asked what he teaches, Senex makes reply,
> "Students," with a lewd twinkle in his eye;
> And woe to those who study, in his class,
> If not a Chiron, then a horse's ass.

[Unsigned]

---

1   Elbert Hubbard's *A Message to Garcia* (East Aurora, NY: Roycrofters Press, 1899) is, as one source has it, an "inspirational" essay about a soldier who "takes the initiative to accomplish a daunting and difficult task, and who, without questions or objections, graciously accomplishes his task."

[186]

[WLM]
April 4th, 1978
25 Henshaw Avenue, Northampton, Massachusetts 01060

[Letter, typed on a Fogg Art Museum, Harvard University, Cambridge, Massachusetts 02138, letterhead, posted in an envelope with the sender's address given as Baby LeRoy, 25 H / 01060, addressed to Sig. Anthony Hecht, Mkaer / Braeker of Rules, 19 East Boulevard, Rochester NY 14610]

God's Feet!

I'd hoped that Nick & B[arbara] would come along, and that we would drive, but as I said, I'll almost certainly be alone. Thus I fly, and I find that the only flight on the 27th, Thursday, that would work is Allegheny 365 early in the morning, arriving in Rochester at 8:02 a.m.. The alternative would be to take that flight the next day, go right to the lecture, and then join you. What do you think? If I did the latter, I'd stay over Friday night & come back Saturday. It is I suppose risky to fly out on the day of the lecture, so perhaps 8 a.m. on Thursday the 27th is in the cards ...

The situation with regard to Dale is confusing. Her sister calls and says the end is near, that someone of us must be there; the MD says she will live a year or two and Noel, who just came back from Denver, says the real problem is that the chemotherapy affects her so strongly that she cannot eat properly. He and I and Nick will sit down tonight and talk things out; Noel is just back & not quite recovered from night coach flights that go to Denver by way of Anchorage, or somewhere.

Did I tell you about <u>The Message to Garcia</u>? (<u>A Message</u> ...?). If I did not, please ask, with a SASE. Whoops,

Publius Invidious Nasal

[Handwritten note on back of envelope]

+ Thanks for the AA+S <u>Bulletin</u> clipping on translating architectural history. [Hank] Millon, in charge, is an old friend, but he's not communicated with me. I want to translate Cleo's comments on Anthony's accommodations for her ... Nick has borrowed "Venetian Vespers," which he loves, so soon you will be famous at U. Mass.!

[187]

[WLM]
April 11th, 1978
25 Henshaw Avenue, Northampton, Massachusetts 01060

[Blank postcard, typed, addressed to Mr and Mrs Anthony Hecht, 19 East Boulevard, Rochester NY 14610]

Dear Helen & Tony,
Would you ask Leon Satkowski, Prof. Archit., Univ. Syr., 103 Slocum Hall, Syracuse 13210, to dinner on the night of the 27th? Great tall, 30's, bright archt/arch'l historian, a bit angular, a good friend, a Vasari expert, e un vero italiano. I <u>think</u> you'd like him, though I'm bound to say he's a bit eccentric (but well-mannered) ... Dale was operated on again yesterday and the news is not good. The boys are beginning to show signs of strain. Noel was just with her 8 days back. Prognosis unclear as we await detailed word which should come today ... Looking forward immensely to seeing you.
                    Love,
                    Sixtus V Peretti

[188]

[AH]

[Some time between April 13th and 23rd, 1978]
[19 East Boulevard, Rochester, NY 14610]

[Letter, typed on an Iowa Memorial Union, University of Iowa, letterhead, with enclosure]

[Enclosure: clipping]

Ya gotta be livin' in a pretty fuckin' sophisticated community to get ads like this one. And always remember, – incest, like charity, begins at home. We have invited your crazy Polish friend from Syracuse. He hasn't answered yet; probably looking for someone to read the letter to him. Which reminds me, did I write you about the Pole who flung himself to the ground, and missed?

I think yer best plan is to show up with the rosy-fingered dawn the day before yer talk. Remind me again of yer arrival time. There's a new I. M. Pei bldg. here I think you'd like; I'm told it's a small version of his thing for the National Gallery in Washington.

       Frobenius

[189]

[WLM]
[April 23rd, 1978]
25 Henshaw Avenue, Northampton, Massachusetts 01060

[Blank postcard, typed, addressed to Anthony Hecht, Boulevardier extraordinaire,
19 East Boulevard, Rochester NY, 14610]

Eminenza,

 I'm bringing a bowl of goldfish to be named by your buddy. OK? And yes, I'm arriving early, 8:02 a.m. the day before*. Allegheny no. 365. Can't figure out any other way to do it, so you're stuck with me. Nick & I, had he been able to come, would have driven out together; he's taken a leave from college & is now in Denver with Dale; last night he told me that he thought she'd prob. never leave the hospital. I assume my lecture is still on. I never had any communication from Mrs [Jean] France other than that first telephone call; I hope she got my note about the title, etc. Looking forward, etc.

      Yours in florbity,
      Billy the Boy Artist

* 27th

Just back from Texas, where I saw Frank & J[ackie] [Brown], where the azaleas have already gone by ...

[190]

[AH]
May 2nd, 1978
[19 East Boulevard, Rochester, NY 14610]

[Letter, typed on a Brandeis University, Department of English and American Literature,
Waltham, Massachusetts 02154, letterhead]

Dear Right Honorable,

 We were delighted to have you here, howsoever briefly; but now that you know there is something of architectural interest hereabouts maybe you'll stay longer on your next visit. Meanwhile know that all three of us were gratified by your visit, and I have monopolized your gift of the Book of Lists. More of that in a moment.

The lines from the poem you inquired about are the last half of the fourth stanza of a twelve-stanza poem by Auden, titled "A Summer Night," of which the first line goes, "Out on the lawn I lie in bed." You should have no trouble finding it; it's on page 69 of the <u>Collected Shorter Poems</u>.[1]

As for the book of lists, it has encouraged me to manufacture a few lists of my own, of which one is a list of errors in the book itself. On the whole they are rather cagey, and avoid being caught out by presenting "random" lists, like, "Ten Great Barbers," as contrasted with The Ten Greatest, etc. Still, they are guilty of a number of bloopers. But their concluding request for help from their readers is so disarming that I'm inclined to rush to their aid, and in this respect I seek your help. What they clearly need almost as much as anything is a list of our lecture topics. Of these I seem able to recall only four at present: GREAT HATS I HAVE WORN, THE PHLOGISTON THEORY: IS IT MAKING A COMEBACK?, LITTLE-KNOWN FACTS IN THE SEX-LIFE OF HARRIET BEECHER STOWE, and FAMOUS STREETCAR ACCIDENTS. I hope you can somehow lay your hands on the rest of that fine list; I want to send it to them in both our names, and with an outline of our lecture circuit plans. I shall also try to send as much as I can recall of Robert Graves's list of great literary non-swimmers.

It is much too late now to hope for any good news from Denver. And I know that you and your sons have before you only crisis and grief. I wish there were some useful, or even graceful, thing to be said or done. Lacking all that, I send my love.

Tony

---

1 W. H. Auden, *Collected Shorter Poems: 1930-1944* (London: Faber & Faber, 1950). The lines WLM must have been inquiring about read as follows: "The lion griefs loped from the shade / And on our knees their muzzles laid, / And Death put down his book."

[191]

[WLM]
May 2nd, 1978
[25 Henshaw Avenue, Northampton, Massachusetts 01060]

[Postcard, with a photograph of Edward S. Bartholomew's sculpture, "Repentant Eve," handwritten, addressed to Mr + Mrts Anthony Hecht, 19 East Boulevard, Rochester NY, 14610]

↗ disconsolate student who got a C–

Dear Helen and Tony –

It was awfully good to be with you for two days, and I am grateful for your hospitality. What a fine thing it is to have good friends. And I much enjoyed looking at buildings, esp. the Frank Lloyd Wright house. A small thank-you gift is on the way to you, in affectionate friendship and with warmest greetings.

Yours,
Bill

[192]

[WLM]
May 13th, 1978
[25 Henshaw Avenue, Northampton, Massachusetts 01060]

[Letter, typed on a Tom Sawyer Motor Inns, Albany, New York, letterhead, posted in the same company's envelope, addressed to Anthony Hecht, poetaster, 19, East Boulevard, Rochester NY 14610]

Dear Customer,

Is it true that you are being considered for the Chair of Polish Culture at Kanakee State Teachers'? I heard that in New York at Le Pavilion …

The titles you want, in addition to the memorable ones you have listed in yours of the 2nd inst., are

LITTLE Women

Oops, that's the only one I can recall now. Perhaps there were only five titles. As I remember it we were going to offer various package deals, expensive yes, with one option where we both spoke at once or, at the refined kind of joint, a kind of stichomythia thing, speaking our alternate lines like the Gondolier kings …

Noel has gone to Denver for a few days but none of us has hope of knowing any more than we do now.

Thanks for the Auden reference; I couldn't remember where I'd seen and more or less learned it from (How's that for a sentence?). Someone has sent me a new book by a scholar claiming to be Helen Gardner, and it's all about the mss. of Eliot's 4 Quartets.[1] At first I was a little put off by the minutiae, but I really got interested in the parts about Cape Ann & Gloucester, where as you know I spend some time every summer. I'd no idea that Hayward et al. were responsible for so many (good) alterations, even lines. But the book costs a half-zillion dinars, so don't buy it. You can rent my copy.

Love to you all,
J. P. Schwartz

---

1 Helen Gardner, *The Composition of Four Quartets* (Boston, MA: Faber & Faber, 1978).

[193]

[WLM]
[? May 15th, 1978]
[25 Henshaw Avenue, Northampton, Massachusetts 01060]

[Postcard, with a photograph of the Old Heidelberg Restaurant, New Haven, Connecticut, addressed to A. E. Hecht, polymath, 19 East Blvd, Rochester NY, 14610, with enclosed clipping, and beneath it, WLM's handwritten comment]

14 The properties of phlogiston were first described by G. E. Stahl, of Cavorite by H. G. Wells, of vril by Bulwer Lytton, of mithril by Tolkien and of ice-9 by Kurt Vonnegut.

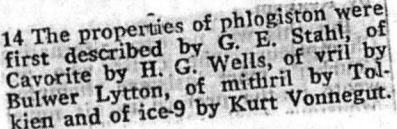

and Filboid Studge?[1]

[Unsigned]

[194]

[WLM]
May [28th], 1978
25 Henshaw Avenue, Northampton, Massachusetts 01060

[Blank postcard, typed, addressed to Mr and Mrs Anthony Hecht, 19 East Boulevard, Rochester NY 14610]

Monday

Dear Helen & Tony,

Just a line to say that Dale died yesterday morning. Noel had gone out Friday so both boys were there with her. They are holding up very well so far, but from experience my guess is that it hasn't hit them fully yet. Noel's wedding will go on quietly as planned, next Sunday. I'm all right, but if it weren't for Noel and Nicholas I'd be worse off.

Love,
Bill

---

1 "Filboid studge" is the name of a breakfast cereal which figures in Saki's short story of the same name.

[195]

[AH]
May 31st, 1978
[19 East Boulevard, Rochester, NY 14610]

[Letter, typed on a The University of Rochester, Department of English, letterhead]

Dear Bill,
 I know that just now you must be deeply concerned with how Noel and Nick are bearing up. But if after seeing them through this critical period you feel the need of company yourself, either to talk with, or simply to be with silently, I hope you know we would welcome you. Meanwhile, I send love to you and your sons.
Tony

[196]

[WLM]
June 6th, 1978
25 Henshaw Avenue, Northampton, Massachusetts 01060

[Blank postcard, typed, addressed to A E Hecht, 19 East Boulevard, Rochester NY 14610]

Dear Tony,
 Thanks so much for your sweet note of the 31st. Things have gone well. The boys handled everything in Denver magnificently; being kept so busy helped. They flew back Friday last and in a whirl we got Noel married Sunday; he is now resting with Ellen on some Bermuda beach and Nick and I are fine. There has not been a great deal of grief, partly because the end was expected for so long and for Dale to live would have been unthinkable. Now I must go to California to see my oldest friend, Lanny Larson, who is dying of cancer. I don't know how long I'll be gone. His wife is largely incoherent on the telephone but wants me to come; a son is near so they are not without support. Nick takes me to the plane now,
 Again, thanks, Tony.
Bill

[197]

WLM
[June 20th, 1978]
25 Henshaw Avenue, Northampton, Massachusetts 01060

[Message, handwritten on a flier originally addressed to WLM, but re-addressed by WLM to Anthony Hecht + Co., 19 E. Boulevard, Rochester, NY 14610]

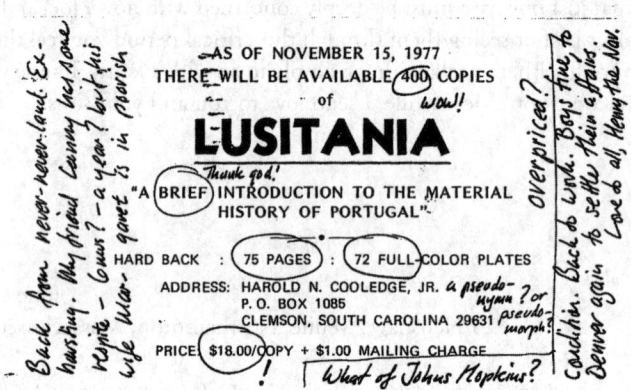

[198]

[AH]
July 6th, 1978
19 East Boulevard, Rochester, NY 14610

[Letter, typed]

Dear Consumer,

I came across a text I thought you might not know of, and might like. It comes from the <u>Legenda Aurea</u> by Jacobus de Voragine,[1] who throve and wrote in the thirteenth century. "When the Romans were masters of the whole world, they built a very large temple, in the middle of which they set up a statue of their own god, and placed the gods of all the provinces in a circle about him, with their faces uplifted to the god of Rome. If at any time one of the provinces rebelled, it is said that instantly, by the Devil's magic, the idol of that province turned his back upon the god of the Romans, as if to show that he had defected from his lord. The Romans then made haste to dispatch a large army to that province, and reduced it to subjection. But

---

1 Jacobus de Voragine, *The Golden Legend*, translated by William G. Ryan and Helmut Ripperger (London: Longmans, Green & Co., 1941).

the Romans were not content to have the idols of all the provinces in their city. In addition, they built separate temples to each of the gods, as if honoring them for having made Rome the conqueror and mistress of the whole world. Yet since it was not possible for each and every god to have a temple, the Romans, the better to show forth their folly, erected one temple higher and more wondrous than all the others, dedicated it to all the gods, and called it the Pantheon, which name means "all the gods," and comes from pan, which means all, and theos, god. For the priests of the idols, in order the more fully to delude the people, pretended that they had received a command from Cybele, the mother of all the gods, that if they wished to obtain victory over every people, they should erect a magnificent temple to all her children. The foundation of this temple was circular, to signify the eternity of the gods. But since it seemed to them that the vault of the building would be too wide to be supported, as soon as they built up the walls to a certain height, they filled the whole interior with earth, and threw coins in with the earth; and so they proceeded until the edifice was complete. They then declared that anyone who wished to carry away the earth that was in the temple might keep what money he found; whereupon the crowd right speedily emptied the building of earth. Finally the Romans constructed a gilded bronze battlement, and set it at the summit of the temple. And it is said that upon this battlement they placed statues representing each of the provinces, so that anyone who came to Rome might know in which direction his province lay. In time, however, this battlement collapsed, and left an opening in the roof."

Love,
Debussy Fields

[199]

[WLM]
July 12th, 1978
25 Henshaw Avenue, Northampton, Massachusetts 01060

[Letter, typed, addressed to Anthony Hecht (Martial reincarnate),
19, East Boulevard, Rochester NY 14610]

Julius Caesar's 2,080th birthday, & my 57th, god help us all]

Dear Junior Citizen,

The poem in the TLS[1] is perfectly placed, and very good and funny. Congratulations. I'm sure the dons are all a-chuckle. It's awfully good. And not just funny.

I knew the salted-earth story about the Big Dome, but not in the version you so kindly typed out for me. Many thanks; I'm sure I'll make use of it, with a credit

---

1 "An Old Malediction" was printed in the July 7th, 1978 issue of the *Times Literary Supplement*, and was subsequently collected in *The Venetian Vespers*.

line to my heroine, Miss Modene Gunch of Lubbock, TX, who was as you probably know Miss Vacant Lot of 1976 (I'm not joking).[1] The details about the battlement and the provinces are very fine; I've not yet had the chance to check to see whether the works of my old pal Tillmann Budenseig (again I'm not joking; I know you wish I were) at the Frei Universität in Berlin, who writes on the Big Dome in the Middle Ages now and again, has this material. If he doesn't, I'll wise him up.

When will "Venetian Vespers" appear? Or is it out arreddy?

Here things are fairly calm. Nick and Noel got back from the last trip to Denver pulling a big U-Haul trailer full of furniture and such; both are working for Smith; poor Noel has not even yet heard from any law schools, which we cannot understand but which I must say he is taking in good order. Barbara comes out now & again – we are going to Maine this coming weekend where I'll attend the 40th reunion of my High School class, perhaps for only ten minutes – and our relationship is sort of resting and sorting itself out a little.

Love to yawl,
A. Pismo Clam

P.S. When next you write, would you give me the bibliographical & page data on the Jake de Vee passage? All honor to thee.

[200]

[AH]
July 16th, 1978
[19 East Boulevard, Rochester, NY 14610]

[Letter, typed]

Hail, Caesar (and Happy Birthday!)

Thanks for your note about the Malediction. I've just translated another poem, this one by Ronsard, and called, "Invective Against Denise, a Witch,"[2] and Helen has pointed out to me that, what with all these poems attacking women, even though they are translations everyone will assume that our marriage is on the rocks, or at least that I am an obsessive M. C. Pig. As for "Venetian Vespers," <u>Poetry</u> has

---

1 WLM had first mentioned Ms Gunch in letter #95, dated October 15th, 1973, and he will mention her again in letter #353, dated August 29th, 1984, so it may be worth correcting a few small errors in his account: the winner was Modine (not Modene) Gunch, her full title was Miss Vacant Lot of the World (not Miss Vacant Lot), and she secured it in 1973 (not 1976). The inquisitive reader may also be gratified to learn from the April 26th, 1987 issue of *The Victoria Advocate* that Ms Gunch "received international acclaim for her efforts, which, according to news accounts and an article in *Playboy* magazine, included standing on one hand, upside down, while twirling a hoop from one leg to the other, dressed in a skimpy halter top and wearing hot pants." The whole article can be read online at http://news.google.com/newspapers?nid=861&dat=19670426&id=HLUdAAAAIBAJ&sjid=_FgEAAAAIBAJ&pg=6737,6210420

2 The poem was first published in *The American Scholar*, 48:4 (Autumn 1979), pp. 499-501, and was subsequently included in *The Venetian Vespers*.

decided to hold it till their October issue, for make-up convenience of their own. I don't really mind, because the chances are that if it came out in the summer no one much would see it. I've also written another long (419 line) poem, this one set in Amurikuh with a woman for its central figure.[1]

As for your inquiries about old Jacobus, let me say that the passage I quoted was from the comparatively modern (1941) translation by Granger Ryan and Helmut Ripperger, published by Longmans, Green & Co. The great and famous translation is, of course, Caxton's, of 1483, which I believe is published in the Temple Classics Edition. In both cases the passage occurs in the section on All Hallows (November 1) and in the Longmans edition this begins on page 640. I hope you have no trouble finding it (I'll be glad to make a Xerox of my own copy, if that will help) and I hope you can make good use of it.

We are all well, and happy, and I am to be one of the three judges in poetry for the National Book Award this year.

Love,
Timon of Buzzard's Gulch

[201]

[WLM]
July 20th, 1978
25 Henshaw Avenue, Northampton, Massachusetts 01060

[Blank postcard, typed, addressed to A. E. Hecht, genius, 19 East Boulevard, Rochester NY 14610, with the sender's address given as me/XXV Hen/01060]

Dear Timon,

Thanks for the Jacobus data. "Malediction" gives a lot of pleasure: I've read it to any number of friends and strangers. Is it a translation/paraphrase? If so, of what? Or is it unadulterated Hecht? I'm sure it's the latter, but the wording of your July 16th letter makes me wonder a bit ... Forgot to say that the earth-salted-with-coins story was also told of Brunelleschi's Florentine dome.

I am writing again, which makes me feel Good. Many projects for half-time, which makes me feel Good. So I'm feeling pretty good. Noel still hasn't heard from any law schools, and we are now hearing horror stories about admissions appearing after Labor Day ... Now that you are an NBA poetry judge, I guess I'll submit some of my cherce limericks.

Love to all,
Chuck Kling

---

1 This was "The Short End," which was also included in *The Venetian Vespers*.

[202]

[AH]
July 23rd, 1978
19 East Boulevard [Rochester, NY 14610]

[Letter, typed on a The University of Rochester, Department of English, letterhead]

Dear Breather,

A new News Bulletin from the Academy in Rome carries a lot of up-to-date data on my recent activities. Was that supplied by you, by any chance?

I'm sorry I can't take complete credit for MALEDICTION; it is in fact a mod version of the fifth ode of the first book of Horace.

I finished the second long poem, now titled THE SHORT END, and am off on another in which the speaker is an aging chambermaid in a European resort hotel.[1] What I'm hoping for from all this, of course, is a Hollywood studio snapping up these poems for their plots and characters, and paying me enormous sums, first for the rights to use the poems as the basis for films, and then to turn them into original screenplays. I'll let you know what happens.

Love,
Paracelsus

[203]

[AH]
July 25th, 1978
19 East Boulevard, Rochester, NY 14610

[Letter, typed on a The University of Rochester, Department of English, letterhead]

Dear Bill,

If you could without great inconvenience help me out in a matter concerning a painting I'd be much obliged. The painting is by Renoir, it's dated 1872, and called "Parisian Women Dressed in Algerian Costume." It hangs in the National Museum of Western Art in Tokyo. The best reproduction I can find of it, which leaves much to be desired, is in black and white, and appears in <u>Mnemosene: The Parallel Between Literature and the Visual Arts</u>, by Mario Praz.[2] There are a lot of things in that picture I can't read, partly for lack of color, no doubt from reduction in size. But in the hope that you can lay your hands on a good reproduction among your own books or the Smith archives I have a number of questions to ask. 1) With regard to the woman in the background with her back to the viewer: is she looking

---

[1] "The Grapes," first published in *The American Scholar*, 48:1 (Winter 1979), pp. 61-64, and subsequently collected in *The Venetian Vespers*.

[2] Mario Praz, *Mnemosene: The Parallel Between Literature and the Visual Arts* (Princeton, NJ: Princeton University Press, 1967).

at a painting or a mirror? The woman left foreground is taking at least momentary notice of her in a pause during making up the central woman. If that's a mirror in the background, the woman regarding it has apparently already been made up by the same cosmetic artist, and is now admiring the effect, while the artist pauses to listen to her praise. If a picture, though little enough of it is shown, it might be another exotic, Algerian one (by Ingres? Delacroix?) and the background woman is reporting cosmetic effects to the foreground artist, who is trying to put them into practice on the central subject. 2) What is the curious, fluffy thing on the carpet beside the sandal? 3) What is the pendant that the artist seems to hold in her left hand? 4) What is the background behind the artist? We must assume that the literal setting is a Paris apartment that these women have tried to redesign to resemble a sultry harem or desert tent. 5) Am I right in thinking I see a parquet floor at the lower left?

All these bear upon a poem I'd like to write,[1] and I'd be more grateful than I can say if you could help. I report with chagrin that neither the Rochester Memorial Art Gallery nor the Art Library of the University was able to help me in any way.

We send our love,
Tony

[204]

[WLM]
July 28th, 1978
[25 Henshaw Avenue, Northampton, Massachusetts 01060]

Letter, typed on a Driskill Hotel, 117 East Seventh Street, Austin, Texas 78701, letterhead, posted in the same hotel's envelope, addressed to Anthony Hecht, unequalled, 19, East Boulevard, Rochester NY 14610]

Dear Doktuh Ehkehtuh,

The Committee has had two meetings, with a fairly good black-and-white reproduction in front of it, and has come to the following conclusions and non-conclusions (try <u>that</u> !):

1. We're pretty sure the woman is looking at a painting. It is very large and has a big, heavy frame around it, though nothing of the painting itself is visible. I can't find a color reproduction. We think your theory that the painting-within-a-painting is by Delacroix, and that Renoir is showing us his girls getting up a tableau of that painting, is v. persuasive.

2. The curious, fluffy thing by the sandal, is a feathery ankle bracelet, of the kind beside the left foot of the girl farthest to the right. It is one of a number of costumeries lying about.

3. The pendant the make-up kid is holding in her left hand is, we think, a piece of jewelry, though a) we're not certain, and b) we can't figure out why she should

---

1 The poem became "The Deodand," which was first published in *The Kenyon Review*, 1:1 (New Series), Winter 1979, and was then included in *The Venetian Vespers*.

have it in her hand at this juncture in the proceedings.

4. The background behind the artist is two more or less Algerian hangings, blowing in toward the girls. The diamonds atop and the border below are much like an Algerian hanging (a blanket) right in front of the Committee as it sat in my living room, one I bought (the blanket, not the living room) in the Aurès mountains in 1967 no kidding.

5. The floor under the two rugs is definitely a quadrillage, but whether it is parquet or flagging we can't be sure; the pattern, however, and the size of its elements, cause us to lean toward stone flagging or tiling.

Our reprod. is in Francois Posca, <u>Renoir: His Life and Work</u>. Prentice-Hall 1962, p. 36.

The long poem has come but I've not had a chance to read it yet. Finally, I want to say that this stationery comes from the Driskill, a fact that might have escaped your attention.[1]

      Yours in Christ Our Mother,
      A. Pismo Clam

Academy Bulletin, new style: No, source not me!

[Handwritten note on reverse side of the envelope]

Dinner w/ Ralph + Fanny [Ellison], Wilburs, Russell Lyneses last night – many compliments to you + Helen; Ralph loud.

[205]

[AH]
July 30th, 1978
19 East Boulevard, Rochester, NY 14610

[Letter, typed on a Brandeis University, Department of English and American Literature, letterhead, with a now missing enclosure]

May it please Your Majesty,

I suppose you came across the enclosed splendid picture yourself in today's <u>Times</u>, and that even if you missed it crowds of colleagues and local types have clipped and sent it to you.[2] But just to be safe, here it is; and a gorgeous thing, too.

I've been reading all sorts of books at the same time, some for fun and some for duty. The duty has to do with serving on a literary jury that awards prizes in fiction,

---

1 The Driskill name is repeated in large display type seventeen times down the left margin of their letterhead.

2 Several trawls through the 351-page *New York Times* for this day have unearthed no obvious candidate for the cutting AH refers to here.

non-fiction and poetry.[1] For IT I am currently reading a Best Seller – which is not my normal run of reading – called <u>The World According to Garp</u>.[2] I am astonished at how thin it is. By contrast, for fun I am reading Peter Blake's <u>Form Follows Fiasco</u>.[3] He is witty, makes sense and writes well. And since he writes on a serious subject, it virtually follows that his book is NOT a Best Seller. In addition to the jury above mentioned I have agreed to be on the poetry jury of the National Book Awards for this year. I figure it will probably not involve much extra reading, since I have to read poetry for the jury I'm already on anyway. But this looks like a busy year.

The week of August 20th we three are going to NYC, there to spend a week or ten days in the apartment of some friends who are out of town for the summer.[4] No doubt it will be hot and hateful and just the sort of weather New Yorkers strive to avoid. But it's not always we are offered a large, well-situated apartment free. Is there any crazy possibility that business or pleasure might bring you to the city during that time? We would offer you some very good food and drink, though I fear we could not in fairness offer you the hospitality of our own hosts – viz., a place in their apartment. But in order to make the proposal the more attractive let me add that Helen is presently engaged, in collaboration with a friend and neighbor of ours and mother of one of Evan's schoolmates, in writing an original cook book. To that end she has prepared a great array of splendid fare, and talks with excitement of stunning our friends in NY. If you could contrive to come in while we were there it would be a fine thing.

Richard the Chicken-Livered

[206]

[WLM]
August 11th, 1978
25 Henshaw Avenue, Northampton, Massachusetts 01060

[Blank postcard, typed, with the sender's address given as Hadrian Caes Imp, XXV Henshaw, 01060, addressed to Mr & Mrs A. E. Hecht, 19 East Boulevard, Rochester NY 14610]

Dear Helen & Tony,
All set for the 24th. Should I have a name on a button / mailbox? I've noted the

---

1 The committee in question was the Literary Awards Committee of the American Academy of Arts and Letters.

2 John Irving, *The World According to Garp* (New York: E. P. Dutton, 1976). This was Irving's fourth novel. Its hardback edition was a finalist for the National Book Award for fiction in 1979, and its paperback edition won the same prize in 1980.

3 Peter Blake, *Form Follows Fiasco: Why Modern Architecture Hasn't Worked* (Boston, MA: Little Brown, 1977).

4 The apartment belonged to Hays and Linda Rockwell.

address, 320 E. 72nd St.

And thanks for the clipping. I had seen it in the <u>Times</u>, but it is good to know that you are alert out there in Roch., keeping my interests in mind. No, didn't have anything to do with the Hecht entry in the snazzy new Academy bulletin; don't know who did that. Met young John Peck, poet, who goes now to the Academy. Yes, Peter Blake is smart and readable. I've not read <u>Form Follows Fiasco</u>, but did read his <u>Le Corbusier</u>[1] & learned & liked.

Nick wanted to come to NY with me, but I felt he shouldn't take so much time off from his job, & promised him a weekend there in the fall. My friend Lanny is v. ill, probably won't be able to make the trip East, judging from a pathetic letter than came today from his wife.

Love to all,
Marta Thatcher

[207]

[AH]
August 14th, 1978
19 East Boulevard, Rochester, New York 14610

[Letter, typed on a The University of Rochester, Rochester, New York 14627, Department of English, Morey Hall, letterhead, with a now missing enclosure]

Dear Bill,

I thought you might like to see the poem you were good enough to help me with.[2]

I'm now at work on a little song. It's not finished yet, but the ending goes,

> O say does that star-spangled banner yet wave
> O'er the pools of the rich and the homes of the swave?

We hope you can meet us in NY later this month.

Where, by the way, did that august dinner with Wilburs, Lyneses and Ellisons[3] take place?

C. T. Onions

---

1 Peter Blake, *Le Corbusier: Architecture and Form* (Baltimore, MD: Penguin, 1960).

2 AH had enclosed a draft of "The Deodand."

3 Richard and Charlee Wilbur, Russell and Mildred Lynes, Ralph and Fanny Ellison.

[208]

[WLM]
August 19th, 1978
25 Henshaw Avenue, Northampton, Massachusetts 01060

[Letter, typed on a Santa Barbara Biltmore Hotel and Cottages, Montecito, Santa Barbara, California letterhead, addressed to Anthony Hecht, 19, East Boulevard, Rochester NY 14610, with two enclosures, one now missing]

O Seer:

Jess run yore finner over that there printin', Bub …

Off to The Hub to see D'Oyly Carte's <u>Iolanthe</u>. Was it not the patter song therefrom that brought us together in Yehudi [Wyner]'s studio that night in '54?

I like the Deodand, but can't quite connect the title with the poem.[1] The only (v. tiny) thing that I question is "the old queen": I know of course what you mean, but the uneducated masses will think of her as old in years, perhaps …?[2]

I look forward to seeing you in New York next week. Sounds like good fun.

The dinner with the Ellisons & Co. was at Ralph's and Fanny's very nice hideaway in the Berkshires, in Plainfield, actually, perhaps forty minutes from here. There was still another couple there, the Nathan Scotts, he a black Prof. from some big southren university or other. He was almost as noisy as Ralph. It was a good evening, and we were glad we went, but I was just a little itchy about Ralph's shouting, esp, at Fanny. Dick and I sat quietly through part of it, talking about Owen Barfield.

The news from San Jose is very bad, and I am beginning to think about another trip out. I don't quite know how to handle it, but then, no one would.

My own work goes along well, but more of that in The Big Apricot.

Soon, then,
Aunt Tizzy Payshun

[Enclosure: a message typed on the back of a library index card]

Antoninus (Pius?):

Would you when you have an opportunity criticize this for me, as if I were one of your duller students?[3] All thanks. In Cassius Dio[4] 49.9 we are told that Hadrian had the First Batavians swim the Danube, to the consternation of the barbarians.

---

1 WLM must have seen a draft of AH's poem "The Deodand."

2 AH does seem to have taken WLM's advice on this, replacing the draft version's "old queen" with the published version's "once queen."

3 The missing enclosure was a poem. All attempts to track this down have unfortunately proved fruitless.

4 Cassius Dio's *Roman History*, which covers the last years of the Roman Republic and the early years of the Roman Principate.

Yours,
Mc

[209]

[AH]
September 1st, 1978
19 East Boulevard, Rochester, NY 14610

[Letter, typed on a The University of Rochester, Department of English, letterhead]

Dear Bill,

I'm delighted by your poem, "Hadrian Orders the First Batavians to Swim the Danube." Whatever delay there may have been in this letter of mine I hope you will excuse on the grounds that, after our frenetic week in New York, I returned to accumulated mail that demanded instant attention, along with the making out of syllabi for my courses, and I have only just waded past the worst of these duties. So at length I can turn to more pleasurable tasks. The poem, as I say, is fine. The first part of it seems to me especially successful, <u>exactly</u> conveying that insufferable arrogance of high-ranking officers who, under the guise of undertaking no more than the enlisted men, show off with useless feats of strength or daring – though always in matters of their own choice, and at their chosen time and place (as contrasted with being ordered to do something you don't feel like doing, or that you are simply incapable of doing) and supremely without regard to the cost in life to others of such heartless ostentations. The smug, vain, unawareness of Hadrian, the decent compassion of the veteran who speaks, are both clear and telling.

I am, however, less certain of the propriety of the <u>tone</u> in the last part. The propriety, that is to say, of the explicit <u>complaint</u>. After all, when a soldier signs up, he is, for the term of his service, putting his life itself on the line whenever it's called for. No doubt it can be called for foolishly, to no great purpose, merely for the convenience of the top brass. You and I both know of such behavior from our own war experiences. I myself remember a particular example. My regiment was stationed on the west bank of the Rhine, across from Cologne. The east bank of the river was fortified by a very high, immensely thick wall of reinforced concrete. Orders came down from, not merely Division, but from Corps or perhaps even from Army, to send out scouting expeditions at night in rubber boats, to reconnoiter the far side of the river. Two companies (not my own, thank God) were chosen, in both of which I had friends, to perform this foolish, pointless and costly errand. They went out at night in rubber boats, were spotted by enemy searchlights above those walls, and were ruthlessly machine-gunned in the middle of the river. This happened not once or twice but time after time, and there was no information to be gotten, even had the enemy not fired a shot, except the fact that there was a thick concrete wall on the far side – a fact which you could tell by looking across the river in the day time. This, however, took place during our division's first three weeks of actual combat; and the speculation throughout my own company on the reason for this mindless massacre was simply that our Division Commander, who had himself never committed any troops to combat, was too scared to disobey one of his first combat orders – to conduct reconnaissance of a specified kind. It was my first real insight into the way wars are regularly waged. Outraged, however, as my feelings were then and still are, it would never occur to me, in a mild and reasonable tone, to argue with the general on what he has a right to do, on what we've signed up for, on Justice. What I guess, after all this palaver, I'm getting to is perhaps merely the excision of about two and a half lines. I'm happy with everything up through "rivers even broader / Than the Danube; swifter, too." I would be happy to take up again with, "There's no Leander here in camp / Nor any Hero past the swell." It's the intervening lines that a little bother me with their attempt at adjudication, at ironic reasonableness, and so on. I'm sure you can supply an easy ligature for the incision I've made if you think it worthwhile. Anyway, my quibble is small, and your poem is a strong and fine one.

Our stay in New York was busy and happy and came to a frenzied conclusion in the most unexpected of ways. I was walking north one morning, alone, on Madison Avenue, towards the Whitney, and across the Avenue in an art store window I spotted what looked like a large painting of Venice. I crossed the Avenue the better to see it, and from nearer by it looked like a Guardi. From nearer still it looked like an imitation Guardi, but there was also an icon in the window, though not a very good one, but in any case I wandered in to look around. Inside the store I saw what appeared to me an extraordinarily fine icon, and from then on the rush of events was headlong. I wanted Helen of course to see it and confirm my enthusiasm. There was the nervous-making topic of price. There was the even more nervous-making topic of authenticity. Suffice to say that, we stayed over an extra day, and bought the icon, and showed it to a lady we know, Mrs. [Ray] Schaffer, who with her son runs A La Vieille Russie, that modest little shop at the corner of the Sherry Netherland; and she confirmed that it was a Kiev icon from the early eighteenth century. We are eager to have you come to see it. I'm still rather breathless about it.

We send our love
Tony

[210]

[WLM]
September 6th, 1978
[19 East Boulevard, Rochester, NY 14610]

[Letter, typed on a Charing Cross Hotel, London, letterhead, posted in a Syracuse Airport Inn, Hancock Airport, New York, envelope, addressed to Maître Antoine Hecht, 19 East Boulevard, Rochester NY 14610]

Dear Maître,

You can I'm sure imagine my pleasure at your approval of my effort. I think you are rather too kind, but having said that I return to basking in your kindness. I see what you mean about the last lines, and I will tinker about somewhat. All thanks for taking the time to write to me about it. And what is the name of the man in charge of perms at the TLS? I might as well start collecting rejection slips (I always think, on hearing that phrase, of a vast pile of pastel-colored garments on the floor of some great House's cabine …).

You state that you have been busy, and have given some reasons. But I know, just between us, that a lot of your time has been spent sitting lazily at your desk, running your fingers over the masthead of the Santa Barbara Biltmore paper I wrote on recently.

I can't wait to see the icon. I'm all excited about it. You may know that I have a few, two or three of them rather good. One expert put my Saint George as "Early XV cent., Novgorod," but since he said that years ago I've come to believe he was about a century or a century and a half too early. And I confess to dying to know what you paid for yours, because it's hard to know what my good ones are worth in order properly to insure them. Don't tell me, though, he said coyly; I'll check rather on mine in New Yawk.

And speaking of the Big Apricot, that was a very nice evening you and Helen set up. I enjoyed your friends immensely, and even the old Wellington was comfortable after all the fine booze and wine.

Back to the icon. Your timing must have been, as they say, exquisite. Good, old icons are v. hard to find and v. expensive; worse, there are a lot of v. good fakes about, and I was much encouraged to learn you had yours authenticated. Trottenberg got a little taken a few years ago, but luckily he didn't spend much.

I am mired in the intricacies of the National Endowment for the Humanities application. It makes the 1040[1] and its many sub-forms seem like child's play. But, being encouraged by the Washington project chief, I'm going ahead. A few prayers, sir, on your part would I think be in order. Me, I pray to the Divine Trajan; you may prefer Marta Thatcher,[2] or even H. Lester Cooke …

While I think of it, when you see the Browns across the street, do thank them for me for allowing of such a good, thorough visit. It meant a lot to me, and I learned a lot. They may wish to know, if they don't already, that the house is accurately entered in the new, full catalogue of Frank Lloyd Wright's works. Bye the bye, if you have any taste for such things, the biography of FLW by Twombly is really very good;[3]

1 The 1040 is one of the forms on which Americans are required to make their annual tax returns.

2 Though he uses "Marta Thatcher" as an allonym on several occasions, this is the only letter in which he appears to be using the name properly, to refer to a person. The question is, *Who is it?* Could he be meaning the British politician Margaret Thatcher? In 1969, when he first used the name, she was still a little-known back-bench MP, but she had spent some six weeks in the USA in 1967, and while there had met several prominent figures, including Paul Samuelson, Walt Rostow, Pierre-Paul Schweitzer, and Nelson Rockefeller. The only other candidate – an equally good, and possibly better one, so far as I can see – is a certain Marta K. Thatcher, about whom all it has been possible to discover is that she was the author of a poem entitled "Uneasy Lies," which was published in the March 8th, 1958 issue of the *National Review*.

3 Robert C. Twombly and Donald Walker, *Frank Lloyd Wright: An Interpretive Biography* (New York: Harper & Row, 1973).

very un-specialist and the better, I think, for that.

The College has decided that I maybe know something, and I am to give The Lecture, the Katherine Asher Engel Lecture, in November, and have settled on the sources of Piranesi's architectural imagery. Great fun, plenty of new material.

Love to you all,
Sidonius Apollinarus

[211]

[AH]
September 9th, 1978
19 East Boulevard, Rochester, NY 14610

[Letter, typed on a Brandeis University, Department of English and American Literature, letterhead]

Share Mounseer (that's French),

First with regard to your puzzle over the fitness of the title of "The Deodand." The <u>OED</u>, which I happen to have handy, defines it as "A thing to be forfeited or to be given to God … a personal chattel having "been the immediate occasion of the death of a human being, was given to God as an expiatory offering …" and also, "<u>loosely</u>, the amount to be forfeited as the value of a deodand." I take it those meanings ought to cover the sort of human expiatory sacrifice, the personal chattel, which is the role of the Legionnaire in the poem. The expiation, as the <u>OED</u> makes clear in parts I didn't quote, may be made under civil law to the crown or the temporal authority – not simply to God. And my Legionnaire is sacrificed to some obscure law of historical necessity, or perhaps to the laws of "tragic necessity" as they appear in Racine, and in all classic drama. So much for that.

All my dealing with the <u>TLS</u>, both for poems I've sent and for reviews I've done, has been through John Gross, the very witty and civilized head of the whole thing. I'm sure he will know your name because of the splendid review your Yale book got there. You're of course welcome to mention my name if it will assist in introductions.

The icon. I fear I misled you if I claimed we had it "authenticated." We did, as I think I wrote you, show it to kindly Mrs. Schaffer, doyenne of A La Vieille Russie. She looked at it; no more. Not even with a magnifying glass, and certainly subjected it to no special scrutiny. But from our point of view her examination, if you can call it that, of the icon was valuable in that she seemed not for a moment to question that it was anything but what it was described as being: an early eighteenth-century icon from Kiev. She went on to say of it that it was sufficiently damaged here and there with cracks and peelings in the paint for her to feel she would not have bought it herself, since, for her purposes, it would only be bought to be sold again, and the cost of the restoration required would be so high as to make the whole venture too extravagant. You must not suppose from this that ours is in very bad shape; it is rather that that fancy store deals only in almost perfect works, or pays to restore them to perfection when they are moderately marred. In any case you must see ours.

As it happened, Helen once gave me as a gift a booklet-catalogue from Parke-Bernet of an auction in 1975 of items of Russian art that included a good many icons. The catalogue has a rather obscure black & white photo reproduction of an eighteenth-century icon which obviously has the same subject matter as ours. The obscurity is of course partly due to the reduction in size; but this is the more noticeable in that both icons are composed of many very small figures. In fact, along with Mrs. Schaffer not batting an eye at the early eighteenth-century, Kiev, claim, goes my conviction that, so minute and painstaking and many are the details in this icon that, had it been a forgery the forger would have asked more money for all his time and pains. We paid, to come to the bald fact at last, $1500.

The subject is what our catalogue calls "The Complete Resurrection." It contains a central panel surrounded by twelve smaller panels, all rectangular, the whole thing measuring 14½ × 11½, including a broad border of an inch and a half around the whole thing. As you can surmise from this, the figures, the details of their dress, the architecture behind them and the lettering in their haloes has to be extremely small. The scenes along the top are: The birth of the Virgin; the presentation of the Virgin at the temple; the Annunciation; the nativity of Christ. The four panels, two on the left and two on the right of the larger central one, are, reading left, right, left right, and going down: The presentation of Christ at the temple; the baptism by John; the entry into Jerusalem; the Transfiguration. The four bottom panels are: The finding of the True Cross (with Constantine in the picture, but <u>not</u> his mother); the Resurrection; a panel which I surmise has something to do with the establishment of the ritual of the Eucharist – three angels are seated around a round table on which is placed a chalice or grail. One of the angels is seated on some sort of dais, but another appears to be seated on a closed book. To each side of this group is a saint, their names unintelligible, but each holding in his hands an irregular brown shape that might be a loaf of bread. The last of the small panels is the Dormition of the Virgin. And the larger central panel represents Christ, alive as a man, preaching to two of his disciples; Christ after his death and descent into Hell, saving crowds of souls that include Moses, David and Solomon (their names recognizable, the last two wearing crowns as well as haloes – please note that I've boned up on Cyrillic) and finally, presiding over all, Christ as God among the angels in heaven. None of even the smaller panels but has some four or five full length figures in it, and the central panel has huge crowds of the saved and the angels. I could of course be wrong, but I should think a <u>modern</u> forger would want a lot more money than I paid for so much meticulous work on so many figures.

Both Helen and I wish we could hear, not merely read, your forthcoming Piranesi lecture. If we could persuade Jean France to bring you to give it here, would you be so willing? If so, could you indicate when in a rough way? Good luck to all your projects.

Going back to teaching is hell after a productive year of writing.

St. Pincas the Bland

[212]

[WLM]
September 12th, 1978
[25 Henshaw Avenue, Northampton, Massachusetts 01060]

[Letter, typed on a Syracuse Airport Inn, Syracuse Hancock International Airport, N. Syracuse, N.Y. 13212, letterhead]

Dear flâneur,

I read in the TLS that a certain lady was thought to be a bad 'un, and one of the reasons given was that she took hotel stationery home with her.[1] What a shock! I thought everyone did it! I thought that's what hotels were for …

And, speaking of the TLS, thanks for the name of Mr Gross, to whom I will send that Batavian effort, all ligatured up. I am, I repeat, much indebted to you for your criticism and help. You will, natch, be inundated with poems of middling to grand quality; you should have refused, when you had the chance, to have anything to do with my poetic side …

The icon sounds magnificent. I was rude indeed to ask you the cost, and after mailing the letter shuddered at my embarrassingly direct way of doing things. But you handled it properly, and deftly, as you would, and the information is helpful to me. No, you did not say that Mrs Schaffer authenticated it; I guess I used the word when I wrote to you. All is clear. The last one I bought was in Istanbul, at Fengor's in the Bazaar in 1975. It is probably Greek provincial, XIX cent., and I paid, after much dickering & oceans of tea, three hundred dollars for it. Now that I've had it on the wall for three years I'm beginning to have some doubts about it, very slight doubts, to be sure, but doubts nonetheless … I agree with your ideas about many small figures being an unlikely format for a forger. My Scenes from the Life of the Virgin, said to be Novgorod, late XV cent., but probably much later, has some similarities to yours: many scenes, small figures, but without the actual internal frames or smaller panels you describe. I've been looking in my books on icons and have come up pretty much with the kind of thing you have. It sounds wonderful, and I look forward to seeing it. Your Cyrillic is indeed impressive.

The Piranesi effort has come down to "Piranesi's Carceri: Sources of Invention," and will deal with the tangible sources of the motives in that great series. And yes, I'd love to bring it to Rochester, should such a possibility surface.

The NEH application, which has kept me at the table for weeks now, is almost ready to go to Washington, 25 copies of everything. Obviously the Feds are in the

---

1 The lady in question was Lady Victoria Sackville-West, mother of Vita Sackville-West, and WLM had read about her behavior in a review of Susan Mary Alsop's *Lady Sackville: A Biography* (New York: Doubleday, 1978) which appeared in the June 30th, 1978 issue of the *Times Literary Supplement*. The review, by Violet Powell, included the following admonishing passage: "Until this period Mary Alsop is successful in convincing the reader that Victoria's charm outweighed her tempers and magpie meannesses which manifested themselves in stealing stationery from hotels. Now, however, it becomes impossible to conceal the deterioration of her character …"

pocket of the International Paper Co.
Love to you all,
Bill

P.S.: Speaking of Mrs S's remarks about the cost of restoring icons, my classmate Carroll Wales, as good as there is in that business, & the proprietor of Oliver Brothers in Boston, a celebrated joint, many years ago quoted me $1600 to clean and repair my 2 best icons, both of which, to my eye, are in good to very good condition ... Needless to say, I didn't act.

[213]

[WLM]
October 12th, 1978
25 Henshaw Avenue, Northampton, Massachusetts 01060

[Letter, typed on a New Omayad Hotel letterhead, posted in the same hotel's envelope,
with the sender's address given as Mehmet-ben-Fella Bella, addressed to Prof. Dr. Ing. A. HECHT,
19, East Boulevard, Rochester NY 14610, États-unis]

Oct, 12, MCMLXVIII

Distinguished Docteur!

Pleasing us to make Informations about advertsing your splendids book, MILLIONS TINY SHADES, here in great Muslim world. Oil shieks prefer billions; next volume could you oblige your Muslim followers?

Our secretary, Mile Farta, says their is a Club of Fans already in Muscat and Oman, song = Muscat Ramble.

With a copy of advert applied below, we close and remain, Dear Docteur, your humbled

Sevrantes,

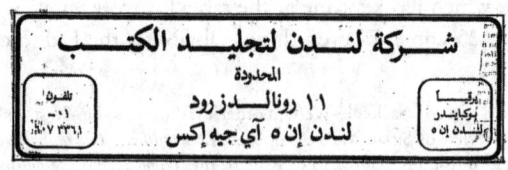

[214]

[WLM]
October 27th, 1978
25 Henshaw Avenue, Northampton, Massachusetts 01060

[Blank postcard, typed, addressed to Anthony E. Hecht, Poet, 19 East Boulevard, Rochester NY 14610]

Dear Commisar,
    A question: Is the Cutler Union, on the University of Rochester Campus, a sort of Yaley Gothic Revival structure with a tower? If not, does a University building that is not a religious one answer to that description? I've some slides, and that one I'm not able properly to label [please note the → elegant phrasing].
    Many thanks for the copy of <u>Poetry</u>. The poem,[1] re-read, is as good as one thought it was: that is, splendid. One of your very best, I'd say.
Love to all,
A. Bakunin

[215]

[WLM]
November 5th, 1978
25 Henshaw Avenue, Northampton, Massachusetts 01060

[Blank postcard, typed, with the sender's address given as Where M sits, that's the head of the table: 25 Hen / 01060, addressed to A E Hecht, mixologist, 19 East Boulevard, Rochester NY 14610]

Dear debtor,
    Thanks for the info about yr local Harkness; I thought I had it right but wasn't sure. And are you preparing a "Billions" book for your Arab fans? I hope so. Lots of petro-dollars there (that word always conjures up for me a vision of Peter the Great and Pieces of Eight; – that's a joke, son). Things here are fairly all right; the Piranesi lecture & show keep me hoping and that's nice, but I'm somewhat lonely part of the time. There are nice people hereabouts but somehow they don't <u>satisfy</u>, you know? Penalty of a rich full life? Many chuckles from Kingsley Amis' new <u>OxBookLightVerse</u>,[2] esp. a fine tourist perm by Graves.[3] No Mervin Peake, though, which perplexes me. Invitations to the Piranesi lecture should go out in a few days. Helen, love, were you able to use any of the Balsdon stuff?[4]

---

1 *Poetry* magazine had just published "The Venetian Vespers."

2 Kingsley Amis, *The New Oxford Book of Light Verse* (New York: OUP, 1978).

3 Robert Graves, "¡Welcome, to the Caves of Arta!," ibid, p. 232.

4 Helen Hecht is unsure what WLM was referring to here, though it might have been one of the books written by the ancient historian J. P. V. D. Balsdon – *Roman Women: Their History and Habits* (London:

Heaps to all,
Blumenthal + Strauss

[216]

[AH]
[November 7th, 1978]
[19 East Boulevard, Rochester, NY 14610

[Canadian postcard, with a photograph of the lid on an elaborately carved Ming Dynasty box, addressed to Wm. MacDonald O.M., 25 Henshaw Ave., Northampton, Mass. 01060]

Dear Archdeacon –
I've got a new lecture title for our distinguished series: Civilization and its Discotheques. M[arilyn] Lavin was hot stuff on Piero's Baptism. Irving came with her. They go to Rome in Jan., the lucky stiffs. A nice note from Dick Wilbur about "Vespers."[1]

St. Francis

[217]

[WLM]
[November 11th, 1978]
25 Henshaw Avenue, Northampton, Massachusetts 01060

[Letter, typed, with the sender's address given as Marta Thatcher, Room 39, A[merican] A[cademy] [in] R[ome], 25 Henshaw / 01060, addressed to Antonio Conte Hecht, 19 East Boulevard, Rochester NY 14610]

Armistice Day
beng / beng

My dear Abbott,
Glad you saw the Lavins, Oiving: at least. I like him. We took a course or two together at the Fogg Way Back When. He's very smart. She I can take or leave. It's a kind of toughness that ain't ezackly to my taste. She condescends to me massively,

Bodley Head, 1962), perhaps, or *Life and Leisure in Ancient Rome* (London: Bodley Head, 1974).

1 Wilbur had written to AH on October 28th: "Dear Tony, About three weeks ago I wrote to John [Frederick] Nims about something, and said that under his editorship Poetry was making a great comeback; a few more events like 'The Venetian Vespers,' and Poetry will once again be where everyone would like to display his best. It's a splendid and sustained work. Regardless of what's in focus, the character of your traumatized hero, with his need of suspension, of vacancy, of death-in-life, continually transpires; you manage thereby to knit together plain passages and fits of baroque, St. Mark's and Lee & Perrins, the voice that says 'silicate fragility' and the voice that says 'Soon as he could …' If I praised all that I relish, I'd exhaust us both; at the moment, I think that the effect which seems most brilliant to me is the transition from the hero's momentary self-forgetting in St. Mark's to the Heavy Weapons corporal's discovery of a dream of order in Emily Post. Bravo, old man, Yours, Dick." (Anthony Hecht Papers, Box 74, file 40.)

and I can't figure out the Why of those Art Bulletin displays of hers. It's a kind of art history that I don't follow ... dumb, I guess.

I forgot to ask you how the Zajac bash was. I have a new accomplishment. It is almost going to New York. I am now extremely good at it. Plans are made, sometimes people are informed, but at the last hour I don't go. I thought I'd go down this week to the Opening*, as three of the artists are friends of mine (Greg & Fran Gillespie live near me and he has taught in the Smith's Art Dept). But, in full form after the Zajac thing, I only almost went ... Then next week there's a reception at the Architectural History Foundation ...

Re "Vespers," of which you said Dick was complimentary. I've now read it through three times, once in the final Poetry version you kindly sent me. I not only feel about it as I wrote some months back, but that feeling has grown. At first one of its qualities I missed was the smoky or hazy remove of its reality, its allegorical presence, so to speak. And each time its woven quality, its density in the sense of the interconnections of its meanings, seems greater and more remarkable. Last night, after taking Nick out to dinner and in the midst of a long conversation about Life, we returned to one of his two favorite topics, poetry (he is very well read), and took note of the inclusion of "The Dover Bitch" in Amis' OxLite. Then we began talking again about "Venetian Vespers," and Nick said "It's the best poem of modern times I've ever read," and proceeded to talk about it at some length. In fact, the poorly-expressed opinions of mine above are a mix of his and mine. He however did much better than I have here; he's better on poetry than I am, and better educated, too, in respect of Littrachoor.

Life is fairly all right. Have been wrapped up in the Piranesi show that will open the night of my Engel lecture. Museum shows are an awful lot of work, but exhilarating to prepare.

Love to U 2,
Fornicatus IIII

* American Academy. Rome painters' show

[Handwritten note on the back of the envelope]

P.S. I hope you heard from your Arab agents. They wrote me for your address.

[218]

[WLM]
[November 14th, 1979]
[University of California, Berkeley, Department of Architecture,
Wurster Hall 232, Berkeley, California 94720]

*[Postcard, with a reproduction of Henry Fuseli's painting, Here I and Sorrows Sit ...,
(but bearing the caption "Here We and Sorrows Sit"), handwritten, addressed to A.E. Hecht,
19 East Boulevard, Rochester N.Y. 14610]*

Jimmy,

Petersson is sojourning in Rome – for too brief a time, I fear – and I just had a card from him. It says "recently satisfied myself about the way space works in the piazza and basilica of S. Pietro, also in the Campidoglio piazza ..." I thought you'd want to know this Right Away, so you could Spread the Word. Krautheimer, Ackerman, et al., look to your laurels!

Bert

[219]

[AH]
[Mid-November, 1978]
[19 East Boulevard, Rochester, NY 14610]

*[Letter, typed on a The University of Rochester, Rochester, New York 14627,
Department of English Morey Hall, letterhead]*

Dear Vicar,

I intend to oblige my Arab fans by a due inflation of my titles from here on in. In fact, my next book will be called, "The blessed Damosel leaned out / From the gold bar of Heaven; / Her eyes were deeper than the depth / Of waters stilled at even; / She had three lilies in her hand,/ And the stars in her hair were seven hundred and sixty-seven billion, four hundred and twenty-eight million, eight hundred and thirty-nine thousand, four hundred and one."[1]

I am grateful for the high esteem in which you and Nick hold "Venetian Vespers."

[Unsigned]

---

1 AH is making play with the first stanza of Dante Gabriel Rossetti's poem, "The Blessed Damozel," which reads: "The blessed damozel lean'd out / From the gold bar of Heaven; / Her eyes were deeper than the depth / Of waters still'd at even; / She had three lilies in her hand, And the stars in her hair were seven."

[220]

[AH]
November 23rd, 1978]
19 East Boulevard, Rochester, NY 14610

[Letter, typed on a letterhead in Arabic script, addressed to William MacDonald (Infidel), 25 Henshaw Ave., Northampton, Mass. 01060]

Dear Vestryman,

I've just made a quick trip to check up on my Arab fans, and despite their current preoccupation with multiples of billions they assure me they'll go on being my loyal readers even if my next volume should be called, "The One And Only." They have, on the other hand, reserved comment on common or vulgar fractions.

We were grateful to receive an invitation to your Piranesi lecture and the reception afterwards, but we shall be unable to make it. But Smith traditionally publishes such lectures – at least they published Dimock's – so we entertain some hope of getting hold of a copy in the future. Of course, a lecture on prisons is full of all sorts of amusing possibilities, and we are sure your native wit will find happy occasions to scintillate.

We have sent you, under separate cover, a little gift for the holiday season. It is not meant to intimidate you with uneasy sensations of obligatory reciprocity; if you inspect it carefully you will notice sooner or later that it was produced by my very own publisher, and, seeing it lying about on his desk, I had only to express my keen interest in offering it to someone who was knowledgeable about its subject to have been given the thing forthwith.

It occurs to me that half-time teaching might in some ways be even more painful than full-time, since it gives you a keener and continuous sense of how your time might be better employed. I feel that this year, after a particularly fertile sabbatical. Teaching, and all the little wearisome committees and deliberations and earnest, necessary labors in evaluating junior colleagues, and all those soul-searching meditations about grades and the future of the department and the library holdings and God knows what else – it all seems like the sort of misapplication of energy that so characterized army life, where mathematical prodigies were automatically assigned to the infantry and professional second storey men to the MP's,

We send our love,
Barka da Buzzard's Gulch

[221]

[AH]
[Late November, 1978]
19 East Boulevard, Rochester, NY 14610

[Letter, typed on a The University of Rochester, Department of English, letterhead, enclosing a copy of Ned Bradford's Boston's Locke-Ober Café: An Illustrated Social History with Miscellaneous Recipes *(Boston: Atheneum, 1978)]*

Dear old Sergio,
    This is intended to bring back fond memories, and to convey to you our warmest Christmas greetings.
    It is also to let you know that if we should show up unexpectedly at Henshaw Avenue it would be thoughtful if you whipped up the Escargots Bourguignon (p. 126) and the Filet Mignon Rossini (p. 155). In actual fact, I prefer Rossini's food to his music.

Timon of Akron

[222]

[WLM]
December 1st, 1978
25 Henshaw Avenue, Northampton, Massachusetts 01060

[Letter, typed, addressed to The Hechts (mmmmm …), 19 East Boulevard, Rochester NY 14610]

Dear Helen & Tony,
    Thanks for all the nice things that have been coming this way from you. Now that the Engel lecture is over, I've time to answer letters that have been reproaching me from a pile on my worktable. The lecture was great fun, a good house in spite of bad weather, then the opening at the Museum of my show of the <u>Carceri</u> & my photos. I was able to convince the Powers that we [should] have there an open bar, so things were merry. [Jill] Conway gave me a gracious introduction, and many old friends were on hand. So.
    First, the recipe. Helen, I've not tried it, being on a diet of sorts, but when I lose enough poundage it will be first on the list. It sounds delicious. And the Locke-Ober book is quite wonderful. It has been not only fun to scan the recipes, but to read about figures that were demigods when I was young, Even "my" old waiter, Carlo, is there; a socialist who harangued the young Harvard men on the assumption that they were all rich. We used to save for months to go there, and I remember many a happy night so spent. The ex-men's wine-room looks almost exactly the same as it did when my father first took me there in the late 30s. I don't know, though, whether the waiters still fold their greatcoats and put them into the enormous sterling soup tureens that line the broad shelf behind the counter.

But I've a note of jealousy, too – your Arab stationery. I've only two pieces of my precious Hotel Omayad stuff & <u>you</u> turn up nonchalantly with something better ... I may cry, but, on second thought, perhaps I can carefully erase and white out the typing and use it again.

The Guggenheim poem is splendid[1]; many have noticed it & talked about it. The pooh-pooh-ers of the <u>TLS</u> aren't as strong around here as they used to be. I never heard from Mr Gross about my "Batavians" poem, which is disappointing, as I wanted to frame his notice or letter of rejection alone: with my testimonial from Sally Keith, the former four-tassel lady of Scollay Square.[2]

The boys are fine. My work goes well. My old friend Lanny Larson, with whom I flew in the war, died of cancer the day before Thanksgiving. All had been waiting for it. I didn't go out, as there was no service; I'd seen him a couple of times during the summer.

Love to you all.
William the Inextinguishable

P.S. Lecture will be published, will send.

[223]

[AH]
December 27th, 1978
[19 East Boulevard, Rochester, NY 14610]

[Letter, typed on a The University of Rochester, Department of English, letterhead, addressed to William MacDonald (an obvious alias), 25 Henshaw, Northampton, Mass. 01060]

Dear Friend of Nature and Wildlife,

All of us here at the American Pancreas Association want to wish you a joyous holiday season, and hope you are doing all you can to support the microbes and bacteria that depend so much upon us all. Just a little bit of decay can go such a long way to making millions happy and content. We feel sure that just at this time of year you may want to give special help to endangered species of paramecia that are only really safe and comfortable in a generous American pancreas.

With warmest seasonal good wishes,
Epictetus

---

1 "Application for a Grant" was first published in the November 24th, 1978 issue of the *Times Literary Supplement*, and was then included in *The Venetian Vespers*.

2 Boston's Scollay Square, home to burlesque theaters, tattoo parlours, barrooms, shooting galleries and hotdog stands, was very popular with Harvard students, amongst others. A striptease dancer famous for her tassels, Sally Keith was one of the Square's great attractions.

[224]

[WLM]
January 4th, 1979
25 Henshaw Avenue, Northampton, Massachusetts 01060

[Blank postcard, typed, with the sender's address given as Oxford Companion to Architecture, William L. MacDonald, 25 Henshaw Avenue, Northampton, Mass. 01060, addressed to Anthony Hecht, bather, 19 East Boulevard, Rochester NY 14610]

O Seer!

We here in the Pancreatic League have long known about the voyages we must take into the Gut and to Bladderville. But we are glad to have your strictures, and we obey.

Isn't Auden's "Fall of Rome"[1] fun?

Went to the Capital to be on an National Endowment of the Humanities panel & was impressed by the care and thoroughness with which they process applicants. I like Washington.

I think you ought to look up the definition of espichellite in the unabridged dictionary. It's quite catchy. If you can use it in a poem – the word, not the def. – you will get in the mail a Grand Surprise.

Yr svt, Sir,
Ivan Idea

[225]

[AH]
January 6th, 1979
[19 East Boulevard, Rochester, NY 14610]

[Letter, typed on an Imperial Hotel, Tokyo, letterhead, posted in the same hotel's envelope, addressed to William MacDonald (The Sage of Henshaw), 25 Henshaw Ave., Northampton, Mass. 01060]

Now see here, Fenwig,

What sort of bloody unabridged dictionary do you consort with when you find the term "espichellite"? Not, certainly, the <u>OED</u>. Possibly some wop dialect volume, which refers to the <u>espichellity</u> of the house, as, spaghetti alle vongole, perhaps? If you have vulgarities of this sort in mind you can bet your bottom yen I won't be using them in a perm, no matter what the bribe.

The dear old Imperial is not what it used to be, now that it's torn down. One misses the silent glide of the waiters, the perfect service. And yet when I gaze from my balcony at Mt. Fuji, and consider that it may be one of the largest orifices in the world, some deep-seated ambition or yearning rises within me. A sense of the

---

1 W. H. Auden, "The Fall of Rome," in W. H. Auden, *Another Time* (New York: Random House, 1940).

AH, 1943

AH, third from right, with other members of C Company, 386th Infantry Regiment, 97th Division, 1944
Photograph courtesy of James W. Fitzpatrick ©

WLM with Lanny Larson, Smyrna, TN, 1944

AH, 1946 or 1947

WLM, California, 1948

AH, Ischia, 1950

WLM, early 1950s

The American Academy in Rome

Seal of the American Academy in Rome

WLM with Dale MacDonald, Patricia Hecht, and AH,
in front of the American Academy in Rome, 1954 or 1955

WLM in front of the dome of St. Peter's, Rome, 1954 or 1955
Photograph by Alice Sedgewick ©

AH at the Villa d'Este, Tivoli, Rome, 1955

Members of the AAR and their wives look down from the roof of the Pantheon in Rome, 1954 or 1955

This photo was included by WLM on page 133 of *The Pantheon: Design, Meaning, and Progeny*, and prompted the following observation from AH: "[W]ith the assistance of a lens I thought I was able to make out ... the lineaments of the author [standing to the right of the photographer], his then wife [third from the left, leaning over the edge of the oculus], and a genial poetic type named Wilbur [first from the right leaning over the oculus]. So that rather adroitly, in the manner of Alfred Hitchcock (not Henry-Russell) you have contrived to insinuate yourself into your own work in an unexpected way." See letter #115, May 11th, 1976.

Dale MacDonald with WLM, near Alanya, Turkey, 1955

232 vii

WLM, Rome, 1963

AH, mid-1960s
Photograph by Rollie McKenna ©

Dale MacDonald with WLM and their sons Noel and Nick, Guilford, Connecticut, 1964

WLM with unidentified companions, "Thrace," 1965

WLM conducting a tour of the ruins of Leptis Magna, Khoms, Libya, 1966

W. H. Auden with AH, backstage at the 92nd Street Poetry Center, New York, 1967
Photograph by Jill Krementz ©

WLM, 1969

Helen Hecht and AH with their son Evan, 1972

WLM with unidentified companion, Greece, early 1970s

AH, 1970s

AH, Library of Congress, Washington, D.C., 1981
Photograph by William Stafford ©

AH teaching at the University of Rochester, 1977
Photograph courtesy of the Department of Rare Books and Special Collections, University of Rochester Library ©

WLM, Northampton, MA, 1982

Helen Hecht, 1983
Photograph by Nancy Crampton ©

AH with James Merrill and Mark Strand, Library of Congress, Washington, D.C., 1990
photograph courtesy of the Library of Congress ©

WLM, 1990s

Helen Hecht with AH, Sewanee Writers' Conference, Tennessee, 1992
Photograph by James R. Peters ©

sublime, it may be; of something far more deeply interfused, like the solid-state wirings of a Sony transistor. I get quite carried away.

What can you tell me about Rodolphe Bresdin, Belgian engraver (1825-85)? Baskin admires him, as you may know. I believe he went mad.[1] It is about his madness that I'm curious. I want to find out if it's connected to the obsessive thickets of detail in his work. Have you any notion where I can look or ask? Bear always in mind that art historical materials here are not of the best. A. M. Hind's <u>History of Engraving and Etching</u>[2] lists him, but nothing more. (This inquiry is toward another poem.)[3]

I have just "translated" another poem by Brodsky, this one called "Lagoon" and set in Venice. So it will find a fitting place in my own book as well as his.

Not necessarily,
Walter Ego

P.S.: Never fully realised before that you were an Oxford Companion to Architecture. Must be a chilly sort of job, keeping the old halls propped up, cheering up the cellars.

[226]

[WLM]
January 9th, 1979
25 Henshaw Avenue, Northampton, Massachusetts 01060

[Blank postcard, typed, addressed to Count Anthony de Hecht (Eastern Boulevardier), 19, East Boulevard, Rochester NY 14610]

III days after XII night

O Rhymer:

The thought of you without a copy of <u>Webster's International Unabridged Dictionary</u>, 2nd edition[4] (<u>never</u> the 3rd! it's awful) moved me to tears of pity. Buy now, they're getting hard to find in good condition. Got one for Barbara a couple of years ago for $45. I've lived with mine for twenty-seven years now and feel that it

---

1 Bresdin was French, not Belgian, and he was born in 1822, not 1825. Though he was certainly an eccentric figure, I have been able to discover no evidence that he went mad, and the suggestion that he did seems to derive from the fantastical and disturbing nature of his work without actually explaining it.

2 A. M. Hind, *A History of Engraving & Etching: from the 15th Century to the Year 1914: Being the 3rd and Fully Rev. Ed. of "A Short History of Engraving and Etching"* (New York: Dover, 1978).

3 It is not clear what poem Hecht had in mind here, and it is quite possible that it came to nothing. Later on, and at Baskin's prompting, he and AH collaborated on "The Presumptions of Death," a sequence of poems which formed Part I of AH's next-but-one collection, *Flight Among the Tombs*. One might speculate that what lay behind the project was Baskin's interest in Bresdin's sometimes death-haunted work. See, for example, *The Comedy of Death* (1854) or *The Hunters Surprised by Death* (1857), or *The Bather and Death (1857),* which, together with many other of Bresdin's works, can be viewed at http://cargocollective.com/Kunstkabinett/Rodolphe-Bresdin.

4 *Webster's New International Dictionary of the English Language*, 2nd edition, unabridged (New York: G. & C. Merriam Co., 1951).

is one of the greatest books of all time. It is not a substitute for the <u>OED</u>, any more than the <u>OED</u> is a substitute for it. After you get your copy we can talk about the differences. But hurry. Espichellite: a lamprophyre containing phenocrysts of olivine (it goes on at length this way and then comes) The plagioclass may have orthoclass borders (can you believe it?), and there may be secondary analcite. Well, there you are. Good augury, Sir.

P. Oblivius Nasal

Our art history committee is at work on your request.

[227]

[WLM]
January 11th, 1979
25 Henshaw Avenue, Northampton, Massachusetts 01060

[Blank postcard, typed, addressed to His Excellency Antonino ter Hecht,
19 East Boulevard, Rochester NY 14610]

Excellency,

    I can't dig up nothing about your buddy Bresdin. The reference volumes give a fact or two, + ancient bibliography unobtainable here; and there's no monograph listed in the card catalogue. A colleague who might be helpful is in Patagonia, or Hamburg, or somewhere, and when he returns after Interterm I'll quizz'm.

    Your longing for Fuji's orifice puts me in mind of a Neapolitan waiter who told me years ago that he had heard of an energetic English tourist who hoped for an affair with Vesuvius. Not only that, there was recently in the Personals column of the <u>New York Review of Books</u> an ad from a lady saying she wanted to cuddle up with someone who was into Bach, Baskin, and Baryshnikov. Maybe <u>she</u> knows about Bresdin. I've other grand stories, but they'll keep.

Thine in heliophany,
Apollo, Bel Vedere

[228]

[WLM]
March 1st, 1979
25 Henshaw Avenue, Northampton, Massachusetts 01060

[Letter, typed on the back of a library index card, with the sender's address given as The Grand Master of the Knights of Cabiria, 25 Henshaw Avenue, 01060, addressed to Mr Anthony Hecht, Seer, 19 East Boulevard, Rochester, NY 14610, and enclosing an invitation to join the National Social Directory, together with a two-page questionnaire and a covering letter which states that, "Published annually, [the National Social Directory] contains in one volume thousands of noteworthy families and individuals in America ...," and goes on: "Please do not send your check with the enclosed form. Upon the acceptance of your name by the Advisory Committee for inclusion in the directory, you will be asked to pay a $40.00 listing fee which entitles you to a copy of the next edition of the National Social Directory."]

O Titan!

I've had some peachy ideas about filling this out, but then I realised that you haven't anything to do all day except read <u>Hustler</u> and so I decided to give you a treat. I've no doubt but that if you put your mind to it you can send them the classiest applikation they've ever had.

Yours in the undergraduate sense,
Admiral Dewey

[229]

[AH]
March 10th, 1979
19 East Boulevard, Rochester, New York 14610

[Letter, typed, posted in a The University of Rochester envelope, addressed to Mr. William MacDonald (Guru of Henshaw), 25 Henshaw Ave., Northampton, Mass. 01060]

High and Mighty (or, at least, High),

There are times when I muse upon the anomalies of divine justice – that, in the words of the psalm, the wicked should prosper, and, as in The Book of Job, the good and the innocent should suffer. I find those texts the substance of much meditation, and they have been richly enlarged by a two-page spread in the March issue of <u>House Beautiful</u>. There, in a series of ravishing color shots, are displayed various aspects of the estate, named "Calithea," of Mr. and Mrs. Richard S. L. Pearman, who reside in Bermuda. The house, designed around a central, tree-planted atrium, with wings and appendages flying off in orbit around it, and interspersed among manicured lawns and a turquoise-bottomed pool, is a pure coral white; and the exterior sides of the quadrilateral plan each give upon a patio terrace of its own. The lawns incline gently to balustraded steps that descend directly into an Atlantic tinted an almost artificial blue, its superb, untroubled breadth visible, across the pool, from the main, or dining, terrace, which is decorated in vivid pinks and greens, planted begonias in white porcelain baskets, a lotus-shaped Lucite salad bowl filled with crisp greens, and shaded by a thick-leaved almond tree. Standing cheerfully beside their luncheon table are Mr. and Mrs. Pearman themselves, he in, appropriately, Bermuda shorts. They are remarkably young, and appear to have undergone no strain whatever in arriving at their stately condition. And what do you think it is that Mr. Pearman does? I venture to suppose that you would not guess, no matter how many chances I gave, so I will tell you. He is the United States lawn croquet champion. There is even a picture of the bar, finished in a dazzling oriental wall paper, where his indubitable trophies are displayed. It is enough all by itself to convert one to instant Marxism or ferocious prayer in the manner of David at his most agitated. The "Consume them in wrath, consume them, that they may not be" sort of thing. And the truth is that I cherish no love whatever for Mr. and Mrs. Pearman (and their five children) who appear to be able to get along fairly well without it. He favors a deep maroon tie with matching hankie in his seersucker breast pocket, and has the authentic, paunchy build of a croquet champion. Though he has five children he looks young enough to be a graduate student. A bad one. Lucky for him indeed he isn't one of mine. And so with these fine, scriptural thoughts I lapse back into the torpor of spring vacation. Almost half a term still to go. But we have plans, and hopes of going to Europe this summer for 45 days. Leave end of June. First Rome, then Florence, Venice and London. Any chance of your being over there then? How fine it would be if we could join forces, however briefly. Surely there must be some crumby Roman building you need to look at. Perhaps even a baroque church or two, as well as a taverna or a pub. Let us know. Our books, Helen's cookbook and my perms, will be out in September, both from Atheneum.

        Richard the Pigeon-Toed

[230]

[AH]
June 3rd, 1979
19 East Boulevard, Rochester, New York 14610

[Letter, typed on a The University of Rochester, Department of English, letterhead]

Caro amico,

  Last time we spoke I made mention of some article on Piranesi in the Harvard Bulletin that pointed out that most of his "views" were shown from a vantage point some twenty-five or thirty feet above the ground. I remember finding this striking and odd, yet by now it strikes me as altogether plausible. In the interval I have read Kenneth Clark's <u>Landscape into Art</u>,[1] and while he makes no mention of Piranesi, he makes much of the early painters' problem in dealing satisfactorily with "the middle distance," and indicates convincingly that their initial way of overcoming this problem

---

1 Kenneth Clark, *Landscape into Art* (New York: Harper & Row, 1979).

was to represent a foreground scene, say of a Madonna and Child, with saints and donor, in a sort of elevated loggia, through the arches of which could be viewed the remote and distant landscapes. Clearly, to get a view of any distance one must view from a vantage point, even if an imaginary one. Some of Canaletto's city scapes are viewed from normal eye-level above the ground, and this serves well when the street scenes themselves prevent a distant view; but he is by no means consistent about this, and one view of the Piazzetta which looks out across the Lagoon to include San Giorgio is painted from what must be an angelic platform some forty feet in the air in front of St. Mark's. All this floods up because of two happy facts: I have been reading proof on the new book, <u>The Venetian Vespers</u>, which will be out in the fall; and our little family, Helen, her mother, Evan and I, are going abroad this summer. We go straight to Rome in late July, and spend ten days or two weeks there; then a week or more in Florence, and nearly two weeks in Venice; and we conclude with ten days in London. Only recently have I been able to contemplate this as a reality, and a pleasant one at that. As I think you know, I have had a hiatal hernia for several years; till recently it attacked me whenever I ate or drank, and was extremely painful. But as of about a month ago I have been given a medication that seems completely to have eliminated all attacks.

Now that you are a gentleman of semi-leisure, is there any chance research will take you to Europe this summer? How fine if we could meet in Rome or Venice! Dimitri [Hadzi] is going to Greece first, and then to Rome, but our schedules don't coincide. He, by the way, has done some six or eight etchings about which he is very enthusiastic (I have not yet seen them) which are to accompany the text of "The Venetian Vespers" (that one poem) in a limited, deluxe, impossibly chic and expensive edition that David Godine will bring out.[1] Also in the fall, I believe.

Milton of Saudi Arabia

[231]

[WLM]
June 6th, 1979
[25 Henshaw Avenue, Northampton, Massachusetts 01060]

[Letter, typed on a Royal Motor Inns, 325 E. Main St., Walla Walla, Washington, letterhead, posted in the same company's envelope, with the sender's address given as Madame Lepescu, addressed to Anthony Hecht, or whoever reads to him ..., 19 East Boulevard, Rochester NY 14610]

D-Day '79

Hey there Miltie!

That's wonderful news about your medication, and about your forthcoming trip, I espek to be right here all summer, writing away with any luck. Things have been moving along well so far. But do salute the Romans and Venetians for me; the hell with

---

1 David Godine issued the book in tall octavo format, with quarter morocco and pictorial boards and a glassine dust jacket in a limited signed edition of 165 copies. Hadzi contributed six leaves of plates.

the Fiorentini. Saw Dimitri [Hadzi] at the Fogg when I lectured there on Piranesi, and we vowed to get together, but that never seems to happen for one reason or another. I mean get together for a weekend; we do see each other now and again for a meal & I gather things are going very well for him,

Speaking of Piranesi, my printed lecture should have appeared by now. The Stinehour people keep saying "next week"' – you know how it is. It looks nice, I think: conservative, neat, even austere – a little like me. Will send a copy along as soon as the printer obliges.

Did you know that the first drive-in movie theatre in the world opened in Camden, New Jersey, in June 1933? I thought not.

Yeah, ole P. did get up in the air about things, like the Harvards said, though not for the <u>Carceri</u>. I liked the <u>H. Mag.</u> piece about the intestines a lot, and am amused by the letters about who had tea with whom, Literate mag., that.

Finishing up the Small Baths, after some ten years of fucking around. It's been refused by a couple of editors, and I've rewritten it twice now. I hope to hell the current enthusiast takes it, and as is. It's the best I can do, and I think It contains some of the best analytical writing I've done. The drawings, which are not mine, sono ottimi.

Pat[1] has bought a house in Northampton and I've run in to her on the street. She looks well.

My very old friend Charlie Groves, who has been sliding downhill at an alarming rate – broke, deep alcoholic, etc. – was beaten within an inch of his life Monday night in a Boston dive. He lies in the Tufts Medical Center, unconscious, and only his sister and I really care anything about him. I find I can handle these things better as time passes and I experience more of them. The poor bastard might be better off dead. I never thought I'd ever say such a thing about anybody, but …

More cheerful things: the boys are fine, I've pretty much adjusted to living the way I do – many friends about, plenty of good company. I want to "retire" soon, get a little condominium in say Washington, a city I like. '82? '83? Just hope I can keep on writing. Health robust, sort of looking for a nice lady who could understand my quaint ways and opinions.

     Love, to you all, & have a great trip.
       Père E.A.
       (je sparcle)

---

1 Patricia Harris, AH's first wife.

[232]

[AH]
July 9th, 1979
[Florence, Italy]

[Italian postcard, with a reproduction of a drawing of the Piazza della Signoria, Florence, handwritten, addressed to Prof. Wm. MacDonald, 25 Henshaw Ave, Northampton, Mass 01060, U.S.A]

I meant to ask you: do you have a copy of a book called <u>The Lost Treasures of Europe</u>, published by Pantheon?[1] It's a picture book about the mainly architectural works destroyed by WWII. If you don't have it, I have a copy for you. We have run into Leon of Syracuse[2] here, who speaks of you with reverence.

Love
Hechts

[233]

[AH]
July 11th, 1979
[Florence, Italy]

[Italian postcard, with a reproduction of a painting from the Venetian School of Man's Three Ages, handwritten, addressed to Prof. Wm. MacDonald, 25 Henshaw Ave, Northampton, Mass 01060, U.S.A]

"Hark! The Harold Bloomers sing:
'Hermeneutics is my thing!'"

Timon of South Bend

[234]

[AH]
July 15th, 1979
Venice, Italy

[Italian postcard, with a reproduction of a nativity scene by a painter of the Cretan School, mid-16th century, handwritten, addressed to Prof. Wm. MacDonald, 25 Henshaw Ave, Northampton, Mass. 01060, U.S.A]

Dear Bill –

This icon brought yours to mind. I hope this barrage of postcards from glamorous Italian cities does not appear to have an edge of cruelty about it. We

---

1 Henry La Farge, *Lost Treasures of Europe – 427 Photographs* (New York: Pantheon, 1946).
2 Leon Satkowski.

will meet more friends here in Venice. John M. Brinnin, poet and author of books on Dylan Thomas + Gertrude Stein, and David Kalstone, critic of poetry. Also perhaps the Robertses, if they are here. The prices in Florence (for restaurants) were far higher than Rome; and in Venice they are strikingly higher than Florence. Still, tomorrow night – Back in the Basilica. Last night – fireworks on the Lagoon for the feast of the Redentore. And scampi and funghi. O Boy.

Irving da Fiesole

[235]

[AH]
July 19th, 1979
[Rome, Italy]

[Italian postcard, with a reproduction of Ippolito Caffi's painting, Panorama, handwritten, addressed to Prof. Wm. MacDonald, 25 Henshaw Ave, Northampton, Mass 01060, U.S.A]

Groggy with jet-lag, tramping through streets & forum, we are also groggy with awe and pleasure. Prices, of course, are higher than ever. But the Pantheon, the Aventine, are splendid as ever. We will dine with the Zajacs this evening. We missed your company & knowledge this morning as we made our way through the forum. One forgets how good Italian food & wine taste.

Giulio Cesare

[236]

[WLM]
July 21st, 1979
[25 Henshaw Avenue, Northampton, Massachusetts 01060]

[German postcard, with a photograph of the Oberammergau Passionstheater, handwritten, addressed to A. E. Hecht, World Hitchhiker, 19 East Blvd, Rochester NY, 14610]

Your cards are making me green with envy. Yes, with all thanks, I do have <u>Lost Treasures</u>, which I picked up in Cambridge when it first came out. Valuable. Am writing quite steadily, which is nice. And even losing a bit of weight.

Love to all,
Ann Tomorrow,
Lindbergh

[237]

[WLM]
July 25th, 1979
25 Henshaw Avenue, Northampton, Massachusetts 01060

[Blank postcard, typed, with the sender's address given as 25 Hensh., 01060, addressed to A E Hecht, 19 East Boulevard, Ro-chester NY 14610]

25th Iulii *79*

My dear Doctor,

While you have been cutting a swathe through the flesh-pots of Yerp, we here have been sweltering. It is not, perhaps, as easy to do as some think. You have to get a swelt that is, so to speak, worth your time. Many are backward and disorganized and, frankly, many of us feel that the popular mauve, fur-bearing variety is not all it is crunched up to be. But of course it isn't often that you have – how shall I say – the kind of Thing that can both sing "Hurray for Captain Spaulding!"[1] and give you a cube root at the snap of your fingers. I've planted some of mine's – I call him Eddie – and the flowers have a kind of logarithmic grace. He (it? – shows no interest in other sexes) sleeps outside, and right now I have him / it counting all the gerunds in the <u>Britannica</u>, He thrives on gerunds. Maybe he's a Professor of Engl. Lit., gone to ground.

Yours,
Frobenius

[238]

[AH]
August 9th, 1979
19 East Boulevard, Rochester, NY 14610

[Letter, typed on a The University of Rochester, Department of English, letterhead]

Dear Bill,

We just got back a few days ago, and of course I have found waiting for me your Piranesi lecture,[2] along with some genial cards from you. I've had a chance to read the lecture through once with care, and to browse in it here and there as well before writing to thank you. It strikes me as so dense and suggestive that it should more properly be acknowledged with a long, discursive letter of thanks. I was reminded, for example, of a recent book of photographs of Freud's home in Vienna, and especially the room he used for his practice of therapy. It was filled, as

---

1 The song originally performed by Groucho Marx in the 1928 Marx Brothers' stage and film musical, *Animal Crackers*.

2 *Piranesi's Carceri: Sources of Invention*.

no doubt you know, with ancient artefacts, most of them fragments, many of them Egyptian, as well as Greek and Minoan. His archeological interests were clearly a symbolic parallel to the dredging up of the unconscious or the buried personal past. And in Piranesi there is not only the same archeological bias, but, as you make clear, a keen interest in foundations, in unadorned underground structures and a focus which is usually looking up from below. Those cellarages do suggest the terrifyingly large and unsuspected dimensions of a buried and hidden life; they cast something of the same spell as the enclosed spaces (The Cask of Amontillado, The Pit and the Pendulum) in Poe. This is not to side with those who call Piranesi a romantic or drugged hallucinator – though he did consciously romanticize some of those scenes in their later states, as you point out. But for now I can only send my very grateful thanks for your rich, provocative work.

Tony

[239]

[WLM]
August 12th, 1979
25 Henshaw Avenue, Northampton, Massachusetts 01060

[Letter, typed on WLM's own letterhead]

Dear Doctor Hecht,

I am glad you are all back safe and sound from your trip, which must have been a splendid one. As time passes I have less and less interest in going to Italy again, though I count myself fortunate in having been able to spend several years there. What I want to do now is see the United States, and have taken a first step in that direction by agreeing to teach the fall quarter at Berkeley, leaving here toward the end of September. I know California pretty well, but want to explore it more thoroughly, partly because of the Oxford Companion, partly because the U.S. intrigues and mystifies me. I don't quite understand how it holds together.

I'm delighted that you read the Piranesi piece. You say it is dense, and I know what you mean. I'm forever trying to put everything into whatever I write. Barbara, who is an excellent if fierce critic, returns again and again to my tendency to condense, to think what is elliptical is clear. But the Piranesi piece is probably as good as I can do. It is attracting attention and will be reviewed, in an omnium gatherum of Piranesi things, by Robin Middleton of Cambridge, who is a very good man.[1] A couple of experts have written to say that it is about time the nonsense that has been written about the Carceri [...][2] and have praised the architectural arguments I offer. That's nice.

---

1 The review appeared three years later, in the *Journal of the Society of Architectural Historians*, 41:4 (December, 1982), pp. 333-344.

2 WLM has omitted a word or words here.

I've been working on my cities book and am now pushing to have the text at least Yale[1] before I go West (I don't mean that in the sense that my mother's generation spoke of people "going West," meaning dying; did you hear that one when you were young? I wonder what the origin of it is: "He's gone West" – accent on "gone" …). It is coming along, painfully, by and large, because I've not even now thought out carefully enough what it is I want to say. I'm flooded with ideas, some of them I think very good, but it is difficult for me to get them into a reasonably flowing, clear English.

Howja like my snazzy stationery? First in 30 years; printed by the nice lady who will do your VV for Godine as I understand it, Carol Blinn of Easthampton. Meanwhile I am sending you a couple of fairly well housebroken swelts, and solemnly inform you that the next Oxford Companion is that for California … I've seen the galleys. Oh, yes: the TLS finally got around to returning my Hadrian poem; I've now sent it to the Massachusetts Review.[2]

Love to you all,
Stilicho
(Magister utv. in praes.)

[240]

[WLM]
October 2nd, 1979
[University of California, Berkeley, Department of Architecture,
Wurster Hall 232, Berkeley, California 94720]

[Postcard, with a photograph of San Francisco by night, handwritten, addressed to
The Hechts, 19 East Boulevard, Rochester NY, 14610, with enclosure]

[Enclosure: clipping]

DEAR DR. MILLER: When I asked our veterinarian how often our pet crocodile needed his teeth cleaned, he said "Never!" Is this true, or was it just because he didn't want anything to do with Smiley's teeth? – H.A.

---

1 WLM had begun work on his "Cities book" in 1962-63. The publisher to whom it was under contract at that time was Atheneum, who had asked for delivery of the manuscript in 1965. WLM had run into serious problems with the book, however. As he later wrote: "An early attempt at such a study [i.e. a study of Roman buildings in the context of their cities and towns] proved inadequate. Further research and travel, as time and resources permitted, as well as editorial and other work … broadened my knowledge and helped me see the shape of the book more clearly; the new draft that followed was the basis for this book." We know from letter #93 that Atheneum cancelled their contract for the book in 1973, but at some point between then and the writing of this letter, a new one was issued by Yale University Press. At some point between then and the summer of 1986, when it was eventually published, the "Cities book" became Volume II of *The Architecture of the Roman Empire*, subtitled *An Urban Appraisal*.

2 The poem did not appear in *The Massachusetts Review*; and there is no record of its having been published anywhere else.

Dear H.A. – <u>Please</u> stop bothering me. I've told you that's not a crocodile, but a Prof. of Comp. Lit.

Dr Miller

[241]

[WLM]
October 15th, 1979
University of California, Berkeley, Department of Architecture,
Wurster Hall 232, Berkeley, California 94720

[Letter, handwritten]

Dear Tony,

A tacky, strange place with pretty good students. Here until ca. 1 Dec., "doing" the Fall Quarter. Restaurants can be interesting, + the buildings are very much so; each weekend I make a giro to one area or another around the Bay or beyond it. Raining, can't see the GGate bridge from my tiny room. Old California is nice, new California dull and a little frightening.

Before I left Northampton I think I made something of an enemy of [Robert T.] Petersson. My own fault. He asked me to read a 20/30 p. ms. of his on the Piazza S. Pietro ("I've got the space solved") + like a <u>fool</u> I said I would. Then, instead of reading it quickly, I went into my compulsive copy-editing routine, for his English was bad to terrible, + on top of that he simply doesn't know about, or understand, architecture. Vaguely realizing what I might be getting into, I slowed down around p. 6 or so, but –

He called, came over, + somewhat belligerently told me he <u>did</u> know what a sentence is,* etc. I smoothed it over as best I could, loaned him some good b/white negatives of Bernini's work, and there it stands. It's a poor paper. When will I learn? But the whole thing may have an advantageous result: he'll not keep buttering me up the way he has for years. He's a decent man I think, but (to me) not interesting, tho' he thinks he is. Ah well – I've had too much academia, I guess. Being a Visiting Prof. is quite nice, as you know. Some red carpet, no meetings <u>at all</u> (Yippee!), and a degree of respect. <u>And</u> the dough, v. good, for not much work. I needed the change of pace; + these Quarters are short.

L. + K.
Nicholas Pevsner, III

*That, however, is not true –

[242]

[WLM]
October 17th, 1979
University of California, Berkeley, Department of Architecture,
Wurster Hall 232, Berkeley, California 94720

*[Blank postcard, typed, addressed to Anthony Hecht, Cardinal of Isk,
19 East Boulevard, Rochester NY 14610]*

My dear Principe,

That's nice, Limestone.[1] Bravo for spilling [Vincent] Scully into the drink. The last sentence of his you quote is preposterous.[2] I love Auden's personal Eden, new to me. I've a 1935 ms. in which I seem to have designed an Empire with a few similar characteristics. Varia: Do you suppose A. knew [Jorge Luis] Borges' Encyclopedia schema, where animals were divided as follows: 1) those owned by the Emperor; 2) pigs; 3) those that look like flies when seen from a distance; 4) others; etc.?[3] "Gennel" new to me. Someone in the <u>Times</u> wanted info. about Allen Tate so I sent (modified) my Rome journal entry about the night he & Auden led the famous confederate march through the Academy corridors. O'Gorman, the questioner's name was; never ack'd my contribution. Could he have been annoyed that Allen was plastered?[4] ... Did you get the crocodile information? All's well; eating lotuses. Hot.

---

1 WLM is responding to a copy of AH's essay, "On W. H. Auden's 'In Praise of Limestone'," first published in Vol. 2, No. 1 of the *New England Review* in autumn 1979, and subsequently included in AH's *Obbligati: Essays in Criticism*.

2 The passage in question, from Vincent Scully's *Modern Architecture: The Architecture of Democracy* (New York: G. Braziller, 1974), pours scorn on the Baroque. Its last two sentences give the flavour: "It is a paternal, or, perhaps better, maternal architecture, and creates a world with which, today, only children, if they are lucky, could identify. This may be the reason why, since the Second World War, Baroque Rome has become a Mecca for some literati who would escape maturity...." In quoting the more extended passage, AH is contrasting Scully's distinctly negative view of the Baroque with Auden's distinctly positive view of it: "The very features of the Baroque that Scully singles out for opprobrium – those spaces which give the illusion of freedom while really serving as protections and safeguards – are in fact exactly the ones that Auden means to embrace. But while Scully, with the contemptuous tone of a very superior adult admonishing a backward and regressive child, can see in a modern person's taste for this period style only some immature perversity, some unwillingness to grow up and face facts, Auden very explicitly selects the style as 'edenic,' as part of a mythic and psychic landscape of our own licensed invention, not meant to correspond to any harsh realities of this world, but, on the contrary, to evoke some prehistorical perfection." *Obbligati: Essays in Criticism*, p. 46.

3 In the very same month that this letter was written, AH received from the Nobel Committee of the Swedish Academy a letter inviting him to nominate a candidate for the 1980 Nobel Prize for Literature, and two months later he wrote back, nominating Borges, whom he described as "a poet and fiction writer of international renown and incomparable attainment." The nomination was unsuccessful, and when Borges died, in 1986, he did so regretting that he had been never been rewarded with this, the most prestigious literary prize available.

4 The poet Ned O'Gorman began work on a biography of Allen Tate in 1979, and ran adverts and wrote letters soliciting information from people who had had dealings with him.

Yrs.
Samra Binowitz

[243]

[WLM]
October 18th, 1979
University of California, Berkeley, Department of Architecture,
Wurster Hall 232, Berkeley, California 94720

[Blank postcard, typed, with the sender's address given as Prince Torlonia KC, Wurster 232 UCal, Berk 94720, addressed to A E von Hecht, 19 East Boulevard, Rochester, NY 14620]

My dear Cavour,

Enchanted by my own wit & flow of words, I forgot to give you on yesterday's card the only, and tiny, criticism I have of "Limestone": Bramante was a High Ren,, as we say, architect, not Mannerist or Barock. He dies I think in the 1540s, just as the Council of Trent is being packaged.[1] The article is however very rich and satisfactory, and as always I marvel at your learning and your ability to connect successfully literature from periods and cultures so widely spread in time and space (You may quote me, four shillings the word, each use).

Yours in revolt,
Ole Red Shirt

---

1. In the version of this article which AH sent WLM, he had written as follows: "'In Praise of Limestone' combines rather curiously (and rather like Michelangelo's famous tondo, or round painting of the Holy Family, with young male nude athletes lounging around in the background), a serious religious concern, indicated at the very least by references to 'the blessed' and 'the life to come,' with a particularly worldly sensuality. And in this it resembles a good deal of Italian baroque and mannerist art. Both that art and this poem envision an antipuritanical ideal, and the art was part of the deliberate achievement of the Counter Reformation. It had been the Reformers, of course, who so violently divided pleasure from piety; and here in this poem, as in those paintings of Michelangelo, those statues and buildings of Bramante and Bernini, we have 'modifications of matter into / Innocent athletes and gesticulating fountains, / Made solely for pleasure. ....'" When AH reprinted the essay in *Obbligati: Essays in Criticism*, he acted on WLM's criticism and replaced the reference to Bramante with one to Borromini.

[244]

[WLM]
[October 24th, 1979]
University of California, Berkeley, Department of Architecture,
Wurster Hall 232, Berkeley, California 94720

*[Letter, typed, addressed to Professor Anthony E. Hecht, Department of English,
The University of Rochester, New York, 146XX, with enclosure]*

[Enclosure: clipping]

SPLAG — (shpläag), n., pl., the splaggies. (A.S. splagat, a ggarthe or similar farkle = D. splage, a word or momfret = Icel. splague, the common curlew. = G. splach, identity papers = Celt, splash, whiskey.) Orig, a typical spawl or wiven;- but now refers to the ordinary nurdle or similar grond. I. *Heral.* an escutcheon bearing an invisible farole or transparent plagent to confuse the villain. II. *Theol.,.* that dogma that deals with general principles and espouses the tenet that man is composed of body, soul and yeast; any Trappist carnival. III. *Geol.*, noting or pertaining to rich ore and the land adjacent to it, esp. belonging to others. IV. *Polit.*, the former National Assembly of Serbia or the former khedive of Clifton, N.J. V. *Obs.* a sowern or blind pig (as Chaucer, *Canterbury Tales*, "Filoke cithern and vertheth in sowern and splag.") -VI. *Pathol.*, a somewhat mild pediatric condition of the lower extremities ("a dose of the old splag."; Motley's *Rise of the Dutch Republic*.) VII. Any Incan beaker, Jewish month, obscure part of a cathedral, minor Scandinavian goddess, word in Low German, a popular name for "the thane of Crawford, So. Dak., and collectively, all S.E. Asian turpentine gatherers. VIII. *Arch.*, an edifice constructed entirely of marzipan. IX. A casual gesture of contempt made by placing knees on buttocks and grimacing humorously, or any such merry gesture, viz.("... the splag was cast towards Genghis Khan by his late vizier known to history as "Timor of a Thousand Deaths ..." De Quincey, *Revolt of the Tartars*.) X. *Naut.*, any irregular rippon, snard or other riculette used by carlmen and fiagens for waining, hence, in general, any fannion, whord or steapsin used in foc'lin'. XI. Sexual congress with palm trees or the avoidance of such. ("Prince Albert observed wryly that the Pathans prefer a woman for childbearing, but he was not amused at their excessive splag.' Parkman, *The Oregon Trail*). The family name of King Zog of Albania and, to some extent, a sect of roach worshippers ...[1]

---

1 The cutting is from the February 7, 1972 edition of *New York* magazine, and is the submission of a

Sage: This is to help you with your research – any research at all. I enjoyed the Beethoven V building, and hope to use it in my article "Music and Architecture" in the OxCompArch, as we call it. Seriously. So don't feel unloved, up there in the cold northeast. Your work, maturated, will bear fruits. Mail is coming through in semi-monthly bags, via Pony Express. God, but this is a strange place.

Yours in transcended meditation,
Ahmed, at the sign of the Persianburger
(cor. Dwight + Telegraph)

[245]

[AH]
October 31st, 1979
19 East Boulevard, Rochester, New York 14610

[Letter, typed, posted in a The University of Rochester envelope, addressed to William MacDonald (Bishop of Diss), Wurster 232, Department of Architecture, University of California, Berkeley, California 94270, with a now missing enclosure]

Dear Major Upset,

Sorry to hear you responded with innocent good will to Ned O'Gorman's letter in the Times, requesting help on a biography he said he was "appointed" to write about Allen Tate. We were in Europe when that letter appeared, but news of it reached us even there. In Venice Laurance Roberts told me he had received a personal letter from O'Gorman, requesting a personal interview about Tate. Laurance knew nothing of the Times letter, and nothing, of course, of O'Gorman himself, and so he asked me if, since we were shortly to return to the States, I would find out whether this whole thing were a legitimate enterprise. I already had reason to doubt that it was, knowing something of O'Gorman already. He is a stunningly bad poet, and someone with no scholarly qualifications whatever, nor has he ever published a solitary piece of criticism. On that basis alone he is spectacularly ill-equipped for the job. He is a very pious Roman Catholic with what I suppose must be an admirable Goody-Two-Shoes aspect to his character since, for a good part of his adult life, he has run a store-front library for the poor and illiterate in Harlem. Anyway, it was not, as I said, from Laurance that I heard of the Times letter; it was from James Merrill, who also appeared in Venice while we were there. I promised Laurance to find out what was going on, and after a few failed attempts to get in touch with Allen's widow, Helen, I succeeded. It appears that at least four years before his death Allen had selected and appointed a man named Robert Buffington, of the University of Georgia Press, to be his official biographer, and for those four years he worked with Buffington to assist him. Buffington is apparently a very careful, painstaking scholar

certain Jack Ryan of NYC for a competition whose entrants had to invent and then define a word containing the letters SPLA.

who works slowly, but who has access, by Allen's express permission, to examine the Tate archives at Princeton, which are otherwise closed to public inspection. It goes without saying that Buffington also has the blessing of Helen Tate. But apparently O'Gorman has the cooperation of Allen's two disgruntled ex-wives, Caroline Gordon and Isabella Gardner, as well as Allen's daughter by Caroline, Nancy Tate Wood (whose son, incidentally, has just published a book about having been brainwashed by the Moonies.) Helen Tate knows that O'Gorman cannot possibly write a "responsible" biography since so many important archives are closed to him, and since Allen chose and worked with another man. She is therefore convinced that O'Gorman is likely to be prompted chiefly by the vindictiveness of resentful ex-wives and the loyal daughter of one of them, and that Simon and Schuster, which contracted the book, is not concerned with either scholarship or accuracy but merely a sensational exposé that will beat Buffington's careful labors into print. Everything I have been able to find out about this suggests to me that Helen Tate is right. At the very least it may be said (quite without prejudice) that O'Gorman is a loyal and long-standing friend of Caroline's. I let Laurance know all this in due course, and he seemed grateful to be spared an audience he thought he might have had to grant.

O'Gorman also wrote to me asking for help, which I have not offered.[1]

Incidentally, while we were with him in Venice Laurance complained of how badly the Academy was managed under the presidency of Bill Lacy, who, as I think I understood it from Laurance, seemed to take upon himself both posts of President in New York and Director in Rome, travelling back and forth throughout the year. Well, Bill Lacy just quit to take over Cooper Union, as I suppose you know; the Academy is soliciting nominations for a new President. I have nominated you, and also Bobby White. Having the opportunity conveniently at hand, I also echoed Laurance in stating that I did not think one man could successfully fill both posts, and that I thought you (or Bobby) would best serve in Rome. There is no need for you to tell me how grateful you are right away; but I think we would be very comfortable in the little mezzanine apartment at the back of the Academy as soon as you

---

1 In fact, AH had at one point offered to help, but it was an offer he subsequently withdrew. O'Gorman had written to him on May 25th, 1979, explaining that he was beginning work on a biography of Tate and asking whether AH would be willing to write to him, sharing any memories of Tate he might have. AH did not receive this letter until after his summer, and at a time when, as he explained to O'Gorman, he was too busy preparing for a new year of teaching to try to write up his many memories of Tate, someone he had known well since the late 1940s. O'Gorman wrote again on August 24th, 1979, assuming that AH was refusing all co-operation, and expressing the hope that AH would reconsider: "It seems a grim thought that you will not see me." AH wrote back the next day, pointing out that he had not refused to see him, that O'Gorman had only asked him to put his memories down on paper, not asked whether he would be prepared to record an interview. He concluded by saying "If you ... wish to tape some conversation with me here in Rochester I will do all I can to assist you." (Anthony Hecht Papers, Box 55, file 2.) However, and as the present letter to WLM makes clear, after getting through to Helen Tate, and discovering that, contrary to what O'Gorman's *Times* advert had claimed, the proposed biography was unauthorised, AH repented of his offer to help, and O'Gorman never got to interview him. It is worth adding that a note in the O'Gorman archive in Georgetown University's Special Collections states that, despite receiving "voluminous responses" to the adverts and letters he sent out asking for memories of Tate, his biography "was stopped short and never published."

can arrange it.

I enclose an interesting and puzzling picture which presents a number of problems.[1]

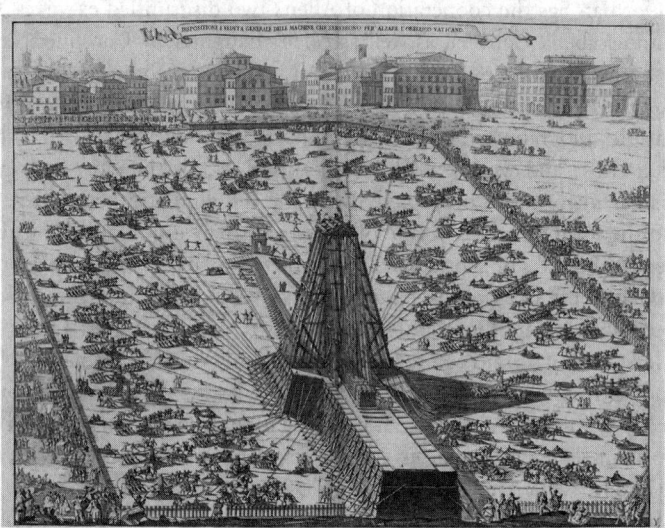

The obelisk, the article informs me, was raised in front of St. Peter's by Carlo Fontana in 1586. This <u>veduta</u> by Specchi (of the Spanish Steps?) could therefore, given his dates, not be based on personal eye-witness. It could nevertheless be based on a good deal of reliable second-hand information. How did they arrange for all those scattered windlasses to wind at the same rate so that all forces were equalized? It must be the top of the obelisk that points toward the viewer in this picture, though it certainly doesn't look like the top. If, on the other hand, it were the bottom, the top would be lying right at the foot of the tower of scaffolding, and they would probably not be able to raise it to more than a thirty-degree angle. I remember your telling the story of putting water on the ropes, but I would be glad to hear from you in more detail about how this whole thing was engineered.

I assume you will not be teaching next term; neither will I. We will both, of course, have our even more serious projects to advance. But Helen joins me in hoping you can come, bringing some work with you, for a visit.

My book[2] is out, in a manner of speaking. Like all books of poetry, it emerges undetectably, like a silent fart. It may well be a year or more before any reviews appear. A few copies of the book have made their way to Rochester, but Atheneum's methods of distribution are so peculiar that I have no idea whether it can yet be obtained in a New York bookstore. In any case, I may say of it without any taint of vanity that it is an extremely handsome job of book-making, and a copy has been

---

1 Though the reproduction AH enclosed is now missing, this is the engraving he wished to discuss.

2 *The Venetian Vespers.*

addressed to you in Northampton. Helen's book, with a long excerpt from it in the November issue of Gourmet, is also out.¹ I assume you know that in collaboration with a neighbor she has composed a cookbook of food gifts one can make at home in a book called Gifts in Good Taste. Not only is Gourmet featuring it but the Cooking and Crafts department (a new one) of the Book-of-The-Month-Club has taken it for half of their February choice, the other half being Erma Bombeck (if that's how she spells her foolish name.²)

Do not let those sunny skies corrupt you; California is dangerous.

Epaminondas

[246]

[WLM]
November 17th, 1979
[University of California, Berkeley, Department of Architecture,
Wurster Hall 232, Berkeley, California 94720]

*[Postcard, with a photograph of the Frontier Hotel, Las Vegas, Nevada, handwritten, addressed to
Anthony Hecht, Phrenologist, 19 East Boulevard, Rochester NY, 14610]*

O'Gorman, from what you say, will in the end I'd say get his just due. I am much touched by your nomination of me for the AAR post. I'll take it, install you in the Bellacci³ + we'll show them really how to live.* Went to Vegas – strange, wonderful. Barbara, whom I've not seen in 6-8 months, arrives today for a week's inspection of CA.

[Unsigned]

*Student construction

[247]

[WLM]
December 4th, 1979
25 Henshaw Avenue, Northampton, Massachusetts 01060

*[Letter, typed on a The Waldorf-Astoria Hotel, New York, letterhead, posted in a
The Dunfey Family's Parker House envelope, addressed to Anthony Hecht, Famous Man,
19 East Boulevard, Rochester NY 14610]*

Heigh Ho, etc.

1 Helen Hecht, *Gifts in Good Taste* (New York: Atheneum, 1979).
2 Her first name was actually spelt with an I rather than an E.
3 The Villino Bellacci is one of the buildings which belong to the American Academy in Rome.

Auden's "gennels," as you probably know, are not in the Big Webster's, but the OED came through in good style as usual. I am trying to be renitent about new words ...

The Times review was heart warming.[1] I've still not had time to sit down and read the book through. Coming home after a fair absence seems to require a week's extra work or more. But as soon as I can curl up with it – I think I've read three of the poems in journals – I will send on a critical report. Of course I will consult Petersson before writing.

Seeing the Zajacs was a high point of my recent jaunt. I'd no idea they were in Santa Cruz, which made it doubly delectable. They've a nice house on the ocean, and I'm sure you know what that means (aren't Victoria's letters fun, with all that underlining?). My students were good, I gave a couple of full dress lectures, and Barbara came out for a week for her first view of California; but the best part was looking at, and photographing, buildings.

Now lessee. The etching of the obelisk charivari may well be by Specchi, but it is from what I have always known as Fontana's own book. I'll look further into the matter and let you know. F. did a number of etchings of his exploit, which took place in 1589 as I recall. And what is RIT? That is, where is the Beethoven V building of which you so kindly sent me a clipping? I need this information in order to complete my files on Frozen Music, etc. Seriously. Thanks for the clipping; Birdseye is fine, but as to the actual photograph, I would venture that Wormseye would be better, but of course it won't sell.

Nothing from the AAR. I was asked – in May or so – if I was interested in the Prof-in-Charge job, but replied that I am not qualified; that was from Lacy, by the way, who has not in my judgement done all that bad a job. A friend of mine who knows a great deal about the Academy's situation and administration places some blame for the current state of affairs on the Trustees. In any event, thanks for your ever so kind thought in nominating me. If I hear anything I'll be in touch directly ...

The book you want is Bern Dibner, Raising the Obelisk, MIT Press 1970 – woops, it's Moving the Obelisks, I find. A good starting point. I think maybe the caption in the clipping is wrong. But, as I said, I'll look into it further. There's a fair amount of writing on and by D[omenico] Fontana (not to be confused with C[arlo], an architect a century later), so I ought to be able to clear the matter up.

Trottenberg has returned to Harvard, and I expect to dine with him in Cambridge next week. The Archaeological Institute is celebrating its 100th birthday in Boston after Christmas; maybe I'll go in & see who's there,

So, you see, life progresses, or at least continues.

Love to all,
Edna May Oliver

---

1 Christopher Ricks, "Poets Who Have Learned Their Trade," *New York Times Book Review*, December 2nd, 1979.

[248]

[WLM]
December 10th, 1979
[25 Henshaw Avenue, Northampton, Massachusetts 01060]

[Blank postcard, typed]

Dear Mag. Mil. Utr. in Praes.,

The clipping is correct. That particular view of the obelisk caper is from Carlo Fontana's Il Tempio] Vaticano of 1694, work by the same Specchi who, as you say, designed (in part?) the S[panish] Steps. But most of the obelisk frolic scenes are from Domenico Fontana's <u>Della trasportatione dell'obelisco vaticano</u> of 1590, and I for a bit confused the two works; I should have noted the stylistic differences. Dibner's book, though amateurish in some ways, is clear on all this. When I say "most of the ob. scenes" I mean the ones commonly reproduced in modern times. So.
With all good wishes for Saint Somebody's Day, & love to all,
Meyer Sharp-hero

(P.S. With a little ingenuity, you can use this card again –)[1]

[249]

[AH]
December 19th, 1979
19 East Boulevard, Rochester, NY 14610

[Letter, typed, posted in a The University of Rochester envelope, addressed to Prof. William MacDonald (in excelsis), 25 Henshaw Ave., Northampton, Mass. 01060]

Dear Parishioner,

Here beginneth the First Lesson, in the Revised Standard Version, of course. Moses and his staff were leading the Children of Israel out of Egypt, but the staff were worried, especially the PR man. He kept saying, "They're gaining on us," and "Haven't ya gotta plan?" and "Whatta ya gonna do, fer God's sake?" And Moses answered him, saying, "We're gonna take a short-cut to the Red Sea, and when we get there, I'm gonna part the waters so we can march right through." And the PR man said, "Terrific, but they're catching up so fast they will march through right behind us." And Moses answered him, saying, "But when we reach dry land on the other side I will let the sea fill right up again, and they'll all drown." At which the PR man smiled and said, "Moses, baby, if ya can bring that off I can getcha four pages in the Old Testament."

The reason I'm writing to you today is that I have all my term papers and final

---

1 WLM had left the postcard unaddressed, enclosing it in a now missing envelope.

exams to correct and I can't face them. Forty-eight little blunderers in Shakespeare alone; actually, a few of them are rather good, and one of the better ones, I rejoice to say, is a medical student.

You will be amused to know that a young man, an assistant prof, and a very good young poet at Yale, named Robert Shaw, whom we got to know during my term there, asked me to write a commendation for his dossier, which I was happy to do, and to get it written in time for it to be sent off to places that were considering him for appointment – though, of course, my commendation was to be sent to the Yale Placement Office, and not directly to the places considering him. I hastened to meet that deadline, and was duly thanked by him, and told that his dossier had been sent off to Berkeley and to Tufts. Oddly, Tufts is also considering me. Anything you may know about it, by the way, will be of interest to us. Actually I know nothing of it whatever, and am not especially inclined to move unless they can make some irresistible offer. Its only superficial attraction is Boston/Cambridge. Still, even if nothing comes of it, the offer may shake up some people around here to good purposes.

Best
Al (minor prophet)

[250]

[WLM]
December ???, 1979
[The Bronx, New York]

[Letter, typed on a Society of Architectural Historians letterhead, addressed to Mr. Anthony Hecht, 19 East Boulevard, New York 14610]

"Small Baths," after a score of delays, chiefly on the part of my draughtsman-collaborator, Michael Boyle, and the Editor of the <u>American Journal of Archaeology</u>, who rejected it with a curt note saying "we don't publish surveys" (which they have been doing for ninety years), and numerous re-writings to suit another editor, is, at long last, in print, that is, in galleys, which I passed last week, which event has lifted my spirits considerably.[1] (You may use that sentence in any of your future works, with or without credit, as you see fit.)

Barbara came out to San Francisco for a week, her first trip to the Lotus Land. I'd not seen her since last April. We had a good time, moochng about the city & environs. She is to come here for New Year's eve, etc. Jobless again, but not too sad. We're friends in a kind of wary way. Of course I think nothing will ever come of it, which is rather comforting. But, on the other hand, I've no one else, though I

---

1 "The Small Baths at Hadrian's Villa" was published in the *Journal of the Society of Architectural Historians*, 39:1 early in 1980.

have to say that the Ada Comstock Program[1] here (invented by my close pal Allen Weinstein [Perjury])[2] has produced some fine, interesting women that I have begun dinner-once-in-a-while kinds of beginnings with. All three divorced, 35?-ish?, smallish kids ... beautifully determined to finish college.

Lovely letters from Meyer Schapiro & Richard Krautheimer about my Piranesi piece.

Do you want, think about, Tufts? Trott is back at Harvard & would be a fine weapon if needed. When Bundy left the Ford Foundation, Trott left too. At the Faculty Club a few days ago I said "Well, Arturo, how are you?" And he replied, "I'm 5'3." I'm Jewish. I have huge, protruding ears. Also, I became the managing Vice President of the Ford Foundation. That's how I am."

Love to all,
Onopodius of Nicea
(not Nicaea)

Gore Vidal: "It's not enough to succeed. Others must fail."

[251]

[WLM]
December 27th, 1979
[25 Henshaw Avenue, Northampton, Massachusetts 01060]

[Letter, typed on Syracuse Airport Inn, Syracuse Hancock International Airport, letterhead]

(Swabian day of S/Heil. Flätyewlenz)

Dear Cappadocian,

A few years ago the Spaniards published a thick, very good volume simply entitled LEGIO VII GEMINA, a kind of Festschrift, slightly delayed, for the military machine that kept order in Hispania and Lusitania in the I–III centuries, and brought civilisation to the edges of the earth (well, one edge, anyway). Perusing it the other day, I got an idea for a story: scene, Field Officers Club & Bar on the Olympian slopes, chief characters, a few Old Soldiers, colonels of the line of VII Gemina, men who knew every hectare of ground. One of them has checked LEGIO VII out of the Clouds Circulating Library, and has read it with increasing exasperation. "Look here, mates, this utter fool says that at the investiture of Barraca the Iberians had no artillery? Can you believe that? Mother of the Dioscuri (or whatever), I'd like to have had that bastard there with me under fire. No artillery? These damnable historians act as if they knew something, when they don't know anything at all." Assent, all round, and another round. "And there's an article here called "Hadrian the intellectual." In-

---

1 The Ada Comstock Scholars Program was established at Smith College to enable women of non-traditional college age to study for Bachelor of Arts degrees.
2 Allen Weinstein was the author of *Perjury: The Hiss-Chambers Case* (New York: Knopf, 1978).

tellectual, my rosy ass. I can remember when he was a green tribune and didn't know one end of a pilus from the other! Read a lot of books, I suppose, but anything he knew he learned from the likes of us, right? Right!" Etc ... moving to a more serious vein as Ammianus walks in for his afternoon Falernian and lectures them gently on the problems of writing history, the whole winding up with A's assessment of the problems, using LEGIO VII as his sounding-board. I.e. the serving man vs. the military historians. Reading Manchester's <u>MacArthur</u>,[1] and comparing notes with Nick, who is also reading it (though not at exactly the same time as I am) uncovers a lot of such problems. "Persian Colonels," that wonderful poem, also comes to mind. I've been looking for some way to write about my vast knowledge of military events, and more particularly about how one evaluates military matters and, within that frame, how great commanders manage the huge, often defeating, political side of their jobs, assignments, and careers ...

Tufts: not knowledgeable. Good place I think. Will check in Beantown when I next go in if you want me to. Would of course be wonderful to have you next door.

<u>Venetian Vespers</u>: haven't yet been able to give it a proper reading – like you, term papers (Berkeley) to do, Xmas, etc. Still warmed by the thought of Ricks' review. What of that RIT / Beethoven's V building. RochInst Technol? Or?

[Unsigned]

[252]

[AH]
January 8th, 1980
[19 East Boulevard, Rochester, NY 14610]

[Letter, typed on a The University of Rochester, Department of English, letterhead, with a now missing enclosure]

Dear Ol' Fred,

Bet you didn't know that the Iranians have established a university abroad in Italy. They have a pretty good football team, and their cheer for it begins, "Ayatollah U. Once, Ayatollah U. Twice ..."[2]

I enclose some deathless observations by Ada Louise [Huxtable], who strikes me as especially bright on Philip Johnson's A.T.&T. project, and on Bob Venturi, bless her soul.[3]

---

1 William Manchester, *American Caesar, Douglas MacArthur 1880-1964* (Boston, MA: Little Brown, 1978).

2 The references to Iran in this letter and its predecessor were clearly prompted by the hostage crisis which had begun on November 4th 1979 when a group of students stormed the American Embassy in Teheran, taking dozens of US staff hostage. Another year would go by before the hostages were released.

3 A. L. Huxtable, "The Present: The Troubled State of Modern Architecture," *Bulletin of the American Academy of Arts and Sciences,* 33: 24–37, January 1980, and reprinted in the *New York Review of Books,* May 1st, 1980. About Johnson, Huxtable wrote: "[M]uch as I admire Philip Johnson's taste and intel-

Your powers of divination are unblemished: that Beethoven-inspired wall is a fixture of the campus of the Rochester Institute of Technology.

I'm feeling rather piqued today at not having received the National Book Critics' Circle Award, which would have come in very handy.[1] The more so because an inside tip informs me that I'm out of the running for the Pulitzer, both because I've won it once already, and because the jurors (whose identities are supposed to be unknown but are known to my informant) have other favorites; and because I've already made up my mind to refuse an award from the newly constituted American Book Awards, which is to make its first appearance this spring. So it looks dishearteningly as if The Venetian Vespers will go unhonored.[2]

Went to the White House[3] reception for poets (and Patrons of The Arts) which was quite pleasant, though it was difficult to understand how the guest list of poets was made out. Most of the really good ones were not there (not invited or refused?) while some partial or total creeps were on hand.

The snow's begun.

Reverently,
Billy Graham, the Chilly-Assed Chiliast.

lect, I cannot take a standup joke like his AT&T Building in New York seriously—or his PPG Industries Building, Pittsburgh, either. No, I take that back. I take them very seriously, because they are such shallow, cerebral design and such bad pieces of architecture. The impressive care and cost with which they are detailed does not really make them any better. It takes a creative act, not clever cannibalism, to turn a building into art. It must do more than satisfy a roving eye. Unfortunately, these buildings are flying the flag for post-modernism all over the place, in the name of such things as historical allusion, because this kind of superficial shocker that doubles as a calculated crowd pleaser is so beloved by the popular press." And about WLM and AH's old friend Venturi, she wrote: "The work of Venturi and Rauch represents a difficult rather than an easy eclecticism. Their addition to Cass Gilbert's classical Oberlin College Art Museum is a much riskier and much more rewarding kind of design. In 1966 Robert Venturi wrote and the Museum of Modern Art published the ground-breaking treatise on today's new eclecticism: Complexity and Contradiction in Architecture—"a gentle manifesto." Almost a classic text ten years later, it was reissued in 1977. The book dealt with the "inclusive" rather than the "exclusive" environment; complexity and contradiction were seen as aesthetically and urbanistically desirable. Robert Venturi and his wife, Denise Scott Brown, immortalized the Pop environment in Learning from Las Vegas and Levittown. And they translated it all into a language of symbols and signs that gave instant intellectual cachet to suburbia and the strip. Theory, however, is always passed through Venturi's very refined and sensitive eye for what might be called a synthetic eclecticism in a subtle act of design that manages to transcend the theories he espouses."

1 The award went to Philip Levine for *Ashes* (New York: Atheneum, 1979). Hecht's fellow finalists were John Hollander, for *Blue Wine and Other Poems* (Baltimore, MD: Johns Hopkins University Press, 1979), Dave Smith for *Goshawk, Antelope* (Urbana, IL: University of Illinois Press, 1979) and Howard Moss for *Notes From the Castle* (New York: Atheneum, 1979).

2 The winner of the 1980 Pulitzer was Donald Justice, for his *Selected Poems* (New York: Atheneum, 1979); the only other finalist was Dave Smith, for *Goshawk, Antelope* (Urbana, IL: Illinois: University of Illinois Press, 1979).

3 The reception, thrown by President Jimmy Carter's White House, was held on December 27th, 1979. Some eighty poets were present and there were 500 or so guests.

[253]

[AH]
January 9th, 1980
[19 East Boulevard, Rochester, NY 14610]

[Letter, typed on a The University of Rochester memorandum slip]

Post scriptum to my note of yesterday –

Spectacular congratulations on the compliments you got from Meyer Shapiro and Richard Krautheimer on your Piranesi essay. Praise from them is worth the price of gold.

I've called things off with Tufts. By which I mean that in describing my situation here I have shown them that either they cannot or do not care to better it …

Charles the Overweight

[254]

[WLM]
January 23rd, 1980
25 Henshaw Avenue, Northampton, Massachusetts 01060

[Letter, typed, with the sender's address given as Golden Arches, XXV Hen, 01060, addressed to Anthony Hecht, DD (DMD?), 19 East Boulevard, Rochester NY 14610]

Well, Bub,

You get my award, anyway. It's a wonderful book, filled with delights and depths. Of the poems new to me I like "The Short End" and "Still Life" the best; but as time passes positions will shift. The Quill is sold out; people can't get the book; they've reordered. One point so minor that it barely qualifies for mention: Isn't "Malediction" (a marvelous thing) missing from the list of places where some of the poems were originally published? Didn't we first see it in the TLS?[1]

Could you tell me when you have a moment where the useful remarks of A. L. Huxtable appeared? ("Stated Meeting Report"). Tanks.

I can understand about Tufts. Selfishly, it would be just wonderful to have you all nearby.

Had a long talk with Hank Millon, who is on the committee to choose the Academy President. He said my name was before his gang, along with a number of others, and he asked if I was serious. I thought it over, back home, for a day or two and decided to ask them to take my folder out of circulation. It's not my kind of thing, and would keep me from my real work. As the sixty mark approaches I try to concentrate my efforts, sometimes successfully, sometimes not. I was, and am, touched by your tender of my name, and I hope you will understand my reasons for withdrawing. It could be an excit-

---

1 WLM was right: the poem had appeared in the July 7th, 1978 issue of the *Times Literary Supplement*.

ing job, but I've put so much time into my architectural studies, and have not yet begun to produce from them the way I wish to, that I cannot, I think, change work now.

Now something Really Important. It is clear to me, from Helen's splendid book,[1] that the Regents of the Double-D Society have forsaken their ***** New York Restaurant for the picnic glades of Rochester. I see a whole genre growing from this – the composition of Important Works through gastronomic stimulus. I will guess, now, that your next book will have an introduction in which a group meets in Battle Creek to discuss matters over dehydrated astronaut glunk. Or at the Hosteria dell'Orso?

Your letters, complete with envelopes, are filed in my correspondence drawers between Harvard and History, and that ought to make you feel good. Grand, inclusive headings, eh?

Meanwhile, and still and all, I am
Yours in K 421,[2]
Frankie

[255]

[AH]
January 28th, 1980
[19 East Boulevard, Rochester, NY 14610]

[Letter, typed on a The University of Rochester memorandum slip, addressed to Dr. William MacDonald (Eudemonist), 25 Henshaw Ave., Northampton, Mass. 01060]

Comrade,

Been in bed with a virus, and not even a sexy one, for several days. What really gets me is that some strain of puritan resistance invariably sees to it that I never get sick when I'm teaching; I reserve it all for holidays and leaves. I'm on leave this term, which is to be devoted to completing, with the aid of God and William Arrowsmith, the translation of Oedipus at Colonos. God's in his heaven and Arrowsmith is in Baltimore, and I shall be visiting the latter some time next month, I expect, for a week or more. After that there may be some NY meetings, and perhaps he will visit us during the summer. In any case, I want to get the damned play done with once and for all; and, once it is done I will confine myself to my own work henceforward.

The remarks by Ada Louise appeared in the Bulletin of the American Academy of Arts and Sciences fairly recently, though I can't tell you which issue.

I can understand your decision about via A. Masina, 5.[3] Aside from any considerations about your own professional projects, which clearly must take precedence over anything else, there is the sad fact that in this era of financial troubles

---

1 WLM had sent Helen Hecht a handwritten, but now largely illegible letter, on December 19th, 1979, thanking her for her cookbook, *Gifts in Good Taste*.
2 Presumably a reference to Mozart's String Quartet No. 15 in D. Minor, op. K421.
3 The street address of the American Academy in Rome.

to which no one is able to foresee a clear ending the job in Rome will consist more and more of passing the hat and economizing and behaving in a generally unpopular way. It would take the sort of zeal of a reformer, or else the sort of brazen vanity that makes for a presidential candidate in these troubled days. Can you imagine Jerry Brown believing he has a cure for any of our ills?

I've got this problem. When a body says, "I'm plumb tuckered out," how do you spell "plumb," and why?

Frank Machiavelli
(no relation)

[256]

[WLM]
January 29th, 1980
25 Henshaw Avenue, Northampton, Massachusetts 01060

[Blank postcard, typed, with address given as Top O'the Dome, 25 Hens/01060, addressed to A.E. Hecht, Obeliskoid, 19 East Boulevard, Rochester NY 14610]

Well, Gov,

The Truth about Moving the Obelisks is out, & I've permission from the Reverenda Fabbrica[1] to spill it. Specchi used Domenico Fontana's actual plates, from the <u>Trasportazione dell'Obelisco</u> of the 1590's, when he, S., did his <u>Templum Vaticanum</u> a century later. Either that, or S. had D. F.'s plates copied; one of the two. S. was Carlo Fontana's right-hand man, so Domenico's plates may either have come down in the family, or Carlo had easy access to them. They were used by other makers of illustrated books than Specchi, it turns out.

So there.

Yours in

[2]

P. P. Lord Cardinal, Rev. Ap. Fabbr. S.P.s
— Onofrio —

---

1 In 1523, Pope Clement VII appointed a committee of experts whose responsibility it was to maintain St Paul's Basilica in Rome. This committee later became independent, and was known as the Congregazione della Reverenda Fabbrica di San Pietro. It was presided over by the basilica's Cardinal Archpriest.

2 The Chi Rho, an ancient symbol adopted by some Christians since it superimposes the first two letters of Christ's name as spelt in Greek: ΧΡΙΣΤΟΣ.

[257]

[WLM]
[February 15th 1980]
[25 Henshaw Avenue, Northampton, Massachusetts 01060]

[Letter, typed on a The Byzantine Institute Inc., letterhead, with a now missing enclosure]

The Ides, Yes
M C M L X X X

Ole Hoss,

I enclose a photograph I had made of myself by BackRack the other day. I send it along to you, knowing that you savor your friends' successes; and what could be a greater signal of success than to have one's picture taken in one's study, surrounded by leather, velvet, and Karastan (where is Karastan? In New Jersey?[1]) You will by now have noted that the picture is suitable for framing; I will expect it to be on your wall when I come on my next tour of inspection.

"Surrounded" makes me think of a (true) experience of mine many years ago. Sir Bruce Ingram, then editor of the <u>Illustrated London News</u> (in the days when the cover of that grand mag was Something) had condescended to see me on the matter of a possible article on the Institute's work in Istanbul. He gave me tea in an oak-paneled office that in appearance and effect came dangerously close to a brilliant stage-set I once experienced in a straw-hat circuit performance of "Fumed Oak," that grand play. Sir Bruce patiently explained, after a bit, that what his <u>News</u> liked best to publish, in order of preference, was royalty, archaeology, and animals and, with respect to the last-named, dogs in particular. Now comes the good part, and you have to recall that I was then quite young, say twenty-nine. I replied that I thought his precedence, and indeed his subject-matters, admirable, and could suggest a story on the excavation in Sicily of the site of Morgantina, being conducted by the Swedes, which could be illustrated with pictures of His Majesty Gustav VI Adolf, at work on the site, surrounded by his hunting dogs. H. M. was a very good archaeologist, you may recall. Not bad, eh? You may tell this story to selected guests and friends. (You will notice that I do not make the vulgar assumption that those two categories always coincide.)

Barbara and I have been seeing something of each other since I came back from California. Last week we went to New York to hear a very good lecture at the Morgan, on Piranesi, by John Wilton-Ely from Hull, the pre-eminent authority. Dinner with him afterwards, a splendid evening for me. We went to the Cooper-Hewitt, which has such consistently good shows, to see the current Ocean Liner exhibit, and it was quite wonderful, though the curators could not have counted on the fact that I, who know quite a great deal about Ocean Liners, would come and notice errors. Then B. got a bit ill, so we came home. I've mixed feelings about her. I enjoy, by and large, her company, for she is v. intelligent, v. quick-witted, and we tend to worship at the

---

1   The name is that of a fine carpet and rug maker.

same shrines, but she is pretty cracked, too. Not too important, as we are no longer lovers, which is something of a relief. Her antics no longer upset me; peace.

The only other news is that after prolonged deliberation, and full discussions with my sons, I've resigned from Smith, effective at the end of the next academic year (I must come back next fall, as I am on an earned sabbatical term now, & not to return would be Very Bad Form). Ms [Jill] Conway, whom I have come to think highly of, and with whom I am on a very friendly basis – for some reason, she thinks I'm the cat's pyjamas – says I can stay here at 25 Henshaw for a few years, and since working conditions are nearly ideal here it will give me a chance to finish the Oxford tome almost unhindered. I'm exhilarated by the decision – it seems Right – and a bit pleased, albeit blushingly, with myself at being able to throw away over a quarter of a million clams. Finances all OK, won't have to go near TIAA/CREF[1] and indeed will I think be able to continue to sweeten it. Don't know where I'll move to eventually; things will be so much different in five or so years that it strikes me the only thing to do is to keep on writing, and let the future, for the nonce (what the hell is a nonce?) look after itself.

"The Small Baths," after all these years, are about to appear in print in a longish article; I passed galleys last December. An offprint, with the plans of which you can make comparisons with your own baths, will be in the mails to you fairly soon.

Love to you both,
Gide

P.S. You may from the photograph recall my part in <u>Gidget goes to Hawaii</u>.[2] Another story: a Radcliffe contemporary of mine, mad for Gide, rang at his door in the XVIme. The house-man eyed her dubiously; prepared for this, she recited a line of Gide's about "welcoming the world with open arms." Whereupon the houseman, as he shut the door, replied "Gide has changed his mind."

[258]

[AH]
March 21st, 1980
19 East Boulevard, Rochester, NY 14610

[Letter, typed on an Ocean Manor Resort Hotel letterhead, and posted in the same company's envelope, addressed to Dr. William MacDonald, Philoxenist and Nice Guy, 25 Henshaw Ave., Northampton, Mass. 01060]

Dear Sachem,
I am plumb impressed with your retirement plans. And mystified and envious.

1 The acronym for the Teachers Insurance and Annuity Association – College Retirement Equities Fund.

2 *Gidget Goes Hawaiian* (sic) was a musical comedy film first released in 1961. Had the photograph not gone missing, we might be able to guess which part WLM was joking about – not that of the film's eponymous heroine, presumably, but whether it was that of Eddie Horner, Russ Lawrence, or "Moondoggie" Matthews, is likely to remain a mystery.

Don't see how, in these days of what former President Nixon once publicly called "Flation," you can manage to slip so gracefully into the ranks of the leisure class. Be warned lest you be arrested for vagrancy on the charge of having no visible means of support. If questioned by the authorities in this matter you should maintain that you enjoy the <u>invisible</u> support of the Holy Ghost and the Ford Foundation, along with a little innocent blackmail of former colleagues. Also, it is interesting to hear that you will maintain your Northampton residence. I suppose that, mortgage rates being what they are, it would take a particular inducement to leave. This is something I myself have given a moment's thought to. Having led a fairly peregrine life as an academic, I almost suspect I am beginning to calcify if I stay any place too long; and while I am quite happy here at Roch. and well treated, the notion of beckoning gestures from selected places has occurred to me from time to time. In this regard Dimitri, with whom I converse from time to time regarding the Godine edition of <u>Vespers</u>, remarked wistfully how nice it would be if I were teaching there in Cambridge. And since Harvard has recently lost both Lowell and Elizabeth Bishop, and it further occurred to me that they might wish to replace at least one of them, I suggested to Dimitri that he sound out Robert Fitzgerald along those lines. Which he did, and reported to me in due course that Fitzgerald declared I was "too old." It's hard to know what that means, but it does make me feel elderly. It could be a tactful way of saying that my reputation lacks the luster of Lowell's or Bishop's, which is true enough. It could mean that if Harvard is going to replace one or both of them it wants somebody who will be around longer than I would be; or somebody they could get away with paying less. Incidentally, I think I wrote you that Tufts had expressed interest. Well, in trying to indicate to them what would be needed to lure me away from here I told them that I owned a large and comfortable house with a 7½ % mortgage; whereupon they wrote to say they couldn't match my present circumstances. Anyway, it is interesting in itself to know that you intend to stay in Northampton, and there is the odd additional interest that it is where Pat and my boys have taken up residence. For Pat nothing could more definitively constitute a return to the scene of the crime [...]

I rarely hear from the boys [...] Do you ever see anything of them? ... As for your portrait, I immediately recognized your shirt, which is rendered with great fidelity. We have sent it to the framers where it is likely to remain indefinitely. I may add that Hadrian's small baths are as nothing to my small baths. "In and out in a jiffy" is my motto, and I work with a stop-watch. When you declare, regarding small baths, "I passed galleys last December," what I want to know is, was it painful? As may be the case where you are too, things have warmed up considerably here. A night and day of rain have washed away the last of the snow – it is warm, vaguely steamy and springlike, and high time you considered a visit. By way of inducement let me tell you that Helen is making enormous progress toward the completion of a new cookbook which will utterly eclipse and diminish the last one, and having savored a good deal of this new work I can testify to its quality. By the way, have you ever noticed that there is virtually no prose so precious, so easily capable of rousing radical political fury along outright communist lines, as a description of an elegant meal at a fine restaurant in, let us say, the back pages of an old issue of Gourmet? This is curious. It is quite possible to read of someone's unusually sumptuous and gorgeous home, an architectural extravagance, or their collection of polo ponies or any of the other accoutrements of wealth, with an almost tolerant amusement. But a baroque and affected paragraph on the only wine suitable to accompany oysters Rockefeller can send me straight to the communist underground, begging to sign-up. Anyway, we got some good food here, and lots of room. Come see us.

Love,
Sam Trismegistus

[259]

[AH]
March 25th, 1980
[19 East Boulevard, Rochester, NY 14610]

Letter, typed on a The University of Rochester memorandum slip]

Cute Sir,

Not so long ago the name of Samuel Putnam was revered as one of the best of translators of Renaissance texts in the Romance Languages. He did a famous Rabelais,[1] for example. He has also translated some dialogues of Pietro Aretino, and in the introduction to that volume[2] he regrettably quotes from a novelized biography of Michelangelo by Dmitri Merejkowski, who, though he wrote in either Polish or Russian (which Putnam might be excused for not knowing) had his novel translated into the French, as "Michel Ange, Roman, Traduit du russe (I neglected to look ahead as I wrote this) par Dumesnil de Gramont, Paris, Artheme Fayard & Cie, 1926," and it is from this French text that Putnam supplies the English that begins thus: "On the day set by Julius II, that is to say, on Monday, Michelangelo betook himself once more to the palace. He had been given to understand that the Pope was leaving on a hunting expedition in the Albanian mountains." Sic! There is a magnificent inflation of the Alban hills. And from a skilled translator.

Bert the Areopagite

---

1 *The Portable Rabelais* (New York: Viking Press, 1946).

2 *The Works of Aretino*, translated into English from the original Italian, with a critical and biographical essay by Samuel Putnam, illustrations by the Marquis de Bayros, in two volumes, Volume I (Chicago, IL: Pascal Covici, 1926).

[260]

[WLM]
April 8th, 1980
[25 Henshaw Avenue, Northampton, Massachusetts 01060]

[Letter, typed on a The Michigan League, 227 South Ingalls, Ann Arbor, Michigan 48104, letterhead, addressed to Anthony Hecht, psuedo-anaymous, 19 East Boulevard, Rochester NY 14610, with enclosure]

Old Soldier,

I can understand that you are plumb impressed with my plans. Ekshul, it's simple: I have very few needs and unlike most of my friends am not keeping up a fairly big establishment. Nick has only one more year of college to go. Such factors, combined with the fact that I have been hustling for years and investing the money, let me do it. I carefully avoid the word retirement; I've just resigned my professorship, that's all. It's exhilarating. Truth is, if I never saw another classroom I wouldn't much care. But I'll do the winter quarter of '81 at Emory to help them get rid of some of that Coke money[1] ... I will be writing all I can.

Hard to know what Robert Fitzgerald meant. At Berkeley a student said (a pretty woman student) that I "look like everyone's father." That hurt a little; I don't know why; she meant well; she was talking about how open the students found me, implying (correctly, I think) that the other teachers there were not so. Smith is planning a big architectural museum bash for me in May of '81. I tried to head it off but without any luck; it embarrasses me. But yes, I am staying here for the time being. If I can finish the Oxford book it is possible that I'll be swimming in money. Anyway, I'm not looking very far down the road, just sticking to the work-table. Not going to touch TIAA-CREF until I have to, which with luck will be about when I would have anyway. Have been sweetening those accounts from time to time but now I find that money-market funds etc. are much better. All dull and in a way stupid, but I do like books and travel.

I've seen Pat a couple of times but not since nearly a year ago. She came with the Dimocks to my Piranesi lecture, and later I went to see her house. Her daughter was there,[2] and Adam; I didn't see Jason. Later on she called me saying she needed help, but I begged off, not wanting to get involved. I feel a bit guilty about not responding, but I knew I couldn't handle it. My five sentences with Adam left me with an impression of an attractive and cheerful young man. I am friendly with the Dimocks, but George is on sabbatical this year and as a result I haven't seen them and gotten any information they might want to impart. They did see Pat off and on when she lived in Ware or wherever it was; I don't know about more recent times.

---

1 Emory College was transformed into Emory University in 1915 after a sizeable injection of funds and the gift of valuable real estate in the city of Atlanta, GA, by the founder of Coca-Cola, Asa Candler. Since then, Coca-Cola's ongoing support for the university has helped to make it one of the country's top research establishments.

2 Johanna, born to Pat and Philippe Lambert in 1962.

[Enclosure: clipping]

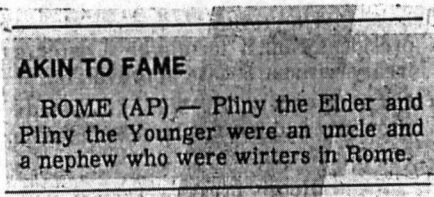

Speaking of seeing/not seeing people, I haven't seen or heard from the Wilburs in a year and a half. Very mysterious. I'm experienced enough not to put much weight on it but I do miss having an evening with them now and again.

Reading '30s stories by Graham Greene. Some, like "When Greek Meets Greek," "A Ride in the Country," and "The Innocent" strike me as being exceptionally good. But then, I'm a sucker for entertainment, and can't see literature in terms of an argument about meaning, symbols, and such. I'd have never made a Professor of Englitch.

I've an idea for an ad to be put in the Positions Wanted circulars of the professional societies I belong to. I'll sketch it out for your criticisms and suggestions:

> Mature SWM has slides, will travel. Wants term/quarterly visits to co-ed, well-formed places. Send 'phone, SASE, photos. No freaks or fatties.

Howzat?
Humbly,
Lucian K. Truscott V

[261]

[WLM]
[June 30th?, 1980]
25 Henshaw Avenue, Northampton, Massachusetts 01060

[Blank postcard, typed, with the sender's address given as Wille Macke, XXV Hensh, 01060, addressed to Anthony Evan Hecht, Author & C., 19 East Boulevard, Rochester NY 14610]

late June 80

Comrade,

Did you know that Darwin had a trombonist play an hour a day to a row of string beans?[1] Jee-zus. Many thanks for the 3½ x 5" girl. She fits neatly into my

---

1 WLM had first asked AH this question eight years earlier. See letter #70, February 16th, 1970.

Small Baths; though as for her g ..... l p ..... n I can't say much, being Big myself. News: Cohn-Haft is writing a book, on Marriage in Antiquity. Like the rest of us, he has some modern experience to help him out. His wife Betty is nice. What of the B[oylston] C[hair] of R[hetoric] & O[ratory]? Anything new? I have sacrificed to the Divine Trajan for you; he's mah buddeh. Nice letter from F[rank] E. B[rown] about the Baths piece, which he liked. He took it out to the Villa, he says, and spent a half day pacing about with it. Me, I'm working along, expect to summer here. Am avoiding Ankylosis, you'll be glad to know; and have 48 penny rockets for next Friday, courtesy of Nick. Yale to reprint my '65 book in both cloth & paper, which puts me Up.

                Yours on the Column of Life,
                  [Signature illegible]

[262]

                                                              [AH]
                                                   July 7th, 1980
                            19 East Boulevard, Rochester, NY 14610

                [Letter, typed]

Dear Primate (of the church, of course),
    There are those who, when trying either to butter you up or make a secret mockery of you, incline to tell you tales they know you would like to hear, quite aside from whether the tales have any foundation in truth or are simply the fruit of spontaneous invention. It was thus, I fear, with that rumor I so foolishly retailed about the B. C. of R. & O. It was handed to me, like a spread of caviar, by Mark Strand, who did not venture to explain how he came by it. There has been nothing since, and I strongly suspect that this is not simply because I'm here in Rochester where we are largely in the dark about what goes on in the world.[1]
    If Cohn-Haft is writing on Marriage in Antiquity perhaps it is about his first marriage. She was quite statuesque and handsome, and bore the daunting name of Athena. I'm surprised he wasn't fixed to a wheel.
    I wonder whether you can, should the occasion present itself, make a very discreet inquiry for me. I have sent two copies of <u>The Venetian Vespers</u> to Dick Wilbur, the second one being sent after a long interval when there had been no response about the first. There has now been no response about either one. It seems to me unlikely that neither copy reached him, and if they arrived while he was in Florida he must by now have had time to notice them. Can it be that he doesn't like the book and is embarrassed about writing? Needless to say, I don't want you to put him on the spot or let him know I'm inquiring. But I am puzzled.

1 The Boylston Professor of Rhetoric and Oratory at this point was Robert Fitzgerald, but Fitzgerald, who had been elected to the position in 1965, was due to retire in 1981. His successor was to be Seamus Heaney, who was elected in 1984.

I'm at work on a light-hearted poem in many parts, based on a Haydn quartet, with four voices assigned to the four lovers (Hermia, Lysander, Helena, Demetrius) of <u>A Midsummer Night's Dream</u>.[1]

Where did you find that item about Darwin having a trombonist play to his beans?

If you're going to be at Emory in their spring quarter you should have Richard Ellmann, the distinguished literary critic, historian and biographer, as a colleague. He's a don at Oxford but comes every spring to Atlanta.

Helen has finished a new cookbook, <u>Cold Cuisine</u>, which is all her own work, and enormous. It has been accepted for publication by Atheneum and will be out in about a year.

St. Polycarp

[263]

[WLM]
July 11th, 1980
25 Henshaw Avenue, Northampton, Massachusetts 01060

[Letter, typed, addressed to Sehr Gehlehrter Herr Professor Ord. Mag., Antonius De Hecht, 19 East Boulevard, Rochester NY 14610]

Plumber (of depths, that is):

The Darwin/trombone thing is something I've had rattling around in my brain for a long time. If I had to go to the wall, I'd say it came from one of Logan Pearsall-Smith's <u>Trivia</u> books, but I'd not be sure & might lose my balls.[2]

Wilburs: I never see them, as I may have mentioned before. Sad; and I'm damned if I know anything about it other than to say that we used to have drinks & dinner here or there, go to the movies, &c. They used often to stop by. Then they sort of evaporated – oh, say two years or more ago, then there came apologetic-ish notes – "you know we love you," & "it's sad that we teach in the same place & don't see each other," &c. Then that too stopped. I sent them the <u>Piranesi</u> piece & never heard anything. I go on a bit about it because it's a curious thing, and now that it may be happening to you it may be that they are changing directions, so to speak, with regard to friends. People do, and it's a little hard on the friends. I had gotten in

---

1 The poem AH was working on was "A Love for Four Voices: Homage to Franz Joseph Haydn," which was first published in *Poetry*, 138:1 (Apr., 1981), pp. 1-12, was later published in a fine press edition (Hitchin, Hertfordshire, UK: The Mandeville Press, 1983), and then collected in *The Transparent Man*.

2 WLM's attribution does seem to be mistaken, and in two important respects. The only source for the story I have been able to find is J. E. Littlewood's *A Mathematician's Miscellany*, which mentions it in connection not with Charles Darwin but Charles's grand-father Erasmus: "Erasmus Darwin had a theory that once in a while one should perform a damn-fool experiment. It almost always fails, but when it does come off is terrific. Darwin played the trombone to his tulips. The result of this particular experiment was negative." J. E. Littlewood, *A Mathematician's Miscellany* (London: Methuen, 1953). Whether this was WLM's actual source is unclear.

the mid-70s to like Charlee. I found I could talk to her about almost anything. I've always liked and admired Dick, while knowing that he was keeping his distance. So I can't help regrets. I'm not at all upset about their behavior, though I may sound that way. I don't care much anymore about that sort of thing, and rather expect it sometimes; a function of entering my sixtieth year? (Tomorrow.)

Just finished a peachy article for the Festschrift for Henry-Russell Hitchcock, on how Italian types of the '30s made use of ancient Roman architecture for the official fascist buildings,[1] another step in my Quest for the reasons for the Persistence of Classicism. Now to revise the '65 Roman arch. book for a new edition, then back to the OxComp.

Lessee, that's about it. Emory will be fun, and I look forward to meeting Ellmann, as I supp. I will, Em. being a sm. place. Tell Helen that I think she should now come to WGBH and take over from J ... a C ...d,[2] who after all is too TALL.

Thine,
Stroker, of the Queen's Ass

[264]

[WLM]
[September 1st, 1980]
[25 Henshaw Avenue, Northampton, Massachusetts 01060]

[Letter, typed on a The Halloran House Hotel, New York, letterhead, posted in the same hotel's envelope, addressed to The Rev. Dr. A.E. HECHT, S.O.S., 19 East Boulevard, Rochester NY 14610, with enclosure]

Labor Day
MCMLXXX

My dear doctor,

We wish to know if you will review the following for our journal, The Distinctive Howard Johnson's Hotel Review:

[Enclosure]

ERLICH, Zipora. On Centralized Bus Transportation Systems with Poisson Arrivals.

We are particularly interested in this work because of both the transport and the fish. We deal with both. Our honorarium will consist of free postage for all your business letters to Madagascar for twenty days. Please, do not write on more than two sides of the paper. Our readers will want to know a lot about the way the fish arrive, and

---

1 The article was entitled "Excavation, Restoration, and Italian Architecture of the 1930s."

2 The reference is to Julia Child, the chef, author and television presenter, whose *The French Chef* series premiered on the Boston television station WGBH in 1962, and was thereafter syndicated to 96 stations throughout America.

what their attitudes are when they arrive. But then, having long been connected with things fishy, you will know how to deal with this. We can send you Ms Erlich, too, if you wish; she has a lot of Zip, as you can tell.

<u>Very</u> truly yours,
Ed. Wilson

[265]

[AH]
September 6th, 1980
19 East Boulevard, Rochester, New York 14610

[Letter, typed, with a now missing enclosure]

Dear Lord Chesterfield,

I've been trying to keep an eye on your son for you, and he and I have gotten to be rather good friends – like, we visit the same cat houses and get smashed at one another's homes, and like that. I want you to know that I think he's a real good guy, but he's bugged by your endless letters of advice. They rub him the wrong way, ya know what I mean? It makes him surly, and he usually tries to take it out by slugging a cop or something. Twice I've had to bail him out of the can after a dust-up of that kind. So if you'd care for some friendly advice for yourself, I'd say, put a sock in it. Your son works himself into a crimson fury at the mere sight of a postman, and it's bad for his heart.[1]

I enclose a recent string quartet of my own composition[2] which I hope will amuse you. I offer it in lieu (i.e., in loo) of the review you requested "On Centralized Bus Transportation Systems with Poisson Arrivals." While such a review would doubtless be challenging to write, the time involved in interviewing all those fish is more than I can spare just now. The term has, dammit, begun; and for almost the first time for me the term "term" has a penitentiary ring to it. At least my mood contrasts strikingly with the general lightness with which the quartet was composed. And the last few weeks have seen a considerable innovation in all our lives. Adam[3] has come to live with us. He has moved in, registered for courses of an elementary sort at Monroe Community College, and begun his first week of work. His morale is high – he's unbelievably relieved to be out of his mother's menage (she, by the way, is about to sell her house and move to an apartment) and his motivation toward college is touchingly high. We are deeply touched by his gratitude and his sense of true familial comfort with us, but I am privately concerned about finances, and have

---

1 Philip Dormer Stanhope, 4th Earl of Chesterfield, wrote some 400 letters to his son, mostly intended to instruct him in subjects as various as geography, history, literature and politics, but also in how he should conduct himself in polite society.
2 A draft of "A Love for Four Voices: Homage to Franz Joseph Haydn."
3 The younger of AH's two sons by Patricia Harris.

already asked the university to make adjustments. [...]
                                    Rutyard Coupling

[266]

[WLM]
September 12th, 1980
25 Henshaw Avenue, Northampton, Massachusetts 01060

[Blank postcard, typed, with the sender's address given as Somewhere on Henshaw, 01060, addressed to A. E. Hecht (not Housman), 19 East Boulevard, Rochester NY 14610]

Dear Tonino,

That's good news about Adam. I deeply hope it will all, if gradually, come out well. I've enormous faith in our young uns. Thanks for the poem, which I've put aside until the term (my last! my last!) gets well underway.[1] I've been saddled with the direction of the survey course (jealous colleagues?) and it's a lot of work and of course everything is fubar.[2] Yes, Athena, ex-Cohn-Haft, is as statuesque as ever, happily married to an ex-printer, a quiet and I think nice man. Meanwhile Lou has finished his monograph on marriage in antiquity, his first work in 20+ years, and he's way Up. Ran into Dick W[ilbur] briefly, polite words only ...
                     Love to all,
                  Prince William of Mauve

[267]

[AH]
September 19th, 1980
19 East Boulevard, Rochester, NY 14610

*[Letter, typed, addressed to Prof. William MacDonald (for President),
25 Henshaw Avenue, Northampton, Mass. 01060]*

Ragazzo mio,

Here are two brief cheery items. I've been invited to read my perms in mid-October at Oxford, Cambridge and in London, and will get all that done in the neat compass of one week. Cambridge Oct. 15; Oxford Oct. 17; and London Oct. 19; by which schedule I will miss only one of my regular classes, there being a holiday that week.

And I have written as follows to Donald E. Peterson, President of the Ford

---

1 WLM wouldn't respond to "A Love for Four Voices: Homage to Franz Joseph Haydn" until late in December. See letter #269, December 26th, 1980.

2 Military slang, meaning: fucked up beyond all recognition.

Motor Company.

>Dear Sir,
>   In behalf of all the members of my family, I want to thank you for the unlimited cheer you have brought us through the simple candor and humility of your current television advertising campaign. All of us, as we wander about the house or pass on the stairs, greet each other with the stirring motif of "Ford, That's Incredible!" You cannot imagine how lighthearted it has made us all. That one of the major industrial organizations in our nation, one of our manufacturing giants, should so forth-rightly characterize itself as "incredible," i.e., unbelievable, viz., not to be trusted, is a turn of events quite unforeseen and genuinely breath-taking.
>   For a moment, our youngest, who is eight years old, entertained the cynical suspicion that the Ford Motor Company was so contemptuous of the public intelligence as to suppose it was too ignorant to recognize the force and weight of so frank a corporate confession. But this attack of biliousness, which may well have been due to a Big Mac, passed quickly with the aid of a little bicarbonate of soda, and the general family gaiety was restored.
>   We rejoice not only in the candor of your admission, but look forward to a whole new era in advertising technique, the possibilities of which are mind-boggling, and in which Ford may rightly claim pride of place as a pioneer in that risk and daring for which all industries traditionally seek appropriate tax incentives from the federal government.
>   Most sincerely, etc.

I'm as puzzled as you by Wilbur's remoteness these days. He is currently working on a translation of Racine, a selection from which appeared recently in <u>Poetry</u>. Doubtless that is quite preoccupying. But still ...
                                Irving of Arimathaea

[268]

[AH]
October 13th, 1980
19 East Boulevard, Rochester, New York 14610

[Letter, typed]

Dear Friend of Coot and Hern,[1]

You will be pleased to know that I got a response, a cordial and amused response, from the Ford Motor Co. in the person of one B. E. Bidwell, Vice President of the Car and Truck Group, to whom I wrote in turn as follows -

> Dear Mr. Bidwell,
> This is to acknowledge with warm thanks the courtesy and good humor of your reply to my letter regarding the, as it now seems, abandoned thematic motif of "Ford, That's Incredible!" I find myself already missing its relentless reassertions, its hypnotic, almost hallucinatory invitation to abandon rational thought in favor of that sort of mystical ecstasy that declares in a high state of transport: <u>Credo quia incredibile</u>. I have come to feel almost as if I could write commercials for you myself; and if the time should come when you care to call upon my services you have only to let me know.
> With warmest good wishes,

I suppose it will mean moving to Dearborn[2] for a short while, just to get a look at the product; but I expect to persuade them that I can nowhere produce the sort of commercials that will sell their wretched cars so well as in the serenity and quiet of the Cipriani Hotel in Venice, always assuming I can turn to my family for companionship and support whenever I need. Once established at the Cipriani, we will ask you over, and reserve a suite for you in advance if you let us know your arrival date. After all, if Ford wants the best, they must be prepared to pay for it. I hope your taste for caviar has remained intact.

Fritz of Cappadocia

---

1 Tennyson's poem "The Brook" opens with "I come from haunts of coot and hern," a line which inspired James Thurber's *New Yorker* cartoon for August 19th, 1939.
2 Dearborn, Michigan, home to the Ford Motor Corporation's World Headquarters.

[269]

[WLM]
December 26th, 1980
[25 Henshaw Avenue, Northampton, Massachusetts 01060]

*[Letter, typed on a Santa Barbara Biltmore Hotel letterhead, addressed to
Les Hechts, tout court, 19 East Boulevard, Rochester NY 14610]*

Dear Elena e Antonio,

A fair chunk of yesterday morning was spent in the arms of W. B. Scott, whose pieces[1] made me laugh again and again which, given the fact that I have the grippe, or the 'flu, or whatever, probably loosened me up and speeded my recovery. They don't care much for laughter here in Santa Barbara[2] (there's a sign at the registration desk that warns that "Gentlemen with Unusual Haircuts will not be Registered"; and there's a tent-card on the bureau that says "Guests attending Conventions Will Kindly Not Wear their Identification Badges in the Bar or Other Public Rooms.").* So your splendid gift is all the more welcome.

I plunged into the book at the middle, as is my (sad) wont (I still read the NYTimes Mag & Book sections from back to front, a habit of forty-five years' standing – do you think I'm all right?), and so discovered to my pleasure that friends of mine – Carl Condit, for example – get Scottched. Only later did I get the preface down, to find out who Scott is. Nice.

In retaliation, I need an answer to this question: Why is it that a chain of modest motels around here is called "Susse Chalets"? It's beginning to bug me. A Swiss Dr Seuss? Please advise.

Scott's etymologies are sometimes hilarious. Please collect all my cards with "Etymologies for Humble Folk" and send them back so I can edit them for immediate publication. By the way, [William] Safire is wrong I think 22.7 % of the time: He missed nurd almost entirely, forgetting Mortimer Snurd, for example.[3]

I see to my great pleasure that "Ostia Antica" is featured in A Roman Collection,[4] though why they didn't include my piece on "S. Messalina in Flagrante: Some Peeks at the Real Action," I don't know.

"Organ involuntaries" indeed.[5] I think I am equipped, because of my shady past, to

---

1 The reference is to Scott's *Chicago Letter & Other Parodies*, published just two years earlier (Ann Arbor, MI: Ardis, 1978).

2 WLM's "here in Santa Barbara" seems to be a jest prompted by the letterhead; The letter was posted in Northampton, and was almost certainly written there too.

3 In 1979, Safire inaugurated a column in the *New York Times Magazine* – the "On Language" column, as it was called – in which he and others discussed etymology, usage, pronunciation, and other linguistic matters.

4 *A Roman Collection: Stories, Poems, and Other Good Pieces*, edited by Miller Williams (Columbia, MO: University of Missouri Press, 1980) contained two of AH's poems, not just "Ostia Antica" (from *The Hard Hours*) but also "The Gardens of the Villa d'Este" (from *A Summoning of Stones*).

5 The reference is to a line in part I of "A Love for Four Voices," and it is this poem that WLM is re-

read Lysander; do keep that in mind. The whole thing is springy and sharp at the same time; I particularly like the last three pages. Perhaps it is because we are about the same age and share so many interests that I strongly feel and savor your "once," your sense of the past, which to me suffuses the great "Martini" poem.[1] Old men – and I feel a bit old now and again – have to feel that if they've had any kind of life I guess. Lest it sound short-handed, I hasten to say that evoking "once" truthfully is one of your fortes (as the kids say); and by the way, who was that dumb bastard that suggested you didn't have enough passion? Fuck him.

Off to Atlanta in a week. Looking forward to it. Have lined up a number of Southland lectures while I'm there. And am about to sign up as the Clark Visiting Prof. at Williams for the Spring of '82, so 1) the larder will stay full, and 2) my estimate of the Visiting Prof. market was sound. Work moving along, offspring fine except that Nick is having something of a delayed reaction to his mother's death. But he's basically all right.

Love, and buon' anno to you all.
Orville Rong

* Gospel

sponding to in the ensuing lines.

1 "The Ghost in the Martini," from *Millions of Strange Shadows*.

3. 1981–1992

One hundred and forty-five letters and postcards have come down to us from the last twelve years in which Hecht and MacDonald corresponded with each other, a little more than half the number that have survived from the previous twelve years. The drop-off is not hard to understand, for by the fall of 1985 the two men were once again living in the same city,[1] and not only that but just a short walk from each other. Up till then, they had continued to write at the old rate, but now they could meet up whenever they wished it was only to be expected that they would write less frequently.[2]

The same high spirits that were such a prominent feature of their earlier exchanges are as much in evidence in these later ones. The very first letter from this period, sent by MacDonald shortly after he quit his job at Smith and arrived in Atlanta to take up a visiting position in Emory's Art History Department, lifts off with a joke about the four-times-married-and-four-times-divorced film-star John Barrymore, whom some affected to believe was gay. More jokes would follow, and the jesting, the ribbing, and the capering would still constitute the norm, but there would also be plenty of more serious departures, especially when it came to talk about their health, their reading, and their work.

Both men were getting on in years, but neither had any inclination to slow down or ease up. Indeed, each man still felt he had a lot to strive for. It was for this reason that MacDonald had resigned his chair at Smith: he was not retiring, as some supposed, but freeing himself of administrative responsibilities, and escaping what he will describe as "the petty and quite depressing side of academic life,"[3] so as to devote himself more fully to his writing, lecturing only when and where he wanted to, and on subjects of his own choosing.

Hecht wouldn't be able to give up full-time employment until his retirement, more than a decade hence, and in August 1981, after receiving another letter from MacDonald exulting in his new-found independence, we find him consoling himself with the thought that he will be on sabbatical leave throughout the following year. "I pray that I may make great inroads towards a new book. It is borne in on me

---

1 The last time had been in Rome, thirty years earlier.

2 Once again, I have chosen not to include all of the one hundred and forty-five items here. Eleven have been excluded, roughly the same proportion that was excluded from the years 1969–1980, and for the same general reasons.

3 Letter #278, September 15th, 1981.

that I am fast approaching sixty, when few poets are expected to perform with any success at all, and one points to the exceptions, like Yeats and Hardy and Sophocles, with gratitude precisely because they are exceptions."[1]

In that same letter, which was written shortly after he and Helen had returned from a two-month sojourn in Europe, we catch a whiff of Hecht's mounting dissatisfaction with life in Rochester, about which – if we disregard his complaints about the city's brutal winters – he has hitherto been quite positive. "Perhaps the saddest part of the shock of coming back from such a trip as we took," he writes, "is the feeling that sets in in less than a week's time that we have never been away ..."[2] "Rochester and home seem the locale of habit, familiar and comforting and dreary and repetitious, from which serious work will be the best escape, though I have not yet begun it." But then, after going on to tell MacDonald that he has been given an honorary degree by Georgetown University, he strikes a rather different, and in its way more troubling, note: "It is sad to say that this will not please some of my colleagues." Who these colleagues were, and what the basis of their anticipated displeasure was, is never made clear; but it is hard not to be put in mind of Gore Vidal's bitterly funny admission, "Whenever a friend succeeds, a little something in me dies."[3]

As well as the honorary degree from Georgetown, 1981 had brought Hecht the English Speaking Union Award for "A Love for Four Voices: Homage to Franz Joseph Haydn." 1982 had a still bigger honor in store for him, however – an invitation to become the thirty-seventh Consultant in Poetry to the Library of Congress (a post whose title would be changed just four years later to Poet Laureate Consultant to the Library of Congress). Hecht might have had misgivings about accepting a position which required him to start three-quarters of the way through his sabbatical, but the LOC's demands of its Consultants are kept to a minimum precisely so as to leave them as free as possible to pursue their own work, and besides this, the prospect of escaping from Rochester to Washington, D.C. for two years would have been a seriously enticing one.

Now that he no longer taught at Smith, MacDonald was also thinking about making a move. Northampton's winters were as uncongenial to him as Rochester's were to the Hechts, and in the months following his resignation we see him musing about where he might go. As early as June 1979, when he was still only thinking about resigning, he had talked about finding an apartment in Washington, D.C. some time in 1982 or 1983, but D.C. was only one possibility, and in February 1981 we find him talking about another destination altogether – Tallahassee, in Florida. Then something happened which obliged him to put on hold any thoughts about moving. The previous September, he had been able to tell Hecht that he was feeling "very well," and that, even though he had recently

1 Letter #276, August 10th, 1981.

2 The Hechts had left for Europe in early June. Their first month away was spent visiting London, Rome, Florence, and Venice; their second was spent in Asolo, an ancient town nestling in the foothills of the Dolomites which had once been home to Robert Browning, Eleonora Duse, Freya Stark, and Gian Francesco Malipiero. They had returned to the US on July 31st.

3 Quoted in *The Sunday Times* (London), September 16th, 1973.

turned sixty, he didn't "seem to have lost much energy."[1] But just two months later, he reports that he is only feeling "pretty well," and is having "a bit of eye trouble," for which he is undergoing tests. Characteristically, he makes light of the whole thing, describing the tests as "great sport,"[2] but as well as seeing double, he has been falling over and having difficulty talking, and when the test results come through, they are not good: "Diagnosis is miasthenia (sp.?) gravis, more tests this afternoon; a muscular disorder. Serious. Ho-hum."[3] Hecht, never having heard of the disorder, not being told about the symptoms, and mistaking MacDonald's tone, sends off what he subsequently calls an "utterly frivolous" response, and is only made to realise how big a thing the diagnosis is as a result of a telephone conversation the two men have in early February. This conversation prompts one of the most touching exchanges the two men ever had, one in which their deep fondness for each other is made perfectly explicit.

There is no cure for myasthenia gravis, but MacDonald responded well to treatment, and although he was never entirely free of its symptoms, and during these first several months often felt quite poorly, he refused to let the illness interfere with his life. In January, only weeks after receiving the diagnosis, he flew to Arizona to deliver two lectures and then do some sightseeing. Shortly after that, he fulfilled his obligations as Robert Sterling Clark Visiting Professor of Art at the Clark Institute in Williamstown, Massachusetts, doing a day's teaching each week throughout the spring. In April, he gave the three Amy M. Sacker Memorial Lectures he'd been invited to deliver at Mount Holyoke College in South Hadley, Massachusetts. In addition to his teaching, MacDonald was hard at work on his writing, contributing a dozen articles to the twenty-four volume *Macmillan Encyclopedia of Architects,* and endeavouring to finish *The Architecture of the Roman Empire, Vol. II: An Urban Appraisal,* the earliest version of which he'd been supposed to deliver to Atheneum all the way back in 1965. In 1982, he had two books to his credit: a revised edition of *The Architecture of the Roman Empire,* now subtitled *An Introductory Study,* was published by Yale, and The Smithsonian Institution's National Museum of Design published his pamphlet, *Columns in the Collection of the Cooper-Hewitt Museum.*[4]

That September, the Hechts closed up their house in Rochester and moved to a house on East Lenox Street in Chevy Chase, some eight miles to the north-west of the Library of Congress on Capitol Hill. MacDonald was able to visit them just a few weeks later, when he was in town to give two lectures at the Smithsonian, which the Hechts attended. Writing to them afterwards, MacDonald told them that they looked not just "well-installed" but also "well-connected."[5] This visit, and another

---

1 Letter #277, September 5th, 1981.

2 The three quotations are all from letter #281, November 18th, 1981.

3 Letter #284, December 13th, 1981.

4 A digital facsimile of this pamphlet can be viewed online at https://archive.org/details/columnsincollect00coop.

5 Letter #305, October 28th, 1982.

MacDonald made in November, when he returned to give a lecture at Georgetown University, almost certainly helped to reawaken in him thoughts about making D.C. his new home.

The next few years were active ones for both men. In the first few weeks of January 1983 Hecht heard that he had won Yale's prestigious Bollingen Prize for Poetry (a prize he would share with his old friend, and co-editor of *Jiggery-Pokery*, John Hollander), he was awarded another honorary degree (this time from Towson State University), and he became a Trustee of the American Academy in Rome.

Not long after Hecht took up his position at the LOC, Father Timothy Healy, SJ, the President of Georgetown University, asked him to consider leaving Rochester and joining the Georgetown faculty. Though gratified by this expression of interest, Hecht declined, thinking that he was well situated in Rochester. But as the months went by he underwent a change of heart, and in February of 1983 he told Father Healy that he could be open to an offer. Life in the capital was proving very agreeable to him and his family, and the prospect of going back to "familiar and comforting and dreary and repetitious" Rochester must have seemed even more unappealing than it had after their return from Europe in the summer of 1981.

In May 1983, MacDonald was back in D.C. again, this time to give a lecture at the Catholic University of America, but he had another reason besides, for he had definitely made up his mind to move to the city, and wanted to do some serious apartment hunting. He succeeded, too, finding a comfortable two-bed condominium at 3811 39th Street NW. Remarkably enough, he was ensconced there a mere two months later.

In February of 1984, Georgetown offered Hecht the position of University Professor. He had four months remaining in his term as Consultant in Poetry, and felt obliged to return to Rochester for a final year of teaching, but he gladly accepted, and rang MacDonald to let him know what had happened. "The news you gave me on the Ameche," MacDonald wrote afterwards, "is just great. I'm getting to know my students there and they are O.K."[1]

In August 1984, preparing for the new term at Rochester, Hecht learned that he was to be the first poet to receive the Librex-Guggenheim Eugenio Montale Award, and that the award would be made on the stage at La Scala, Milan at the end of September. Hearing that a singer would take to the stage after the award had been conferred, MacDonald teased: "I've been trying to plan your singing programme for La Scala and have hit some snags, but will send it along when I put it together. I'm pretty sure that it will include "Hut Sut Rawlson on the Brawla Brawla Sewit," and probably "O Promise Me."[2] The prize, which was worth $5,000, was conferred by Joseph Brodsky and Stephen Spender.

MacDonald was keeping himself remarkably busy, so busy that it's hard to imagine he could still find time to work on his other projects. In the four weeks of October 1984, he gave lectures at Yale, Wheaton College, and the Smithsonian – *twenty of them*. A younger and fitter man might have found this schedule pretty punishing,

---

1 Postcard #328, February 15th, 1984.

2 Letter #348, August 13th, 1984.

but MacDonald seems to have thrived on it, and in letters written in subsequent years we hear about many other public appearances: a presentation to a Joint Meeting of the Classical Association of the Atlantic States and the Washington Classical Society; a talk for the Historic American Buildings Survey; a series of lectures and seminars for the University of South Carolina at Chapel Hill; a lecture for the University of Texas; a lecture for Harvard ... Somehow, he was still able to find time for plenty of other activities as well – serving on prize-giving juries, reviewing books, writing introductions to exhibition catalogues, and undertaking sightseeing tours, all the while chipping away at his nearly completed "Cities" book.

Hecht was hard at it, too – teaching, of course, but also trying to make headway with his and William Arrowsmith's translation of Sophocles's *Oedipus at Colonos*, giving readings, serving on literary juries, writing reviews, dealing with a steadily growing volume of correspondence, responding to requests from younger poets for help with their work, and to requests from publishers for blurbs, and reading, reading, reading. He was also making frustratingly slow progress with his next collection of poems, the "great inroads towards a new book" he'd prayed for in Letter #276 having eluded him, and the poems only coming slowly and intermittently.

It had looked as though Hecht and MacDonald would start to see a lot more of each other once the Hechts returned to D.C. in September 1985, but in March of that year MacDonald was offered a prized scholarship by the John Paul Getty Museum, and his acceptance of this obliged him to take up residence at the Getty Center for the History of Art and the Humanities in Santa Monica, California, beginning in September, just before the Hechts reappeared, and not ending till the following June.

MacDonald put his time in "Lotus Land" to good use, doing solid work on his next big project, a book about Hadrian's Villa, an architectural landmark which had long fascinated him. He also found time to carry on teaching, giving, as he told Hecht, "a slew of lectures from February through May, mostly up and down the California coast, but penetrating Arizona and Texas as well."[1] When he wasn't working, he visited with old friends, such as Spiro Kostof and Jack and Corda Zajac, and made a good many new ones too, amongst them the architect Frank Gehry, the architectural critic Charles Jencks, the English philosopher Stephen Toulmin, and Hecht's former student, Jonathan Post, who had been teaching in UCLA's English Department since 1980.

1986 saw publication of MacDonald's long-gestated *The Architecture of the Roman Empire, Vol. II: An Urban Appraisal*, and the quarter of a century he'd spent on it was richly rewarded with praise. Leon Krier wrote that it was "Simply the best book on Roman urbanism [that] I know ... a formidable breakthrough. It brings to life the genius of Roman urbanism and reveals its continuing relevance for present urban planning and architecture."[2] Henry V. Bender agreed: "Lucid and articulate, MacDonald has once again produced a learned work of significant value to the

---

1 Letter #379, January 5th, 1986.
2 *Architects' Journal*, 183, March 1986.

general reader as well as to the informed scholar ... A unique talent for making the complex comprehensible, a scholarly command of the subject, and a facile style of writing enable MacDonald to achieve his avowed purpose: 'to interpret imperial architecture by analyzing its urban purposes and content.' A fine book, against which all future works of its type must be measured."[1] And Martin Henig, writing in the *Times Literary Supplement*, was equally unstinting: "In this very fine book ... William L. MacDonald lays before the reader the physical evidence of what a Roman city was like for its inhabitants ... The illustrations ... are superbly chosen, illuminating the text as well as being interesting in themselves ... It is a joy to find a book so attractively designed, worthy of both its author and its subject."[2] The book went on to win the coveted Society of Architectural Historians' Alice Davis Hitchcock Award for the most distinguished work of scholarship in architectural history, previous winners of which included Richard Krautheimer, Rudolf Wittkower, James Ackerman, Kenneth John Conant, and Henry-Russell Hitchcock.

We start to see the drop-off in the two men's exchanges that I mentioned earlier after the Getty Scholarship ends and MacDonald is back in D.C. Between then and September 1990, we know of only sixteen more items, five of which are brief postcards. Between September 1990 and April 1992, there will only be three more postcards and one very brief letter. I shall confine to an afterword what I have to say about those last four items. But in the space left to me here, I should like to continue with the narrative, for now that the two men were near neighbors and their correspondence is on the point of drying up, their exchanges leave a great deal unmentioned.

In 1986 Atheneum published a 330-page gathering of Hecht's more extended prose pieces entitled *Obbligati: Essays in Criticism*. He had mentioned some of these pieces and his hopes for the book in his letters to MacDonald, but after publication he said no more about it. We know that Hecht was disappointed with the book's critical reception, for in a letter to Harry Ford, who had been his editor at Atheneum, he later lamented that "*Obbligati* may be said to have been received with stifled yawns. I still think there is much good in it, but I feel more and more lonely about this as time goes on."[3] One critic, Bruce Bawer, did indeed yawn, and at some considerable length, before ending a review for the *New Criterion* with these damning words: "*Obbligati* is, on the whole, a substantial disappointment. At a time when major American publishers tend to consider essay collections unmarketable (as they did short-story collections a decade ago) and consequently issue very few of them, one cannot help finding it ironic that Atheneum should publish so critically flawed a volume by a man celebrated not for his prose but for his poetry. It seems, in some way, a shirking of obligations."[4] But Ford could have reminded Hecht of other,

1 *The Classical World*, 81:1 (Sep–Oct, 1987), pp. 60-61.

2 *Times Literary Supplement*, April 3rd, 1987, p. 369.

3 Letter of May 10th, 1991, *The Selected Letters of Anthony Hecht*, p. 241.

4 "A Critic's Obligations," *The New Criterion*, 5:2, October 1986, p. 75. The review can be read online at: http://www.newcriterion.com/articles.cfm/A-critic-s-obligations-6075

much more positive responses. The eminent critic, John Gross, writing for the *New York Times,* was clearly impressed: "Most good poets are also good critics, and Anthony Hecht is very much a case in point ... For the most part Mr. Hecht proceeds at a leisurely pace. He quotes generously, lets his points sink in, and pauses when he wants to alert you to a particular felicity or a feature of the landscape you might have overlooked ... But he doesn't allow the details to distract him from the major issues, and he is at his best ... when he is discussing an extended argument ... Mr Hecht's essays are not only stimulating but also beautifully written."[1] William Pratt, writing in *World Literature Today,* was every bit as enthusiastic: "Good criticism is as rare as good poetry; it should be no surprise, then, that it often comes from poets. Reading Anthony Hecht's collection of essays, garnered from two decades of writing of and about poetry, calls to mind writers like Randall Jarrell and John Berryman, who were distinguished poets and critics, and at ease in both roles. As a critic, Hecht is not as trenchant as Jarrell or as passionate as Berryman, but he is their peer in his wide-ranging erudition and his unabashed love for the literature he chooses to criticize. He also shares their audacity, because any critic who undertakes to explore works by Shakespeare, Marvell, Keats, Ruskin, Dickinson, Auden, and Lowell in the same volume is hunting big game."[2]

In 1987, Ecco Press released *The Essential Herbert*, which Hecht had edited and for which he wrote the introduction. This was the fifth volume in Ecco's *Essential Poets* series, the nine other volumes of which featured Philip Levine's selections from Keats, Galway Kinnell's from Whitman, Robert Penn Warren's from Melville, Stanley Kunitz's from Blake, Seamus Heaney's from Wordsworth, Paul Muldoon's from Byron, Charles Simic's from Campion, Amy Clampitt's from John Donne, and W. S. Merwin's from Wyatt. The series was welcomed by Paul Mariani, who closed his omnibus review with words from Hecht's introduction: "'If this book finds its way into the hands of some grateful readers who had never met with Herbert's work before,' writes Hecht, ending his introduction to Herbert with ... generosity and grace, 'it will achieve everything its editor can hope for it. Introducing me to the works of certain poets has been one of the greatest services that a few other poets, teachers and friends have done for me, and I should be proud to have done as much for others, and not least for total strangers.'"[3]

Several more awards and honors came Hecht's way between 1987 and 1992. In 1987, *Poetry* magazine gave him the Harriet Monroe Award, and the University of Rochester, which he had served for eighteen years, gave him an honorary degree. In 1988 *Poetry* magazine awarded him the Ruth B. Lilly Poetry Prize, and in 1989 the University of the South gave him the Aiken-Taylor Award for Modern American Poetry, and St. John Fisher's College gave him yet another honorary degree.

In 1989 MacDonald also received an honor when MIT's School of Architecture

---

1 *New York Times*, September 12th, 1986. The review can be read online at: http://www.nytimes.com/1986/09/12/books/books-of-the-times-312786.html
2 *World Literature Today*, 61:2 (Spring, 1987), p. 289.
3 *New England Review and Bread Loaf Quarterly*, 12:3 (Spring 1990), pp. 313-320.

and Planning bestowed on him one of its newly-established Kevin Lynch Awards, given in recognition of his contributions to "Preservation and Change in City Image."

In the spring of 1990, and wholly unexpectedly, Hecht's younger brother Roger died. The only mentions of him in these letters occur in 1982, and suggest that their relationship was not without its difficulties, but in the eulogy he delivered at his brother's memorial service Hecht made it clear that the loss had touched him deeply: "Jobs and geographical destiny ... kept us apart from one another. And yet we were brothers, the children of the same parents, and our closeness was of long standing and of greater intimacy than anyone can guess at ... Such was the nature of our brotherhood, and the intensity of the bond between us, that his own life was sometimes disrupted in sympathy with the disruptions in mine."[1]

Hecht's next two books, *The Transparent Man* – his first collection in eleven years – and *Collected Earlier Poems* – which gathered everything he wanted preserved from his first four books – were released simultaneously by Knopf in the States in 1990 and then by OUP in the UK in 1991.[2] Reviewing both books for the *New York Times*, William Logan wrote: "In the late witness of our century, no poet has been more austere in his imaginative engagements than Mr. Hecht, or purer in his sense of pacing and weight; his poetry at times approaches the condition of sculpture. Some poets are saved by grace, others by will. Mr Hecht began as a poet of convenience and charm, of difficult form and baroque extravagance ... Scarred by a history whose lessons will be ignored, and whose lessons will murder us, he has become our only poet who is able to horrify ... The beauty of his language is stilled by the horror of knowledge ... [H]is dry and melancholy authority has been a brilliant counterirritant to the wastage of our language. The best poems in *The Transparent Man* equal the difficult achievement of *Collected Earlier Poems* in elegance, in cold pity, in the harsh, unamenable, cruel condition of life."[3] Reviewing the UK editions of both books for the *Times Literary Supplement*, Lachlan Mackinnon wrote: "Anthony Hecht is one of the best poets now writing ... It is time for the startling, unostentatious originality of his work to be celebrated beyond a small world of isolated ardent connoisseurs."[4]

---

1 Anthony Hecht Papers, Box 109, File 8.

2 The move from Atheneum to Knopf came about as a result of Harry Ford's leaving the one for the other three years earlier, and taking Hecht (and others) with him.

3 "When Beauty Shows No Mercy," *New York Times*, July 22nd, 1990. Reprinted in William Logan, *Reputations of the Tongue* (Gainesville, FL: University of Florida Press), pp. 148–152. The whole review can be read online at http://www.nytimes.com/1990/07/22/books/when-beauty-shows-no-mercy.html?pagewanted=1

4 *Times Literary Supplement*, July 26th, 1991, p. 4.

[270]

[WLM]
February 2nd, 1981
Emory University, Art History Department, Atlanta, Georgia 30322

[Letter, typed, with the sender's address given as Erwin-Panofsky-Jones, addressed to Anthony, Baron Hecht, 19 East Boulevard, Rochester NY 14610, with enclosure]

My dear Saint Anthony,

It seems that Jack Barrymore, at a drunken party in Hollywood in the early thirties, was accosted by a lady who insisted that they had had a fling a few years before. Barrymore, sloshed, denied this, whereupon the woman arched her back and said, "Now do you remember?" Barrymore did not. So she undid her blouse and revealed a shapely breast. Barrymore, a bit more interested, peered at it a bit and then an expression of recognition appeared. "For God's sake … Wiley Post! You old son of a gun!"

A newly-made friend told me that the other day and I've decided it ranks with those two great stories, Gielgud doing Shakespeare monologues, and the grand fence-mender/steamboat captain stories.

As you can see, I am in the Old South. It is nice; sometimes balmy. Much hospitality, but that's partly because I go around the countryside, strewing fragrant lectures hither and yon. I hear Sherman's name twice a week. Atlanta was struck head on by the twentieth century about 1955 or so and it is a huge and quite interesting city. Home ca. mid-March, then off to Victoria BC to give a paper, then to Ohio State (Charlie Babcock) for a week, etc. My new career is fun, and lucrative. <u>Pantheon</u> coming out in paperback next month, revised ed. of the <u>Architecture of the Roman Empire</u> in the fall; reprinting the Northampton book myself so I need all the lecture fees I can get!

One course at Emory (The Persistence of Classicism (in architecture)), good students, have a small apartment not far from the campus. Nick is in Oregon still, Noel and Ellen snug in their "new" house in Florence MA. Barbara went to Berkeley last September to the Business School, but I've not heard from her since Nov. and am a bit anxious about her.

    Thou? Thine?
    Accept, my dear Doctor Engineer Knight's
    Cross, my most profound and holy respects,
    with the request that you write a play
    about me soon,
        Faustus Minor

[Enclosure]

THE ART HISTORY DEPARTMENT
OF EMORY UNIVERSITY
PRESENTS

ON UNDERSTANDING HADRIAN'S VILLA

A Lecture By

William L. MacDonald
Professor of Art History
Smith College

TUESDAY
MARCH
THIRD

8:00 P.M.
208 WHITE HALL

RECEPTION AND OPENING OF PRINT EXHIBITION FOLLOWING THE
LECTURE IN THE GALLERY OF THE ART HISTORY BUILDING

[271]

[AH]
February 6th, 1981
19 East Boulevard, Rochester, New York 14610

[Letter, typed on a The University of Rochester, Department of English, letterhead, posted in a The University of Rochester envelope, addressed to Prof. William MacDonald (Vitruvius Redivivus), Art History Department, Emory University, Atlanta, Georgia 30322]

Dear Professor,

It seems to me in the end the best policy to come right out and say plainly that Hadrian was a dirty-old-man, and that's why there was such an abundance of baths in his damn villa. And what, for God's sake, are we to make of the United States' Post Office tribute to lesbian couples, as represented by the stamp on the enclosing envelope?[1]

Every year poor Helen finds herself ticketed to do something to raise funds for Smith,[2] usually in connection with a "house tour," in which some of the fancier houses of Rochester open themselves for public inspection, and a fee is collected from the visitors. It involves an enormous amount of work, with reliable docents to guide and instruct and protect, and be relieved at proper intervals by others, and what not. This year her duties are a little lighter than they have been in the past, but I have offered to help in my small way. A handy little brochure is published each year for the tour; a memento of sorts, and a brief comment on each of the houses offered for inspection. I've offered to compose one for this year, and presented a specimen description for consideration. "The Annabelle Philpotts House on East Cumberland is a converted comfort station once visited by President Taft during a fleeting stop at Rochester. Its main features, in an unusual marriage of the Federal and Baroque styles, have fortunately been preserved by the tireless efforts of the Landmark Society; and one may view the original urinal, honored with a commemorative plaque bearing tasteful sentiments composed by Dr. Rowland Collins, sometime chairperson of the Landmark Society. The house itself, though

1
2 Helen Hecht is an alumna of Smith College.

somewhat cramped for space, is currently occupied by Bess Flitch, who shares it with the boyfriend, a young free-thinker named Daryll Briscomb, of her former husband, Mac. It is Briscomb who made the lovely macrame bedspread, the hooked rugs, and the antimacassars that adorn the Eames chairs. The one burner range and the leatherette barstool are especially to be admired. Watch your step going out."

You are welcome to incorporate this passage into any lecture of yours, always with proper credit of course.

Joe of Cusa

[272]

[AH]
[February 13th, 1981]
[19 East Boulevard, Rochester, NY 14610]

[Letter, typed, posted in a The University of Rochester envelope, addressed to Prof. Wm. MacDonald (kunsthistorischewissenschaftlicher Kerl), Art History Department, Emory University, Atlanta, Georgia 30322]

The Power of Love

"The most eloquent essay – Mr. Kissinger's oration at the funeral of his patron and friend, Nelson Rockefeller – stands alone, quite out of character with the rest of the book. Here Mr. Kissinger recalls that Rockefeller in his final years, 'would say, because I needed it, but, above all, because he deeply felt it: "Never forget that the most profound force in the world is love."'"

– Gaddis Smith, in a review of <u>For The Record</u> by Henry Kissinger, in the <u>New York Times Book Review</u>, Feb. 1, 1981.[1]

Great heart, Nelson, lover of Art, of Beauty,
Things transcendent, Governor, we revere you,
Prize that sentence Kissinger has reported,
    Love's very adage.

Words to live by, words to rebuke the doubter,
Whether raised with, laved by a family fortune,
Or, like most, just struggling with a mortgage,
    Here is a motto.

---

1 Gaddis Smith's article was entitled "A Guide to Realpolitik."

> May our statesmen, following your example,
> Stake their claims in Cythera, just as you did,
> Love's bold champion, who, as its latest martyr,
> Died in its service.

Dear Comrade,

I thought you might like to see these Sapphics, prompted by a review in a recent Times Book Review. I bet it's nice and warm down your way, you lucky stiff. Six above here right now. Have you gotten to know Richard Ellmann, who is also at Emory just now? If Pantheon is coming out in paper, will you be able to insert that tale from the Golden Legend about the coin in the dirt inside it? (I'm eager to appear in the list of credits.) Have you seen the Dover book on Palladio's Architecture and its influences?[1] Lots of dandy pictures. I like the Barrymore story, but don't think I know the other two (Gielgud or fence-mender).

Irving, Procurator of Teaneck, N.J.

[273]

[WLM]
February 20th, 1981
Emory University, Art History Department, Atlanta, Georgia 30322

[Letter, typed on an Emory University, Art History Department, letterhead, posted in an Emory University envelope, with the sender's name given as P. Oblivious Naso, addressed to Sir Anthony Hecht, Bart (Bay Area Rapid Transit), 19 East Boulevard, Rochester NY 14610]

William L. MacDonald

<u>Public lectures given during the Winter Quarter 1981:</u>

January 27, at the University of Georgia, Athens: "On Understanding Hadrian's Villa"

February 3, at Emory University, Graduate Institute of Liberal Arts: "Hadrian's Villa"

February 5, Atlanta Chapter. Archaeological Institute of America, Agnes Scott College: "Hadrian and Architecture"

February 10, The State University of Florida: "On Understanding Hadrian's Villa"

February 11, The State University of Florida: "The Rational and Irrational in Piranesi: A Reappraisal"

February 25, Georgia Tech. School of Architecture: "The Persistence of

---

1 Joseph C. Farber and Henry Hope Reed, *Palladio's Architecture and Its Influence: A Photographic Guide*, (New York: Dover Publications, 1980).

Classicism"

March 3, Emory University, Art History Department lecture: "On Understanding Hadrian's Villa"

Dear Uncle Harry:

Now that you're not a missionary now, in the words of the grand old Noel Coward song, I thought you'd like to see a list of <u>my</u> missionary activities. Lecturing all the hell and gone around; fun; S. hospitality is not hard to take, and the women (read "wimming," as in the "Shakespeare" song in <u>Kiss Me, Kate</u>; I'm sorry not to get the footnotes at the bottom of the page, but my secretary, Laurel, is busy on the 'phone) are often very taking, winning, &c.

Loved your Sapphics on Ole Nelson, that shithead; I wish they could be published. Quarter here rushing to a close. Parties, lectures, dinners everywhere; putting on weight. Fun. Went to Tallahassee for a couple of days and was much taken by it. Place to move to in a couple of years? Possible repetitions: Clark Professor (GREAT HONOR) at Williams, Spring of '82, ideal because I drive up and stay over one night, each week; reprinting <u>Northampton</u> out of my own pocket, having finally gotten the City to transfer the rights to me; <u>Pantheon</u> coming out now in paperback, grâce à the Harvards, bless them; Yale reissuing the 1965 <u>Roman Empire</u> book in a revised paperback & in hardcover, too; bless <u>them</u>, also. So I'm feeling pretty good about publications; writing away, between vodka marts and aggressive kisses.

Kisses make me think of Barbara, who survived the first purgatorial term at the Berkeley School of BusAdmn where she seeks an MBA. She sounds less haunted than in the past, and I am glad for her. I miss her company sometimes, she's so damned bright, but not the hassles ... Another person, a man I much respect, told me that Petersson's <u>Ecstasy</u> is a good book ... that's <u>two</u> who've said it! Can we be Wrong?

Glad you liked the Barrymore story; best I've heard in a long time. The Gielgud I'm sure you know; the fence-mender and the ferryboat captain is probably the greatest story ever told, but it will have to wait until we are seated in a dark bar in Smyrna, Tennessee; I can't get it right on paper, I'm afraid. There! That'll (Aztec word) keep you on pins & needles ... Home about March 15th or so, then on a lecture jaunt to British Columbia (!), Columbus Ohio, &c., all for the sweet long green. Christ, resigning was a grand idea. Then there's the marvelous stimulus of remembering that I threw away some six hundred thousand bucks. The people who want to know How I Did It but who can't bear to ask outright are sometimes pretty funny. So far, only an old friend in Tallahassee has asked for exact instructions as to how it can be done. NO MEETINGS! NO ENTANGLEMENTS! ... foreign or domestic. Administrators love me: no fringe benefits to pay, not around long enough to become a nuisance, and they can parade me around & brag, waving my c.v. about. I'm expensive as hell, but so far no one has balked. Try it, you'll like it. Don't miss Smith at all, almost never think of it.

Love to all,
Postum, Postman, Pestum

Gielgud story, en short: London music hall, G. doing solo turns from Shakespeare. Drunk in topmost balcony, during first turn, leans dangerously far out over the rail, with its tattered, faded, red velvet cover, and shouts: "Sing 'Melancholy Baby'!" His friends pull him back and quiet him, but when G. comes on again, with Polonius' speech, the drunk breaks loose and shouts, more loudly even, "C'mon; SING 'MELANCHOLY BABY'!" Again his pals retrieve him. G. pays no attention to either interruption, needless to say, but when he, after a Quick Change, comes back on to woo Giullietta, our friend will not be denied. Leaning out still another time, he shouts in great indignation: "Awright, you Bastid! If you can't sing 'Melancholy Baby,' show us your pecker!" (...... with credits to A. D. Trottenberg)

Can't resist immodestly telling you that Richard Oliver, a very bright man, curator of architecture at the Cooper-Hewitt, told Joseph Polshek,[1] Dean of the Columbia School of Architecture, that "MacDonald is the best lecturer on architecture in the country." So.

[274]

[WLM]
[June 11th, 1981]
[25 Henshaw Avenue, Northampton, Massachusetts 01060]

[Postcard, with a photograph of the Onthank Home, Beaufort, South Carolina, handwritten, addressed to Anthony E. Hecht, 19 East Boulevard, Rochester, NY, 14610, with enclosure]

[Enclosure]

My dear Sir –

We are located in the attic here, looking for work to publish. Do you have anything, preferably dank to send us? We are High, + Classy. Yours in metric enthusiasm,

F. X. Odorono

---

1 WLM has misremembered Polshek's given name, which is James.

[275]

[WLM]

July 27th, 1981
[25 Henshaw Avenue, Northampton, Massachusetts 01060]

[Letter, typed on a The Blue Horizon Town & Country Inn letterhead, posted in an Ohio Staters, Inc., The Ohio State University, envelope, addressed to Rev. mo Ill. mo Antonio Principe Hecht, 19 East Boulevard, Rochester New York 14610]

My dear Prince,

I can see that the prayer rug did its job & got you to Italy, Don't use it (the rug) too often.

We at the Armhole Press await your inspired work. Don't forget, dank-like is the word,

Dick Wilbur called me a couple of days ago, about Babylonian sheep (true). First time I'd had any congress with him in nearly three years, except for a wave on the campus. He took our long interlude lightly, saying that we ought to dine together at the Fort in Springfield sometime.

Freedom, it's wonderful. Keep getting flirtations about visiting teaching, so my thoughts on that score were correct. Off to Washington for a lecture at the Catholic University ("Genuine Genuflection; or, Pensive Pendentives") and a couple of days of sightseeing and condominium-checking. The more I think about it, the better Washington appears. Want to leave here in a year or two, after I get a couple of books finished.

Thine,
Waltraut Thiesinger

Evelyn Waugh's Letters[1] are marvellous. Several friends & acquaintances of mine get it good ("dim"; "bogus"...)[2]

Much interest in Jiggery-Pokery. Reprinting? I hope so. Have you seen the dactyls2 in the Saturday Review? If not, advise, + I'll forward a zeerocks. – W.T.[3]

1 *The Letters of Evelyn Waugh*, edited by Mark Amory (New Haven, CT: Ticknor & Fields, 1980).

2 The classicist John D'Arms would seem to be one of the people WLM was referring to here. In 1960, D'Arms had proposed to, and would go on to marry, Waugh's daughter, Maria Teresa, and was described by her underwhelmed father as "a very poor American," "a studious, penniless American," and "dim and studious." (See *The Letters of Evelyn Waugh*, edited by Mark Amory (New Haven, CT: Ticknor & Fields, 1980), pp. 455-457.

3 *Jiggery-Pokery: A Compendium of Double Dactyls*, co-edited by AH and John Hollander, had been published in 1967. The February 1981 issue of the *Saturday Review*'s "Diversions" page invited submissions of double dactyls, offering three prizes of $25 each. What WLM appears to have seen is the magazine's May issue, which printed the winning poems and told readers that "The Double Dactyl contest brought in an unexampled onslaught of entries." The relevant page can be read online at http://www.unz.org/Pub/SaturdayRev-1981may-00092

[276]

[AH]
August 10th, 1981
19 East Boulevard, Rochester, New York 14610

[Letter, typed, addressed to The Very Reverend William MacDonald, 25 Henshaw Avenue, Northampton, Mass. 01060, with a now missing enclosure]

Honored Sir,

I enclose a reservation for the second seating, reminding you that if you are not prompt your place may be assigned to someone else.

In addition, here is a majestic new work not yet widely circulated among my admiring public:

> A peculiarly plain Dame of Sark
> Was persistently heard to remark:
> "Men may not make passes
> At girls who wear glasses,
> But all cats are gray in the dark."

This has, of course, a beauty of its own (with its deft quotations and rich literary resources) and at the same time serves to let my readers know that my talents are not confined to long, narrative poems.

Perhaps the saddest part of the shock of coming back from such a trip as we took is the feeling that sets in in less than a week's time that we have never been away, or that the trip blends all too easily and strangely with one we took two years ago, and seems equally remote. Rochester and home seem the locale of habit, familiar and comforting and dreary and repetitious, from which serious work will be the best escape, though I have not yet begun it. I have a heavy teaching schedule in the fall, but come Christmas vacation, I begin a full calendar year's leave. I pray that I may make great inroads towards a new book. It is borne in upon me with more and more exquisite anxiety that I am fast approaching sixty, when few poets are expected to perform with any success at all, and one points to the exceptions, like Yeats and Hardy and Sophocles, with gratitude precisely because they are exceptions. But the odd fact is that my knowledge of my age, a purely cerebral matter, though it is confirmed by any number of physical frailties and symptoms of age, is almost entirely set aside by instinctive feelings about myself as curiously youthful. A pathetic though useful illusion, no doubt. Auden used to make a great event of his birthday, not, as one might suppose, out of egotism or self-regard, but as a way of reminding himself of the indisputable fact of his age; and he felt it was particularly perilous for a <u>writer</u> to pretend to himself that he was younger than in fact he was. I remember how very difficult it was for me as a child of, say, six or seven, to assess the age of anyone beyond sixteen. A sixteen-year-old looked college-age to me (quite rightly, since that was my age when I entered college), which age was to me indistinguishable from general young adulthood (which meant anyone who was not exhibiting visible signs of decay), and young adulthood was a vast, elastic class, running from sixteen to perhaps the late forties or middle fifties, somehow distinguishable from children and from the elderly. It was the class that contained parents, one's own and other children's parents, whose age and physical appearance seemed to remain fixed. Eheu, fugaces …

Did I tell you before that Georgetown University gave me an honorary degree? It is sad to say that this will not please some of my colleagues.

Let me recommend with unstinted enthusiasm a book I have just finished reading. It is <u>The Genesis of Secrecy</u> by Frank Kermode, the Charles Eliot Norton Lectures at Harvard in 1977–78, and available as a Harvard Press paperback.[1] I am unable offhand to recall another book I have admired so much. Do not be put off by the fact that the book appears to be about the problems of interpreting the Gospel According to St. Mark: while it is undeniably that, it is in fact about our capacity to "read" or interpret anything – works secular as well as religious, and, I would suppose, works of art other than literary ones, and ultimately the world itself. I am myself almost always reluctant to take up such recommendations from others; partly out of doubt that our tastes are bound to coincide, but more usually because I am convinced beforehand that whatever it is will too much divert me from whatever serious and committed work I have at hand. As a consequence, I sometimes buy the book in question, but set it aside to be read when leisure permits. I would be ashamed even to try to guess how many books on my shelves were bought for that reason and remain unread to this day. In any case, it is a frame of mind that accounts for my having come to this Kermode book so long after both its appearance and its many laudatory reviews.

Erwin Panofsky

---

1 Frank Kermode, *The Genesis of Secrecy: On the Interpretation of Narrative* (The Charles Eliot Norton Lectures) (Boston, MA: Harvard University Press, 1979).

[277]

[WLM]
September 5th, 1981
[25 Henshaw Avenue, Northampton, Massachusetts 01060]

[Letter, typed on a The Michigan League letterhead, posted in a Gramercy Park Hotel, envelope, addressed to Professor Doctor HECHT, 19, East Boulevard, Rochester NY 14610, with two enclosures]

[Enclosure 1]

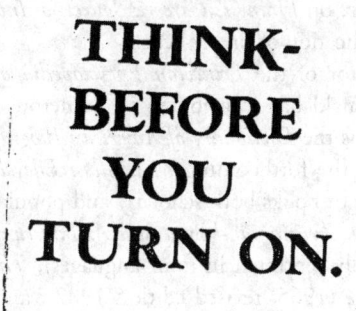

Comrade:

The enclosed Turn On is, believe it or not, from a southren fundamentalist college, and is handed out to the students to make them conscious of electricity usage. Honest.

The other enclosure is to ensure that you salute when you think of me. Nick had a good line after reading it: "'Enraptured'? Doesn't she mean 'stupefied'?"

[Enclosure 2: article from a Smith College publication]

William L. MacDonald

In January of this year, William L. MacDonald, Alice Pratt Brown Professor of History of Art, resigned from his teaching post in order to devote more time to independent projects of scholarship and publishing. A member of the Smith faculty since 1965, Professor MacDonald has won the affection and respect of students, alumnae, colleagues and the general public with his enthusiastic and penetrating publications and lectures on architecture. Although his major field is Roman art and architecture, buildings from every historical period have long fascinated Professor MacDonald, who studies their fabric and social context as well as their aesthetic and symbolic qualities. He has lovingly opened our eyes to the meaning and character of the built environment from North Africa to Northampton, and his superb photographic skills make his experience the more vivid to enraptured readers and audiences.

William MacDonald received the A.B. (1949), A.M. (1953) and Ph.D. (1956) from Harvard University. He has been resident at the American Academy in Rome as a Rome Prize Fellow (1954–1956) and Morse Fellow (1962–1963). He joined the Yale University faculty in 1956 and has taught at Harvard and Emory Universities, as well as at the University of California at Berkeley and the Massachusetts Institute of Technology. In 1979 he gave the Smith College Katharine Asher Engel lecture on *Piranesi's Carceri: Sources of Invention*, which is available as a publication of the College.

Associate Editor of the *Princeton Encyclopedia of Classical Sites*, Professor MacDonald has contributed to numerous journals and to compendia such as the *Dictionary of American Biography*, *Readings in Art History*,[1] and the forthcoming *Macmillan Encyclopedia of Architects*. He is author of books both scholarly and popular, among which are included *Early Christian and Byzantine Architecture* (first published in 1962; repeatedly reprinted in four languages), *The Architecture of the Roman Empire* (1965; revised edition 1982), and *The Pantheon: Design, Meaning, and Progeny* (1976, 1980). His Bicentennial book, *Northampton, Massachusetts: Architecture and Buildings*, which first appeared in 1975, has recently been reissued in a paperback edition that is coveted by alumnae and town residents alike. Scheduled for publication in 1983 is *Roman Cities and Towns*[2]; in preparation is *Roman Architecture and the History of Architecture*.[3]

This spring Professor MacDonald will be Robert Sterling Clark Visiting Professor of Art at the Clark Institute in Williamstown. For the time being, he will continue to make his home in Northampton, and his many friends will hope to see him frequently on the Smith campus.

HELEN SEARING, *professor of art*

Reciprocity, like compound interest one of the Great Things of Life, requires that I send the following in response to your Dame of Sark ditty. My title is "On the Nile":

1 *Readings in Art History*, edited by Harold Spencer (New York: Scribner, 1976).

2 This was the provisional title of what became volume II of *The Architecture of the Roman Empire*, which bore the subtitle *An Urban Appraisal*.

3 This volume was never completed.

>   There once was a youth named Antinuous
>   With Praxiteles curves oh so sinuous
>   He fell in the drink
>   And quickly did sink
>   Now he sleeps in the deep midst the minnuous
>
>   When Hadrian got the bad news
>   He felt like a poet sans muse
>   "Alas, and alack
>   My life's out of whack
>   We should never have taken this cruise."

Well, now that I re-read them, I guess I should have not sent them. Anyway, they're not by me, but by a gorgeous ex-student, who used to write me fairly often.

You remember Tom Schumacher? Well, he's at the University of Virginia now, and last month I saw him in Washington. He's written a brief book that I've not seen yet,[1] has been through 2 or 3 wives.

I'm serious about Jiggery-Pokery. I hope they reprint it. People want it. You could reprint it yourself, as I have done with the Bicentennial book (50 % profit...)

* * * * * *

Yes, feelings of youth. I can't relate to my gray hair, my fairly long life (sixty this last July), very well. I feel fine, thank god; that awful chapter with the surgeon in '77 was I hope my only experience, birth to death, of that kind. Yes, youthful, say 33 or so. Why don't other people notice this about us? I'm just this year beginning to see little hints of the thought "He's old" in the conversations and speculative glances of others. I don't mind it as much as I thought I might because I really can't ask any more of life than I have, except for a good companion. And anyway, what do youngsters know anyway? And it's good to be in a field that is cumulative, knowing more than ever and still eager to do it (now and then, which is enough). Death doesn't concern me much, but on the occasions when it does it also fails to frighten me as much as I thought it might. I like being sixty, and don't seem to have lost much energy. I however have cut down on the booze, though food is another matter.

Leonardo said that "old age is a state of mind." I know what he meant, but I'm not sure I'm going to be able to handle it that way. Right now, other than the lady problem, what concerns me is where to move to. It seems like an adventure, and it isn't threatening, but I sure as hell want to be sure to avoid the wrong place.

My feelings about others' ages are much like yours. I rarely can tell how old anyone is unless there is some contextual indication: student, classmate, married in '56, 3 kids, etc. At one time I was awfully alert to ages, to relative chronologies

---

1 *Il Danteum di Terragni* (Rome: Officina Edizioni, 1980), later translated into English as *The Danteum* (Princeton, NJ: Princeton University Press, 1986).

among people, esp. among groups of which I was a part. But that too has drifted away from me. As Frederick the Great said, "Responsible People should concentrate on the essentials," and, to the degree that I'm responsible, I'm trying to do that, which means trying to write every day, which I've by no means been able to stick to, but I'm better at it than I was, and that I guess is something.

This letter keeps veering over to Me, when I want to remark on what you've written. <u>Very</u> unusual, what?

What really is on my mind is wishing to write better, more powerful things about architecture. What I've written in the past isn't bad, and one or two pieces are pretty good, but not good enough. The problem occupies me night and day, esp. that part of it that niggles: maybe I can't do any better, find then of course there's the age-old, normal, and good: I'll show those bastards. I don't see architectural history and criticism the way they do, and it's evident to me from time to time that they find me likeable but not very serious. Fuck them.

Busy fall with lectures all over hell. Thought I'd saturated the ground forever, but that's not so, apparently. Writing a series of biographies for a <u>MacMillan Encyclopedia of Architects</u>, and that's fun and well paid. Then back to <u>Roman Cities</u>; it seems like forever that I've been working on it; might finish it by next winter or spring. Of course, I've finished it before ...

You speak of ailments, and that makes me apprehensive for you. I hope they are minor. If I didn't have so many Appearances to make this fall I'd get in my car and drive out for a weekend; but with no salary check I keep hopping, which is a damned good thing. People here are awfully funny about my quitting. They keep saying I'm retired, which burns my ass, but I've given up explaining that I traded one job for another. They just can't understand that, I guess. I'm glad I don't have to deal with them any more. With a very few exceptions they're not very interesting.

And on that tolerant, judicious note, I will stir my great Beef Stew for Noel, Ellen (a marvelous young woman), and Nick, who will descend on me about six o'clock and lower the level of liquids and food by an astonishing degree. Thank god they are all here in town.

Vale, princeps
Marcius Quintus Turbo
Praefectus Praetorio
(a real person my newest hero)

[278]

[WLM]
September 15th, 1981
25 Henshaw Avenue, Northampton, Massachusetts 01060

[Blank postcard, typed, with the sender's address given as XXV Hensh, 01060, addressed to Eminenza Anthony Hecht, 19 East Boulevard, Rochester NY 14610]

Antoninus:

That's disgusting about your colleagues, some of them, feeling the way they do about your hon. degree. It describes the petty and quite depressing side of academic life that I am so glad to be able to do without. Some reactions here to my resignation have been most peculiar. But in any event, heartfelt congratulations, Doc.

I will look up the Kermode book when I go to the Liberry. I promise to do my best. If it is about "literary criticism" I may not make much way with it, for I just don't understand the subject; like philosophy, it defeats me, seeming to be either obvious or so arcane as who cares. But from your words I may be in for a gt. surprise.

Up, the Navy!
Lord Fisher

[279]

[AH]
September 17th, 1981
19 East Boulevard, Rochester, NY 14610

[Letter, typed, posted in a The University of Rochester envelope, addressed to The Celebrated William MacDonald (hic!), 25 Henshaw Ave., Northampton, Mass. 01060, with now missing enclosures]

Caro gentiluomo

The chief merit of this missive may well lie in the stamp.[1] Anyway, it includes some valuable tickets and prizes, suitable, as they say, for mounting; plus a few random works of my own, and, as a special bonus, a little-known opus by Kingsley Amis, I'll give you the Amis first.

1

> The fellow who screwed Brigid Brophy
> Was awarded the Kraft-Ebbing trophy,
>   He won eighty quid
>   For the thing that he did,
> Which many declared was a low fee.[1]

To which I add some modest labors of my own:

> A coming young pro from Alsace,
> Whose patrons were all lower class,
>   Remarked, "I deplore
>   The soubriquet, 'Whore';
> It's a genuine pain in the ass."

and,

> Proust wrote in his "Recherche" one day:
> "There is nothing so cute, I must say,
>   At least to my mind,
>   As a young boy's behind, –
> If one's given to derriere pensées."

and,

> There was a young Gaul from the Somme
> Whom sexual ennui made glum,
>   At such moments he'd sigh,
>   With a tear in his eye:
> "Il n'y a que des femmes et des hommes."

Arthur Garfield Hays

---

1 This is a slightly reworded version of a limerick jointly composed by Kingsley Amis and Robert Conquest after Brophy had given a novel by Amis a bad review. Their version reads as follows:

> The first chap to fuck Brigid Brophy
> Was awarded the Kraft-Ebbing Trophy,
>   Plus 10,000 quid,
>   Which, for what the chap did,
> Will be widely denounced as a low fee.

See Zachary Leader, *The Life of Kingsley Amis* (London: Jonathan Cape, 2006), p. 291.

[280]

[WLM]
September 29th, 1981
25 Henshaw Avenue, Northampton, Massachusetts 01060

[Blank postcard, typed, addressed to F. M. General Antoninus d'Hecht, OM, OBE, OK, SMOM, &c &c , 19 East Boulevard, Rochester NY 14610]

My Dear King Harry,

I am about third or fourth on the College Library's waiting list for the Kermode book, so I'll probably get to it about Flag Day. A former student that I like, mid-30s or so, called last night & said she'd like to come & spend the weekend. Probably just needs reassurance. Off to Richmond to look at buildings and give a lecture "On Understanding Hadrian's Villa," one of my better productions … I know Kaplan is a pal of yours, at least I think he is, but I am perplexed by his reviews. The one in the <u>Times</u> of the biography of O'Hara[1] struck me as not useful and distinctly off. [O'Hara] was a bastard, no doubt, but so? What he wrote seems to me to be well toward the top of the second rank, and significant in a kind of documentary sense. K. will have none of him, & avoided really saying anything about his work. Same as the lady? who did the awful review of Saki: not a word about the work.[2]

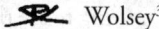 Wolsey[3]

Long letter from Barbara, who sounds more secure & confident than ever before.

---

1 WLM had misremembered the name of the reviewer, which was Kazin, not Kaplan. Alfred Kazin, who was known to AH but not a friend of his, had reviewed Frank McShane's *The Life of John O'Hara* (New York: E. P. Dutton, 1981) and had been highly critical of its subject – "What is amazing about [O'Hara], as I read him now, is how much demonism without moderating intellect he brought to his special accomplishment" – and not a lot less critical of its author. See Alfred Kazin, "A Rage to Record," in *The New York Times*, January 18th, 1981. The article can be read online at http://www.nytimes.com/1981/01/18/books/a-rage-to-record.html?pagewanted=1#h[]

2 The lady in question was the biographer Victoria Glendinning, who had reviewed A. J. Langguth's *Saki: A Life of Hector Hugh Munro, with Six Stories Never Before Collected* (New York: Simon & Schuster, 1980). Like Kazin, Glendinning had some sharp things to say about the subject of the book she was reviewing – "Although a fascination with the erotic and the horrible were subordinated to the comic in [Saki's] stories, which made it all palatable, a closer look reveals a bloodlust, a taste for cruel practical jokes, a fear of women and undercurrents of what Mr. Langguth calls 'a genuine, if faintly nasty desire' for beautiful boys with dark Mediterranean skins and few clothes" – and, again like Kazin, was not overly enthusiastic about its author. See "Schoolboy Cruelty" in *The New York Times*, August 16th, 1981. The article can be read online at: http://www.nytimes.com/1981/08/16/books/schoolboy-cruelty.html?module=Search&mabReward=relbias%3Ar

3 WLM's handwriting is hard to decipher here, but the Chi Roh symbol preceding the name and the fact that "King Harry" was one of the familiar names given to King Henry VIII, strongly suggest that WLM was intending to sign off as Cardinal Wolsey.

[281]

[WLM]
November 18th, 1981
25 Henshaw Avenue, Northampton, Massachusetts 01060

[Letter, typed, with the sender's address given as XXV henshaw, 01060, addressed to Prof. Dr. Anthony Hecht, idle aedile, 19 East Boulevard, Rochester NY 14610]

My dear Quintus,

It was in February, '08, I think, when the unwordly Bishop found himself sharing a second-class carriage from London to Manchester with a group of young ladies who were taking a production of <u>Dick Whittington</u> to the provinces. The bishop passed round his bag of Blackpool Rock and asked the girls which parts they took in the play, discovering Sarah, the Maid, and so on. Then he asked, "And who takes Dick?" "Oh," said one of the girls, "We all do … but not just for Blackpool Rock!"

How are you? I'm pretty well, though with a bit of eye trouble that hasn't been resolved. X-Rays, dilation, etc.; great sport. Been plastering the east coast with lectures, including star performances at Charlottesville, where I saw Tom Schumacher, and Washington, where we had a grand get-together for Frank [Brown]. Last Thursday he gave a paper, which was excellent, tho' his aphasia has increased since I last saw him. It is moving to see that tower of strength paw about in his mind for an ordinary word. Then cocktails and dinner, courtesy of the National Gallery, where the clambake was held. Next day a closed-door session for about 30, with topics for discussion arranged in advance (Frank had picked as one of them my work on the Small Baths), and that was a success also. I think that format is the best for scholarly gatherings now that I've experienced several of them.

Afterward a half-dozen of us were taken by Frank to the super-chic Cosmos club for martinis, and from there we all went off to a <u>very</u> expensive, <u>very</u> bad restaurant where we continued to have a fine time. Frank got pretty tight – and he was not the only one – so that I had to walk him back to the Club, arm in arm, rather slowly. Mid-evening he asked for news of you, and repeated three times that he'd like to see you while he is in the country; I believe they return in January to Rome; Jackie [Brown] is as you know in Chicago for work on her hands.

Next morning Frank, showing no trace of wear from the previous evening, and I spent two or three hours together and that perhaps was best. He has mellowed, as you know, and is much less inclined to more or less delicately phrased scorn than he was, and he shows many signs of appreciating the extraordinary value of affection given by and to others. I asked his permission to dedicate my next book to him, which he gave with some signs of emotion. We embraced warmly at the gallery doors, and he gave me his blessing …

Fr. [Timothy S] Healy, President of Georgetown University, is a great admirer of yours, I learn from my friend Allen Weinstein (<u>Perjury</u>, &c), who has just gained a University Professorship there. Allen now becomes editor of the <u>G'town 4ly</u>, or whatever it's called,[1] and he and Healy hope for a poem or some poems from you.

Did you see the Playboy cartoon of Abraham on the mount, aggressively questioning the deity? "Now let me get this straight. You mean you want us to cut off the ends of our dicks ?"

Please pay your taxes: Caesar has his eye on you ...

Tigellinus

[282]

[AH]
November 22nd, 1981
[19 East Boulevard, Rochester, NY 14610]

[Letter, typed]

Dear Ulfric the Magnanimous,

It's a sign of the culturally impoverished conditions in which we live here that I have not heard a good joke, not even a clean one, within the reaches of a fairly reliable memory. Add to this that there's snow all over the fucking ground, I'm up to my ear lobes in bad grades from illiterate papers, and you have an index of the sort of desolation that obtains in these crummy parts. It was recently topped off, as with a maraschino cherry, by poor Helen's coming down with the most rabid case of poison ivy I've ever encountered. She was trying to save me labor, and when a face-cord of fire-wood was delivered to the house, but stacked neatly outdoors, she carried it armload by armload down to the cellar, an afternoon's work that cost her 25 trips or more, and would have been cheap at the price, since she broke out in flaming red welts and an agony of discomfort on Friday the 13th, and is only now, according to our doctor, reaching the summit and apex of the infliction, after which there is to be a slow, stately and interminable decline. A corollary, if minor, problem has to do with whether it is safe to use any of that wood for the fire. One can, of course, be fastidious enough about hauling it upstairs from the cellar, but the real question has to do with whether the fumes of any poisonous matter could not start the whole thing up again. This happened to Helen once before, and the first time we were quite bewildered by how she might have caught poison ivy in mid-winter. The first time, though very unpleasant, it was not nearly so severe, and in due course, by a dredging of memory and shrewd inference, we figured out what the cause must have been.

We have seen, as who has not, the tarring and feathering Smith took in a recent

---

1 The magazine's title was in fact *The Washington Quarterly*, and it was published by Georgetown University's Center for Strategic and International Studies. Weinstein served as its Executive Editor between 1981 and 1983.

issue of, I think, Harper's.[1] (I confused it with the Stockman exposé in The Atlantic.[2]) I am a little surprised by what appears to be Jill Conway's imperturbability as regards this smear. There seems no evidence that she made any attempt to prevent the article from being published, or to offer a rebuttal once it had appeared. If, like Woodrow Wilson, she is too proud to fight, she may have a very impaired sense of the powerful effect that article has had. Helen was very distressed by it, and has more or less decided not to continue contributing to the Alumnae Fund (not, I may add, chiefly because of the evidence of rampant lesbianism, but because of the shocking decline in academic standards.) Nursing my by no means happy recollections of my teaching years at Smith (which held for me bitternesses comparable to your own at Yale) this seems to me a domestic economy I will particularly enjoy effecting. Helen's editor, another ex-Smithy, wrote Helen, "Is there any way to transfer after you've graduated?" The whole things is a sad and sorry mess, and while I know that the college has dealt decently (and perhaps generously) with you, I'm glad that you are officially severed from it, since all this very bad publicity can only mean that things are going to be bad for quite a long time to come.

The lesbianism angle bothers Helen only slightly less than the lowering of academic standards, and I must say that I find it the more shocking because of Smith's brutal corporate behavior with regard to Newton Arvin and the two other very gifted male faculty members when, in 1960 (?) a scandal broke over their receiving dirty pictures in the mail.[3] They were branded and dismissed by an act of the Board of Trustees; or, more accurately, Newton was allowed to retire prematurely in public and undisguised shame, of which he died shortly after[4] – Ned Spofford fortunately was able to escape the country to the American Academy in Rome, which, though quite aware of the scandal attached to his name, refused to penalize him on that

---

1 The article to which AH is referring was Barbara Grizzuti Harrison's "What Do Women Want? Feminism and Its Future," which had appeared in the October 1981 issue of *Harper's Magazine*. The author had spent a week on the Smith College campus questioning students about their hopes and ambitions. Although the troubles which had afflicted college campuses in the 1960s had passed Smith by, Grizzuti Harrison claimed that the institution was "no longer so ladylike." "There are still Friday afternoon teas, but few people are shocked and even fewer surprised when they become the occasion for 'lesbian workshops.'" The article made Smith sound like a hotbed of lesbianism.

2 The December 1981 issue of *The Atlantic Monthly* contained an 18,246 word article by William Greider, "The Education of David Stockman," in which Stockman, who was President Reagan's Director of the Office of Management and Budget, was quoted as expressing serious misgivings about the administration's economic policies. "None of us really understands what's going on with all these numbers," he was quoted as saying. The article was hugely controversial, and although he wasn't fired, Stockman was "taken to the woodshed" by his boss. (The article can be read online at: http://www.theatlantic.com/magazine/archive/1981/12/the-education-of-david-stockman/305760/)

3 It *was* in 1960, just as AH remembers. Newton Arvin, a Professor of English at Smith, author of well-received studies of major American authors, the recipient of a National Book Award, a former Guggenheim fellow, and a trustee at the Yaddo Writers' Colony, was arrested in 1960 on charges of trafficking in pornography. (AH might have forgotten that he and his first wife had had the MacDonalds to dinner with Arvin four years before the scandal broke. See p. 28 above.)

4 The recorded cause of death was pancreatic cancer.

account[1] – and Joel Dorius may have had to suffer the worst fate of all, being unable to find any teaching job whatever at any level at all, even including grade-school and high-school in this country, and forced to teach for years in Germany before sneaking back to an undesirable teaching job at, I think, San Francisco State during the student riots when nobody much wanted to be teaching there.[2] Meanwhile, back at the ranch, a not inconsiderable portion of the Smith faculty continued to be made up of rather mannish spinster ladies who took an unusually intimate interest in the work and the lives of their students, and all this seemed to be officially regarded as perfectly standard, if not natural.[3]

It was said of Toscanini in his last years, when he was recording the whole cycle of Beethoven Symphonies for RCA, that his tempi seemed to get faster and faster, perhaps out of anxiety that he wouldn't live to complete them. In my case things work quite the opposite way. I have never found myself teaching Shakespeare with such delighted and meticulous attention to detail; and the effect of this is that I've covered scarcely any ground at all. The students seem to like it, and I like it too; but come the end of the term we will, with luck, have studied four plays. I find I must rush to complete Othello as fast as possible to leave what will doubtless be insufficient time for The Tempest.

Glad to hear in this circumlocutious way that Fr. Healy still thinks well of me. I had my doubts because he has not replied to two letters of mine. It's not that I suppose that the busy head of a middle-sized university has nothing better to do than to keep up a cheerful but unproductive correspondence with me, but that he suggested last summer that he would like to have me down to talk with his students about poetry and Life and Truth and other pithy topics. At the time I had to say that my teaching schedule seemed to make a visit in the fall term unlikely. But then, when the term began, I was able to effect some changes which allowed me to finish my teaching duties on Wednesday. I wrote him to that effect, and receiving no reply, wrote again on a different but related topic, and got no reply to that, either. This provoked a tiny bout of paranoia, during which I wondered if I had given him any cause to be offended. Since then I noticed in The Times that he is one of those under consideration for the Chancellorship of City College of New York. So he is doubtless a busy man.

Looks as if a meeting with Frank or Jackie or both is not in the books for this winter; at least I don't see how it can be managed. But if you see either of them again, give them my love.

Ethelred, the Moderately Well-Prepared

---

1 Edward W. Spofford led a successful career after returning from Italy, teaching Classics at, first, Cornell, then San Francisco State, and, finally, Stanford Universities, retiring in 1988.

2 Joel Dorius, who had taught English at MIT, Harvard and Yale before going to Smith, remained at San Francisco State until his retirement in 1984.

3 Smith College never issued a formal apology for its treatment of the three men, but in 2002 it did establish the $100,000 Dorius/Spofford Fund for the Study of Civil Liberties and Freedom of Expression as well as the Newton Arvin Prize in American Studies, which offers a $500 annual stipend.

[283]

[WLM]
November 26th, 1981
[25 Henshaw Avenue, Northampton, Massachusetts 01060]

[Letter, typed on a The Byzantine Institute Inc., letterhead]

Dear Helen & Tony,

What a strange and unfortunate coincidence! I hope, Helen, that you are completely recovered, or so nearly so that the worst is far behind you. A close friend once was similarly afflicted, and he suffered dreadfully, so though I've never had an attack, I've some idea of what it is like. I wish I could spend a weekend with you; perhaps in the Spring when, being already in Williamstown one day a week to teach, I could drive the balance of the distance, but my lecture book is almost filled.

I haven't read the Harper's article, but I'm told by rational friends that it was sadly mistaken and quite inaccurate. It's true that lesbianism is more in the open than it was, and I suppose that is the case in most colleges and universities nowadays. But the vast majority of the students are, I believe, heterosexual and gladly so. As for lowering of standards, I can only say that it seems no worse here than elsewhere, and though I have no obligation to Smith other than to acknowledge that I was treated fairly and paid generously, I do feel that it is still a good, perhaps very good college. I don't know why Jill Conway failed to respond – she's on sabbatical; perhaps she feels, as I do, that engaging in polemics accomplishes little or nothing. Or perhaps she will yet speak up. I hope you won't be too downcast by the whole thing. The college is I think quite healthy.

As for the broader issues about academic life Tony's letter raises, I couldn't agree more. Getting well away from close involvement with it has confirmed my long-held opinion that it is a snake pit, where the lack of proper balance makes a great deal of trouble. Except for some warm and very bright individuals, it ain't for me. I did 21 years of teaching, 1952–80, and that was enough. Visiting is just right, and anyway, I only do it on my own terms. As you know, I'm trying to change my life in some ways, to simplify it, to concentrate on what I love most and what (I hope) I do best, and the challenges are exciting. Next big move will be to move....

I hear John Gross is leaving the TLS for Weidenfeld & Nicholson. Off to New Hampshire to my brother's place for a big family hootnanny.

Much love,
Bill

[284]

[WLM]
December 13th, 1981
[25 Henshaw Avenue, Northampton, Massachusetts 01060]

[Letter, typed]

Id. Dec. MCMLXXXI

Excellency:

I wonder what mysterious mechanism causes one to buy, usually fairly early on in life, books that seem a bit interesting at the time but are left unread for decades, only to be found useful or even inspirational much later on? It has happened to me repeatedly in recent years, and though I tend to reject fancy explanations of such things I can't help but feel that the Victorians' mysterious Providence is hovering around somewhere. The most recent case is William Gaunt's <u>Victorian Olympus</u>,[1] bought about 1952, which has been carted all over hell, left unread, dusted off every few years and now, today, devoured for its information on those XIX cent. painters of classical scenes who are the butt of so many art historians and pundits – of those, at least, who can bear to speak of such things. Gaunt writes well, has a good story to relate, and gives the kind of information (on Leighton and Alma Tadema) that I find very hard to get: what their sources were, why they chose the subjects they did, how their production – and that, I think, is the right word – proceeded as it did, and so on. All this anent work on the Persistence of Classicism, on which I now lecture often, and about which I have constructed a course that I tried out in Berkeley and Atlanta and will soon give, in more polished form, at Williams, and which I hope will someday become a Book. Gaunt may now and then put his tongue in his cheek, but he never demeans these people, whose hope was to entertain and instruct. They never thought themselves Rubens or Tintoretto; when Whistler, master of invective, tried to cut A-T down to size and said he couldn't paint at all well, A-T said cheerfully and with some dignity that Whistler was right, that he had a different purpose.

And then yesterday, taking down from the shelves for reasons completely unknown to me, Nancy Mitford's <u>Noblesse Oblige</u>,[2] I found to my great surprise that there was a Waugh piece in it,[3] something I'd entirely forgotten, and as W's architecture and interiors are a continuing project with me – notebook growing ever fatter – here was not just an addition to my bibliography but more evidence for the foundations of W's point of view about such matters. I had a tag sale in October, and put my finger on every book in the house except the more precious scholarly ones,

---

1 William Gaunt, *Victorian Olympus* (New York: Oxford, 1952).

2 Nancy Mitford, Editor, *Noblesse Oblige: An Enquiry into the Identifiable Characteristics of the English Aristocracy* (New York: Harper & Brothers, 1956).

3 Waugh's contribution, "An Open Letter to the Hon[ble] Mrs. Peter Robb (Nancy Mitford) on a Very Serious Subject from Evelyn Waugh," asked, in semi-serious fashion, what right Mitford had to address the subject of the English upper classes, since she was only just a member of that class and was now living in a foreign country.

and came up with about 500 to sell, mostly trash, with some publishers' "gifts" and the like thrown in. The art books and the serious stuff sold well, the trash hardly moved; took it to the local 2nd-hand man. Peculiar.

It is very early and my eyes are working pretty well.

Diagnosis is miasthenia (sp.?) gravis, more tests this afternoon; a muscular disorder. Serious. Ho-hum. Nick is here to cart me around. The whole thing has made me rush to my work and commitments in a semi-fury, the kind I wish I had conjured up earlier. What uninstructable (sp.? again) creatures we are!

Finally, I recall with a touch of dissatisfaction with myself that when I wrote to you and Helen about the Harper's stuff I used the word "rational" with respect to friends who had given me their opinions of the piece. After I mailed the letter I realised that the word could suggest, to sensitive and intelligent readers such as you and Helen, that I was implying or might be implying that your reaction was not rational. I hasten to say that no such thought ever crossed my poor old mind, and that I fully understand and sympathize with your reaction to what seems to me to be an inaccurate but very disturbing article.

We plan to go to the great Red Lion Inn in Stockbridge for Christmas dinner, weather permitting (I see that you all in Roch. have been getting your share). Unusually, I have some January lectures, one in Phoenix where I plan to take a long break and look at Wright's Taliesin[1] and Soleri's Arcosanti[2] and the like. But all that waits on what the MDs say.

I hope H. has fully recovered from her unwelcome visitation, recovered fully. And that you are all well and flourishing.

Al bocca di lup'
Giuseppe at the Gate

[285]

[AH]
[December 27th, 1981]
[19 East Boulevard, Rochester, NY 14610]

[Letter, typed]

Dear Critter,

I've been given this extraordinary machine[3] by Helen for Christmas, and I'm not very good at it yet – which is to say, it takes me four or five times as long to operate on this as on a regular typewriter – and there are lots of gadgets on it I don't yet quite know how to deal with. I'm counting on the theory that 1 will eventually become

---

1 Taliesin West, the house Frank Lloyd Wright built in Scottsdale, Arizona.

2 An experimental town in the Arizona desert, built to explore the Italian-American architect Paolo Soleri's concept of arcology, which attempts to harmonize architecture and ecology.

3 An electric typewriter.

habituated to it; it's a fancy and sensitive instrument, and while I don't care if I batter away at my little Olivetti portable as though it were a Piñata [I trust you're duly impressed], I feel a respectful nervousness at this keyboard which, even though it has devices to cancel errors, invites much intimidating reverence. Besides, I happen to be supremely a typist of imprecise aim, and this instrument is especially apt at picking up my imprecisions. Vediamo.

Curious that you should mention William Gaunt. While I can't claim to know much of his work, The Aesthetic Adventure (which I have in a Pelican paperback)[1] is a favorite book of mine. There are, in fact, certain passages I especially cherish. "The craving for sensation, the fastidious and patrician research for strange refinement, the jealous cultivation of art as a thing removed from the common affairs of men constituted the prevailing atmosphere of the 'brilliant' period which was now beginning – the Second Empire. By a series of republican (and even Bohemian) revolutions, assisted that is to say by 'vagabonds, disbanded soldiers, discharged prisoners, fugitives from galleys, sharpers, jugglers, professional beggars, pickpockets, conjurers, gamesters, pimps, brothel keepers, porters, men of letters, organ grinders, rag pickers, knife grinders and tinkers, Charles Louis Napoleon Bonaparte, third son of the King of Holland made himself Emperor of the French. The description of his helpers is that of Karl Marx who, it will be seen, places 'men of letters' somewhere between porters and organ grinders; who further described Bohemia as 'the scum, offal, and detritus of society.'" Again: "Frederick Goodall, R. A., had received two thousand guineas for an Egyptian composition – The Ploughman and Shepherdess. To make himself familiar with Egyptian sheep ('different from our European breeds') he imported a whole flock which he kept at a farm at Harrow WEALD." Perhaps best: 'Our unfortunate century was born middle-aged. It had none of the ardors and ideals of youth. Genial, false, and well provided with the world's goods it ate, drank, and was frivolous after an elderly fashion. Hence there was in many of its productions a queer vacancy, a bonelessness, an absence of aim – manifest, for instance, in the art nouveau, the 'new art', in which solid forms disappeared in amazing twists and contortions, ornaments of glass dripped cloudy tears, ashtrays looked like spent dum-dum bullets. This aberration came from Vienna under the inspiration of the English arts and crafts movement and left traces in every home."

Since you put in a good word for a Gaunt book, let me recommend The Forbidden Experiment by Roger Shattuck.[2] It's available in paperback, and I found it impressive and suggestive and very moving. It's subtitled: The Story of the Wild Boy of Aveyron.

WHEN ARE YOU GOING TO COME VISIT US?
                    Aunt Fidget Wonkham-Strong[3]

---

1 William Gaunt, *The Aesthetic Adventure* (Harmondsworth, Middlesex: Pelican, 1957).

2 Roger Shattuck, *The Forbidden Experiment: The Story of the Wild Boy of Aveyron* (New York: Farrar Straus Giroux, 1980).

3 A character in Russell Hoban's children's books, *How Tom Beat Captain Najork and His Hired Sportsman* (New York: Atheneum, 1974) and *A Near Thing for Captain Najork* (New York: Atheneum, 1976).

[286]

[WLM]
January 9th, 1982
25 Henshaw Avenue, Northampton, Massachusetts 01060

[Blank postcard, typed, with the sender's address given as xxv hensh / 01060, addressed to A. E. Hecht, rhymist, 19 E. Boulevard, Rochester NY 14610]

Dear Sergeant:

Your letter & quotes took me back handsomely to the time (30 yrs ago?) when I read the <u>Aesth. Adv.</u>, a book that introduced me to all kinds of new things. Can't find my copy but will get the Penguin, and read it all again. Finishing up some entries for the forthcoming Macmillan dict. of architects[1]; I rather enjoy doing that sort of thing, and it pays well, which may influence me somehow. Off to Arizona presently to give two lectures, after which I will hang around a bit in the sun, & try to see Taliesin & Arcosanti and suchlike marvels. Into the Piranesian Massachusetts General for test after test: turns out to be myasthenia gravis, which I can't recommend at all. See double, OK with girls, not good for typing, driving exhilarating to say the least. Cohn-Haft & new, nice wife had a v. good party recently; he's changed, is more confident, & is back at work.

Thine,
Calypso, Countess von Klättensmund-Hallensmörd

[287]

[AH]
January 16th, 1982
19 East Boulevard, Rochester, NY 14610

[Letter, typed on an Albert D'Alessandro[2] letterhead, addressed to Señor William MacDonald, Procurator of Sheboygan, 25 Henshaw Avenue, Northampton, Mass. 01060]

Comrade General Ivan Ivanovitch,

Well sir, I'm sixty years old today. It feels genuinely creepy to state it outright like that. I enjoy celebrating my birthdays; I like having a fuss made, but I seem to have gone out of my way to keep from noticing just which birthday it was, at least until this milestone came and clobbered me. I wish I could say that it gave one pause, because that would slow things down. Mortality, in the Wodehouse phrase, "gets in amongst one," in the guise of various <u>faiblesses</u> such as we both now seem to have fallen heir to. Nothing of mine can yet be called <u>gravis</u>, but I have been officially warned not to shovel snow by my doctor, who detected a

---

1 *Macmillan Encyclopedia of Architects*, edited by Adolf K. Placzek (New York: The Free Press, 1982).

2 This letterhead had belonged to Helen Hecht's late father, a New York lawyer.

murmur several years ago, and now I find myself grotesquely standing by while Helen, frail and lovely thing that she is, gets the shovel and digs us out. There has been plenty of digging to do, and I feel the more invalided because when I turned in my grades and papers for last term I began a full calendar year of leave. I am now home all the time, and certainly around when the chores need doing. And even the weather reminds us of our frailty, as if we needed reminding. We were planning a trip to the big city for this very weekend, and then the snow walloped New York, and we were advised that it would be wiser not to come. I'm sure the advice was right. When you live there, you simply stay home in bad weather; when you visit, you make a schedule of appointments that you like to think of as inflexible, and if you have to scratch an item your visit is by that much impaired. We had made ourselves a very heavy schedule of lunches and dinners and even a play (the playwright was to have set aside complimentary tickets for us; the play is The Curse of an Aching Heart, by William Alfred) but the telephoned advice from friends in the city was terrifyingly reinforced by that plane crash into the Potomac.[1] So I am sitting here at home, counting my blessings, of which my wife and youngest son are the chief. But a few new ones were added as birthday gifts. Of these, one is a small (8 × 5¼) Piranesi engraving of the front (seen from an angle) of the Pantheon. It was printed in Paris from the original plate in 1810. I will have it framed one of these jolly days when the weather lets up enough for us to emerge. Not that there isn't plenty to keep me occupied indoors. I still have standard detritus to dispose of: letters of recommendation, blurbs for publishers, correspondence, and the rest of it. In that line, I just sent in an article requested by the NY Times Book Review for their series on, as they call it, "the making of a writer." I still have more junk to clear away, but then I have two major projects. The first is the most obvious: to work hard and productively on a further book of poems. I think I have roughly a quarter to a third of a book in hand. The other is to write an essay, possibly a long, windy and detailed one, on The Merchant of Venice. My excitement and enthusiasm about this has nothing whatever to do with its Venetian setting. It's that, having read the play since sixth grade, and having taught it for perhaps twenty years, I have just discovered what it is really about; and what is most exciting is that nobody else knows! I can't say that with total certainty of course, because I haven't read all or even much of the commentary on the play. But I am absolutely certain that I am right, and I'm eager to clear the decks and get under way. My certainty is not merely heady vanity, though doubtless there is a measure of that in it. The point is that I think I can persuasively solve a whole collection of puzzles about the play that other people have either failed to solve, or when they have addressed one or two have ignored the rest. Some of the puzzles seem minor in comparison with others, but by my solution they are all related to a central design with I think is inescapable once it is pointed out. The main puzzles, large and small, are these. This is the

---

1 On January 13th Air Florida Flight 90 from Washington National Airport to Fort Lauderdale crashed into the 14th Street Bridge over the Potomac River, with serious loss of life.

only one of Shakespeare's plays that has been presented both as a comedy and a tragedy; in the eighteenth century especially, it was offered as a tragic play. How do we account for this? Next, the merchant of the title is Antonio, perhaps the most passive and easily the most uninteresting character in the play. When great actors from Kean and Garrick to Olivier elect to tackle the play, they invariably play Shylock. There is no question about who is the central character in Hamlet or Macbeth. Then why is this play named for Antonio? And what is the meaning of Antonio's very first line, which is the first line of the whole play: "In sooth I know not why I am so sad"? It is never explained at any point in the play. Three other questions. Why does Shylock really want that pound of flesh, why did Portia's father bind her to the absurd conditions of his will, and how does Portia (who as far as we can tell has had no legal education) get to know more law than anyone else, and why should no one else know what she knows? I've had to transfer to another machine because of ribbon problems. Anyway, I have a set of answers to all those problems (and a few others) and my answers all fit together with one another and make an absolutely convincing pattern. By dint of some fooling around I fixed my fancy machine. So there you have it; a project I look forward to with some pleasure – though imagine how I should feel if some son-of-a-bitch had already come up with my discovery? The reason I'm so confident that no one has done so is that the latest essays by careful and responsible scholars still flounder around, whereas the solution, once it's found, is like "The Last Chord"; it sums up everything, and would have to be recognized. – I hope that you will so arrange things for yourself as to schedule lectures in some decent climate. These days, that doesn't leave much choice. Perhaps southern California or the tip of Florida. I wish we could bring you here some way, though there's nothing in the way of the weather that would entice anyone. Keep in touch. I find myself much concerned about you, not merely on account of the troubling news you report but because you are alone, and because of my great affection.

William of Magenta

[288]

[AH]
January 17th, 1982
19 East Boulevard, Rochester, NY 14610

[Letter, typed on an Albert D'Alessandro letterhead]

Comrade, etc …

Read t'other letter first. This is no more than a postscript.

Well, sir, you could have knocked me over with a feather. I wrote my garrulous letter to you yesterday afternoon, bitter cold outside and suitable for staying home and writing letters. It was Saturday, and too late for the mailman who comes to the door, and too cold to journey out to find a mailbox. Best just to seal and stamp it, and hold it for posting on Monday. Which is what I did. And it will go out at the same time as this. But somehow later that afternoon I bethought myself, and got out my little pocket calculator, and by cold, numerical computation concluded that I am in fact only a mewling fifty-nine years old. So I now withdraw all my observations on mutability, and ask you to reserve them for around this time next year. My error in this matter should only serve to confirm my remark that while I like celebrating my birthday I'm content to leave it obscure as to just which birthday it is.

Dazedly,
Calixtus, anti-Pope

[289]

[AH]
February 5th, 1982
19 East Boulevard, Rochester, NY 14610

[Letter, typed, addressed to William MacDonald, Archimandrite,
25 Henshaw Avenue, Northampton, Mass. 01060]

Dear Bill,

At the time that you wrote me what can only be called your "jocular" postcard about myasthenia gravis I had no idea at all what it was, as you must clearly have recognized by my utterly frivolous response. It was only as a consequence of our phone conversation that I realised how serious the matter is, and I seem to feel that while you are entitled to jest about the matter, and may be most at ease in dealing with it jestingly, it is not a privilege that I can take, nor one I wish to. I have discussed this with Helen, I've made inquiries of a general nature among some of our medical friends, and was even able to find the term listed in the latest supplement of the <u>OED</u>. Of course, everything must wait and hang upon the further findings of Mass. General, but we have given the matter more than a little serious thought, and it seems not unimportant for you to know that it was Helen who first uttered the proposal that you come here to live; though in speaking she did no more than pronounce what was in my mind, too. Read on a bit further before you start spluttering protests. One of the things that concerns us both is that you are alone. And while I know that you have two sons who must love you, and would want to be first among those who offered any help, they are, quite simply, less well situated to do so than we are. Ours, as you may remember, is a rather ample house, and one of its former owners in fact had intended to divide it into separate apartments and rent them out. You could, therefore, have a suite of small rooms of your own, including, of course, a private bath. And there would always be someone around to help or drive or attend in whatever way. Rochester, it may be said, is neither Boston nor New York as regards hospitals or medical facilities, but it is miles beyond Northampton, and it seems to me likely that you could put yourself in very responsible hands here. In fact, the only serious impediment to this plan as I see it is the fact that we could not furnish shelf space for your vast collection of books. I'm not sure I know how to deal with that matter, but it must come second to our first proposal. It is important that you should understand quite firmly that this is a very seriously intended proposal, which is not made in the expectation of elaborate thanks and a refusal. Everything, of course, is contingent on what the doctors recommend; and it may be a good long time, as I sincerely hope it will be, before you need to take advantage of this offer. It is, in any case, there for you and your doctors to consider; and doubtless your doctors in Boston can also advise you about whether there are competent people here in Rochester to deal with your condition. In thinking about the matter I beg you not to forget that this invitation comes from both of us.

Tony

[290]

[WLM]
February 10th, 1982
25 Henshaw Avenue, Northampton, Massachusetts 01060

[Letter, typed, addressed to Professor and Mrs Anthony E. Hecht,
19 East Boulevard, Rochester NY 14510, with enclosure]

Dear Helen and Tony,

Your offer of a place to live touches me deeply. Friends, old friends, good friends, are the most precious things in life. They really are the only people who can help. The children want to, often, but through no fault of their own they can't in any serious way.

The situation is as follows: I stay on the present regimen of drugs for another month or two, giving the doctors a chance to observe and meditate. I am, then, in a sort of stasis, waiting that part of it out. I had planned to move next June, to a warmer climate, but I'll now stay somewhat longer so that moving doesn't have to be added to other things. And I really do want to get out of these winters. So although my appreciation of and thanks for your offer, one of the nicest things that has ever happened to me, know no bounds, I really think I should find a more southern latitude.

Yes, I joke about it. For me it is the way to handle it. And I am not ill in the sense of pain, just somewhat restricted as to what I can do and how much of it. Furthermore, I am adjusting to it somewhat. I'm not much of a worrier, which in some ways is a stupid condition, but in this case may help. And it is, to me, funny: our helplessness, the irony of so much of our lives. I know you know what kind of funny I mean. So naturally your reaction was proper and apposite and there is no way, anyway, that I could be offended by what you say.

I guess I can say this to you, since we are close: I'm not upset particularly. I don't like falling down when I can't tell where the surface is that my foot is supposed to marry, but that's only happened four or five times. I'm driving to Williams this morning for my seminar; slowly, VERY carefully, but driving nevertheless. I don't feel at all courageous, and my condition is so insignificant compared to that of some of my friends and family both here and gone that it doesn't, in balance, seem like much. My book on Roman cities, that I have been working on for so long, is slowly coming to its conclusion, the end product of so many years of work, study, and travel, and that does wonders for my morale. All in all, a long way round to say to you splendid friends that I'm pretty much all right, and that the m.g. is not life-threatening.

I've not read your <u>Times</u> piece[1]; Nick, one of your admirers, has & he liked it.
Bless you both, and much love from
Bill

Stationery (c) [copyright] WLM 1982. You type it twice along the long side of a sheet & take that to the xerox people, have them do it on rag-ish paper, then cut the new sheets down the middle. Clever, eh? You may use the idea without paying any royalty.

[Enclosure]

You are cordially invited to attend
The 1982 Amy M. Sacker Memorial Lectures

PROFESSOR WILLIAM L. MacDONALD

Sorting Out Classical Architecture

April 15 — *A Revisionist View of Antiquity*
April 22 — *Renaissance and Baroque Transformations*
April 29 — *The Persistence of Classical Forms*

MOUNT HOLYOKE COLLEGE

Gamble Auditorium, 8 P.M.   *South Hadley, Massachusetts*

---

1 "Masters of Unpleasantness," *The New York Times*, February 7, 1982. This appears to be the article AH referred to in his letter of January 16th, where he spoke of having been commissioned by the "<u>NY Times Book Review</u> for their series on, as they call it, 'the making of a writer'." In the article, AH explains, amongst other things, why "vanity, paranoia [and] selfishness" seem to him to be "characteristic afflictions, amounting almost to professional deformations, of most poets." "I recognized them instantly in myself," he writes, "and, after a moment's thought, in most other poets I know." The article can be read online at http://www.nytimes.com/1982/02/07/books/masters-of-unpleasantness.html?module=Se arch&mabReward=relbias%3Ar

[291]

[AH]
March 7th, 1982
[19 East Boulevard, Rochester, NY 14610]

[Letter, typed]

Éminence chartreuse,

"The peculiar ambience of the [Washington, D.C.] Metro stations results from the fluorescent lamps hidden under floor-level soffits reflecting light and shadow on the ceiling coffers. (Ambience is the atmosphere that surrounds you; soffits are the underside of any building element, in this case the base of the overhanging arch; coffers are the deeply recessed rectangular or polygonal panels sunk into the surface of a ceiling.) The lights are sunken even below floor level where the arch curves under the platforms – as at the Rosslyn and Metro Center stations – placed so they are easy to service but safe from vandalism.

The prototype of the coffered ceiling is the Pantheon in Rome, which was also the inspiration for the Jefferson Memorial. Sir Banister Fletcher, in the 20th edition of his History of Architecture,[1] describes the ceiling of the Pantheon thus: 'The coffers not only ornament the surface of the dome, but serve also to reduce its weight. The lighting in the crown of the dome ... produces the most solemn and impressive effect. It is a matter of no small surprise that from a single source light should be thrown round all parts of the building.' That gives some idea of what Harry Weese means when he says, 'The Russians did it with marble; we did it with shadows.'"

Harry Weese's inspiration for these vast cellar depots seems to have drawn on a timeless geometry, partly the colossal prisons and grottoes of Piranesi, partly the futurist landscape of Star Wars."

The author of these interesting observations is a fella named E. J. Applewhite,[2] who set them down in a book named Washington Itself.[3] (Knopf paperback). This Applewhite fella is an innerresting guy. He went to Washington in 1947, and in 1970 retired from the CIA "where he held executive positions." Since then "he was co-author with R. Buckminster Fuller of Synergetics (1975)[4] and Synergetics 2 (1979),[5] and the author of a book about working with Fuller, called Cosmic

---

1 Sir Banister Fletcher, *Sir Banister Fletcher's: A History of Architecture* (New York: Prentice Hall, 1975).

2 Edgar Jarratt Applewhite, (1919–2005), American, retired CIA officer, and writer, who called himself a "taxophilist," i.e. a collector and classifier of thoughts, interests and obsessions.

3 E. J. Applewhite, *Washington Itself: An Informal Guide to the Capital of the United States* (New York: Knopf, 1981).

4 E. J. Applewhite and Buckminster Fuller, *Synergetics: Explorations in the Geometry of Thinking* (New York: Macmillan, 1975).

5 E. J. Applewhite and Buckminster Fuller, *Synergetics 2: Further Explorations in the Geometry of Thinking* (New York: Macmillan, 1979).

Fishing.[1]

As for me, I have just finished a longish essay that will quite simply demonstrate for good and all that nobody has ever understood the real meaning and integral design of <u>The Merchant of Venice</u> except Shakespeare and me. It will come to the world as a genuine revelation. And so before bringing it to the public's attention, I am arranging for northern lights to appear, and am about to hire a brass band.

Can Grande della Scala

[292]

[AH]
May 16th, 1982
19 East Boulevard, Rochester, NY 14610

[Letter, typed, addressed to Prof. William MacDonald (Big Mac to all his friends!),
25 Henshaw Ave., Northampton, Mass. 01060, with a now missing enclosure]

Noble Sir,

I've always felt that the best letters are those most copiously illustrated, and preferably pornographic as well; but dirty pictures being in short supply around here just now, I send instead a couple of Roman views taken from a catalogue called <u>Old Master Drawings from Chatsworth</u>,[2] which I recently picked up second hand. In the picture of St. Peter's, it looks much as though Maderno modeled his fountains on one that had been there before. And in the other, the little houses in the Forum are odd and unexpected.

I feel sure I must have told you I had been working on a critical essay on <u>The Merchant of Venice</u>.[3] Well, at last I've finished it, and it runs on to seventy blessed pages with nine pages of notes. A highly improbable length from the point of view of publication: too long for virtually any journal, not long enough for a book. Nevertheless, and very surprisingly, the <u>New York Review of Books</u> asked to see it in spite of its length, and promised a decision in a week's time. By now they have had it two and a half weeks, and I'm getting fidgety. I may add that I'm extremely pleased with it, and am convinced that once it appears it will prove definitive as regards the major themes and the meanings of the play.

I imagine that by now you have heard from a guilt-ridden Hank Millon. I phoned him with regard to some Washington topic, and we got on to chatting about you. I mentioned your illness, in a general and undefined way, and he seemed to be unaware of what was going on, and asked for particulars, which I

1 E. J. Applewhite, *Cosmic Fishing: An Account of Writing Synergetics with Buckminster Fuller* (New York: Macmillan, 1977).

2 James Byam Shaw, *Old Master Drawings from Chatsworth: A Loan Exhibition from the Devonshire Collection* (Washington, D.C.: International Exhibitions Foundation: National Gallery of Art, 1969).

3 The essay in question was entitled "*The Merchant of Venice:* A Venture in Hermeneutics" and it was first published in AH's essay collection, *Obbligati: Essays in Criticism*.

gave him. He listened to me in total silence, and I tried to be as careful and detailed as I could. When he finally spoke he was overcome with remorse. He told me he had asked you to perform some chore and you had declined, naming your ailment. The name of it meant nothing to him, and he supposed that this was merely your odd way of saying you didn't want to be diverted from tasks you had set for yourself. He felt ashamed of himself for not realizing how serious the matter was; and I in turn felt that I had somehow exposed him to a sort of humiliation. I tried to explain to him that were we not, here in Rochester, surrounded by many friends who were physicians, I would certainly not have known what myasthenia gravis was. This did not appear to console him much; he heaped blame upon himself for not inquiring further. Anyway, I hope the whole matter has been straightened out.

And of course I hope that the big wheels at Mass. General have weighed and balanced all things in such ways as to allow you to lead a decent and pleasant and fruitful and long life.

Myshkin

[293]

[WLM]
May 21st, 1982
[25 Henshaw Avenue, Northampton, Massachusetts 01060]

[Letter, typed, with the sender's address given as Q. Marcius Turbo, Praefectus Praetorio, Porticus Octaviae, Reg. XI Aug., Caput Mundi, addressed to Anthony Hecht (a.k.a. Doge & Patriarch, 19 East Boulevard, Rochester NY 14610]

My dear Doge,

Venice and you are so happily allied, that I'm sure you can get me a cut rate at the Reale Danieli (where I once stayed for three nights when I was leading a tour group in '58, I think it was; it was quite wonderful. I remember dining on the roof, with captains bringing me bottles of splendid wines because I was the capo … the boats strung with lights … ahhhhh …). So when you get things arranged, let me know. I thought that when there I would have VV engraved on 69 bronze plaques, which will be set into the piers of the grand Piazza … however, if you are against this, do let me know and I'll think of something else, no doubt.

But seriously, that's great news about Merchant. Our work keeps us going, and still excites us; I don't know what I'd do without mine. I can't do it every day, and I can't always feel enthusiastic about it, but much of the time I can and do. I look forward very much to reading your analysis. It is not a play I know at all well, nor, as I recall, understand well either. I will read it this summer in order to be ready.

Sorry you got caught in the middle with Hank. Knowing your great sense of delicacy I'm sure you handled it just right. And I can understand his reaction, for he and I are close friends of long standing. I did indeed beg off something or other … I forget what … and in the process mentioned that I had a new companion, m.g. He is one of the busiest, and most peripatetic, of men and I quite understand how he took my note; I very likely would have done the same. I've not heard from him, but he and Judy will be going to New Hampshire with the children one of these days and that will be the time he will stop by, or they will call and ask me to Peterborough for a visit. It will all come out well, I assure you.

Some gent, named Parish, named by the TLS as a don who is an Americanist, reviewed McFeeley's great biography of Grant in a most grudging way.[1] Not that he didn't make good observations, he did, but he set himself up as a great authority, and with Grant that's a dangerous thing to do. He (P.) said that Grant had no political ability at all, but the Whole Point of his generalcy, I've decided after decades of reading and mulling, is that he was politically savvy, unlike his predecessors, a man who could understand Lincoln's needs (and, of course, L. reciprocated). G. dealt with the damned political generals with a sure touch … again and again … and if that isn't political savvy, I don't know what is. Few great commanders have been able to handle that kind of problem, which always exists in war, as well as he; Wellington could, but his charisma (forgive me) was greater. Worked myself up to a letter about it, but subsided, as the TLS never pays any attention to what I say.

Cities is in its last weeks. I can no longer tell if it is a great book or a humdrum one. Viscerally, I feel it is the former, but I'm old enough & smart enough, &c … Dedicating it to F[rank] E B[rown] and Sterling Dow, my old Harvard teacher & friend. Tried to say some things that are fresh and new and imaginative about cites, while correcting the utterly retardataire study of the buildings, mostly XVIII century in conception. It is the broadest and brainiest thing I've ever done, and the long delay in getting it together bothers me not at all. Meanwhile, proofs of the revised edition of Big Red, my 1965 Vol. I, have been passed, and a paperback and hard cover will appear in September or October. Also, I've written a fairly long article on how the excavations at Ostia affected the Italian regime architects in the 1930s; it will appear in a Festschrift for H-R Hitchcock which will appear soon; will send you an offprint as I know you want it badly.

Cheers,
Q. Marcius Turbo

---

1 P. J. Parish, "The Career of an Enigma," a review of William S. McFeeley's *Grant: A Biography* (New York: Norton, 1981), appeared in the February 12th, 1982 issue of the *Times Literary Supplement*.

[294]

[AH]
June 14th, 1982
19 East Boulevard, Rochester, NY 14610

[Letter, typed on a J. B. Borreau letterhead, addressed to Dr. William MacDonald, Inspector of Drains, 25 Henshaw Avenue, Northampton, Mass. 01060]

My Old,

    I would have written sooner, if only to show off this classy letterpaper, but for a viral invasion that came down upon me like the British fleet, arriving several weeks ago, along with the gipsy moths. It was a forceful invasion, developing into bronchitis, and I'm not yet over it, though somewhat improved. By an odd turn of fate, it hit me at the same time as a strangely deep depression (doubtless contributing its infected share) that was the vastly overdetermined reaction to the loss of a book. Perpend. When my parents died they left their New York apartment to my brother, Roger, who had shared it with them all his life, having been wholly dependent on them because of grave physical disabilities that have been with him from birth. Not only the apartment itself but all its appurtenances and furnishings remained for his use, though it was understood that he could not dispose either of the apartment itself or of any valuables without consulting me, since, though he had exclusive use of all, they were half mine. Among the possessions left were my parents' books; not an extensive library, but in some ways choice, since, at the time they married they told their friends they wished to collect fine books, and accordingly received some very fine things as wedding presents. However, in terms of sheer volume Roger's continuing, life-long purchases (chiefly of paperbacks) that were one of the very few pleasures of a crippled and retiring man, had expanded well beyond the shelving space of his own room, and at length, in consultation with me, he decided to dispose of such parts of our parents' library as neither he nor I cared to keep. It was left to him (alas!) to find somebody to appraise and dispose of the rest. Of all the gloomy parts of the story, the fact that he was handed a paltry hundred dollars for superb, leather-bound sets of books is the least of it. I had sent Roger a list of the things I wanted set aside for me until such time as I could come to New York to claim them. They included a three-volume, first edition, set of <u>Tom Jones</u>. When, on June 3rd, I finally found myself in the city and able to bring back some books, it was discovered that volume one of the Fielding was missing. Roger had disposed of what he had not kept fully a year before, could not remember the name of the person who had taken the books, had idly thrown away the receipt, and could not even remember who had recommended this factor to him. My reaction to this has been abnormally strong, and I recognize the feelings as those with which I have not been afflicted for many years, but which were remarkably common during my first marriage. But not only at that time. They are generated by that kind of remarkable, seeming unwittingness which, even if it were pure, would betoken a lack of concern with the feelings of others; but which is more likely to be mixed with an incalculable portion of either conscious or unconscious malice. Roger's feelings about me could not fail to be painfully complicated with admiration and envy, and what most stunned me was that, after sifting through the books twice over in search of that missing volume, and failing to find it, I sought Roger out in a state of great agitation. He had retired, during my rummaging, to his own room. I asked him whether there was the slightest chance that whoever had taken away the other books could somehow have taken the missing Fielding volume as well, and without an instant's hesitation, with an alacrity that was breath-taking, he said, "Yes." Not, "Good heavens, is something missing?" Not, "My God, it never occurred to me that anything of the sort might happen." Just "Yes." Since there has been nothing else whatever in the way of family heirlooms that has come my way or that I cared to have, this is a matter that I am struggling to cope with, and finding more difficult than the plain, literal events warrant in themselves.

Between the lost book, the virus and the gipsy moths I have been pretty well out of things, and have little else to report. My long essay on The Merchant of Venice was returned by both the New York Review of Books (as being too long for them) and by Vintage Books (as being unsuitable for them). I have no idea where to send it next. We have found ourselves a Home in Washington, though. It is a three-bedroom, unfurnished house on the Maryland side of the D.C. border of Chevy Chase, near Chevy Chase Circle. This is a very convenient location as regards getting Evan to school, there being no buses for that purpose; and it will put me at the end of a bus line that can take me right to Capitol Hill.[1] We plan to take household necessaries and a little furniture and have them shipped; and to purchase frugally and furnish sparely when we arrive, and hope to resell when we depart. My chief diversion during the viral episode has been reading J. E. Neale's biography of Queen Elizabeth I.[2] Not the least of its pleasures was in recognizing the peculiar, twisted temperament of Mary Queen of Scots. It's a good book when you're laid up, though I suspect that like almost all history, it is given to the brisk and easy simplifications of hindsights. Still, I find more and more that when I seek reading for diversion I invariably turn to non-fiction, and many recent purchases of fiction have remained unread. This is an odd embarrassment, since many of our friends here have their choice of reading virtually governed by the best-seller list or some equivalent thereof; and a few worthy persons almost always manage to ask in a friendly, expectant way (the more expectant precisely because I am supposed to be a "literary" type) "Have you read [D. M. Thomas's] The White Hotel?" Or [John Irving's] Garp? Or the latest Updike, Bellow, Barth or whatever? And I never have. Sometimes I have gone so far as to buy the books with a genuine mind to reading them. But they evade me, and find their ways to the shelves. Helen shares my bias, for the present at least, and I find myself recommending to her

---

1 AH had been appointed to the two-year position of Consultant in Poetry to the Library of Congress, the Library of Congress being situated on Capitol Hill.

2 J. E. Neale, *Elizabeth I and Her Parliaments* (New York: Norton, 1966).

biographies I have enjoyed. She's now reading one on the Sitwells.

Let me say that I was much heartened, and hope I was entitled to be, by the general spirit of cheerfulness of your last letter. I hope it means that some metabolic equilibrium has been established. May it be so.

Joseph of Arimathea (not the Joseph of Arimathea; another one).

[295]

[WLM]
June 20th, 1982
[25 Henshaw Avenue, Northampton, Massachusetts 01060]

[Letter, typed, with enclosure]

Father's Day MCMLXXXII

Principe,

How awful for you. Perhaps the book will turn up. How is it that experiences like that reach into our vitals and twist them horribly? I've even now, at 61, without any defences to speak of against such things. I've a litany of rational thoughts that I tell like beads, and it helps some, as does the thought that all things end, but cold comfort there. It is always the thing with which we are certain we ourselves had nothing to do; though when the Second Act is finished I suspect for myself at least that I had a lot more to do with it than I had imagined and that the thought of having nothing to do with it was an unconscious mechanism to ward off something very unpalatable; I sense you may be suggesting something similar. Also, an experience like that makes us ask what we really do hold precious and why. I wish I could offer solace; I can only say I know precisely, exactly, what you are going through. It cannot be much if any comfort to know that the experience is truly common, shelved by most of us as being all but incommunicable. I won't add to your concerns by retailing any of my experiences, but I mention that I have had them in order the better to project my heartfelt sympathy.

I've just noticed what piece of paper I picked from my "use it up" pile, an old resumé. Hardly a match for your glorious sheet.

I too purposefully overlook the current works by Successful Novelists; I can say happily that I've been in that frame of mind for decades. Later on, sometimes, I'll pick up the paperback, and sometimes that pays off. But then, I've never been able to finish To the Lighthouse. I read some thrillers (liked the first 3/4 of Gorky Park) and a lot of history and biog.; began with them about 1930 or so and have never stopped. When I look into a White Hotel or a Garp I find little I didn't know, which I can say without false modesty, and little of worth for my own life. I do read collections of short stories by authors I like (Cheever, Greene, &c), and read and re-read what I love – Waugh, Compton Mackenzie, Trollope, Yourcenar, James (some of), Patrick White, Lampedusa and, more or less at the head of the list, Stendhal – the Roman contes, the Journals, in particular. I can't seem to warm to Dickens –

perhaps it's time to try again – but I love George Eliot and Hardy. But I return again and again to history, ancient and modern, to good biography – liked Powell, tho.

Work moving along fairly well. The handbook for myasthenics says they tend to become reclusive, embarrassed by their condition, but I'm going to Fight That. I'm not running scared, but if at this time next year the symptoms have not been much cut back I probably will be. Some of the literature is scary. A little catalogue I did for the Cooper-Hewitt – a fine place which of course you know – is in the mail to you.[1] Lots of other stuff, much of it minor, in proof or about to be, and <u>Cities</u> takes up my good hours (6–noon) most days.

I hope you saw the piece in the <u>Times</u> about the benefits of studying Latin. The reporter ended his up-beat paragraphs with the stirring statement that it was wonderful to see enthusiasm "for the great writers in the language, Virgil, Horace, and Homer." How nice! How nifty!

Love to you all,
Marcus Agrippa · Cos. III.

[Enclosure: WLM's "old resumé"]

<u>William L. MacDonald</u>

A. P. Brown Professor of the History of Art
Smith College, Northampton, Massachusetts 01063

<u>but all mail, please, to</u>: 25 Henshaw Avenue
Northampton, Mass. 01060

Telephone: 413.584.3284. Social Security number: 006-12-8540
Harvard A.B.(1949), A.M.(1953), and Ph.D. (1956) Rome Prize Fellow, The American Academy in Rome (1954-1956); Morse (Yale) Fellow at the Academy (1962-1963); Executive Secretary, The Byzantine Institute (1950-1954)

Publications

<u>A Selected Bibliography of Architecture in tho Age of Justinian</u>

<u>Early Christian and Byzantine Architecture</u>

---

1 *Columns in the Collection of the Cooper-Hewitt Musem.*

The Architecture of the Roman Empire:
I <u>An Introductory Study</u>
II <u>Cities and Towns</u> (forthcoming)
III <u>Roman Architecture and the History of Architecture</u> (in preparation)
<u>Northampton Massachusetts Architecture & Buildings</u> (a Bicentennial book)

<u>The Pantheon – Design, Meaning, and Progeny</u>

<u>Piranesi's Carceri: Sources of Invention</u>

Chapters and articles in: <u>The Architect, Chapters in the History of the Profession</u>; <u>Readings in Art History</u>; the <u>Princeton Encyclopedia of Classical Sites</u>; the <u>Dictionary of American Biography</u>, and various journals

Associate Editor of the <u>Princeton Encyclopedia of Classical Sites</u>

[296]

[AH]
June 24th, 1982
19 East Boulevard, Rochester, NY 14610

[Letter, typed on a Henry Chavigny, Blois, France, letterhead, addressed to William MacDonald, Plenipotentiary, 25 Henshaw Avenue, Northampton, Mass. 01060]

Honored Sir,
    You know how Keats felt when he first looked into Chapman's Homer. Pretty good; much as if he'd stumbled upon something really keen. Well, I have come across what strikes me as indisputably the best poem about masturbation I've ever seen, and I am eager to impart this information to the world at large. Indeed, the only thing that astonishes me is that the poem has not been more widely recognized and anthologized. Pray look it up in the Clarendon Press edition of the poems of Lovelace.[1] It is called, "Love Made in the First Age: To Chloris," and its first line is "In the Nativity of time …" Quite seriously, I think it's an exceptionally good poem; as good, I think, as any of Lovelace's, and it has some memorable lines, one of which, describing the Edenic innocence of sexual love and naked beauty before The Fall, declares: "No palace to the Clouds did swell; / Each humble Princess then did dwell / In the <u>Piazza</u> of her hair."
    Thank you for your very compassionate, generous and understanding letter. I

---

1 *The Poems of Richard Lovelace*, edited by C. H. Wilkinson (Oxford: Clarendon Press, 1968).

am happy to report that I am by now quite over the shock – and it was shock more than anything else that so stirred me. I knew at once that the loss was almost entirely symbolic, though the knowledge did not in the least diminish my Gordian knot of rage, guilt, and other violent emotions that I had thought pretty well buried for good. In fact, the chief shock was to find myself experiencing feelings that had blissfully been banished for so long, but which had once festered in ulcerous silence for years. Anyway, while I would still like to retrieve the book, and some efforts are still going forward to that end, I have been restored to calm and good spirits. Your letter was wise and thoughtful, and agreed in many of its insights with intuitions of my own. It is curious how long it takes us, how much pondering and ruthless self-inquisition, to come anywhere near understanding ourselves, and how we turn out to be the most subversive and resistant witnesses in all such inquiries. And it is no less curious that both Socrates and Freud should have thought self-knowledge was the ultimate kind. In this the two of them stand opposed to all that empiric and positivistic sciences profess to honor as the only kind of knowledge – impersonal and quantifiable. I once annoyed my Dean here, who also teaches psychology, by referring to that field as "the softest of the sciences," in a paper I was giving. When he raised his objection at the end, I merely said that by calling it the softest I meant it was the most literary. Since I was a literary type myself, he could not proceed to object, but he was not happy. Anyway, the way we disguise our deepest truths from ourselves is the subject of my poem, "Green: An Epistle,"[1] which was prompted by, first, an insight into symbiotic family ties, and later into myself. It's a better poem, I think, than has so far been noticed by those who are supposed to notice such things – except for Allen Tate, who wrote me a warm and generous detailed letter about it when I sent him a copy shortly after finishing it.[2] It is no longer a poem that I am much interested in, though in some ways it may be one of the most personal I've written.

Bill Arrowsmith and I must be engaged in the most protracted, amiable collaboration over a work of literature on record. I can no longer remember how many years we have been "in the process" of translating Oedipus at Colonos, and we are only a little better than half-way through what will doubtless prove to be the antepenultimate draft. If we're lucky. The celebrated unfulfillment of this project is due in no small part to the fact that he keeps shifting ground, and always shifts to somewhere far away. Now that I'm going to Washington, he is planning to be at Emory during their spring term, and in New York during the fall; with summers in Connecticut and Martha's Vineyard. Still and all, we've gotten some respectable work done, of which a specimen follows. It's a passage I'm sure you know.

1 Included in *Millions of Strange Shadows*.

2 In a letter dated September 4th, 1970, Tate had written AH as follows: "Dear Tony, Till a few days ago I was trying to catch up with myself, after the intensive three weeks abroad. I've been in and out of 'Green' for more than a month: now I am <u>with it</u>. Unless this old man is much mistaken, it is one of the great 20th century poems. It is so completely and brilliantly finished that I can now only stare at it. It has all the mystery of great poetry. The last paragraph gives me a <u>frisson</u> – so simple and so strange it is." Tate went on briefly to express some dissatisfaction with the title, but then signed off "Affly, Allen."

```
          What is unwisdom but the lusting after
          Longevity: to be old and full of days!
          For the vast and unremitting tide of years
          Casts up to view more sorrowful things than joyful;
          And as for pleasures, once beyond our prime,
          They all drift out of reach, they are washed away.
          And the same gaunt bailiff calls upon us all,
          Summoning into Darkness, to those wards
          Where is no music, dance or marriage hymn
          That soothes or gladdens. To the tenements of Death.

          Not to be born is, past all yearning, best
          And second best is, having seen the light,
          To return at once to deep oblivion.
          When youth is past, and the baseless dreams of youth,
          What misery does not then make man's acquaintance,
          Join him as a companion, share his hearth:
          Betrayal, envy, poverty and bloodshed
          Move in on him, and finally Old Age --
          Infirm, despised Old Age -- joins in his ruin,
          The crowning taunt of his indignities.

          So is it with that man, not just with me.
          He seems like a frail jetty facing North
          Whose pilings the waves batter from all quarters;
          From where the sun comes up, from where it sets,
          From freezing boreal regions, from below,
          A whole winter of miseries now assails him,
          Thrashes his sides and breaks over his head.
```
                                                       [1]

(You can't expect every sheet of letterpaper to be as dazzling as the first one.[2]) I had almost concluded this letter to you without thanking you for your splendid Cooper-Hewitt Lecture on Columns. I wish I wrote things like that, with all them pictures. I thought you were a trifle hard on poor Vitruvius, who was only trying to be helpful, after all.[3] With regard to him, you may be interested in what I think is an allusion to him (or perhaps to Leonardo's drawing of Vitruvian Man) in the sixth stanza of Andrew Marvell's "Upon Appleton House." The whole poem, I may add, though a dazzling and difficult one, ought to have special interest to anyone interested in architecture, and to the architecture and landscape architecture of English country houses in particular. Perhaps you know it well, and find these comments insufferably condescending. If so forgive me. If not, you will perhaps be interested in the stanza

---

1 This is an early draft of "Chorus from *Oedipus at Colonos*," which, when it was published in AH's fifth collection, *The Transparent Man*, nine years later, had undergone some changes. The poem is all that survives of AH's second attempt to translate the whole of Sophocles's *Oedipus at Colonus*, an attempt which foundered when, in 1992, his collaborator, the classicist William Arrowsmith, died. The earlier attempt, made in collaboration with another classicist, George Dimock, had come to nothing in the mid-1970s, though it too produced a single poem, "Praise for Kolonos," which was included in *Millions of Strange Shadows*.

2 Succeeding pages of this letter were typed on blank paper.

3 WLM described Vitruvius's ten-volume *De Architectura* as an "inordinately influential" treatise, and went on to say: "Today we know that Vitruvius, far from representing fairly the architecture of his time, was a very conservative man, proud of the knowledge he acquired in the field and in the library, but hardly receptive to the striking innovations of his day." *Columns in the Collection of the Cooper-Hewitt Museum*, pp. 17-18.

(an architectural word in the original) in question, which goes thus:

> Humility alone designs
> Those short but admirable lines,
> By which, ungirt and unconstrained,
> Things greater are in less contained.
> Let others vainly strive t'immure
> The circle in the quadrature!
> These holy mathematics can
> In every figure equal man.

It is an interesting coincidence that you should have sent me this lecture of yours just at this time, because I recently bought Sir John Summerson's The Classical Language of Architecture,[1] and in writing the honorary degree citation for I. M. Pei, I quoted Sir Henry Wotton on architecture as combining Commodity, Firmness and Delight. Wotton has much to say about the orders, of course.[2]

Edward the Superfluous

---

1 John N. Summerson, *The Classical Language of Architecture* (Cambridge, MA: MIT Press, 1982).

2 AH delivered the citation when, in 1982, the University of Rochester conferred a doctorate on the architect, I. M. Pei. The quotation from Wotton is from his translation of Vitruvius's *de Architectura*, and reads in full: "Well building hath three conditions: firmness, commodity, and delight."

[297]

[AH]
[July 10th, 1982]
19 East Boulevard, Rochester, NY 14610

[Draft of a poem, apparently sent without a covering letter, addressed to Wm. MacDonald, Haruspex Maximus and Adviser, 25 Henshaw Avenue, Northampton, Mass. 01060]

A Bountiful Harvest

> The Rev. Elisha Fawcett,..a Manchester
> Evangelist,..devoted his life to teaching
> the natives of the Admiralty Islands the
> Commandments of God and the Laws of Cricket.
> Too poor to purchase a monument to this
> good man, his parishoners erected his wooden
> leg upon his grave. In that fertile clime
> it miraculously took root and for many years
> provided a bountiful harvest of bats.

As if mistaking a foghorn for The Last Trump,
This risen limb, come forth before its time,
Dryadic, out of a turned and varnished stump,
A Lazarus with one foot still in the grave,

(To whom some shameless newsman presses his query,
"What was it like...I mean...you know...down there?"
And with all the sad reserve of the truly weary,
The leaves signal their dignified "No Comment")

This umbrageous Evangelical Christmas tree
Is festooned with a troupe of gymnasts all in gray
Instead of with globes and tinsel, a filigree
Of bats, or acrobats, hung upside-down

As if to receive a well-timed fling of wrists
Or ankles, and known as "The Flying Pipistrelli."
Their capes wrapped close about them, these aerialists
Let their blood pool in their tiny frontal lobes

And dream they are now, in the words of the secular Pope,
"The light Militia of the lower Sky,"
Attendant Sprites, cruising through stroboscope,
Slow-motion frames of inner loops and dives,

Guided by sonar wit or the saintly folly
Of those who the World at large describe as "batty,"
Raising their little, high-pitched, melancholy
Sqeaks in a Chapel hymn by Isaac Watts.

The Commands of God and Ordinances of Cricket
Meshed and were married in the good man's sermon
Titled, "The Straight Gate is a Sticky Wicket,"
Still quoted with approval at church picnics,

And all the parish point with ordinate praise
To the leafy witness of the life that died
And rose again in green (with some scattered grays.)
That went forth, was fruitful, and multiplied.[1]

---

[1] This poem, with the second line of its antepenultimate stanza corrected to read "Of those the World at large describe as 'batty,'" was first published in the November 28th, 1982 issue of the *Washington Post Book World*, and was included in AH's next collection, *The Transparent Man*.

[298]

[WLM]
July 21st, 1982
[25 Henshaw Avenue, Northampton, Massachusetts 01060]

[Letter, typed on a The BostonPark Plaza Hotel and Towers, Arlington Street at Park Plaza, Boston, Massachusetts 02117, letterhead, with a now missing enclosure]

My dear Fellow Tourist,

Rush now to your photographer, have a picture taken of your ear (left), and compare. Are you Common? I am.

Haven't written as I've been in a slump. May be coming out of it. Lunch in Hartford yesterday with a former Yale student of mine, now a prof. of archit. there, who wants me to give a series of lectures next Spring. With him was another prof. who would alternate with my lectures for reasons that are not clear; I'd never met him before. He set out in crackling fashion to Impress Me: Cartesian logic, obscure English architects, an essay by Pevsner I'd never heard of, the significance of carved foliage in Hindoo art, &c. Saves them up, these topics, I suppose. I was of course my usual pleasant, urbane, witty, accommodating self … but driving home I realised that I will get myself in with a boob, one of those people I rarely see anymore, widely-spread, erratically read, filled with unrecognized pretensions and no self-awareness whatsoever. Depressing. And, he will climb on me …

Is my memory going bad, or have I read the splendid wooden leg poem before?[1] Have you published it? I like it a great deal – neat, precise, funny, allusive. Don't answer my q.; you'll be Washingtoning and all. I see I have two lectures at The Smithsonian Institution booked on October 25th. If I feel up to it I'll drive down so I can nose about a bit & stop on the way back to visit Noel and Ellen.

And that's fascinating about Marvell; will pursue. Lovelace I've not had a chance to check but will. Sorry you thought I was hard on Vitruvius. Not at all, in my judgement. He is in many ways a figment of yearning Renaissance imagination; in Architecture he counts for very little. I like him, but his arch-conservatism and his utterly accidental survival put him in a place that he neither earned nor deserved. Useful, yes; important (in himself), hardly.

Yours in the faith,
Margery Main

---

1 WLM *had* heard the story of the Rev. Fawcett before – AH had brought it up in Postcard #173 and Letter #176, written in early 1978 – but this seems to have been the first time he had been shown "A Bountiful Harvest."

[299]

[WLM]
[August 20th, 1982]
[25 Henshaw Avenue, Northampton, Massachusetts 01060]

[German postcard, with a reproduction of an eighteenth-century icon featuring Saint Paraskeva, handwritten, addressed to THE HECHTS, 19 EAST BOULEVARD, ROCHESTER, NY, 14610]

This icon makes me think of Fanny Ellison's remark as I took her into the crypt of S. Clara in Assisi + showed her S. Clara's mummy: "Bill – you didn't tell me she was one of ours!" Thanks for the addresses + all good luck with the move. I'll be in Wash. in late Oct. to give lectures at the Smithsonian but it may be an in-and-out fast sort of thing. Can't bear to leave this almost finished ms. for very long. Back to the Mass. Gen'l in 2-3 weeks for a check-up etc. Feeling fairly well much of the time.

                    Love to you all,
                         Berthe Marti

[300]

[AH]
[September 22nd, 1982]
The Library of Congress, Washington, D.C. 20540

[Letter, typed on a The Library of Congress, Washington, D.C. letterhead, posted in a Library of Congress, Poetry Office, envelope, addressed to Prof. William MacDonald, 25 Henshaw Avenue, Northampton, Mass. 01060]

Admired Sir,

I think I may have won the battle of exclusiveness with this crested stationery. As contrasted, for example, with White House letterpaper, which is used by countless throngs, this is available only to some very few. I am reserving for another occasion a similar small sheet that has, in addition to the Library of Congress inscribed upon it, the legend, Poetry Room. That is perhaps the most exclusive of all, being as it is confined to the use of the Poetry Consultant (li'l ol' Io) and his two splendid and efficient secretaries: a breath-taking total of three. I think that must deserve some sort of prize, don't you? I shall await your judgment with impatience.

Let me add that our address now is 1 100 110 East Lenox St., Chevy Chase, MD 20815; and our new phone number is (202) (301) 652-9185. I'm not used to this IBM Selectric yet.

I notice that you are going to be chatting at the Smithsonian on Monday, Oct. 25th. What plans have you for socializing and being jolly? Before, after? How long will you be staying in Washington? Please let us know.

I hope Mass. General has been reassuring.

Continued on home machine. Just attended a fancy reception of the President's Committee on the Arts, at which I met S. Dillon Ripley of the Smithsonian, and we spoke of you. He's rather a remarkable man: an old Yale prof. whose actual field, I learned, is ornithology, but who lectured on Biology, Latin America, social science and history. A great friend of Frank Brown's, having been at Jonathan Edwards [College, Yale University]. Met Nancy Hanks, too. And I found among that august company a former student of mine, who used to work for National Endowment for the Arts.

> Keep in touch with us.
> Guthrie of Cappadocia
> (a rare signature)

[301]

[WLM]
[September] 25th, 1982[1]
[25 Henshaw Avenue, Northampton, Massachusetts 01060]

[Letter, typed on a Hôtel de Crillon, 10, Plaçe de la Concorde, Paris, France, letterhead, posted in a Gramercy Park Hotel envelope, addressed to Field Marshal Dr. (h.c.) Anthony Hecht, The Poetry Office, The Library of Congress, Washington, D.C. 20540, with enclosure]

My dear St. Pancreas,

Well … I'm not so sure you've won the stationery sweepstakes. The L C Poet's Corner is damned impressive, and I agree about the White House jazz (O for a friend that would steal some for me, but that's by the way), but I have to say that I do think that this sheet has a grand eclat, or eclair, or something. Rub your thumb lightly along that there printing, then do it on your stuff. No, I'll go along with a draw, though in my heart of hearts I think I'm winning. If you want to put it out to an independent jury, do so. I've another entry – the Hotel New Omayad (air mail) in Damascus – but I really don't think I'll need it. Just to fool you, I've put this in a fairly pedestrian (get it? USPS, etc.?) envelope.

Washington late Oct. plans depend on how I'm feeling. Well, stay a bit; poorly, fly in and out. Will advise. Mass. General put off to 19/20 Oct. Two secretaries! Send one to me (the prettier). Down E. Capitol St. 10 blocks or so from you is The Carbarn, a re-habbed bit of brick Victoriana with apartments in it that look good to me. If you're ever in the area checking out the bars, take a look at it, will you?

Nick ran into Jason at a local joint and they talked successfully. Several friends and well-wishers have sent my name in to the Academy Committee for appointing the new Mellon Professor.[2] The deadline is 15 Oct. and I'm thinking about it. But I doubt I'll put myself forward (formal applications are required) because much as I'd like the job in some, perhaps many, ways, it is a Big Piece of Work; the specifications are lengthy. Since I worked like hell to separate myself from much of that, I don't think I want to get into it. On the other hand, if they'd go for 3/5 of the job at 3/5 of the salary, well … D'Arms, I gather, would be the big competition.[3] Off to dine with the Trott[enberg]s.

Cheerz,
The Old Muffin

---

1 WLM misdated this letter as August 25th. Its contents, but also the date stamp of September 27th, and the Library of Congress Poetry Office's date received stamp of September 30th, make it clear that this was a slip.

2 The Andrew W. Mellon Professor in Charge of the School of Classical Studies in the American Academy in Rome.

3 In the end, no appointment was made, and the position remained open until 1984, when the job was taken by Russell T. Scott.

[302]

[AH]
October 7th, 1982
[110 East Lenox Street, Chevy Chase, MD 20815]

[Letter, typed on a Claridge's Hotel letterhead, addressed to King William (of Orange) MacDonald, 25 Henshaw Avenue, Northampton, Mass. 01060]

Dear Boy,

I find it touching that you should be so impressed with the simple embossings of the Crillon as to fail to notice the cheap white stock so thin it can be seen through on which it appears. It is also worth pointing out that it is so parvenu an outfit that its address – 10 Place de la Concorde, Paris (yet) – is set down below the name with the obvious nervous anxiety of a firm that fears it has never been heard of. The simple truth of the matter, of course, is that the Crillon has got to keep reminding people of its address because anyone in that neighborhood instinctively thinks of, and goes to, the Ritz.

There's a journal published up in your neck of the woods, name of <u>English Literary Renaissance</u>, issuing from University of Massachusetts, Amherst, with a fellow named Arthur Kinney for editor. They are currently considering for publication that piece of mine of improbable length (75 pages of text, plus ten of notes) on <u>The Merchant of Venice</u>. They write me very encouraging notes while not deciding things one way or the other. But I believe that from their point of view there are two problems involved. The first is financial: I gather Kinney subsidizes the journal out of his own pocket, and has to raise funds from time to time, especially if he plans to bring out an irregular issue. And I gather that the length of my piece would demand a special issue. This, in any case, is my imperfect sense of how things stand. If you have any renaissance pals at U. Mass. who might have any inside tips on how things stand I would be most grateful.

Hank Millon and his very charming wife came to a fancy "inaugural lunch" given in my honor by the Library – and came to my reading that same evening. He seems to be a splendid man, and could not have been more cordial and friendly. Bernard Knox also came to the lunch (though not to the reading). The reading seemed to go pretty well, but I'm afraid I had been spoiled only two nights before by the size and enthusiasm and manifest alertness and attention I got from an audience at the University of Virginia in Charlottesville. They are, in fact, in the business of trying to woo me. I feel vaguely awkward about this because the U. of R. has been especially obliging in a whole bunch of ways, including not inconsiderable financial ways, in regard to this two-year stint of mine in Washington. And they assume that decency at the very least, to say nothing of company loyalty and team spirit, would dictate my return to the fold. Given my age, I am not likely to want to make many moves in the future: if I do not in fact remain in Rochester, I think there is only time for one further move before my retirement. And there is Evan's schooling to think of, and the discomforts he is obliged to undergo with any such uprooting.

But Virginia has a number of things to recommend it to us. It happens, to begin on a purely selfish note, to have a very good English faculty. And the next thing about it is the wonderful mildness of the winters. If we moved, I would imagine that Helen's mother, who lives a quarter of a mile from us in Rochester, would move too. All this winter mildness would please her, too; but she is very happy now in Rochester, where she has made many friends of her own age, and where she has a pretty independent life. As you can see, the topic is loaded with imponderables. For the present, it is up to Virginia to see if they can produce sufficiently attractive terms to make them seem to me irresistible. And meanwhile, of course, mum is the word as far as my Rochester pals are concerned.

          Von Wrangle

[303]

                            [WLM]
                        October 19th, 1982
         [25 Henshaw Avenue, Northampton, Massachusetts 01060]

[Letter, typed on a New Omayad Hotel letterhead, addressed to Anthony Evan Hecht, Esq, National Treasure, Treasured Nationally, 110 East Lenox Street, Chevy Chase MD 20815]

My dear Mr Ekt:

I now realise the depths of your cunning. You wrote to me on that Class III L.C. Poetry Office stuff knowing I'd reach into the bottom of my drawers and produce something splendid like the Crillon material, and THEN you hit me with Claridge's, in order that I would be FORCED to produce this, the GEM of all GEMS. Now before you criticize it I wish to warn you that should it turn out that you cabled instructions, as has been rumored, upon receipt of my splendid and aforementioned Crillon airmail (a point you missed, that!) sheet, to your agents in Moscow, Tuscaloosa, and Bangkok, to get for you by fair means or false, examples from the Dim, the Pachyderm, or the Crash, for you to use anon – or, as it may well be, that you 'phoned London for the Claridge's slip, poor thing though it is, for of course they print no address, in the hope that no one will come and they will not have to polish the silver backings of the brushes in the Gentlemens' Retreats – then, as I say, I should warn you that I will memorialize the Regents to bar you from the National Competition, not to mention the up-coming XXXVIII International. You should reflect for an hour or two on what this would do to your reputation, not only in Caribou, Maine, but in the nation's capital where, very likely, those now warming to you slightly will take the sage cheese out of your elevenses sandwiches. Which would serve you right, though admiring what you now hold in your hand is probably punishment enow.

Now this glorious specimen is special in another way. I have STAYED in the New Omayad. You hint you have stayed in the great Crillon, the slipping Ritz (yes! sad!), and Porridge's ... oh, uh ... Claridge's, I guess. But, Sir, I've doubts you ever stayed in any of them. My Venetian factor did report once that you sashayed into the Reale Danieli bar, for I think it was, a Kir. A Kir! I will send my affidavits to the Regent's Secretariat, including of course other documents of proof such as a Xerox of my "Preparez ma chambre SVP"* card from the N.O. M'shallah, Sir, or, Don't Mess with My Djinn!

If we are eating in Sunday evening, as they say, please tell dear Helen that I eat very little. Seriously.

Up the Navy!
Omar Kye Am

(*I translate for you from the Arabic.)

[304]

[AH]
October 27th, 1982
[110 East Lenox Street, Chevy Chase, MD 20815]

[Letter, typed]

Dear Mr. MacDonald,

We, here at the Grove Press, have been looking over your stuff, which we certainly respect. I mean, anyone who can write that much about Roman and Byzantine buildings is obviously a brain, and we appreciate it. But a little birdie tells me that your sales are not exactly enormous, right? You're not up there with John Irving, say, or Joyce Carol Oates. And it's a shame, because a nice guy like you, brainy, with all those Harvard degrees, deserves a little more of the cake than you've gotten so far.

Now normally the Grove Press wouldn't touch any book of yours with a ten-foot pole; but we are a pretty "creative" outfit when it comes to marketing, and I think we may have a proposition that ought to interest you, and make you a little bundle on the side. What we have in mind is a coffee-table, glossy volume to be called, <u>Dirty Buildings</u>. Something sexy, that will catch attention and have a wide appeal. We feel sure that a man with your qualifications will be able to think up some lubricious angles (and curves, ha! ha! ha!) that will arouse a suitably lecherous interest; and we are prepared to set aside a handsome budget for the illustrations. The sort of thing we have in mind, to be quite frank, involves a photograph of Jane Russell, say, or Rita Hayworth, lying on their back, seductively arched and emphasizing their bosoms, neatly juxtaposed with a view (in color, of course) of the domes of San Marco. The text we would leave entirely to you.

I hope you find this an attractive notion, and one you would like to work on with us. We are convinced that it is a virtually unexplored (or "virgin," ha! ha! ha!) field.

We look forward to hearing from you.

Mel Kizzadeck

[305]

[WLM]
October 28th, 1982
[25 Henshaw Avenue, Northampton, Massachusetts 01060]

[Letter, typed on a Harvard Club of Boston letterhead, posted in an Ohio Staters, Inc., envelope, addressed to Mr and Mrs Anthony Hecht, 110 East Lenox Street, Chevy Chase MD 20815, with a now missing enclosure]

Dear Helen and Tony,

I got up very early this morning & set up the ironing board and heated the iron, in order to press the raised lettering here down flat, in order that you not think I'd gotten above myself or given myself airs that would offend you. I simply can't help it if I'm superior.

Well, that was a marvelous visit if all too short. You all looked splendid and fit, well-installed and already well-connected in Washington, as I knew you would be. I enclose, Helen, a little something for you to put casually on the kitchen counter when a certain kind of guest is in the house – you know, those who pretend not to be impressed by your great savoir faire – so you can make a note or two at just the right time. Or, you could get someone, Evan perhaps, to write out a recipe & sign it Olivez de Montillado y Caballeros, which if it isn't the name of the master chef at the Madrid Ritz, it ought to be. Another, weightier gift follows, which from time to time should be warmed in the hands and turned in the sunlight. No, it is <u>not</u> Hamilton Jordan!

Thanks. You will get a pro forma invitation to the Georgetown Nov, 16th Pantheon lecture. Tony, sorry to leave you in the rain on Constitution Avenue Monday night, but I felt I couldn't refuse John Jessup's offer of a ride to the airport. After all that, the plane left an hour late. We could have been in a snug bar …

Roscoe Karnes

[306]

[AH]
December 6th, 1982
[110 East Lenox Street, Chevy Chase, MD 20815]

[Letter, typed on a The Library of Congress letterhead, with a now missing enclosure]

My dear fellow,

I am sending the enclosed advertisement for Judith Krantz's book[1] because it includes such a fetching picture of her, and I know how you lust after literary celebrities.

We will be returning to Rochester for the Christmas holidays, leaving here on the

---

1 *Mistral's Daughter* (New York: Crown Publishers, 1982).

17th and returning on the 2nd. Rochester will be cold, and very likely snowbound, but it is still home to us all – where Evan has his best friends and his treasured possessions, where Helen's mother lives, and so forth. I guess you must have told me when you were next coming to Washington and planning to stay at the Millons, but I have forgotten. I hope we will not be away when you come.

I have just finished writing three Guggenheim recommendations, as well as furnishing some valuable information to the Charles and Catherine MacArthur Foundation, so I am feeling almost disgustingly noble at the moment. Don't worry; it will pass.

Avicenna

[307]

[WLM]
December 7th, 1982
[25 Henshaw Avenue, Northampton, Massachusetts 01060]

[Letter, typed, addressed to Anthony E. Hecht, Infinitely Laureate,
110 East Lenox Street, Chevy Chase MD 20815]

Dear Tony,

I've just read your readings selection and am deeply touched by your reference to the Pantheon book. Your kindness, combined with your authority in all matters of reading and thinking, makes your statement the best I've ever had about any of my work. You know how much a compliment from the right person buoys one up. Buoyed I am; every kind of thanks ...

And you should get the Association of Patient Attenders of Lectures (APAL) first award for sitting through not one but two of my spiels. I will attempt to satisfy the Grove people's request for a book, but first must take a chartered yacht through the Med, with an appropriate lady crew aboard, to test, so to speak, the water. Jayne Mansfield and the Hagia Sophia? Or? Meanwhile, I will try to make sure you aren't APALled again in the near future. Thought the Pantheon lecture so-so; didn't jell; B? B - ?

Please note that I am the on-board authority for a Smith Alumnae cruise next Sept. in the Aegean and Black seas. Why don't you and Helen come along? We'll sing off-color songs in the ship's bar late at night, and be civilised in many other ways as well ...

I've not thanked you for the zeerockes of the Roman vedute. There are things to say about them which, if they don't dazzle your mind, will perhaps be a mite interesting. But they'll have to wait, as I must get a ms. into the mail to Yale ("Into the Mail to Yale" will probably give you a chance to get going on a Great Poem; no thanks needed). Meanwhile,

Love to you all from
Guglielmo at the gate

P.S.: Did you know that D'Annunzio, on his estate in the north of Italy, had the front parts of a naval cruiser, complete with guns, mounted in his garden, so he could fire off salutes when he wished? Ponder that ...

[308]

[AH]
January 20th, 1983
110 East Lenox Street, Chevy Chase, MD 20815

[Letter, typed on a The Library of Congress, Poetry Office, letterhead]

Tovarisch!

Though I am late to acknowledge it, I have read your splendid article, "Excavation, Restoration, and Italian Architecture of the 1930s"[1] with enormous pleasure, profit and excitement. What I think pleased me most came as almost a revelation. Here and there in Italy I had seen, like everyone else, those rather stark modern buildings that seemed to repudiate felicity of line and delicacy of ornament – that were somehow insistently large, blank shapes and spaces, defiantly bold and intimidating in their apparent unwillingness to conciliate anything in the eye's petition for loveliness. Such as your illustration 20. When I thought about these buildings at all, I set down their relentless spareness to considerations of frugality. So your article came as an absolutely convincing illumination, tying together in perfect and handsome demonstration the grand forms of unadorned Roman ruins and the jingoistic revivalism of arriviste fascism. The whole piece, moreover, is written with an ease and elegance and calm command that makes Henry-Russell lucky indeed to have had you among the contributors to his Festschrift. I am very grateful to you.

We went to the White House, stood in line and shook hands with the President and First Lady (both beamed and muttered courtesies) on Martin Luther King's birthday.[2] We were there because the Eastman Philharmonia Orchestra (of the University of Rochester) was to premiere a work composed to honor the memory of King,[3] and so a lot of Rochester people got invited. The concert, later, at the Kennedy Center (where us VIPs were given dinner beforehand) was a great success. But the day was memorable for a number of other reasons. For one thing, it was definitively confirmed, though not yet made public, that a former student of mine from Harvard, a splendid young poet named Brad Leithauser, whose first book,

---

1 This paper, which WLM had mentioned in Letter #263, of July 11th, 1980, had been published in *In Search of Modern Architecture: A Tribute to Henry-Russell Hitchcock*, edited by Helen Searing (Cambridge, MA: MIT Press, 1982).

2 The event took place on January 15th, 1982, in the East Room of the White House. Ronald Reagan had been in office for a little over one year.

3 The composer was Joseph Schwantner, and the piece, for narrator and orchestra, was *New Morning in the World*.

published by Knopf,[1] was enthusiastically reviewed everywhere, was going to win a MacArthur Fellowship – that subsidizes you for five years. And on the same day a cheerful fellow who introduced himself to me on the phone as one David Schoonover, phoned from Yale to say that John Hollander and I were awarded the Bollingen Prize, an announcement of which is scheduled to be made, I believe, today. The following day was my 60th birthday, and Brad, with his brother Mark and sister-in-law Bryan Leithauser all came to dinner, with plenty of cause for general celebration. Moreover, just the day before, in fact shortly before leaving for the White House, I finished a Canzone, the most difficult and demanding poetic form I have ever tried.[2] I know only of four modern ones – by Auden, James Merrill, L. E. Sissman and my own.[3] I think Merrill's is the best of these, and mine is next.

I have also written, on commission, a review of the new biography of Robert Lowell, by Ian Hamilton,[4] that will appear in a journal called Grand Street, which is published in New York.[5] It was a large and time-consuming task, but I have found that I shall be allowed to make two different uses of it. One of my duties as Consultant here is to offer an annual lecture. The Library of Congress later publishes these lectures, so they normally do not like to have material that has been published elsewhere. But they have given me permission to use most of my review – which in any case would have to be enlarged to become an hour lecture – and since it is scheduled for periodical publication in early April, and my lecture will take place on the second of May, it is not likely that a large segment of the audience will be acquainted with my text. This is a wonderful economy for me, since it will allow me much more time for poems without having to worry about that damned spring lecture.

All this good news was the more welcome because it followed an episode that greatly alarmed me, and terrified Helen. And which I hasten to say has turned out okay. As you know, I was recently elected to the board of trustees of the American Academy in Rome. I was to have gone to New York to attend my first meeting of the board, when, very early on the morning of the day I was to depart, I passed enormous quantities of blood as an unremittent diarrhea. There was no pain involved, and at first I thought I would simply say nothing to Helen, and go off as scheduled. But I must have lost a good deal of blood, and began to feel weak. What followed was a hospital sojourn (during which I was scared out of my wits by overhearing some stupid and uninformed nurses gossiping about me at a time they thought I was fast asleep) and a further hospital visit later on. They removed a polyp from somewhere in

1 Brad Leithauser, *Hundreds of Fireflies: Poems* (New York: Knopf, 1981).

2 The canzone was entitled "Terms," and AH included it in his next collection, *The Transparent Man*, where it was dedicated to Derek Walcott.

3 Auden's "Canzone" was first collected in *The Collected Poetry of W. H. Auden* (New York; Random House, 1945); Merrill's "Samos" first appeared in "Scripts for the Pageant," Book III of his *The Changing Light at Sandover* (New York: Atheneum, 1980); and Sissman's "Canzone: Aubade" first appeared in his *Dying: An Introduction* (Boston, MA: Little Brown, 1967).

4 Ian Hamilton, *Robert Lowell: A Biography* (New York: Random House, 1982).

5 "Robert Lowell" appeared in *Grand Street*, 2:3, Spring 1983, and was later included in AH's *Obbligati: Essays in Criticism*.

the intestinal tract that proved to be benign, and cauterized an area of distended veins which may have produced the bleeding. Though the bleeding may also have come from an hiatal hernia that I have had for years. The main point, however, is that the bleeding stopped, and that nothing of a grave order was discovered. I must go easy on drinking these days, and eliminate caffeine. Since I was never much a coffee drinker, this second consideration leaves me untroubled. But the other matter will be harder. My doctor is very good, very candid and open in explaining matters, partly, I think, by way of securing my confidence after I had heard those nurses talking to one another at midnight, and saying that my case was so grave the doctors had decided not to tell me the truth about my condition. Anyway, things turned out all right in the end. And if you think about that last sentence for a moment you will doubtless appreciate how apposite it is.

I was being fished for by the University of Virginia, but a committee of deans decided to economize and make a junior appointment instead. It is, I think, just as well. While Virginia has one of the best English Departments in the country these days (far better than Rochester) Charlottesville, for all the merit of its gentler climate, is not the sort of town either Helen or I would want to move to. If I move at all, given my stage of life and the likelihood that the move would be my last, I think only New York, Boston or Washington would serve.

Polyphemus (Perverse)

[309]

[WLM]
January 27th, 1983
25 Henshaw Avenue, Northampton, Massachusetts 01060

[Letter, typed, addressed to Anthony Hecht, le profond, 110 East Lenox Street, Chevy Chase MD 20815]

xxvii Ian MCMLXXXIII

Hecht –

> a knight with an ebony pie-pan
> rode by on a quizzical mare,
> and said, "the flora on Saipan
> are waving at José Ferrer."

You see, anyone can do it. I'm having trouble with another, and I know your sense of honor will cause you to send me a sealed packet of rhymes for "babe" something exotic? I've astrolabe, of course:

> Tsimmis, tsauris
> Uncle Morris
> Married to
> An Irish babe

It needs, a little work, I think …

Have you ever thought about dividing xlvii by, say, ccviii?

I will be wearing gloves when I next see you, knowing what you've been up to with Ronnie Baby.[1]

Thank god you are all right. You'll recall that I'd heard you'd been in hospital, and called. Those nurses should be sent to the galleys. When I was in Cooley-Dickinson in '77 they were all quite wonderful, solicitous and efficient and smart; I guess some are not that way. Do take care of yourself all round. I've laid way off on the booze and try to save it for getting together with friends. So far, pretty good. Feel better, too, I think. But now and then, when I'm lonely, I have 2 or 3 instead of one and that's Not So Good. Yes, the hell with coffee. Like you, I'm not interested. But tea, Christ, I'm addicted.

It's good news that you have such a compassionate and intelligent MD. Later, perhaps you'll give me his name.

I am dazzled by your approval of the fascismo piece. I read it through when it appeared and it seemed viscous and overcooked (can a thing be both? – oh yes, it can; visiting ladies, saying "I'll cook," have produced such). And since you called a couple or three notes have come from here and there also approving; one from a very good scholar said I'd put the study of the stuff on a new footing.[2] It is all part of my pursuit of the persistence of classicism throughout architecture; I'm peddling, or trying to peddle, a book on the subject to the Harvards. They love me, but so far have shied away from my bed.

A lovely lady, smart and funny and good company, looked me up last fall. We'd known each other some years back, then she married an MD and we lost track. I've seen her a couple of times, like her husband, and am happy to say that although I like her a lot, and were she not married might well be camped on her doorstep, can handle it easily and calmly. Victory!

I agree about the Univ. of VA. I go there to lecture and have good friends there. It's a good place, with some charm left yet, but as you say not the place either of us would wish to live.

---

1 An indication of WLM's feelings about Ronald Reagan.

2 This appears to be a reference to the Cambridge-based architectural historian David Watkins, who, in a review of the Hitchcock Festschrift, described MacDonald's article as "the most original and stimulating piece in the whole book," and went on to say that "[its author] shows how Italian architects of the Fascist period looked back not to 'the grand tradition of the classical orders,' but more often 'turned to a style characterised by primary geometric shapes, largely unadorned that had flourished during the Roman Empire, a style the regime's vast programs of restoration revealed in quantity.' In describing the products of a fruitful union between archaeology and architecture, which reminds one of 18th- and early 19th-century neo-classicism, he unveils a style of timeless classicism. Like the current designs of Leon Krier, this suggests that it is about time we called off the 'Search for Modern Architecture.' Otherwise, we might resemble the man in the detective story by Edgar Allen Poe who searched everywhere in the house for a missing letter except in the one obvious place where it was all the time, the letter-box inside the front-door." *Journal of the Society of Architectural Historians*, 42:3 (October, 1983), pp. 304-305.

I'm quite excited about moving to Washington. To my considerable surprise I find myself looking forward to selling, throwing out, and giving away a fair part of the stuff that I have squirreled away in this place. A grand book dealer comes next month to look at a couple of dozen folios that weigh tons and that I don't need and don't want to move; paid $1-20 for them years ago and they are worth thousands. Hot damn!

What is a single malt whiskey? Used to have double malts at Saul Shalit's drugstore in the '30s ...

I'll be driving down about the 17th or 18th of March and will let you know the details well ahead. The order of the day will be apmnt hunting in NW; lunch w/Don Freeze Mon. 21st, big NatGallery lecture late that afternoon with all the trimmings afterwards; seminar all day the 22nd, home early on the 23rd. A couple of those nights the Natgall puts me up downtown. I have specified the Gralyn, a dusty and quite wonderful, inexpensive old place ... don't give that dope out to just anybody, please.

Three-thirty a.m.. Sleep for three or four hours, get up and work for two or three, go back to bed. Don't really know what a canzone is, but will hit the books and find out. But it's good news that you are so happy with it. Thank god we picked work that can go on, from which there is no retirement and can be none – something we'd never settle for.

Northampton, goodbye! Should have done it before this. Quitting Smith, a place I find as good any institution I've rubbed up against, was the best thing I've done in decades. Lots of stuff coming out; will send this and that along now and then. A huge <u>Macmillan Enc. of Architects</u>, 26 vols (I call it the Big Mac), 4 vols., have appeared, and I have a dozen entries in it; some long – the Mansarts, Vignola ... looks nice.

a presto, & love to Helen & Evan.

As for you, poet, all my affection, and best hopes for full health forever.

MacDonald

[310]

[AH]
[February ?, 1983]
[110 East Lenox Street, Chevy Chase, MD 20815]

[Letter, typed on a Saunier, "Enterprise de Déménagements pour La France a L'Étranger," Angers, France, letterhead]

Mon vieux,

Went to see the Vatican show at the Metropolitan Museum of Art[1] – a very odd exhibit, that left me feeling irritated and dissatisfied. It is very uneven, and along with painting and sculpture includes church vestments and fancy candlesticks and crucifixes and similar objects of virtu and art. Moreover, much work was badly exhibited or poorly lit, and I continue to wonder at some of the choices. What

---

1 "The Vatican Collections: The Papacy and Art" only opened to the public on February 26th.

seemed best to me was a sort of predella by Raphael, with three scenes; a similar two-scene St. Nicholas predella by Fra Angelico; a Sassetta, and two brilliantly animated sculptured sketches in sepia-tinted plaster by Bernini. Striking among the peculiarities was a very large statue of Antinous as an Egyptian god in the whitest, most chilling marmoreal, funerary marble I've ever seen – a very deadly thing. The little descriptive plaque declared unambiguously and unequivocally that in order to appease some adverse omen that seemed to offer a threat to the well-being of Hadrian, Antinous voluntarily drowned himself as a propitiating sacrifice. Now I thought that idea was the novelistic creation of Miss Yourcenar, and that in fact there was no real evidence about how Antinous died, except that it happened during a visit he and Hadrian paid to Egypt. This is a little like taking Robert Graves as a responsible historian, and labelling a painting of Mary Magdalen as Mrs. Jesus Christ.

We were there because of an American Academy of Rome bash at which I saw, among many others, Charles Babcock, and we spoke of you, insultingly, of course. Also present in that huge throng was Russell Lynes, an old friend, and one who happens to head the search committee for a new director. So I was able then and there to drop Babcock's name with your endorsement. It dropped like a lead weight, though. It appears that they have found someone to take over the directorship of classical studies, and therefore want someone connected with the arts or humanities to serve as director, and thus balance the slate. Their problem, as Russell tersely states it, is to find someone with impeccable credentials in the field of art, music, or art history, who gets on well with everyone and can entertain in a style befitting the Villa, and who will as well be able to take on the plain drudgery of book-keeper cum file clerk, supervising the plant, the salaries of employees, the plumbing and the whole sorry mess that belongs to any landlord, and is bound to be a little more difficult abroad. God knows where they will seek. But I feel sure they would be grateful for any tips, if you have any.

Hank Millon was to have been at that bash, but I don't think he showed. It was held, after the showing at the Met, in the Doris Duke mansion, now the Institute of Fine Arts of NYU at Fifth and 78th St. A very splendid building indeed, with the drinks and excellent dinner for what must have been a crowd of perhaps two hundred catered by a fancy caterer called Glorious Food. The drinks, in the words of Pepys, were noble and enough. The canapés included small squares of dark pumpernickel bread with slices of smoked salmon topped with caviar. There was a small group of musicians, who could scarcely be heard once the bulk of the crowd arrived, but who up until that time played lovely Renaissance and 18th century music. Helen wore a very handsome new dress and looked terrific. We are all, I am pleased to report, reasonably well, though the correcting ribbon on my machine here has run out, and yesterday when we returned from a chilly New York we arrived in a snowbound Washington, where overnight we accumulated some five inches. I think I was prepared to believe that we would have no snow at all this winter, the first part of it having been so benign around here, at least. O yes, one more item. We had Tim Healy here for dinner (a splendid job of Helen's, as usual) and without mincing words I let him know that I was prepared to receive overtures from him.[1] He minced no words either, and said I would be welcome any time I wished to come. It is not, of course, as if there were no further complications, and the change may never come about. But it is nice to have that card up my sleeve. I am now trying to write a poem about a man who attempts to fuck a duck.

Sophocles

[311]

[WLM]
February 5th, 1983
25 Henshaw Avenue, Northampton, Massachusetts 01060

[Blank postcard, addressed to A E Hecht, 110 East Lenox Street, Chevy Chase MD 20815]

Tonino:

A friend, a Fellow, who has a very large fund of Academy information, told me last night that Charles Babcock's wife doesn't like Rome, doesn't want to go there; that when Charles wished to accept a three-year appointment as summer school professor, she wouldn't go … sounds odd, but my friend, David Grose, a classics prof at UMass., usually knows whereof he speaks. Just finished a piece on Augustan empire imagery in architecture for something called <u>Archaeologica Transatlantica</u>.[2] Friends have word processors; they look great. Buy?

A presto,
Antinu

[312]

[AH]
[February ?, 1983]
[110 East Lenox Street, Chevy Chase, MD 20815]

[Letter, typed on a United States Senate memorandum slip]

Dear Constituent,

Not to worry. Turns out that Babcock wouldn't suit them even if his wife were not an obstacle. It seems that they have a director of classical studies all lined up, though I have no idea who; and they want a "humanist" type, an art historian perhaps, to balance the slate.

All of us here in the Senate want you to know that just because we voted ourselves a raise we were not ignorant of the plight of the national economy, nor

---

1 Father Timothy Healy, S.J., was the President of Georgetown University in Washington, D.C.

2 "Empire Imagery in Augustan Architecture," in *Archaeologica Transatlantica*, V (1985).

insensitive to the problems of others, but merely trying to adjust to the rising costs of living. Please remember that in pursuit of a careful policy on federal spending we also voted to freeze the salaries of all federal employees, except for ourselves. So you may relax in full confidence of our fiscal probity. And we all plan to run again next election.

Those word processors are instruments of the devil. Did Shakespeare have one? Did Goethe? Have you ever looked to see how many feet of shelf space are occupied by the complete works (including correspondence) of Voltaire? Can you bear to imagine how much that would be enlarged if he had had a word processor to fiddle with? Enough of this folly.

R. Krautheimer

[313]
[AH]
[February 8th, 1983]
110 East Lenox Street, Chevy Chase, MD 20815]

[Letter, typed on a The Helmsley Palace Hotel, New York, letterhead, addressed to Prof. William MacDonald, Fermentarian, 25 Henshaw Avenue, Northampton, Mass. 01060]

> Here lies a famed physician, whose best skill
> Could not at last evade The Bitter Pill.
> No one was sure, but someone thought he sighed,
> "Enema, fibula, glandular," as he died.

Please take note that this crested letterpaper is not merely embossed, like the crummy French stuff you once employed, but is two-toned and gilded and altogether regal. I could tell quite easily how unnerved and overcome with anxiety you were about just where you stood in our sadly one-sided competition when in desperation you introduced the highly irrelevant declaration that you only used letterpaper from hotels you had actually stayed in. It shows a pathetic literalness of mind with which one can only commiserate.

Eryximachus

[314]

[WLM]
February 12th, 1983
[25 Henshaw Avenue, Northampton, Massachusetts 01060]

[Letter, typed on a The Boston Park Plaza Hotel and Towers letterhead, addressed to ANTHONY HECHT, ODOLATOR, 110 E. Lenox St, Chevy Chase, MD, 20815]

My dear Hotspur,

The Chevy Chase snow removal authority just called and said that I should tell you to get your driveway shovelled out, now. But I suppose you kept up with that right through the storm. The disaster merchants here said 4"; we got four times that, natch. Beautiful, though.

The poor old Academy. I don't see how its problems can be solved without a single, energetic, bright, strong, youthful person,* paid very well and given a free hand except for some kind of last-ditch removal system. I won't bore you with tales of incompetence, and indeed rudeness, in both Rome and New York. My name has come up many times for various posts, and though that is flattering, I must say that those that handled the matter didn't have a clue. I do not know [Sophie Chandler] Consagra, but those that do that I in turn know and trust have grave doubts …

That's good news about Healy's carte blanche. Good for you. I will be lunching with [Don] Freeze on 21 March to discuss a visit to their faculty. From Freeze's choice of words in the past, it sounds as if I will be able to write my own ticket by and large; but we'll see.

It may be that I will not do my apartment-hunting, phase I, when I come down then. The Cities book is my whole life – well, much of it – and I may well put off an apartment hunt until later in the Spring. I'll let you know.

Reading of the Vatican Show in the Times did not move me to move my butt to see it[1]; anyway, I'm tired of art and the frenzy and foolishness that surrounds it so often today. I have some radical ideas about public changes in attitude toward museums and art that I feel pretty certain are in the offing, and not for the better for the curators and historians … and anyway, I've seen all those things, most many times.

Too bad the Antinous label dignified the gossip. Yourcenar did not invent it; the story began not long after A's death and has never stopped circulating. But the emperor himself wrote that the drowning was accidental, and I'll stick with him. A. Garzetti, in one of the best, perhaps the best, of the books I've ever read about Rome (From Tiberias to the Antonines[2] p. 399), makes this very clear, When I write

---

1 Michael Brenson had previewed the show several months earlier. See "Major Vatican Show Planned at Museum" in the June 11th, 1982 issue of the *New York Times*. The article can be read online at http://www.nytimes.com/1982/06/11/arts/major-vatican-show-planned-at-museum.html

2 Albino Garzetti, *From Tiberius to the Antonines: A History of the Roman Empire*, AD 14–192 (London: Methuen, 1974).

my novel about Q. Marcius Turbo, H's right-hand man, I'll get it all straight for everyone,

About the AAR: it is plagued with amateurs. Six requests for money in as many months, some from professors who should be kept light-years from administrative matters – Ackerman, for example. Two requests duplicates, had already sent a check to the first requestor ... etc., etc. [Bill] Lacey a total flop, [Calvin] Rand not much better. I love the old place, and owe it a lot, and if I were younger and not a myasthenic, I'd go down to NY and say Here I am, I can do it, I know almost everyone, but you have to give me authority and you have to pay me well ... pipe-dreams ...

I like your thought about the duck poem. And am glad it's never been done before.

In the hope, professor, of getting an A, or A– from you,
I am,
yours infinitely,
Roscoe Kearns

---

* In charge overall.
I too know Lynes and like and admire him. I don't know him well, but well enough to think him a man of parts. But isn't he and his crowd a bit too old and too successful to have so much authority? That worries me; I've seen it happen for years now. Nice, older, establishment people, who don't understand the real problems, which don't have ready labels of the kind such people use so readily, and who inevitably, however good their intentions, are quite out of touch. Above all things, the Academy needs leadership, leadership that can keep NY just an office, nothing more; anything else bleeds Rome ... Money raising, sure, but no Rome-bossing. The Getty business scares me; I know something about those people. Millon thinks it's all OK, though, but I've doubts ...

[315]

[WLM]
February 22nd, 1983
[25 Henshaw Avenue, Northampton, Massachusetts 01060]

[Letter, typed on a Hotel Ritz, Madrid, letterhead, posted in a Hotel Sacher, Wien I., Philharmonikerstrasse 4, envelope, addressed to Prof. Dr. A. E. Hecht, Odometer, 110 East Lenox Street, Chevy Chase MD 20815]

Honestly, My Dear Sir,

Your love of flash and lack of interest in True Substance is a matter of deep concern here at ASS (Associated Stationery Stealers). It may be that we will have to take you off the rolls. A Director saw that Helmsley Palace stuff [1] and was ill on my Bokhara

---

1 WLM is referring to the letterhead of Letter #313, of February 8th, 1983.

runner (he's all right, though ... they're made of strong material, those Bokharas).

The reason the Director was sick was that your paper made him think of that awful woman in the <u>Times</u>' ads, a kind of fattish Ponchartrain sporting house boss; and, come to think of it, that's probably what the Helmsley Palace is. For me, what is so disappointing is your fixation on what you think is quality lettering. We just can't have you going around stealing notepaper if you don't know declassé raised lettering; yours seems to have been made by gnats manipulating pastry cones. Look above, and learn. The Real Thing, Truly Regal, the Right Stuff. You can carry this around with you as you pop in and out of hotels, reticule at the ready. Just whip this out, cross-check, and grab or not, knowing that you are OK and All Right.

Yours in engraved sentiments,
Chas. Ritz

[316]

[WLM]
March 14th, 1983
25 Henshaw Avenue, Northampton, Massachusetts 0106

[Blank postcard, typed, with the sender's address given as XXV Henshaw, 01060, addressed to Ill. mo Prof. Dott. A. E. Hecht, 110 East Lenox Street, Chevy Chase MD 20815]

Etymologies for Humble Folk — # 14:

ANACOURSE

as in the TV weatherperson's "... anacourse these wins will overspread the Grate Plain States ..."

The word comes from the name of a small island off the WSW edge of Corsica (Corse), where all the women females are named Anna. As you know, TV weatherpersons are ex-Air Force meteorologists, and while in AF training they had to memorize the maps of the Mediterranean (MemMed 1). Taken by this island name, and <u>its</u> etymology, the word has come into our language, helped no doubt by extensive R & R on Anacourse by the 6th fleet, and the helpful example of Anacapri.

[Unsigned]

[317]

[AH]
March 30th, 1983
The Library of Congress, Poetry Office, Washington, D.C. 20540

[Letter, typed on a The Library of Congress, Poetry Office, letterhead, addressed to Mr. William MacDonald, 25 Henshaw Avenue, Northampton, Massachusetts 01060]

My dear sir:
    It should cheer you immensely to know that the Marechale de Luxembourg, on reading the Bible remarked: "Quel ton! Quel effroyable ton! Ah, Madame, quel dommage que le Saint Esprit eût aussi peu de goût!"[1]
                  Yours,
                Anthony Hecht
              Consultant in Poetry

[318]

[WLM]
April 21st, 1983
25 Henshaw Avenue, Northampton, Massachusetts 01060

[Blank postcard, typed, with the sender's address given as XXV Henshaw, 01060, addressed to Dr Prof Anthony Evan Hecht Esq, Poetry Office, The Library of Congress, Washington, D.C. 20540]

My dear Monsignor,
    I hope you are spreading my etymologies thru' Congress and the Dept of Sanitation.
    I suppose you know that Quintin Hogg, a formidable figure in his Lord Chancellor's gown and wig, when he espied Neil Marten MP, his friend, behind a group of American Tourists beside the Palace of Westminster, and cried "Neil!," that they all did?
    Washington apmt-hunt put off until mid-June, when I've another Cath. U. lecture. I suppose, alas, that you will have Gone North by then.
    All's well. Two more, long, chapters of the Cities book now go to the Yales, who like it.
    (Surely you noticed in a recent TLS that my work was spoken of as "brilliantly innovative" (!))[2]

---

1 French = "What tone! What appalling tone. Ah, Madame, what a pity the Holy Spirit had so little taste!" AH is quite possibly quoting from Lytton Strachey's *Books and Characters: French & English* (New York: Harcourt, Brace and Company, 1922), p. 94.

2 Reviewing Frank Sear's *Roman Architecture* in the February 25th, 1983 issue of the *Times Literary Supplement*, Margaret Lyttelton had described the book as "clear, concise and readable rather than … comprehensive and encyclopaedic, like the books of Crema and Ward-Perkins, or brilliantly innovatory,

Your
Marten

[319]

[AH]
May 1st, 1983
110 East Lenox St., Chevy Chase, MD 20815

[Letter, typed on a Hyatt Regency Hotel, 223 Promenade des Anglais, F-06200, Nice, France, letterhead]

(Power to the <u>right</u> People)

Most Noble Sir,

We had an extremely nice weekend in New York. I gave a reading at Columbia on a bright, hot, afternoon, and being early I had time to wander around the grounds outside the Low Memorial Library, in front of which a demonstration was going on in protest against Reagan's Central American policies; though perhaps after the 1960's "demonstration" is too strong a term. There were lots of cops, and a fair-sized crowd that was both sympathetic and apathetic. There were P.A. systems, mikes and speakers (human) preaching to the converted, and a number of photographers, though no TV cameras that I could see. I wandered into Philosophy Hall, where I had studied in 1950, when I took an M.A., vaguely hoping that it would seem suddenly and brilliantly familiar. It was nothing of the kind; it looked like a place I had never seen before in my life. The reading went very well, though the room was small and crowded and badly ventilated. But I felt cheerful, had a drink with some friends, and then met Helen and Evan at our hotel – where they had arrived by a later plane so that Evan would not miss school events. We went to Elaine's[1] for dinner, where I was welcomed like a long-lost-son, and where we were given special attention and made much of. But best of all, not long after our drinks were ordered, Evan leaned across the table in a very conspiratorial way, and asked if the man seated at the adjoining table just behind me was Woody Allen. There was no question about it; it was he. So Evan asked if I had pen and paper for an autograph. I had a pen but only my appointment book for paper, so one of the latter pages, ostensibly to be devoted to notes, is signed by Woody Allen, and Evan will surely be showing it off to his friends tomorrow. Next day we went to the Met, and while Evan and Helen went to see whatever it was they wanted to see (which covered a great deal of ground, including Egypt and the Middle Ages) I saw a really splendid Constable show,[2] which I revisited the next day. Also a number of Renaissance items I hadn't seen for a long time and acquaintance with which it was high time I renewed. But at one point, being ahead of time for a rendezvous in an appointed gallery, and

like that of W. MacDonald."

1 A bar and restaurant located on Manhattan's Upper East Side, popular with figures prominent in the arts. It closed shortly after the death of its famed owner, Elaine Kaufman, in 2010.

2 *Constable's England*, Metropolitan Museum of Art, April 16th – September 4th, 1983.

seated on a bench near three Panini paintings, I had time to observe them with more care than I had thought to give them before. One of them is a gallery of paintings of ancient Roman monuments, and it contains within the same Panini painting both interior and exterior views of the Pantheon. But the picture that most disturbed me was an interior of St. Peter's. The pattern of quadrilaterals in the marble floor descend at a precipitous angle from right to left, an angle pronounced enough to suggest that a billiard ball placed at one side of the nave could not fail to roll across it starting from a stationary position. The line of sight is admittedly along the left side of the nave, yet there is nothing to suggest that the floor would have begun an upward curve if the painting had been wider. And the perpendiculars at both sides were perfectly plumb and correct.[1] The effect, however, of the painting on the viewer is really disconcerting and unbalancing as, in a different way, the interior of the Pantheon is in the large single painting that you so often employ, and which violates one's sense of the sphericality, and even the circularity, of the building.[2] We saw a number of old friends, and dined unusually well. Helen chose the portrait photograph she wants for the new book (which will be out in late August) a masterful shot taken by me, and turned it in to the publisher. Tomorrow I give my final lecture for the year (on Robert Lowell) at the Library,[3] and the next day take a class at Georgetown (a gratis performance) on Frost and Keats (the unlikely combination being their choice). And perhaps most interesting of all, I have heard unconfirmed reports that someone who cordially detests me has recently become an advisor on poetry applicants to the Guggenheim Foundation, a situation that could easily explain why none of the four worthy poets I recommended were chosen, and why some others of no consequence (or talent) were preferred. I have well-placed friends now trying to find out for certain whether there is any truth to this report. If there is, I shall simply not recommend anyone I admire until this son-of-a-bitch has been purged from the penetralia of the foundation.

Dogwood is now in full blossom here, and I am astonished to see what I have never seen before: two-tone dogwood trees, like saddle shoes, with pink dogwood apparently grafted smoothly onto a white dogwood tree (or vice versa). There were brilliant yellow tulips all the length of Park Avenue's traffic divider in New York. All this is very cheerful, and a good note to end on.

Aurore Dudevant
(a rare signature)

---

1 Giovanni Paolo Panini, *Interior of Saint Peter's Rome* (after 1754), Metropolitan Museum of Art, New York.

2 Giovanni Paolo Panini, *Interior of the Pantheon, Rome* (circa 1750), National Gallery of Art, Washington, D.C. The painting is used as a frontispiece to WLM's *The Pantheon: Design, Meaning, and Progeny.*

3 "Robert Lowell," delivered at the Library of Congress on May 2nd, 1983.

[320]

[AH]
May 10th, 1983
The Library of Congress, Poetry Office, Washington, D.C. 20540

[Letter, typed on a Library of Congress, Poetry Office, letterhead, addressed to Professor William MacDonald, 25 Henshaw Avenue, Northampton, Massachusetts 01060]

Most Esteemed and Reverend Sir:

On the 14th of March, 1978, you wrote to me as follows: "Did you know that Elbert Hubbard's <u>Message to Garcia</u>, which sold some fifty million copies, was once distributed to the entire Japanese Army? I lie about thinking about this. It is probably the single most staggering fact I've ever possessed. Let me have your reactions to it."[1]

I suppose you might claim that I have been slow to react, and indeed I have been bothered from time to time by the thought of you, restless and unable to sleep as you lie about, preoccupied with this mystery. But, like the laggardly hero of Zeno's problem, I am at last prepared to furnish a solution that will allow you to sleep restfully and at peace once again.[2]

Let me tell you at once that my source for this information is no one less than the Librarian of the Library of Congress himself, Daniel Boorstin, a very distinguished historian and sometime professor of history at Chicago University. Though not himself a great Elbert Hubbard fan, his father was, and his father kept pressing wretched books by Hubbard upon him during his defenseless early years. With a noticeable twinge he remembers the <u>Message</u>, and, fully aware of the facts that you imparted, and adding to them the information that at a later time, and for much the same reasons, the book was distributed to Russian troops, described the volume somewhat as follows: They've got to get this message to Garcia, so they ask for volunteers. The first one asks how far away Garcia is, and is, in consequence, scratched from the list. The second asks where Garcia is, and is similarly scratched. The third asks at least that Garcia's general direction be indicated, but is dismissed out of hand. Finally some guy shows up to bear the message, and prepared to do so with no questions asked; he doesn't care where Garcia is, what the dangers are, how far away his goal nor how long it will take him. As a model of imbecile obedience he is clearly high calibre, and just what the Japs, and later the Russkies, were eager to inculcate in their troops. Hence the wide distribution. I hope this will set your mind at rest.

V.
Verse an' Getorix

---

1 See postcard #183.

2 WLM could have told AH that he'd ignored not just one appeal for a reaction to the story about *Message to Garcia* but two. See letter #186, of April 4th, 1978 for his follow-up.

[321]

[WLM]
May 12th, 1983
[25 Henshaw Avenue, Northampton, Massachusetts 01060]

[Letter, typed on a The Mayflower Hotel, 1127 Connecticut Avenue, N.W., Washington, D.C.20036, letterhead]

Kind Sir,

In the throes of throwing out stuff, selling books and prints, and generally slimming down – wish it were that easy to do the same with my waistline & satisfying, but gets in the way of writing, which has been in something of a slump lately. I find I have until August 15th to get out of here; will try for earlier that month in order not to pay in two places.

Speaking at Catholic U. on the 14th of June and will extend the trip in order to apartment-hunt. Will you have gone to the City by the lake, or will you yet be in Residence?

Nick should just now be getting off the midnight train from Roma in Brindisi, where he meets a pal coming from Greece; they then go round Sicily together.

My non-lady friend lady friend arrives in a couple of hours to go through her computer program for Norman church doorways with me, so today ought to be nice; been cold as hell (odd phrase). I know what you mean about word processors, but when I get to Wash. I think I'll lease one to see if I want to buy. I can't type, and the w.p.s I've been checked out on seem to fit the bill; I like the ms. pp. that come out of the better printers.

Baskins return here shortly. Ran into Lisa in the fruit store. L[eonard] burned every beam of every bridge when he left, so it will be interesting to see how things go … Am[erican] Ac[ademy], Roma called again to ask if I wanted to stand for the Directorship. 4th, 5th time? Guess they don't keep records. Told them politely why it wouldn't do. Harry Cobb and I had a ½ lunch on it at Harvard the other day; I sugg. my former, student, Spiro Kostof, prof. at Berkeley, as a candidate …

Will you consider Georgetown seriously?

Would you please write a novel?

Nick and I particularly liked the picture of you on the Lowell lecture flyer – a touch of impishness, indeed of cheerful slyness, we thought — very suitable for L. Evan & Woody Allen fine; Nick had just read that A. when at Elaine's is importuned by autograph-seekers …

Meanwhile, sir, we are all working on getting you a sinecure on the Marquis of O's staff (get it?).

A presto,
Ciano

Did you know Mussolini gave D'Annunzio ½ a battleship, which was <u>towed</u> <u>up</u> <u>into</u> D'A's gardens, so he could fire salutes whenever he wished?

[322]

[WLM]
June 8th, 1983
25 Henshaw Avenue, Northampton, Massachusetts 01060

[Blank postcard, typed, addressed to Anthony Hecht, an ancient mariner, 19 East Boulevard, Rochester, NY 14610, but re-routed by the US Postal Service to Hecht, 110 East Lenox St, Chevy Chase MD 20815]

8 Juin 83

Fellow Deliquescent,

   Called the Chevy Chase house a couple of times, perhaps at the wrong hours, but I suspect you are back in Rotch Esther for the summer. Well, Burstein (sp) is right up to a point. I read the great <u>Message</u> when I was fifteen or so, & B. has the plot right, but failed to tell you that it is set in the Spanish American War, or some other Latin fling; I forget now; and that adds a lot to the whizz, or verve, of the thing. Is it true that Boorstin will give me a room or cubicle at the LofC? A novelist pal, who just moved to DC, claims he got one. No, I didn't think your remarks about <u>Message</u> unduly delayed. And I've still to comment on the Rome vedute of a couple of years ago, or on important matters pert. to Aurore Dudevant. Off to DC next Tues, to lecture & apartment hunt. Meanwhile, never mistake asthma for passion (Life Rule #7)

St. Bill

[323]

[WLM]
July 4th, 1983
25 Henshaw Avenue, Northampton, Massachusetts 01060

[Letter, typed on a Tom Sawyer Motor Inns letterhead, posted in an Ohio Stater Inn, 2060 North High Street, Columbus, Ohio 43201 envelope, addressed to Anthony Hecht, measurer of balconies, 110 East Lenox Street, Chevy Chase MD 20815]

Indep. Day '83

Mon cher probist:

   That's very encouraging about the dear old Academy, and reassuring about La Consagra.[1] Friends have not been impressed by her, to say the least, and it is good to have an optimistic view. I hope it all works out, especially the financial side.
   I am a bit disappointed that you have air conditioning, not only because it deprives me of lording it over you, but because it surely must be bad for the muse, who loves hot weather as you know. And shouldn't creative people suffer in order to create? I

---

1 A reference to Sophie Chandler Consagra, who was Director of the American Academy in Rome from 1980 until 1984, President from 1984 until 1988, and Vice Chair-Special Projects from 1988 until 1990.

believe that opinion is firmly held. But I guess it will be all right if you cool off, since I so clearly have the upper hand in the matter of elegant stationery.

It will be great to be nearby, to mull and churn about the antics of our masters and their minions, to be sure that each understands the lofty and utterly original thoughts of the other. My apartment is new – I will have to hire an F-100 pilot to check me out on the stove controls – and on two floors. I have a living room to make into a study, and a big loft for a living room. I've never lived in a new building before and may be somewhat shy about it at first. Wall-to-wall, previously thought an abomination, looks good (I chose a reddish-brown to match the icons) and I must say I look forward to all the modern conveniences. I'll have to learn how to run a washer-dryer? perhaps you have some gorgeous young female instructor in mind, of the kind that brandishes handsome containers of Fix, DeBlot, Whoops!, and the like at you on the T.V. … ?

Have been selling things I don't want; a surprising amount. Slimming down is an unanticipated pleasure of the whole affair. About ¼ or so of my books are no longer needed, and to my pleasure they have been fetching good prices, esp. the old architectural folios that I bought here and there many years ago for five to thirty dollars. Much squirreled-away junk has gone – god only knows why I saved some of it. I am very much ready for a change. If I don't like it, I can go somewhere else, but I fully expect the whole thing to be a success.

I believe that it will be the first time since 1955 or so that we will living in the same town (that sentence seems a bit weak, doesn't it? Well, I've been packing books, and so can be excused).

Any further thoughts or actions with regard to our friendly Jesuits? Would you entertain an offer as they say? Offers like many pillows, and generally stay prone during their entertainment …

A presto,
William of Washington

On a serious note (I love those abandoned, wild, unserious notes, don't you? The kind that float about, giggling and cavorting?) I might add that a splendid neuromuscular disease man, trained by my austere, elderly protector at the Massachusetts General Hospital, is in Washington. He is said to be tops, as we say, and approachable …

[324]

[AH]
July 29th, 1983
19 East Boulevard, Rochester, New York 14610

[Letter, typed, addressed to WLM at 3811 39th Street NW, #F-90, Washington, D.C. 20016, with enclosure]

Dear Voter,

This is as much an experiment in reaching you at your new address as it is a gallant communication. Observe, if you will, the enclosed reproduction of a photograph of the classiest cemetery in Buenos Aires. It bears a striking resemblance to an illustration of a so-called Tragic Scene in Sebastiano Serlio's Libro primo d'architettura[1] which Panofsky reproduces in Meaning in the Visual Arts.[2] Doubtless you will remember that there are two scenic settings, one tragic and one comic, the comic one being distinctly more asymmetrical than its opposite. Books on the history of the theater abound with such conventional stage sets for comic and tragic theater, but it's odd to find one put to such practical use as in the photograph.

Henry-Fréderic Amiel

[Enclosure]

A reproduction of a photograph with the caption "Opulent mausoleums and eerily lit effigies fill La Recoleta, "City of the Dead," resting place of Argentina's rich and famous."

[325]

[WLM]
December 11th, 1983
[3811 39th Street NW, #F-90, Washington, D.C. 20016]

[Letter, typed]

Most Reverend Lord Bishop,

You will I think be as pleased as I am to know that at least one famous streetcar accident turned out to be a fake. After all, our lecture would be somewhat lugubrious, would it not, with a litany of casualties (you'll notice that I use "litany" in an improper and therefore crowd-pleasing sense)?

It seems that the late Carl Laemmle, Sr., founder of Universal Studios and, as you will well know, one of the grander motion picture tycoons, wishing to undo the stranglehold of the Motion Picture Patents Company on the hiring of stars for their Biograph pictures, undid them properly. He lured its most popular player, Frances

---

1 Sebastiano Serlio, *Libro primo d'architettura* (Venice, Italy: 1551).

2 Erwin Panofsky, *Meaning in the Visual Arts* (Chicago, IL: University of Chicago Press, 1982), p. 242.

Lawrence, away from them; she had been known everywhere as The Biograph Girl. He then "planted a report in the Newspapers that 'The Biograph Girl' had been killed in a streetcar accident. The following day he came out with an indignant advertisement denouncing the malicious report and announcing that Miss Lawrence, now 'The Imp Girl' [Independent Motion Pictures], was alive and well and working for him." [Ephraim Katz, The Film Encyclopedia, 1979, p. 677.]

Makes one feel good, doesn't it?

All took place in 1910 which, as Franklin P. Adams used to say, was before my time. The only streetcar accident I ever witnessed, in the winter of either 1933 or 1934, on the main street of Sanford, Maine, was fatal to a town drunk who was mangled under the wheels of the car that had just come in from the north from Springfield. This was not the same drunk who a couple of years later said to my mother, when she informed him that she would no longer put out her garbage for him, together with the customary quarter, because I (who had just obtained an ancient Chevrolet truck for $28 (actually it was an ex-roadster, 1927 model, that someone had ripped the rumble seat out of in order to install a home-made truck bed) was going to take over his garbage collection route, at least along School and West Elm Streets, that that was fine with him, adding, as he swayed at the foot of the back stoop, his ancient, blinkered horse standing patiently behind him – a famous horse in town because no matter how pickled Curly (his name was Curly Wood) got, the horse always got him home to his shack beside the town dump – "that's how I got my start; good for him!"

That's A True Story and you may use it as you wish.

As you can easily see, I should have been a writer.

I've curled up some lately with John Gross's Oxford Book of Aphorisms.[1] It's fun, but not a patch on the one by Auden and Kronenberger of some years back.[2] As you know, you can't read many aphorisms at a sitting or, in my case, at a lying; that brings on indigestion. But when you do leaf about, reading the short and very short ones, you realise that these people, witty and clear-thinking one and all, are actually building blocks for a strong wall around themselves, and that their self-irony and such are only means of distancing themselves from those foibles, or worse, that they so clearly see. Once in a great while an aphorismer sees this in turn, but it's a rare thing.

The National Geographic, with which I lunched in mid-week, may want a short book on Herculaneum, in which its Board has gotten very interested, indeed involved. The price that was murmured to me was vast. 160 pp!* I doubt anything will come of it, but if you hear I've gone off to Pago Pago, and there seems to be a dearth of handsome women on the Metro and in the Shops, you'll know what happened.

Try pink! You'll like it!

Yours in S. Accacia's tears,
A. Pismo Clam

*typed

---

1 *The Oxford Book of Aphorisms* (New York: Oxford University Press, 1983).
2 *The Viking Book of Aphorisms: A Personal Selection by W. H. Auden and Louis Kronenberger* (New York: Viking Press, 1962).

[326]

[AH]
December 16th, 1983
110 East Lenox Street, Chevy Chase, MD 20815

*[Letter, typed, addressed to Wm. MacDonald, Leader of Men (& Women),
3811 39th Street. N.W., Apt. F90, Washington, D.C. 20016]]*

My dear Seneschal,

Over the years it has occurred to me that there may indeed be more famous streetcar accidents than at first I supposed. Am I not correct in believing that it was just such a vehicle that did in poor old Antonio Gaudí? It seems to me that it was merely a gross lapse of taste that allowed Tolstoy to let Anna Karenina perish by being creamed by a train rather than by a streetcar. Indeed, I think a sufficiently astute modern novelist might create a sensation by rewriting the Russian novel to give it the proper and dignified ending it calls out for so passionately. In contrast to this the incident about Frances Lawrence and the Motion Picture Industry seems trifling, if pleasant. On the other hand, the story you have to tell about Curly Wood and your mother is a noble tale that I shall treasure.

Your news about writing a new book on Herculaneum is great, and I hope N.G. treats you with respect and generosity.[1] It's an outfit close to the heart of Evan, who loves their bldg. We all leave tomorrow for Rochester for the Christmas holidays, to which Helen and I look forward with unmixed dismay. First of all, reports of the weather up there are uniformly bad. Secondly, Helen's mother will be moving from one apartment to another just about the time we arrive, and we will clearly be involved in all that. Thirdly, the university is changing administrations, and most of the people we like are dropping away. It seems to us both that we have strong ties to very few up there. I suspect that it is more than merely a factor of age that I continue these days to astonish myself at how many Rochester acquaintances and even colleagues I can recall only by physical features but without the identifying label of a name. It is going to make for a good deal of social discomfort during this visit.

I agree with your suspicion of the makers of aphorisms. There is something usually smug and self-satisfied about the form, as though the aphorist believes that everything could be neatly summed up in a trice, without all the fuss and bother that others labored to go through. Mathematical formulas can indeed condense an enormous amount of prior thought and labor without giving the impression that their author is trying to show off by seeming to do something effortless. And witty aphorists are a pleasure, being essentially against pretension.

Have a splendid holiday season; I'll be in touch when we return.

Galla Placidia

---

1 This project never materialized.

[327]

[WLM]
January 5th, 1984
3811 39th Street NW, #F-90, Washington, D.C. 20016

[Letter, typed, addressed to The Most Honorable A. Hecht, 110 East Lenox Street, Chevy Chase MD 20815]

X a. Kal. Ian. MCMLXXXIV

Honour'd Gent.,

One of my admirers – they are as common as Bloomingdale's branches, as you know – has sent me the following :

> Higgledy Piggledy
> Emperor Hadrian
> Ordered the Pantheon
> Built for his fame.
>
> But for MacDonald's book,
> Architectonically,
> Who in the hell would re-
> Member his name?[1]

All is not lost: I see there is a Le Pavilion restaurant in Washington. Perhaps a Rump Session, or Rear Echelon, of the Regents could meet here some time? Review the rules, carouse, and talk about Mutual Funds? Failing that, you could join my International Association of Tolerant Aardwolves (Ayatollah), but the dues are steep.

Today is the hundredth anniversary of the first performance of Princess Ida.[2] I do not know why I know this.

I've not played my delicious D'Oyly Carte recording in years, but I thought I would have a martini and put it on and let Gilbert put me on.

I remain, nice gent., one of your perfervid admirers.

J. Fleb (or Flerb)

---

1 A double dactyl, the verse form invented by AH and Paul Pascal when both were fellows at the American Academy in Rome in 1951. This particular example was sent to WLM by Judith Testa, who was then Professor of Art History at Northern Illinois University.

2 *Princess Ida* was premiered on January 5th, 1884; this fact, together with the letter's postmark of January 6th, 1984, makes WLM's Roman calendar date – X a. Kal. Ian. MCMLXXXIV – puzzling. January 5th, 1984 ought to have been rendered as Non. Ian. MCMLXXXIV.

[328]

[WLM]
February 15th, 1984
3811 39th Street NW, #F-90, Washington, D.C. 20016

[Blank postcard, typed, addressed to M. le duc Antoine de Hecht,
110 East Lenox Street, Chevy Chase MD 20815]

My dear duc,

A line to thank you for the Lowell lecture,[1] about which I will be writing more fully later on. I'm on the prize committee for the Hitchcock medal, the award in the history of architecture,[2] and have been putting off examining the fifty-odd entries and now must pay the piper (that piper must be damned well off!). The news you gave me on the Ameche about G[eorgetown] U[niversity] is just great.[3] I'm getting to know my students there and they are O.K.

Yours,
devant d'Hier

[329]

[WLM]
March 11th, 1984
3811 39th Street NW, #F-90, Washington, D.C. 20016

[Letter, typed, addressed to Dr Anthony Hecht, Out in the Left Field,
110 East Lenox Street, Chevy Chase MD 20815]

My dear monophysite friend,

The simplest way to state my reaction to your very informative and readable <u>Lowell</u> is to say that I never knew that he was a good poet. I'm sure many others never knew either, intelligent people like me. Any comment of mine on your critical observations would be presumptuous, but I can say that you make him accessible to me, and because of that I hope the lecture reaches a wide audience. I think that, as so often happens, I reacted negatively to those poems of his that I read and tried to understand because I'd no sense of context – and, of course, little sense of the art of poetry (though ample sense of the appreciability and value of it). Nor did I have any sense of his learning; now I have.

But I must say I come away from contemplation of his life and work with a

---

1 *Robert Lowell* (Washington, D.C.: Library of Congress, 1983); later included in AH's *Obbligati: Essays in Criticism*.

2 The Alice Davis Hitchcock Award, named after the mother of Henry-Russell Hitchcock, and awarded annually for "the most distinguished work of scholarship in the history of architecture published by a North American scholar."

3 AH had heard that he was to be offered a chair at Georgetown.

kind of sadness. I could never agree with Auden's willed madness, but I can't escape the impression that Lowell did desire to be great and though I can't say whether or not he became great, it does seem to me that he also hurt himself by that and other maladies of ambition. On the other hand, I know several men well who think they are great and who, unhappily, do not know they are not and never will be.

For me, knowing you but not Lowell, the most important thing in the lecture is your ability to explicate: you must be one of the very best. Your analogues and explorations of meaning are cumulatively the best kind of argument; as I am methodologically in a rather similar business I can admire your clarity and effectiveness in these matters the more.

Finally, it turns out that Lowell and Noel and Nick are related as they – N. + N. – are, as you may know, direct descendants of Jonathan Edwards.

The Georgetown students are squarish, with a veneer of with-it-ness, hard-working, a bit cocky (the men), just realizing they're smart (the women). My class of fifty did quite a bit better on their hour examination than I would have guessed beforehand. I have been able to get a third of them to speak up, to react audibly, and that seems after thirty-odd years of coaxing and trying everything to be a good fraction; I hope to raise it some after vacation. My guess is that a class of seniors in literary criticism would be pretty good provided they'd done the kind of reading earlier on that we would think minimal.

I look forward to seeing you all here four days after the Ides. The erotic slides will appear toward the end of the show.

Yours in cosmic simplicity,
Sarah, Duchess of Marlboro Lights

[330]

[AH]
March 18th, 1984
[110 East Lenox Street, Chevy Chase, MD 20815]

[Letter, typed on a The Library of Congress, Poetry Office, letterhead, with now missing enclosure]

My dear Iconodule,

I enclose a few distinctly savory items that should go a long way to convincing you that this region we both now so happily inhabit is unexpectedly rich in cultural and intellectual resources. Social Studies 596, for example, offered in conjunction with the Department of Anthropology, ought to interest many students, and Home Ec. 218, though potentially fattening, should also attract large crowds. The chief problem, however, lies in Psychology 220. Clearly it is addressed to those who habitually procrastinate; but the problem lies in how to overcome their lethargy about signing up. We have got to get the dean to give serious thought to this matter.

Thank you for your appreciative letter about Lowell. The things about him that put you off, or repel you (I've misplaced your letter for the moment, and cannot exactly recall your tone) were undeniably a part of his character: there was a huge, overwhelming vanity that inclined to diminish the importance of everyone else on many occasions. It is clearly there in the poetry, too. But almost as a corollary he was capable of great respect for others, almost a tenderness, and a touching eagerness to be liked and approved. A puzzling man, and, generally speaking, a very unhappy one. Even his triumphs were, in a sense, spoiled by being manic – that is, governed by chemical or metabolic shifts in his system. This provided him with his periodic "highs," of course, but they were somehow unrelated to reality; and even when they were related, they were too often a sign of illness. I remember hearing that just before he went on stage at the Poetry Center in New York to give one of his first readings (just after WWII) he was given word that he had just won the Pulitzer Prize. Someone, however, told me this, described his elation, in words that really stunned me. I remember them (not word for word, of course, but their impression) vividly because it seemed to me at the time that I myself had never been that happy; and when much later I won the Pulitzer, though I was undeniably very happy indeed, that account of Lowell's delirium came back (again, wordless, but vivid) because I knew that what happened to me was not what had happened to him.

I have been reading The Selected Letters and Journals of Byron, edited by Leslie Marchand; Harvard Press paperback.[1] I recommend it enthusiastically, though it tends to make all other letter-writers feel they should confine themselves to Western Union.

Publius Ovidius Naso

---

1 *Lord Byron: Selected Letters and Journals*, edited by Leslie A. Marchand (Cambridge, MA: Belknap Press of Harvard University Press, 1982).

[331]

[AH]
March 31st, 1984
[110 East Lenox Street, Chevy Chase, MD 20815]

[Letter, typed on a Rogier & Cie, "Dentelles & Guipures Noires & Blanches," Paris, France, letterhead]

My dear chap,

There is nothing, you may take my word for it, nothing whatever that so guarantees the enduring importance of a scholarly book as the choice and selective list of obligations and notes of indebtedness that normally appears in tiny print somewhere at the tail of the author's preface. Long after the reader has tired of the text, long after he has dismissed the laborious arguments put forth, he can still turn to those names with a renewed and invigorated pleasure, if only they have been chosen with flair and imagination. I have been giving much thought to this matter since I am on the point of completing a volume, not of poetry this time, but of critical prose – which will allow me, as poetry would not, a suitable profusion and dropping of names. And I furthermore find myself still smouldering with resentment at having been beaten to the draw by Hugh Trevor-Roper, who, with an easy and familiar calm, expressed himself as obliged to Laetitia, Lady Lucas-Tooth. There is a name worth relishing, and just the sort of thing that would make any work of Trevor-Roper's worth preserving, no matter how tiresome or wrong-headed (as he was, of course, about Anthony Blunt) the main body of the text might be.[1] I have in

---

1 In 1979, Sir Anthony Blunt, a renowned art historian and Keeper of the Queen's Pictures, had been exposed by Prime Minister Margaret Thatcher as someone who had spied for the Soviet Union during WWII. Blunt had confessed to this as early as 1964, but only in return for its being kept an official secret and his being given immunity from prosecution. After publication in 1979 of Andrew Boyle's *Climate of Treason,* which, although it hadn't named Blunt, had awoken (or in some cases re-awoken) suspicions about him, Thatcher had decided to make his identity as one of the Cambridge Spies public, thereby prompting a hue and cry. AH's charge, that Trevor-Roper had been "tiresome" or "wrong-headed" about Blunt, would seem to be based on the position taken by Trevor-Roper in an article he wrote for *The Spectator*: "What have we gained from the exposure of Blunt? Apart from the pleasure of a public scandal, and

consequence been casting about among the list of those cited by the Shorter Oxford English Dictionary, and am pleased and reassured to have winkled out the following largely neglected names: Dionysius Lardner, Vicesimus Knox, and Mountstuart Elphinstone. If one is able to convey, ever so casually, that one pals around with the likes of these, an air of worldly assurance and sophistication is imparted to the work that cites them in suitably modest small print that is always used for such occasions.

You would be wrong to suppose that the two ladies whose seated portraits appear above are maiden aunts of mine. They are nothing of the sort; they are instead allegorical figures. What looks like the fine-feathered hat of one of them is actually a nest of serpents, and she is a Medusa-like representation of Wrath. Her companion, wearing an overturned soup-bowl on her head, represents penitence, and is all wet and uncomfortable, as well as smelling strongly of New England Clam Chowder. The work as a whole is very edifying, and I commend it to you for spiritual uplift and downdraft.

We went off on a little excursion to Amherst, where I gave a reading at U. Mass., and where we saw the Baskins. Leonard was his gentlest and most friendly, and I was quite touched by his kindliness as well as his enthusiasm for my poems. He would like to do another emblem book with me, and while I would be delighted to collaborate with him again, I would not want to go back to the writing of verse epigrams, which is what usually accompanies emblematic designs. Anyway, we had a very pleasant visit with friends, took a tour of the Smith campus, which brought back no cheerful memories to me, but which was a small excursion into nostalgia for Helen. We have heard rumor (new to us, though perhaps you are familiar with it) that Jill Conway will shortly resign her presidency in order to go back to teaching. We also were shown over the Emily Dickinson house, both of us for the first time. One can no longer go up to the cupola, of which Dick Wilbur has written so splendidly,[1] because the house is currently lived in by a widow of a sometime trustee, and bats have sneaked into the cupola, and she has had to seal off the top of the house to keep them from entering her domain. She was the soul of courtesy and charm with us, and we enjoyed the visit enormously. Tomorrow we go to view the house we are going to buy here in Washington, assuming that all goes well. The other interested party has been checked, and discouraged from any intentions to sue, and it looks as if we are on the way to a clear title. Such, indeed, is the premise of the owner, who has invited us tomorrow to give us as much information as he can about the technicalities of maintenance: who to seek in the line of plumbers and painters, and all such practical tips. What still remains to be worked out in precise detail has to do with the financing of the deal by Georgetown, and just what the interest terms on the mortgage are to be. The house, whose present owner has lived in it for thirty-seven years, is beautifully furnished, very obviously with furnishings

---

the evacuation of tribal resentments, precisely nothing. What would we have lost if Blunt had remained unexposed, with his dead past sunk in secret memory? Equally, nothing. What will we gain if, like the Americans, we effectively dismantle our security service? Less than nothing." "Blunt Censured, Nothing Gained," *The Spectator*, November 24th, 1979.

1 See Richard Wilbur's "Altitudes," in his *Things of This World* (New York: Harcourt, Brace & Co, 1956).

carefully acquired over time and just for the places they so aptly occupy; while we will be faced with the nearly impossible task of fitting what we already own into places we had never dreamed of before.

The Library of Congress has scheduled a rather impressive set of programs, one every week until I conclude the series in May with a lecture on the Pathetic Fallacy. The first, on Monday the 2nd (very likely before this reaches you) will present Richard Ellmann lecturing on Yeats. On April 9th Bernard Malamud will read, and it may be that tickets for him have already been exhausted; I do know they were in great demand. On the 16th Joseph Brodsky will read; on the 24th Northrop Frye will lecture on "The Social Authority of the Writer." On the 30th of April and 1st of May there will be a series of programs on George Orwell and <u>1984</u>. And I do my act on the 7th.

Galla Placidia Augusta

[332]

[AH]
May 9th, 1984
[The Library of Congress, Poetry Office, Washington, D.C. 20540]

[Letter, typed on a The Library of Congress, Poetry Office, letterhead, addressed to Mr. William MacDonald, 3811 39th Street. N.W., Apt. F90, Washington, D.C. 20016]

My dear young fella:

I hope you were paying close attention to my lecture the other evening, and that you learned a good deal from it.[1] One of the things that should have impressed you was that the whole thing was done without resorting to pictures, that lame and feeble device invariably employed by art and architectural historians, who are almost always at a loss for something to say, and who hope to distract the attention of their audiences by this Fourth Grade "Show and Tell" expedient. Audiences at these gatherings are a docile lot, and there are even those who attend such programs – it would unduly dignify them to call them "lectures" – in the hope of seeing some dirty pictures, or any sort of pictorial exhibit jazzy enough to distract them from the invariable drone that comes from the dark recesses "off camera," as they say in the motion picture industry. But even the most docile attenders will learn sooner or later that any such presentation, even if open free to the public with little dry biscuits served afterwards, will not stand comparison with your standard, grade-C soft-porn flick, even when the box office levies a duty of fifteen clams. I point this out to you for your own good, and because it is high time that people like you and Krautheimer and Lavin wised up to the fact that we're living in the Michael Jackson era, man, and this tame stuff won't wash any more. I mean, if you've seen one Roman bath you've

1 WLM had attended AH's lecture, "The Pathetic Fallacy," delivered at the Library of Congress on May 7th. The lecture was published as *The Pathetic Fallacy* (Washington, D.C.: Library of Congress, 1985), and was later included in AH's essay collection, *Obbligati: Essays in Criticism*.

seen them all, as Spiro Agnew once magnificently said. Besides, there's something downright indecent about such searching inquiries into Hadrian's baths, to say nothing of Caracalla's. There are ways in which scholarship can be carried too far.

So I hope to hear that you have reformed your ways, and abandoned these cheap devices, which lack even the merit of sensationalism; and that you will bone up on your vocabulary, and attempt to master some elementary form of articulate discourse.

Thine evermore,
Fred
Anthony Hecht
Consultant in Poetry

[333]

[AH]
June 18th, 1984
110 East Lenox Street, Chevy Chase, MD 20815

[Letter, typed on a Jean Vidal, "Marchand de Bois et de Charbons en Gros et en Detail," Paris, France, letterhead, addressed to William MacDonald, Cyclopousseur, 811 39th St. N.W., Apt. F90, Washington, D.C. 20016]

18 Juin, 1984

Great Jumping Jehosaphat,

My final duty here in Washington has been to compose my Annual Report, and given the pressure of events I have made it mercifully brief – brief enough to offer it to you here.[1]

ANNUAL REPORT

> I terminate my appointment as Consultant in Poetry to the Library of Congress with a keen sense of pleasure in the two years of my tenure, and regret that they have come to an end; though I am pleased to think that the position will be ennobled and strengthened by my successor. It is an act of self-abnegation nearly heroic in proportions to relinquish

---

1 The report which follows appears to have been sent to WLM twice, on this occasion by AH himself, but at a later date by AH's Library of Congress secretary, Nancy Galbraith. The second copy is undated, but it contains a handwritten correction that is incorporated in the first, which makes it reasonable to assume that the second was a draft and the first a fair copy made from it. At the top of that second copy, Ms Galbraith has penned a note: "Bill: He closed his 1st term, 1982–83, with a 'straight' annual report: highlights of his time, what he'd done, reflections on the experience ... The usual annual report. He decided to do this instead for his 2nd term. If it matters to your purposes to have facts, this piece was Tony's portion of The Annual Report of the Manuscript Division, its destinations 1) The desk of the Assistant Librarian for Research Services, ultimately 2) The files of the Library of Congress. Cordially, Nancy." It seems likely that WLM had mislaid the copy sent him by AH and had asked Galbraith for another, prompted to do so by AH's suggestion that he contribute something to a collection of essays on his work that Sydney Lea had proposed in a letter of May 12th, 1984. (See WLM's letters #339 and #340 of July 19th, 1984 and July 22nd 1984, respectively).

the dictatorial powers over American Poetry that have been mine during the length of my term of office. One acquires, it may be said, a taste and relish for power, and grows used to it in a remarkably short time; and, Lord Acton to the contrary notwithstanding, I have not found it in the least corrupting. One may take simple pleasure in the ceremonial parades, the firework displays, the popular ovations, the devotion of literary groupies, the constant round of talk-shows and autograph seekers; as well as in the public execution of those guilty of laxness in their meters (checked by a diligent staff of meter-maids) – a matter which, prompted by Ben Jonson's strictures on the metrics of John Donne, I am pleased to claim to have revived and put into settled practice.

Then there are what may be called the perquisites and garnishes of the job: the publishers' bribes – though some who are by nature niggardly have pleaded inflation. And, not least, there is the cringing servility of all the nation's poets, and their total conformity and abject meekness in adopting those themes and forms the Consultant designates as the official ones for the nation during his administration. During my own period as Consultant poets were limited to writing sestinas, rondeaux and rhyme royal on the Persian Gulf Crisis, post-coital sadness, and the National Geographic Society. Deviations either in materials or forms were dealt with instantly and mercilessly, and it is with a genuine sense of regret that I turn in the boot, the rack and the official thumb-screws of office. They were, along with the incomparable work of the office staff, Nancy Galbraith and Jenny Rutland, nothing less than indispensable.

I am pleased to claim that, besides driving the <u>vers libristes</u> underground, virtually stamping out their pathetic journal, <u>Free Feet</u>, and infiltrating the Black Mountain School with long-haired double-agents, I was able, with the aid of my wife, to design a special garment to be worn by all recognized American poets. There is first of all the floppy, Wagnerian velvet hat, black for major poets, magenta for minor ones. Then the waterproof Inverness cape, lined in yellow silk, with a large manuscript pouch at one side. Special attention has been paid to shoes and boots, and any poet who lays claim to a variable foot is liable to immediate amputation. Reviving a vestment worn by John Skelton at the court of Henry VIII, there is, for the younger members of the Consultant's entourage, a red, white and blue satin bowling jacket, with the name "Calliope" inscribed across the back in cheerful Day-Glo orange. These devices tend to call the attention of an otherwise comparatively indifferent public to the presence of poetry in its midst.

I can do no less than point out to my successor that anyone who takes upon himself the role of Caesar must expect the attendant risks. There were the usual assassination attempts. We had been warned that Robert Bly was planning a coup. But in fact the real danger came from another quarter entirely. A plot was uncovered in good time at the headquarters of the Concrete Poets, an underground bunker in Iowa, but the apprehended have not yet been brought to trial, so details are still confidential.

During my tenure 62% of the nation's poets fell in love, well over half of these with themselves; 17% divorced; 24% watched five or more hours of TV a day; 31% were declared mentally unsound, and 8% failed to have their drivers' licenses renewed. This is a healthy trend, considering the wretched material one has to work with. It is, however, worth noting that not a few modern poets are quite comfortably situated, and I plan to live in luxurious retirement in Venice on an annuity furnished by about sixty of the most craven of the poets under my recent authority; and I suggest to my successor that he take similar steps in planning for what the rest homes so amiably call "the golden years."

Clement of Alexandria (VA)

[334]

[WLM]
June 24th, 1984
3811 39th Street NW, #F-90, Washington, D.C. 20016

[Postcard, illustrated with a drawing of a Tuscan order column, typed, addressed to
Dr & Mrs A E Hecht, yeah!, 19 East Boulevard, Rochester NY 14610]

Mes share colleagues,

Zoja Pavlovskis, in her splendid <u>Man in an Artificial Landscape</u>* (Brill, Leiden, 1973, p. 53, n. 129) shows that she has heard of you. Speaking of the mannerist blurring of the natural and the artificial, she says "Even in the utilitarian first half of the 20th century, accomplishments such as Frank Lloyd Wright's "Falling Water" ... (show) the trend to obliterate the dividing line ... and, to descend to ... popular culture, everywhere in the U.S. (& probably elsewhere) one can observe groups of mass-produced plastic ducks and ducklings ... displayed on their lawns by suburban lovers of illusion who have, however, never heard of Statius or Pliny."

CUPH (Comm. for Upkeeps of Poetic Houses) will get more swans which will be <u>in situ</u> when you return.

Yours in illusion,
A. Cygnet Ring, Chair

* I feel it necc. to say, because of the modicum of kidding we do, that this is for real.

[335]

[AH]
July 1st, 1984
19 East Boulevard, Rochester, NY 14610

[Letter, typed on a Minoterie D'Albi, France, letterhead]

Dear Gentleperson,

Well, we made it, and I am still mildly astonished. The car was packed as tightly and intricately as a Chinese puzzle, and if we had had to change a tire it would have meant a major operation. Nervous and tense as we were about whether we had correctly sorted out what was to be left in the Washington house and what brought with us, we lost our way (I was driving) to the Baltimore beltway (a poor start) and lost a good deal of time having to make our way through the heart (if that's the right organ) of that city, being misdirected by friendly natives along the way. Just outside of Harrisburg I stopped for gas. Now, we have bought a locking cap for our gas tank because so many lockless caps were stolen from us in Washington. Therefore, at this gas station I unlocked the cap, and set it neatly on the edge of the rear bumper while I filled the tank. I paid, Helen took over the driving, and drove some eighty-five miles, to Williamsport, where we stopped for the night. And where I discovered that the cap for the gas tank, the keys still in it, was still wedged against the rear bumper. Next day we stopped at the glass museum in Corning, which has some genuinely interesting stuff in it, especially the exhibits of ancient glass from Egyptian and Roman times to the Venetian era; after that it seems to get gross and vulgar. And we made it here by mid-afternoon. Unpacking was no inconsiderable task, and occupied several days. But I was overcome by a fit of sustained panic when, believing I had opened all the cardboard cartons, I was unable to find the manuscripts to my two books (essays and poems) and so was forced to assume that, since I remembered having packed them, I must have left them in Washington. But, mercifully, there was a carton I had overlooked, and the manuscripts were found. But this little event confirmed my feeling that during this strange transition I did not have my wits about me much of the time.

So now we are back in Rochester, and it's easy to tell it's Rochester. Word has just got out here that T. S. Eliot is responsible for a musical smash hit, and everyone here is agog. As people around here have heard it, the play, which is called "Katz," is about a Jewish tailor who makes vestments for the Archbishop of Canterbury. His opening number is especially appealing.

> My name is Sammy Katz
> And my game is vests and spats;
> If you're really in the know
> Give the miss to Savile Row;
> Get your gaiters and your hats
> From Sam Katz.

Coming back has had other stunning effects. We had forgotten, after two years away, how extraordinarily spacious and ample is our Rochester house. And it is disheartening to imagine accommodating our furniture to the more modest dimensions of the new house. This is all the more unnerving because of an event that took place the day of our departure. The moving men showed up to move our heavy furniture from East Lenox Street to the Nebraska address.[1] It was our intention that everything be stored on the third floor, leaving the first and second floor free to be occupied by anyone Georgetown was able to find. Well, the movers calmly informed us that out double-bed, as well as a bureau, and the big Tiepolo that hung in the dining-room, were too large to get up the last flight of stairs to the top. There followed a good deal of scurrying back and forth because it seemed worth trying to see whether the removal of the door to the stairs would make the necessary difference; but I had lost my screwdriver, and had to drive to a neighbor to borrow one. The door was removed, but the difference was negligible; and now what couldn't be gotten up those stairs has been left oddly scattered on the second floor. This will perhaps annoy Georgetown, but it annoys us still more. That third floor was to have been given over to two guest rooms, and since the rooms are small it seemed best to put double-beds in them, which could accommodate either a single person or a couple; for the rooms are really too small for twin beds. We are now wondering whether a good carpenter could disassemble a box spring and reassemble it on the third floor.

We are grateful for your latest postcard, with its learned information on the mannerist character of plastic ducks and flamingos, and want to assure you that we do not intend to stop there. If a thing is to be done at all it had better be done right, and Rochester seems just the place to pick up the sort of items we need to lend a truly mannerist sense to the front lawn. A fellow is coming around tomorrow to show us samples of "the wee folk," little green leprechauns, some of them fishing in plaster pools, others carousing adorably with small plaster mugs of ale upon some green plaster turf on which is inscribed, "Welcome to our Happy Home." This fellow also carries large mirror globes set upon pedestals, which would go well with the flamingos. We shall see. Meanwhile I can report that it is really blessedly cool here, and we put on sweaters in the evenings.

Carpocrates the Lewd

---

1 The Hechts had bought a house at 4256 Nebraska Avenue NW, a short walk from WLM's apartment at 3811 39th Street NW, in readiness for their move from Rochester to Washington, D.C.

[336]

[AH]
July 7th, 1984
19 East Boulevard, Rochester, NY 14610

[Letter, typed on a The Dana-Palmer House, Cambridge, letterhead, posted in a Secretary to the Corporation, Harvard University, Cambridge, Massachusetts 02138 envelope, addressed to William MacDonald, Fluxionist, 3811 39th Street. N.W., Washington, D.C. 20016, with enclosures]

Dear Author,

Knowing how heady and self-satisfied you must feel these days, after just having finished the second volume of your Roman Architecture, I offer a salutary take-me-down, a salubrious deflation that should set you well back on your heels. It consists merely of a list of words. Define the following: lampromeirakiodia; tygendis; technikrym; tolutiloquent; contorpultation; fumicables; zaimph; aseity; purrothrixine; and banaysically. You get two points if you so much as know what author they come from.

As a consolation prize, which I dare say you will badly need, I enclose not only a valuable coupon, but a still more valuable ticket which, in 1958, would have allowed you to see John Wain himself ride across the stage of the Coolidge Auditorium in his ten-gallon hat while cheerfully shooting off his six-shooters at the audience.[1]

Kropotkin

[Enclosure 1]

---

1 AH is joking: the person WLM would have seen, had he been able to use this ticket, was the English poet John Wain, who was not known for riding across the stages on which he appeared, nor for wearing a ten-gallon hat, nor for firing off six-shooters, in these respects being quite different from the American actor John Wayne.

[Enclosure 2]

[337]

[WLM]
July 9th, 1984
3811 39th Street NW, #F-90, Washington, D.C. 20016

[Austrian postcard, from the Wiener Rathhausekeller, with a painting showing revellers in flight from the Devil, while a figure to the side warns "Man soll den Teufel nicht and die Wand Malen," which can be glossed as "Do not invite trouble by talking like that," typed, addressed to A E Hecht, Lost, 19 E Boulevard, Rochester NY, 14610]

Look here, Bub,

Whuddyuh think I am, stupid? Frederick Rolfe, Baron Corvo. And it's not I believe fumicables but fumificables (though I do not have the books at hand [so] I cannot be sure);[1] & you left out some good ones, like fylfot. As for definitions, since you know them, why should I tell you? If you <u>don't</u> know them, look them up. I very much like the J. Wain ticket, but demand more because of your splendid condescension.

       Thine,
       Marta Thatcher.

---

1 WLM was right about the word's spelling.

[338]

[AH]
July 18th, 1984
19 East Boulevard, Rochester, New York 14610

[Letter, typed on a The Prince of Wales Hotel letterhead]

dear old wastrel,

    I realise that you are probably still smarting from the humiliation of having received all those difficult words from me in my latest note, and so to spare you further pain I take off on a new tack. I've long since found it useful to read my classes Vitruvius on temples, which never fails to astonish both them and me. The beautiful idea of the proportional relationships of architecture to the human body is in itself splendid, but it seems to carry an added and sophisticated meaning probably unconscious to the author: that we react to beautifully proportioned buildings out of an unconscious recognition of what ideal proportions must be, and these derive from an ideal human body, and that we all share this instinctive recognition. Moreover, the correspondence is purely an esthetic one, and bears no special or concealed doctrine within it. I wonder whether the text was known by St. Augustine, because in De Civitate Dei he offers another example of the correspondence between architecture and the human anatomy. In Book XV, chapter 26, he writes: "The actual measurements of the ark [i.e., Noah's], its length, height and breadth, symbolize the human body, in the reality of which Christ was to come, and did come, to mankind. For the length of the human body from the top of the head to the sole of the foot is six times its breadth from side to side, and ten times its depth, measured on the side from back to belly. I mean that if you have a man lying on his back or on his face, and measure him, his length from head to foot is six times his breadth from right to left, and ten times his altitude from the ground. That is why the ark was made 300 cubits in length, fifty cubits in breadth, and thirty in height. And the door which it was given in its side surely represents the wound made when the side of the crucified was pierced with a spear. This, as we know, is the way of entrance for those who come to him, because from that wound flowed the sacraments with which believers were initiated …" From this point on Augustine departs from his starting point, the human body, and proceeds with churchly and theological parallels that obviously have no resemblance to Vitruvius. And even insofar as there is any resemblance at all, Vitruvius is far more detailed in his outline of proportions, and far more interested in the sheer geometrical designs involved; he is, quite simply, both more artistic and more scientific than Augustine. Nevertheless, it is curious to find such unexpected unanimity. (I should add, to revert to an earlier point, that when I read Vitruvius to my classes it is by way of discussing the character, value and nature of "form" itself, a topic the young find academic and wearying.) I suppose it's too late for you to make use of this in your latest volume on Roman architecture (alas) and the consequent note of indebtedness to me. I don't suppose you were ever able to make use of The Golden Legend's account of the building of the Pantheon over piled earth with coins concealed inside it, another of my useful tips. I figure that if I fail to achieve immortality on the basis of my own work, I may always show up in a footnote of yours.

Give my best to the Leithausers if and when you see them.

Lorenzo Valla

N.B.: The signature here is very rare and valuable, since Valla normally signs his letters "Larry."

[339]

[WLM]
July 19th, 1984
[3811 39th Street NW, #F-90, Washington, D.C. 20016]

[Letter, typed on a The Park Plaza Hotel, 155 Temple Street, New Haven, Connecticut 06510, letterhead, addressed to Anthony Hecht, Polymodulate, 19 East Boulevard, Rochester NY 14610]

My dear Archimandrite,

Your tale of the keys put me in mind of a trip to New York a few years back. I found early on that the best way to get to the City from Northampton was to drive to New Haven, leave the car in the commodious public parking lot there, and take the train on in. Once, upon detraining at New Haven, while walking toward my car, I reached into my pocket for my key ring to find only change and my pen knife. You know the feeling – cold terror, then a rapid scramble through other pockets and the briefcase: no keys. I walked on, thinking about the local locksmiths, the Ford garage, the nearest 'phone booth, when I arrived at the car. You may remember it – an elderly, bright red convertible. I stood on the driver's side, rather upset, looking across the top of the canvas roof toward the station, when I saw a pile of little metal things on the roof. The day before, when I had arrived, I apparently put the keys up there as I withdrew my case from the back seat, pushed down the locking button, and walked off. The thieves of New Haven, being an ignorant and loutish crowd, missed them, and I drove home filled with the knowledge that fools are, indeed, watched over by divine providence … It is only fair to add that there have been a lot of experiences of that general kind in my life; I think I'm ahead of the game. There's the time I put my glasses in the refrigerator when I went for a glass of juice; the ensuing hunt I think broke all records; I now have a duplicate pair of specs. Of course geniuses like us <u>do</u> do such things.

Do you happen to know what "Besame Mucho" means? If, indeed, that's the proper spelling. It is for me the Tune of the Month, that is, I can't get it out of my head.¹ Last month it was "Thou Swell."² Retribution for an ill-spent youth?

I wrote Sydney Lea along the lines we discussed, but he has not had a chance to answer yet.

I don't envy you all the back-and-forthing, but can bring a measure of comfort to you by saying that after next summer I plan to have a clutch of grand parties for you, given, I hasten to add, over at your place. I plan to invite the boys' choir of S. Nicholas church on Wisconsin Ave., to sing "Lydia the Tattooed Lady"³ and other morsels, as well as the Loyal Order of Moose's moose. Meanwhile, and, as the English novelists love to say, still and all, do call on me for odd chores here while you are what I think of as "away."

Where <u>did</u> the <u>New York Times Book Review</u> get that picture of Muriel Spark?⁴ Taken about 25 years ago?

I am knee-deep in footnotes, illustrations lists and orders, and the like, pleasurable work by and large. I dread all the changes my (superb) editor will find necessary, and the readers' reports, which I find hard to read. Nick and Noel both came for my birthday, Noel staying over a night and Nick a few days, all a great pleasure for me. They lowered the beer level of the District noticeably (I helped a bit). The social wheel has slowed and I look forward to the balance of the summer with a good deal of pleasure, hoping to mop up the cities book and then start on the Villa book⁵ in the fall.

Meanwhile, keep in mind what Pascal said: "A father is a banker provided by nature."⁶

Yours in Christ (is there room there for <u>all</u> of us?)
A presto,
Prospering Merry May

---

1 "Bésame Mucho" (Spanish = "Kiss me a lot") is a song written in 1940 by the Mexican songwriter Consuelo Velázquez.

2 "Thou Swell" is a Richard Rodgers and Lorenz Hart show tune, written for the 1927 musical *A Connecticut Yankee*.

3 A song written by Yip Harburg and Harold Arlen in 1939, and which became one of Groucho Marx's signature tunes.

4 The photograph accompanied a review of Spark's *The Only Problem* (New York: Putnam, 1984) by Anita Brookner, which appeared in the July 15th, 1984 issue of the *New York Times Book Review*.

5 The projected book was *Hadrian's Villa and Its Legacy*, which turned into a collaborative venture, WLM's co-author being John Pinto. The book was eventually published in 1995.

6 The saying *is* French, but seems not to originate with Pascal.

[340]

[WLM]
July 22nd, 1984
3811 Thirty-ninth Street NW Washington, D.C. 20016

[Letter, typed on WLM's own letterhead]

Dear Sebastie,

    I've just had this new stationery printed and honor you with the first letter written on it. You will see that it is not showy like the stuff you like, no raised print or gaudy colors, but a simple, manly, clear-cut kind of thing – just like me. It cost $0.391 for each suite of envelope and a piece of paper, and you can remit by either personal check or money-order.

    Also, please fill in the following blanks. As you will of course wish to keep the original now in your hand, so that your archive will reveal that you were corresponding with people – or at least with one person – of taste and consequence, a xerox copy for me will be sufficient. The object is to give the correct pronunciation of these words; you may use the diacritical marks of <u>Webster's Unabridged</u>, ed. 2, or those of Vizitelly, if you wish. I rarely if ever hear the words pronounced properly; like mineralogy and genealogy they get battered by one and all. Now go:

    FALCON:_____

    RABIES:_____

    HOMOSEXUAL:_____
(hint: the BBC announcers/readers do know how to pronounce this word; here in the US apparently nobody does because they have in mind the wrong root word for the first two syllables)

    COLLATE:_____
    (certainly the IBM people have no clue about this one)

This is a serious quiz. Do not peek into your paperback collegiate speller's dictionary!

    It is with profound pleasure that I imagine your groans of envy when you see this stationery. Feel free to copy it at your bespoke printer's, though you must change the name.

    I've cut the daily drug intake by 1/3 and am thinking of going to 1/2. Huzzah!
                  Your servant, Sir.
                  Hayley Mills

P.S.: I heard from S. Lea and he wants me to submit a piece on your "humor."

[341]

[WLM]
July 25th, 1984
3811 39th Street NW, #F-90, Washington, D.C. 20016

[Letter, typed, with a now missing enclosure]

Imagine, Sir,

my great pleasure and surprise when at Braddock and Crawford's in London the other day I obtained at their annual auction of authors' memorabilia the enclosed. They are the <u>original writing pens of William Shakespeare</u>!

You can tell they are authentic because they have his name on them; no doubt he hoped that Bacon and others would be caught with them.

I bought them, at extraordinary cost, for you, in the thought that they would inspire you of an evening when the Muse, temporarily, has gone over to Ginsberg's place. Just think! He penned the (pened?) folios with them! I will alert the Department of English at Georgetown about this, so you may expect a hero's welcome in the fall of 1985, not because of your work, but as the possessor of these unique artifacts. Guard them well!

If you decide to sell them, I get 50%.

Locked in them somewhere, of course, are secrets about Dark Ladies, fair-haired Earls, and the like. You will note S. always wrote in blue ink, and this will allow you to get up articles (c) A. Hecht for the <u>TLS</u>, <u>PMLA</u>, <u>DRUNK</u> (Disgusting Revelations Unknown Nor Known), and so on. Also, the hexagonal shape is crucial: a gloss on the coffee-house bill in the BM's first folio of <u>The Tempest</u> speaks of "young Johnny's (var. Jonnie) six-sided whonkus." In any event, the possibilities are positively unextinguishable.

Don't bother to thank me. It is such a privilege to know someone as Grand as you are.

If you need help working on the work that will come about from having these precious, and indeed precocious, pens, you might ask Bob Petersson or, better yet, Joan Rivers.

Yours as a collector,
Patience!
C. Aubrey Smith

[342]

[AH]
July 26th, 1984
19 East Boulevard, Rochester, New York 14610

[Letter, typed on an Albert D'Alessandro, Counsellor at Law, letterhead, with now missing enclosures]

My dear Thraso,

Never have I known anyone to be so vainglorious about his stationery – but let it go. As for those words, I naturally pronounce them all correctly, especially RABIES, who are Jewish clergymen, as almost anyone knows. Far more important is catching what seems an important oversight in the Oxford English Dictionary. Now I have the greatest regard for old Murray and his minions, and I very much enjoyed reading his biography, Caught in the Web of Words, by his devoted grand-daughter,[1] though it's written in a spirit of moist-eyed veneration and Victorian primness. On the other hand, I know nothing like it for an account of an auto-didact's self-instruction in foreign languages. But when it comes to the OED entry on HOCUS-POCUS, abundant as are the citations, interesting as are the conjectures, I suspect that the main point has been missed. For this a lot of blame must be placed on their reliance upon the authority of Archbishop Tillotson, a good man in many ways, of course, but here very likely in error. The editors say, "Appears early in 17th c., as the appellation of a juggler (and, apparently, as the assumed name of a particular conjuror) derived from the sham Latin formula employed by him: see below, and cf. Grimm,[2] Hokuspokus. The notion that hocus pocus was a parody of the Latin words used in the Eucharist rests merely on the conjecture thrown out by Tillotson … 1694 Tillotson, Sermon XXVI, 'In all probability those common juggling words of hocus pocus are nothing else but a corruption of hoc est corpus, by way of ridiculous imitation of the priests of the Church of Rome in their trick of Transubstantiation.'" There follows a good deal of stuff, including three main definitions of the term as a noun (it is also used as a verb.) The nouns are: a conjuror or trickster; a formula used in conjuring or magical incantation; and the trick itself, sleight-of-hand. For the second of these, [John] Fletcher is cited among others thus: 1772 Fletcher Logica Genevensis. 201. The hocus pocus of a popish priest cannot turn bread into flesh." There is of course much more stuff cited. But I shall let it go at this.

Now my theory is that the old archbishop and those who follow him, including certain editors, are all wet. They might have done better if they had remembered the popular tradition of "rhyming cant" which they do remember and make use of when they come to "hugger-mugger." About this term they say: "This is the commonest of a group of reduplicated words of parallel forms and nearly synonymous meaning, including … holy-moke [sic]. Nothing definite appears as to their derivation or origin

---

1 K. M. Elisabeth Murray, *Caught in the Web of Words: James A. H. Murray and the Oxford English Dictionary* (New Haven, CT: Yale University Press, 1977).

2 Jacob Grimm and Wilhelm Grimm, *Deutsches Wörterbuch* (Leipzig: Verlag Von S. Hirzel, 1854).

…" Rhyming cant shows up in Shakespeare as well as in modern demotic speech, and is usually a covert way of saying something that is forbidden as indelicate or impious, but which can also be employed as a sort of "code" language, meant for initiates, or as a demonstration of wit. In the case of hocus-pocus, the point is that the words do not simply rhyme with one another; they rhyme with a third term that has been omitted, but known to those who are insiders. The full term, which I myself used to hear as a child, is hocus-pocus-malocus. The suppressed term, which is the one that bears all the potency, is derived from malocchio, and is exactly what magicians were thought to possess, and what gave them their sinister authority, and their ability to perform demonic tricks. Consequently, the third word of the dangerous trinity was not to be pronounced, unless in jest, and instead it was generally to be inferred from the two rhymed words that were spoken, and which implied by rhyme the unspoken third.

I can say of my theory that it looks to me at least as plausible as the bishop's and that "rhyming cant" operated in this way. Present my theory to your lexicographic friends, and let me know what they think.

Enclosed, as a token of my esteem, are two valuable tickets.

Gabriel Harvey

P.S.: According to Jean Lemaire de Belges, in his <u>Les illustrations de Gaule et singularitez de Troye</u>,[1] Noah became the father of many children after the Flood and conducted a college in which he taught religion and astronomy. In extracurricular moments he studied agriculture and discovered the art of fermentation.

[343]

[AH]
July 30th, 1984
19 East Boulevard, Rochester, NY 14610

[Letter, typed on a The Library of Congress letterhead, addressed to William MacDonald, Oneirocrite, 3811 39th St. N.W., Washington, D.C. 20016]

See here,

I've known a number of smart-asses like you, who like to show off and pretend they've read everything, and so forth; and let me tell you, they always come to a bad end. It was just luck, in all probability, that led you to Frederick Rolfe in answer to my questions. But anyway that was just a preliminary or warm-up, so to speak, and doesn't really count since it regards a Baron. Instead, consider the following: 1) Smalt, 2) Thalassocrat, 3) Griffonage, 4) Agniology, 5) Piss-prophet, 6) Forquidder, 7) Uprist, and 8) Emunctory. Now I am prepared to admit that these do not all come from one author, but they should give you paws.

Watteau! What Ho!

---

1 Jean Lemaire, *Les IIllustrations de Gaule et singularitez de Troye* (Lyon, France: 1549).

[344]

[AH]
[August ?, 1984]
19 East Boulevard, Rochester, NY 14610

[Letter, typed on a Harvard University, Department of English and American Literature and Language, letterhead, with now missing enclosures]

Dear Inspector,

    Furthermore, in his <u>Observations on Popular Antiquities</u>, John Brand writes as follows: "Winstanley, in his <u>Historical Rarities</u> writes: 'The Italians, when they intend to scoff or disgrace one, use to put their Thumb between two of their Fingers, and say, "Ecco, la fico;" which is counted a Disgrace answerable to our English Custom of making Horns to the Man whom we suspect to be a Cuckold.' He proceeds to account for it thus: 'In the time of the Emperor Frederick Barbarossa, anno 1161, Beatrice, the Emperor's Wife, coming to see the City of Millian in Italy, was by the irreverent people, first imprisoned and then most barbarously handled; for they placed her upon a mule, with her face toward the Tail, which she was compelled to use instead of a bridle: and when they had thus shown her all the Town, they brought her to the Gate, and kicked her out. To avenge this wrong, the Emperor besieged and forced this Town, and adjudged all the people to die, save such as would undergo this Ransome. Between the Buttocks of a skittish Mule a bunch of Figs was fastened; and such as would live must, with their hands bound behind, run after the Mule, till, with their Teeth, they had snatched out one or more of the Figs. This Condition, besides the hazard of many sound kicks, was, by most, accepted and performed."[1]

    And even with such historical fictions as these are false etymologies bred. The word "fico" turns up a lot in Shakespeare, as do the biting of thumbs, and both carry a good deal more vulgar energy than the rather laundered Victorianism, "I don't give a fig for so-and-so." The obvious point of the word, which has nothing to do with Barbarossa or his wife, is that the bottom, or blossom, end of the fruit (opposite the stem, and of course when fresh, not when dried) looks more like a rectum than anything else on earth except the real thing.*

    I like the pens, and am very grateful for them. I plan to use them to flunk everyone. They will carry needed authority. I have even told Evan that he may take one to school, where I hope it will properly impress both students and faculty.

*The trouble with Brand, as well as with most of the commentators he cites, is that he insists on this arbitrary connection between "fico" and horns of cuckoldry, when in fact the term usually means "up yours" in a general sort of way, and has nothing to do with one's marital status. Such are the follies of scholarship. Don Cameron Allen

---

1 John Brand and Henry Ellis, *Observations on Popular Antiquities: Chiefly Illustrating the Origin of Our Vulgar Customs, Ceremonies, and Superstitions* (London: Chatto and Windus, 1913).

records: "Augustine thinks that Noah did not take fish or insects on the Ark, because the first lived in water and the second were bred from putrefaction. He also states that the carnivores probably ate fruit and chestnuts during the voyage, but other commentators thought that Noah had to ship a cargo of fresh meat for them. Hugo of St. Victor's stalls for the amphibians were probably the result of discussions by Alcuin, Rabanus Maurus, and others concerning the fate of frogs, seals, and sirens."[1] Once again I enclose items of immeasurable worth.

Isidore of Westchester

[345]

[AH]
August 6th, 1984
19 East Boulevard, Rochester, NY 14610

[Letter, typed on a The University of Rochester, Department of English, letterhead]

Most Esteemed Sir,

As I'm sure you know, Garry Wills, in his careful account of The Declaration of Independence,[2] takes pains to address almost every phrase of the document, and pays specific attention to "the pursuit of happiness," which Jefferson derived in part from George Mason's Declaration of Rights for Virginia, 1774. Mason's statement went, in part: "All men are by nature equally free and independent, and have certain inherent rights of which, when they enter into a state of society, they cannot, by any compact, deprive their posterity; namely the enjoyment of life and liberty, with the means of acquiring and possessing property, and pursuing and obtaining happiness and safety." A claim has been made that in an early draft, Jefferson proclaimed human rights as encompassing Life, Liberty, and the pursuit of Property. There appears to be much in the way of eighteenth century political philosophy of a libertarian tone that virtually equated the owning of private property with the possession of political freedom. At that time, Socialism in any of its forms having been no serious threat to stable society, the importance of private property must have been predicated on the danger of its possible confiscation by any kind of tyranny, either royal or ecclesiastical. Doubtless it furnishes some of the ground for Max Weber's identification of Protestantism with Capitalism. Anyway, I found this interesting notion cropping up again in a papal encyclical of 1891, as recounted in a new biography of Hilaire Belloc (which I am now reading off and on between other things.) Leo XIII issued an encyclical, <u>Rerum novarum</u>, which categorically castigated the evils of laissez-faire capitalism, the callousness of employers and the greed of unrestrained competition. At the same time the document is as fiercely

---

1 Don Cameron Allen: *The Legend of Noah: Renaissance Rationalism in Art, Science & Letters* (Urbana, IL: University of Illinois Press, 1949).

2 Gary Wills, *Inventing America: Jefferson's Declaration of Independence* (Garden City, New York: Doubleday, 1978).

anti-socialist as it is opposed to capitalism. "The basis of society was, it insisted, the family; and the encyclical views 'the stable and permanent possession' of <u>property</u> as the essential ingredient of human freedom." I find it quite striking that Jeffersonian deism and papal fideism should be of one mind about private property and human freedom.

    I have some good news, though obscure, as if from a Delphic Pythoness. What I mean is that it came in the form of a phone call from Venice, and as yet I have no written confirmation of any sort. It comes, I was told by a nice-sounding lady who spoke excellent English, from the Peggy Guggenheim Collection in Venice, an outfit that had written and wired me at my Chevy Chase address with, of course, no hope of response. It was finally a phone call to the Library of Congress that located me here in Rochester. Now here is where the news becomes a trifle cloudy, due in some part to my giddy agitation in hearing it on a very long-distance phone call. One would have supposed, purely from the name, that the Peggy Guggenheim Collection referred to that lady's superb collection of modern art: paintings, sculpture, and graphics. But it appears (obscurely) that they are now handing out prizes. I believe this is a fairly new undertaking, and, as I currently understand it, they are planning to give a prize every two years, and to have that prize rotate among three arts: poetry, painting and music. I have no idea how long this has been in operation, whether any prizes whatever have been awarded before, or in what fields or to whom. But I do know that I have just won the poetry prize, and that they are going to fly me to Milan (I will be bringing Helen with me) where, on September 29th, the presentation and announcement will be made at La Scala. (I seem vaguely to recall that Bernard Shaw once addressed a group of liberal minded ladies from the stage of the Metropolitan Opera House in New York, and began by saying something like, "Finding myself as I do upon this stage, I am overcome by an irresistible impulse to sing.") I can also inform you that I was told who composed the jury that chose me: Stephen Spender, John Ashbery, and Joseph Brodsky. I was told that I should be in Milan at least two days in advance of the ceremonies for publicity purposes, and that an Italian publishing house was connected with the whole fandango. So our plan is to take a full week. We are planning to go straight to Venice for a few holidays before moving to Milan at the required time. I've cleared all this with my chairman, who has given me permission to leave. I figure I'll miss one week of classes; perhaps I'll be able to make them up. We each day expect mail regarding this matter to be forwarded from Chevy Chase – the post office there has our forwarding address – but nothing has turned up, so I am really uncertain of the background information. I may add that the prize is not enormous in financial terms, but the fact that they are flying me to Europe for it has some quality of glamour about it. Also, I am struck by the fact that they want me there two days ahead of time "for publicity purposes," which sounds like a major promotional job, though I have never heard of this prize before. They did ask on the phone that I immediately send them a vita, a photograph and a copy of my last book, which, they said, would be used for translation into Italian so that a specimen of my poetry in Italian could be read that evening at La Scala. It all sounds, as I said, a little like what you would expect of some woman overcome by the fumes issuing from a fissure in the earth over which she had placed her tripod stool. If and when some solid, written information shows up, and it turns out to be mortifyingly different from the above, I will let you know. But I can at least confirm that it is not a hoax. I was given a Venice phone number, and I actually phoned back to let them know about our plan to go to Venice first. They knew who I was, and all about the prize. So I was not dreaming.

Hugh of St. Victor

[346]

[WLM]
August 9th, 1984
3811 39th Street NW, #F-90, Washington, D.C. 20016

*[Blank postcard, typed, addressed to A E Hecht, Monophysite Salesman,
19, East Boulevard, Rochester NY 14610]*

O Sage!

Our corresp. puts me in mind of the old, beloved joke about the call Mr Jones put in to Mr Smith's office. S's secretary said S was not in, would the gentleman leave his name. "Jones," was the reply. "Sorry, I didn't get that, sir." "Jones, JONES, J-O-N-E-S!" "Could you repeat that, please, sir?" "Jesus, lady ... J as in Jabberwocky, O as in Onomatopoeia, N as in Nephrites, E as in Epiphytotic, S as in Sesquipedalial." The secretary said, "Thank you; but O as in what?"

Marvelously hot. Hunting for plastic animals for your lawn and have a good lead down in Fairfax county. Muzzy from footnotes but by no means unhappy

Yours indeed,
Hi! – Lee Sell Assie

[347]

[AH]
August 11th, 1984
19 East Boulevard, Rochester, NY 14610

*[Letter, typed on a Hyatt Regency Hotel, Nice, letterhead, posted in a The University of Rochester envelope,
addressed to William MacDonald, shond, 3811 39th St. N.W., Apt. F90, Washington, D.C. 20016]*

Right Honorable,

I've just received the most extraordinary gift from one Arthur Ross (a name, so far as I can recall, quite unknown to me) with an attached card saying, "No acknowledgement required." The book to which the card was attached is called <u>Letarouilly on Renaissance Rome</u>, by John Barrington Bayley,[1] published by

---

1 *Letarouilly on Renaissance Rome: The Student's Edition of Paul Letarouilly's Edifice de Rome moderne*

Architectural Book Publ. Co, as one of a series called, The Classical America Series in Art and Architecture. The book is edited by Henry Hope Reed, and has a preface by Arthur Ross. It is exceptionally handsome, with superb drawings of, among other things, the Campidoglio (with pictures of the Senatorial Palace before Michelangelo got to it, and the same with the Palazzo dei Conservatori) and most of the great palaces, piazzas, courtyards, villas, domes and vault decorations in Rome (with a few American and Florentine additions), not excluding St. Peter's and the Vatican. It is absolutely stunning. The series projects publication of The Architecture of Ancient Rome and of the Renaissance, by J. Buehlmann, and has already published a book on McKim, Mead and White. I observe, moreover, that the publisher appears to be jointly the Architectural Book Publishing Company, Classical America, and the Arthur Ross Foundation. It is a paperback. Fingering my way through it with delight, I came upon a photograph of the main entrance of the J. Paul Getty Museum in Malibu. It manages to be both Roman and Californian at once. All the details authentically Roman, but with a kind of ostentatious use of marble that cries out its considerable cost. And the caption declares, "Norman Neuerburg, design consultant." So you can see that an Academy Fellowship [can] really get someone places.

News of my forthcoming prize continues to trickle through in brief and costly phone calls from Italy without so much as one written word having reached me. It appears that I am the first poet to receive the award. Two years ago it was given to an American composer named Davidowski (sp?)[1] and two years hence will be given to a painter; whereupon the cycle of composer, poet, painter will repeat itself in rotation with the two-year interval between awards. This year the prize is being given jointly with a prize to an Italian poet (I don't know who) in honor and in the name of Eugenio Montale.[2] The two of us will read from our poetry (which will also be read in translation) on the stage of La Scala in Milan on the 29th of Sept., after which some operatic bozo will sing some arias. I am apparently welcome to tell this news to friends but not to the press, since they are planning a giant publicity bash in Milan. I have finished the Belloc biography, and have ended up not only detesting him, but his biographer as well.[3] I say this in the strictest confidence, since the book is published by my own publisher, Atheneum.

Alexander Poop

and Le Vatican et la Basilique de Saint-Pierre, edited by John Barrington Bayley, Henry Hope Reed, and Nicholas King, (New York: Architectural Book Publishing Company, 1984).

1 Mario Davidovsky was born in Buenos Aires and did not emigrate to the United States until 1960. He is an Argentine-American rather than an American composer.

2 The prize was the Librex-Guggenheim Eugenio Montale Award for Poetry, and the Italian poet who was its joint winner that year was Carlo Betocchi.

3 A. N. Wilson, *Hilaire Belloc* (New York: Atheneum, 1984). In a letter to John Hollander on August 23rd, AH repeated the point, and slightly enlarged on it: "Harry [Ford] just sent me a new biography of Hilaire Belloc, and by the time I finished reading it I was uncertain whether it was Belloc or his biographer (and rather disingenuous apologist) I most detested." See *The Selected Letters of Anthony Hecht*, p. 217).

[348]

[WLM]
August 13th, 1984
[3811 39th Street NW, #F-90, Washington, D.C. 20016]

[Letter, typed, addressed to A E Hecht, Guggenheimable, 19, East Boulevard, Rochester NY 14610]

13th day of Augustus' very own month, '84

My dear Senator,

That's grand news about the Guggenheim prize, and particularly about the first-class flight. I find first class very, very enjoyable. This winter, when I go to Penn. six times or whatever, I intend to ride the Metroliner chair car, my idea of grand luxe; anyway, they said they'd pay.

I've been trying to plan your singing programme for La Scala and have hit some snags, but will send it along when I get it all put together. I'm pretty sure, though, that it will include "Hut Sut Rawlson on the Brawla Brawla Sewit," and probably "Oh Promise Me."[1]

But seriously, that's awfully good news. And out of the blue, instead of a sweating session of four months or a year, as so many decisions taken about us seem to use up. I'm greatly pleased for you, and envious of the trip. It does seem to me that your career is in marvelous condition, that you are at the height of your powers, where you will I hope long remain, and that you are increasingly recognized as a great artist. The reaction of the audience to your farewell address at the Library seemed, in its own way, proof of that. Savoring friends' success is sweet.

For some reason or other I'm re-reading after many years Anthony Powell's Venusberg,[2] probably as an antidote to watching the Olympic games between bouts of manuscript shuffling. It is very funny, and, as always, I find his style and clarity very instructive, besides giving me fits of jealousy. The bit about people not being able to open the hotel door is a jewel.

I have, you will be glad to hear, arranged to have the Tenleyville[3] Metro stop opened before you come back. It is at the corner of Albemarle and Wisconsin, at Sears, just around the corner from you. They had free rides the other day, which I missed, being busy checking on my facts on the west cemetery at Wadi Zlem[4] (a genuine fact). From there (Sears, not Wadi Zlem), you will be able to go out into Maryland, quite some distance, which will be nice in case you want to Get Away For A Bit; or bomb right on on the red line of which our Metro is a part.

On a different note, a man was shot trying to get into the Library of Congress

---

1 "The Hut Sut Song," by Leo Killen, Ted McMichael, and Jack Owens dates back to 1941, and "Oh Promise Me," written by Reginald De Koven and Clement Scott, dates all the way back to 1887.

2 Anthony Powell, Venusberg (New York: Popular Library, 1978).

3 WLM has misremembered the name of the stop, which is Tenleytown, not Tenleyville.

4 Wadi Zlem, aka Wadi l-Salam, is an extensive historic cemetery situated in Najaf, Iraq.

the other night (another genuine fact). I assume he thought you were still there, & that he was sent by R[obert] Bly or the Concrete Bunker crowd.[1]

Let us reflect on Augustus' conception, this month, MMXLVII years ago now.

Yours in nictitative anamnesis,

Lillian Gash

[349]

[WLM]
August 14th, 1984
[3811 39th Street NW, #F-90, Washington, D.C. 20016]

[Letter, typed, addressed to A E Hecht, Oomphalist, 19, East Boulevard, Rochester NY 14610]

My dear chap,

You need some help. Fico, fig, doesn't refer to the anus, I believe, but to the female pudenda. I want to get you straightened out on this before you mislead your classes.

Ask any Italian waiter why he giggles so when the blonde transalpine lady orders figs.

The thumb projecting between the index and second finger does not, any more than fico, refer to cuckoldry but to sexual intercourse. The Italian sign for cuckoldry, for a cuckold, is that of the horns: index and little finger up, middle two down, hand up. Hand down = insurance against the evil eye; that is, if you can't touch the person in question. Watch for an hour along the Viale di Trastevere.

I just don't know where you get all your misinformation.

Once, caught in traffic on the Pons Aelius in my tiny 600, I was inches away from a huge, hissing bus. It was hot as hell. The bus driver and the man in front of me, who was in a snazzy convertible, got into a heated discussion. I couldn't follow all of it, but I did catch a grand sally by the bus driver: You have more horns than a basket full of centipedes. Lovely, eh? Viva Roma!

Yes, Norman Neuerburg worked long and hard on the Getty Museum and he did a hell of a job. Old Man Getty, as you know, never came to see it, so Norman would make suggestions by letter and in person in England. He has written his work up nicely in Classical America, the journal of the people who sent you the book. Norman put several of his favorite Roman locales into the Museum, including a marvelous tomb out in the back end of nowhere that he once took me to. He has never had proper credit for his work, got into a thing with the haughty Getty administrators, and now has left Roman art and archaeology for

---

1 "Two U.S. Capitol police officers shot and killed a man early yesterday after he allegedly took the gun of a Library of Congress special police officer and fired at them, according to a D.C. police spokeswoman. The suspect, a former St. Elizabeths mental hospital patient identified as Milton Smith, 25, of Brooklyn, N.Y., was discovered about 2:45 a.m. trying to enter the Library of Congress' Jefferson Building, 100 Independence Ave. NE, police spokeswoman Lania Bryant said." *The Washington Post*, August 11th, 1984.

the restoration of Mission churches and art. To go through the Getty with him is a special treat.

Off to Dallas to lecture, consult, and be a juryman for a bunch of U[niversity of T[e]X[as] students who have just spent six weeks in Roma.

A presto,

P. Invidious Naso

I did see Mary Lou(?) Leithauser at the Supermercato – Brad was in Iceland –[1]

[350]

[AH]
August 16th, 1984
[19 East Boulevard, Rochester, NY 14610]

[Letter, typed on a J-B. Huet, "Éclairage," 25 Quai Napoléon, (près du Vieux-Pont), France, letterhead, posted in a The University of Rochester, Department of English, envelope, addressed to William MacDonald, pisciculturist, 3811 39th St. N.W., Apt. F90, Washington, D.C. 20016]

Mon cher Guillaume,

I've just received your warm and generously enthusiastic letter about my Guggenheim prize, and I'm both grateful and touched by your kindness. The only thing that puzzles me is how I conveyed to you the notion that we were going first class. Nothing of the sort. We will be traveling incognito among the peasantry of Alitalia, in order to avoid the tiresome intrusions of photographers and reporters. I have already ordered some dark glasses and a slouch hat, and Helen is getting herself [an] auburn wig with ringlets in the Empire style. We will mingle with the basest of the base, and have every hope of remaining undetected. The curious thing, though, is that as of this date I have still not received one written word from those people in Italy. I suppose that's standard Italian befuddlement, and if I hadn't confirmed the announcement with several overseas phone calls I could easily suppose the whole thing was a hoax. My phone calls have come from two very nice young people there, a man (English) named Philip, and a woman named Alessandra Allaria, who have been the souls of courtesy, and have tried to supply as much information as they could, though there was much they didn't seem to know. The third person who phoned me was an outrageously imperious woman, who gave me no information at all, phoned chiefly to ask for information from me, and chided me for not having received any of the written materials (letters, a wire) she claimed to have sent me. She claimed that if this stuff hadn't reached me it was my fault, and that I'd better set about tracking it down. I did in fact phone the Chevy Chase post office, and they assured me that all first class mail had been

---

1 This note – which refers to Mary Jo Salter, who was then married to Brad Leithauser – was handwritten by WLM on the back of the envelope.

forwarded according to instructions.

I wrote earlier about John Barrington Bayley's edition of Letarouilly. Bayley was an Academy Fellow, and, if his text is any indication, one of the most pompous stuffed shirts on record. Hear this: "The chief role in art, let me repeat, is that of the Patron. All he has to do is pay for what he wants, and talent will produce it. It is very much in the classical vein, which is supremely objective, to be putting art with money. Art, ineffable and subjective, is for intellectuals." That's the sort of man I would enjoy clobbering.

Défense de Rougemont

[351]

[AH]
August 17th, 1984
19 East Boulevard, Rochester, NY 14610

[Letter, typed on a Claridge Hotel, Tucumán 535 - 1049 Buenos Aires, Argentina, letterhead]

My dear varlet,

I no sooner finished writing to you than your strangely ill-informed and bewildering letter arrived concerning the word fico. a) you write, "I just don't know where you get all your misinformation." I thought I had supplied full annotation on that matter. With regard to the topic of cuckoldry, I quoted to you from John Brand's Observations on Popular Antiquities, and he in turn quotes from Winstanley's Historical Rarities. I am perfectly aware of the normal modern way of making the sign of horns; I am simply quoting from learned sources. b) as for your curious insistence that fico refers exclusively to heterosexual intercourse (a notion in which you are gravely mistaken) it would, if you were right, not be applied between men themselves. But it has been, and by Shakespeare. In Henry V, III, vi, Pistol says, "Die and be damned! and figo for thy friendship!" This is the equivalent of "fuck you"; and if you can construe Pistol's phrase (he is speaking to Fluellen) as relating in any way to "the female pudenda," as you so astonishingly claim, you will have performed a transsexual miracle!

I am preoccupied these days with Shakespeare, in part because I shall begin teaching the plays again any day now. But my preoccupation has been interrupted by frequent phone calls from the editor of Oxford University Press in NY in behalf of Bill Arrowsmith. As perhaps you know, Arrowsmith and I are a little better than half-way through a translation of Oedipus at Colonos. We've been stuck at that point for some time because we have not been able to work out a schedule for working together; either he is free and I am not, or the reverse. Then too, little ego problems get in the way as regards who shall go or come to visit whom if a meeting can be arranged. Bill likes me to come to him; but he has no family, as I have, and Helen does not want me to leave her, while Bill can be very stuffy about the whole thing. In spite of what must sound like a difficult relationship between prima donnas, we really get on splendidly together when we actually get down to work. However, that has not been for some time, and OUP, our publisher, cannot wait much longer, or put up with more shilly-shallying. Hence, these mediating phone calls – of which nothing has come so far. But I go into all this because I asked the editor, a diplomatic young man named Curtis Church, whether Oxford would be at all interested in my collection of essays, and he said most emphatically that they would be. This was chiefly precautionary on my part. The book is currently being considered at Atheneum, and I have no reason to supposed they won't take it. But it's always possible that they might not. Such books are not likely to sell very well – unless, of course, they are written by the likes of Edmund Wilson or Lionel Trilling. And precisely because Atheneum is a small firm it is less easy for them to risk a volume that may not sell. (Poetry, of course, is a separate consideration.)

I've had a letter from the new chairman of the English department at Georgetown, who, without by any means appearing to be stiff and inflexible seems to want me to teach freshman composition; and I am doing what I can within the limits of friendliness and courtesy to resist. With only eight more teaching years before me after I move to Washington, and with more years of dutiful drudgery behind me (three of the grimmest at Smith) than I care to think of, I do hope I can, without seeming to demand special considerations, avoid that sort of task.

I have just reread Strachey on Cardinal Manning,[1] and it is brilliant and devastating. Strachey is not normally notable for impartiality, but with regard to the dogma of Papal Infallibility he is wonderfully lucid and disinterested. He is also quite clear on a number of other difficult theological puzzles. I went back to Strachey's Manning because the cardinal was a key teacher of Hilaire Belloc, and they both shared some bigotries, and were rather hateful in the same ways.

St. Thomas Aquinas

[352]

[WLM]
August 19th, 1984
[3811 39th Street NW, #F-90, Washington, D.C. 20016]

[Blank postcard, typed, addressed to A E Hecht, Prophylian, 19, East Boulevard, Rochester NY 14610]

Tasso:

Bayley gave a lecture on the survival of Roman architecture when I was an undergraduate at Harvard, & I ran across the notes I took then when I was sorting out things in Northampton; I think I had kept them as a record of a truly bad lecture. I don't think he was an Academy Fellow – he's not in Valentine's list,[2] & that

---

1 Lytton Strachey, *Eminent Victorians: Cardinal Manning, Florence Nightingale, Dr. Arnold, General Gordon* (New York: Harcourt, Brace and World, 1980).

2 Lucia and Alan Valentine's *The American Academy in Rome: 1894-1969* (Charlottesville, VA: University Press of Virginia, 1973) has an appendix listing all of the Fellows of the Academy. Bayley's name doesn't

is curious to me because just the other day a man was here who proudly said he was a Fellow and I know damned well he isn't; I said nothing. The Classical Association people are an odd lot. I agree with much they do, and am a member, but as they say that Classical architecture is the only architecture, rather than that it is a great architecture needing our understanding, I keep my distance. Reed wrote a book you may know, The Golden City,[1] a hymn to classicism, with many astute observations but with the same blind side …

Yours in Ionic contemplation,
M. Vitruvius Pollio

[353]

[WLM]
August 29th, 1984
3811 39th Street NW, #F-90, Washington, D.C. 20016

[Letter, typed on a Sheraton Airport Inn, Sky Harbor Airport, 2901 East Sky Harbor Blvd., Phoenix, Arizona 85034, letterhead, addressed to Anthony Hecht, Defectivator, 19 East Boulevard, Rochester NY 14610]

Dear Plebeian,

A time of anniversaries. Thirty years ago Dale and I, married a year or so, sailed on the Liberté for England and drove then through the home counties, then France, Germany, and Austria, to cross the Grossglöckner to Venice, which neither of us had seen before, and on to Rome to take up residence in the Academy. It seems sometimes like a hundred years ago. Being at the Academy was a very great experience; none of the petty things that went on seem to have lessened that. In a way I've been living off the capital acquired during that experience, and travels from 1951 through 1975, ever since.

And it was three years ago that I was diagnosed as having Myasthenia Gravis. The first year was difficult – falling down, unable to speak clearly, many other difficulties. I tried to adjust to the fact that I might always be that way, and the doctors, for reasons one can understand, did not suggest otherwise. Then came your offer and Helen's of a place to live in your house, one of the two or three nicest and kindest things that have ever happened to me.

And it was fifteen years ago that Dale and I parted, and started the ghastly experience of divorce with all of its attendant misery. Like you, I don't particularly want to think about the past, but I can't help it. The binding chain is very strong and I'll never break it. I am however able to look at it now with some degree of judgement and relaxation …

I see that Bill Pritchard (sp?) has sprungboard from you in the Times; I've not

appear there; nor does it appear in the more comprehensive listing given in *The Centennial Directory of the American Academy in Rome*, edited by Benjamin G. Kohl, Wayne A. Linklater, and Buff Suzanne Kavelman (New York and Rome: American Academy in Rome, 1995).

1 Henry Hope Reed, *The Golden City* (New York: Norton, 1971).

read it through yet.[1]

Tom Schumacher was denied tenure at the University of Virginia Architecture School. That surprises me. The chairman, a one-time student of mine at Yale, was, I thought, on Tom's side. He and Patty, his new wife, will be at the University of Maryland next year; that is, this coming one.

I could get a false beard and sneak in and teach Freshman English for you. Always wanted to insist on gerunds as the central core of universal thought and expression. How foolish of them to expect you to do that. More proof of the peculiarities of academic life. Nearly every day I give thanks to the Divine Trajan, who watches over me, that for once I made a sound decision when I left Smith and regular employment in that world. I'd reached the point where not only did I have little if any interest in what most of my colleagues said and did, but often couldn't figure out why they were so exercised about some insignificant point. Probably they felt the same way about me. There were few true professors among them, from my point of view.

As for the figs, Colonel, I guess it will have to be very ripe ones at five or six paces, provided that, if by any chance you win, you will announce clearly to the crowd that because I am older than you, I'm smarter.

The weather has for two weeks been beautiful: hot, dry, and clear. I've been tramping about, partly in the hope of losing some weight, looking at this city which is filled with exciting things for me, photographing, talking to people, getting what I always get out of studying buildings, a sense of the value of my work, and a renewed interest in those essential questions of my professional life – what is architecture, exactly? what makes it look the way it does? This has cut back a bit on my ms. work. I have to check every sentence, every fact, the spelling etc. of all place names, every citation; and it takes time. Some more drawings have to be made, and some others corrected, and there's always the question of leaving Modene Gunch out of the acknowledgements, or putting her in …

So things go along well, and I have no engagements until the end of September, a speech here in Washington to a grand assembly of classicists, where I share top banana billing with B. M. W. Knox.[2] October is nearly filled with lectures, at Yale, Wheaton, and the Smithsonian, twenty in all.

I realise that you have been waiting anxiously for all of this important information; if you wish to edit it before handing it in to the Rochester <u>Daily Gregarian</u>, that's OK, but don't cut too much.

Please give Helen my love, and tell her that the cleaning lady, obtained through

---

1 William Pritchard, "Pleasures of the Poison Pen," in the August 26th, 1984 issue of the *New York Times*. The article takes as its starting point AH's "Masters of Unpleasantness," which had appeared in the *New York Times* in 1982 (see AH's Letter 314 and WLM's Letter 318). It can be read online at http://www.nytimes.com/1984/08/26/books/pleasures-of-the-poison-pen.html

2 This was a joint meeting of the Classical Association of the Atlantic States and the Washington Classical Society to be held at the Hotel Washington on September 28th and 29th. WLM's address, entitled "Hadrian and Architecture" was to close the first day, and Bernard M. W. Knox's address, entitled "Fiction and Autobiography: Archolochus and Hipponax" was to close the second.

her helpfulness, is named Vilma. For six months I thought She was Beulah, which shows how well we understand each other. She brought her mother with her last week and I would have said that V. was the mother, who was a handsome, be-jeaned, up-to-date Murkan Lady. Mom speaks pretty good the Eengleesh, but whether she will return next time is unknown.

Yours in the lap of
Jayne Mansfield,
Percy Kilbride

[354]

[AH]
August 31st, 1984
19 East Boulevard, Rochester, NY 14610

[Letter, typed on a Yale University, Department of English, letterhead, posted in a Yale University envelope, addressed to William MacDonald, Jovinianist, 3811 39th St. N.W., Apt. F90, Washington, D.C. 20016]

Off-White Eminence,

Early in his career Noel Coward found himself stranded and short of cash in Naples in the company of one Gladys Calthrop. They "were forced to ask an unwilling British Consul for enough money to get them home to England. After a long bombardment of Coward charm the Consul succumbed and agreed to accept a cheque and left them while he went to get the money. 'Who shall I make it payable to?' Noel called. 'Summers Cox.' 'And some hasn't,' Gladys added."

It doesn't surprise me in the least that you are still asking yourself such questions as "what is architecture, exactly? and what makes it look the way it does?" But given the fact that you've been teaching the goddam stuff so long, and are scheduled to give twenty fucking lectures in October alone, I think you would be wise not to let it be too widely known just how ignorant you are. Show them lots of pictures, and they may not notice. And, if you care for a tip from me, you might do well to make them pictures of <u>buildings</u>. I can offer, by way of helping you along, a note I composed in behalf of our local Preservation Board. (The "Dr. Rowland Collins" referred to is an English Department colleague of mine.) "The Annabelle Philpotts House on East Cumberland is a converted comfort station once visited by President Taft during a fleeting stop at Rochester. Its main features, in an unusual marriage of the Federal and Baroque styles, have fortunately been preserved by the tireless efforts of the Landmark Society, and one may still view the original urinal, honored with a commemorative plaque bearing tasteful sentiments composed by Dr. Rowland Collins, sometime chairperson of the Landmark Society. The house itself, though somewhat cramped for space, is currently occupied by Bess Flitch, who shares it with the boyfriend, a young free-thinker named Daryll Briscomb, of her former husband, Mac. It is Briscomb who made the lovely macrame bedspread, the hooked rugs, and the antimacassars that adorn the Eames chairs. The one-burner range and leatherette barstool are especially to be admired. Watch your step going out." (That last sentence was stolen from Finnegans Wake.)

Your feelings about your Smith colleagues are precisely what I feel about mine here. It's a curious business, and more peculiar in my case, I suspect, than in yours. For most of my professional life I cherished the belief that what all of us English Professors did was to teach English (and American) literature, and we did this because we loved it, or at least a good deal of it. But this was not actually the case, as it took me far too long to discover. My colleagues were only nominally interested in works of literature. Since their professional lives required of them that they should publish, and what was expected of them in the way of publication was literary criticism, it became instantly clear to them, while dawning only slowly upon me, that from a purely practical point of view they had more to learn as regards the advancement of their careers from the reading of other critics, and the criticism of the literature of their own "fields," as distinct from the literature itself. After all, other critics were their models, or rivals, or guides to the only kind of academic success they could aspire to – while I could make my career as a poet and quite apart from this whole enterprise. I began by being astonished at how completely they seemed to command, off the tops of their minds, so it seemed, the up-to-date critical bibliographies of the authors within their jurisdictions. I should not, of course, have been so surprised at this because I took a graduate course at Columbia from a man named Clifford[1] in Pope and Dryden, and all he did was hand out and discuss mimeographed bibliographies up until the very last class, when he actually got around to reading and commenting on a few of the poems. I had taken the course because at that time those poets were pretty much terra incognita to me, or at least their charms eluded me; and I sincerely hoped that Clifford would open some sort of window and show me what I was missing. Nothing of the sort happened, of course. He addressed us as if we were just what he hoped we were – potential "scholars," which being translated means persons who would themselves someday publish criticism, and would therefore wish to be acquainted with the most important criticism of the eighteenth century. It was still further borne in on me here at Rochester, where, I may add, some of my colleagues are very decent men who do really love literary works; though every once in a while I fear that the love is partly mere gratitude for the opportunities of professional parasitism. It has always been one of my committee duties here to plan the readings of visiting poets, as well as some writers of fiction, and over the years I am proud to say I have been responsible for bringing Robert Lowell, Elizabeth Bishop, John Ashbery, Ralph Ellison, Dick Wilbur, James Wright, Joseph Brodsky and Derek Walcott to the campus. Many of these readings have been very well attended by the students, and when Allen Ginsberg came there were mobs, of course. Not a few of these readings were also quite well attended by faculty, but, alas, not by faculty of the English Department. Poetry lovers, lovers of literature were to be found among the Professors of Chemistry, and Physics, among the Professors of foreign languages and of History. But the colleagues in my department

---

1 Professor James L. Clifford.

had almost always more important things to concern themselves with, and if they hoped to get ahead there was no point in wasting the hours of an evening listening to some creep read poems. This wonderful parsimony about valuable time they were gleefully willing to set aside, however, any time a genuine "critic" came to lecture. They all showed up – and urged their graduate students to show up – to hear what were not infrequently vacuous and fearfully dull lectures. But in these cases they were witnessing somebody doing the very thing they were trying to do, whereas they were of course not really interested in writing poetry or fiction themselves, and so could not take much interest in a poet or novelist. There are, certainly, critics I enormously admire, and many I have read or listened to with profit, but I have never been able to like them to the exclusion of the materials they write about.

Pseudo Justin
(a rare signature)

[355]

[WLM]
September 13th, 1984
3811 39th Street NW, #F-90, Washington, D.C. 20016

[Blank postcard, typed, addressed to Anthony, Lord Hecht, 19 East Boulevard, Rochester, NY 14610]

Splendidissimo,

Could you send me the names of your realtors? They have gone out of my head. Friends are house-hunting, as they will be moving here from San Francisco almost certainly, and I recall how pleased you were &c.

Washington notes: I have never heard anyone whistle here. There are very few ants on the many miles of sidewalks I trace each week. I have only seen one funeral home on all my voyages. Ponder that.

In sweet relish,
Bobbie Petersson

[356]

[AH]

September 17th, 1984
[19 East Boulevard, Rochester, NY 14610]

[Letter, typed on a Dubai Inter-Continental Hotel, United Araba Emirates, letterhead, posted in a The University of Rochester, Department of English, envelope, addressed to Wm. MacDonald, Hugotontheonbiquiffinarian, 3811 39th St. N.W., Apt. F90, Washington, D.C. 20016, letterhead, with now missing enclosures]

Most Venerable,

Our realtors are Keene and Nancy Taylor; they have an office on Connecticut Avenue, near the Piccadilly Restaurant, just below the circle; and they live on Tennyson St. We regard them as the souls of courtesy, efficiency and honesty. I hope they can help your San Francisco pals.

I cannot explain your dilemmas about whistling or ants; but I can clear up the puzzle about what you regard as the strange absence of funeral parlors. This is a very delicate southern gesture to the sensibilities of the general populace. The Baskin-Robbins ice-cream stores are actually fronts for these parlors, and if, when someone comes round to take your order, you simply ask for the caskets, they conduct you straight into a back room where all their wares are on display, among suitable potted palms, soft, piped organ music, and gentlemen in striped trousers and morning coats.

We went this afternoon to buy our travelers' checks, but I have not yet allowed myself to realise that we are going to Venice and Milan on the 20th. I am too busy thinking about the classes that lie immediately before me. Tomorrow I will be teaching the central part of <u>Othello</u>, and beginning Gerard Manley Hopkins's poem, "The Wreck of the Deutschland." My renewed thinking about <u>Othello</u> for this course will, I hope, lead to a further essay for my book, which, by the way, Atheneum agreed to publish.

I enclose some items, a few of genuwine value.

It has been cold enough here for us to have built some fires in a fireplace of an evening, and, more dramatically still, to have turned up the heat on the thermostat. Alas. But it's for our final year in this climate.

I know how impressed you are going to be with this letterpaper, and how sullen, resentful and envious you will no doubt feel for days to come. Doubtless it's a good thing we're leaving the country for a while, and by the time we return perhaps you will have regained a portion of your equanimity.

[357]

[WLM]
October 27th, 1984
[3811 39th Street NW, #F-90, Washington, D.C. 20016]

[Letter, typed on a Twentieth Century-Fox Film Corporation, Box 900, Beverly Hills, California 90213, letterhead, addressed to Anthony E. Hecht, Coupleteer, 19 East Boulevard NY 14610]

Dear Mr Hekt,

My colleagues and I are hot on making a film bio of you now that you are famous. We have had several brainstorming sessions and would like to fly you out here in the company jet at our convenience. One of our people saw you in Milan and she was impressed by your carriage and hauteur, and carriage and hauteur are just what the flicks need these days. Believe me.

Some of our thoughts include: a hologram of Christ Our Mother, played by Claudia Cardinale (Jesus!), motionless; a hologram of millions of strange shadows (we're not sure just how to make them strange, but there are a lot of strange people in this racket and when you meet some of them I'm sure we'll work out a solution); bit parts for those pals of yours – Lear, Simpson, Hadzi, McDougall, Beau de Lair, and so on, who could be featured in the Special Effects we've in mind, such as the Rescue of Poetry from the Fulton Street Express, or some such.

Naturally you will have ideas about this, but we would ask you, in fact we do ask you, to keep them to yourself. Shortly you will receive our standard Bio Film Questionnaire, which you will fill out together with the blanks in our standard Poet's Contract Form (you will note it is written in rhyming couplets, but then, in California anything is possible). We did start a film on Mary McQuester Fulrd, who wrote some poems for the Abilene (Kansas) Daily Trick in the 1930s – you probably know them – but it has never been finished; one of your jobs out here will be to flesh out the script for that (Ms Fulrd was my father's aunt).

Oh, I almost forgot. You'll hafta shave off your beard. Beards are out, bards are in. You won't actually appear on the screen, but you'll hafta come to my place out in the Hills and up the Springs and I can't afford to be seen around with no Beards. Pay? Forget it. Plenty of marts, though, and a nifty steam bath. % and residuals, too …

Yours eternally,
Ziggy S.
Zygmunt Saltonstall

[358]

[AH]
[November 20th, 1984]
[19 East Boulevard, Rochester, NY 14610]

[Message typed on a The Cosmopolitan Club, 122 East 66th Street, New York, N.Y. 10021, New York, postcard, addressed to Mr. William MacDonald, Grueller, 3811 39th St. N.W., Apt. F90, Washington, D.C. 20016]

Dear Bishop,

Latest word from the Post says that they will run the review (of the Eliot biography) in the Dec. 9th issue.[1] Much rearranging had to be done because of their annual Christmas issue. So don't hold your breath. It is down in the 20s here today, and I'm doing everything I can to resist building a fire, since we have two cords of new wood but I don't want to run through it too fast. I serve again this year on the Richard Rodgers jury, which awards a huge sum for the best unproduced musical show; we convene in NYC on December 20th – Arthur Miller, Stephen Sondheim and John Hollander are on the jury too.[2] It should be fun.

[359]

[AH]
December 5th, 1984
[19 East Boulevard, Rochester, NY 14610]

[Letter, typed on a The University of Rochester, Department of English, letterhead, addressed to William MacDonald, divagator, 3811 39th St. N.W., Apt. F90, Washington, D.C. 20016]

Your Grace,

With the advent of Advent I begin casting my eyes over the ads in the hope of lighting upon notions for Christmas gifts, and I have come upon one especially festive, holiday-spirited and desirable. The only hitch is that it can only be enjoyed in Rochester and its suburbs; at least I suppose that there is no equivalent elsewhere. The ad is tastefully bordered with swags of holly and white poinsettia, and, "ALL YOURS FOR <u>ONLY</u> $89," it offers "Karate For Christmas." (Association fee not included, but then the following items all <u>are</u> included: finest facilities – I suppose

1 "Three Who Made a Literary Revolution," a review by AH of Peter Ackroyd's *T. S. Eliot: A Life*, in *The Washington Post*, December 9th, 1984.

2 Administered by the American Academy of Arts and Letters, the $65,000 Richard Rodgers Production Award for 1984 went to Andrew Cadiff, Peter Larson and Josh Rubens for *Brownstone,* and the $10,000 Richard Rodgers Development Award for the same year went to Andrew Teirstein for *Papushko*.

that's toilets – three months of lessons, Karate uniform, day and evening classes, men-women-kids, expert instruction, easy payment plan, total value $180, start classes anytime.) There's also a drawing of an oriental male, young and ferocious, with a forearm like Superman's, a Karate belt and jacket, and jet-black hair, who is slugging forward towards the reader in true Christmas spirit. It occurred to me that this would make a very attractive gift for a number of my colleagues, in particular a liberated female professor who hates men and is fiercely competitive, resentful and haughty. It might be nice to have her classes begin on Christmas Eve.

I am actually quite astonished to discover that I have only four more meetings of each of my classes before the term ends. I omit mention (and even the thought) of papers and grades. But I am astonished at how quickly this term has vanished – and pleased. Next term I will teach a seminar on Yeats, and (heaven help me) a poetry-writing workshop. On the whole I detest poetry-writing courses; my students at Rochester have never been any good at all. I taught for one semester at Harvard in 1973, and for one semester at Yale in 1977. In those two brief periods I had excellent students in poetry-writing courses; from my Harvard days, one student has published his first book with Knopf, won a MacArthur Fellowship, and is about to publish his first novel (Brad Leithauser),[1] and another (Nicholas Christopher) is about to produce his second book of poems with Knopf, his first novel with Viking, and has won an Amy Lowell Travelling Fellowship.[2] From my Yale days, a fine young poet (Norman Williams) has won an Amy Lowell Fellowship, and will bring out his first book with Knopf in a month or so.[3] By way of contrast, I will have been on the faculty of Rochester for eighteen years, come May. And in that time I have taught a poetry-writing course every year I have taught here. And I have never had any student who could write worth a damn, much less get published.

In the Christmas spirit, I enclose herewith some particularly rare and attractive items, viz. a toothpick from IL BUCO, and assorted documents.

Pendragon Rex

---

1 Brad Leithauser's first poetry collection was *Hundreds of Fireflies* (New York: Knopf, 1982), and his first novel was *Equal Distance* (New York: Knopf, 1986).

2 Nicholas Christopher's first poetry collection was *Tour with Rita* (New York: Knopf, 1982), his second, published by Viking, not Knopf, was *A Short History of the Island of Butterflies* (New York: Viking, 1986); and his first novel was *The Soloist* (New York: Viking, 1986).

3 Norman Williams, *The Unlovely Child* (New York: Knopf, 1985).

[360]

[AH]
January 21st, 1985
[19 East Boulevard, Rochester, NY 14610]

[Letter, typed on a The University of Rochester, Department of English, letterhead, posted in a University of Rochester, Department of English, envelope, addressed to William MacDonald, Eminence Puce, 3811 39th St. N.W., Apt. F90, Washington, D.C. 20016]

Eminence Puce,

The weather is a topic of conversation here. That in itself is unusual, because native Rochesterians are revoltingly hardy types, who feel that to complain of meteorological disturbances is to give way, in Samuel Johnson's words, to the play of "the imagination upon luxury." I've just finished a careful reading of Walter Jackson Bate's biography of Johnson,[1] and he seems to me easily one of the most admirable men who ever lived. But as regards the weather, it is 35 below here today if the wind-chill factor is taken into account, and it was nearly that cold last night, when we gave a cocktail party to which some 57 people were invited. It was not just the cold that was forbidding. Squalls and flurries, winds and drifting snow made stepping outdoors a species of folly. We seriously contemplated phoning everyone and cancelling, but we knew that the hardier members of the group fully intended to come, and we decided, after a number of people phoned to say their cars wouldn't start, or that they were sure they wouldn't be able to drive up the incline of their own driveways, to let the guests themselves decide whether to come or not, and go ahead as scheduled. The bash was to begin at 6 and to last till about 8. At 5:15 the bartender, a university student, phoned to say that none of the cab services she was counting on to bring her to our house was operating, and that her sorority sister, who had just come back from the airport, having driven someone there, reported the roads as impassible, the visibility nil, and refused flatly to offer a lift. So the bartender smoothly apologised and hung up. Anyway, thirty people showed up, and I made the first round of drinks, after which they were invited to help themselves. Helen had made all kinds of things to eat: a delicious paté, a rare, sliced, cold filet of beef, seasoned pecans, bread sticks lightly coated with melted cheese, along with assorted cheeses and other things. They gorged themselves shamelessly, seemed to enjoy themselves and left reasonably promptly (probably concerned about driving home). So, on the whole, it turned out successfully, rather more successfully than the inauguration down your way, if what we hear be true.[2] I may add, in the words of my father, that we never had weather like this under Roosevelt.

I enclose a number of especially valuable coupons.

Ptolemy Euergetes II

1 Walter Jackson Bate, *Samuel Johnson* (New York: Harcourt Brace Jovanovich, 1977).

2 President Ronald Reagan's second inauguration, which took place on the day this letter was written, was the coldest on record; the oath of office had to be moved inside to the Capitol Rotunda and the customary parade cancelled.

P.S.: The seriousness of the weather here last night may be gauged by the fact that hospitals cancelled all surgery except emergency work, and there was a vast overload of that kind, due to innumerable car accidents. One of our guests was to have been a surgeon, who cancelled for just this reason.

[361]

[WLM]
[January 27th, 1985]
[3811 39th Street NW, #F-90, Washington, D.C. 20016]

[Letter, typed on a University of Pennsylvania, Department of Art History, Leo Steinberg, Benjamin Franklin Professor of the History of Art, Philadelphia 19104, letterhead, addressed to Cousin Anthony Hecht, KCB, OBE, MAYBE, 19 East Boulevard, Rochester NY 14610]

A person of my distinction doesn't need dates

My dear Feel-Marshal,

I have changed my name and decided to write about Sex in Art; but not around it, <u>in</u> it. I am putting a lot of direct effort into that personally.

I like to think my new name, "Lion Stone Mountain" or, as it will probably soon become, Lionstone Mountain, (pron. LYNstn) will bring in a raft of new readers, especially from the Comanche and Nez Pierced tribes, who have as you know given up finger painting and basket plaiting pretty much and now buy paperbacks (the reason is that the finger has been given to the Bureau of Indian Affairs, and plaiting has been forbidden ever since the plaiters read Mark Twain's splendid story about the man who got woven into sixty-six feet of carpet).[1]

In other words, I've done my first stint at Penn., where my pals gave me Leo's office in which to meet students, goof off, etc., the way you professors do. I'd send some of this stuff to you, but I'm not sure you could handle it.

Getting 69.4% of your invited guests at -40° (I just love that little ° thing) was pretty good. At one point, according to one of those voices that come out of the furniture, we had a W/C factor of -40° here, too. I can't be sure, as I keep my W/C (00) to you) in the house.

Speaking of houses, the work installing the pink fluorescent lights up under the

---

[1] "The Story of Grandfather's Old Ram," collected in *Roughing It* (Hartford, CT: American Publishing Company, 1872): "Parson Hagar belonged to the Western Reserve Hagars; prime family; his mother was a Watson; one of his sisters married a Wheeler; they settled in Morgan county, and he got nipped by the machinery in a carpet factory and went through in less than a quarter of a minute; his widder bought the piece of carpet that had his remains wove in, and people come a hundred mile to 'tend the funeral. There was fourteen yards in the piece. She wouldn't let them roll him up, but planted him just so–full length. The church was middling small where they preached the funeral, and they had to let one end of the coffin stick out of the window. They didn't bury him–they planted one end, and let him stand up, same as a monument. And they nailed a sign on it and put–put on–put on it–sacred to–the m-e-m-o-r-y–of fourteen y-a-r-d-s–of three-ply–car—pet—containing all that was–m-o-r-t-a-l–of-of–W-i-l-l-i-a-m–W-h-e–."

eaves of your Washington place is nearly finished. I went over the other night and turned on the ones already connected and was pleased, and you will be, to note that they spelled SH T. If you want me to keep them this way, or can think of a letter to put in the blank spot, call.

Still speaking, this time about Mark Twain, I want to inform you that I've read most of J. Kaplan's shorter book on Mark Twain,[1] which is a hell of a lot more readable than his Twain / Clemens work.[2] Come to think of it, I didn't finish the latter, so actually I read about the same amount in both books, which means that because I finished the shorter, and better, book, I'm ahead of the game; I recommend to you, that when you get two books by the same author, you read only the shorter of the two (that thought is probably in Dr Johnson's works, too).

Have you ever browsed in Ambrose Bierce's <u>Devil's Dictionary</u>?[3] Many splendid entries, and a rich course of perms.

Yours in the Madonna's lapp,
Thos. of Schenectady

[362]

[WLM]
January 28th, 1985
3811 39th Street NW, #F-90, Washington, D.C. 20016

[Blank postcard, typed, addressed to Anthony, RRev. Card. Princ. Hecht,
19 East Boulevard, Rochester NY 14610]

Yeminentz,

The old count of Urbino: "His terrible profile, disfigured by a sword blow in a tournament that cost him his right eye and the bridge of his nose …" (Frederick Hartt, <u>History of Renaissance Painting</u> [New York, Abrams, 1974], p. 243). I'm inclined to think that in such matters, H. knows what he is talking about. I can't find anything else on the topic.

As you probably know, the Great Duke of Wellington said, "Make water when you can"; it's the only saying attributed to him in John Gross's anthology of aphorisms. As I grow older, I often think of it.

Yours in the lap of Mary,
Sidney Toler

---

1 Justin Kaplan, *Mark Twain and His World* (New York: Harmony Books, 1983).
2 Justin Kaplan, *Mr Clemens and Mark Twain: A Biography* (New York: Simon & Schuster, 1968).
3 Ambrose Bierce, *The Devil's Dictionary* (New York: Dover, 1980).

[363]

[AH]
February 1st, 1985
[19 East Boulevard, Rochester, NY 14610]

[Letter, typed on a Hotel Excelsior, Dubrovnik, Yugoslavia, letterhead]

Most noble and esteemed good sir,

When I returned to my office at the university after an absence of about two years the evidence of its occupancy by others was clear enough. I had agreed to let the space be used at the discretion and convenience of the English Department. To have found some old blue books and exam forms lying about did not disturb me, and it was but the work of a moment to rid myself of this debris, along with an extra and unwanted desk and chair. There remained a number of books, dog-eared and paperbacked for the most part, but what surprised me was to find the 1978–79 two-volume edition of Who's Who in America.[1] It was not marked as the property of any individual, nor did it bear the marks of belonging to the English Department or to the university. I let it sit there on my shelves for the whole first term, supposing that its owner and abandoner might yet return to pick it up. But no claim was made upon it, and as I have never owned such a thing myself, feeling the price to be ridiculously high, and having no real use for it as a reference tool – having in fact no other interest in it but the standard one of personal vanity, I decided at long last to bring it home (to, in the old military terminology, "liberate" it) and browse about.

It has turned out to be more revealing than I had supposed, and in very unlikely ways. It contains a wholesale trade executive, a professional baseball player, and a chess player. On the other hand it does not list Laurance Roberts, nor Charles Reiskamp,[2] the head of the Morgan Library in New York. F[rank] E. B[rown] is there, and you and I, but I'm really quite astonished by the conspicuous absences, to say nothing of those accountants and heads of food chain stores who contribute little enough to the glory of the nation. It's like joining a club, and then finding out who the other members are. This happened to me recently, and I may have written you about it. I was, after a long probationary waiting period, elected to the Century Club of New York, largely through the sponsorship of William H. Whyte and Russell Lynes. It is supposed to be a club of professionals and amateurs of the arts, and it is true that I do seem to know at least the names of some of the eminent members. But among the membership roster is listed – prepare to shudder – Caspar Weinberger. One must suppose him to be among the amateurs, and it taxes the imagination to consider which of the arts he practices, but my considered opinion is classical ballet. Anyway, my initial impression of Who's Who is so disappointing

---

1 *Who's Who in America*, 40th edition, 1978-1979 (Chicago: Marquis, 1978).

2 AH had been looking in the wrong place. The Director of the Morgan Library was Charles R*y*skamp, not Charles R*ei*skamp, and the 40th edition of *Who's Who in America* did in fact contain an entry for him.

that unless I dig up some pretty interesting material soon I may very well wipe out my entire career as a thief and bring the damn thing back to where I found it. As you know, biographees (as we are so hideously called) are invited to contribute pearls of wisdom, by way of letting the world know what it is that made them the important people they so obviously are, and I must admit that I do rather enjoy these fatuities. They are a sort of very welcome bonus. Take, if you will, the remarks of Stanley Roger Smith, professional tennis player: "God has given me certain talents. I feel a great opportunity and responsibility to develop and use these talents to their fullest on and off the tennis courts. I see great potential in our country and especially in our youth today, and I hope to provide some leadership and direction that this youth will need to develop their potential constructively. God has given me a great life so far and I plan to rely on His guidance to take me the rest of the way." And then there is the almost biblical wisdom of Richard A. Nunis, amusement park executive: "Do the best job you can with the job you are given to do. Those who look over the hill never climb the mountain." Mr. Nunis has a real way with words, and it is clear that he deserves the eminence to which he has risen. Some of the most stupid and pretentious statements, alas, come from persons identified as "educators." In fact, come to think of it, you and I might collaborate on a new parlor game, like Trivial Pursuit, that could sweep the nation and make us rich. We would cull the quotations from <u>Who's Who</u> and challenge the reader to guess the profession of the author of each. Some, of course, like the tennis player, are dead give-aways, but there still may be enough to make it a going thing. So I'll hold on to my stolen property for a bit.

Stephanus Baluzius
(a very rare signature)

[364]

[WLM]
March 4th, 1985
[3811 39th Street NW, #F-90, Washington, D.C. 20016]

[Letter, typed on a The Park Plaza Hotel, New Haven, Connecticut, letterhead, with enclosure]

Dear Senator,

The only thing that <u>Who's Who</u> ever did for me was to bring, early on, a flurry of calls from New York bond salesmen, rubbing their hands in their boiler rooms at the thought of all those naive doctors out there. But Noel and Nick liked seeing their names in print when they were fairly small. Who is not in the book is interesting: some grossi pezzi obviously have their names taken out. I don't think being in there has ever done any good, though I did mention it (the only time I have, other than to Noel and Nick) to the rental agent here who seemed uneasy at the thought that I was not connected with any company or institution. She brightened right up and said that a letter of recommendation from my lawyer would do. And it did.

The nuggets of Eternal Wisdom that you quote make me think of the paragraphs that one's classmates feel obliged to include in their quinquennial college reports. Stupefying nonsense, though I suspect sometimes they are the result of utterly unsuspected senses of humor.

I enclose some crucial literature. I think the TLS phlogistenic cut is from Eric Korn's column, often worth reading.

Have finished my stint at Penn. which I enjoyed. The students were good and lively, and even the auditors spoke up. Since I don't teach the usual art history line, I like to think I stimulated the kids some. They were all Ph.D. candidates, and I expect some good papers. Saw a lot of my old friends the McCoubreys (great admirers of yours) who among other things are sane, a rare condition. Had dinner with Bob Venturi and Denise [Scott-Brown], and what with the short Metroliner commute, as they say, it was a good experience. Being overpaid didn't hurt, either.

I am somewhat plagued by waiting to see things I've written. There are five or six articles out there somewhere, two written in 1981, that call me Dad. A Smith Museum catalogue essay may amuse you, and that will be out next month and I'll send a copy along. The Roman book lay untouched at Yale throughout the strike, and now that the strike is settled I await news of motion which, alas, has yet to come through. But, valiant and strong, of course, I keep on working. Have I confessed to you that I want to try to write a novel? Yes, the idea makes me laugh, too. But why not? Can't be any worse than some of that stuff out there. But come to think of it ... Nice to see that your protegé Brad L[eithauser] has gotten some nice notices.[1] A few weeks back I invited Bryan and Mark [Leithauser] to dinner, but on the day itself I felt a bit unstable and had to call it off. I'll try again. They do like cold pizza and Pennsylvania red, don't they? Nice people, in any event.

Sometimes I sit around trying to figure out what to do with my life. I'm not often unhappy (which may be due to insensitivity, or a lack of brain power), but there doesn't seem to be much to do except try to write. I'm about to chuck most of the freight of scholarly requirements – in fact, the Roman book has very few footnotes – and strike out toward a different audience. All this is part of leaving institutional life, which I don't care for. But writing, which I find difficult and rewarding, is hardly a whole life. Luckily, I keep very busy; what "retired" people do I've no idea; it would drive me to mild madness or worse.

We vacillate here between 79° temperatures and bitter cold winter days. The regulatory agencies are, obviously, failures.

---

1 The reviews were of Leithauser's first novel, *Equal Distance*. Christopher Lehmann-Haupt's in the January 3rd, 1985 issue of the *New York Times* was especially positive: "This is a perfect epiphany of contemporary Japan, but then everything upon which Mr. Leithauser casts his antic eye seems to transform itself into its essence, be it comic or pathetic, ugly or beautiful. His appetite for the world appears to be insatiable, and his capacity to make it into language, entirely without limit. 'It was an absolutely immense stroke of good fortune on your part to run into me,' Greg says to Danny early in their friendship, only half kidding himself. Mr. Leithauser could say the same thing to his readers, but in all sincerity. And we look forward immensely to the next encounter."

[Enclosure]

lished by the Denver Chemical Manufacturing Company (of New York, curiously) in the interests of spreading about the globe (Drogueria "Standard", 2 Strada Zorilor, Bucharest; Muller and Phipps [Malaya] Ltd, 26 Gang Passer Baroe, Batavia) the Good News about Antiphlogistine. Antiphlogistine was a sort of dove-grey therapeutic artificial mud, with which sufferers from divers ills were comprehensively poulticed, and had little to do with Phlogiston, except that today both are equally unfashionable (nothing is so powerless as an idea whose time has gone), except again that while Phlogiston never did exist, never rising above the rank of postulant postulate or apprentice hypothesis, Antiphlogistine demonstrably did and I still bear the scar of an over-zealous dose. (It looked, come to think of it, rather the way I've always imagined *hyle*, the primal matter of the Aristotelians; a universe of medicated clay is no harder to imagine than a universe of quarks.) "Bloodless Phlebotomist", I suppose, is a good thing to be, even if it does sound like a rather refined term of Parliamentary abuse.

My interest in the crossword, an early example of the form, petered out when I realized I was ineligible for the prize of a clinical thermometer, but I noted with relish – we snatch, as I said, at whatever distinction we can – that 19 down BIN was, for surely the only time in history, clued as "Bismuth Subnitrate (abbrev), 3 letters".

[365]

[WLM]
March 4th, 1985
[3811 39th Street NW, #F-90, Washington, D.C. 20016]

[Letter, typed, with a now missing enclosure]

My dear Doctor Eye Kew,

1 As WLM thought, this is an excerpt from Eric Korn's "Remainders" column, and comes from the August 10th 1984 issue of the *Times Literary Supplement*.

You can see from the enclosed what great strides the history of art is making. I always liked Roden, didn't yew? Rodent, maybe. But I particularly have always been au fond of the Segmatura Chapel. I think probably, though, they mean the Smegmatura Chapel, don't yew? You know how Sancho, I mean Sanzio, Raphael <u>was</u>! Always fucking up.

Additional strides are being made also by the dogs, which we are going to. $500 to get there, supporting; like a fire hydrant, maybe?

A basic problem here in The Most Powerful City in the World is that we're gradually being flooded. I think it is because so many politicians are throwing out babies with the bath water. After decades of trying, they now have the phrase approximately right (Yew'll recall that they used always to refer to "throwing out the baby with the bath") and are off and running with it. The amount of bath water slung out of the House of Representatives last week alone was enough to fill the Gatun Locks[1] several times over. It flows down the hill at the west side of the Capitol and then spreads out along Pennsylvania. Luckily I'm up high. But the real problem is that we are running out of babies. Can you help? Not babes, babies.

I hope to get the baby concession for the Congress. Bath water is easy; you can fake it. But babies are something else, short supply. Inventor and I are starting on a plastic baby product, good for throwing out with; millions in it, probably.

Yours unplugged,
Patty O'Furniture

[366]

[WLM]
March 19th, 1985
[3811 39th Street NW, #F-90, Washington, D.C. 20016]

[Letter, typed on a Sheraton Airport Inn, Phoenix, Arizona, letterhead,

My Lord,

A thing has befallen me somewhat like your telephone call last year about the Venice Prize. Out of a moderately clear blue sky, one morning recently, the 7th, to be exact, I had a call from a young man I know, Paolo Polledri, a Venetian by birth but now an architectural historian in California. He is an assistant to an old friend, a distinguished art historian, Kurt Forster, who is now the head of the newly formed J. Paul Getty Center for the History of Arts and the Humanities, now installed in Santa Monica, but only temporarily, until the 780 acres of land Getty once bought in the Brentwood section of northern LA has been cleared and supplied with millions of dollars' worth of buildings that have been designed by one Richard Meier, as hot a ticket in Modern Architecture as you could hope to locate.

Well, Paolo said, "You know, Beel (Venetians talk that way, as <u>you</u> know), I've been

---

1 The Gatun Locks are one of the three sets of locks servicing the Panama Canal.

hoping to get you out here; and I'm calling to see if you want to be here next year at the Center." He went on to mention a free, furnished apartment, travel money, research money, research assistance, Washington-LA-Washington expenses, and a large* salary in addition, plus a number of other things that in my astonishment I failed to jot down. I told him yes, I was interested†, and the next morning, the 8th, at 9 a.m., a Federal Express deliveryman handed me a very large red, white, and blue envelope which I signed for and carried upstairs in a most excited mood (also in my hands), for I had never received a Federal Express envelope before and knew from the television ads that all important people get them. The envelope, however, was difficult to open.

But once inside it I found a formal letter from Forster, making a genuine, and bona fide, offer just as Paolo P. had said he would. Plus more money to ask people to come to the Center!

I think I'll go. All that money and the beach, plus all those California girls. I have to give them a bibliography of my work, state a project, and that's it. When I asked PP what I had to do besides think and write, he replied "Nothing." That's all right, isn't it? At last I will be able to prepare my monograph on the grand church of S. Messalina in Flagrante ("sempre aperto"), of which of course you have heard.

I must say it is nice to be asked, and just as nice to be asked without warning. I had never thought of such a thing, for when PP, on a postcard, had said earlier that he was "waging a discreet campaign" to get me out there, I thought of course that he meant the usual, a lecture or two. There are to be a dozen or so scholars from Yerp 'n Murka in residence, late Sept. / early June.

Forster wants I think to make it The Place of Its Kind in the World, and now that he's got me, success for him is in sight.

Working on the Hadrian's Villa book. Not a peep from the Yale Press, though I was supposed to have a copy editor some time back. I'm not particularly worried, but I'm beginning to think a query is in order. They waited so long, and with such graceful patience, for the ms., that I can't say much, or anything in a loud voice.

Warming here. There?

Yours in the bowels of Our Saviour, Buzzy Osmond
B. Osmond

* <u>Very</u> large

† Which will surprise you

[367]

[WLM]
March 27th, 1985
3811 39th Street NW, #F-90, Washington, D.C. 20016

[Letter, typed, addressed to Anthony, Baron Hecht, 29 [sic] East Boulevard, Rochester NY 14610, with enclosure]

Dear Tony,

Thought you might like to see the enclosed, sent to me by the Pintos.

Jim Ackerman was here for dinner a week or two ago and spoke of having resigned from the Academy board of Trustees. Does that signify? From the latest printed matter, it looks as if the old place is doing fairly well. Two young people I know have won the prize, one, a son of my college roommate, for the present year, in art history, another, a junior professor at the University of Virginia, in landscape architecture, for next year.

I've decided to go to lotus land in September.[1] I'm surprised at how much will have to be done to effect the move; nothing, of course, compared to the effort you and Helen must summon. But of course you are young and stalwart (what an odd word that is).

I must now go downtown to the Historic American Buildings Survey, a worthy, underfunded subdivision of the Department of the Interior, and talk about classicism in architecture to the staff. Nice people, free lunch. My consulting business is beginning to grow a little, with the National Geographic and the Smithsonian tossing me a few jobs. One, on the Vatican, is great fun. Like all institutions with research departments, those places don't know much.

My health has on the whole been acceptable, though I still have unaccountable lapses in energy levels, resulting in much sleep and lounging about, a sore body, and so on. They last one or two days and occur every three or four weeks. In themselves they are annoying but not serious, though the last one, just over, scared me a little as I began to think about the rapidity with which a myasthenic's condition can change for the worse ... But I am now my bouncy, charming, resistible self again.

It is warm and sunny, with 70/75° forecast for the day. The cherry blossoms are promised for April first.

Thine,
A Herald, In Italy

---

1 WLM had been awarded a Getty Scholarship, which required that, between September 1985 and June 1986, he reside in "lotus land," i.e. California. As the Getty Foundation's website explains, "Getty Scholar Grants are for established scholars, or writers who have attained distinction in their fields. Recipients are in residence at the Getty Research Institute or Getty Villa, where they pursue their own projects free from academic obligations, make use of Getty collections, join their colleagues in a weekly meeting devoted to an annual research theme, and participate in the intellectual life of the Getty."

[Enclosure]

The Department of Classics
The University of North Carolina at Chapel Hill

is pleased to announce a lecture series

ROMAN ARCHITECTURE: CLASSICISM FULFILLED

by

William L. MacDonald

Historian of Architecture
Washington, D.C.

Last Rites for Vitruvius

A conservative whose studies enshrined the past, Vitruvius helps only marginally in understanding subsequent Roman buildings. His fame to the contrary, meaningful Roman architecture is not Vitruvian; the archaeological evidence and his text do not match. Normative analysis gains little ground because Roman architecture was evolutionary and so diverse, so to understand its meaning and persistent influence other views are needed.

Tuesday, April 9

Connection and Passage

Urban needs and civic pride produced fulfilled Roman architecture. The character of the cities and towns was established not by town-planning but by suitably functional and symbolic buildings. These were the essential, interdependent parts of urban configurations, members of civic families rather than of stylistic groups. This is seen in the means provided for circulation and urban articulation: thoroughfares, plazas, and the fountains, arches, exedras, and the like met along the way.

Wednesday, April 10

Empire Imagery

Classicism in the Greek sense, already altered in hellenistic times, was shifted once again under the empire. The orders were liberalized and, more important, deployed in novel ways. In combination with Roman spatial innovations, they formed the cardinal compositional themes of Roman imagery. Such themes, executed often in a quite untraditional way, spread across the empire and at times approaching baroque modes, were Rome's tectonic emblems.

Tuesday, April 16

Form and Meaning

Fulfilled classicism was popular, urban, and impure, an architecture of town purposes and town life. It is not a style in the traditional art-historical sense, and not as is sometimes said a language. Rather it is the purveyor of a visual narrative, its ultimate product the visible, usable town: it is an architecture of content rather than of style. Its buildings did not stand alone but belonged together, linked by their own versions of ancient classicism.

Wednesday, April 17

All lectures will be held in the Art Classroom and Studio Building, Room 121 (ground floor), on the UNC-Chapel Hill campus, at 8:15 p.m.

In addition, two seminar sessions are scheduled with the following topics for discussion:

The Role of Architecture in Roman Urbanism
Thursday, April 11, 1985, 4:30 p.m.

The Architecture and Planning of Luxury Villas.
The Nature of Imperial Architectural Imagery
Thursday, April 18, 1985, 4:30 p.m.

Both Seminars will take place in Room 117 of the Art Classroom and Studio Building

[368]

[AH]
April 20th, 1985
[19 East Boulevard, Rochester, NY 14610]

[Letter, typed on a The University of Rochester, Department of English, letterhead, with enclosure]

Esteemed good sir,

    I have one more week of classes to go, and, believe me, I am grateful. You may cast your mind back on lousy work that students turned in to you some time in the past, but I'll wager you never had anything to match a sentence written for me last semester, which is so breath-taking that, while I never bothered to copy any of the monstrosities I encountered in the whole of my teaching career, which began in 1946, I have decided to enter this in my commonplace book, so as never to forget it. It demands a sort of immortality, and you are welcome to quote it on solemn occasions. It will have the more impact if it is pointed out that it was written by a senior English major.

    "Each of these objects are used in an extremely opposite manner than that which they were originally devised."

    No one yet has made an offer on our house, and we are getting mighty nervous.

                  Love,
                  John Tzimisces, Imp.

[Enclosure]

> **CARDIOLOGY AND INTERNAL MEDICINE**
> **PROFESSIONAL ASSOCIATION**
> 5530 WISCONSIN AVENUE   SUITE 505
> CHEVY CHASE, MARYLAND 20815
>
> JACK P. SEGAL, M.D., F.A.C.C.
> STANLEY M. SILVERBERG, M.D., F.A.C.C.
> RECEP ARI, M.D., F.A.C.C.
> GARY P. FISHER, M.D., F.A.C.C.
> LEWIS C. LIPSON, M.D., F.A.C.C.
> SEAN M. DWYER, M.D.
>
> Telephone 301 - 656-9070
> Answering Service 301 - 251-8191
>
> **DISABILITY CERTIFICATE**
>
> DATE _____
>
> TO WHOM IT MAY CONCERN:
>   William
> I HEREBY CERTIFY THAT _____
>   MacDonald
>
> ~~HAS BEEN UNDER MY PROFESSIONAL CARE AND~~ WAS:
> ☒ TOTALLY INCAPACITATED
> ☐ ~~PARTIALLY INCAPACITATED~~
> FROM _dawn_ TO: _dusk_
> REMARKS: Due to his crude habit of switching back and forth between vodka martinis and French 75's.
>
> SIGNED _Anton Chekhov, M.D._

[369]

[WLM]
May 11th, 1985
3811 39th Street NW, #F-90, Washington, D.C. 20016

[Letter, typed on an Ohio Stater Inn, Columbus, Ohio, letterhead, addressed to H. E. Lord Hecht, 19 East Boulevard, Rochester NY 14610, with enclosures]

Yessirree bob,

That's the hell of a sentence all right. As good as any of that "life reeked with joy" stuff, taken from student papers, that circulates so widely. It is a bit much, though, that your student should have taken such pains to imitate you …

I'm sorry about the anxiety caused by the problem of selling the house. Perhaps by now some action has, as we say, presented itself. I wish some kind of action would present itself to me, if you get my drift.

Four clear months ahead of me, with no engagements of significance, in which to work on the Hadrian's Villa book. Some progress has been effected. The book at Yale is being copy-edited by one of those c-eds "in diapers," as Jimmy Casson says. She wants to change my meaning at times, and is in love with her own "not wholly unexceptionable style," as she puts it. And the editorial people want to change my illustrations references, so I had yesterday to compose a two-page letter rehearsing all my reasons and strategies, and putting my dainty little feet down firmly. But at least, after all this time, it's in the works; publication, they say, next Spring.

Wrote a little piece for a Smith Museum show of photos, and if the niggardly staff up there ever gets around to sending me my copies of the catalogue in which the piece appears,[1] I'll send you a copy. Free, of course.

Had a fine time with Hadzi and his lady Cynthia when lecturing at Harvard recently. He's going strong.

The shape of the Getty plot slowly unfolds. I now have the list of G[etty] Scholars, as We Are Called, and know only one, a woman from Brown. [Jan] Kott,+ the Bologna [i.e. Carlo] Ginzburg, are the only names I recognize; there are a dozen in all; publicity release, with the usual errors, due out any day now.

On my own I've cut back on the drug and symptoms have not increased. Mysterious business; feel pretty good most of the time.

I enclose a real L. A. ballot from the recent municipal election. I thought you might like to know of the Part Time Clerk. I am taking surfing and roller-skating lessons, and am buying second-hand copies of <u>Oui</u> and <u>Gash</u> so I'll be able to recognize people when I get out there.

Yours in the bowels of Happiness,
Andrew, Fool for Christ's Sake

---

1 Chester Michalik, *Photographs*, with a foreword by Charles Chetham, and an introduction by William L. MacDonald (Northampton, MA: Smith College Museum of Art, 1985). The catalog was to accompany an exhibition at Smith held between April 4th and June 16th, 1985.

[Enclosure 1]

SAMPLE BALLOT

**CITY OF LOS ANGELES
PRIMARY NOMINATING ELECTION
AND CONSOLIDATED ELECTIONS
APRIL 9, 1985**

INSTRUCTIONS TO VOTERS

Punch ballot cards with punching device attached to vote recorder. Do not use pen or pencil.

To vote for a candidate of your choice, punch the ballot card in the hole next to that candidate's name. Vote for only one candidate for each office. To vote for a person not on the ballot, write both the title of the office and the candidate's name in the blank space left for that purpose on the gray ballot envelope.

[Enclosure 2]

MUNICIPAL BALLOT
City of Los Angeles Primary Nominating Election
Tuesday, April 9, 1985

FOR MAYOR

Vote for one

EILEEN ANDERSON – Singing Dancing Candidate	5 →
SAL GENOVESE – Community Advisor/Educator	6 →
JAMES E. HARRIS – Auto-worker	7 →
JUDY L. HUFFMAN – Consultant	8 →
WILLIAM LOSKA – Baker	9 →
TOM BRADLEY – Mayor	10 →
WALTER "BUCK" BUCHANAN – Political Activist	11 →
VENUS DE MILO – Part Time Clerk	12 →X
JOHN FERRARO – Member, City Council	13 →

[370]

[AH]
May 18th, 1985
[19 East Boulevard, Rochester, NY 14610]

[Letter, typed on a The University of Rochester, Department of English, letterhead]

Eminence beige,

My career here at the University of Rochester, after seventeen years, has ended on a rather sour note. But then, at least officially, and possibly personally as well, there seems to be some puzzle about how they ought to feel about my departure. Much has been made, in an official sort of way, about the fact that I am adopting the plan of "early retirement," and I've received two formal notices to the effect that nothing less than the Board of Trustees has voted me into "emeritus" status. (From the university's point of view, this has the merit of allowing them to keep my name in the catalogue and anywhere else they care to use it.) At the same time, they know very well that I am going to take up full-time teaching duties elsewhere, and there is a good deal more resentment about this than I expected to encounter or was prepared for. And it came like a blow in the solar plexus.

Last year, when we were still in Washington, one of my best-known colleagues, a Dickens scholar named George Ford, arrived at the year of his retirement, and there was a huge fandango in his honor. Since he had also written a book on D. H. Lawrence, a composer at the Eastman School set a passage of Lawrence to music for voice and orchestra, and a full evening's concert program was devised to honor the occasion. Moreover, on another evening, distinguished scholars in his field, as well as friends from other institutions, came to lecture on their respective fields, and salute the retiring guest of honor. And this year, another of my colleagues retired, and something of the same was done for him. In fact, we put up as overnight guests some who came to honor him. There were, as before, personal tributes, a huge cocktail party and dinner for 250, and a concert, though a smaller one in this case. But smaller though it was, preparations for it began last September. Well now, on the 18th of March my chairman wrote to me asking if I would like to have some sort of gala in my own honor. Please recall that this was about a month before the close of the academic year. He suggested a poetry reading by me, and by some poet-friends I might care to invite from elsewhere, to be followed by cocktails and dinner. He specifically suggested the name of Wilbur. I was able to tell him immediately that Wilbur was in the south of France, translating Racine, difficult to reach and unlikely to accept. I was able further to point out that so late in the course of the academic year it would be very difficult for any poets who were also teaching to get away from the burdens of end-of-term to come here on such short notice. He seemed embarrassed by having brought the proposal up so late, and asked me to let him try to work out something anyway. I never heard from him on the topic again. The university contrived to allow my retirement to pass unnoticed, and I have been really quite hurt by this. It has, however, at least the beneficial effect of making me look forward with uncomplicated eagerness to leaving here.

Out of as near a facsimile to a clear, blue sky as one can hope for in Rochester, I received a letter from one Edward Klein, editor of the New York Times Magazine, asking me to write an article for them. By way of indicating the sort of thing he had in mind, he sent me a back issue with a cover article on Nicaragua by the Peruvian novelist, Mario Vargas Llosa.[1] It certainly was a spectacular spread, but not, of course, the kind of thing I could do. So I pondered about what I could possibly attempt, and wrote back explaining about our move to Washington this summer, but saying I would greatly like to write for them. Since then, we have had a very cordial phone conversation, and he seems eager to get me to write, and is willing to send me abroad or anywhere else for that matter. I've proposed a number of topics to him, of which the one he embraced with the most enthusiasm was a profile of Ted Hughes, now the English laureate, whom I knew when he was married to Sylvia Plath and they were both in Northampton. Another topic, which he took note of for future reference, had to do with the celebrations planned for 1986, when the Statue of Liberty reappears with suitable fanfares, including a text by Wilbur set to music by William Schuman.[2] Since speaking to him on the phone a couple of other topics have suggested themselves. 1) What's going on in the Getty camp in California, 2) new methods of restoration now being employed in Italy on canvases and on such frescoes as the Sistine Chapel. But I am a little daunted not only by the prospect of our move, but by the expectation of receiving any day now the proofs of my book of criticism, which should run to about 300 pages, and which I want to attend to with care. So I may have to ask Mr. Klein to let me postpone accepting his invitation till a later time.

I found out about the imminent arrival of the proofs at the annual bash of the American Academy and Institute of Arts and Letters in NY, where Helen and I spent a couple of days. We heard Daniel Aaron lecture very well on Ben Franklin at the NY Public Library, and the next day went to the bash, where we, too, saw Dimitri [Hadzi] and Cynthia [von Thuna], who spoke of you, and who are to be married at the Harvard College Chapel pretty damn soon. I'm delighted.

Even as I write this letter people are wandering through our house with an eye to possible purchase. May it come to pass.

Rural VI

---

[1] Mario Vargas Llosa's article, "In Nicaragua," appeared in the April 28th, 1985 issue of the *New York Times Magazine*. It can be read online at http://www.nytimes.com/1985/04/28/magazine/in-nicaragua.html

[2] *On Freedom's Ground*, a cantata by William Schuman. The text appeared under the same title in Richard Wilbur's *New and Collected Poems* (New York: Harcourt Brace, 1987).

[371]

[WLM]
May 21st, 1985
3811 39th Street NW, #F-90, Washington, D.C. 20016

*[Letter, typed on WLM's own letterhead, addressed to Anthony E. Hecht, Orbiter dictum,
19 East Boulevard, Rochester NY 14610]*

O Sage, Can You See?

Your description of the University's sad inability to do right by you confirms one of my cherished opinions, that one ought not place much faith in institutions, if any. Some are miffed that you have chosen to go elsewhere, and are too small to rise above that and be grateful that they had you in their midst for so long. You brought honor to them, and they know it but feel jealous and insecure and thus cannot act. That, coupled with the lack of all memory and emotional capacity that characterizes institutions, has done you wrong; plus, of course, the notorious inability of most humans to show gratitude. I forget in whose essay – Goethe's? – this is explained in part by a concomitant embarrassment and feeling of inferiority ...

At Smith a few years back I felt this but had prepared myself for it as best I could. Few actually said anything, but it was in the air: so he thinks we're not good enough for him, eh? One young man, a bright classics person (of course they didn't keep him) said when half in his cups that some regarded my decision to leave as displaying disdain for Smith. That shocked me until I marshalled my hard-won knowledge about academic life and institutions and saw the light: one should never show gratitude to an institution just as one should never expect it. To the credit of a few, a museum show was to have been mounted in my honor; I scotched that quickly, mustering as much tact and smooth[ness] as I can manage (which isn't much); that left them a bit nettled but it was the best I could do. I don't like to be the center of attention, don't know how to handle it and, after long reflection, recognize that although my attitude is lame and quirky, I'd rather be this way than otherwise.

You're absolutely right about the emeritus business. I didn't have to deal with that at Smith because I left so early. I'm overly sensitive on that point and ask sponsors and publicity people not to use the word or to say that I'm retired. I've disappeared entirely from Smith's printed matter, I believe, though I am an honorary member of the Alumnae Association, which gives me a nice chuckle now and then; they were able to say thank you thus, for I had done my share for the AA and we are quits.

All this because your letter brought forward in my mind matters of great moment: success, the individual versus the group, institutional allegiance, and going to the office. My first large book was pooh-poohed by the "experts"; now they eat out of my hand. How hard it is to be original, which I think I can fairly say my best work is. Old Sigfried Giedion, pissed off that I had written some pretty good stuff in a field he was (unwisely) burrowing into, wrote some such phrase as "MacDonald, summarizing the work of others"; and Ward Perkins put me down in print and in conversations (the kind that always get back to you; they are what Ashbery's messenger is carrying ...¹). Hard stuff to take, but I feel much better now, first about the value of my work, and second because I am getting recognition. This latter doesn't amount to much, but not to want a little of it would be inhuman. Not being a joiner, not wishing to belong to groups, I've probably stood in my own way, and that has I assume slowed things down ... The work moves, and that is paramount (isn't it?).

I've bought a rowing machine, and though at first I felt silly sitting on it rowing away, glad that no one was there to watch, it really is a wonderful thing. I feel better, I'm losing a little weight, and now I enjoy doing it (first thing on getting up). I still walk a lot when I can, but that tends to bring on the coughing and other respiratory admonishments that myasthenia gravis is ever ready to supply. For some reason, rowing – thus far – doesn't raise the beast.

Had a swell evening with Cynthia and Dimitri. Their coming marriage was toasted, Cynthia made a video tape (she's good at it) of Dimitri and me talking about the day we all went to the Trajanic forum and markets with Rothko at R's request; memorable affair to say the least.² I'm delighted with Dimitri's success and as always marvel at his energy and solidity. He took me to all three of his studios the next day – I stayed over with them – and I came away refreshed and feeling as always lucky in my friends.

That's good news about the proofs in spite of the work. I am struggling with an over-zealous copy-editor but am at the same time making rather good headway with my part of the Hadrian's Villa book; my dream is to get a draft finished before leaving for lotus land. The Getty sent a copy of the official announcement of Us Greats who will be there but I don't see newspapers much and couldn't find anything in last Sunday's <u>Times</u> so who knows if the tree fell in an unoccupied forest?

<u>Smithsonian</u> magazine, <u>National Geographic</u> (where a good friend, now senior, is trying hard to raise the content level and the quality of the writing) both want articles from me; I'm not sure I can write that kind of stuff but we'll see. Big thing of the moment is to get ready for the daily opening of the bank vault in my study in Santa Monica and decide how much walking-around cash I'll need. I'm trying to find out what daily helicopter and Hispano Suiza rentals are so that I can handle the matter easily and quickly.

In the hope of a better world and more nooky,
J. Walter Thompson

---

1 A reference, presumably, to the figure described in "At North Farm," the opening poem in Ashbery's then most recent collection, *A Wave* (New York : Viking Press, 1984): "Somewhere, someone is traveling furiously toward you, / At incredible speed, traveling day and night / ... But will he know where to find you, / Recognize you when he sees you, / Give you the thing he has for you?"

2 The Rothko mentioned here was the painter Mark Rothko. He was passing through Rome in the summer of 1966, just as WLM was also passing through, on his way to spending a month with his family on board the MS Argonaut, from which he conducted tours of Roman and Byzantine sites.

[372]

[AH]
May 27th, 1985
[19 East Boulevard, Rochester, NY 14610]

[Letter, typed on a J. B. Borreau, "A La Fiancée," France, letterhead]

Memorial Day

Meinherr,

    Do you ever read trash for fun, or haven't you time for that sort of thing? Because if you would enjoy some diversion, I would recommend a book I think will amuse you; indeed, you may have read it. It is called, The Caravaggio Conspiracy, it's published (in paper) by Penguin, and written by one Peter Watson.[1] A note on the author, which appears at the front of the book (first published by Viking in this country) reads, in part, "Peter Watson was born in 1943 and educated at the universities of Durham, London, and Rome. After postgraduate work in psychology at the Tavistock Clinic in London, … he became a member of the 'Insight' team of the London Sunday Times, …" and [has] written for the (daily) London Times, and has been that paper's New York correspondent. These sound like decent credentials. The book itself is a rather exciting tale about an attempt (successful) to trap a group of art thieves, smugglers and forgers, in which the author, Watson, assumes a false identity as one A. John Blake, a knowledgeable art-dealer of questionable ethics who would not be averse to buying art works he knows to be stolen. The story is offered to us as solid, documentary investigative reporting. In fact, the book is prefaced by a brief author's note which reads in its entirety, "This is a true story about an attempt to recover stolen old master paintings. For legal reasons, and because of the threat of reprisals, two names have been changed. They are indicated by asterisks at appropriate points in the story." Clearly, this is the sort of thing that ought to entertain us both. Among other things, it begins with Watson's attempt to provide himself with enough art-historical know-how to fool the crooks he expects to deal with; and with regard to Caravaggio at least, he does seem to have found out that Walter Friedlander is an authority to be reckoned with. But what I think you may find most charming of all is how spotty, shaky and false is the facade Watson, alias Blake, contrives for himself. His characterizations of the styles and manners of the more famous painters is always, or almost always, gross and "popular," and often enough he gets things wrong even when he is showing off how knowledgeable he has become. For example, "In English, the standard work on art forgery is Otto Kurtz's book Fakes,[2] which examines archeological objects, prints, glass, furniture and tapestries as well as paintings. I was agog and read it through from cover to cover at a sitting." If that book can be read cover to cover at a sitting, it can't be the last word on the topic, upon which, as you must know, Gisela Richter has written

---

1 Peter Watson, *The Caravaggio Conspiracy: How Five Art Dealers, Four Policemen, Three Picture Restorers, Two Auction Houses, and a Journalist Plotted to Recover Some of the World's Most Beautiful Stolen Paintings* (New York: Penguin, 1985).

2 Otto Kurtz, *Fakes* (New York: Dover, 1967).

a vast, two-volume work dealing with fake Roman and Greek antiquities alone. Of Caravaggio's The Seven Acts of Mercy (which I saw at the National Gallery during our stay) the author says, "It is a marvelous composition." It seems to me one of the most frantically disorganized paintings I can think of. At another point, parading his scholarship, he writes, "The others were talking about Veronese when I arrived. The Venetian painter had been called before the Inquisition in the late sixteenth century and accused of heresy, of putting animals and (Protestant) Germans in a Last Supper he was painting. Veronese had given a good account of himself, saying he felt free to put into his pictures what he wanted, though in the end he changed the title of the picture to a secular one." This is, as doubtless you know, a ludicrous error. The painting in question is the giant one in the Accademia, the text of the Inquisitorial debate is quoted in Elizabeth Holt's famous A Documentary History of Art,[1] the painting's name was changed from The Last Supper to The Feast at The House of Levi, which is not a secular title, whatever it is. But what seemed to cheer me most, as a sort of intellectual bonus, an unexpected dividend from a man who attended three distinguished universities, and then did postgraduate work in psychology, and made a career of writing for the august London Times, was the fact that the author liked to drop casual quotations here and there in his work – little gems and maxims that exhibited the breadth of his reading. I will offer you only one of these, brief but delicious: "'Death takes us piecemeal,' wrote one of the Greeks, Seneca, I think, '… not at a gulp.'" There writes a man who enjoys not only a sound classical education, but scrupulous copy editors for his book, and understanding editors at his paper. The whole book has this kind of authenticity about it. The publisher's blurb remarks that "… it has all the elements of a fictional thriller …" and it has this supremely in its capacity to invite doubt that Watson's cover could possibly have succeeded in fooling anyone at all. I will certainly have gone on too long about this if it's a book you have already read and cast aside. But as a half-assed excursion into a field you know a good deal about, it seems to me something you might get a kick out of. There is, let it be admitted, a good deal of action and suspense. It's not up to the level of Graham Greene or Eric Ambler in this regard, but then, after all, it labors under the handicap of pretending to be the truth, rather than fiction. Sadly enough, it's harder to believe than the works of the novelists. Even Watson's briefly interpolated biography of Caravaggio succeeds in being far more lurid than the equally short one in the Wittkowers' book, Born Under Saturn,[2] which is, after all, a book more or less devoted to the lurid. Great Suffering Catfish, if you or I had made that blunder about Seneca being a Greek what do you suppose would have happened to our reputations, assuming, of course, that the error was not caught before the book appeared in print? It says something about the standards of the London Times, The Viking Press, and Penguin Books.

Bernard of Clairvaux

1 Elizabeth B. G. Holt, *A Documentary History of Art* (Princeton, NJ: Princeton University Press, 1981).

2 Rudolf and Margot Wittkower, *Born Under Saturn: The Character and Conduct of Artists: A Documented History from Antiquity to the French Revolution* (New York: Norton, 1969).

[373]

[AH]
May 31st, 1985
[19 East Boulevard, Rochester, NY 14610]

[Letter, typed on a The University of Rochester, Department of English, letterhead, addressed to William MacDonald, Gymnopædist, 3811 39th St. N.W., Washington, D.C. 20016]

Most esteemed and noble sir,

We are delighted by your gift of the catalogue of Chester Michalik's photographs[1] with your introduction. It is a handsome volume, and, as you say, the pictures are extraordinarily suggestive. In fact, I like it so much that I found I had one objection to its format. What I most enjoy about such a volume as this is to compare or test my own reactions with those of the expert whose commentary accompanies the illustrations. What I should have preferred was a slightly more detailed table of contents; so that, for example, I would be told, with regard to figure 4, that it was a Las Vegas wedding chapel. I would then have been able to react a little more precisely on my own, and without having read your very illuminating and sensitively persuasive text, with which I could then have proceeded to compare my own reactions. As things stand, I am not sure how much my reactions are really my own, and how much they were colored by your text, which I read with great care before looking at the pictures with any care.

Architectural photographs devoid of persons (or with only an unimportant or accidental human – fig. 16) are always strange, eerie, alarming, full of suggestive power. Dorothea Lange's pictures of sharecropper houses, South Dakotan wooden-frame churches, the blank white walls of barns, are examples of what can be found in the work of other American photographers as well. But these pictures by Michalik have a special, added power by virtue of color, and a considerable drama is added thereby. After all, architecture is meant to be inhabited, and when we see it vacant our first impulse is to think of calamity. If there is no real evidence of calamity, our next impulse is to create some scenario to explain the absence of humans. Something of this sort is hinted at in the juxtapositions in figure one. The huge letters, as you rightly said, seem cut-outs of the sky, as well as giving evidence of the irregular surface of the pool. Like the desert scape in figure 8, they are a crude, Hollywood scrim, meant both to initiate the landscape or skyscape beyond, and to be recognized as a cheap fraud by anyone who is not rather drunk. And the message they both convey is that it would be best to be rather drunk, which suits the mood of a resort. In figure 1, however, the huge word MINT, read backward, still insists on money, a principal concern in Las Vegas, and the pathetic little sign, exit, suggests a scenario in which all those deckchairs and the evening sun have been abandoned (this gave the photographer his opportunity) by the compulsive gamblers who are dressing for cocktails and the tables.

---

1 *Chester Michalik: Photographs*, with a foreword by Charles Chetham and an introduction by William L. MacDonald (Northampton, MA: Smith College Museum of Art, 1985).

The stairs and balustrades in fig. 9, have, as you note, their awkwardly improvised air of not quite fitting, but they seem to recall the American turn-of-the-century, Victorian grandeurs of summer hotels at such places as Saratoga and Chautauqua, or at least some pretension to that sort of grandeur. Such steps would lead to an ample porch with wicker rockers, or to a glass-etched, formal door. Here it leads to what we cannot see, but can make a guess at: from the tall lighting posts and fixtures it is probably a parking lot, and possibly the parking lot of a supermarket, making of these steps something wonderfully irrelevant. Unlike you, I have never been in Las Vegas, either with the Christchurch, New Zealand, Fire Brigade, or anyone else. But I have seen such a setting as is conveyed in figure 3, or something equivalent anyway. It was at Rome, when Helen and I were on our return trip by "charter" from Italy. After infinite delays, we were told we could not board the plane, which wasn't working right, and put in a bus which took us to a vast, modern "pilgrimage" hotel on the outskirts of Rome. It was as impersonal, ugly and huge as a convention center (which in effect it was) but we were there out of season, when there were no foreign pilgrims, and our little plane-load of passengers were dwarfed by the size of the place. We could look out onto a terrace with a huge, filled swimming pool that was lit at night (in rather more severely modern style than the Art Deco of the cover photo) but with regular plantings of flowers and shrubs. Again, it was a place that suggested that being drunk (either with booze or with religious fervor) would make the sheer inhuman part of it tolerable. The cover picture (not mentioned by you) I take to be a roof-top pool; and I take the vertical and horizontal structures upper left to be antennae, their wire shapes and textures and colors wittily parodied in the metallic pipes around the pool. There seems to be a hideous little nympheum at the back, center, plus a travesty of a temple of Vesta, all roughly lit, to the right. The tiny awning at left leads to the essential BAR. The most moving of all the pictures, for me, was fig. 10. As you said, the Mexican pictures are "more humane, less desiccated physically and spiritually." There is a candor about the juxtapositions of buildings and colors, blunt destruction and delicate grille-work. And by the sad pilaster cut across by electrical wires. But chiefly it is the quality of the late afternoon light on this uninhabited scene that I find terribly poignant, and that I was trying to capture myself in a passage about deserted buildings in the opening section of "The Venetian Vespers," even to the isometric shadows of ironwork (in my case a fire-escape) against a building. Figure 15 has something Aztec, something of a sacrificial ziggurat about the way the steps move in opposing directions; though of course it is this barbaric theme perversely domesticated to the tamest and bleakest of living quarters. Its blue color is a litmus test of the mood of its inhabitants. Figure 16 reminded me most of Cartier-Bresson when he uses architecture in surrealistic ways, as in some of his pictures of Spain. As perhaps you may have guessed, I've hogged the book so far, but I will now give poor Helen a chance. Meanwhile, I send thanks for us both.

[374]

[WLM]
[June 6th, 1985]
[3811 39th Street NW, #F-90, Washington, D.C. 20016]

[Letter, typed on a Brookhollow Inn, letterhead]

D-Day 1985

My dear Bishop,

I've not read the art-historical romance you speak of, but it sounds good. Can you tell who any of the main characters are, i.e. Robert Hecht (I see from the AAR Directory of Fellows he has settled in Paris)?[1] Do I read trash? Mostly, excluding architectural trash, of which there is a fair amount available. Right now I'm struggling with Iris Murdoch's Black Prince[2] which, though it may not be trash, is awfully dense, or so it seems to me, willfully so. Perhaps I'll never finish it, and it will go on the pile of books with markers in them, mostly somewhere between pages 30 and 80, that accumulates upstairs.

Your comments on the Michalik piece again show how closely you look and read. I liked the Aztec reference. I think the MINT isn't so much money as cool, blue spearmint-flavored advertising – soothing, suckling. The comparison with the anonymous barn in Rome made me think again of my strong reaction to motels and chain hotels – Jesus, I need a drink, where's the bar, please? I think as hard as I can about the meaning of place, as you'll see in my next book; I think that's why I like Chester's photographs so much. One intelligent woman I know said either my words were bullshit, or the pictures, she didn't know which. I agree about a Table of Contents or, better still, for such a minor, short effort, captions under the illustrations. But I had nothing to do with that, and was limited to 3000 words. The cover photo, which you penetrate so skillfully, came as a surprise with the first batch of finished catalogues. You know how it is. The person in charge didn't even bother to send me proof! The actual photographs are very large and magnificently printed. Negotiations are underway to bring the exhibition to Washington, so perhaps you'll be able to see the originals next year.

I've just spent a few days in Virginia looking at buildings. I'd never been to Yorktown, or to the great Tidewater plantations. To stand where Washington stood when the British marched past, their band (perhaps) playing "The World Turned Upside Down" was a thrill, as was standing for a few moments in the tiny cubical building at Tuckahoe Plantation where Jefferson learned his ABC's. Arrangements had been made in advance

---

1 Robert E. Hecht (who was no relation of AH's) was a much respected dealer in antiquities whose involvement in the $1 million sale of a Euphronios krater to the Metropolitan Museum of Art in 1972 brought him to international attention, the Italian government accusing him of having acquired the piece illegally. He was eventually acquitted of this in Italy's Supreme Court of Cassation, but many years later, in 2005, he was once again indicted by the Italian Government for conspiracy to traffic in illegally acquired antiquities. The case again failed, this time because of the expiry of a statute of limitations.

2 Iris Murdoch, *The Black Prince* (New York: Penguin, 1983).

to see the interiors of all the houses, some of which were splendid by any standards. But most of all I was taken by the settings – the great gardens, some beautifully restored and kept (Brandon, for example) and, above all, the huge reaches, lawn or garden, between the main house, in every case, and the James [River] (much broader than I had expected). We were royally entertained at one or two places. The chatelaines came forward and took us around, usually very well informed, in spite of having gone to Sweetbriar (Sweet Briar? – what a name!). The husbands, their bright red hacking jackets hung in the corners of immense halls, seem all to have gone to Princeton. All in all a restorative and exciting trip, the kind of thing I like so much and that does so much for me. It wasn't at all diminished by a stay at Williamsburg, which I'd not seen for a dog's age and which in its own way was rewarding, though I don't have to go back again soon. The best part, as you probably know, is the untouristy William and Mary campus. The motel was one of Those Places, clean, sterile, anonymous to the point of invisibility, lousy food, lousy postcards, fake this and that. But it was in a quiet and very beautiful pine grove which someone had the wit to preserve, so early in the morning I went for a long walk and felt, as I had the day before along the James, rather human in spite of all attempts to prevent it.

In a Yorktown antiques shop I indulged in a bit of impulse buying, two early Victorian brass measures in the form of tankards, one pint-sized, the other a quart-er. Beautiful – a rich orangey-gold; heavy; satisfying.

It is important that you keep in mind always that essentially Hegelian dictum of our times: Lift tab to open.

> "… fled gilded dukes and belted earls before me;
> Ah me, ah me,
> I was a fair young curate then"

Prompted by a PBS TV [Gilbert & Sullivan] <u>Sorcerer</u> that was very good indeed.[1]

---

1 The lines are from Dr Daly's first "Ballad," which reads as follows:

> Time was when Love and I were well acquainted.
> Time was when we walked ever hand in hand.
> A saintly youth, with worldly thought untainted,
> None better-loved than I in all the land!
> Time was, when maidens of the noblest station,
> Forsaking even military men,
> Would gaze upon me, rapt in adoration –
> Ah me, I was a fair young curate then!
>
> Had I a headache? sighed the maids assembled;
> Had I a cold? welled forth the silent tear;
> Did I look pale? then half a parish trembled;
> And when I coughed all thought the end was near!
> I had no care – no jealous doubts hung o'er me –
> For I was loved beyond all other men.
> Fled gilded dukes and belted earls before me –
> Ah me, I was a pale young curate them!

Yours in the deep home of the early return of antidisestablishmentarianism,
"Armadillo Jack" Nussbaum

[375]

[AH]
July 11th, 1985
[19 East Boulevard, Rochester, NY 14610]

[Letter, typed on a The Century Association, 7 West Forty-Third Street, New York, N.Y. 10036, letterhead]

Dear Mr. MacDonald,

Our College of Augurs and Heralds has been at work uncovering your family escutcheon, and a pretty picture it presents, you may be pleased to know. The quartered shield is supported by two lions with measles, and still in the contagious stage. The shield is surmounted by twin crests: helmets topped on sinister by mailed hand writing a check with a large, ostentatious and awkward pen (possibly supplied by the Getty Foundation) and dexter by a bull foolishly attempting to urinate behind a pathetically insufficient sapling. The Motto, <u>Per Mare, Per Terras</u>, means "Towards Mother by way of the Terrace."[1]

A tasteful, three-color, glowing neon reproduction of this noble device may be purchased to adorn your establishment at a breathtakingly modest price. Our glass-benders are among the most skilful to be found anywhere, and we can assure you that the effect of the urinating bull will be unsurpassed in realistic effect. A soundtrack can be provided at slight additional cost.

       Your most sincerely,
       Meister Eckhardt
       Dean of the College

---

1 AH's spoof translation is of a piece with his spoof description of the coat of arms. The MacDonald clan's Latin motto in fact means "By Sea, By Land." An undated draft of this letter's first paragraph is to be found in the Woodruff Library's archive (Box 110, file 10), and AH has inserted as a handwritten continuation of the second sentence the words "who are performing what appears to be the carioca" [the carioca being a dance known today only because it was the first one that Fred Astaire and Ginger Rogers performed together on screen].

It is maybe worth pointing out here that WLM's paternal forebears were McDonalds, not MacDonalds, and that it was WLM's father who started to style himself a Mac rather than a Mc so as to give the impression that his was a Scottish and Protestant background rather than an Irish and Catholic one.

[376]

[WLM]
September 10th, 1985
[3811 39th Street NW, #F-90, Washington, D.C. 20016]

[Letter, typed on a The Motor House, Williamsburg, Virginia, letterhead, with a now missing enclosure]

My dear budding thinker,
    Keep pruned!
    I enclose a less-than-court quality xerox of an article of mine on fascismo. Note 30 is probably the high point. I hope I will have enlivened a happy hour on the Metro, or in Riggs' vaults.
    I keep forgetting to tell you, probably because of a touch of embarrassment, that when Mr Lea wrote me a kindly, brief note this summer, asking when he might expect my contribution to his book about you, that I found I had to reply that, although I had given the matter much thought, I'd not been able to locate a concetto and had not been able to produce anything. I suspect that perhaps the presence, in the final volume, of distinguished poets and critics may also have influenced me, by way of my subconscious. I'd like to send something in, and perhaps lightning will strike. Books of that kind take a long time to prepare (the Hitchcock affair went on for years), so perhaps your kind suggestion that I contribute may yet bear fruit. But first I've got to have an Idea.[1]
        Yours, sir, in the harmony of the spheres.
            Intelligently,
            William the Conqueror
            (a common signature)

[377]

[WLM]
October 12th, 1985
The Getty Center for the History of Art and the Humanities,
401 Wilshire Boulevard, Suite 400, Santa Monica, California 90401-1455

[Letter, typed on a The Getty Center letterhead, addressed to Professor Anthony E. Hecht, Curopalates, 4256 Nebraska Avenue, Washington, D.C. 20016]

Columbus' Day 1985

My dear Corinthian,
    I got this paper all on my own. Please run your finger over the embossed printing, gently, and reflect on my grand life.

---

1 WLM ended up not contributing to the book, which was to appear four years later. See *The Burdens of Formality: Essays on the Poetry of Anthony Hecht*, edited by Sydney Lea (Athens, GA: University of Georgia Press, 1989).

And grand it is. Nice young pages, wearing long white immaculate coats, bring books to the scholar from the Library; the pages look like youthful Paul Munis in Microbe Hunters.[1] Nothing is beyond the Getty's capacity in satisfying one's merest whim, and I am coddled and waited on, which I rather like. I've spectacular views of the Santa Monica Hills and a good angle to the Ocean itself; below me the lines of great palm trees lean into the Pacific breeze. 75°, crystal clear, low humidity … Hectic two weeks getting settled in and finishing galleys for the Yale Press; the last batch went off Friday and I turn now to the fleshpots of the thousand-odd square miles of greater Los Angeles. Perhaps I'll even do a little work. The insubstantiality of California, which I feel every time I'm out here, has set in once again, but perhaps this time I'll overcome it. There is so much to see and do that I will have to work out a proper program.

The Center thus far has proven quite bearable. Two of the other scholars have engaged me in useful conversations, and a couple of the others look promising. One is left quite alone, in an excellent study, if one wishes it, though there have been several rather nice lunches and dinners. In other words, I'll stay for a while.

I have a computer, which fact I hope won't damage our friendship. Some kid with a few graduate degrees has tried hard to teach me how to use it – he is a remarkably good teacher – and I've grasped just enough to practice on my own. I'm still not convinced that I need or even want a computer, but I'm going to give it a fair trial. I have to admit that even at my elementary state of knowledge the thing does do some astonishing things … will I be lost to Kultur forever?

I hope that you and Helen and Evan thrive and that all is well. I will much miss our evenings together. They mean a lot to me.

Thine,
John D. Rockefeller II

[378]

[AH]
[Early November, 1985]
4256 Nebraska Avenue N.W., Washington, D.C. 20016

[Letter, typed on a Fudan University, Shanghai, People's Republic of China, letterhead]

Decadent bourgeois capitalist no-goodnik,

We here in the intellectual circles of the People's Republic hold your embossed stationery in utmost contempt. It suggests to us that your jockstrap is lined with chinchilla, and that, in the cheering words of Spengler, the untergang of the abendlandes[2] [is] advancing at a hearteningly rapid pace. We look forward to your

---

1 The film to which WLM is referring was *The Story of Louis Pasteur*, directed by William Dieterle, in which Muni played the part of Pasteur. *Microbe Hunters* was the title of a book by Paul Henry de Kruif which seems to have been one of the inspirations for the film.

2 *Der Untergang des Abendlandes* (*The Decline of the West*) was the title of Oswald Spengler's two-volume

imminent collapse, aided and abetted by the San Andreas fault, any day now.

In actual fact, there have been something in the way of natural calamities in the Washington region, which you may have read of, if you are ever diverted from your rounds of heady pleasure-seeking. Floods have hit the region, warnings have been issued about the wickedness of the Republican administration, arks are being built by the Boy Scouts and travel agents are taking reservations. Your own apartment, though on the top floor, has taken in about 2½ feet of water, moistening the books.

The big thing around here these days is the English Country House show (and, of course, the arrival of the Prince and Princess of Wales in connection with it.)[1] I have never seen so much publicity about any show before. All the papers, as well as the magazines, including National Geographic and the Smithsonian, have had extended coverage or general articles upon the homes themselves; and there has been unanimous praise for Mark Leithauser in all the most prominent ones. He appears to be solely responsible for designing the interior constructions that imitate either rooms themselves or walls and fireplaces. The rounds of parties that he and Bryan have already attended in connection with the show staggers not only the mind but simple sobriety. Bryan, having to attend formal dinners on two successive nights, and not having a sufficiently various wardrobe, wore her evening dress backwards on the second evening for the sake of variety, and to give the impression that it was a different dress. They had us to dinner the other evening with a few British types: Gervase Jackson-Stops (a curator of the National Trust, and the chief Brit. to assist in arranging this show) and his boyfriend, Simon [Blow], who was a reincarnation of Aubrey Beardsley in appearance. Also one John Harris, who seems to be chief architectural renderer for houses in the Trust, and an exhibition of whose drawings will be on view at the Octagon House while the show runs. He vaguely resembled a slightly mad Patrick Moynihan.[2] He seems to be a good friend of Jon and Jill Stallworthy, who are due to visit us a week before Thanksgiving.

Slowly, ever so slowly, things are beginning to take shape. It was clear from the first that I would not be able to shelve what I had shelved in Rochester. So much in the way of journals and papers has been boxed away in the attic; new bookshelves have been acquired; and by now almost all the important books have been unpacked and shelved. And we have gotten rid of numberless cartons that were cluttering our rooms, waiting to be unpacked. The top floor, upon which Helen has expended herself, is now in really attractive condition, and has what is manifestly the choicest bathroom in the house: the largest and the most attractive. You will have noticed that I have said nothing so far about Georgetown. I have tried to keep my mind open and my figurative mouth shut on that topic until I had a chance to assess things carefully.

work of world history.

1 *The Treasure Houses of Britain: Five Hundred Years of Private Patronage and Art Collecting* exhibit was held at the National Gallery in Washington, D.C., where it ran from November 3rd till the following April 13th.

2 The reference is almost certainly to Daniel Patrick Moynihan, who in 1982 had been elected for a second term as the Democrat Senator for New York, not to Patrick Henry Moynihan, the Republican member of the House of Representatives, who had died in 1946, nor to the British politician, Patrick, the 2nd Baron Moynihan, who had died in 1965.

And by now I guess I can say that I like my colleagues a great deal; they seem kind and interesting. But the students, with some exceptions, are very poor.
Bertie de Born

[379]

[WLM]
January 5th, 1986
The Getty Center for the History of Art and the Humanities,
401 Wilshire Boulevard, Suite 400, Santa Monica, California 90401-1455

[Letter, typed on a The Getty Center letterhead, addressed to Professor Anthony E. Hecht, Opthamologist, 4256 Nebraska Avenue, Washington, D.C. 20016]

My dear Bishop,

You will understand that I can with equanimity (nice kid, Eq) praise your flimsy Chinese stationery, righteous in my position as a user only of stationery I've purloined myself (save for the XX Cent. Fox sheet, like the San Andreas an inexcusable but comprehensible fault). In fact, think as you run your fingertips lightly over the heading above, of the heights to which I have now risen, and sniffle a bit. (snaffle?)

If the John Harris of your Leithauser dinner party is the man I think he is, he is indeed mad. I sat across from him one night in a Washington crab-house and was stricken by his determination with the crabs, of which he ate a goodly dozen, talking the while, as we great writers often say. I will be in the Great White City in April for the Architectural Historians' annual meeting, and will see the Brit. show then; everyone here who has seen it has nothing but praise for the installation. I note with joy that Mark's name is given in more than one review.

The news that your colleagues are kind and your students poor comes as no surprise. My students, perhaps partly due to luck, though not really good students, were all right, and, as I think I've said before, two or three would pass muster as very bright anywhere. As for colleagues, I almost never saw mine and had the feeling that they felt there was some gap between us, if they thought about the matter at all. Now that I look back on it, aided by your remarks, I suspect that they were good people who may, in some cases at least, have felt (improperly) a bit apologetic about their situation. But I may be wrong; I was wrong once before, in '47 I think it may have been. The oddity for me at Georgetown was Freeze's handling of his (not my) request to return. But that was a minor matter and I'm hardly even curious about it (for this construction, cf. John Wayne's frequent riposte "Not hardly!").

I read Helen's nice note with pleasure and am glad she likes the book. It struck me that given your Italian experiences she might already have the book, but as it is not your run-of-the-mill bookstore item, I took a chance. We all gathered in Princeton – my god but it was cold – and had a fine and truly merry time over the Christmas week. I cannot get over people who don't want children – I can just barely understand it. But then, there are millions of other things I can't understand at all, for example why the Yellow Pages designers keep putting "Who to call" and "Where to find it" in quotes.

Life here is good. The uprooting was easier to take than any such previous experience. I'm glad I came. The Villa project moves forward, and now and then I try to do a bit on my classicism in architecture project. Ironically, offers keep coming in, or, more strictly, offers of offers. I will make a small, elegant selection and then try again to sell my two-weeks-or-a-month format which, to my pleasure and surprise, seems to be attractive to administrators and colleagues alike (they're never the same, as you will know well).

I've a slew of lectures from February through May, mostly up and down the California coast, but penetrating into Arizona and Texas as well. I just can't seem to say no. I guess I need them, though I'm not quite sure why, considering all the lectures I've already given.

Just finished Reyner Banham's <u>Los Angeles</u> (Penguin paperback)[1] and found it excellent. It makes sense out of L.A. and it contains many sharp observations and convincing suggestions. He is terrific on modern architecture here. With all its horrors, the city is fascinating. I've been here many times before but never for more than a few days. The place is not at all like the image of it I used to carry in my mind – it is much more vital, far less silly, and much more comprehensible to me than before.

Health OK, almost off the drug! Ladies abound but I've not yet done any more than take a couple of them to lunch (one at a time). The Center is well run and I am awash in money and perks. Ha!

Your moderately humble Servant, Sir.
Guglielmo Maccadonalda
"Il Villegiatore"[2]

[380]

[WLM]
January 6th, 1986
The Getty Center for the History of Art and the Humanities,
401 Wilshire Boulevard, Suite 400, Santa Monica, California 90401-1455

[Blank postcard, typed, addressed to Anthony Hecht, mahjongg champ,
4256 Nebraska Avenue, Washington, D.C. 20016]

Holiness:

I forgot to say, with my recent bull, that I met Jonathan Post at a University of California at Los Angeles shindig and we had a chance to talk some. Your name came up, I <u>think</u> in a complimentary way. I liked him & hope to see him again.

---

1 Reyner Banham, *Los Angeles: The Architecture of Four Ecologies* (Middlesex: Penguin, 1971).

2 Italian = The holiday-maker.

Had a grand thought last night: an update and extension of Pausanias' Description,[1] giving me a chance to describe/discuss the Roman Empire; could attribute the work to Hadrian's right-hand man, Q. Marcius Turbo, about whom I've long wanted to write …

70°, sunny, sonny

Persius the Pertinent

[381]

[AH]
January 11th, 1986
4256 Nebraska Avenue, N.W., Washington, D.C. 20016

[Letter, typed on a Croisière de Musique à bord de Mermoz letterhead, addressed to William MacDonald, conicopoly, The Getty Center for One Thing and Another, 401 Wilshire Boulevard, Suite 400, Santa Monica, California 90401-1455]

Illustrious One,

It seems to me pathetically clear that even the briefest residence in California corrupts, just as Lord Acton said it would. As if your own letter, with its touching approval of L. A. architecture, were not evidence enough, there is the book, light but pointed, I am currently reading, by Paul Fussell, named Class.[2] He quotes one Roger Price as saying "in Southern California even newscasters say 'wunnerful' and 'anna-bi-od-dicks' and 'in-eress-ting.'"[3] This kind of talk he characterizes as "prole," and goes on to state: "A writer in the London Sunday Times not long ago testified to hearing that attempts were made to pervert a strike, and that somewhere a priest had been called in to circumcise a ghost. 'Readers notify me of the lady with a painful "Ulster" in her mouth; the shrines you can see in Catholic countries in commemoration of "St. Mary Mandolin"; the police at the scene of a crime, who threw "an accordion" round the street; the touching sight of the deceased George V lying in state on a "catapult"… the student who always was to be found "embossed" in a book; the pilot who left his aircraft by means of an "ejaculation seat"; the drowning swimmer who was revived by means of "artificial insemination"; and the rainbow which was said by an onlooker to contain "all the colors of the rectum."' This, though it come from a British paper, sounds very Californian to me, and indicates the depths to which you have sunk. I plan to get the Banham book (I've already ordered it) to confirm my sad suspicions.

Helen is delighted by your gift. She is presently reading proofs of the newest

---

1 Pausanias's *Description of Greece* is a ten-volume account of his travels in the Peloponnese and central Greece, cataloguing the temples and shrines of the region and describing its myths and cult practices.

2 Paul Fussell, *Class* (New York: Ballantine Books, 1984).

3 Fussell is quoting from Roger Price's *The Great Roob Revolution* (New York: Random House, 1970).

book, called Simple Pleasures.¹ It has an elegant still life for the jacket, chosen by me: a painting by William McCloskey of oranges on a black background. Once that is out of the way she will start casting about for the germ of a new book, and your gift suggests to me that she might well consider a dish called Caccia venti-due.²

Very good news about your health. I am only now soothing myself out of a bout of anxiety, since I have given myself up to complete medical and dental checkups, the results of which are not yet in. I have distracted myself from worry by roughing out a lecture I will give at the Folger [Shakespeare Library] in a few days, titled, "Houses as Metaphors: The Poetry of Architecture." I am sending you a notice in the mail.³ It has been fun to work at, and has also distracted me from the disappointment I felt with my students of the first term. This coming term, which begins fairly shortly, may be better; one of my courses (a poetry-writing workshop) is a graduate course, and the other is one I can nearly teach in my sleep, and may find it wise to so conduct it.

You cannot make me envious by casual notes about the climate and temperature. Even when it's cold here we are so grateful for the sunshine we can scarcely contain ourselves. There has been only one day of snow so far this winter in Washington, and it had all melted by the next morning. By contrast Rochester has been having almost constant snow since well before Christmas I'm glad you and Jonathan Post have met, and I'm sure you'll like one another. I conclude with an unusually rare autograph.

Pio No-No

---

1 This was published as *Simple Pleasures: Casual Cooking for All Occasions* (New York: Atheneum, 1986).

2 Italian = Hunt twenty-two.

3 The lecture was given on January 13th, and was subsequently included in *Obbligati: Essays in Criticism*.

[382]

[AH]
[4256 Nebraska Avenue, N.W., Washington, D.C. 20016]

[An invitation from The Council of the Friends of the Folger Library to AH's lecture "Houses as Metaphors" posted in a Folger Shakespeare Library envelope, addressed to Wm. MacDonald, gaberlunzie, The Getty Center for This and That, 401 Wilshire Boulevard, Suite 400, Santa Monica, California 90401 - 1455]

The Council of the Friends of the Folger Library
cordially invites you to
a talk by
Anthony Hecht
Houses as Metaphors
The Poetry of Architecture

Following the talk, Friends and guests are invited to a reception in the Great Hall.

This program is being presented by the Evening Poetry Series in conjunction with the National Gallery of Art's "Treasure Houses of Britain" exhibit.

During the 16th and 17th centuries, the English Manorial estate represented a locus of social and ethical norms celebrating decorum, plentitude, utility, and clearly defined relations between individuals. The poets Ben Johnson, Andrew Marvell and Robert Herrick were prime practitioners of country house literature.

Anthony Hecht is an eminent poet and scholar in his right, winner of both the Pulitzer and Bollingen prizes for poetry, former Consultant in Poetry to the Library of Congress, and professor of English at Georgetown University. Mr. William Claire will introduce Mr. Hecht.[4]

---

[4] AH will almost certainly have winced at the misspelling of Ben Jonson's name.

[383]

[WLM]
January 14th, 1986
The Getty Center for the History of Art and the Humanities,
401 Wilshire Boulevard, Suite 400, Santa Monica, California 90401-1455

[Blank postcard, typed, addressed to Il Hecht, 4256 Nebraska Ave NW, Wahington D.C. 20016]

I11.mo egg.mo poeta,

It is marvelous what you have done for me. I have saved all the bar bills, museum tickets, etc., that you have sent, and am applying them to my tax deductions. I now have a total of lire It. 67840 in hand, or $37.89, in receipts for my tax manager. Thanks, bub! Classical music station announcer called Don Giovanni a "rue"; and in Washington, a lady (local) TV news announcer said once that a Druid chieftain had been killed in Lebanon. Spent the whole weekend looking at buildings; marvelous. Will have plenty of slides for you to sleep thru.

Pseudo-Anonymous

Hope the talk went well yesterday; couldn't make it!

Why weren't you at the Chicago M[odern] L[anguage] A[ssociation] meeting?

[384]

[AH]
January 25th, 1986
4256 Nebraska Avenue, N.W., Washington, D.C. 20016

[Letter, typed on a Hyatt Regency Hotel, Nice, letterhead, posted in a University of Rochester, Department of English envelope, addressed to Mr. William MacDonald, drawcansir, The Getty Center for Nearly Everything, Suite 400, 401 Wilshire Boulevard, Santa Monica, California 90401]

Sahib,

Though national and international news is conventionally grim,[1] the interstellar stuff has riveted me with delighted attention because everyone from newscasters to eminent scientists has been wracked with convulsions of Mrs. Grundyism. After months

---

1 For several months, the news had been full of terrorist outrages. On January 21st, a car bomb in Beirut had killed 27 people; on December 12th, 1985, an Arrow Air Douglas DC8 had crashed, killing all 256 people on board, and a terrorist attack had been suspected; on December 11th and November 15th, 1985, the so-called Unabomber had struck again, killing a research assistant at the University of Michigan and a computer store owner in Sacramento; on November 23rd, Egyptian commandos had stormed an Egyptair Boeing 737 which had been hijacked by members of the Abu Nidal terrorist group, and 58 people had died; on October 8th, Leon Klinghoffer had been murdered by the PLO terrorists who had hijacked the cruise ship Achille Lauro.

of embarrassed equivocation, a consensus seems to be forming to the effect that, given a very unhappy choice, it is probably more seemly to refer to the newest planet on the path of Voyager II as sounding like "urinous" rather than like "your anus." Responsible dictionaries offer both pronunciations, deriving from Greek by way of Latin, and related to the muse of Astronomy about whose name, Urania, there is little dispute as to pronunciation. I envision the corporate heads of the major networks volunteering to cooperate in this matter of finding the least humiliating solution to a name they cannot responsibly avoid, brow-beating and threatening the scientific community into submission to whatever their board of advisors (which has sampled the reactions of viewers in secret polls) declare to be the least offensive solution. It is things like this that take my mind off terrorism and the like. With regard to "the like," there has been a local crime in the district you are not likely to have been apprised of out there. It is really horrible, but horrible in a truly classic way. A young black woman, quite an attractive one it would seem by the photographs, got high on PCP[1] and proceeded to decapitate and disembowel her seven-year-old son, who, again, from the photographs, looked especially attractive and intelligent. What astonished me about this story is that in its local context it is sordid, ugly in a tabloid sense, and inextricably bound up with grim sociological facts: the poverty of blacks (which they pathetically try to forget through drugs), the prevalence of unwed black mothers, black ghetto life, the victimization of blacks by the whole system, etc. And yet the Euripidean play has manifest grandeur, presumably because the chief characters are maturely responsible for the choices they make, however tragic the results may be.[2]

My Folger lecture went well, though I took an instant dislike to the new director there, one Werner Gundersheimer (a cultural historian of the Renaissance) who tried to one-up me on several points in my lecture in conversation at the reception when it was over. He wanted me to understand that his casual knowledge was superior to my prepared presentation. For example, he told me that my statement that Knole[3] had 365 rooms, one for every day of the normal year, was wrong, and that while this was commonly said about Knole, it simply meant that there were too many rooms to count, and that I had been too literal about interpreting what was in fact a sort of figure of speech.[4] He found a number of other points to grudge me, and he seems to be like a lot of Washingtonians on the make: determined to push themselves forward at the expense of everyone who is not specifically in the position to aid them. But others were kinder. I've now gotten hold of the Banham book on LA, and have read as far as the epigraphs.

1 Phencyclidine, a recreational dissociative drug, more commonly known as "Angel Dust."

2 The case AH is referring to was that of Erica Mendell Daye, who, just ten days earlier, had been charged with the murder of her five-year-old son, William Lawrence Deloach. She was to plead guilty and be sentenced to a prison term of twenty years.

3 Knole House, near Sevenoaks in Kent, is one of the UK's largest houses, whose construction dates back to the 15th and 16th centuries.

4 AH seems to have been better informed than Gundersheimer. The National Trust, which owns and maintains Knole, believes that it was once a so-called "calendar house," meaning that it had 365 rooms, 52 staircases, 12 entrances, and 7 courtyards. The number of rooms is still approximately 365, but it has fewer than 12 staircases as a result of restructuring and renovation.

Out where you are now they probably think that crêpe de chine is elegant for dogshit.

Ulrich von Hutton

P.S.: If you're one of these perverts who like to "feel" stationery, here's your big chance.

[385]

[WLM]
February 23rd, 1986
The Getty Center for the History of Art and the Humanities,
401 Wilshire Boulevard, Suite 400, Santa Monica, California 90401-1455

[Letter, typed on a The Getty Center letterhead, posted in the same institution's envelope, addressed to A E Hecht, Obfoliast, 4256 Nebraska Avenue, D.C. 20016, with two enclosures]

My dear Copronymos,

You'll recall a ditty by Milton, "Haste thee nymph / And bring with thee / Jest ..." etc.[1] It is one of the few memorization passages from grammar school and high school I can recall now. I know a bit more of it than "Is this a handle that I see before me?" and something about a little horse stopping somewhere. You know the kind of thing.

Well, I've never quite understood why I remember things like that, things one had to learn, as opposed to the acres of G&S, doggerel, stirring hymns, etc., of which I can still recall almost every line, and sometimes feel a little sad about in that no one seems to know them or care anything about them. All this is in the service of an extraordinary experience I had Friday last, when "Haste thee ..." came to life with a bang, and my keeping of it for fifty or more years was at last explained to me; & I made use of it.

Picture if you will the hills of Santa Monica, stuffed with the rich and famous, splashed with swimming pools, quite splendid views (canyons below, and sometimes the great Pacific), and, to be truthful, some of the most beautiful trees, shrubs, and flowers I have ever seen anywhere, partly supplied by nature, partly by the r. & f. One of these places belongs to Charles and Maggie Jencks, he an architectural critic and historian, a kind of gadfly of the contemporary scene, and she a landscape architect. They divide their time between LA and London; mid-forties I'd say, bright and funny and very attractive. I've read a fair amount of his work – he's prolific – and though I thought his foundations shaky, I liked his irreverence and his energy.

On the Friday, then, I found myself at their gate, a latticework design of a stylized palmtree with the word TERRA lettered across its facade four times. Jencks met me, gave me a glass, and asked if I wanted to look the place over. I did, very much; and it turned out that the extensive grounds, beautifully planted, were arranged according to Milton's poem and the principles of Earth, Air, Fire, and Water. It was, as we say, devilish clever, but not at all cute, and carefully thought out. It only became frivolous,

1 The lines are from Milton's "L'Allegro."

and most amusingly so, at the terrace with the swimming pool. The latter is large but in the outline shape of California. The major cities have each a different colored light just under the water's surface, but the drain, just above the mid-point, is black and large, and that is the state capital, Sacramento. Trees, sculpture, an openwork temple, and other events are inscribed with the Miltonic

(One of the great letters, page two)

phrases. I realised that were I rich I would do something like that, but probably more along the lines of the dirty parts in the Church Fathers and other early Christian writers (I know you are familiar with this material, but I enclose an aide-mémoire, the contents of that volume in the great Migne Patrologia[1] dealing with such things; I expect you will find a good deal of poetic inspiration therein).

So, when the tour began and I grasped what was taking place, I broke out in song, "Haste thee nymph ...," and as I did so, mildly surprising my hostess and host and a couple of other luncheon guests, I realised why I had remembered those lines for so long: because the Jenckses would ask me to lunch at their Miltonian estate. In truth I hadn't thought of the poem for perhaps ten or twenty years, nor had I read it again since childhood. It was a fine experience, knowing that one's powerful memory was not useless even in its most obscure contents, and that was good for me, for I often wonder what to do with all the miscellaneous information I've collected. The poem will of course be an intimate part of your life, but much as I like it, human and humane though it is, and beautiful, it is not something I feel is part of my everyday life. A good experience, warming and somehow very satisfying in its bringing round of a thing in a circle.

* * * *

Gundersheimer surely is a cousin of a couple of people I know. One of the marvels of our kind of life is that there are people who, after one's lecture, explain one's work to one. One-upping is a dismal occupation; I confess to it, when I was less secure about myself and my work. But today I can actually keep quiet – at least for a while. Tell G. from me that he can drop dead.

I was knocked out by the flu, almost betook (ha!) myself to the hospital, lost two weeks' time, &c. OK now. I hope your book of essays is in the works. My book, after a nearly knock-down fight with the Yale Press over the butchering of my Index by a stupid copy editor, has passed page proof and though there may be more trouble on the horizon, they promise bound copies in June. I have a bright red Mazda – don't ask me what it looks like, all those Japanese look alike to me – and it is a splendid machine. Nick (who is doing well, back in College) will come out and drive back with me, a trip I am much looking forward to; in Washington ca. 22 June.

Working on the Villa, have much new material on its influence upon modern architects.

Ciao,
Zymont Saltonstall

1 The *Patrologia Graeca*, a collection of writings in Greek by the Christian Church Fathers and various secular writers, published in one hundred and sixty one volumes by J.-P. Migne's Imprimerie Catholique in Paris between 1857 and 1866.

(your pal)

[Enclosure 1]

pecunia quæ per usuram acquiritur, in peccato et per peccatum habetur. — 465 : Hic leguntur Alani carmina contra avaritiam.
INNOCENTIUS III, papa, CCXVII, 719 : De venditione justitiæ. — *Ibid.*: De insaiiabili desiderio cupidorum. — 720 : De falso nomine divitiarum. — *Ibid.* : Exempla contra cupiditatem. — 721 : De avaritia. — *Ibid.*: Cur avaritia sit servitus idolorum. — *Ibid.*: De quibusdam proprietatibus avaritiæ. — 722 : De iniqua possessione divitiarum. — *Ibid.* : De licitis opibus. — 723 : De incertitudine divitiarum. — 727 : De ambitioso. — *Ibid.* : De nimia concupiscentia ambitiosorum. — *Ibid.*: De ambitionis exemplo.

CLXXI.

INDEX

DE PROFANIS ET ILLICITIS VOLUPTATIBUS,

SENTENTIAS, DICTA, SERMONES, TRACTATUS,

ET IPSOS LIBROS SS. PATRUM ET OMNIUM SCRIPTORUM PATROLOGIÆ LATINÆ COMPLECTENS.

MONITUM.

Primo in limine oculis subjicimus rerum capita quæ eo indice tractantur juxta ordinem numerorum infra scriptorum :

I. Amor profanus ex concupiscentia seu libidine procedens. — II. Cantus lascivi, cantilenæ cantiones, turpes fabulæ, poemata erotica, libri obsceni. — III. Corporis cultus inordinatus, luxus vestium et ornamentorum. Pulchritudinis, vultus falsa et inanis æstimatio. — IV. Ebrietas. — V. Epulæ inordinatæ, seu gula. — VI. Lascivorum consortium et colloquia. Adulatio. — VII. Ludi lucrum sorte facientes ut alea, tesseræ, pila, etc. — VIII. Mulierum frequens conversatio et peccata inde derivantia. — IX. Mundi pompæ, luxus domesticus, gloriæ et divitiarum vana cupido. — X. Mundanæ voluptates festa gentilitia, saltationes. — XI. Oculorum petulantia et curiositas picturæ et imagines minus honestæ. — XII. Spectacula, comœdiæ, tragœdiæ, theatra, histriones. — XIII. Vaniloquium, scurrilitas. — XIV. Venationes tumultuosæ, sumptuosæ et indecentes, tornamenta, etc.

I. — *Amor profanus ex concupiscentia seu libidine procedens.*

TERTULLIANUS. — Nihil amari potest sine eo per quod est id quod est, II, 759. — Dilectio perfecta est fugatrix dæmonum et animatrix confessionis, 147. — Decor naturaliter invitator libidinis, I, 1317. — Non de integra conscientia venit studium placendi per decorem, *ibid*. — Pulchritudinis usus et fructus, luxuria, 1319.
ARNOBIUS. — Mentem excæcat libido, exempla dantur, V, 1207. — Ad libidinem homines proni atque ad voluptatum blanditias naturæ infirmitate proclives, 1044.
LACTANTIUS. — inflammantur (juvenes) libidine, quæ aspectu maxime concitatur, VI, 711. — De tactus voluptate et libidine, 716. — Maximiani Herculii abominanda libido, VII, 207. — Multi dum existimant nulli Deo nos esse curæ, aut post mortem nihil futuros, totos se libidinibus addicunt, 354. — De Sodomia exclamat : Non potest hæc res pro magnitudine sceleris enarrari... vincit officium linguæ sceleris magnitudo, VI, 707. — Qui voluptatibus indulgent, qui libidini obsequuntur, ii animam suam corpori mancipant ad mortemque condemnant, 718.
EUSEBIUS PAMPHILUS. — De Maxentii tyranni libidine insatiabili, VIII, 24. — Nobilis femina Christiana ipsi tradita se gladio perimit, *ibid*. — Hujus tyranni mors tragica, 26.
HILARIUS (S.) Pictav. — Carnis humanæ labes aboleri penitus non potest in hac vita, IX, 842. — Concupiscentiæ lucta in regeneratis, 876, 877. — Caro nostra Babylonis et confusionis est filia, 785. — Carnis vitia cruci configenda, 605. — Dei recordatione comprimuntur, 403. — Delectatio corporis animam inficiat, 402.
ZENO (S.) Veron. — Necessario unicuique sinceri amoris est noscenda proprietas... est enim et alius amor sanæ saluti nostræ contrarius,... lineamento puerili depingitur, lascivo vultu, nudus, pennatus, telis constructus et cæcus, XI, 276. — Iste amor jocatur, ludit, suspirat, obsequitur, tentat, decipit, blanditur, furit, 277. — Semper exæstuans libidinis turpitudo aut veritate aut imagine perpetratur, 292.

AMBROSIUS (S.). — Libidinis commotiones plerumque excitantur a diabolo, XIV, 1025. — Homo avertere debet oculos animæ, ne videant sentiam libidinem, XV, 1268. — Libidini quisquis subditus est, servus est, XIV, 650. — Carnis natura disciplinæ repugnat, quia voluptati obtemperat, XIV, 363. — Caro semper exæstuat, 568. — Ejus fragilitas describitur, 167, 168, 825. — Corde qui uritur, comburetur corpore, 891. — Multa de cavenda libidine, *ibid*. — Sævus criminum stimulus libido est, quæ nunquam quietum manere patitur affectum; nocte fervet, die anhelat, de somno excitat, a negotio abducit, a ratione revocat, aufert consilium, amantes inquietat, lapsos inclinat, castis insidiatur; potiendo inflammat, usuque accenditur, 538. — Tenera est amoris titillatio, quæ improvisum affectum excitat, XVI, 1318. — Non est vehementior natura ad diligendum quam gratia, 50. — Quid tam insitum naturæ, quam ut diligentem diligas, 113? — Lascivia plerumque latet sub tristi amictu mentis, 1318. — Ærugo nostra lascivia est, ærugo nostra luxuria est, 742. — Libido velut festuca, cito accenditur, propere consumitur, 1045. — Juvenilis levitas obnoxia est mundi cupiditatibus, 296. — Voluptas sola nos paradiso exuit, 1195.
HIERONYMUS (S.). — Amor impudicus quid agit, XXII, 1195 *seqq*. — Amare aliquid necesse est, 405. — Verba dulcia amantium, 532. — Blandas et dulces litterulas sanctus amor non habet, *ibid*. — Amare et amari sæpe evenit magicis artibus, XXVI, 415. — Amor amore expulsus, XXII, 1089. — Illiciti amores in sene evelli difficile, 937. — Libidinosa mens ardentius inhonesta prosequitur, *ibid*. — Nemo potest duobus amoribus possideri, si carnis amator es, amorem spiritus non capis, XXIII, 1121. — Fomenta libidinis, 555. — Amatorum misera conditio, 1071. — Idolis servire, quid, XXII, 350. — Idolum uniuscujusque id quod diligit, 400.
AUGUSTINUS (S.). — Amatores lubrici, ut sint formosi fallaces, non curant reprehensores veraces, XXXVI, 282. — Semper se et suum corpus amat homo, XXXIV, 27, 29. — Amor pondus est quo animus fertur, XXXII, 859 ; XXXIII, 677 ; XLI, 342. — Amate, sed quid ametis videte, XXXVI, 260. — Amor aut ascendit, aut descendit,

INDEX DE ILLICITIS VOLUPTATIBUS.

XXXVII, 1629. — Amor, cum pravus est, vocatur cupiditas aut libido, XXXVI, 121. — Est amor qui ad omne recte factum, et amor qui ad omne peccatum ducit, 1026. — Amare non sic debemus homines, quomodo gulosi turdos, XXXV, 2058. — Creatura, si diligatur ab homine qui Deum negligit, fit pœnalis dilectori suo, XXXII, 158. — Vitia quæ sunt in amore. XLI, 632. — Amor rerum inordinatus, non ipsa res in vitio est, 356. — Inordinatus amor creaturæ est peccatum, XXXVIII, 145. — Amor rerum temporalium viscum est pennarum spiritalium, 646, 1418. — Amor illicitus, XXXIX, 1550. — Amor tartareus, XXXVII, 1816. — Deum esse amorem turpis et vitio favens fingit libido, XLII, 574. — Vis amoris impuri, XXXVIII, 584, 883. — Quantas molestias habeat, XXXVII, 1551. — Amor immundus in ima præcipitat, amor sanctus ad superna levat, 1618. — Quisquis amat carnaliter, necesse est ut cum zelo pestifero amet, XXXVI, 310.

Libido quid sit, XL, 496. — Voluptas est sensuum, XLIV, 770, 771. — Libido vulgo de obscenis motibus corporis intelligi solet, XLI, 624. — Libidines discernendæ a sensibus, XLV, 1367, 1368. — Libidinis auctor diabolus, XLIV, 801. — Malum peccati originalis, 142. — Mala est libido spiritui resistens, XLV, 1101. — Morbus, XLIV, 469, 765. — Vulnus naturæ, 752. — Pœna peccati, 120, 287. — Latibulum quærit, XLI, 426, 427. — Præ cæteris cupiditatibus turpis est, XLIV, 756. — Merito pudet, XLI, 425, 428, 451. — Quare, 431; XLV, 1161. — Libidinis motus cur aliis magis pudendus est, XLI, 427, 450. — Libidinis morbus a nuptiarum negotio distinguendus, XLV, 1090. — Libido non est fami cæterisque molestiis comparanda, XLIV, 773. — Mentem absorbet, *ibid*. — Non sinit sancta cogitare, 808. — Totum hominem commovet ac sibi vindicat, XLI, 424. — Libido etiam inter conjugis frenanda, XLIV, 716, 717. — Cum vincitur, vincitur diabolus, 801. — Libidinis impetus cantus gravitate fra.tus, 798. — Libido pertinet ad naturam pecoris, ad pœnam hominis, XLV, 1560, 1563, 1572. — Libidinosi describuntur, XXXIV, 97.

JOANNES CASSIANUS. — De coll ctatione carnis et spiritus, XLIX, 591, 600. — De libidine, 870. — Libidinis memoria penitus excludenda, 1146.

PROSPER (S.). — Concupiscentiæ malæ languores animæ, LI, 285. — Concupiscentia carnis adversus spiritum minui vel augeri potest, 349. — Cum ea non pax sed bellum esse debet, 656. — Quomodo homines diligendi, 465. — De diversitate humanæ affectionis, 448. — Creaturis non adhærendum, 449.

PETRUS CHRYSOLOGUS (S.). — Pulchritudo corporis non est roncupiscentia, sed formae decus concupiscentiæ me rapuit et perduxit ad lapsum, LII, 518. — Luxuria quæ mala parturiat, 190, 190, 198, 349. — Luxuria desperationi similis, 493 — Qui luxuria ardet, mavult cum ea perire quam redire, 550. — Luxuriosi porci diaboli, 190, Contagio carnis dicitur luxuria, 562. — Vide sermones de filio prodigo, 183, 187, 190, 194; et de impio Herode, 549, 653.

SALVIANUS. — Amor stultus est alterius memor et sui immemor (in rebus salutis), LIII, 215. — Libidinum barathro immorantes se ipsi suis sepeliunt ruinis, 184. — Quomodo quædam illecebræ licebant sub lege, quæ sublatæ sunt ab Evangelio, 195.

LEO MAGNUS (S.). — Cum a licitis abstinetur, facilius illicitis resistitur, LIV, 430. — Mens nulli carnali dedit voluptati, nullius sit captiva mendacii, 431. — Insidiæ diabolicæ inter nostra studia non quiescunt, 449. — Duo amores sunt ex quibus prodeunt omnes voluptates, 448. — Cupiditates diabolo militant, 400. — Ab æstu terrenæ concupiscentiæ et ab omnium vitiorum illecebris abstineamus, 506. — Rationabili moderatione sanctoque proposito frenandæ sunt rebelles 439. — Nec concupiscentiis carnis mens principatus sui oblita consentiat, 147.

MAXIMUS (S.) Taurin. — Quisque post acceptam gratiam gustaverit de lascivia sæculari, accipit boni malique discrimen, LVII, 560. — Dominus noster totius turpitudinis emendator.... præcipiti vigore incentiva lubricæ carnis antevertit, 750. — Quam longe a corde hominis vult abesse luxuriam, qui tanta cautela lascivientes reprimit et castigat obtutus, *ibid*. — Scorpionis libido nos compungit, 340. *Vide* 810.

PRUDENTIUS. (S.). — Insani amoris descriptio, LX, 53.

EUGYPPIUS abbas. — Quid præsertim vitare debeant adolescentes, LXII, 605.

BOETIUS. — Ebrio similis est qui bonis caducis adhæret, LXIII, 724.

FULGENTIUS (S.) Rusp. — Amor inordinatus, initium peccati, LXVII, 167. — Defectus a summo bono ad infimum bonum, hoc est peccatoris proprium et voluntarium malum, *ibid*. — Amor mundanus cur vitiosus, *ibid*.

VITÆ PATRUM. — Amor impudicus amore divino vincitur, LXXIII, 563. — Libido vivit etiam in senibus, 883. — Libidinis tentatio molestiis superanda, 810. — Libidinem dæmones incendunt, 566.

GREGORIUS (S.) MAGNUS. — Voluptatis perfectio frustra quæritur, LXXV, 667. — Omnis descensus est in voluptate, 782. — Deus nos docet carnis voluptates cavere, LXXVI, 563. — Contra mundi voluptates invehitur, 1113. — Diabolus ad tentandum tempus observat, LXXV, 568. — Quanta diaboli in decipiendo astutia, 1047. — Ejus suggestiones variæ, 1065; LXXVI, 716. — Malæ cogitationes, unde procedant interrogandæ et repellendæ, LXXV, 587, 628, 629. — Ab iis nemo immunis, 1146. — Ratio instar dominæ, si redeat, ordini redeunt cordis cogitationes et foris dejicitur immundus spiritus, 546. — Libido carnem et per hanc omnia bene acta consumit, 201. — Luxuria ignis est usque ad perditionem devorans, *ibid*. — Virus libidinis de radice nascitur elationis, 364. — Concupiscentiæ ostiis consensus noster aperuit, unde innumera mala, LXXV, 660. — Cor hominis abyssus, LXXVI, 77. — Custodiæ cordis et vigilantiæ necessitas, 118. — A rebus exterioribus ad cor redeundum, 550. — Humana corda dum terrena appetunt, diabolo conterenda se sternunt, 594. — Luxuriosi cæcitas, quanta, LXXV, 1162. — Luxuriosus tumultuantem cogitationum turpium in se turbam gestat, 667. — Quandiu vivimus concupiscentiæ incendium metuendum, LXXVII, 336. — Quid iis qui concupiscentia repentina peccant faciendum sit, 115. — Voluptas et adolescentia vanæ, 524.

TAIO, Cæsaraug. episc. — De luxuria, LXXX, 945.

ISIDORUS (S.) Hispal. — Amor vehementior qualis sit, LXXXII, 417. — Libido colebatur ab ethnicis, 524. — Quomodo cavenda, LXXXIII, 640. Libidinis motus, 616.

BEDA (V.). — Dum concupiscentiis blandientibus caro enerviter subjugatur jam vitiorum exercitus firmiter adversus animum armatur, XCIII, 52.

PAULINUS (S.). Aquileien. — Nunquam carnalis amor amorem cœlestem excludat, nunquam te, quæso, hujus fluctivagi ac mirabilis sæculi dulcedo decipiat, XCIX, 220. — Nulla te seducat corporis pulchritudo, ne intret mors in animam tuam per fenestras oculorum tuorum, *ibid*. — Quando mors venerit, dic mihi quanta remanebit in corpore pulchritudo, 220.

ALCUINUS (B.). — Castitatis tibi conscius esto, non libidinis, continentiæ, non luxuriæ, sobrietatis, non ebrietatis, C, 161. — Nulla carnalis concupiscentia beatitudinis iter vobis intercludat, 146. — Ubi immunditia est corporis, ibi habitatio diabolici spiritus, CI, 626. — Opponat homo desiderio carnis suæ æternorum flammas tormentorum, *ib*.

SMARAGDUS, abbas. — Adversus concupiscentiam carnis et spiritus invehitur, CII, 415. — Diabolus quando decipere quærit, prius naturam uniuscujusque intendit, inde se applicat, unde aptum hominem ad peccandum inspexerit, 628.

SEDULIUS SCOTUS. — De veterum Romanorum luxuria pruriente, CIII, 20, 21.

AGOBARDUS (S.). Lugd. — De amore visibilium rerum, CIV, 211. — Vita libidini nimis dedita parum apta fit veritati percipiendæ, 220.

HALITGARIUS. — De luxuria, CV, 668. — Remedia adversus luxuriam, 669. — Canones adversus luxuriæ sectatores, 682. — Descriptio luctuosa sacerdotum carnaliter viventium, 692, 693. — Pastores dici volumus nec tamen esse contendimus, auditus noster nihil unde proficiamus admittit.... Seipsos non oves pascunt.... Tantum quid foveat et arguat voluptates nostras attendimus.... Quis ad hæc non infremiscat, *ibid*.

JONAS Aurelien. — De immundis cogitationibus vitandis, CVI, 154. — Sicut volutabra sues palustria, columbæ limpida solent frequentare fluenta, ita cogitationes impuram mentem immundæ perturbant, castam autem spiritales sanctificant, 154?

RABANUS MAURUS. — De concupiscentiæ origine in peccato primi parentis, CVII, 491. — Iniqui dum corde transire ad æterna negligunt et cuncta præsentia fugitiva esse non intuentur, mentem in amore vitæ præsentis figunt, et quasi longæ habitationis in eos sibi fundamentum construunt, 508. — Malorum consortium vitandum, exemplo Lot docetur, 536, 533. — Quomodo lubrica voluptas in prosperis expellenda sit, 632. — Pro carnis voluptatibus, laboriosa hujus vitæ itinera etiam lacrymis plena concupiscunt multi, CVIII, 655. — Immoderatus usus licitarum voluptatum ab .pso Christo arguitur, CX, 425.

EULOGIUS (S.) Toletan. — De impio Mahumeti dogmate, sic habet : Sic fautor immunditiæ et libidinum

[386]

[WLM]
April 24th, 1986
The Getty Center for the History of Art and the Humanities,
401 Wilshire Boulevard, Suite 400, Santa Monica, California 90401-1455

[Letter, typed on the back of a Getty Center for the History of Art and the Humanities, Library, memorandum (see below)]

My dear parsnip,

Please study the instructions on the other side of this sheet. It will help you greatly to know them when the Getty people take over the world (I of course will be Praefectus Praetorio[1]).

I had both dinner and a long leisurely luncheon with Jack and Corda [Zajac] in Santa Cruz last week. They looked much the same as seven years ago and we had a hilarious time reminiscing and telling each other bad jokes. Jack particularly asked that I send you his affectionate greetings. At luncheon they filled our table out with a gorgeous, very bright, funny actress, with whom I was instantly smitten; she is happily married and has several children, drat it!

Noel arrives shortly for a week's stay that I look forward to greatly; we are to do some exploring together. Ellen is fine. September 10th is the date for their child to arrive. Camera-ready copy came yesterday for the book.[2] I found some smallish errors, telephoned the Press, and found that corrections are impossible at this stage. I wonder why they sent me copy at all. The designer has done what I most detest in modern books, left off numerous page numbers either because of aesthetic sensibilities or the placement of illustrations. I have fought this vigorously, to the point of being offensive to some, but it has done no good and I've given up. I lectured them in a long letter about the use of books; for all the good it did I might as well write in the page numbers as copies come off the press. But it is a handsome animal, and I am pleased in all major respects. Anon, varlet.

Paolo Odorono

---

1 Originally, the title given to whoever commanded ancient Rome's Praetorian Guard, but eventually broadened to include those who served as the Emperor's chief aides.

2 *The Architecture of the Roman Empire, Vol. II: An Urban Appraisal.*

```
Getty Center for the History of Art
         and the Humanities
              Library

TO:    Orion Users
FROM:  Ellen Sleeter
DATE:  April 22, 1986

RE:    Scrolling Screens for Orion Patron Userids

Currently all userids that begin EGS3, EGS4, EGJ4 are categorized by Orion as
"patron" accounts. One of the characteristics of these accounts is that the screen
display *scrolls* rather than displays a page from top to bottom. This scrolling is
irritating to some users and presents some problems when using the <Print> key to
get a hard copy of the screen. Currently, after the printing is finished, the cursor
relocates to the top of the screen, and the user must <Clear> the screen before
typing in another Orion command.

Orion Development Office has provided us with a quick solution that you may wish
to try. At any time in your session, after an Orion prompt, type crt=ibm, as below:

       Orion:      ENTER NEXT COMMAND

       User:       crt=ibm <CR>

       Orion:      CRT TYPE (RE)SET TO IBM
                   ENTER NEXT COMMAND
                   \

You will continue to see the backslash \ as part of the Orion prompt. It is a handy
reminder that your terminal will be displaying pages rather than scrolling. Changing
the CRT type will last only for your current session; we unfortunately have no way
to make it automatic for you userid.
```

[387]

[AH]
May 3rd, 1986
4256 Nebraska Avenue, N.W., Washington, D.C. 20016

[Letter, typed on a V^r. Bonnet, "Magasin de Graines, Gros & Détail," France, letterhead, posted in a The Library of Congress, Poetry Office, envelope, addressed to William MacDonald, Dempster, The Getty Center for Luxe, Calme et Volupté, 401 Wilshire Boulevard, Suite 400, Santa Monica, California 90401-1455]

Honored Podsnap,

I'm feeling mighty sorry for myself at the moment, caught as I am in the deluge of term papers, exams and grades. One student of mine wrote on a term paper that John Donne's mother was the sister of Thomas Aquinas. I was really stumped by this, but a little research cleared it all up; what the student meant was that Donne's mother was descended from the sister of Thomas More. A perfectly understandable confusion. But you can see why correcting these things takes time. Wherefore, in the spirit of frivolity and diversion, I write to you in your Lucullan voluptuousness among the Pincian grandeurs of L.A. It went without saying that the briefest sojourn out there would corrupt you, and your newly acquired enthusiasm about California architecture – pissoir mosaic, gas station moderne – is clear evidence. Imagine going to someone's home where the fucking garden is laid out in cryptic relation to Milton's "L'Allegro"! They should have known that the poem refers to New York, not to California. The old song goes: "East Side, West Side, All around the town ... Boys and girls together, Me and Mamie O'Rourke, We'll trip the light fantastic On the Sidewalks of New York."[1] Well, this highly cultured (as it is now called in the current jargon) "intertextual echo" derives from "Come, and trip it as ye go / On the light fantastic toe ..." Nothing Californian about that! Pure pretentiousness on their part. Apropos of Milton's two-part poem, Edgar Wind has something interesting in his book on pagan mysteries in the Renaissance.[2] He says Ficino had "a picture of the smiling Democritus, defying the tears of Heraclitus" in his study to remind him that <u>euthymia</u> (cheerfulness) was a quality becoming a philosopher." Antonio Fregoso wrote a long poem in terza rima (c. 1506) called "Riso de Democrito et Pianto de Heraclito," and Matthew Prior wrote a short poem on the same subject.[3] As to Ficino's conviction that cheerfulness becomes a philosopher, there is a relevant passage in Boswell's life of Johnson. An amiable friend of Johnson's says: "You are a philosopher, Dr. Johnson. I have tried too in my time to be a philosopher; but, I don't know how, cheerfulness was always breaking in." This has its serious application to Johnson, who was a touchingly saturnine person, often supposing his own sanity was vanishing, and doing arithmetical problems to prove himself sane. Walter Jackson Bate's biography is a splendid and moving life. Well, I suppose this is enough diversion; as the French shepherds say, "Back to the fucking sheep."

Marshall Law

[388]

[AH]
May 8th, 1986
[4256 Nebraska Avenue, N.W., Washington, D.C. 20016]

[Letter, typed on a Cornell Club of New York, 155 East 50th Street, New York, N.Y. 10022, letterhead, posted in a Hyatt Regency Hotel, Nice, envelope, addressed to Mr. William MacDonald, Hackbutter, The Getty Center for Otiosity and Repose, 401 Wilshire Boulevard, Suite 400, Santa Monica, California 90401-1455, with now missing enclosures]

Dear Constituent,

I enclose herewith a sample of the California-Style in hamburgers, which shares something of the pronounced vulgarity of the architecture of that state. In fact, there is a close visual resemblance. It may be that you are already too corrupted by your stay out there to be any longer appreciative of the Georgian and Federal styles that are more common in this part of the world; and you may find, once you return to these parts, that you will want to spend more and more time wandering around shopping malls and amusement parks.

---

1 "The Sidewalks of New York," a popular song about New York City, was written by James W. Blake and Charles B. Lawlor in 1894.

2 Edgar Wind, *Pagan Mysteries in the Renaissance* (New Haven, CT: Yale University Press, 1958).

3 "Democritus and Heraclitus," from *The Poetical Works of Matthew Prior, with a Life by Rev. John Mitford, in Two Volumes*, Volume II (Boston: Little Brown, 1860).

It is growing warm these days (nary a drop of rain for about a month; terrible brush and forest fires in Virginia, etc.) and I am near the end of correcting the term papers for my course. Some of them were dreadful (I think I may have written you about the student who claimed that John Donne's mother was the sister of Thomas Aquinas). Once the papers are corrected, I have only the final exam to administer and correct, and then, then there is only commencement.

I also enclose some priceless coupons.
Bessie May Mucho

[389]

[WLM]
May 19th, 1986
The Getty Center for the History of Art and the Humanities,
401 Wilshire Boulevard, Suite 400, Santa Monica, California 90401-1455

[Letter, typed on The Getty Center for the History of Art and the Humanities letterhead, posted in the same institution's envelope, addressed to Professor A E Hecht, Porphyrogenitus, 4256 Nebraska Avenue, Washington, D.C. 20016, with now missing enclosures]

My dear Porphyrios,

Now that I know from your letters that you are enamored of all things Californian and Western, I feel free to send you the enclosed. Going to the Liberace museum would I think strengthen the life force within you, not to say aid in your choice of costume for grand events such as readings in the evenings at the Old Ebbett Grill, or running escort services from your Georgetown University office.

Other materials are enclosed also; I note that they claim success for those up to eighty, which ought to be enough for any man.

My friend John Pinto arrives at any moment; he is collaborating with me on the Hadrian's Villa book. He just published a nice work on the Trevi Fountain[1] (Yale) and is as knowledgeable about Rome as anyone you're likely to meet, even in Rome.

I deeply appreciate the little tokens you send. A few I have varnished and placed in my Memory Book, others I use here on muscle beach to get rid of the panhandlers; they rush to the "Checks Cashed Here – Foreign Exchange" huts that bloom amid the blight. (Blight / bloom makes me think of Nash's fine poem, "Senator Smoot Smites Smut,"[2] which of course you can recite at the drop of a tam, or beret.)

---

1 *The Trevi Fountain* (New Haven, CT: Yale University Press, 1986).

2 The title of Ogden Nash's poem was "Invocation," not "Smoot Smites Smut," which was a widely celebrated newspaper headline. The poem and the headline were prompted by the same thing, however, namely Republican Senator Reed Smoot's 1930 proposal to impose a tariff ban on "improper" books. "Invocation" first appeared in the January 11th, 1930 issue of *The New Yorker*, and its first stanza reads as follows: "Senator Smoot (Republican, Ut.) / Is planning a ban on smut. / Oh rooti-ti-toot for Smoot of Ut. / And his reverend occiput. / Smite, Smoot, smite for Ut., / Grit your molars and do your dut., / Gird up your l--ns, / Smite h-p and th-gh, / We'll all be Kansas /By and by."

The last days reel out. Nick comes soon, explores a bit, and we leave on a Grand Trip by Car Across the Continent. And none too soon; the earthquake last night thudded up through my apartment at 9:16 p.m. as I was reading Calvino's <u>Mr Palomar</u>[1] (come to think of it, the gods may have chosen that method of directing my attention to something rather more worthwhile).

More travels looking at buildings. Yesterday, among other things, I found and assessed the Watts towers. They are truly beautiful. In 1957, urban planners tried to have them destroyed, but the local (poor) people combined with the conservancy groups and they still stand, lacy and improbable but ever so proud and delicate. Then I found 1930s streets all but untouched ... and so on. Such voyages nourish and fulfil me greatly.

A presto,
Billy the Boy Artist

[390]

[WLM]
October 27th, 1986
[3811 39th Street NW, #F-90, Washington, D.C. 20016]

[Letter, typed on a Melody Lane Motel, Raton, New Mexico 87740, letterhead, posted in the same company's envelope, addressed to Anthony La Hecht, Rhymer & Primer, 4256 Nebraska Avenue, Washington, D.C. 20016, with two enclosures]

My dear Doctor Hecht,

We see in the reference books that your doctorate is h.c., which we presume means horse cookies. If you will send us eleven thousand dollars, cash, registered mail, to the office here, we will get you a Real Degree from our Melody Lane School of Prose, Prosody, and Propositions. Only one appearance here will be necessary, for you must, in order fully to qualify, walk down our very own Melody Lane, a thrill you won't wish to miss, for you will hear then Mel Torme, the Velvet Fog, Liberace's own private piano tuner, and the famous all-hermaphrodite Chorus of the Blessed Bifurcation.

Just as important for the Culture of Our Country is the fact that we wish to commission a pope ... er, a poem, and we want it to be about Joanie the Girl Bishop. Please see the enclosed, copied from J. N. D. Kelly's excellent new <u>Oxford Dictionary of Popes</u>.[2] She is a grand subject, as you know, and if you will write the poem we will throw in Master's degrees for all members of your family. If you cannot come out here, we will come to The Great Stone City and buy you an all-the-toppings pizza at Armand's Chicago Shop. If you will foot the bill, we will bring the Chorus with us so that they can sing "Any Which Way, Lord" to the Congress.

1 Italo Calvino, *Mr Palomar* (San Diego, CA: Harcourt, Brace, Jovanovich, 1985).
2 J. N. D. Kelly, *The Oxford Dictionary of Popes* (New York: Oxford University Press, 1986).

After paying you all this attention, we expect a reply to these questions: have you ever heard anyone actually say assiduity? And, have you ever heard anyone actually say wiseacre? We just looked up the pronunciation of the latter and it put us in mind of the old expression, "Gee Whizzakers!," which you'll remember from your youth in Far Rockaway. Is there a connection?

With a modicum, or commode, of respect,
Yours,
Sally-Mae and Fred Davantdier,
Rectoress and Canceller

[Enclosure 1]

APPENDIX
Pope Joan

From the mid-13th to the 17th cent. the tradition that there had been a female pope, commonly but not invariably named Joan, at some date in the 9th, 10th, or 11th cent., was almost universally accepted; it was still furnishing ammunition to attackers of the papacy and the Roman church in the late 19th cent. The story first appears, between 1240 and 1250, in the *Universal Chronicle of Metz* attributed to the Dominican Jean de Mailly, according to which Victor III (d. 1087) was succeeded by a talented woman who, disguised as a man, had worked her way up in the curia as a notary, and had eventually been promoted cardinal. She was betrayed when, mounting her horse, she gave birth to a child, and was ignominiously tied to the horse's tail, dragged round the city, and then stoned to death. The Dominican Stephen de Bourbon (d. *c.*1262) and the Franciscan of Erfurt who wrote (*c.*1265) the *Chronicon minor* give broadly similar accounts of the affair of the 'popess', the one placing it *c.*1100 and the other *c.*915. The tale was given definitive form, however, and very wide diffusion by the later editions of the immensely popular and influential *Chronicle of Popes and Emperors* by the Polish Dominican Martin of Troppau (d. 1297). According to these, Leo IV (d. 855) was succeeded by one John Anglicus, who reigned two years, seven months, and four days, but was in fact a woman. A native of Mainz, she went as a girl, dressed in a man's clothes but escorted by her lover, to Athens, had a brilliant student career there, and then settled in Rome, where her lectures attracted such distinguished audiences and her life was so edifying that she was unanimously elected pope. Her imposture was finally exposed when, riding in procession from St Peter's to the Lateran, she gave birth to a child in a narrow street between the Colosseum and S. Clemente. She died on the spot and was buried there; because of the shameful episode, popes thereafter studiously avoided traversing the street. While Martin gives her name as John (i.e. Joan or Joanna in the feminine), other accounts call her Agnes, Gilberta, or Jutta, or leave her nameless.

The story, often embellished with fantastic details, was accepted without question in Catholic circles for centuries. It was taken up by humanists like Petrarch (d. 1374) and Boccaccio (d. 1375), and influenced iconography; Joan figures among the busts of popes placed *c.*1400 in Siena cathedral. Critics of the papal claims (e.g. John Hus at the council of Constance in 1415) were able to exploit the story without being contradicted. One enthusiastic writer, Mario Equicola of Alvito (near Caserta: d. 1525), even argued that Providence had used Joan's elevation to demonstrate the equality of women with men. Catholic criticism of the legend became increasingly vocal from the middle of the 16th cent., but it was a French Protestant, David Blondel (1590–1655), who effectively demolished it in treatises published at Amsterdam in 1647 and 1657. It scarcely needs painstaking refutation today, for not only is there no contemporary evidence for a female pope at any of the dates suggested for her reign, but the known facts of the respective periods make it impossible to fit one in. The origin of the story, however, has never been satisfactorily explained. Its kernel is generally taken to be an ancient Roman folk-tale which was blown up by a number of circumstances needlessly taken to be suspicious—e.g. the deliberate avoidance of a certain street by papal processions (probably because of its narrowness), the discovery in it of an enig-

[Enclosure 2]

POPE JOAN

matic statue taken to represent a woman suckling a child and of a puzzling inscription near by which could be twisted to support the legend, and the popular belief (from the late 13th cent.) that after his election a pope had to undergo tests that he was really of the male sex. It is likely, too, that the recollection that in the 10th cent. the papacy had been dominated by unscrupulous women like Theodora the Elder, Marozia, and the younger Theodora, helped to give it currency.

MGSS 22, 428 (Martin of Troppau); 24, 184 (*Chron. minor*); 514 (Jean de Mailly); J. J. I. von Döllinger, *Die Papstfabeln des Mittelalters* (2nd edn., Stuttgart, 1890); É. Vacandard, *Études de critique et d'histoire religieuse* (Paris, 1909–23), 4, 13–39; *EC* 6, 482–5 (F. Antonelli).

another excellent subject →

Abelard, 16{
abortion, 32
Acacian schi
    56
Acacius, 46,
Achilleus, 3{
Acoemetae,
Acre, 197, 2
Action frança
Adalbero, 1{
Adalbert of
Adalbert of '
Adaldag, 12.
Adalgar, 114
Adoptionism
    98
Aethelred II
Aethelwulf,
Afiarta, Paul
Agbar of Ed
Agilulf, 66,
Agnes (emp
Agobard of
Aimeric, 16{
Aistulf, 89,
Alaric, 38
Albani, Gio
    291
Albani, Giu:
Alberic I, 1 1
Alberic II, 1
Alberic III,
Albert I, 20{
Albertus Ma
Albigenses,
Albornoz, G
Alcuin, 97
Aldobrandin
Alexander S
Alexis of M{
Alexius I Co
Alexius III /
Alfonso I (P
Alfonso II ({
Alfonso III (
Alfonso V (/
    247
Alfonso VI (

330

[391]

[AH]
[January 9th, 1987]
[4256 Nebraska Avenue, N.W., Washington, D.C. 20016]

[Letter, typed on an English Literary Renaissance, *University of Massachusetts, Department of English, Amherts, Massachusetts 01003, letterhead, posted in an Inter-Continental Hotel, Tehran, envelope, addressed to William MacDonald, influence peddler, 3811 39th Street NW, #F-90, Washington, D.C. 20016, with enclosure]*

Dear Vizier,

Knowing your fondness for the latest in architectural innovations, I send along the enclosed new line of TV cabinets. It's clear that the designer has not even scratched the surface of possibilities here, which accounts, perhaps, for the modesty of his prices. But consider a cabinet shaped like the Albert Memorial; or Theoderic's Tomb. True monumentality, solidity and weight, if you know what I mean. The best part of such cabinets is that you could put little jars of fresh-cut flowers in front of them, small American flags, and little tin votive stamps of arms and legs and internal organs. It would give "character" to otherwise dreary and conventional interiors. You and I ought to get together on this; we could clean up.

Søren

[Enclosure: clipping]

A TOMB FOR THE TELLY

Media criticism perhaps, Christopher Maier's witty architectural TV and stereo cabinets are shapes inspired by New Orleans cemetery vaults. *Above from left:* Classic (74 inches tall), Gothic (90 inches), Crude (78 inches) from $3,800 to $4,800 at the New Orleans design shop Leitmotif, 3814 Magazine St.; (504) 891-7777.

[392]

[AH]
July 1st, 1987
[4256 Nebraska Avenue, N.W., Washington, D.C. 20016]

[Letter, typed on a A. Dutour, "Dépôt des Principales Verreries & Cristaux," Quai des Luisettes, Angers, France, letterhead, with enclosure]

Dear Sir,

Feeling certain that you were unable to keep abreast of events in this country while you were abroad, we engaged a clipping service to record leading events. But since even such services incline to prolixity, we have conveniently reduced what they sent to a single headline, and will summarize the substance of the ensuing article below:

[Enclosure]

Cranberry Fungus Is Watched [1]

Mr. Shlomo Fitzhugh of Teaneck, N.J. was advised by his physician that a cardiac irregularity necessitated his pursuing a very much modified routine of life, and particularly the elimination of the customary stimulations he was up till then in the habit of enjoying. Fitzhugh had for years been a devoted fungus watcher, but his doctor felt that this was too exciting a habit to be allowed to continue unchecked. Nevertheless, the physician was touched by the deep dejection into which this prohibition cast the poor patient, and so a small concession was agreed upon. It was to be permitted to Fitzhugh to watch only cranberry-colored fungi, and since these are unusually rare, it is confidently hoped that excitement will be reduced to a minimum. When the New York Times covered this remarkable story, Fitzhugh had actually gotten hold of a cranberry-tinted fungus, and was actively engaged in watching it. The reporter was only able to stick around for half an hour or so, during which Fitzhugh refused to be interviewed, wishing to give his entire attention to the fungus.

We rejoice in being able to fill you in on what otherwise might have escaped your notice.

Tancred, the Cantankerous

---

1 The whole story – unembellished by what AH goes on to say – can be read online at http://www.nytimes.com/1987/06/28/us/cranberry-fungus-is-watched.html

[393]

[WLM]
October 25th, 1987
[3811 39th Street NW, #F-90, Washington, D.C. 20016]

[Letter, typed on the back of an incomplete photocopy of WLM's entry for Thomas Whittemore, scholar, archaeologist and founder of the Byzantine Institute of America, in the Dictionary of American Biography, *Supplement 4, 1946-1950, pp. 890-91 (New York, Scribner, 1974), with one enclosure]*

Viii p. kal. Nov.
MCMLXXXVII

My dear lord prince Cardinal,

We here at Andy's are not sure if you <u>actually</u> have a Gutenberg Bible, and if you don't it's OK; not to worry. What we suggest is that you buy our page and then from time to time pick up the other pages. Our page is a flat million, postage extra.

If you already have a full copy, buy the page anyway, as a spare. You know the economy can't survive unless we all have all kinds of spares. I've got one, right around my middle.

Did you know that Gutenberg was ennobled toward the end of his life? And thus called Sehr Gut? Ha, ha – little joke there. And that his wife made a special dish for him, chopped beef on a bun, that he loved, that it was called in the household a Gutenberger?

We throw this scholarly detail in free. Imprints of time. Lagniappes of culture. Now that we're all moveable types.

A. Stewart
(not <u>the</u> Stewart)

[Enclosure: clipping]

[394]

[WLM]
January 16th, 1988
[3811 39th Street NW, #F-90, Washington, D.C. 20016]

Postcard, with a reproduction of "Nereid Riding a Bull," an Egyptian wool tapestry from the Dumbarton Oaks Museum in Washington, D.C., handwritten]

Anthony –
    I thought you'd like to see this recent picture of me.
Xxxx
Marta Thatcher

[395]

[AH]
August 31st, 1988
[4256 Nebraska Avenue, N.W., Washington, D.C. 20016]

[Letter, typed on a Georgetown University, Department of English, Washington, D.C. 20057, letterhead]

Dear Bill,
    Much has passed since last we saw each other, and now, with the usual suddenness I am plunged back into the thick of the academic year, feeling very startled and unprepared, as I have ever since I first began teaching. There's something curious and unfair about this. When I began in the forties I assumed that in time I'd grow accustomed to the routines and duties, but this has never happened, at least to

me. I'm perfectly aware that it has happened to others; I had a colleague at Bard in history who taught a course called "The History of the Trans-Mississippi West." He very proudly told me that he maintained two sets of lecture notes, one in his office and one in his home, in case either should go up in flames. This prudence was an index of another sort as well; he felt no need to read any further in his field, and his notes served him without variation for pretty much the length of his teaching career.

Anyway, our summer seemed especially brief, and crowded with, largely happy, event. Evan had six wonderfully successful weeks in Oxford, studying French and Elizabethan drama (Shakespeare and Middleton) from which he profited and which he enjoyed. All by itself this is a major consideration, since he would not normally have been inclined to study during the summer, and usually resents his regular homework, or at least does it grudgingly. So his election to work during his summer vacation, and to do so enthusiastically, and to join a program in which all the others, faculty and students, were total strangers, is very heartening. Helen and I followed him over, arriving at the end of his term. We spent two days in Oxford, staying with friends, and then the three of us went to London for a splendid week in which the weather was perfect, though the English were constantly apologizing for the 70-degree heat. We saw Cats (famously well designed, but otherwise a bore), Noel Coward's frothy, amusing and inconsequential Easy Virtue; Tom Stoppard's first-rate Hapgood; and Middleton's The Changeling. We trudged about a good deal, had some marvelous meals, saw the Queen's Collection, and Sir John Soane's House. I got a glimpse of the National Gallery (with a huge billboard next to it announcing the new wing by Venturi and Scott-Brown) and we did a certain amount of visiting stores. The prices were not merely forbidding but terrifying. When we returned Helen was overcome with severe pain (this was only after a few days back home) and had to be rushed to the hospital at five in the morning. It turned out to be nothing, and she recovered quickly and completely, but it scared us both. Then I came down with one of the more uncomfortable viruses, causing aches in feet and legs, among other regions, and this has largely, though not completely, disappeared.

I saw Larry Richardson's book[1] displayed on the shelves of Calliope's Bookstore on Connecticut Avenue, and picked it up simply to see what acknowledgements of indebtedness he makes, and could find none whatever (though I suppose there might be some at the end of the book, where I did not look.) I will be giving a reading for the American Academy in Rome later this fall at the Morgan Library, just before the Literary Lions Dinner at the New York Public Library. And, praises be, I have next term off, so I already begin to feel cheered.

Summer, apart from our trip, was cluttered with oddly assorted chores. Helen worked remarkably hard and long at her interior design tasks, and we put a lot of thought into the projected extension of the kitchen. I wrote some assorted essays and lectures: on the first eighteen lines of The Waste Land (to be delivered at a T. S.

---

1 Lawrence Richardson, *Pompeii: An Architectural History* (Baltimore, MD: Johns Hopkins University Press, 1988).

Eliot centenary in St. Louis in October);[1] on a memoir about W. H. Auden by A. L. Rowse, the Shakespearean scholar, for the New York Review of Books;[2] and on the Epistle to the Galatians, for a collection of essays on the New Testament by writers, which is still in the process of revision.[3] So in various disorderly ways all three of us got something done. In England Helen found some wallpaper for our bedroom, which seems to be the next project she has set for herself. The house is gradually beginning to take shape, and once she starts on our bedroom we will have to sleep on the third floor to avoid the smell of paint. That will not be too bad, and will certainly be brief, in contrast to the time we will have to survive without the use of a kitchen, once the renovations get underway. The Millons went through something of the same sort not long ago. Anyway, I think this will more or less bring you up to date on our goings and comings. And I hope we will be seeing you quite soon.

      Best,
      Arthur Pendentive, Rex

[396]

[WLM]
September 12th, 1988
[3811 39th Street NW, #F-90, Washington, D.C. 20016]

[Letter, typed, addressed to Anthony Hecht, Borogrove, 4256 Nebraska Avenue, Washington, D.C. 20016]

Dear Tony,
 Your summer was full and successful. I knew Evan would have a grand time and am delighted to have the thought confirmed. I stayed right here, worked on my book – profitably, I think, as a couple of friends, experts in Roman history, have found the work sound. Getting ready for Harvard has as you will understand taken a lot of time but that's all done now. I leave in a few days and will stay up there for a while to get settled in. I find myself almost excited at the prospect of a change of place, and I've almost always enjoyed teaching. Boston I love.
 It is odd to leaf through the Harvard catalogue and find that I know almost no one on the faculty. One in English ([Helen] Vendler), one or two in classics, three in Architecture, and, of course, a few (only) of the Fine Arts people. Time has so many

---

1 "The First Eighteen Lines of 'The Waste Land'" was delivered as part of the "T. S. Eliot: A Centennial Appraisal" conference sponsored by Washington University, St. Louis, Missouri, and held between September 30th and October 2nd, 1988. It was published a year later in the September 1989 issue of *The Yale Review*, and was reprinted as "Uncle Tom's Shantih" in AH's *Melodies Unheard: Essays on the Mysteries of Poetry*.

2 The review was of Rowse's *The Poet Auden: A Personal Memoir* (New York: Weidenfeld & Nicholson, 1987) and appeared in the December 21st, 1989, issue of the *New York Review of Books*.

3 "St. Paul's Epistle to the Galatians" was published in *Incarnation: Contemporary Writers on the New Testament*, edited by Alfred Corn (New York: Viking, 1990), and reprinted in AH's *Melodies Unheard: Essays on the Mysteries of Poetry*.

courses that I have some difficulty adjusting to change, particularly as my Harvard experiences over the years have ranged from good to extremely good. I'm stuck in the past in some ways.

Richardson thanks no one, front or back. His references to the work of other scholars are few. But the book really is his own. It is a site he has mastered (and written quite a lot about). The book isn't about architecture but about buildings (a distinction few classicists understand, and one of the reasons for the radical nature of my last book). It reads easily and well, and is jam-packed with information. Poorly illustrated, though. He has just finished a huge book on the topography and buildings of ancient Rome.[1] The last one is 59 years old and used by everyone who touches the subject, and that's a hell of a lot of people. I'm a consultant for R's press on the matter of illustrations and bibliography. The book will be on call for decades.

My colleague John Pinto was here for two days and we had at it with a will. I've done articles with others but never a book. John is mild and modest, with a spine of steel. We agree however on most things, and our negotiations on the balance have so far been successful. Our architect's drawings are splendid, our photos are splendid, and I now have color transparencies of major Villa sculptures in the Vatican, Terme, etc. The book will be a whiz I think. I thought John would balk at eliminating footnote numbers by putting all references etc. in the back, page-keyed, a system I think works well. But he likes it …

Hadzi's visit was a great success. His vitality is enormous; seeing the Gauguin show[2] with him was a special treat. He wanted to have dinner in Georgetown on a Saturday night; we did.

A presto,
Suetonius, Tranquillus

[397]

[AH]
[March 23rd, 1989]
[4256 Nebraska Avenue, N.W., Washington, D.C. 20016]

[Blank personalised postcard, typed]

Dear Subscriber,

I think it worth pointing out that our baths around here are even <u>smaller</u> than Hadrian's small baths, and deserve mention in consequence … We are planning a rematch with you and Howard Nemerov sometime in mid-April, as I seem to recall; we will, if you cooperate, let you know about it. "Cooperate," by the way, is a word derived from the practice of James Fennimore Cooper, who refused to Cooperate

---

1 Lawrence Richardson, *A New Topographical Dictionary of Ancient Rome* (Baltimore, MD: Johns Hopkins University Press, 1992).

2 *The Art of Paul Gauguin*, an exhibition which ran at the National Gallery in Washington, D.C. from May 1st to July 31st, and displayed 280 of the painter's catalogued works.

with Mark Twain.

Comparable Max

[398]

[AH]
February 25th, 1990
4256 Nebraska Avenue, N.W., Washington, D.C. 20016

[Letter, typed on a Georgetown University, Department of English, letterhead]

Dear Bill,

    I stayed up all night and just finished Sir Banister Fletcher's <u>History of Architecture</u>,[1] and it confirms a theory of Helen's that our destinies are determined by our names, so that it follows that anyone named Krankheit ought to be a doctor, and anyone named Banister would have something to do with architecture. It's a really good book, and like all this art-history stuff, it has great pictures that keep you diverted when the writing gets dull.

    Seriously, though, it is quite extraordinary, and I have looked up the entries on Palladio and Lutyens and a few others, including Wren. I even noticed a glancing reference to Ernesto Rogers, whom I had met at the Academy in Rome. The pictures, including the drawings, are remarkable; though, like most architectural pictures, difficult to "read," by which I mean that I would have great trouble grasping what a certain building that I have actually seen is like from an illustration of it. Many of the entries are so terse (for example, the one on S. Ivo in Rome) that one is disappointed in not having more. But it certainly looks as if he has covered the whole surface of the earth, and left no stone unturned. The sheer breadth of learning and cultural embrace is astonishing. We are very, very grateful to you.[2]

Love,
Tony

---

1 *Sir Banister Fletcher's A History of Architecture,* edited by John Musgrove (Boston, MA: Butterworths, 1989).

2 WLM had sent the Banister Fletcher volume to AH as a present for his 67th birthday.

[399]

[WLM]
March 1st, 1990
[3811 39th Street NW, #F-90, Washington, D.C. 20016]

[Postcard, with a photograph of the United States Capitol, typed, with the sender's address given as S Cody Grasshopper, Nebraska 72727, addressed to A Hecht, 4256 Nebraska Ave., Washington, D.C. 20016]

My dear Hecht,
    I feel I must tell you, since I am a doctor, that the last person to read Fletcher through at one sitting came down with a very serious case of entasis, and broke out all over with a case of large voussoirs; he is now on a strict diet of boiled archivolts.[1] It puts me in mind of the sad case of R. T. Petersson, who read all of <u>Paddington Bear</u> at a gulp; he came down, as you'll recall, with zeugma gravis and has had to drink a 20% solution of litotes every day ever since.
                  With kind regards,
                  Sherwin C.

[400]

[WLM]
[September 13th, 1990]
[3811 39th Street NW, #F-90, Washington, D.C. 20016]

[Postcard, with an 1896 photograph taken in front of the Plaza Hotel, 5th Avenue at 59th Street, New York, handwritten, addressed to The Hechts, 4256 Nebraska, Ave, NW, Washington, D.C., 20016]

Dear Helen and Tony,
    Nice evening. I thought Jason an intelligent and likely person – he'll do well, I'd

---

1 The book is 1,621 pages long.

think.[1] Tony, is that you, obverse, furthest right? Thanks again.
                                Billy the Boy Artist.

[401]

[WLM]
November 13th, 1990
3811 39th Street NW, #F-90, Washington, D.C. 20016

[Blank postcard, typed, addressed to Anthony Hecht, 4256 Nebraska Ave NW, Washington, D.C. 20016]

Tony,
   I suggest a long moratorium, after which we might talk if both of us wish to.
                                Bill

[402]

[WLM]
February 1st, 1992
3811 39th Street NW, #F-90, Washington, D.C. 20016

[Blank postcard, typed, addressed to Anthony Hecht, 4256 Nebraska Ave. NW, Washington, D.C. 20016]

Tony,
   I'll be out of circulation for some time.[2] Your letter has been put aside, unopened, with other things to be attended to later on.
                                Bill

[403]

[WLM]
April 16th, 1992
3811 39th Street NW, #F-90, Washington, D.C. 20016

[Letter, typed, addressed to Anthony Hecht, 4256 Nebraska Ave NW,
4256 Nebraska Ave NW, Washington, D.C. 20016]

Dear Tony,
   Thanks for your note of long ago. I am almost fully reanimated, as the medics say, and am back at work at last. It was in some ways a horrible experience, brightened

1 The Hechts had hosted a small dinner party for WLM. Jason, the other guest referred to here, was a friend of Evan Hecht's from his Grade School days, and was now a student at the American University in Washington, D.C., which was very close to the Hechts' house on Nebraska Avenue N.W.
2 WLM had had to undergo triple bypass heart surgery.

by the care of the hospital nurses and staff.
                              Yours,
                              Bill

Afterword

Janus-headed herm bust

Detail of an etching by Johann Adam Schweickart, 1743

Readers who have come this far will be wondering what can have happened to bring this correspondence to such an abrupt close. The answer is that the friends had had a serious falling out.

During the dinner party for which MacDonald thanked his hosts on September 13th, 1990, a subject came up which was of interest to both men – this being Trajan's column, the 115' monument whose erection in the center of Rome was completed around AD 113. MacDonald's interest in the column was that of an architectural historian who had made ancient Rome his speciality; Hecht's was that of a poet who had placed it at the center of one of his best-known poems.

"The Cost" had first appeared in *Encounter* in July 1971, and Hecht had included it in his 1977 collection, *Millions of Strange Shadows*. He hadn't just included it, however; he had given it prominence by making it the very first poem in the book. We can take it from this that he was pleased with what he'd written – as he had reason to be, since it is a highly accomplished piece of work, both formally and imaginatively – but he almost certainly placed it where he did for another, more important reason, this being that it announced a theme which would reappear throughout the collection.

Hecht's poem describes a young couple circling the column on a motor-scooter:

> Instinct with joy, a young Italian banks
>   Smoothly round the base
> of Trajan's column, feeling between his flanks
>   That cool, efficient beast,
> His Vespa, at one with him in a centaur's race,
>   Fresh from a Lapith feast,
>
> And his Lapith girl behind him.
>
> [...]
>
> Look at their slender purchase, how they list
>   Like a blown clipper, brought
> To the lively edge of peril, to the kissed
>   Lip, the victor's crown,
> The prize of life. Yet one unbodied thought

>   Could topple them, bring down
>
>   The whole shebang ...

For the *motociclisti*, wholly absorbed in what they are doing, the column is nothing but a giant traffic-island, something they need to go round if they are to get to where they are headed. But of course it is a great deal more than that, for

>   around the column
>   There also turn, and turn eternally,
>   Two thousand raw recruits
>   And scarred veterans coiling the stone in solemn
>   Military pursuits

The 600' spiral frieze described here shows scenes from Trajan's campaigns against the tribes of Dacia (a region to the north of the Danube which had been giving Rome trouble since before the days of Caesar). Those campaigns, which the poet tells us lasted for fifteen years, would have taken an extraordinary toll on the legionaries who took part in them, but it isn't thoughts about what the soldiery had endured which the poet imagines upending the couple; rather it is thoughts about what those "raw recruits" and "scarred veterans" came to:

>   All of that youth and purpose is, of course,
>   No more than so much dust.

If this thought were suddenly to strike the couple, if they were vividly and inescapably seized with it – the column no longer a traffic island but a giant *memento mori* – their smooth and joyful progress could easily be interrupted.

To lead tolerable lives – lives which contain their fair share of contentment, happiness, even joy – we must be able not to attend to certain things, something we can do either by virtue of being *inattentive*, and simply not seeing them, or else by virtue of being *disattentive*, and deliberately shutting them out. Is there anything wrong with this? The last stanza of this poem – written, it should be said, at the height of the Vietnam War – appears to suggest that there isn't, or needn't be:

>   And why should they take thought
>   Of all that ancient pain,
>   The Danube winters, the nameless young who fought,
>   The blood's uncertain lease?

We surely wouldn't want to see the couple thrown from their Vespa, after all. But not attending to things sometimes exacts a cost, and the cost can be exorbitant. Here it will be as well to quote the whole of that last stanza:

> And why should they take thought
>   Of all that ancient pain,
> The Danube winters, the nameless young who fought,
>   The blood's uncertain lease?
> Or remember that the fifteen-year campaign
>   Won seven years of peace?

At some point during the dinner party conversation about Trajan's column, MacDonald told Hecht that the Dacian Wars had only taken two or three years to complete – the first having been waged between AD 101 and 102, and the second in 105 – not, as Hecht had supposed, fifteen. Hecht was taken aback by this information, shocked even. How could he have got this so badly wrong?

Poets do sometimes make mistakes, of course. Shakespeare has Cassius telling Brutus "The clock hath stricken three," when in BC 44 there were no clocks, let alone clocks which chimed; Keats stations Cortez "Silent upon a peak in Darien," when it should have been his compatriot Balboa; and Elizabeth Bishop includes an 80-watt light bulb in one of her poems, when light bulbs only ever came in 40-, 60-, or 100-watt varieties. But not all mistakes are as minor as these, and it is clear that Hecht was straightaway convinced that if the Dacian Wars had lasted a mere two or three years, his mistake in thinking that they had last a full fifteen was far more damaging to "The Cost" than Shakespeare's mistake was to *Julius Caesar*, or Keats's to "On First Looking into Chapman's Homer," or Bishop's to "Faustina, or Rock Roses."[1]

If he was shocked by what MacDonald told him, he was also at a loss to understand why his friend hadn't said anything about the matter before. MacDonald had seen the poem shortly after it was first published in *Encounter* in 1971, and all he'd done was compliment him on it: "The column poem is great," he'd written, only adding "I have slides somewhere of couples on Vespas rounding the Col. by Santa Maria di Loreto, + once from atop the Col. I saw a 2-Vespa crash. Learned, experienced."[2]

MacDonald could have pleaded embarrassment. How was he to tell Hecht that a poem with which he was so pleased contained so big an error? Instead of this, he told Hecht that the reason he'd not said anything was because he didn't think the mistake mattered. This was a poem, after all, not a treatise, and different standards surely applied. Hecht was dismayed. For him, a poem that is trying to get at the truth about something, and whose argument depends upon statements advanced as historically accurate, cannot survive unscathed the discovery that those statements are false. It belittled the importance of poetry to suppose otherwise.[3]

---

1 It was AH who first noticed this mistake of Bishop's, mentioning it in "Awful But Cheerful," the review of her *Geography III* which he wrote for the August 26th, 1977 issue of the *Times Literary Supplement*.

2 Postcard #68, December 6th, 1971.

3 Christopher Ricks has set out a very powerful case for agreeing with Hecht on this question. "When a work is acutely consonant with the facts which it adduces, it is praised for fidelity; when it lapses from its claims, the idea of infidelity is held to be farcically solemn and inadmissible. This is not criticism but

Afterword | 463

Although he tried to disguise his feelings, Hecht was impatient for the dinner to be over and the guests gone so that he could go up to his library and track down his source. According to Helen Hecht, he stayed up all night, and did eventually locate the volume he'd relied on; but if he felt partially vindicated – he hadn't simply imagined that the Wars had lasted fifteen years – he also realized that the source was an unreliable one, and that he'd been unwise to rely on it.

This would have been painful for him, given that the argument of his poem depended on the wars having lasted as long as he'd said – or considerably longer than they had, at any rate – but making it even more painful would have been the realization that, just as the young couple he'd written about could only delight in "their headlong lurch and flatulent racket" for as long as certain things escaped them, so he'd only been able to delight in his fluently written and carefully crafted poem for as long as certain things had escaped *him*. This was a bitter irony, and contemplating it Hecht must have felt more like the "stricken deer" than the "hart ungallèd" of the poem's epigraph.[1]

Hecht rang MacDonald the next day, and the conversation did not go well. Indeed, it seems to have gone quite badly, and when the call came to an end, it did so with both men feeling upset and aggrieved.

Though Hecht's last letters to MacDonald have gone missing, we know that he tried on at least three separate occasions to get back on terms. But MacDonald's responses – one sent in November 1990, another in February 1992, and the third in April 1992 – show him firmly resisting, with the result that a friendship which had lasted for thirty-six years, and seen the two men through fat years and lean, good times and bad – was sadly, perplexingly, at an end.

---

public relations." See "Literature and the Matter of Fact," in Christopher Ricks, *Essays in Appreciation* (Oxford and New York: Oxford University Press, 1998), pp. 280–310. T. S. Eliot seems to have seen it the same way. After Horace M. Kallen pointed out a geographical error in "Journey of the Magi," saying "There is no way that men travelling with horse and camel can pass from snowline to vegetation overnight and reach Bethlehem …There is no snow nearer than [Mt] Hermon, to the north, several camel journey away," Eliot replied as follows: "I am much interested to hear your criticism of my geographical ignorance. Theoretically, I believe one ought to make verse as watertight as prose on such points." However, he then sought to sidestep Kallen's criticism, availing himself of the same sort of defence that apologists for Keats and Bishop have used, arguing that his poem was not to be understood literally: "if I had bothered about the topography and archaeology of Asia Minor, I should have had to omit a good deal of detail which really is meant to be symbolical." *The Poems of T. S. Eliot: Volume 1: Collected and Uncollected Poems*, eds. Christopher Ricks and Jim McCue (London: Faber & Faber, 2015), p. 760.

Not everyone sees the relation between literature and the matter of fact as Ricks does and as Eliot did. As Ricks himself acknowledges, eminent figures have taken a different view, amongst them no less a scholar than M. H. Abrams, who, in an essay on Keats, wrote that the poet's mistake about Cortez "matters to history but not to poetry." See M. H. Abrams, "John Keats," in *The Norton Anthology of English Literature*, revised edition, ed., M. H. Abrams *et al* (New York: W. W. Norton & Co., 1968), 2:504, note 1.

1 Hecht quotes the first two lines of Hamlet's first four to Horatio as soon as the play within the play is over. In full, those lines read as follows: "Why, let the stricken deer go weep / The hart ungallèd play, For some must watch / While some must sleep, / Thus runs the world away. *Hamlet*, III.ii. 271-274.

In the years that remained to them – Hecht was to die twelve years later and MacDonald six years after that – each man continued to work hard, producing more books, giving more lectures, undertaking more travels, and receiving more honors. They also experienced more losses, and had to endure more bouts of ill-health, some of them serious. One can only imagine how each must have felt when, prompted by one of these developments, a choice letterhead, a good joke, or a quirky headline, they had to check a powerful impulse to dash off a "Dear Boy" or an "Admired Sir," a "Dear Bill" or a "Dear Tony."

We do know that, whatever prevented him from responding to Hecht's entreaties, MacDonald ended up greatly regretting what had happened, and that when he heard of his old friend's death, in October 2004, the news deeply saddened him. Not long afterwards, he wrote to Helen Hecht, letting her know that he had held onto her late husband's side of their correspondence, and that he would be returning it to her for safe keeping.

We should be grateful that he did.

Chronology

1921	William Lloyd MacDonald is born in Putnam, Connecticut, on July 12th, to William Lloyd MacDonald, Sr. (1883–1963) and Susan MacDonald (née Elrod, 1886–1961). He has one elder brother, John Elrod MacDonald (1914–2005).
1923	Anthony Evan Hecht is born in New York City, on January 16th, to Melvyn Hahlo Hecht (1893–1978) and Dorothea Grace Hecht (née Holzman, 1894–1979).
1926	AH's brother Roger is born.
1927	AH arrives at the Dalton School, Manhattan, and remains there until 1930.
1930	AH attends the Collegiate School in Manhattan, and remains there until 1936.
1936	WLM attends the Governor Dummer Academy (now the Governor's Academy) in Byfield, Massachusetts, but leaves in 1937.
	AH attends the Horace Mann School for Boys, Manhattan, and remains there until 1940.
1937	WLM arrives at the Sanford High School, Sanford, Maine, and remains there until 1939.
1939	WLM enters the University of New Hampshire, but withdraws after one term.
1940	WLM moves to Boston, where he finds work in the ticket office of American Airlines, and meets and courts Betsey Adams Schadt.
	AH attends Bard College, Annandale-on-Hudson, New York.
1941	WLM moves to Bangor, Maine, and marries Betsey Adams Schadt.
1942	WLM enlists in the US Army Air Corps, and is trained as a Bombardier/Navigator. He serves as an Air Inspector and as a Bombardier Instructor, first at Kirtland Field in Albuquerque, New Mexico, then at Smyrna Air Base near Nashville, Tennessee, and finally at Santa Ana Air Base in Costa Mesa, California, where he rises to the rank of First Lieutenant. He is honorably discharged in 1945.
1943	AH enlists in the US Army, and is assigned to the 386th Infantry Regiment, C Company, 3rd Platoon. He sees action on the German front in April 1945, and is stationed in Japan in the fall-winter of 1946. He is honorably discharged on March 12th, 1946.

1944   AH is awarded his B.A. by Bard, *in absentia*.

1946   WLM and his wife divorce. He enters Harvard on the GI Bill, where his favourite subjects are history and geography, and his most admired teachers are Kenneth John Conant and Robert Pierpoint Blake, whom he later credits with having inspired his love of buildings and travel. At Harvard he makes a number of lifelong friends, amongst them Arthur Trottenberg and Gerry Gillerman, Budd Sweeney, Rick Peale, Ray Considine, J. P. Young, Dave Register and Don Blake.

AH attends Kenyon College in Ohio, having enrolled as a "special" (i.e. non-matriculating) student. He studies with John Crowe Ransom.

1947   AH starts teaching at Kenyon College. Poems of his appear in print for the first time, chosen by Ransom for the *Kenyon Review*. In the fall, he is employed as a graduate teaching assistant at the State University of Iowa, where he befriends Flannery O'Connor. He suffers a nervous breakdown and is hospitalized in New York. After being discharged, he enters psychoanalysis and studies privately with Allen Tate. Tate recommends that AH take over his teaching duties that fall at New York University. He meets Robert Lowell and Jean Stafford. In the summer he returns to Kenyon, where he studies with William Empson, F. O. Matthiessen, and Austin Warren.

1948   AH's poems appear in *The Hudson Review*, *Poetry*, and *Furioso*, and he wins the *Furioso* Poetry Award.

WLM is made a Veterans National Scholar by Harvard.

1949   WLM graduates from Harvard, having majored in history, and drives his parents all the way to California to visit relatives. He takes a summer job as Assistant Manager at the Ahwahnee Lodge in Yosemite National Park, and begins graduate studies at Harvard.

AH spends the summer traveling in France and Italy and returns to the US to enter Columbia University as a candidate for the Master's Degree in English literature.

1950   AH is awarded his M.A. by Columbia, and returns to Europe for the summer. In the fall, he moves to Ischia, where for the first time he encounters and gets to know W. H. Auden.

WLM starts lecturing on the history of architecture at the Boston Architectural Center, and is appointed Executive Secretary of the Byzantine Institute.

1951   WLM travels to Europe, and spends time in Paris, where he stays with a wealthy American family who invite him out for an evening at the Ritz Hotel. There he finds himself seated beside Humphrey Bogart and opposite Lauren Bacall. His article, "The Uncovering of Byzantine Mosaics in Hagia Sophia," is published in the Summer issue of *Archaeology*.

AH, still on Ischia, is awarded the first ever Rome Fellowship in Literature by the American Academy of Arts and Letters, the grant from which enables him to spend a year at the American Academy in Rome, which commences that October.

1952   AH, returned to the US, begins work as an instructor at his alma mater, Bard College, teaching freshman English, poetry writing, Renaissance poetry, and Shakespeare. His colleagues include Saul Bellow, Irma Brandeis, and Heinrich Blücher.

WLM meets Dale Lorraine Ely, then working as a junior editor for Little Brown, at a party in Cambridge, Massachusetts. Dale was also a divorcee, having been married in the late 1940s to Douglas Conner, a pilot.

1953 WLM and Dale Lorraine Ely get married. He is taken on as an instructor at Wheaton College in Norton, Massachusetts, where he teaches classics. Harvard awards him his M.A., and he becomes a candidate for the Ph.D.

1954 AH marries Patricia Anne Harris, a model. His first collection of poems, *A Summoning of Stones* is published by Macmillan, and he is awarded a Guggenheim Fellowship, the grant from which enables him to return to the American Academy in Rome, taking PH with him.

WLM is awarded a Rome Fellowship, and he and DM cross the Atlantic on board the SS Liberté, spend some time touring the English home counties, and then drive down through France, Germany, Austria, and northern Italy, arriving in Rome in the last week of September.

The Hechts meet the MacDonalds for the first time, probably in early October.

PH discovers that she is pregnant.

The Hechts and MacDonalds move in the same circles, spending time with Dimitri Hadzi, Robert Venturi, Richard Wilbur, Yehudi Wyner, and Jack and Corda Zajac, amongst others. Later on, the circle will widen to include Al Blaustein, Ralph and Fanny Ellison, and visitors to the AAR such as W. H. Auden and Allen Tate.

PH has a miscarriage in late November.

1955 WLM submits his Ph.D dissertation to Harvard in mid-March, and shortly thereafter he and DM set off on a nine-and-a-half week, 8,000 mile road trip to "the Byzantine east." In Istanbul, they meet up with Robert Venturi, with whom they ascend to the dome of Agia Sophia. They are also joined by John Ward-Perkins, Director of the British Academy in Rome, who accompanies them as far as Baalbek in the Lebanon. Other countries they take in are Greece, Syria, Iraq, and Israel. They return to Rome at the end of May, and learn that WLM's Ph.D dissertation has been rejected. WLM resolves to write another.

PH returns alone to New York, sailing from Naples in mid-June. AH, who had accompanied her to Naples, goes on to Ischia, where he spends the rest of the summer, before returning to Rome for the fall.

The MacDonalds spend five days with AH on Ischia, and then return by themselves to Rome.

DM discovers that she is pregnant in early December.

AH sails for New York in mid-December.

1956 AH is appointed as an instructor by Smith College, Northampton, Massachusetts, and teaches freshman English.

WLM and DM's son Noel is born in July. The family leaves Rome for the US in August. WLM's second dissertation – "The Hippodrome at Constantinople" – earns him his Ph.D from Harvard, and he begins work as an instructor at Yale University.

AH and PH's son Jason is born in November.

1957 DM discovers that she is pregnant again in May.

WLM and DM's son Darius born in December.

1958 Darius MacDonald dies in January.

AH is promoted to Assistant Professor at Smith, and his and PH's son Adam is born in October.

1959 AH files for separation from PH in August, and is awarded a second Guggenheim fellowship.

WLM and DM's son Nicholas born in November, and WLM is promoted to Assistant Professor at Yale.

1960 AH is awarded a Ford Foundation fellowship.

1961 AH's divorce from PH is finalized.

WLM's mother dies.

1962 PH marries Baron Philippe Lambert, a banker, and moves with Lambert to his native Belgium, taking Adam and Jason with her.

AH is hospitalized for depression in Gracie Square Hospital in New York, and remains there for three months. After being discharged he spends time recuperating with the MacDonalds at their home in Guilford, Connecticut. AH is appointed Associate Professor at Bard College.

WLM is awarded a Morse Fellowship by Yale, and returns for another year at the American Academy in Rome, taking his family with him. His *Early Christian and Byzantine Architecture* is published by Braziller in New York.

1963 WLM is promoted to Associate Professor at Yale. His father dies.

1965 AH receives the Brandeis University Creative Arts Award.

WLM's second book, *The Architecture of the Roman Empire*, is published by Yale University Press, and he moves from Yale to Smith College, where he has been appointed full Professor in the History of Art.

1966 AH joins the editorial board of *The Hudson Review*, advising on poetry submissions, and is promoted to full Professor at Bard.

WLM is presented with a Dean William Emerson Fund Award.

1967 AH takes part in Poetry International at the Queen Elizabeth Hall in London. The other poets engaged to read include Yehuda Amichai, W. H. Auden, John Berryman, Yves Bonnefoy, William Empson, Allen Ginsberg, Hugh MacDiarmid, Pablo Neruda, Ann Sexton, Giuseppe Ungaretti, Andrei Voznesensky, and Yevgeny Yevtushenko. He is awarded a Rockefeller Foundation fellowship, and the Lillian Fairchild Award. He leaves Bard to take up a full professorship at the University of Rochester in upstate New York. His second collection of poems, *The Hard Hours*, is published by Atheneum, who also publish *Jiggery-Pokery: A Compendium of Double Dactyls*, which he has co-edited with John Hollander.

1968 AH receives the Pulitzer Prize, the Russell Loines Award, and the Miles Poetry Prize for *The Hard Hours*, and the Honorary Fellow grant from the Academy of American Poets. He is named John H. Deane Professor of Rhetoric and Poetry at the University of Rochester, and, on leave, he returns to the American Academy in Rome, where he works with Helen Bacon on a translation of Aeschylus's *Seven Against Thebes*.

1969 WLM and DM separate. WLM, who has maintained his connection with Harvard, and still teaches graduate courses there, meets the undergraduate John Pinto, who will become a friend, colleague, and collaborator.

AH is named a Fellow of the Academy of American Poets.

1970 AH is awarded an honorary degree by Bard, and becomes a member of the National Institute for Arts and Letters.

WLM and DM divorce.

1971 WLM gives a series of eight lectures at Harvard.

AH meets and marries Helen D'Alessandro, a former student of his at Smith College who has been working as an editor for Doubleday and Walker & Co. in New York. He is appointed a chancellor of the American Academy of Poets, and is Visiting Hurst Professor at Washington University, St. Louis, Missouri.

1972 AH is awarded a lectureship in American literature by the US State Department, and represents his country at an international literary conference held in São Paolo, Brazil. He and HH's son Evan Alexander is born.

WLM starts seeing Barbara Satz, a journalist working for the *Holyoke Daily Transcript-Telegram*.

1973 DM moves to Oregon, taking Nicholas and Noel with her.

WLM is Kea Distinguished Professor at the University of Maryland, where he delivers four lectures.

AH is a visiting professor at Harvard University, where he spends time with Elizabeth

Bishop. His and Helen Bacon's translation of Aeschylus's *Seven Against Thebes* is published by Oxford University Press.

1974   WLM is appointed Alice Pratt Brown Professor of History of Art at Smith College.

1975   AH is elected a fellow of the American Academy of Arts and Sciences.

WLM's *Northampton, Massachusetts: Architecture and Buildings* is published by the Northampton Bicentennial Committee.

1976   WLM's *The Pantheon: Design, Meaning, and Progeny* is published by Harvard University Press in the US and by Penguin Books in the UK. *The Princeton Encyclopedia of Classical Sites*, for which he has been an associate editor, is published by Princeton University Press.

1977   AH's *Millions of Strange Shadows* is published by Atheneum in the US, and by Oxford University Press in the UK. AH takes part in the Salzburg Seminar in American Studies, and is visiting professor at Yale University.

WLM undergoes surgery for an obstruction of the digestive tract.

1978   WLM gives the Katherine Asher Engel lecture at Smith College. His lecture is entitled "Piranesi's Carceri: Sources of Invention."

Dale MacDonald dies.

AH's father dies.

1979   WLM befriends V. S. Pritchett, who first went to Smith as a writer in residence in 1966–1967, and has had a series of appointments there ever since. They will go on to correspond on a regular basis. WLM's *Piranesi's Carceri: Sources of Invention* is published by Smith College.

AH's mother dies. His *The Venetian Vespers* is published by Atheneum in the US.

1980   AH's *The Venetian Vespers* is published by Oxford University Press in the UK, where it receives a Poetry Book Society Recommendation.

WLM gives Smith notice of his intention to resign his chair at the end of the academic year, hoping to devote more time to independent scholarship and publishing.

1981   AH is given the English-Speaking Union Award by the Junior Board of the ESU in Chicago for "A Love for Four Voices: Homage to Franz Joseph Haydn," and is awarded an honorary degree (Doctor of Humane Letters) by Georgetown University, Washington, D.C.

WLM is a visiting lecturer at Emory University, and at the end of the year is diagnosed with Myasthenia Gravis.

1982   AH receives the Flint Kellogg Award in Poetry from Bard College. He is named Consultant in Poetry to the Library of Congress, an office he will hold for two years.

WLM is Robert Sterling Clark Visiting Professor of Art at the Clark Institute in Williamstown, Massachusetts. His *The Architecture of the Roman Empire: An Introductory Study* is reissued in a revised edition by Yale University Press, and his *Columns in the Collection of the Cooper-Hewitt Museum* is published by The Smithsonian Institution's National Museum of Design.

1983   AH shares Yale University's Beinecke Library's Bollingen Prize with John Hollander. He is awarded an honorary degree (Doctor of Humane Letters) by Towson State University, Baltimore, Maryland, and is made a Trustee of the American Academy in Rome.

WLM moves from Northampton to Washington, D.C.

1984   AH receives the Librex-Guggenheim Eugenio Montale Award for Poetry.

1985   AH is named University Professor at Georgetown University in Washington, D.C., and moves to the city.

WLM is appointed a Getty Scholar by the Getty Center for the Fine Arts and the Humanities, Los Angeles, California, where he befriends another Getty Scholar, the philosopher Stephen Toulmin, and the architect Frank Gehry. Smith College's Museum of Art publishes *Chester Michalik: Photographs*, with an introduction by WLM.

1986   WLM's *The Architecture of the Roman Empire: Volume II: An Urban Reappraisal* is published by Yale University Press, and the book receives the Society of Architectural Historians' Alice Davis Hithcock Book Award.

AH's *Obbligati: Essays in Criticism* is published by Atheneum.

1987   AH is awarded *Poetry* magazine's Harriet Monroe Award, and receives an honorary degree (Doctor of Humane Letters) from the University of Rochester. Ecco Press publishes *The Essential Herbert*, which he has edited and introduced.

1988   AH is awarded *Poetry* magazine's Ruth B. Lilly Poetry Prize.

1989   AH receives the University of the South's Aiken-Taylor Award for Modern American Poetry, an honorary degree (Doctor of Humane Letters) from St. John Fisher College, Rochester, New York, and a grant from the National Endowment for the Arts.

The Burdens of Formality: Essays on the Poetry of Anthony Hecht, edited by Sydney Lea, is published by Georgia University Press.

WLM receives the Massachusetts Institute of Technology's Kevin Lynch Award.

1990   AH's *The Transparent Man* and his *Collected Earlier Poems* are published by Knopf in the US. He is awarded a Rockefeller Foundation fellowship and spends six weeks in residence at the Villa Serbelloni in Bellagio, Italy, where he befriends another resident at the Villa, Edmund White. AH's brother Roger dies.

1991   AH's *The Transparent Man* and his *Collected Earlier Poems* are published by Oxford University Press in the UK. He ceases to be a Trustee of the AAR and instead becomes a Trustee Emeritus.

1992   WLM is appointed to the committee charged with selecting an architectural firm to take responsibility for renovating the Getty Museum in Malibu, CA. For this, he and other members of the committee – amongst them Ada Louise Huxtable – visit many firms in the US and Europe. It is WLM's last visit to Europe. He undergoes triple by-pass heart surgery.

          AH and WLM's correspondence comes to an end.

          The classicist William Arrowsmith dies, bringing his and AH's collaboration on a translation of Sophocles's *Oedipus at Colonos* to a premature end.

          AH delivers the A. W. Mellon Lectures in the Fine Arts at the National Gallery of Art in Washington, D.C..

1993   AH's *The Hidden Law: The Poetry of W. H. Auden* is published by Harvard University Press. In May, he retires from Georgetown University, and later in the year is a Rockefeller Foundation resident at the Villa Serbelloni, Bellagio, Italy.

1995   WLM and John Pinto's *Hadrian's Villa and Its Legacy* is published by Yale University Press.

          AH's *On the Laws of the Poetic Art* is published by Princeton University Press.

1996   AH's *Flight Among the Tombs* is published by Knopf in the US.

          WLM and John Pinto's *Hadrian's Villa and Its Legacy* receives the Alice Davis Hitchcock Award of the Society of Architectural Historians.

1997   AH is awarded the Academy of American Poets' Dorothea Tanning (now Wallace Stevens) Prize. AH's *Flight Among the Tombs* is published by Oxford University Press in the UK. He receives the first of three Bogliasco Fellowships for residence at the Centro Studi Ligure in Liguria, Italy.

1999   AH receives the second of his three Bogliasco Fellowships for residence at the Centro Studi Ligure in Liguria, Italy, and is awarded the Centenary College of Louisiana's Corrington Award. Between The Lines publishes *Anthony Hecht in Conversation with Philip Hoy*.

2000   AH is awarded the Poetry Society of America's Robert Frost Medal, and undergoes pancreatic surgery.

2001   AH's *The Darkness and the Light* is published by Knopf in the US.

2002   AH receives the Ambassador Book Award from the English Speaking Union, and his archive is established at Emory University's Robert H. Woodruff Library. *The Darkness and the Light* is published by Waywiser in the UK.

2003   AH's *Collected Later Poems* is published by Knopf in the US, and his *Melodies Unheard: Essays on the Mysteries of Poetry* is published by Johns Hopkins University Press.

2004   AH receives the third of his three Bogliasco Fellowships for residence at the Centro

Studi Ligure in Liguria, Italy. His *Collected Later Poems* is published by Waywiser in the UK. He is guest of honor at the Sewanee Writers' Conference, hosted by the University of the South in Sewanee, Tennessee. Papers on his work are delivered by Philip Hoy, Richard Kenney, Brad Leithauser, Wyatt Prunty, and and Mary Jo Salter. He gives his last ever public reading at the conference. *Collected Later Poems* receives the *Los Angeles Times* Book Award. He dies of lymphoma, October 20th, and is buried in the cemetery at Bard College. A memorial is held at the Folger Shakespeare Library in Washington, D.C., where the speakers are Michael Dirda, B. H. Fairchild, Dana Gioia, Joseph Harrison, and Greg Williamson.

2005   A second memorial for AH is held at the Guggenheim Museum in New York City, where the speakers are Shirley Hazzard, John Hollander, Philip Hoy, J. D. McClatchy, and Hays Rockwell. He is posthumously awarded the National Medal for the Arts by President George W. Bush, and an honorary degree by Ohio Wesleyan University.

WLM's brother John dies.

2008   WLM moves into an assisted living facility in Washington, D.C. in November. The 4,465 architectural photographs he has taken since the 1950s – many of them of sites now largely inaccessible or seriously changed – are sold to the Visual Resources Collection of the Department of Art and Archaeology at Princeton University.[1]

2010   WLM dies of natural causes, March 6th. His ashes are scattered in Rome, Italy, and in Astoria, Oregon, where a version of Trajan's Column he greatly admired had been erected in 1926.

2011   The American Academy in Rome hosts "Paradigm and Progeny: Roman Imperial Architecture and Its Legacy," a two-day conference, organized by John Pinto, Diane Favro, and Fikret Yegül, commemorating the work of WLM. Pinto, Favro and Yegül each presents a paper, as do Corey Brennan, Elizabeth Fentress, Sandra Gatti, Pierre Gros, Lothar Haselberger, Tom Howe, Guy Métraux, Eugenio La Rocca, Tom Morton, James Packer, Gianni Ponti, Marcello Spanù, and Mark Wilson-Jones.

Anthony Hecht: Selected Poems, edited by J. D. McClatchy, is published by Knopf, and AH's *Interior Skies: Late Poems from Liguria* is published by Two Ponds Press in a limited fine press edition of 75 copies. The book is illustrated with engravings by Abigail Rorer, and has a foreword by Philip Hoy.

2013   *The Selected Letters of Anthony Hecht,* edited with an introduction by Jonathan Post, is published Johns Hopkins University Press.

2015   The papers presented at the "Paradigm and Progeny: Roman Imperial Architecture and Its Legacy" conference are published in a supplementary volume of the *Journal of Roman Archaeology.*

---

1 Princeton University has collaborated with the Artstor Digital Library, and the photographs can now be viewed by Artstor subscribers at: http://www.artstor.org/content/william-l-macdonald-architecture-princeton-university

Glossary of Names

Aaron, Daniel (1912–2016), American writer and educator, who helped found the Library of America. He taught at Smith College for three decades and at Harvard from 1971 until 1983. It was Aaron who suggested the title for one of AH's most frequently anthologized poems, "The Dover Bitch." He was the husband of **Janet Aaron**.

Aaron, Janet (née Summers, 1915–2003), American political activist, who served on the Northampton City Democratic Committee for many years and was a member of Americans for Democratic Action. She was the wife of **Daniel Aaron**.

Abrams, M. H. (1912–2015), American literary critic, author of numerous studies, and general editor of *The Norton Anthology of English Literature*.

Ackerman, James S. (1919–), American architectural and art historian. He was a Fellow of the American Academy in Rome in 1952, a Resident of the Academy in 1975, and a Trustee and then Trustee Emeritus of the Academy from 1967 until 1984.

Ackroyd, Peter (1949–), British novelist, short-story writer, biographer, literary critic, and dramatist.

Acton, Lord (John Dalberg-Acton, 1834–1902), English Catholic historian, politician, and writer.

Adams, Franklin P. (1881–1960), American columnist, radio personality, author, poet, and translator.

Adler, Mortimer J. (1902–2001), American philosopher, author, and educator.

Aeschylus (BC c.525–c.456), Greek playwright and soldier.

Agnew, Spiro T. (1918–1996), American politician, who served as Vice-President to President **Richard Nixon** from 1969 until 1973, when he became the only person so far to have resigned that office as a result of facing criminal proceedings.

Alcuin (c.735–804), English scholar, churchman, poet, and teacher.

Alfred, William (1922–1999), American playwright and educator.

Allen, Don Cameron (1903–1972), American scholar and educator, who specialized in 16th- and 17th-Century literature.

Allen, Woody (1935–), American film-maker, actor, comedian, and musician.

Alma-Tadema, Lawrence (1835–1912), Dutch-born British painter.

Alsop, Susan Mary (1918–2004), American author and society hostess.

Ambler, Eric (1909–1998), British novelist.

Ameche, Don (1908–1993), American actor.

Amis, Kingsley, Sir (1922–1995), English novelist, poet, critic, anthologist, memoirist, and educator.

Angelico, Fra (Guido di Pietro, 1395–1455), Italian painter.

Antinous (AD 111–130), Bithynian Greek, who was the favorite – perhaps also the lover – of the Emperor **Hadrian**, who had him deified after his untimely death.

Applewhite, Edgar Jarratt (1919–2005), American, retired CIA officer and writer, who called himself a "taxophilist," i.e. a collector and classifier of thoughts, interests, and obsessions.

Aquinas, Thomas (1225–1274), Italian philosopher and theologian.

Arendt, Hannah (1906–1975), German-born American political theorist, and educator. She was the wife of **Heinrich Blücher**.

Aretino, Pietro (1492–1556), Italian author, poet, and playwright.

Arlen, Harold (1905–1986), American composer of popular song music.

Arrowsmith, William (1924–1992), American classicist, editor, educator, and translator. He was a Fellow of the American Academy in Rome in 1957, and until his death was collaborating with AH on a translation of **Sophocles**'s *Oedipus at Colonus*. AH's *On the Laws of the Poetic Art* is dedicated to his memory (as well as to the memory of O. B. Hardison).

Arvin, Newton (1900–1963), American literary critic and educator, who achieved distinction as a writer on 19th-Century American authors. He was one of three gay members of faculty at Smith College – the other two were **Raymond Jules Dorius** and **Edward Spofford** – who were caught up in a scandal involving pornography, as a result of which he was suspended from teaching but kept on at half-salary until his retirement.

Ashbery, John (1927–2017), American poet, novelist, translator, and artist.

Atkinson, Brooks, Justin (1894–1984), American theater critic.

Auden, W. H. (1907–1973), Anglo-American poet, playwright, librettist, essayist, critic, anthologist, and educator. He was the dedicatee of AH and **John Hollander**'s *Jiggery-Pokery*, and the subject of AH's *The Hidden Law: The Poetry of W. H. Auden*.

Augustine, St. (354–430), Numidian Christian theologian and philosopher, one of the most important Church fathers of Western Christianity, best known for his *Confessions* and *City of God*.

Augustus, Emperor (Gaius Julius Octavius, BC 63–AD 14), the first Roman Emperor, who ruled from BC 27 until his death.

Aurelius, Marcus (AD 121–180), Roman Emperor from 161 until 180, a practitioner of Stoicism, and author of one of Stoicism's best-known works, the *Meditations*.

Aurelius, Victor, Sextus (4th Century AD), African, author of *Caesares*, a history of imperial Rome from Augustus to Constantius.

Babcock, Charles L. (1924–2012), American classicist and educator, who taught at Cornell University, the University of Pennsylvania, and Ohio State University. He was a 1955 Fellow of the American Academy in Rome, a Resident in 1986, a Trustee from 1981 until 1983, a Trustee Emeritus thereafter, and from 1988 until 1989 was Acting Mellon Professor-in-Charge. He was the husband of **Mary A. Babcock**.

Babcock, Mary A. (née Taylor), American classicist and educator. She was a Fellow of the American Academy in Rome in 1954, and was the wife of **Charles L. Babcock**.

Bach, Johann Sebastian (1685–1750), German composer and musician.

Bacon, Helen (1919–2007), American classicist and educator, who taught at Smith College from 1953 until 1961, then joined the faculty of Barnard College in New York City, where she remained as Professor (and Chair) of Classics until her retirement in 1989. She was a Resident of the American Academy in Rome in 1969, and collaborated with AH on a translation of **Aeschylus**'s *Seven Against Thebes*.

Banham, Reyner (1922–1988), English architectural critic.

Barbarossa, Frederick (1122–1190), Duke of Swabia (as Frederick III) from 1147 until his death, and German King and Holy Roman Emperor from 1152 until his death, He was the husband of **Beatrice I, Countess of Burgundy**.

Barfield, Owen (1898–1997), British man of letters, and founder of the Anthroposophy movement in the English-speaking world

Barrymore, Ethel (1879–1959), American actress. She was the sister of **John** and **Lionel Barrymore**.

Barrymore, John (1882–1942). American actor. He was the brother of **Ethel** and **Lionel Barrymore**.

Barrymore, Lionel (1878–1954), American actor. He was the brother of **Ethel** and **John Barrymore**.

Barth, John (1930–), American novelist and short-story writer.
Baryshnikov, Mikhail (1948–), Russian-born American dancer and actor.
Baskin, Leonard (1922–2000), American artist, illustrator, engraver, print-maker, sculptor, typographer, book maker, writer, and educator. He founded the Gehenna Press in 1942, was Professor of Art at Smith College from 1953 until 1974, and then, after a decade spent in England, returned to America, where, from 1984 until 1994, he was Professor of Art at Hampshire College in Amherst, Massachusetts. He collaborated with AH on a number of projects, illustrating "The Seven Deadly Sins," "The Presumptions of Death," and "The Gehenna Florilegium." He was the dedicatee of AH's poem "Behold the Lilies of the Field." He was the husband of **Lisa Baskin**.
Baskin, Lisa (née Unger, 1943–), American bibliophile, activist, collector. She was the second wife of **Leonard Baskin**.
Bate, Walter Jackson (1918–1999), American biographer and literary critic, best known for his lives of **John Keats** and **Samuel Johnson**.
Bawer, Bruce (1956–), American poet, and literary, film, and cultural critic.
Bayley, John Barrington (1914–1981), American architect and editor, who founded the Classical America architectural group in 1968, and was its president from then until 1979.
Beardsley, Aubrey (1872–1898), English illustrator and author.
Beatrice I (1143–1184), Countess of Burgundy from 1148 until her death, and Holy Roman Empress by marriage to the Holy Roman Emperor **Frederick Barbarossa**. She was crowned Holy Roman Empress in 1167, and as Queen of Burgundy in 1178.
Bell, Anne Olivier (née Popham, 1916–), British editor, who was responsible for the five-volume edition of *The Diary of Virginia Woolf* which was published in 1979. She was married to Virginia Woolf's nephew, Quentin Bell.
Belloc, Hilaire (1870–1953), Anglo-French Catholic writer and historian.
Bellow, Saul (1915–2005), Canadian-born American novelist and short-story writer, who won the Nobel Prize for Literature in 1976.
Benchley, Robert (1889-1945), American humorist, newspaper columnist, and actor.
Bender, Henry V. (1945–), American classicist and educator.
Bennett, Joseph D. (1922–1972), American literary critic and co-founder of *The Hudson Review*.
Berenson, Bernard (1865–1959), Lithuanian-born American art historian, who was a leading authority on art of the Renaissance period.
Bernini, Gian Lorenzo (1598–1680), Italian sculptor, artist, and architect.
Berryman, John (1914–1972), American poet, scholar, and educator.
Bessie, Mike (1916–2008), American publisher who helped to found the Atheneum publishing house and was its president from 1963 until 1975.
Betocchi, Carlo (1899–1986), Italian poet and writer.
Bidwell, B.E. (1927–2011), American Vice President of the car and truck group of the Ford Motor Company's North American Automotive Operations from 1978 until 1981, when he left Ford to become Chief Operating Officer of The Hertz Group.
Bierce, Ambrose (1842–1914), American journalist, short-story writer, and satirist.
Bigsby, Christopher (1941–), British literary theorist, novelist, and radio presenter.
Bishop, Elizabeth (1911–1979), American poet, short-story writer, artist, and educator, who served as Consultant in Poetry to the Library of Congress from 1949 until 1950. During the 1970s she taught at the University of Washington, Harvard University, New York University, and the Massachusetts Institute of Technology.
Blake, James W. (1862–1935), American songwriter and author.
Blake, Peter (1920–2006), American architect, architectural theorist, and author.
Blake, Robert Pierpont (1886–1950), American authority on Byzantium, and scholar of Armenian and Georgian cultures.
Blake, William (1757–1827), English poet, painter, and printmaker.

Blinn, Carol J. (1946–), American letterpress printer, graphic designer, and publisher, who, since 1973, has run the Warwick Press from Easthampton in Massachusetts. She had been a letterpress apprentice at **Leonard Baskin**'s Gehenna Press, and was chosen by **David R. Godine** to design, create the decorated paste paper for, and carry out the printing of Godine's limited fine press edition of *The Venetian Vespers*.

Bloom, Harold (1930–), American literary critic, writer, and educator, who, since 1955, has taught English Literature at Yale University, and, from 1988 until 2004, was also Berg Professor of English at New York University.

Blow, Simon (1943–), English author and playwright.

Blücher, Heinrich (1899–1970), German poet, philosopher, and educator. Second husband of **Hannah Arendt**.

Blunt, Anthony (1907–1983), British art historian, who in 1964, after being offered immunity from prosecution, confessed to having spied for the Soviet Union. His identity as a member of the "Cambridge Five" was made public by Prime Minister Margaret Thatcher in 1979, and he was stripped of his knighthood immediately thereafter.

Bly, Robert (1926–), American poet, author, and activist.

Bogan, Louise (1897–1970), American poet, who served as Poetry Consultant in the Library of Congress from 1945 until 1946.

Bombeck, Irma (1927–1996), American humorist, newspaper columnist, and writer.

Boorstin, Daniel (1914–2004), American historian and educator, who served as the twelfth Librarian of the United States Congress from 1975 until 1987.

Borromini, Francesco (1599–1667), Italian architect. A leading representative of Roman baroque architecture.

Boswell, James (1740–1795), Scottish lawyer, diarist, and author, best known for his *Life of Johnson*.

Bowen, Charles (1835–1984), English judge.

Boyle, Andrew (1919–1991), Scottish journalist and biographer, best known for his book *The Climate of Treason*, which led to the exposure by Margaret Thatcher of **Anthony Blunt** as the "Fourth Man" in the "Cambridge Five" Soviet spy ring.

Boyle, Bernard Michael (1934–), American architectural historian, educator, and author, who taught at Yale, Smith College, Dartmouth College, the University of California, Berkeley, the Southern California Institute of Architecture, and, from 1969 until 1999, at Arizona State University, where he is now Emeritus Professor. He collaborated with WLM on the article "The Small Baths at Hadrian's Villa."

Bramante, Donato (1444–1514), Italian architect, who was responsible for introducing Renaissance architecture to Milan and High Renaissance architecture to Rome.

Brand, John (1744–1806), English antiquarian, author, curate, and Secretary to the Society of Antiquaries of London from 1784 until his death.

Brandeis, Irma (1905–1990), American literary scholar. An authority on Dante, and one-time mistress of the Italian poet, **Eugenio Montale**.

Brenson, Michael (1943–), American art critic, curator, writer, and educator.

Bresdin, Rodolphe (1822–1885), French draftsman and engraver.

Brinnin, John Malcolm (1916–1998), American poet and literary critic.

Briscoe, Herman T. (1893–1960), American editor, who served on the editorial board of *Webster's New World Dictionary of the American Language*. He was the husband of **Orah C. Briscoe**.

Briscoe, Orah C. (1908–1972), American editor, who served on the editorial board of *Webster's New World Dictionary of the American Language*. She was the wife of **Herman T. Briscoe**.

Britten, Benjamin (1913–1976), English composer, pianist, and conductor. He was the partner of **Peter Pears**.

Brodsky, Joseph (1940–1996), Russian poet and essayist, two of whose poems – "Cape Cody Lullaby" and "Lagoon" – AH translated. He was the dedicatee of AH's poem "Exile," and the subject of AH's elegy "A Death in Winter."

Brooks, Gwendolyn (1917–2000), American poet, who served as Consultant in Poetry to the Library of Congress from 1985 until 1986.

Brougham, Lord Henry Peter (1778–1868), British statesman who became Lord Chancellor of Great Britain.

Brown, Frank E. (1908–1988), American archaeologist and educator. He was the dedicatee of AH and **Helen Bacon**'s *Seven Against Thebes*, and the joint dedicatee, with **Sterling Dow**, of WLM's *The Architecture of the Roman Empire*, Volume II: *An Urban Appraisal*. He was the husband of **Jackie Brown**.

Brown, Jackie (1915–1988), American wife of **Frank E. Brown**.

Browning, Robert (1812–1889), English poet and playwright. He was the husband of **Elizabeth Barrett Browning**.

Browning, Elizabeth Barrett (1806–1861), English poet. She was the wife of **Robert Browning**.

Brunelleschi, Filippo (1377–1446), Italian architect, sculptor, and engineer.

Buckminster Fuller, Richard (1895–1983), American architect, designer, inventor.

Buddensieg, Tilmann (1928–2013), German art historian.

Buehlmann, Josef (1844–1921), German architectural historian and author.

Buffington, Robert Ray (1933–), American author and editor, and the official biographer of **Allen Tate**.

Bullock, Hugh (1898–1996), American investment banker. He was the husband of **Marie Bullock**.

Bullock, Marie (1911–1986), American founder and president of the Academy of American Poets. She was the wife of **Hugh Bullock**.

Bundy, McGeorge (1919–1996), American Foreign and Defense policy expert, who served as United States National Security Advisor to Presidents John F. Kennedy and Lyndon B. Johnson, and from 1961 until 1966 was president of the Ford Foundation.

Burroughs, William (1914–1997), American author.

Burrus, Sextus Afranius (AD 1–62), Roman prefect of the Praetorian Guard, who, together with Seneca the Younger, was an advisor to the Emperor **Nero**.

Byron, Lord George Gordon (1788–1824), English poet and politician.

Cahn, Walter (1933–), German-born American art historian and educator.

Calthrop, Gladys (1894–1980), British artist and stage and costume designer.

Calvino, Italo (1923–1985), Italian novelist, short-story writer, essayist, and journalist.

Cameron, H. D. (1934–), American classicist and educator.

Campion, Thomas (1567–1620), English composer, poet, and physician.

Candler, Asa (1851–1929), American businessman, and founder of the Coca-Cola Company.

Caracalla (Marcus Aurelius Severus Antoninus Augustus, AD 188–217), Roman Emperor, who ruled jointly with his father, Septimus Severus from AD 198 until AD 211, and alone from then until his assassination.

Caravaggio, Michelangelo Merisi (1572?–1610), Italian painter.

Carr, J. L. (1912–1994), English novelist, teacher, publisher, and founder of Quince Tree Press.

Cartier-Bresson, Henri (1908–2004), French photographer, sometimes called the father of photo-journalism.

Casaubon, Isaac (1559–1614), French classical scholar and philologist.

Cassius Dio, Lucius (c.155–235), Roman statesman and historian.

Chapman, George (c.1559–1634), English dramatist, translator, and poet, best known for his translations of **Homer**'s *Iliad* and *Odyssey*.

Charles, Prince of Wales (1948–), English aristocrat, heir apparent to the British throne. He was the former husband of **Diana, Princess of Wales**.

Cheever, John (1912–1982), American novelist and short-story writer.

Chetham, Charles S. (1930–1995), American art historian, who served as Director of the Smith

College Museum of Art from 1962 until 1988.
Child, Julia (1912–2004), American chef, author, and television presenter.
Christopher, Nicholas (1951–), American novelist, poet, and critic.
Clampitt, Amy (1920–1994), American poet and author.
Clark, Kenneth (1914–2000), American psychologist and educator, who served as Dean of the University of Rochester from 1963 until 1980.
Clark, Sir Kenneth McKenzie (1903–1983), British art historian, writer, and broadcaster.
Clark, Louis M., Jr., American, and former owner, with his wife **Joan Clark**, of the 1908 Edward E. Boynton House in Rochester, which was designed by Frank Lloyd Wright.
Clark, Joan, American, and former owner, with her husband **Louis Clark**, of the 1908 Edward E. Boynton House in Rochester, which was designed by Frank Lloyd Wright.
Clifford, James L. (1901–1979), American educator and author, who wrote two biographies of **Samuel Johnson** as well as other works on the subject of biography.
Cobb, Henry N. ("Harry," 1926–), American architect and educator. He was a founding partner, with **I.M. Pei**, of Pei Cobb Freed & Partners, and, from 1980 until 1985, served as chairman of Harvard University's Department of Architecture.
Coffin, Charles M. (1904–1956) American literary critic and educator. He was an authority on John Donne.
Cohn-Haft, Athena (née Capraro, later Warren, 1920–2010), American, and first wife of **Louis Cohn-Haft**.
Cohn-Haft, Louis (1919–2011), American historian and educator. He was an authority on ancient Greek history, who taught at Smith College from 1953 until 1987. He was a former husband of **Athena Cohn-Haft**.
Cohn-Haft, Betty (née Schlerman), American. **Louis Cohn-Haft**'s second wife.
Collins, Dr Rowland (1934–1985), American educator. He was an authority on Old English literature and literature of the Victorian era.
Conant, Kenneth John (1894–1984), American architectural historian. He was an authority on medieval architecture.
Condit, Carl (1914–1997), American historian of urban and architectural history, writer, and educator.
Connors, Joseph (1945–), American architectural historian and educator, who specialized in Italian Renaissance and Baroque architecture.
Conquest, Robert (1917–2015), British-American historian, poet, and novelist.
Consagra, Sophie Chandler (1927–2017), American academic administrator, who was Director of the American Academy in Rome from 1980 until 1984, its President from 1984 until 1988, and its Vice Chair-Special Projects from 1988 until 1990.
Conway, Jill (née Ker, 1934–), Australian-American author and educator, who was Smith College's first female president, serving from 1975 until 1985.
Cooke, H. Lester (1916–1973), American painter and art historian, who served as Curator of Painting at the National Gallery in Washington, D.C. from 1961 until 1973.
Cooper, James Fennimore (1789–1851), American writer, best known for the romantic novel *The Last of the Mohicans*.
Coward, Noel (1899–1973), English playwright, composer, director, actor, and singer.
Crane, Hart (1899–1932), American poet, best known for his most ambitious work, *The Bridge*. He died after (apparently) jumping from the steamship he was on at the time.
Crashaw, Richard (1612–1649), English poet.
Crema, Luigi (1905–1975), Italian historian of art and architecture, and educator.
Daley, Richard J. (1902–1976), American politician, best known for his role as Mayor of Chicago, an office he held from 1955 until 1976.
D'Annunzio, Gabriele (1883–1891), Italian poet, playwright, journalist.
d'Arezzo, Guido (c.990–1050), Italian music theorist, credited with founding modern western

musical notation.

Dando, John (1917–1987), American educator, Professor of English at Trinity College, Hartford, Connecticut.

D'Arms, John H. (1934–2002), American classicist, educator, and author, who was a Resident of the American Academy in Rome in 1972 and 1984, a trustee of the Academy from 1973 until 1976 and from 1981 until 1983, and the Academy's Director and its A. W. Mellon Professor in its School of Classical Studies from 1977 until 1980. He was Professor of Humanities and Professor of Classical Studies and History at the University of Michigan, and also served as President of the American Council of Learned Societies.

D'Arms, Maria Teresa (née Waugh, 1938–), English, the daughter of **Evelyn Waugh**. She was married to **John D'Arms**.

Darwin, Charles (1809–1882), English naturalist, geologist, and biologist, best known for his contributions to the science of evolution. He was the grandson of **Erasmus Darwin**.

Darwin, Erasmus (1731–1802), English physician, natural philosopher, physiologist, and slave-trade abolitionist. He was the grandfather of **Charles Darwin**.

Davidovsky, Mario (1934–), Argentine-American composer.

Daley, Richard J. (1902–1976), American politician who served as Mayor of Chicago from 1955 until 1976.

Daye, Erica Mendell (1961–), American, who was sentenced in 1987 to a twenty-year prison sentence for the second-degree murder of her son while under the influence of the hallucinogen PCP.

de Fine Licht, Kjeld (1931–2014), Danish architect and architectural historian.

de Kay Jr., Ormonde (1923–1998), American writer, poet, editor, translator, and screenwriter.

De Koven, Reginald (1859–1920), American music critic and composer.

Delacroix, Eugène (1798–1863), French painter.

della Francesca, Piero (c.1415–1492), Italian painter.

Democritus (BC c.460–c.370), Greek philosopher.

Demus, Otto (1902–1990), Austrian art historian and Byzantinist.

Diana, Princess of Wales (1961–1997), English aristocrat. She was the first wife of **Charles, Prince of Wales**.

Dibner, Bern (1897–1988), American electrical engineer, industrialist, and historian of science and technology.

Dickens, Charles (1812–1870), British novelist and social critic.

Dickinson, Emily (1830–1886), American poet.

Dieterle, William (1893–1972), German actor and film director.

Dimock, George (1917–2000), American classicist, educator, and author, who collaborated with AH on an unsuccessful attempt to translate Sophocles's *Oedipus at Colonos*. He was the joint dedicatee of AH's poem "Three Prompters from the Wings" (the other dedicatee being his wife, **Mary Dimock**).

Dimock, Mary (née Mesier, 1915–1998), American teacher of English and wife of **George Dimock**. She was the joint dedicatee, with her husband, of AH's poem "Three Prompters from the Wings."

Donne, John (1573–1631), English poet and cleric.

Donoghue, Denis (1928–), Irish literary critic and educator, who, since the late 1970s, has been Professor of English at New York University.

Dorius, Raymond Joel (1919–2006), American educator, who taught English Literature at Smith College. He was one of three gay members of faculty at Smith College – the other two were **Newton Arvin** and **Edward Spofford** – who were caught up in a scandal involving pornography, as a result of which he was fired from his job, fined, and handed a suspended jail sentence. Dorius was able to return to work, teaching in the English Department at San Francisco State University.

Dow, Sterling (1903–1995), American classicist, historian, archaeologist, and educator. He was an authority on Greek history of the fifth and fourth centuries BC, and was the joint dedicatee, with **Frank E. Brown**, of WLM's *The Architecture of the Roman Empire*, Volume II: *An Urban Appraisal*.

Dryden, John (1631–1700), English poet, translator, playwright, and literary critic.

Dudevant, Aurore (Amantine Lucile Aurore, née Dupin; nom-de-plume, George Sand, 1804–1876), French novelist, short-story writer, literary critic, and essayist.

Duke, Doris (1912–1993), American heiress, horticulturist, art collector, and philanthropist.

Dulles, Allen Welsh (1893–1969), American diplomat and lawyer, who became the first civilian, and, to date, the longest-serving, director of the CIA. He was the brother of **Eleanor Lansing Dulles** and **John Foster Dulles**.

Dulles, Eleanor Lansing (1895–1996), American author, educator, and economist. She was the sister of **Allen Welsh Dulles** and **John Foster Dulles**.

Dulles, John Foster (1888–1959), American politician, who served as Secretary of State under President Dwight D. Eisenhower from 1953 until 1959. He was the brother of **Eleanor Lansing Dulles** and **Allen Welsh Dulles**.

Duse, Eleonora (1858–1924), Italian actress.

Edwards, Jonathan (1703–1758), American preacher, theologian, and philosopher.

Ehle, John (1925–), American writer, best known for his novels but also the author of several works of non-fiction.

Eliot, George (Mary Ann Evans, 1819–1880), English novelist.

Eliot, T. S. (1888–1965), American-born British poet, playwright, essayist, literary and social critic, and publisher.

Elliott, George P. (1918–1980), American educator, novelist, short-story writer, poet, and essayist.

Ellis, Henry (1777–1869), English librarian, antiquarian, author, and editor.

Ellison, Fanny (née McConell, 1911–2005), American editor, founder of the Negro People's Theatre, contributor to the *Chicago Defender*, and, later, Director of the National Urban League. Second wife of **Ralph Ellison**.

Ellison, Ralph (1914–1994), American novelist, essayist, and literary critic, best known for his novel, *The Invisible Man*. Second husband of **Fanny Ellison**.

Ellmann, Richard (1918–1987), American literary critic and biographer, best known for his lives of Joyce, Wilde, and **Yeats**.

Elphinstone, Mountstuart (1779–1859), Scottish statesman and historian.

Epictetus (AD c.55–135), Phrygian, Greek-speaking Stoic philosopher.

Epstein, Leslie (1938–), American novelist, essayist, and educator.

Euripides (BC 480–406), Greek tragedian.

Fairchild, B. H. (1942–), American poet and educator.

Ficino, Marsilio (1433–1499), Italian Catholic priest and philosopher. He was a leading figure in the Italian renaissance.

Fitzgerald, Robert (1910–1985), American poet, translator, and literary critic, best known for his translations from the ancient Greek.

Fletcher, Sir Banister (1866–1953), English architect and architectural historian who, together with his father, wrote *A History of Architecture*.

Fletcher, John (1729–1785), Swiss-born English Methodist theologian.

Fluck, Winfried (1944–), German Professor of Cultural Studies, who has a special interest in American literary history.

Fontana, Carlo (1634 or 1638–1714), Italian architect.

Fontana, Domenico (1543–1607), Italian architect.

Ford, George H. (1914–1994), Canadian-born American educator and author, who taught in the Department of English at the University of Rochester, where he was chairman from 1960 until 1972. He was an authority on Charles Dickens and on Victorian literature generally, and was a founding editor of the *Norton Anthology of English Literature*, for which he edited the Victorian sections.

Ford, Gerald (1913–2006), American politician, who, after **Richard Nixon**'s resignation in 1974, served from then until 1977 as the 38th President of the United States.

Ford, Harry (1919–1999), American editor and book designer, who was AH's editor, first at Atheneum, where he worked for 28 years, then at Knopf, where he worked for a further 24 years. He and his wife Kathleen were the joint dedicatees of AH's poem "The Venetian Vespers."

Forster, Kurt W. (1935–), Swiss historian, critic, writer, and educator, who was the founding director of the Getty Center for the History of Art and the Humanities, serving in that capacity from 1984 until 1992.

Foss, Lukas (1922–2009), German-born American composer, pianist, conductor, and sometime educator.

France, Jean (née Reitsman), American architectural historian and educator, and, until her retirement, a professor at the University of Rochester. More recently, she was a consultant on the restoration of the **Frank Lloyd Wright** Edward E. Boynton House in Rochester, NY.

Franklin, Benjamin (1706–1790), American Founding Father of the United States, author, scientist, inventor, political theorist, statesman, and diplomat.

Franklin, Gilbert (1919–2004), American sculptor and educator.

Frederick I, Holy Roman Emperor (*See* Barbarossa, Frederick).

Frederick II ("the Great", 1712–1786), King of Prussia and Elector of Brandenberg.

Fregoso, Antonio (1460–1530), Italian poet.

Freeze, Rev. J. Donald (1932–2006), American Jesuit priest, educator, and administrator, who worked under Fr. Timothy Healy as Executive Vice President of Georgetown University.

Freud, Sigmund (1856–1939), Austrian neurologist who became famous as the founder of psychoanalysis.

Friedlander, Walter (1873–1966), German art historian.

Frost, Robert (1874–1963), American poet.

Frye, Northrop (1912–1991), Canadian literary critic and literary theorist.

Fussell, Paul (1924–2012), American educator, cultural and literary historian, social critic, and author.

Gaddis Smith, George, American historian and educator.

Galbraith, Nancy (1929–2008), American Head of the Poetry and Literature Center at the Library of Congress, and Principal Assistant to the Consultant in Poetry.

Gallienus, Publius Licinius (c.218–268), Forty-first Roman Emperor, and son of **Valerian**.

Gardner, Isabella (1915–1981), American poet and editor. Her fourth husband was **Allen Tate**.

Gardner, John (1933–1982), American novelist, essayist, literary critic, and educator.

Garrick, David (1717–1779), English actor, playwright, theater manager, producer, and pupil and friend of **Samuel Johnson**.

Garzetti, Albino (1914–1998), Italian historian, educator, and author.

Gaudí, Antonio (1852–1926), Catalan Modernist architect.

Gauguin, Paul (1848–1903), French Post-Impressionist painter.

Gaunt, William (1900–1980), British artist and art historian.

Gehry, Frank (1929–), Canadian-born American architect.

George V, King (1865–1936), King of the United Kingdom and the British Dominions, and Emperor of India, from 1910 until his death.

Getty, John Paul (1892–1976), American industrialist and collector of art and antiquities which formed the basis of the J. Paul Getty Museum in Los Angeles, to which he left over $661 million dollars.

Gibbon, Edward (1737–1794), English historian, writer, and sometime Member of Parliament.

Giedion, Siegfried (1888–1968), Bohemian-born Swiss architectural historian and critic.

Gielgud, Sir John, (1904–2000), English actor and theater director.
Gilbert, Cass (1859–1934), American architect.
Gilbert, W. S. (1836–1911), English dramatist, librettist, poet, and illustrator, best known for his partnership with the composer **Arthur Sullivan**.
Gillespie, Fran (née Cohen, 1939–1998), American artist. She was the first wife of **Gregory Gillespie**.
Gillespie, Gregory J. (1936–2000), American painter. He was the husband of **Fran Gillespie**.
Ginsberg, Allen (1926–1997), American poet, who was a prominent member of the so-called Beat Generation.
Ginzburg, Carlo (1939–), Italian art historian.
Giscard d'Estaing, Valéry (1926–), French politician, who served as President of the French Republic from 1974 until 1981.
Godine, David R. (1944–), American independent book publisher, who issued the limited fine press edition of A.H.'s *The Venetian Vespers*.
Goethe, Johann Wolfgang von (1749–1832), German poet, novelist, playwright, author of scientific treatises on various subjects, and statesman.
Gordon, Caroline (1895–1981), American novelist and literary critic. She was the first wife of **Allen Tate**.
Graves, Robert (1895–1985), English poet, novelist, classicist, and critic.
Greene, Graham (1904–1991), English novelist, short-story writer, travel-writer, and memoirist.
Greider, William (1936–), American writer and journalist.
Greenberg, Moshe, American rabbi, biblical scholar, and educator.
Grimaldi, Agostino (1482–1532), Monégasque, Regent of Monaco, Bishop of Grasse, and Abbot of Lérins.
Grimm, Jacob (1785–1863), German anthropologist and author. He was the elder brother of **Wilhelm Grimm**.
Grimm, Wilhelm (1786–1859), German anthropologist and author. He was the younger brother of **Jacob Grimm**.
Grizzuti Harrison, Barbara (1934–2002), American journalist, essayist, and memoirist.
Grose, David (1944–2004), American classicist, archaeologist, educator, and author. He was an authority on early ancient glass from the Roman period, and was a Fellow of the American Academy in Rome from 1972 until 1974.
Gross, John (1935–2011), English man of letters who edited the *Times Literary Supplement* from 1974 until 1981, worked as senior book editor and book critic for the *New York Times* from 1983 until 1989, and was theater critic for the (London) *Daily Telegraph* from 1989 until 2005.
Groves, Charlie (1930?–1979), American friend of WLM's since the late 1940s / early 1950s, about whom little is known beyond the fact that he had been an aspiring writer but eventually became a car salesman, published a paperback guide to buying a used car, and at some point appeared on the popular TV show *To Tell the Truth*. WLM suspected that Groves was homosexual, and that it was his homosexuality which led to his murder, the beating mentioned in letter #231 having caused his death.
Gunch, Modine (1955–), American, who won the Miss Vacant Lot of the World contest in 1973. "The winsome 18-year-old who purportedly won the ... Miss Vacant Lot of the World extravaganza in 1973 and received international acclaim for her efforts." (Description courtesy of *The Victoria Advocate*, April 26th, 1987: http://news.google.com/newspapers?nid=861&d at=19670426&id=HLUdAAAAIBAJ&sjid=_FgEAAAAIBAJ&pg=6737,6210420)
Gundersheimer, Werner (1937–), German-born American historian, educator, author, and administrator. He served as Director of the Folger Shakespeare Library in Washington, D.C. from 1984 until 2002.
Gunther, Hugo, Contributing and Consulting Editor to *Webster's New World Dictionary of the*

American Language.

Gunther, Josephine McCarter, Special and Contributing Editor to *Webster's New World Dictionary of the American Language.*

Gustav VI Adolf (1882–1973), King of Sweden from 1950 until his death, and a keen amateur archaeologist who participated in digs in China, Greece, Korea, and Italy, and founded the Swedish Institute in Rome.

Gutenberg, Johannes (c.1398–1468), German blacksmith, goldsmith, printer, and publisher, who introduced printing into Europe.

Hadrian (Caesar Traianus Hadrianus Augustus, AD 76–138), Roman Emperor from AD 117 until his death, amongst many other things responsible for the rebuilding of the Pantheon in Rome.

Hadzi, Cynthia (née Hoyle, von Thuna by her first marriage, 1938–), English curator of exhibitions who worked at the Carpenter Center for the Visual Arts at Harvard University from the 1960s until her retirement in 1996, after which she supported the artistic career of her second husband, **Dimitri Hadzi**.

Hadzi, Dimitri (1921–2006), American sculptor and educator, who taught studio arts at Harvard University from 1975 until 1989. He was a Fellow of the American Academy in Rome in 1954, and a Resident of the Academy in 1976. Elected into the National Academy of Design in 1990, he was made a full Academician in 1994. He married his second wife, **Cynthia Hadzi**, in 1985, and was the dedicatee of AH's poem "The Origin of Centaurs."

Halpern, John, American businessman and former husband of **Susan Halpern**.

Halpern, Susan (née Uris), American Smith College classmate and friend of Helen Hecht's, heiress, and philanthropist. She is the former wife of **John Halpern**.

Hamilton, Ian (1938–2001), British poet, literary critic, essayist, reviewer, biographer, magazine editor, and publisher.

Hanford, James Holly (1882–1969), American educator. He was an authority on the work of John Milton.

Hanks, Nancy (1927–1983), American administrator, who was appointed Chairperson of the National Endowment for the Arts by President **Richard Nixon** and served under him and his successor, **Gerald Ford**, from 1969 until 1977.

Harburg, Yip (1896–1981), American popular song lyricist.

Hardouin-Mansart, Jules (1646–1708), French architect. He was a great nephew of **François Mansart**.

Hardwick, Elizabeth (1916–2007), American novelist, literary critic, editor, and educator, who, together with **Robert Lowell**, Jason Epstein, Barbara Epstein, and Robert Silvers, founded the *New York Review of Books.*

Hardy, Thomas (1840–1928), English poet, novelist, and playwright.

Harper, Michael (1938–), American poet and educator.

Harris, John (1931–), English curator, historian of architecture, gardens and architectural drawings, and the author of numerous books and catalogues.

Harris, Patricia Anne (1932–), American. She was AH's first wife, and the mother of his first two sons, **Jason** and **Adam**. They were married in 1954 and divorced in 1961, and the following year she married the Belgian banker **Philippe Lambert**, and moved with him and the two boys to Belgium. The marriage to Lambert lasted until 1973, after which she and her children – **Jason**, **Adam**, and her daughter by **Lambert**, **Johanna** – settled back in the United States.

Hart, Lorenz (1895–1943), American lyricist.

Hartt, Frederick (1914–1991), American art historian and educator.

Haydn, Franz Joseph (1732–1809), Austrian composer.

Hayward, John (1905–1965), English editor, critic, anthologist, bibliophile, and close friend of **T. S. Eliot**.

Hayworth, Rita (1918–1987), American film actress, dancer, and pin-up.

Healy, Father Timothy S., S.J. (1923–1992), American, who served as President of Georgetown University from 1976 until 1989, and was then appointed President of the New York Public Library, where he remained until his death. He was the joint dedicatee of AH's *The Hidden Law: The Poetry of W. H. Auden* (the other dedicatee being AH's brother **Roger Hecht**).

Heaney, Seamus (1939–2013), Irish poet, playwright, translator, literary critic, and educator. He taught at Harvard from 1981 until 1997, and was elected Harvard's Boylston Professor of Rhetoric and Oratory in 1984. He held the chair of Professor of Poetry at Oxford from 1989 until 1994, and the following year was awarded the Nobel Prize for Literature.

Hecht, Adam (1958–), American. AH's second son by **Patricia Harris**. He is the joint dedicatee of AH's *The Hard Hours* (the other dedicatee being his brother **Jason Hecht**).

Hecht, Dorothea Grace (née Holtzman, 1894–1979), American. She was the wife of **Melvyn Hecht** and the mother of AH and his brother **Roger Hecht**.

Hecht, Evan Alexander (1972–), American. AH's son by his second wife, **Helen Hecht**. He is the dedicatee of AH's poem "The Odds," and of his *Obbligati: Essays in Criticism*, as well as joint dedicatee, with his mother, of *The Transparent Man* and *Flight Among the Tombs*.

Hecht, Helen (née D'Alessandro, 1939–), American editor, author, and interior designer. She was AH's second wife, and the mother of his son **Evan Alexander Hecht**. AH dedicated *Millions of Strange Shadows*, *The Venetian Vespers*, *The Darkness and the Light* and *Collected Later Poems* to her, and *The Transparent Man* and *Flight Among the Tombs* to her and their son Evan. She is also the dedicatee of his poem "Rara Avis in Terris."

Hecht, Jason (1956–), American. AH's first son by **Patricia Harris**. He is the joint dedicatee of AH's *The Hard Hours* (the other dedicatee being his brother **Adam Hecht**).

Hecht, Melvyn Hahlo (1893–1978), American businessman, who was the husband of **Dorothea Hecht** and the father of AH and his brother **Roger Hecht**.

Hecht, Robert E. (1919–2012), American dealer in antiquities.

Hecht, Roger (1929–1990), American poet. He was the son of **Melvyn Hahlo Hecht** and **Dorothea Grace Hecht**, and the younger brother of AH, and was the joint dedicatee of AH's *The Hidden Law: The Poetry of W. H. Auden* (the other dedicatee being **Father Timothy S. Healy, S.J.**).

Heffner, Hugh (1926–2017), American businessman, magazine publisher, and founder and Editor-in-Chief of *Playboy* magazine.

Henig, Martin (1942–), British classicist and educator.

Henry III, King (1491–1547), King of England from 1509 until his death, and the second Tudor monarch.

Henze, Hans Werner (1926–2012), German composer.

Heraclitus (BC c.535–c.475), Greek philosopher.

Hilb, Horace F. (1917–2009), American librarian, who served on the editorial board of *Webster's New World Dictionary of the American Language*. He was the husband of **Jane G. Hilb**.

Hilb, Jane G. (1917–2006), American, who served on the editorial board of *Webster's New World Dictionary of the American Language*. She was the wife of **Horace F. Hilb**.

Hitchcock, Henry-Russell (1903–1987), American architectural historian, who taught at Smith College, amongst several other institutions, and served as Director of the Smith College Museum of Art from 1949 until 1955.

Hoban, Russell (1925–2011), American novelist, poet, playwright, librettist, and author of children's books.

Hogg, Quintin (1907–2001), English Conservative politician.

Hollander, John (1929–2013), American poet, literary critic, and educator.

Holt, Elizabeth (1906–1987), American art historian and educator.

Homer (8th or 9th Century BC), Greek epic poet, author of the *Iliad* and the *Odyssey*.

Hopkins, Gerard Manley (1844–1889), English poet and Jesuit priest.

Horace (Quintus Horatius Flaccus, BC 65–8), Roman poet.
Hoving, Thomas (1931–2009), American museum executive and consultant, who served as Director of the Metropolitan Museum of Art from 1967 until 1977.
Howard, Richard (1929–), American poet, literary critic, essayist, translator, and educator.
Hubbard, Elbert (1856–1915), American writer, artist, philosopher, and publisher.
Hughes, Carol (née Orchard, 1948–), English. She was the second wife of **Ted Hughes**.
Hughes, Ted (1930–1998), English poet, children's writer, and anthologist. He was the husband, first of **Sylvia Plath**, and later of **Carol Hughes**.
Huxtable, Ada Louise (1921–2013), American architectural critic, writer, and biographer.
Ingram, Sir Bruce (1877–1963), English newspaper editor, successively in charge of *The English Illustrated Magazine*, *The Sketch*, and *The Illustrated London News*, and credited with transforming the last of these by introducing more photography as well as new printing technology.
Ingres, Jean-Auguste-Dominque (1780–1867), French painter.
Irving, John (1942–), American novelist and screenwriter.
Jackson, Michael (1958–2009), American singer, songwriter, and dancer.
Jackson-Stops, Gervase (1947–1995), English architectural historian and journalist, who served as Architectural Adviser to the UK's National Trust for over 20 years, and was responsible for curating various exhibitions.
Jacobs, Steve (1919–1978), American architectural historian and educator.
James, Henry (1843–1916), American-born British novelist and short-story writer.
Jarrell, Randall (1914–1965), American poet, literary critic, children's author, essayist, novelist, and educator, who served as Consultant in Poetry to the Library of Congress from 1956 until 1958.
Jefferson, Thomas (1743–1826), Founding Father of America, and principal author of the Declaration of Independence, who served as the third President of the United States from 1801 until 1809.
Jencks, Charles (1939–), American architectural critic and theorist, landscape architect and designer. He was a former student of **Siegfried Giedion**, and the husband of **Maggie Jencks**.
Jencks, Maggie (1941–1995), Scottish writer, gardener, and designer. She was the wife of **Charles Jencks**.
Jessup, John Knox Jr. (1935–2009), American International Training Officer at the Agency for International Development in Washington D.C., known to WLM through his second wife, the architect Pamela Russell Jessup, who had been a student of WLM's when he taught at Yale.
Johnson, Merle De Vore (1874–1935), American bibliographer, anthologist, book collector, cartoonist, and illustrator.
Johnson, Philip (1906–2005), American architect.
Johnson, Samuel (Dr Johnson, 1709–1784), English essayist, moralist, literary critic, biographer, editor, and lexicographer.
Jonson, Ben (1572–1637), English poet, playwright, and actor.
Jordan, Hamilton (1944–2008), American, who served under President Jimmy Carter as White House Chief of Staff, and who exemplified what his *New York Times* obituary called "the laid-back, informal attitude of much of the president's inner circle, often appearing at official functions in a Navy pea coat and blue jeans." In 1979 he was investigated by a special counsel set up to look into allegations that he had used cocaine during a visit to the Studio 54 nightclub in New York. No charges were ever preferred.
Justice, Donald (1925–2004), American poet and educator.
Kaczynski, Ted ("The Unabomber," 1942–), American mathematician and educator who mounted a bombing campaign in the US which was intended to bring down the industrial-technological complex. He was caught and sentenced to eight consecutive life terms without

parole.

Kahn, Louis (1901–1974), American architect and educator.

Kallen, Horace M. (1882–1974), German-born American philosopher and educator.

Kalstone, David (1933–1986), American literary critic and educator. He was the subject of AH's elegy, "In Memoriam David Kalstone."

Kaplan, Justin (1925–2014), American biographer and editor.

Kazin, Alfred (1915–1998), American writer, literary critic, editor, and memoirist.

Kean, Edmund (1787–1833), British actor, celebrated for his Shakespearean roles.

Keats, John (1795–1821), English poet.

Keith, Sally (1916–1967), American striptease dancer.

Kelly, Reverend Dr. J. N. D. (1909–1997), Scottish priest, educator, author, editor, and university administrator.

Kelly, Walt (1913–1973), American animator and cartoonist.

Kermode, Frank (1919–2010), British literary critic, essayist, anthologist, memoirist, and educator.

Kernan, Alvin (1923–), American literary and social critic, memoirist, and educator.

King, Martin Luther (1929–1968), African-American pastor, activist, leader of the African-American Civil Rights Movement.

Kinnell, Galway (1927–2014), American poet, who served as Poet Laureate for the state of Vermont from 1989 until 1993.

Kinney, Arthur F. (1933–), American writer, educator, and founding editor of *English Literary Renaissance*.

Kirwin, W. Chandler (1941–), American art and architectural historian, and educator.

Kissinger, Henry (1923–), American diplomat and political scientist, who served as National Security Advisor and as United States Secretary of State under Presidents **Richard Nixon** and **Gerald Ford**.

Klein, Edward (1937–), American writer, journalist, and biographer. A former foreign editor of *Newsweek*, he was Editor-in-Chief of the *New York Times Magazine* from 1977 until 1987.

Klinghoffer, Leon (1916–1985), American businessman, who was murdered by members of the Palestinian Liberation Organization during their hijacking of the cruise ship Achille Lauro.

Knox, Bernard (1914–2010), English classicist and author, who served as Director of Harvard's Center for Hellenic Studies in Washington, D.C. from 1962 until his retirement in 1985.

Knox, Vicesimus (1752–1821), English essayist, Anglican priest and headmaster of Tonbridge School in Kent.

Korn, Eric (1933–2014), English antiquarian bookseller and columnist, who throughout the 1980s was responsible for the "Remainders" column in the *Times Literary Supplement*.

Kostof, Spiro (1936–1991), Turkish-born American architectural historian, author, and educator. He was a former student of WLM's who became a close friend, and WLM and **John Pinto**'s *Hadrian's Villa and Its Legacy* is dedicated to his memory.

Kott, Jan (1914–2001), Polish poet, essayist, translator, literary critic, theater critic, reviewer, and educator, who defected from his native country and settled in the United States in 1969.

Krantz, Judith (1928–), American romantic novelist.

Krautheimer, Richard (1897–1994), German-born American art and architectural historian, and educator.

Krier, Léon (1946–), Luxembourger architect, architectural theorist, and urban planner.

Kronenberger, Louis (1904–1980), American novelist, biographer, editor, anthologist, literary critic, drama critic, memoirist, and educator.

Kruif, Paul Henry de (1890–1971), American microbiologist, and writer.

Kunitz, Stanley (1905–2006), American poet and educator, who served as Poet Laureate Consultant to the Library of Congress first from 1974 until 1975 and then again from 2000 until 2001.

Kurtz, Otto (1908–1975), Austrian art historian and educator, who settled in England prior to WWII.

Lacy, Bill (1933–), American architect, who served as President of the American Academy in Rome from 1977 until 1980, then as President of the Cooper Union for the Advancement of Science and Art until 1987, and then as Executive Director of the Pritzker Architecture Prize until 2005.

Laemmle, Carl, Sr. (1867–1939), German-born American film-maker. He was the founder of Universal Studios.

Lambert, Baron Philippe (1930–2011), Belgian banker, and scion of the Rothschild family. He was the second husband of **Patricia Harris** and the father of her daughter, **Johanna Lambert**.

Lambert, Johanna (1962–), Belgian. She is the daughter of **Patricia Harris** and **Baron Philippe Lambert**, and the half sister of **Jason Hecht** and **Adam Hecht**.

Lamour, Dorothy (1914–1996), American actress and singer.

Lampedusa, Giuseppe Tomaso di (1896–1957), Italian writer, famous for his only novel, *Il Gattopardo* (*The Leopard*).

Lanciani, Rodolfo (1845–1929), Italian archaeologist.

Lange, Dorothea (1895–1965), American documentary photographer and photo-journalist, best known for her work in the Depression era.

Lardner, Dionysius (1793–1859), Irish educator and popularizing writer on science and technology, best known as the editor of the 133-volume *Cabinet Cyclopaedia*.

Larson, Lanny (Harlan Ray, 1920–1978), American friend of WLM's since their wartime service in the USAAF.

Lasdun, James (1958–), British poet, novelist, short story writer, and critic.

Lavin, Irving (1927–), American architectural historian and educator. He was the husband of **Marilyn Lavin**.

Lavin, Marilyn (née Aronberg, 1925–), American art historian and educator. She was the wife of **Irving Lavin**.

Lawlor, Charles B. (1852–1925), Irish-born American vaudeville actor, and composer of popular songs.

Lawrence, Frances (1886–1938), Canadian-American actress, often referred to as "The First Movie Star", and, at her peak, when working as a leading lady for the Biograph Studios, known as "The Biograph Girl."

Lea, Sydney (1942–), American poet, novelist, essayist, educator, and founder of the *New England Review*. He edited *The Burdens of Formality: Essays on the Poetry of Anthony Hecht*.

Lehmann, Phyllis Williams (1912–2004), American classical archaeologist and educator, who was on the faculty of Smith College from 1946 until her retirement in 1978.

Lehmann-Haupt, Christopher (1934–), American literary critic, novelist, and journalist.

Leighton, Frederic, 1st Baron (1830–1896), English painter and sculptor.

Leithauser, Brad (1953–), American poet, novelist, and essayist, who studied with AH when the latter was Visiting Professor at Harvard in 1973. He is the former husband of **Mary Jo Salter**, younger brother of **Mark Leithauser**, and brother-in-law of **Bryan Leithauser**.

Leithauser, Bryan (1946–), American. She is the wife of **Mark Leithauser**.

Leithauser, Mark (1950–), American artist, who serves as Chief of Design and Senior Curator at the National Gallery of Art, Washington, D.C. He is the elder brother of **Brad Leithauser**, and the husband of **Bryan Leithauser**.

Lemaire de Belges, Jean (1473–1525), Walloon poet, historian, and pamphleteer.

Leo XIII, Pope (Vincenzo Gioacchino Raffaele Luigi Pecci, 1810–1903), Italian Catholic priest, who reigned as Pope from 1878 until his death.

Levine, Philip (1928–2015), American poet and educator, who served as Poet Laureate Consultant in Poetry to the Library of Congress from 2011 until 2012.

Levit, Herschel (1912–1986), American painter, illustrator, photographer, muralist, historian, educator, and author.

Liberace, Wladzie Valentino (1919–1987), American pianist, singer, and actor.

Lincoln, Abraham (1809–1865), American politician and lawyer, who served as the sixteenth President of the United States from 1861 until his assassination.

Logan, William (1950–), American poet, critic, and educator.

Lovelace, Richard (1618–1657), English poet, who fought on the side of the Royalists during the English Civil War.

Lowell, Robert (1917–1977), American poet, playwright, and educator, who served as Poetry Consultant to the Library of Congress from 1947 until 1948.

Lucas-Tooth, Letitia Helen (*See* Munro-Lucas-Tooth, Laetitia Helen).

Luther, Martin (1483–1546), German monk, priest, and theologian.

Lutyens, Sir Edwin (1869–1944), British architect.

Lynes, Mildred (née Akin, 1909–1999), American art historian and educator, who served as Director of Activities and Membership at the Metropolitan Museum of Art in New York from 1952 until 1962.

Lynes, J. Russell, Jr. (1910–1991), American art historian, photographer, publisher, author, columnist, and editor, who served as a President of the MacDowell Colony, and from 1947 until 1967 was Managing Editor at *Harper's* magazine.

MacDonald, Dale (née Ely, 1924–1978), WLM's second wife, and mother of their three sons, **Noel**, **Darius**, and **Nicholas MacDonald**.

MacDonald, Darius (1957–1958), American. He was the second son of WLM and **Dale MacDonald**.

Macdonald, Dwight (1906–1982), American writer, editor, essayist, film, book, and social critic.

MacDonald, Ellen (1954–), American physical therapist. She is the wife of **Noel MacDonald**.

MacDonald, John (1914–2005), American US Department of State official, stationed at different times in China, Japan, Vietnam, and the USA. He was the son of **William Lloyd MacDonald, Sr.**, and elder brother of WLM.

MacDonald, Nicholas (1959–), American. He was WLM's third son, and the grandson of **William Lloyd MacDonald, Sr.**, and **Susan Elrod MacDonald**. He has worked as a project manager with various environmental consulting companies, as a carpenter, and as a building contractor. He is the joint dedicatee of WLM's *The Pantheon: Design, Meaning, and Progeny* (the other dedicatee being his brother **Noel MacDonald**).

MacDonald, Noel (1956–), American. He was WLM's first son, and the grandson of **William Lloyd MacDonald, Sr.**, and **Susan Elrod MacDonald**. He worked for American Multi Cinema (AMC Theaters), of which he became Vice President, and from which he retired in 2013. He is the joint dedicatee of WLM's *The Pantheon: Design, Meaning, and Progeny* (the other dedicatee being his brother **Nicholas MacDonald**).

MacDonald, Susan (née Elrod, 1886–1961), American wife of **William L. MacDonald, Sr.**, mother of WLM and **John MacDonald**, and grandmother of **Nicholas** and **Noel MacDonald**.

MacDonald, William Lloyd, Sr. (1883–1963), American school-teacher, school superintendent, and banker who, when he retired, was Director of the New Hampshire Savings Bank. He was the Father of WLM and **John MacDonald**, and the grandfather of **Nicholas** and **Noel MacDonald**.

Mackenzie, Sir Compton, (1883–1972), Scottish novelist, biographer, memoirist, and cultural commentator. He was a co-founder (with Hugh MacDiarmid, amongst others) of the Scottish National Party.

Mackinnon, Lachlan (1956–), Scottish poet, critic, and literary journalist.

Maderno, Carlo (1556–1629), Italian architect, who was a key figure in the establishment of Baroque architecture.

Malamud, Bernard (1914–1986), American novelist and short-story writer.

Malipiero, Gian Francesco (1882–1973), Italian composer, musicologist, editor, and educator.
Malraux, André (1901–1976), French author and statesman.
Manchester, William (1922–2004), American biographer and historian.
Mansart, François (1598–1666), French classical architect. He was the great-uncle of **Jules Hardouin-Mansart**.
Mansart, Jules Hardouin (*See* Hardouin-Mansart, Jules).
Mansfield, Jayne (1933–1967), American actress, singer, and pin-up.
Marchand, Leslie A. (1900–1999), American literary scholar. He was a leading authority on Lord Byron.
Maréchale de Luxembourg, La (Madeleine Angéliques, 1707–1787), French society hostess, friend to Rousseau, and described by the Brothers Goncourt as "one of the most original women of the time."
Marten, Sir Harry Neil (1916–1985), English politician.
Marvell, Andrew (1621–1678), English poet and politician.
Marx, Groucho (1890–1977), American comedian and film and television star.
Marx, Karl (1818–1883), German philosopher, economist, sociologist, journalist, and revolutionary socialist.
Mason, David (1954–), American poet, writer, critic, and educator.
Mason, George (1725–1792), American. He was Virginia's delegate to the U.S. Constitutional Convention, and co-author of the Virginia Declaration of Rights.
Masson, Georgina (1912–1980), British author and photographer.
Matteson, Ira (1917–2017), American sculptor and educator.
Maurus, Rabanus (780–856), Frankish theologian, scholar, and monk, who became Archbishop of Mainz. He was the author of many works, including *De rerum naturis* (*On the Natures of Things*).
McClatchy, J. D. ("Sandy," 1945–), American poet, critic, librettist, editor, educator, and AH's literary executor.
McCloskey, William J. (1859–1941), American painter of still-lifes, portraits, and genre scenes.
McCoubrey, Bettsy (née Morse), American clinical and counselling psychologist. She was the wife of **John W. McCoubrey**.
McCoubrey, John W. (1924–2010), American art historian and educator. He was the husband of **Bettsy McCoubrey**.
McKim, Charles F. (1847–1909), American architect. He was a principal of the McKim, Mead & White partnership, and, together with his fellow principals, was instrumental in the foundation of the American Academy in Rome.
McMichael, Ted (1908–2001), American singer, who was one of the founders of the vocal quartet, The Merry Macs.
Mead, William R. (1846–1928), American architect. He was a principal of the McKim, Mead & White partnership, and, together with his fellow principals, was instrumental in the foundation of the American Academy in Rome.
Meier, Richard (1934–), American architect and artist. He was the winner of the 1984 Pritzker Architecture Prize, and designer of the Getty Center in Los Angeles, amongst many other buildings.
Melanchthon, Philip (1497–1560), German theologian, academic, and a leading figure in the Protestant Reformation.
Melville, Herman (1819–1891), American novelist, short story writer, and poet.
Mencken, H. L. (1880–1956), American editor, journalist, literary critic, and controversialist.
Mendenhall, Thomas C. (1910–1998), American historian and educator, who, from 1959 until his retirement in 1975, was both Professor of History and President of Smith College.
Meredith, William (1919–2007), American poet and educator, who served as Consultant in Poetry to the Library of Congress from 1978 until 1980.

Merejkowski, Dmitri (1866–1941), Russian novelist, poet, literary critic, and religious thinker, who was nominated for the Nobel Prize in Literature on nine separate occasions.

Merrill, James (1926–1995), American poet, novelist, playwright, critic, and memoirist. He was the subject of AH's elegy "For James Merrill: An Adieu."

Merritt, Howard (1915–2007), American art historian and educator, who taught at the University of Rochester from 1946 until his retirement in 1976.

Merwin, W. S. (1927–), American poet and ecologist, who served as Poet Laureate Consultant in Poetry to the Library of Congress from 2010 until 2011.

Michalik, Chester (1935–), American photographer and educator, who taught at Smith College from 1978 until his retirement in 2005.

Michelangelo (Michelangelo di Lodovico Buonarotti Simoni, 1475–1564), Italian sculptor, painter, architect, and poet.

Middleton, Robin (1931–), South African architect, architectural historian, and writer.

Middleton, Thomas (1580–1627), English playwright and poet.

Miller, Archie (1930–), Canadian sculptor and educator.

Miller, Arthur (1915–2005), American playwright, essayist, and memoirist.

Millon, Henry ("Hank," 1927–), American architectural historian and educator, whose specialities are the Renaissance and Baroque eras. He was a Fellow of the American Academy of Rome in 1960, a Resident of it in 1966, and its Director from 1974 until 1977. He was the first Dean of the Center for Advanced Study of the Visual Arts in the National Gallery of Arts in Washington, D.C. He is the husband of **Judith Millon**.

Millon, Judith ("Judy," née Rice, 1934–), American architectural historian. She is the wife of **Henry Millon**.

Milton, John (1608–1674), English poet, polemicist, and civil servant.

Mitford, Nancy (1904–1973), English novelist, biographer, and journalist.

Mizener, Arthur (1907–1988), American literary critic, editor, biographer, and educator.

Montale, Eugenio (1896–1981), Italian poet, essayist, editor, and translator, who won the 1975 Nobel Prize for Literature.

More, Thomas (1478–1535), English lawyer, statesman, philosopher, and writer. He was a councillor to **Henry VIII** who went on to become Lord Chancellor, but fell from favour because of his opposition to Henry's defiance of papal authority and his marriage to Anne Boleyn, and was tried for treason and executed.

Morgan, Henry ("Dr I. J., The Mental Fox," 1915–1994), American humorist and radio broadcaster.

Moss, Howard (1922–1987), American poet, dramatist, and critic, who served as poetry editor of the *New Yorker* from 1948 until his death.

Moynihan, Daniel Patrick (1927–2003), American politician and sociologist, who was the US Ambassador to India and then to the United Nations, and subsequently served four terms as Senator for New York.

Mozart, Wolfgang Amadeus (1756–1791), Austrian composer and musician.

Muldoon, Paul (1951–), Irish poet and educator.

Muni, Paul (1895–1967), American stage and film actor.

Munro, Hector ("Saki," 1870–1916), British author and playwright.

Munro-Lucas-Tooth, Laetitia Helen (1926–), English writer on philosophical theology and Christian ethics.

Murdoch, Iris, Dame (1919–1999), Irish-born British novelist, philosopher, and educator.

Murray, Sir James (1837–1915), Scottish lexicographer and philologist, who was the primary editor of the *Oxford English Dictionary* from 1879 until his death. He was the grandfather of **K. M. Elisabeth Murray**.

Murray, K. M. Elisabeth (1909–1998), Scottish author. She was the granddaughter of **Sir James Murray**, and in later life was the Principal of Bishop Otter College, Chichester, UK.

Musgrove, John, British architectural historian, editor, and educator.

Mussolini, Benito (1883–1945), Italian politician, who led the National Fascist Party and ruled Italy as Prime Minister from 1922 until 1943, when he was deposed. He was executed by partisans in 1945.

Nash, Ogden (1902–1971), American poet, best known for his light verse, fourteen volumes of which were published between 1931 and 1972.

Nemerov, Howard (1920–1991), American poet, literary critic, and educator, who served as Poetry Consultant to the Library of Congress from 1963 until 1964, and who served again, this time under the new title of Poet Laureate Consultant in Poetry to the Library of Congress, from 1988 until 1990.

Nero, Claudius Caesar Augustus Germanicus (AD 37–68), Roman Emperor from AD 54 until his death.

Neuerburg, Norman (1926–1997), American art historian, artist, and educator, who served as historical consultant to the J. Paul Getty Museum in Pacific Palisades, Los Angeles.

Nims, John Frederick (1913–1999), American poet, educator, and editor, who edited *Poetry* magazine from 1978 until 1984.

Nixon, Richard (1913–1994), American politician, who served as the 37th President of the United States from 1969 until 1974. He is the only US President thus far to have resigned that office.

Nunis, Roger A. (1932–), American, who served as Executive Vice President of Walt Disney World and Disneyland from 1971 until 1980, and from then until his retirement in 1999 was President of the Outdoor Recreation Division, overseeing Disney World, the Epcot Center and, later, the Disney-MGM Studios Theme Park.

O'Gorman, Edward ("Ned," 1929–2014), American poet, essayist, and educator, who set up a children's library in Harlem in 1966, which then became The Children's Storefront, an independent school, and who, later, after losing control of the Storefront, established the Ricardo O'Gorman Garden and Center for Resources in the Humanities in New York City.

Oates, Joyce Carol (1938–), American novelist, short-story writer, playwright, poet, and memoirist.

Offenbach, Jacques (1819–1880), German-born French composer, musician, and impresario.

O'Hara, John (1905–1970), American novelist, short-story writer, playwright, screenwriter, and newspaper columnist.

Oliver, Richard (1942–1985), American architect, author, and teacher, who for several years served as Curator of Contemporary Architecture and Design at the Cooper-Hewitt Museum in New York, and was a member of the executive board of the Architectural League of New York.

Owens, Jack (1912–1982), American singer, songwriter, pianist, and radio personality.

Paderewski, Ignacy Jan (1860–1941), Polish pianist, composer, and politician, who served as Prime Minister of Poland in 1919.

Palladio, Andrea (Andrea di Pietro della Gondola, 1508–1580), Italian architect and author, who is credited with being one of the most influential figures in western architecture. His *Quattro libri dell'architettura* (*Four Books of Architecture*) is one of the most significant architectural treatises ever produced.

Panini, Giovanni Paolo (1691–1765), Italian painter and architect, who lived and worked in Rome, and is best known for his vistas of the city, particularly its antiquities and ruins.

Panofsky, Dorothea ("Dora," 1885–1965), German art historian. She was the first wife of **Erwin Panofsky**.

Panofsky, Erwin (1892–1968), German art historian and educator, who, because he was Jewish, fled Germany in 1931 and settled in the United States. His first wife was **Dorothea Panofsky**.

Parker, H. M. D. (1894–1971), British. He was a Fellow and Tutor at Magdalen College, Oxford, an author, and, later, Keeper of the Heberden Coin Room at the Ashmolean Museum in Oxford.

Pascal, Blaise (1623–1662), French mathematician, inventor, physicist, and philosopher.

Pasteur, Louis (1822–1895), French chemist and microbiologist, renowned for his discoveries in connection with vaccination, microbial fermentation, and pasteurization.

Pausanias (AD c.110–180), Greek traveller, geographer, and writer, best known for his ten-volume *Description of Greece*.

Pavlovskis, Zoja (now Pavlovskis-Petit, 1936–), Latvian-born American educator and writer, specializing in comparative literature and classics.

Pearman, Jeannie (née Scott), American. She was the second wife of **Richard S. L. Pearman**.

Pearman, Richard S. L (1934–2013), English barrister and sportsman, and the husband of **Jeannie Pearman**.

Pears, Peter (1910–1986), English tenor, and the partner of **Benjamin Britten**.

Pearsall-Smith, Logan (1865–1946), American-born British essayist, critic, autobiographer, and aphorist.

Pearson, Norman Holmes (1909–1975), American author, editor, anthologist, literary critic, and archivist.

Peck, John (1941–), American poet and psychoanalyst.

Pei, I. M. (1917–), Chinese-born American architect. He is the winner of numerous awards, including the 1983 Pritzker Prize.

Pepys, Samuel (1633–1703), English naval administrator, sometime Member of Parliament, and diarist.

Peterson, Donald E. (1926–), American businessman, who served as President and Chief Operating Officer of the Ford Motor Company from 1980 until 1985, and then as Chairman of the Board and Chief Executive Officer until he left the company in 1990.

Petersson, Robert T. (1918–2011), American educator and author, who taught English Literature at Smith College from 1952 until his retirement in 1985, when he became Professor Emeritus. He was the husband of **Suzanne Petersson**.

Petersson, Suzanne (née Straub, 1927–2016), American educator and activist. She was the wife of **Robert T. Petersson**.

Petronius (Gaius Petronius Arbiter, AD c.27–66), Roman courtier of the Emperor Nero, who is believed to have been the author of the *Satyricon*.

Pevsner, Sir Niklaus (1902–1983), German-born British historian of art and architecture, best known for his 46-volume series of guides to the architecture of the British counties.

Pinto, John (1948–), American architectural historian and educator, who was taught by WLM while WLM was a Visiting Professor at Harvard in 1968, was a Fellow of the American Academy in Rome in 1975, and became a colleague and friend of WLM's at Smith College in the late 1970s. Between 1985 and 1995 he collaborated with WLM on what was to be WLM's last book, *Hadrian's Villa and Its Legacy*.

Piranesi, Giovanni Battista (1720–1778), Italian artist, best known for his etchings of Rome, and for his *Carceri d'invenzione* (*Imaginary prisons*).

Placzek, Adolf K. (1913–2000), Austrian-born American architectural historian, librarian, editor, preservationist, and educator, who served as Editor-in-Chief of the four-volume *Macmillan Encyclopedia of Architects*.

Plath, Sylvia (1932–1963), American poet, novelist, and short-story writer, who graduated from Smith College in 1955, and after a two-year Fulbright scholarship to the University of Cambridge in England, returned to Smith with her husband, the poet **Ted Hughes**, to teach. It was during that year that Plath and Hughes got to know AH.

Pliny, the Elder (Gaius Plinius Secundus, AD 23–79), Roman author, naturalist, natural philosopher, and military commander, best known for his *Naturalis Historia*.

Polledri, Paolo (1946–), American writer and designer, who worked at the Getty Center and was founding Curator of Architecture and Design at the San Francisco Museum of Modern Art.

Polshek, James (1930–), American architect, who served as Dean of Columbia University's Graduate School of Architecture, Planning and Preservation from 1972 until 1987.

Pope, Alexander (1688–1744), English poet.

Porter, Peter (1929–2010), Australian poet, who settled in England in the early 1950s.

Portman, John Calvin (1924–2017), American architect and real-estate developer.

Post, Emily (née Price, 1872–1960), American newspaper columnist, novelist, short-story and travel writer, best known for her *Etiquette: The Blue Book of Social Usage*, which was first published in 1922, and has remained in print ever since.

Post, Jonathan F. S. (1947–), American educator and writer. He was a graduate student of AH's at the University of Rochester in the mid-1970s. He edited *The Selected Letters of Anthony Hecht*, and is the author of several books, including the first book-length study of AH's poetry: *A Thickness of Particulars: The Poetry of Anthony Hecht*.

Post, Wiley (1898–1935), American aviator, who was the first person to fly solo around the world. He was killed in an aircraft crash.

Pottle, Frederick A. (1897–1987), American educator, editor, bibliographer, and biographer. He was an authority on **James Boswell**.

Powell, Anthony (1905–2000), English novelist, best known for his twelve-volume work, *A Dance to the Music of Time*.

Pratt, William (1927–), American literary critic, author, and editor.

Praz, Mario (1896–1982), Italian art and literary critic.

Price, Reynolds (1933–2011), American poet, novelist, dramatist, essayist, and educator.

Price, Roger (1918–1990), American humorist, author, and publisher.

Prior, Matthew (1664–1721), English poet, diplomat, and sometime Member of Parliament.

Pritchard, William (1932–), American educator, literary critic, biographer, essayist, and journalist.

Putnam, Samuel (1892–1950), American scholar and translator, best known for his 1949 translation of Cervantes's *Don Quixote*.

Rabanus Maurus (c.780–856), German Benedictine monk and theologian.

Rabelais, François (c.1483–1553), French writer, physician, monk, and scholar.

Racine, Jean (1639–1699), French playwright.

Rand, Calvin G. (1929–), American educator, arts consultant, and philanthropist, who was President of the American Academy in Rome from 1980 until 1984.

Ransom, John Crowe (1888–1974), American poet, critic, editor, and educator.

Raphael (Raffaele Sanzio da Urbino, 1483–1520), Italian painter and architect.

Rauch, John K. (1930–), American architect. He was a former business partner of **Robert Venturi** and **Denise Scott Brown**.

Rauschenberg, Friedrich Wilhelm (1853–1935), German architect.

Rauschenberg, Robert (1925–2008), American painter and graphic artist.

Reagan, Nancy (1921–2016), American film actress. She was the wife of **Ronald Reagan**.

Reagan, Ronald (1911–2004), American film actor and politician, who served as the 40th President of the United States from 1981 until 1989. He was the husband of **Nancy Reagan**.

Reinhardt, Max (1873–1943), Austrian-born American theater and film director, and theatrical producer.

Richardson, Lawrence (1920–2013), American classicist, art historian, and educator.

Ricks, Christopher (1933–), English literary critic, scholar, editor, anthologist, and educator. He is the dedicatee of AH's *Melodies Unheard: Essays on the Mysteries of Poetry*, and gave the first series of Anthony Hecht Lectures in the Humanities at Bard College in 2007, subsequently published as *True Friendship: Geoffrey Hill, Anthony Hecht, and Robert Lowell Under the Sign of Eliot and Pound*.

Rimson, Goldie (1904–1993), American editor, who served on the editorial board of *Webster's New World Dictionary of the American Language*. She was the wife of **Oscar Rimson**.

Rimson, Oscar (1905–1955), American editor, who served on the editorial board of *Webster's New World Dictionary of the American Language.* He was the husband of **Goldie Rimson**.

Ripley, Sidney Dillon (1913–2001), American ornithologist and conservationist, who served as Secretary of the Smithsonian Institution from 1964 until 1984.

Ripperger, Helmut (1897–1974), German author and translator.

Rivers, Joan (1933–2014), American actress, comedian, writer, producer, and television host.

Roberts, Laurance P. (1907–2002), American scholar of Asian art, who served as Curator of the Brooklyn Museum from 1934 until 1938, as its Director from then until 1942, and as Director of the American Academy in Rome from 1946 until 1960. After leaving this last position, and doing a one-year stint as Director of the State Council of the Arts in New York, Roberts and his wife **Isabel Roberts** moved back to Europe, living in Venice, Paris, and London.

Roberts, Isabel (née Spaulding, 1911–2005), American wife of **Lawrence P. Roberts**, who took over from her husband as Director of the Brooklyn Museum while he served as a Captain in Army Intelligence from 1942 until 1946.

Rockefeller, Nelson (1908–1979), American businessman, politician, and philanthropist, who served as Governor of New York from 1959 until 1973, and as the 41st Vice President of the United States from 1974 until 1977.

Rockwell, Hays, The Right Reverend (1936–), American Rector of St. James' Episcopal Church in New York City from 1976 until 1990, and from then until his retirement in 2002 the ninth Bishop of the Episcopal Diocese of Missouri. He is the dedicatee of AH's poem "Gladness of the Best." He is the husband of **Linda Rockwell**.

Rockwell, Linda (1936–), American. She is the wife of **Hays Rockwell**.

Ronsard, Pierre de (1524–1585), French poet.

Rodgers, Richard (1902–1979), American composer, songwriter, and playwright, best known for his collaborations with Lorenz Hart and Oscar Hammerstein.

Rogers, Ernesto (1909–1969), Italian architect, writer, journalist, and educator.

Rolfe, Frederick ("Baron Corvo," aka "Frederick William Serafino Austin Lewis Mary Rolfe," 1860–1913), English novelist, short-story writer, and translator.

Roosevelt, President Franklin D. (1882–1945), American politician and statesman, who served as the 32nd President of the United States from 1933 until his death.

Ross, Arthur (1910–2007), American businessman and philanthropist, who established the Arthur Ross Foundation, and was much involved in the arts, the environment, and international affairs.

Rossetti, Dante Gabriel (1828–1882), English poet, painter, illustrator, and translator.

Rostovtzeff, Michael (1870–1952), Russian-born American ancient historian.

Rostow, Walt (1916–2003), American economist and political theorist, who served as National Security Advisor under President Lyndon B. Johnson from 1966 until 1969.

Rothko, Mark (1903–1970), Russian-born American painter.

Rowse, A. L. (1903–1997), English historian, literary scholar, and biographer.

Rubens, Peter Paul (1577–1640), Flemish painter, scholar, and diplomat.

Rusk, Dean (1909–1994), American statesman and educator, who served as Secretary of State from 1961 until 1969, and then taught International Relations at the University of Georgia.

Ruskin, John (1819–1900), English artist, art critic, social thinker, and philanthropist.

Russell, Bertrand, 3rd Earl Russell (1872–1970), British philosopher, logician, historian, writer, political activist, and winner of 1950's Nobel Prize for Literature.

Russell, Jane (1921–2011), American film actress and pin-up.

Rutland, Jennifer (1950–2014), American, who worked under **Nancy Galbraith**, the Principal Assistant to the Consultant in Poetry in the Library of Congress, and then took over after after Galbraith's retirement in 1993.

Ryan, William Granger (1905–1996), American priest, college administrator, and translator of Jacobus de Voragine's *The Golden Legend*.

Ryskamp, Charles (1922–2010), American administrator, literary scholar, educator, and art collector. He served as a Director of The Frick Collection in Manhattan and as Director of Manhattan's Pierpont Morgan Library.

Sackville-West, Lady Victoria (1862–1936), Anglo-Spanish, the so-called "Lady of Knole," Knole being the great Tudor House not far from Sevenoaks in Kent. She was the mother of **Vita Sackville-West**.

Sackville-West, Vita (1892–1962), English poet, novelist, and garden designer. She was the daughter of **Lady Victoria Sackville-West**.

Safire, William (1929–2009), American author, columnist, journalist, and presidential scriptwriter.

Saint-Simon, Claude Henri de Rouvroy, Comte de (1760–1825), French political, economic, and social theorist.

Saki (*See* Munro, Hector).

Salter, Mary Jo (1954–), American poet, editor, anthologist, and educator. She is the former wife of **Brad Leithauser**.

Samuelson, Paul (1915–2009), American economist and educator, who won the Nobel Memorial Prize in Economic Sciences in 1970.

Sapor I, King (Shapur I, the Great, d. AD 272), Ruler of the Persian Empire from AD 241 until his death.

Sassetta, il (Stefano di Giovanni di Consolo, c.1392– c.1450), Italian painter.

Satkowski, Leon (1947–), Polish-born American architectural historian and educator.

Schadt, Betsey Adams (1919–1982), American. She was the first wife of WLM.

Schapiro, Meyer (1904–1996), Lithuanian-born American art historian and educator, who is credited with transforming his field by forging a much more interdisciplinary approach than had been customary.

Schaffer, Ray (née Kohn, 1911–1993), American antiquarian, who, together with her husband Alexander, founded the Manhattan-based A La Vieille Russie, one of the world's leading outlets for Russian art, jewelry, and antiques.

Scheer-Schäzler, Brigitte, Austrian educator and author, specializing in American literature.

Schoonover, David (1944–), American librarian, who, in 1985, was Curator of Rare Books in the Special Collections Department of the University of Iowa Libraries, which was administering the Bollingen Prize on behalf of Yale University Library. He is now Librarian Emeritus with the University of Iowa.

Schumacher, Emily, American. She was the first wife of **Thomas L. Schumacher**

Schumacher, Patty (née Sachs), American artist, and the second wife of **Thomas L. Schumacher**.

Schumacher, Thomas L. (1941–2009), American architect, architectural historian, and educator. He was a Fellow of the American Academy in Rome in 1969, and a Resident there in 1992. He was the husband, first of **Emily Schumacher**, and then of **Patty Schumacher**.

Schuman, William (1910–1992), American composer and arts administrator.

Schwantner, Joseph (1943–), American composer and educator.

Schweitzer, Pierre-Paul (1912–1994), French financial administrator, who served as Managing Director of the International Monetary Fund from 1963 until 1973.

Scott, Charlotte (née Hanley, 1925–2010), American economist and educator.

Scott, Clement (1841–1904), English theater critic, playwright, lyricist, translator, and travel writer.

Scott, Nathan A. Jr. (1925–2006), American educator, literary critic, and Episcopal priest.

Scott, Russell T. (1939–), American architectural historian, classicist, and educator, who served as Andrew W. Mellon Professor-in-Charge of the School of Classical Studies at the American Academy in Rome from 1984 until 1988.

Scott, Walter Bernard (1907–1980), American educator, critic, and writer, best known for his *Chicago Letter and Other Parodies*, and described by his friend **Richard Ellmann** as "one of the wittiest men in America."

Scott-Brown, Denise (1931–), South-African-born American architect, planner, writer, and educator, and a principal of Scott Brown and Associates in Philadelphia. She is the wife of **Robert Venturi**,

Scully, Vincent (1920–2017), American architectural historian, author, and educator, and an early advocate of the architecture of **Louis Kahn**, and **Robert Venturi**.

Searing, Helen (1933–), American architectural historian, who took over from WLM after he ceased being Alice Pratt Brown Professor of the History of Art at Smith College.

Seneca, Lucius Annaeus Seneca (often known as Seneca the Younger (BC c.4–AD 65), Roman Stoic philosopher, statesman, dramatist, and tutor and later advisor to the Emperor Nero.

Serlio, Sebastiano (1475–c.1554), Italian architect and writer, best known for his *I sette libri dell'architettura* (*The Seven Books of Architecture*).

Shakespeare, William (1564–1616), English poet, playwright, and actor.

Shapur, King [*See* Sapor, King].

Shattuck, Roger (1923–2005), American literary scholar and educator, best known for his books on 19th- and 20th-Century French literature, art, and music.

Sherman, General William Tecumseh (1820–1891), American soldier, educator, businessman, and author, who served with the Union Army during the American Civil War.

Sills, Beverly (1929–2007), American operatic soprano.

Simic, Charles (1938–), Serbian-born American poet, author, and journalist, who served as Poet Laureate Consultant in Poetry to the Library of Congress from 2007 until 2008.

Sissman, Louis Edward (1928–1976), American poet and advertising executive. He was the subject of AH's elegy, "To L. E. Sissman, 1928–1976."

Skelton, John (c.1463–1529), English poet, who served as a tutor to Prince Henry (afterwards **King Henry VIII**).

Smit, Leo (1921–1999), American composer and pianist.

Smith, Milton (1959–1984), American. He was a former patient at St. Elizabeths mental hospital in Washington, D.C., who was shot dead by police after first attempting to enter the Library of Congress and then firing on the officers who had tried to detain him.

Smith, Stan (1946–) American former world number 1 tennis player.

Soane, Sir John (1753–1837), English architect, who was responsible for designing the Bank of England and the Dulwich Picture Gallery, amongst other buildings. He is best remembered for the house AH and his wife visited in 1988, properly called "Sir John Soane's Museum," which is in London's Lincoln's Inn Fields and contains Soane's extensive collection of art works and architectural artefacts.

Socrates (BC c.469–399), Greek philosopher.

Soleri, Paolo (1919–2013), Italian architect, educator, and writer.

Sondheim, Stephen (1930–) American composer and lyricist.

Sophocles (BC 496–406), Greek tragedian, one of whose Theban Plays, *Oedipus at Colonus*, AH and **George Dimock** endeavoured to translate for the Oxford Series of Translations of Greek Plays edited by **William Arrowsmith**. The collaboration failed, as did a subsequent collaboration with **William Arrowsmith**, and all that survives of it is "Praise for Kolonos," collected in AH's *Millions of Strange Shadows*, and "Chorus from Oedipus at Colonos," collected in *The Transparent Man*.

Spark, Muriel (1918–2006), Scottish novelist, short-story writer, poet, essayist, and memoirist.

Specchi, Alessandro (1668–1729), Italian architect and engraver.

Spender, Stephen (1909–1995), English poet, essayist, and diarist, who served as Consultant in Poetry to the Library of Congress from 1965 until 1966.

Spengler, Oswald (1880–1936), German historian and philosopher of history, best known for his *Der Untergang des Abendlandes* (*The Decline of the West*).

Spofford, Edward ("Ned," 1931–2013), American classicist and educator. He was one of three gay members of faculty at Smith College – the other two were **Newton Arvin** and **Raymond Jules Dorius** – who were caught up in a scandal involving pornography, as a result of which he was fired from his job, fined, and handed a suspended jail sentence. After leaving Smith, he did further graduate studies at Harvard, was a Fellow of the American Academy in Rome from 1962 until 1964, taught at Cornell from then until 1971, and from then until his retirement in 1988 taught at Stanford.

Sproull, Robert (1918–2014), American physicist, educator, and administrator, who was President of Rochester University from 1970 until 1984, and thereafter served as Professor of Physics in the same university.

Stallworthy, Jill (1938–2013) English. She was the wife of **Jon Stallworthy**, and the joint dedicatee, with him, and with William and Emily Maxwell, of AH's *On the Laws of the Poetic Art*.

Stallworthy, Jon (1935–2014), English poet, biographer, editor, anthologist, and educator, who had been AH's editor at Oxford University Press. He was the joint dedicatee, with his wife **Jill Stallworthy**, and with William and Emily Maxwell, of AH's *On the Laws of the Poetic Art*.

Stanhope, Philip Dormer (1694–1773), British statesman, man of letters, and wit.

Stark, Freya (1893–1993), Anglo-Italian explorer and travel writer.

Statius, Publius Papinius (AD c.45 – c.96), Roman poet.

Steffens, Henrik (1773–1845), Norwegian-born Danish philosopher, scientist, and poet.

Stein, Gertrude (1874–1946), American novelist, playwright, and poet.

Steinberg, Leo (1920–2011), Russian-born American art historian, art critic, and educator.

Stendhal (Marie-Henri Beyle, 1783–1842), French novelist.

Stockman, David (1946–), American businessman and politician, who served as Representative for the state of Michigan from 1977 until 1981, and was Director of the Office of Management and Budget under **President Ronald Reagan** from 1981 until 1985.

Stoppard, Tom (1937–), Czech-born British playwright and screenwriter.

Stowe, Harriet Beecher (1811–1896), American writer and abolitionist, best known for her book *Uncle Tom's Cabin*.

Strachey, Lytton (1880–1932), English writer, critic, and biographer.

Strand, Mark (1934–2014), Canadian-born American poet and educator, who served as Poet Laureate Consultant in Poetry to the Library of Congress from 1990 until 1991.

Sullivan, Arthur (1842–1900), English composer, famous for his partnership with the librettist, **W. S. Gilbert**.

Summerson, Sir John (1904–1992), British architectural historian.

Sutherland, Sir James (1900–1995), British literary historian, critic, anthologist, biographer, and educator.

Taft, William H. (1857–1930), American politician, who served as the 27th President of the United States from 1909 until 1913, and from 1921 until his death served as Chief Justice of the United States.

Tate Wood, Nancy (1925–2007), American home-maker, peace activist, and founder of the Chiapas chapter of the national environmental protection organization, Pro Natura. She was the daughter of **Allen Tate** and **Caroline Gordon**,

Tate, Allen (1899–1979), American poet, essayist, social commentator, and educator. He served as Consultant in Poetry to the Library of Congress from 1943 until 1944, and was the dedicatee of AH's poem "The Lull."

Tate, Helen (née Heinz, 1934–), American. She was a former student and then third wife of **Allen Tate**.

Taylor, Lily Ross (1886–1969), American classical scholar, ancient historian, and the first female fellow of the American Academy in Rome.

Teirstein, Andrew (1957–), American composer and educator.

Tennyson, Alfred Lord (1809–1892), English poet, who served as Poet Laureate from 1850 until his death.

Testa, Judith (1943–), American art historian and educator.

Thatcher, Margaret (née Roberts, 1925–2013), British politician, who served as leader of the Conservative Party from 1975 until 1990, and as Prime Minister of the United Kingdom from 1979 until 1990.

Thatcher, Marta K. (1908–1989), American. She contributed a poem entitled "Uneasy Lies" to the March 8th, 1958 issue of the *National Review*.

Thomas, D. M. (1935–), English novelist, poet, playwright, and translator.

Tiepolo, Giovanni Battista (1696–1770), Italian painter and printmaker.

Tillotson, John (1630–1694), English divine, who served as Archbishop of Canterbury from 1691 until 1694. Hundreds of his sermons found their way into print after his death.

Tintoretto (born Jacopo Comin, 1518–1594), Italian painter.

Tito, Josip Broz (1892–1980), Yugoslav revolutionary and statesman, who served as his country's first President from 1950 until his death.

Tolstoy, Count Leo (1828–1910), Russian novelist, short-story writer, and social and political thinker.

Tormé, Mel ("The Velvet Fog," 1925–1999), American singer, composer, arranger, drummer, actor, and author.

Toscanini, Arturo (1867–1957), Italian conductor.

Toulmin, Stephen (1922–2009), British philosopher, author, and educator.

Tree, Iris (1897–1968), English poet, actress, and artists' model. She appeared in the 1956 film version of *Moby Dick* and in Fellini's *La Dolce Vita*, and was also the model for numerous artists, amongst them Jacob Epstein, Augustus John, Duncan Grant, Vanessa Bell, and Roger Fry.

Trevor-Roper, Hugh (1914–2003), English historian, scholar, educator, and essayist.

Trilling, Lionel (1905–1975), American literary critic, author, and educator.

Trollope, Anthony (1815–1882), English novelist, short-story writer, and autobiographer.

Trottenberg, Arthur D. (1917–2003), American administrator, who served as Assistant Dean of the Faculty of Arts and Sciences at Harvard University from 1950 until 1968, and from then until 1979 as Vice President of the Ford Foundation. He was the husband of **Margaret Trottenberg**.

Trottenberg, Margaret (1923–2009), American. She was the wife of **Arthur D. Trottenberg**.

Turbo, Quintus Marcius (Early 2nd Century AD), Roman soldier, who rose to be Prefect of the Praetorian Guard, and was a close friend and military advisor to the Emperors **Trajan** and **Hadrian**.

Twain, Mark (Samuel L. Clemens, 1835–1910), American novelist, journalist, travel writer, autobiographer, and public speaker.

Updike, John (1932–2009), American novelist, short-story writer, and literary and art critic.

Valerian, Publius Licinius (AD c.193–260), Roman, who was Emperor of the Roman Empire from AD 253 until his death. He was the father of **Gallienus**.

Van Doren, John (1928–), American historian and educator, who taught at Brandeis University and Boston University. He is the husband of **Mira Van Doren**.

Van Doren, Mira (née Jedwabnik, 1929–) Polish-born American artist and documentary filmmaker. She is the wife of **John Van Doren**.

Van Duyn, Mona (1921–2004), American poet and educator, who served as Poet Laureate Consultant in Poetry to the Library of Congress from 1992 until 1993.

Vargas Llosa, Mario (1936–), Peruvian novelist, essayist, journalist, educator, and politician, who won the Nobel Prize for Literature in 2010.

Vasari, Giorgio (1511–1574), Italian painter, architect, writer, and historian.

Velázque, Consuela (Ciudad Guzmán Zapotlán el Grande, Jalisco, 1916 – 2005), Mexican concert pianist and songwriter.

Vendler, Helen (1933–), American literary critic and educator.

Venturi, Robert (1925–), American architect, and founding partner in the firm Venturi, Scott Brown and Associates. He was a Fellow of the American Academy in Rome in 1956, a Resident of the Academy in 1966, and a Trustee of the Academy from 1969 until 1976. He is the husband of **Denise Scott Brown**.

Veronese, Paolo (1528–1588), Italian painter.

Victoria, Queen Alexandrina (1819–1901), Queen of the United Kingdom of Great Britain and Ireland from 1837 until her death.

Vidal, Gore (1925–2012), American novelist, essayist, playwright, screenwriter, and polemicist.

Vignola, Giacomo (1507–1573), Italian Mannerist architect, and the author of *La Regola degli Cinque Ordini d'Architettura* (*Canon of the Five Orders of Architecture*).

Virgil (Publius Vergilius Maro, BC 70–19), Roman poet best known for his epic, the *Aeneid*.

Vitruvius (Narcus Vitruvius Pollo, BC c.90–c.20), Roman architect, civil engineer, and author, best known for his multi-volume *De Architectura* (*On Architecture*).

Vizitelly, Frank Horace (1864–1938), English-born American lexicographer, etymologist, and editor, who was employed by the publishers Funk and Wagnall, and contributed to their *A Standard Dictionary of the English Language*, as well as to the same firm's dictionaries and encyclopedia. He also had a column in their *Literary Digest* known as "The Lexicographer's Easy Chair."

Voltaire (Francois-Marie Arouet, 1694–1778), French philosopher, novelist, poet, essayist, and polemicist.

Wain, John (1925–1994), English poet, novelist, critic, journalist, and educator.

Walcott, Derek (1930–2017), St. Lucian poet, playwright, and educator, who won the 1992 Nobel Prize for Literature. He was the dedicatee of AH's poem "Terms."

Wales, Carroll (1917–2007), American fine art restorer, and the owner of Oliver Brothers Fine Art Restoration, Boston, MA, from 1968 until 1986.

Ward-Perkins, John (1912–1981), British architectural historian, archaeologist, and educator, who served as Director of the British School in Rome from 1946 until his retirement in 1974. He accompanied WLM and WLM's wife **Dale MacDonald** during their 8,000 mile drive through the Middle East in 1955.

Warren, Robert Penn (1905–1989), American poet, novelist, literary critic, and educator, who served as Consultant in Poetry to the Library of Congress from 1944 until 1945.

Washington, George (1732–1799), American soldier, and statesman. He was one of the Founding Fathers of the United States, and served as the country's first President from 1789 until 1797.

Watkins, David (1941–), British architectural historian.

Watson, Peter (aka A. John Blake, 1943–), English journalist, historian, and author.

Waugh, Evelyn (Arthur Evelyn St. John Waugh, 1903–1966), English novelist, short-story writer, travel-writer, and biographer.

Wayne, John (Marion Mitchell Morrison, 1907–1979), American film actor, director, and producer.

Weber, Max (Karl Emil Maximilian "Max" Weber, 1864–1920), German sociologist, philosopher, and political economist.

Weese, Harry (1915–1998), American architect, who designed Washington, D.C.'s Metro system, amongst many other projects.

Weinberg, Henry (1931–), American composer and educator, who was a Fellow of the American Academy in Rome in 1970.

Weinberger, Caspar (1917–2006), American politician and businessman, who served as Secretary of State for Defense under President Ronald Reagan from 1981 until 1987.

Weinstein, Allen (1937–2015), American historian, educator, author, editor, and administrator, who taught at Smith College from 1966 until 1981, and, after short stints in an editorial capacity at *The Washington Post* and *The Washington Quarterly*, returned to teaching, first at

Georgetown University, later at Boston University, and later still at the University of Maryland. He served as Archivist of the United States from 2005 until 2008.

Weiss, Paul (1901–2002), American philosopher and educator.

Wellington, First Duke of (Arthur Wellesley, 1769–1852), British soldier and statesman.

Wheelock, John Hall (1886–1978), American poet and editor.

Whistler, James Abbott McNeill (1834–1903), American-born British painter.

White, Claire (née Nicolas, 1925–), American poet, novelist, and translator. She was the wife of **Robert W. White**.

White, Robert W. ("Bobby," 1921–2002), American sculptor and educator. He was a Fellow of the American Academy in Rome in 1955, and was the grandson of **Stanford White** and the husband of **Claire Nicolas White**.

White, Patrick (1912–1990), English-born Australian novelist, playwright, short-story writer, essayist, and poet.

White, Stanford (1853–1906), American architect. He was a principal of the McKim, Mead & White partnership, and, together with his fellow principals, was instrumental in the foundation of the American Academy in Rome. He was the grandfather of **Robert W. White**.

White, T. H. (1906-1964), English author, best known for his sequence of Arthurian novels, *The Once and Future King*.

Whitehall, Harold E. (1905–1986), British educator and lexicographer, who served as Etymological and Linguistics Editor on the editorial board of *Webster's New World Dictionary of the American Language*.

Whitehall, Laura Robinson, British editor, who served as Special or Contributing Editor on the editorial board of *Webster's New World Dictionary of the American Language*.

Whitman, Walt (1819–1892), American poet, essayist, and journalist.

Whyte, William H. (1917–1999), American sociologist, urbanist, journalist, and author, best known for *The Organization Men* and *The Social Life of Small Urban Spaces*.

Wiesner, Jerome B. (1915–1994), American educator, who taught electrical engineering at MIT, and was appointed Chairman of President Kennedy's Science Advisory Committee in 1961. He went on to serve as President of MIT from 1971 until 1980.

Wilbur, Charlee (Charlotte, née Ward, 1921–2007), American. She was the wife of **Richard Wilbur**, whom she met in 1941, when she was a student at Smith College and was Poetry Editor of the college's literary magazine.

Wilbur, Richard (1921–2017), American poet, translator, and educator, who was a Fellow of the American Academy in Rome in 1955, and who served as Poet Laureate Consultant in Poetry to the Library of Congress from 1987 until 1988. He was the husband of **Charlee Wilbur**.

Williams, Norman (1952–), American lawyer and poet, who studied with AH while he was a student at Yale Law School.

Wills, Garry (1934–), American author, journalist, and educator, who specializes in history, religion, and politics.

Wilson, A. N. (1950–), English novelist, biographer, historian, and newspaper columnist.

Wilson, Edmund (1895–1972), American literary critic, essayist, editor, and journalist.

Wilton-Ely, John (1937–), English art and architectural historian. He is an authority on Piranesi.

Winckelmann, Johann Joachim (1717–1768), German art historian and archaeologist.

Wind, Edgar (1900–1971), German-born British art historian, best known for his *Pagan Mysteries of the Renaissance*.

Winstanley, William (c.1628–1698), English poet and compiler of biographies.

Wittkower, Margot (née Holtzmann, 1902–1995), German-born British interior designer, furniture designer, art historian, and author. She was the wife of **Rudolf Wittkower**.

Wittkower, Rudolf (1901–1971), German-born British art historian, author, editor, and educator. He was the husband of **Margot Wittkower**.

Wodehouse, P. G. (1881–1975), English author, humorist, and scriptwriter.

Wolsey, Cardinal Thomas (1473–1530), English Roman Catholic cardinal, and statesman, who served as Lord Chancellor under **King Henry VIII**.

Wordsworth, William (1770–1850), English poet, who served as Poet Laureate from 1843 until his death.

Wotton, Sir Henry (1568–1639), English writer, translator, poet, diplomat, and politician.

Wren, Christopher (1632–1723), English architect, anatomist, astronomer, geometer, mathematician, and physicist.

Wright, Frank Lloyd (Frank Lincoln Wright, 1867–1959), American architect, interior designer, writer, and educator.

Wright, James (1927–1980), American poet.

Wyatt, Sir Thomas (1503–1542), English poet and diplomat.

Wyner, Yehudi (1929–), American composer, pianist, conductor, and educator. He was a Fellow of the American Academy in Rome in 1956, and a Resident of the Academy in 1991.

Yeats, William Butler (1865–1939), Irish poet, who won the 1923 Nobel Prize for Literature.

Young, Elizabeth (née Adams, 1923–2014), British writer, researcher, poet, artist, and political campaigner. She was the wife of **Wayland Young**.

Young, Wayland (1923–2009), British writer, politician, and journalist, who, in the early 1950s, was Rome correspondent for *The Observer* (London). He was the husband of **Elizabeth Young**.

Yourcenar, Marguerite (Marguerite Antoinette Jeanne Marie Ghislaine Cleenewerck de Creyencour, 1903–1987), Belgian-born French novelist, essayist, and poet.

Yutang, Lin (1895–1976), Chinese writer, translator, linguist, and inventor.

Zajac, Corda (née Eby, 1934–), American painter. She is the wife of **Jack Zajac**.

Zajac, Jack (1929–), American sculptor and painter. He was a Fellow of the American Academy in Rome in 1958, and a Resident of the Academy in 1969. He is the husband of **Corda Zajac**.

Zonaras, Johannes (12th Century AD), Byzantine historian, canonist, and author of various works, amongst them the eighteen volumes of the *Epitome Historiarum* (*Extracts of History*), a work which purports to chronicle everything from the creation of the world to the death of the Byzantine Emperor Alexios I Komnenos in 1118.

Zosimus (early 6th Century AD), Greek historian, and the author of the six volumes of the *Historia nova* (*New History*), a work dealing with the Roman empire from the time of Augustus until AD 410.

Acknowledgments

My first and largest debt is to Helen Hecht. It was she who first drew my attention to the correspondence contained in this volume when, a little over a year after her husband's death in October 2004, I was a guest at their home in Washington, D.C.

I was in the city to celebrate publication of Morri Creech's *Field Knowledge*, the very first collection to be awarded the Anthony Hecht Poetry Prize, which, with the help of J. D. ("Sandy") McClatchy, Anthony Hecht's literary executor and that year's judge, Waywiser had launched at Chapters bookstore the previous evening. The next day, shortly after Sandy and his partner Chip Kidd returned to New York, Helen invited me to take a look at a gathering of letters and postcards she had boxed up ready for dispatch to the Manuscript, Archives, and Rare Book Library (MARBL) at Emory University, where her late husband's papers were being archived. She had left the box unsealed, thinking that I might enjoy dipping into its contents.

What the box contained was both sides of the Hecht-MacDonald correspondence, and I read through the hundreds of exchanges with mounting excitement. Even before I had reached the end, I told my host that I thought the material should be published, and indicated that I would be only too pleased were she and Sandy to entrust the job of editing it to me. I understood that they had a lot of other things to think about before addressing this proposal, not least helping out with the hugely involved job, entrusted to Jonathan Post, of preparing Hecht's *Selected Letters*. Still, I hoped that once that task was properly under way, the possibility of preparing this more modest volume – which I conceived of as a sort of pendant to the *Selected* – could be revisited.

When, some time later, Helen got in touch to say that she and Sandy would like me to proceed, I could not have been more delighted. I am indebted to both them for the opportunity they afforded me and Waywiser.

I must thank Helen not just for the invitation to work on this correspondence, but also, and more particularly, for the assistance she has given, which has been unstinting. On two week-long stays in Atlanta, she helped me work my way through the original documents, checking everything against the transcripts I had prepared from photocopies supplied by MARBL, puzzling over occasionally illegible handwriting, squinting through a magnifying glass at faint, partial or obscured postmarks, endeavouring to find the right place for undated or misdated items, all of this while doing our best, for the sake of the other library users, to stifle our all too frequent bouts of laughter.

There are a number of other people I especially need to thank. Nick MacDonald has patiently answered a never-ending stream of questions about his father, supplied numerous family photographs, and allowed me to see and quote from the several journals his parents kept between 1954 and 1958. As explained on page 23, he also made me aware of letter #113, a letter whose existence would otherwise have gone unrecorded. Without Nick's help, and that of his brother Noel, my task would have been a great deal harder, and the final text much less satisfactory.

Jonathan Post, a former student of Hecht's who, as well as doing a fine job of editing *The Selected Letters of Anthony Hecht*, and more recently publishing the excellent *A Thickness of Particulars: The Poetry of Anthony Hecht*, the first full-length study of the poet's work, has for many years generously shared his thoughts about Hecht the poet and Hecht the man, while also lending enthusiastic support to my work on this book.

John Pinto, a former student of MacDonald's who went on to become his friend and collaborator, co-authoring their award-winning *Hadrian's Villa and Its Legacy*, has also been remarkably helpful, responding with alacrity to a great many questions, but also putting me in touch with Diane Favro, Guy Métraux, and Fikret Yegül, each of whom had also been taught by MacDonald and had gone on to become his friend. I am grateful to all of them for sharing their memories, and helping to give me a more rounded understanding of the man.

Another of MacDonald's former students who also went on to become a colleague and a friend, and who succeeded to his chair at Smith, was Helen Searing. I should like to thank her for likewise sharing her memories, and helping to throw fresh light on MacDonald's character.

I next need to thank the personnel of several institutions. First and foremost, there are the staff of Emory University's Stuart A. Rose Manuscript, Archives, & Rare Book Library, which houses the Anthony Hecht Papers. Liz Chase, who in 2010 was Coordinator of Research Services, kindly supplied copies of all the exchanges between Hecht and MacDonald that MARBL had in its possession. Kathy Shoemaker, subsequently the library's Reference Coordinator, Research Services, made Helen Hecht and me very welcome on both of our visits, as did her very obliging assistants, Catherine Fernandez and Sara Logue. They were also quick to deal with all subsequent requests for copies of other documents in the Hecht archive. Thanks are also due to the following: the American Academy of Arts and Letters' Executive Director, Virginia Dajani; the American Academy of Arts and Sciences' Director of Publications and Managing Editor of *Daedalus*, Phyllis S. Bendell; the American Academy in Rome's Director, Kimberley Bowes, and its Deputy Director, Cristina Puglisi; Bard College's Executive Assistant to the Vice President of Development & Alumni/ae Affairs, Mary T. Strieder; Harvard University Archives' Researcher, Robin Carlaw; the University of Rochester's Administrative Assistant, Arianna L. Dorschel, and its Librarian, Melissa S. Mead; San Jacinto College North's Librarian, Karyn Jones; and Smith College's Archivist, Nancy Young.

Thanks are due to the following individuals for their responses to my inquiries: Hosea Baskin, Tobias Baskin, Carol Blinn, B. M. Boyle, Charles Brickbauer,

Stas Callinicos, Louis M. and Joan Clark, Susan Davenny Wyner, Stanley Engerman, Leslie Epstein, David Ferry, Jean R. France, Katherine A. Geffcken, David R. Godine, Richard Gordon, Kathy Gowers, Cynthia Hadzi, Martin Henig, George Huxley, Melissa Kunzer, Brad Leithauser, Marianne MacDonald (formerly Mrs Eric Korn), J. D. McClatchy, Hank and Judy Millon, John Onians, Zoja Pavlovskis-Petit, William Pritchard, Clay Risen, Jennifer Roberts, Mary Jo Salter, Leon Satkowski, David E. Schoonover, the late Mark Strand, Judith Testa, the late Richard Wilbur, Michael Wolkoff, Yehudi Wyner, and Stephen Yenser.

I am grateful to my friend and Waywiser colleague Clive Watkins for his careful proof-reading of a much earlier and still incomplete draft of this book.

Lastly, I must thank my wife, Philippa Ibbotson, whose moral support, practical suggestions, inexhaustible patience, and great good humour have been more valuable than I can possibly say.

Index

A La Vieille Russie, NYC, 219, 221
Aaron, Daniel, 99, 177, 416
Aaron, Janet, 177
Abrams, M. H., 464*n*; "John Keats," 464*n*; *The Norton Anthology of English Literature*, 464*n*
Abu Nidal (terrorist group), 434*n*
Academy of American Poets, 53, 76, 93*n2*, 249, 410, 423
Ackerman, James (Jim), 99, 228, 284, 349, 410
Ackroyd, Peter: *T. S. Eliot: A Life*, 399, 399*n1*
Acton, Lord, 369, 431
Ada Comstock Program (Smith College, MA), 255, 255*n1*
Adams Franklin P., 359
Adams, Robert M.: "The High Wire of Faith," 99*n3*
Adler, Mortimer J., 69
Aeschylus, 61; *Seven Against Thebes*, 33, 53, 61
Agnew, Spiro, 51, 65, 65*n1*, 368
Aiken-Taylor Award for Modern American Poetry, 285
Alcuin, 383
Alfred, William, 313; *The Curse of an Aching Heart*, 313
Alice Davis Hitchcock Award (Society of Architectural Historians), 284, 362, 362*n2*
Alice Pratt Brown Professor of History of Art, Smith College, MA, 53
Allaria, Alessandra, 389
Allen, Don Cameron, 382–383; *The Legend of Noah: Renaissance Rationalism in Art, Science & Letters*, 383*n1*
Allen, Woody, 352, 355
Alma-Tadema, Lawrence, 309
Alsop, Susan Mary, 223*n*; *Lady Sackville: A Biography*, 223*n*
Ambler, Eric, 420
Ameche, Don, 120*n*; *The Story of Alexander Graham Bell*, 120*n*

American Academy in Rome (AAR), 13, 14, 16–17, 20, 31, 33, 43, 43*n1*, 89*n2*, 157, 158, 161*n2*, 212, 216, 227, 245, 249, 251*n3*, 252, 258–259, 259*n3*, 282, 298, 306, 325, 334, 341, 345, 346, 348, 349, 355, 356, 356*n*, 361*n1*, 390, 391, 451, 454; Andrew W. Mellon Professor in Charge of the School of Classical Studies, 334, 334*n2*; The Rome Prize, 13, 14, 16, 43*n1*; Villino Bellacci, 251, 251*n3*
American Academy of Arts and Letters (formerly, the American Academy and Institute of Arts and Letters), 14, 189, 189*n1*, 190, 215, 215*n1*, 399*n2*, 416; American Academy of Arts and Letters Award, 190*n*; Richard Rodgers Production Award, 399*n2*; Richard Rodgers Development Award, 399*n2*
American Academy of Arts and Sciences, 53, 256, 259
American Book Awards, 257
American Journal of Archaeology, 254
American Poetry Review, The, 53*n2*
American Scholar, The, 55, 210, 212*n1*
American University, Washington, D.C., 456*n1*
Amichai, Yehuda, 32
Amis, Sir Kingsley, 225, 225*n2*, 227, 301–302, 302*n*; "The first chap to fuck Brigid Brophy," 302, 302*n*; *The New Oxford Book of Light Verse*, 225, 225*n2*, 227
Amory, Mark: *The Letters of Evelyn Waugh*, 294, 294*n1*, 294*n2*
Amy M. Sacker Memorial Lectures, 281; 1982 (WLM), 317
Angelico, Fra, 168, 345
Annabelle Philpotts House, Rochester, NY, 289, 394
Antaeus, 55
Antinous, 116, 116*n1*, 117, 345, 348
Applewhite, E. J., 318, 318*nn2–5*; *Cosmic*

Fishing: An Account of Writing Synergetics with Buckminster Fuller, 318–319, 319*n1*; *Synergetics: Explorations in the Geometry of Thinking*, 318, 318*n4*; *Synergetics 2: Further Explorations in the Geometry of Thinking*, 318, 318*n5*; *Washington Itself: An Informal Guide to the Capital of the United States*, 318, 318*n3*
Aquinas, St. Thomas, 391, 441, 443
Archaeologica Transatlantica, 346*n2*
Archaeological Institute of America, 252, 291
Archaeology, 31, 31*n4*
Architects' Journal, The, 283*n2*
Architectural Book Publishing Company, 386
Architectural Center, Boston, MA, 16
Architectural History Foundation, The, New York, 227
Arcosanti (Paolo Soleri), 310, 310*n2*, 312
Arendt, Hannah, 14
Aretino, Pietro, 264, 264*n*; *The Works of Aretino*, 264, 264*n*
Arlen, Harold, 377*n3*
Arrowsmith, William, 53*n4*, 259, 283, 327*n1*, 390; *The Greek Tragedy in New Translations*, 53*n4*; *Oedipus at Colonos* (Sophocles), 283
Art Journal, 31, 31*n3*, 54*n3*
Art of Paul Gauguin, The (National Gallery, Washington, D.C.), 453, 453*n2*
Arthur Ross Foundation, 386. *See also* Ross, Arthur
Arvin, Newton, 30, 306, 306*n3*, 307
Ashbery, John, 384, 395, 417–418; *A Wave*, 418*n*; "At North Farm," 418*n*
Astaire, Fred, 425*n*
Atheneum (Publisher), 32, 44, 55–56, 63, 63*n1*, 64, 64*n1*, 81, 94, 99, 141*n3*, 145, 236, 243*n1*, 250, 268, 284, 286*n2*, 386, 391, 397
Atkinson, Brooks, 61
Atlantic Monthly, The, 306*n2*
Auden, W. H., 14, 32, 76, 157, 203, 203*n*, 205, 232, 232*n*, 245, 245*n2*, 252, 285, 295, 341, 359, 363, 452; *Another Time*, 232*n*; "A Summer Night," 203, 203*n*; "Canzone," 341*n3*; *Collected Shorter Poems: 1930–1944*, 203*n*; "In Praise of Limestone," 246*n*; *The Collected Poetry of W. H. Auden*, 341*n3*; "The Fall of Rome," 232, 232*n*; *The Viking Book of Aphorisms: A Personal Selection by W. H. Auden and Louis Kronenberger*, 359

Augustine, St., 375, 383; *De Civitate Dei*, 375
Augustus (Gaius Julius Octavius), 116*n3*, 117, 388
Aurelius, Marcus, 148
Aurelius, Victor, 35

Babcock, Charles, 287, 345, 346
Babcock, Mary, 346
Bach, J. S., 234
Bacon, Helen, 33, 53, 61*n3*; *Seven Against Thebes* (Aeschylus), 33, 61*n3*
Bacon, Sir Francis, 379
Balsdon, J. P. V. D., 225*n4*–226; *Life and Leisure in Ancient Rome*, 225*n4*–226; *Roman Women: Their History and Habits*, 225*n4*–226
Banham, Reyner, 430; *Los Angeles: The Architecture of Four Ecologies*, 430, 430*n1*, 435
Barbarossa, Frederick, 382
Bard College, NY, 13, 14, 30, 32, 53, 177, 451
Barfield, Owen, 217
Barrymore, Ethel, 43
Barrymore, John, 44, 279, 287, 291, 292
Barrymore, Lionel, 44
Barth, John, 323
Baryshnikov, Mikhail, 234
Baskin, Leonard, 61, 61*n2*, 73, 73*n*, 85, 89, 91, 94, 96, 99, 118, 145, 233*n3*, 234, 355, 366
Baskin, Lisa, 91, 94, 355, 366
Bate, Walter Jackson, 401, 442; *Samuel Johnson*, 401, 401*n1*
Baths of Caracalla, Rome, 368
Bawer, Bruce, 284; "A Critic's Obligations," 284*n4*
Bayley, John Barrington, 385, 385*n*, 386, 386*n*, 390, 391, 391*n2*; *Letarouilly on Renaissance Rome: The Student's Edition of Paul Letarouilly's Edifice de Rome moderne and Le Vatican et la Basilique de Saint-Pierre*, 385, 385*n*, 386, 386*n* 390
BBC, 378
Beardsley, Aubrey, 428
Beatrice I, Countess of Burgundy, 382
Belloc, Hilaire, 383, 386*n3*, 391
Bell, Anne Olivier, 25; *The Diary of Virginia Woolf*, 25; *Editing Virginia Woolf's Diary*, 25*n*
Bellow, Saul, 14, 50*n4*, 323

Benchley, Robert, 188, 188*n*; *The Treasurer's Report*, 188, 188*n*
Bender, Henry V., 283
Bennett, Joseph, 14
Berenson, Sir Bernard, 104, 163
Bernini, Gian Lorenzo, 81, 164, 244, 246*n*, 345
Berryman, John, 32, 76, 285
Bessie, Mike, 64, 120
Betocchi, Carlo, 386*n2*
Bible, The Holy, 174, 351
Bidwell, B. E., 273
Bierce, Ambrose: The *Devil's Dictionary*, 403, 403*n3*
Bigsby, Christopher, 159*n1*
Bishop, Elizabeth, 76, 157, 263, 395, 463, 463*n1*; "Faustina, or Rock Roses," 463; *Geography III*, 463*n1*
Bishop, John J., 54
Blake, James W.: "The Sidewalks of New York," 441–442, 442*n1*
Blake, Peter, 215, 215*n3*, 216; *Form Follows Fiasco: Why Modern Architecture Hasn't Worked*, 215, 215*n3*, 216; *Le Corbusier: Architecture and Form*, 216, 216*n1*
Blake, Robert Pierpoint, 16
Blake, William, 285
Blinn, Carol J., 243
Bloom, Harold, 55
Blow, Simon, 428
Blücher, Heinrich, 14
Blunt, Anthony, 365, 365*n*–366*n*
Bly, Robert, 369, 388
Boethius, 148
Bogan, Louise, 15, 15*n2*, 76
Bollingen Prize for Poetry, 282, 341
Bombeck, Irma, 251
Bonaparte, Charles Louis Napoleon, 311
Bonnefoy, Yves, 32
Boorstin, Daniel, 354, 356
Borges, Jorge Luis, 245, 245*n3*
Borghese Gallery, Rome, 164
Borromini, Francesco, 164, 193, 246; San Carlo alle Quattro Fontane, Rome, 164
Boswell, James, 442
Bowen, Charles, 174*n1*; "The rain it raineth every day," 174, 174*n1*
Boyle, Andrew: *Climate of Treason*, 365*n*
Boyle, Bernard M.;"The Small Baths at Hadrian's Villa," 158, 158*n*, 238, 254, 254*n*, 262, 267, 304

Boylston Chair of Rhetoric & Oratory (Harvard University, MA). *See under* Harvard University
Bradford, Ned, 230; *Boston's Locke-Ober Café: An Illustrated Social History with Miscellaneous Recipes*, 230
Bramante, Donato, 246, 246*n*
Brand, John, 382, 390; *Observations on Popular Antiquities: Chiefly Illustrating the Origin of Our Vulgar Customs, Ceremonies, and Superstitions*, 382*n*, 390
Brandeis, Irma, 14
Braziller, 31, 38, 245
Breckenridge, James: *Likeness: A Conceptual History of Ancient Portraiture*, 146, 146*n2*–*n3*
Brenson, Michael: "Major Vatican Show Planned at Museum," 348*n1*
Bresdin, Rodolphe, 233, 233*n1*, 233*n3*, 234; *The Bather and Death*, 233*n3*; *The Comedy of Death*, 233*n3*; *The Hunters Surprised by Death*, 233*n3*
Brinnin, John Malcolm, 240
Briscoe, Herman, 69
Briscoe, Orah C., 69
Briscomb, Daryll, 290
British Academy, The, 157
British Museum, The, 379
Britten, Benjamin, 19
Brodsky, Joseph, 233, 282, 367, 384, 395; "Cape Cod Lullaby," 144; "Lagoon," 144, 233
Brookner, Anita: *New York Times Book Review* notice of Muriel Spark's *The Only Problem*, 377*n4*
Brooks, Gwendolyn, 189*n1*
Brougham, Lord Henry, 73
Brown University, RI, 16, 413
Brown, Frank, 15, 31, 37, 38, 61, 63, 70, 72, 89, 140, 163, 163*n1*, 165, 186, 202, 220, 267, 304, 307, 321, 333, 404; *Cosa: The Making of a Roman Town* (The Thomas Spencer Jerome Lectures), 163, 163*n2*
Brown, Jackie, 37, 63, 186, 202, 220, 304, 307
Browne, Sir Thomas, 148
Browning, Elizabeth Barrett, 69
Browning, Robert, 69, 280*n2*
Browning Society, The, 69
Brunelleschi, Filippo, 138, 211
Budenseig, Tillmann, 210

Buehlmann, Josef, 386; *Architecture of Ancient Rome and of the Renaissance*, 386
Buehlmann, Robert, 248, 249
Bulletin of the American Academy of Arts and Sciences, 199, 200, 256, 259
Bullock, Hugh, 93, 93*n1*, 94
Bullock, Marie, 93, 93*n1*, 94
Bundy, McGeorge, 255
Burroughs, William, 87; *Naked Lunch, The*, 87
Burrus, Sextus Afranius, 63
Byron, Lord George Gordon, 285, 364

Cadiff, Andrew: *Brownstone*, 399*n2*; Richard Rodgers Production Award, The, 399*n2*
Caesar, Julius, 44, 87, 209, 305, 369, 462
Cahn, Walter, 77
Calder III, William M., 55
Calthrop, Gladys, 394
Calvino, Italo: *Mr Palomar*, 444, 444*n1*
Cambridge Ancient History, The, 36
Cameron, H. D., 53
Camp David Accords: the signing of, 60*n2*
Campion, Thomas, 285
Canaletto (Giovanni Antonio Canall), 237
Candler, Asa, 265*n1*
Capela dos Ossos, Évora, Portugal, 117, 117*n1*
Caravaggio, Michelangelo Merisi, 419–420; *The Seven Acts of Mercy*, 420
Cardinale, Claudia, 398
Carr, J. L., 193*n2*; *Carr's Dictionary of Extraordinary English Cricketers*, 193*n2*
Carter, Jimmy, 257, 257*n3*; inauguration of, 60*n2*; White House reception for poets and patrons of the arts, 1979, 257, 257*n3*
Cartier-Bresson, Henri, 422
Cary, Max: *Oxford Classical Dictionary*, 35*n2*
Casaubon, Isaac, 35*n1*
Cassius Dio, 35, 217, 217*n4*; *Roman History*, 217, 217*n4*
Casson, Jimmy (unidentified person), 413
Catholic University of America, The, Washington, D.C, 282, 294, 351, 355
Century Club, The, NYC, 404
Chapman, George, 326; *The Whole Works of Homer*, 326
Chapman's Homer. *See* Chapman, George
Charles Eliot Norton Lectures, Harvard University, MA, 296

Charles, Prince of Wales, 428
Cheever, John, 189*n1*, 324
Chetham, Charles: foreword to Chester Michalik's *Photographs*, 413*n*
Child, Julia, 269, 269*n2*; *The French Chef*, 269*n2*
Christina, Queen of Sweden, 135, 135*n*
Christopher, Nicholas, 400, 400*n2*; awarded an Amy Lowell Travelling Fellowship, 400; *A Short History of the Island of Butterflies*, 400, 400*n2*; *The Soloist*, 400, 400*n2*; *Tour with Rita*, 400, 400*n2*
Church, Curtis, 391
City College of New York (CCNY), NYC., 89, 307
Clampitt, Amy, 285
Clarendon Press, The, 326
Clark, Kenneth (Dean of the University of Rochester, NY), 82, 83, 125, 126, 126*n*, 130, 132, 133, 327
Clark, Louis, 139
Clark, Sir Kenneth M., 126*n*, 236, 236*n*; *Landscape into Art*, 236, 236*n*
Classical America, 386, 388
Classical America Series in Art and Architecture, The, 386, 393*n2*
Classical Association of the Atlantic States, 283
Classical Journal, The, 31, 32*n1*, 55*n2*
Classical Philology, 55*n1*
Classical World, The, 53*n1*, 284*n1*
Clemens, Samuel L. *See* Twain, Mark
Clement VII, Pope, 260*n1*
Cleopatra, 44, 87
Clifford, James L., 395*n*
Cobb, Harry, 355
Coca-Cola, 265
Coffin, Charles, 13
Cohn-Haft, Athena, 267, 271
Cohn-Haft, Betty, 267, 312
Cohn-Haft, Louis, 267, 271, 312
Collins, Dr Rowland, 289, 394
Columbia University, NYC, 13, 14, 75, 352, 395; School of Architecture, 293
Committee for Umbrage Not Taken, The 114
Compton's Pictured Encyclopedia, 106, 106*n*
Conant, Kenneth John, 16, 284
Condit, Carl, 54, 171, 171*n2*, 274; review of WLM's *The Pantheon: Design, Meaning, and Progeny*, 171, 171*n2*
Conquest, Robert, 302*n*; "The first chap to

fuck Brigid Brophy," 302n
Consagra, Sophie Chandler, 348, 356, 356n
Constable's England (Metropolitan Museum of Art, NY), 352, 352n2
Consultant in Poetry to the Library of Congress, The, 70, 280, 323n1, 351, 368
Conway, Jill, 230, 262, 306, 308, 366
Cooke, H. Lester, 220n2
Cooley Dickinson Hospital, MA, 159n, 343
Cooper, James Fennimore, 453
Cooper-Hewitt Museum, NYC, 261, 293, 325, 328
Cooper Union for the Advancement of Science and Art, The, NYC, 249
Corn, Alfred: *Incarnation: Contemporary Writers on the New Testament*, 452, 452n3
Cornell University, NY, 53, 67, 68, 307n1, 442
Coward, Noel, 96, 292, 394, 451; "Alice is at it again," 96; *Easy Virtue*, 451; *Noel Coward at Las Vegas*, 96n1; "Piccola Marina," 96
Crane, Hart, 56
Crashaw, Richard, 81
Creese, Walter L., 31, 31n3
Crelly, Walter, 32
Crema, Luigi: *Architettura Romana*, 351n2
Cutler Union, *See under* University of Rochester

Dacian Wars, 462–464
D'Alessandro, Albert, 312n2
D'Alessandro, Helen. *See* Hecht, Helen
Daley, Mayor Richard J., 69
Dando, John, 87
D'Annunzio, Gabriele, 340, 355
d'Arezzo, Guido, 105
D'Arms, John H., 294n2, 334
Darwin, Charles, 104, 266, 268, 268n2
Darwin, Erasmus, 268n2
Davidovsky, Mario, 386n1
Da Vinci, Leonardo, 299, 328
Daye, Erica Mendell, 435n2
de Fine Licht, Kjeld, 31, 31n5
de Kay, Ormonde, Jr., 103–104, 104n1; *Rimes de la Mère Oie: Mother Goose Rhymes*, 103–104, 104n1
De Koven, Reginald: "Oh Promise Me," 387, 387n1
Delacroix, Eugène, 213
della Francesca, Piero, 226; *The Baptism of Christ*, 226
Deloach, William Lawrence, 435n2
Democritus, 442
Demus, Otto, 171, 171n1, ; *Byzantine Mosaic Decoration: Aspects of Monumental Art in Byzantium*, 171, 171n1
Diana, Princess of Wales, 428
Dibner, Bern, 252, 253; *Moving the Obelisks*, 252
Dickens, Charles, 82, 101, 324, 415
Dickinson, Emily, 55, 159, 285, 343, 366
Dictionary of American Biography, 298
Dictionary of International Biography: Bibliographical Record of Contemporary Achievement, 91
Dieterle, William: *The Story of Louis Pasteur*, 427n1
Dimock, George, 53, 53n, 89, 94, 99, 102, 229, 265, 328n1; *Oedipus at Colonos* (Sophocles), 53
Dimock, Mary, 89, 94, 99, 102, 265
Dio, Cassius, 217; *Roman History*, 217
Donne, John, 285, 369, 441, 443
Donoghue, Denis, 55, 55n5, 56, 56n1, 157, 157n1; "Millions of Strange Shadows," 157, 157n1
Dorius, Joel, 307, 307n2
Dorius/Spofford Fund for the Study of Civil Liberties and Freedom of Expression, 307
Dow, Sterling, 321
Downey, Glanville, 31, 31n4
Dr I. J., the Mental Fox. *See* Morgan, Henry
Dryden, John, 395
Dudevant, Aurore, 356
Duke, Doris, 345
Dulles, Allen, 44
Dulles, Eleanor, 43
Dulles, John Foster, 44
Duse, Eleonora, 280n2

Eastman Philharmonia Orchestra, *See under* University of Rochester
Ecco Press, 285
Edward E. Boynton House, Rochester, NY (Frank Lloyd Wright), 139
Edwards, Jonathan, 333, 363
Ehle, John, 159n1
Elaine's, NYC, 352, 352n1, 355
Eliot, George, 325
Eliot, T. S., 205, 371, 399, 452, 464; "The

Waste Land," 451, 452; response to Horace M. Kallen's criticism of "Journey of the Magi, 463n3–464

Elliott, George P., 53, 156n1–n2; "Freshness of the Text," 156n1–n2

Ellis, Henry: *Observations on Popular Antiquities: Chiefly Illustrating the Origin of Our Vulgar Customs, Ceremonies, and Superstitions*, 382n, 390

Ellison, Fanny, 214, 216, 216n3, 217, 332

Ellison, Ralph, 132, 132n2, 214, 216, 216n3, 217, 395

Ellmann, Richard, 268, 291, 367

Elphinstone, Mountstuart, 366

Emily Dickinson House, Amherst, MA, 366

Emory University, GA, 32, 193, 265, 265n1, 268, 269, 279, 287, 291, 298, 327

Empson, William, 32

Encounter, 55, 103n, 461

Encyclopedia Britannica, 68, 69, 70, 100, 105, 106, 169, 170, 241

English Literary Renaissance, 335, 447

English-Speaking Union Award, 280

Enright, D. J.: "Reputations Revisited," 151n2

Epictetus, 148, 231

Epstein, Leslie, 189, 189n2, 190n; *The Steinway Quintet, Plus Four*, 189n2, 190n; "The Disciple of Bacon," 189

Fairchild, B. H., 18n6

Falk, Marcia, 174, 174n2; *The Song of Songs: Love Lyrics from the Bible*, 174, 174n2

Falling Water (Frank Lloyd Wright), 370

Farber, Joseph C.: *Palladio's Architecture and Its Influence: A Photographic Guide*, 291, 291n

Fawcett, Reverend Elisha, 192, 193, 193n2, 331n

Ficino, Marsilio, 442

Fielding, Henry; *Tom Jones*, 322–323

Fields, W. C., 41

Fitzgerald, Robert, 14, 76, 177, 263, 265, 267n

Fletcher, John, 380; *Logica Genevensis*, 380

Fletcher, Sir Banister, 318, 318n1, 454, 455; *Sir Banister Fletcher's: A History of Architecture*, 318, 318n1, 454, 454nn1–2

Flossenbürg concentration camp, 13

Fluck, Winfried, 159n1

Fogg Museum, Harvard University, MA, 111, 154, 200, 226, 238

Folger Shakespeare Library (Washington, D.C.), 432, 433, 435

Fontana, Carlo, 250, 252, 253, 260; *Il Tempio Vaticano*, 253

Fontana, Domenico, 252, 253, 260; *Della trasportatione dell'obelisco vaticano*, 253, 260

Forbes, Bryan, 175n

Ford Foundation, The, 255, 263

Ford, George H., 415

Ford, Gerald, 60n2

Ford, Harry, 55, 56n1, 81, 284, 286n2, 386n3

Ford Motor Company, 271–272, 273, 273n2

Forster, Kurt W., 408–409

Fosca, François, 214; *Renoir: His Life and Work*, 214

Foss, Lukas, 14

France, Jean, 192, 202, 222

Franklin, Benjamin, 416

Franklin, Gil, 18

Frederick II ("the Great"), King of Prussia, 300

Freeze, Reverend J. Donald, 344, 348, 429

Fregoso, Antonio, 442; "Riso de Democrito et Pianto de Heraclito," 442

French, Bryant M., 69

French, Dorothee, 69

Freud, Sigmund, 241, 327

Friedlander, Walter, 135, 419

Frost, Robert, 116, 353; "In going from room to room in the dark," 116; "The Door in the Dark," 116n2; *West-Running Brook*, 116n2

Frye, Northrop, 367; "The Social Authority of the Writer," 367

Fuller, R. Buckminster, 318; *Synergetics: Explorations in the Geometry of Thinking*, 318; *Synergetics 2: Further Explorations in the Geometry of Thinking*, 318

Fussell, Paul, 431; *Class*, 431, 431nn2–3

Gaddis Smith, George, 290, 290n; "A Guide to Realpolitik," 290, 290n

Galbraith, Nancy, 368n, 369

Gallerie dell' Accademia (Venice), 420

Gallienus, Publius Licinius, 36

Gardner, Helen, 205, 205n; *The Composition of Four Quartets*, 205, 205n

Gardner, Isabella, 249

Gardner, John, 159n1

Garland, Patrick, 32

Garrick, David, 314

Garzetti, Albino, 348; *From Tiberius to the Antonines: A History of the Roman Empire, AD 14–192*, 348, 348*n*2
Gaudi, Antonio, 360
Gauguin, Paul, 453
Gaunt, William, 309, 311; *The Aesthetic Adventure*, 311, 311*n*1, 312; *Victorian Olympus*, 309, 309*n*1
Gehry, Frank, 283
George V, King, 431
Georgetown University, Washington, D.C., 280, 282, 296, 304, 305*n*, 338, 346, 353, 355, 362, 362*n*3, 363, 366, 372, 379, 391, 428–429, 443; Center for Strategic and International Studies, 305; Department of English, 379, 391; Special Collections, 249
Getty Foundation, The, 416, 425, 427, 440; Getty Scholarship, 410*n*
Getty, John Paul, 388, 408
Gibbon, Edward, 161
Gide, André, 262
Gidget Goes Hawaiian, 262, 262*n*2
Giedion, Sigried, 417
Gielgud, Sir John, 136, 287, 291, 292, 293
Gilbert, Cass: Oberlin College Art Museum, 257*n*
Gilbert, W. S., & Sullivan, Arthur, 17, 424; *Iolanthe*, 217; "Nightmare Song," 17; *Princess Ida*, 361, 361*n*2; *The Sorcerer*, 424, 424*n*
Gillerman, Gerry, 16
Gillespie, Fran, 227
Gillespie, Greg, 227
Ginsberg, Allen, 32, 379, 395
Ginzburg, Carlo, 413
Giscard d'Estaing, Valéry, 16
Glendinning, Victoria, 303, 303*n*2; "Schoolboy Cruelty," 303, 303*n*2
Godine, David, 237, 237*n*, 243, 263
Goethe, Johann Wolfgang von, 347, 417
Gordon, Caroline, 249
Gourmet, 251
Gowers, Sir Ernest, 41, 41*n*1, 176, 176*n*2; *H. W. Fowler: A Dictionary of Modern English Usage*, 41*n*1, 176, 176*n*2
Gralyn Hotel, Washington D.C., 344
Grand Street, 341, 341*n*5
Grant, Ulysses S., 321
Graves, Robert, 38, 115*n*, 203, 225, 225*n*3, 345; *Proceed, Sergeant Lamb*, 38*n*2; *Sergeant Lamb of the Ninth*, 38*n*2; *Sergeant Lamb's America*, 38*n*2; "¡Welcome, to the Caves of Arta!,*"* 225, 225*n*3
Greenberg, Moshe, 174, 175*n*
Greene, Graham, 266, 324, 420; "A Ride in the Country," 266; "The Innocent," 266; "When Greek Meets Greek," 266
Greider, William: "The Education of David Stockman," 306, 306*n*2
Gretton, R. H: *A Modern History of the English People*, 96*n*3
Grimaldi, Agostino, 39, 39*n*2
Grimm, the brothers, 380; *Deutsches Wörterbuch*, 380, 380*n*2
Grizzuti Harrison, Barbara, 306
Grose, David, 346
Gross, John, 221, 223, 231, 285, 308, 359, 359*n*1, 403; *Oxford Book of Aphorisms*, 359, 359*n*1, 403
Groves, Charlie, 238
Guardi, Francesco, 219
Guggenheim Fellowship, 13, 15
Guggenheim Foundation, 353
Guggenheim Museum (New York), 140
Gunch, Modine, 123, 123*n*, 210, 210*n*, 393; Miss Vacant Lot of the World, 1973, 123*n*, 210*n*
Gundersheimer, Werner, 435, 437
Gunther, Hugo, 69
Gunther, Josephine McCarter, 69
Guralnik, David B. *See Webster's New World Dictionary of the American Language*
Gustav VI, Adolf, King of Sweden, 261
Gutenberg, Johannes, 449

Hadrian (Caesar Traianus Hadrianus Augustus), 67*n*3, 86, 116, 116*n*1, 117, 217, 218, 263, 289, 299, 345, 361, 368, 453
Hadrian's Villa, Rome, 67*n*3, 72, 283, 409, 413, 418, 431, 437, 443
Hadrian's Wall, 63
Hadzi, Cynthia, 413, 416, 418
Hadzi, Dimitri, 15, 62, 176*n*1, 177, 237, 237*n*, 238, 263, 413, 416, 418, 453
Halpern, John, 99*n*2
Halpern, Susan, 99*n*2
Hamilton, Ian, 341; *Robert Lowell: A Biography*, 341*n*4
Hanford, James Holly, 69
Hanford, Ursula, 69
Hanks, Nancy, 333
Harburg, Yip, 377*n*3

Hardouin-Mansart, Jules, 344
Hardwick, Elizabeth, 189$n1$
Hardy, Thomas, 280, 295, 325
Harper's Magazine, 55, 306, 306$n1$, 308, 310
Harriet Monroe Award, 285
Harris, John, 428, 429
Harris, Patricia ("Pat" – Anthony Hecht's first wife), 14, 15, 18, 20, 30, 76, 76n, 90, 91, 93, 93$n1$, 238, 238n, 263, 265, 265$n2$, 270$n3$, 306$n3$
Harrison, Barbara Grizzuti; "What Do Women Want? Feminism and Its Future," 306$n1$
Hart, Lorenz: "Thou Swell," 377, 377$n2$; *A Connecticut Yankee* (Rodgers and Hart), 377$n2$
Hartt, Frederick, 403; *History of Renaissance Painting*, 403
Harvard Bulletin, 236, 238
Harvard University, MA, 13, 16, 53, 55, 76, 91, 100, 117$n4$, 118, 132, 132$n2$, 151, 177, 180, 186, 188, 231$n2$, 252, 255, 263, 283, 296, 298, 307$n2$, 321, 325, 337, 340, 355, 391, 400, 413, 452–453; Boylston Chair of Rhetoric & Oratory, 267, 267n; Carpenter Center for the Visual Arts, 176$n1$; Eliot House, 118; Fogg Museum, 111, 154, 200, 226, 238; Lowell House, 118; Summer School, 132
Harvard University Press, 54, 140$n3$, 296, 364
Harvey, H. P.: *Oxford Classical Dictionary*, 35$n2$
Haydn, Joseph, 268, 270
Hayward, John, 205
Hayworth, Rita, 337
Healy, Fr. Timothy S., S.J., 282, 304, 305, 307, 345–346, 346$n1$, 348
Heaney, Seamus, 267n, 285
Hecht, Adam (AH's second son by first marriage), 30, 62, 76, 76n, 265, 270$n3$, 271
Hecht, Anthony:
ARTICLES AND ESSAYS BY: "Awful But Cheerful" (later entitled "Elizabeth Bishop"), 157, 157$n2$, 463$n1$; "Elizabeth Bishop" (earlier entitled "Awful But Cheerful"), 157, 157$n2$, 463$n1$; "The First Eighteen Lines of 'The Waste Land'" (later entitled "Uncle Tom's Shantih," 451–452, 452$n1$; "Masters of Unpleasantness," 317, 317n, 393$n1$; "*The Merchant of Venice*: A Venture in Hermeneutics," 313, 319, 319$n3$, 323, 335; "The Motions of the Mind" (later entitled "Richard Wilbur"), 157, 157$nn2$–3; "On the Methods and Ambitions of Poetry," 41$n2$–42; "On W. H. Auden's 'In Praise of Limestone,'" 157, 157$n2$, 245, 245$n1$, 246, 246n; "The Pathetic Fallacy," 367; "Richard Wilbur" (earlier entitled "The Motions of the Mind"), 157, 157$nn2$–3; "Robert Lowell," 341, 341$n5$, 353$n3$, 362; "St. Paul's Epistle to the Galatians," 452, 452$n3$; "Three Who Made a Literary Revolution," 399, 399$n1$; "Uncle Tom's Shantih" (earlier entitled "The First Eighteen Lines of 'The Waste Land'"), 452; DISSERTATIONS BY: "Poetry as a Form of Knowledge," 14; LECTURES (GENUINE) BY: "The First Eighteen Lines of 'The Waste Land'" (later entitled "Uncle Tom's Shantih," 451–452, 452$n1$; "Houses as Metaphors: The Poetry of Architecture," 432, 432$n3$, 435; "Little-Known Facts in the Sex Life of Harriet Beecher Stowe," 67$n1$, 102, 102$n3$; "Robert Lowell," 362; "The Pathetic Fallacy," 367, 367n; LECTURES (SPOOF) BY: "Famous Streetcar Accidents," 42, 66, 71, 203; "Great Literary Non-Swimmers," 42; "Little-Known Facts in the Sex Life of Harriet Beecher Stowe," 66, 102$n3$, 203; "The Phlogiston Theory: Will It Make a Comeback?," 66, 72, 74, 203; LIGHT VERSE BY: "And laying his finger inside of his nose," 179; "Asked what he teaches, Senex makes reply," 199; "A crusty old scholar from Leeds," 40; "A peculiarly plain Dame of Sark," 295; "A fruity young Yale art historian," 39; "Here lies a famed physician, whose best skill," 347; "Here lies Priapus Jones who, in his day," 144; "His Highness, the Bey of Baldeen," 35; "A metaphysician named Smith," 37; "My heart, a mere handful of dust," 37; "My name is Sammy Katz," 371; "Proust wrote in his 'Recherche' one day:," 302; "Said Mary to Gabriel, 'Oi,'" 64; "There once was a man named King Henery," 29; "There was a young Gaul from the Somme," 82, 302; LIGHT VERSE QUOTED BY: "Far dearer to me than my treasure," 153; "The rain it raineth every day," 174; "A scandal involving an oyster," 153; "That naughty old Sappho of Greece," 152; "There was a young lady named Gloria," 153; "There was a young

student of Trinity," 153; PLAYS TRANSLATED BY: *Seven Against Thebes* (Aeschylus), 33, 53, 53n4, 61; POEMS BY: "Application for a Grant," 231, 231n1; "Apprehensions," 154n1; "Behold the Lilies of the Field," 36n2; "A Birthday Poem," 196; "A Bountiful Harvest," 193n2, 330, 330n, 331, 331n; "The Cost," 103, 103n, 461–464; "The Deodand, " 213n, 216n2, 217, 217n1, 221; "The Dover Bitch," 227; "The Feast of Stephen," 154n1; "The Gardens of the Villa d'Este," 274n4; "The Ghost in the Martini," 275n; "Gladness of the Best," 143n3; "Goliardic Song," 138; "The Grapes," 212, 212n1, ; "Green: An Epistle," 89, 89n1, 327, 327n2; "Invective Against Denise, a Witch," 210; "It Out-Herods Herod. Pray You, Avoid It," 41n1, ; "A Love for Four Voices: Homage to Franz Joseph Haydn," 268, 268n1, 270, 270n2, 271, 271n1, 274n5, 280; "An Old Malediction," 209, 209n, 210, 211, 212, 258; "Ostia Antica," 274n4; "Peripeteia," 154; "The Power of Love," 290; "The Presumptions of Death," 233n3; "A Roman Holiday," 20, 20n2; "The Short End," 211n, 212, 258; "Still Life," 258; "Terms," 341, 341n2, ; "The Venetian Vespers," 173, 173n, 177, 181, 200, 210, 225, 225n1, 226, 226n, 227, 228, 237, 422; "Who are the wise? Those first Athenian sages," 196; POEMS QUOTED BY: "The Door in the Dark," (Robert Frost), 116; "Upon Appleton House" (Andrew Marvell), 329; POEMS TRANSLATED BY: "Cape Cod Lullaby" (Joseph Brodsky), 144n; "Chorus from *Oedipus at Colonos*" (Sophocles), 328, 327n1; "Lagoon" (Joseph Brodsky), 144n; "Praise for Kolonos" (Sophocles), 53, 328n1; POETRY BOOKS BY: *Collected Earlier Poems*, 286; *Flight Among the Tombs*, 233n3; *The Hard Hours*, 32, 36n2, 41n1, 55, 145, 274n4; *Millions of Strange Shadows*, 53, 55, 56, 57, 89n1, 103n, 138n, 141, 141n3, 143n3, 144n, 153, 156n1, 157, 196, 275n, 327, 327n1, 328n1, 461; *A Summoning of Stones*, 14, 20n2, 274n4; *The Transparent Man*, 193n2, 268n1, 286, 328n1, 330n, 341n2; *The Venetian Vespers* (trade edition), 56, 144n, 209n, 210n2, 211n, 212n1, 213n, 231n, 237, 250, 250n2, 256, 257, 267; *The Venetian Vespers* (David Godine edition), 237, 237n, 243, 263; POETRY BOOKS EDITED BY: *The Essential Herbert*, 285; *Jiggery-Pokery: A Compendium of Double-Dactyls*, 32, 294, 294n3, 299; PROSE BOOKS BY: *Melodies Unheard: Essays on the Mysteries of Poetry*, 452n1, 452n3; *Obbligati: Essays in Criticism*, 157n2, 245, 245n1, 245n2, 246n, 284, 319n3, 341n5, 362, 367n, 432n3; *The Pathetic Fallacy*, 367n; *Robert Lowell*, 362, 362n1

Hecht, Dorothea Holzman (AH's mother), 13, 19, 20n1,

Hecht, Evan Alexander (AH's son by second marriage), 57, 58, 107n, 111, 118, 119, 122, 126, 137, 153, 164, 176, 194, 215, 237, 323, 335, 338, 339, 352, 355, 360, 382, 427, 451, 452, 456n1

Hecht, Helen D'Alessandro (AH's second wife), 50, 56, 99n2, 101, 102, 102n2, 104n, 105, 113, 125, 143, 145, 159, 162, 168, 177, 187, 193n2, 210, 214, 215, 219, 220, 222, 225n4, 236, 250, 251, 251n1, 259n1, 280, 289, 289n2, 305–306, 310, 313, 315, 323, 341–342, 345, 352, 353, 360, 366, 371, 384, 389, 390, 401, 410, 416, 422, 427, 428, 429, 431, 451, 452, 454; *Cold Cuisine*, 268; *Gifts in Good Taste*, 251, 251n1, 259, 259n1; *Simple Pleasures: Casual Cooking for All Occasions*, 432, 432n1

Hecht, Jason (AH's first son by first marriage), 20, 30, 37, 62, 76, 76n, 77, 145, 265, 334

Hecht, Melvyn Hahlo (AH's father), 13, 18, 18n4, 19, 20n1, 57

Hecht, Robert (dealer in antiquities), 423, 423n1

Hecht, Roger (AH's brother), 286, 322–323

Heffner, Hugh, 90

Henig, Martin, 284

Henry VIII, King, 303n3, 369

Henze, Hans Werner, 19

Heraclitus, 442

Herbert, A. P., 137n; "BAKU, or The Map Game," 137; *Siren Song*, 137n

Hilb, Horace, 69

Hilb, Jane G., 69

Hind, A. M.: *A History of Engraving & Etching: from the 15th Century to the Year 1914: Being the 3rd and Fully Rev. Ed. of "A Short History of Engraving and Etching,"* 233,

Index | 527

233n2
Historia Augusta, 35
Historic American Buildings Survey, 283, 410
Hitchcock, Alfred, 140
Hitchcock, Henry-Russell, 140, 269, 321, 340, 362n2, 426
Hoban, Russell: *How Tom Beat Captain Najork and His Hired Sportsman*, 311n3; *A Near Thing for Captain Najork*, 311n3
Hogg, Quintin, Baron Hailsham of St. Marylebone, 2nd Viscount Hailsham 351
Holden, Anthony, 175n
Hollander, John, 14, 32–33, 257n1, 282, 294n3, 341, 386n3, 399; *Blue Wine and Other Poems*, 257n1; *Jiggery-Pokery: A Compendium of Double Dactyls*, 32–33, 294n3
Holt, Elizabeth: *A Documentary History of Art*, 420, 420n1
Holyoke Daily Transcript-Telegram, 57
Homer, 325
Hopkins, Gerard Manley, 397; "The Wreck of the Deutschland," 397
Horace, Quintus Horatius Flaccus, 212, 325
Horner, Eddie, 262
Hourihane, Colum, 32; *Romanesque Art and Thought in the Twelfth Century: Essays in Honor of Walter Cahn*, 32n2
House Beautiful, 235
Hoving, Thomas, 123n; the Euphronios Krater (aka"Hoving's Jug"), 123, 123n
Howard, Richard, 14, 55
Hoy, Philip: *Anthony Hecht in Conversation with Philip Hoy*, 14n, 53n3
Hubbard, Elbert: *Message to Garcia*, 198, 199n, 200, 354, 354n2, 356
Hudson Review, The, 14, 36n2, 42n, 55, 70n2
Hughes, Carol, 99
Hughes, Ted, 32, 99, 416
Hugo of St. Victor, 383
Hustler, 235
Huxtable, Ada Louise, 256, 256n3, 258, 259; "The Present: The Troubled State of Modern Architecture," 256, 256n3, 258

IBM, 378
Illustrated London News, 261
Ingram, Sir Bruce, 261
Ingres, Jean-Auguste-Dominique, 174, 213
Institute of Fine Arts. *See* New York University (NYU)

Iran hostage crisis, 60n2, 256n2
Irving, John, 215, 215n2, 323, 337; *The World According to Garp*, 215, 323, 324
Ipsus, Battle of, 68, 68n2
Issus, Battle of, 68, 68n2

Jackson-Stops, Gervase, 428
Jacobs, Steve, 67
James, Henry, 97, 139, 324
Jarrell, Randall, 285
Jefferson Memorial, Washington, D.C., 318
Jefferson, Thomas, 383, 423
Jencks, Charles, 283, 436–437
Jencks, Maggie, 436–437
Jessup, John, 338
John F. Kennedy Center for the Performing Arts, Washington, D.C., 340
John H. Deane Professor of Rhetoric and Poetry, University of Rochester, 32
John Paul Getty Center for the History of Art and the Humanities, 283, 408, 418, 427, 430
John Paul Getty Museum, 283, 386, 388
Johnson, Merle: *More Maxims of Mark*, 66n1
Johnson, Philip, 256, 256n3; A.T.& T. Building, 256, 256n3, 257n; PPG Industries Building, Pittsburgh, PA, 257n
Johnson, Richard A., 32, 32n4
Johnson, Samuel, Dr., 401, 403, 442
Jonathan Edwards College. *See* Yale University
Jonson, Ben, 369, 433n
Jordan, Hamilton, 338
Joseph's Restaurant, Boston, MA, 118
Journal of American History, The, 54n1
Journal of Architectural Historians, 31
Journal of the Society of Architectural Historians, 31, 31n5, 158n, 242n1, 254n, 343n2
Joyce, James, 20; *Finnegans Wake*, 395
Julius II, Pope, 264
Justice, Donald, 257n2; Pulitzer Prize for Poetry, 1980, 257n2; *Selected Poems*, 257n2

Kahn, Louis, 143; The First Unitarian Church of Rochester, 143, 143n2
Kallen, Horace M., 464n
Kalstone, David, 240
Kaplan, Justin, 403; *Mark Twain and His World*, 403, 403n1; *Mr Clemens and Mark*

Twain: A Biography, 403, 403n2
Katherine Asher Engel lecture, 55
Kaufman, Elaine, 352n1
Kavelman, Buff Suzanne, 392; Centennial Directory of the American Academy in Rome, The, 391n2
Kazin, Alfred, 303, 303n1; "A Rage to Record," 303, 303n1
Kean, Edmund, 314
Keats, John, 285, 326, 353, 463, 464n; "On First Looking into Chapman's Homer," 463
Keats-Shelley House (Rome), 18
Keith, Sally, 231, 231n2
Kelly, J. N. D.: Oxford Dictionary of Popes, The, 444, 444n2
Kelly, Walt, 194n1
Kenyon College, OH, 13
Kenyon Review, The, 13, 15, 15n1, 213n
Kermode, Frank, 296, 296n, 301, 303; Charles Eliot Norton Lectures, 296, 296n; The Genesis of Secrecy, 296, 296n, 301, 303
Kernan, Alvin, 37, 37n2, 41; The Cankered Muse, 37, 37n2
Kevin Lynch Award (MIT, School of Architecture), 286
Killen, Leo: "Hut Sut Song, The," 387, 387n1
King, Martin Luther, 340
King, Nicholas, 386n; Letarouilly on Renaissance Rome: The Student's Edition of Paul Letarouilly's Edifice de Rome moderne and Le Vatican et la Basilique de Saint-Pierre, 386n
Kinnell, Galway, 285
Kinney, Arthur, 335
Kirkus Reviews, 154, 154n1
Kirwin, W. Chandler, 129
Kissinger, Henry, 290; For The Record, 290
Klein, Edward, 416
Kleopatra. See Cleopatra
Klinghoffer, Leon, 434n
Knole House, Sevenoaks, Kent, UK, 435, 435nn3–4
Knopf (publisher), 286, 286n2, 318, 341, 400
Knox, Bernard M. W., 335, 393, 393n2; "Fiction and Autobiography: Archilochus and Hipponax," 393n2
Knox, Vicesimus, 366
Kohl, Benjamin G., 392; Centennial Directory of the American Academy in Rome, The, 391n2
Korn, Eric, 406, 407; "Remainders," 407, 407n

Kostof, Spiro, 32, 283, 355
Kott, Jan, 413
Krantz, Judith, 338, 338n; Mistral's Daughter, 338n
Krautheimer, Richard, 228, 255, 258, 284, 367
Krier, Leon, 283, 343n2
Kronenberger, Louis, 359, 359n2; The Viking Book of Aphorisms: A Personal Selection by W. H. Auden and Louis Kronenberger, 359, 359n2
Kruif, Paul Henry de: Microbe Hunters, 427, 427n1
Kunitz, Stanley, 285
Kurtz, Otto: Fakes, 419, 419n2

La Farge, Henry: Lost Treasures of Europe – 427 Photographs, 239, 239n1
La Scala, Milan, 384, 386, 387
Lacy, Bill, 249, 252
Laemmle, Carl, Sr., 358
Lambert, Baron Philippe, 30, 76n, 91, 93, 93n1, 265n2
Lambert, Johanna, 265n2
Lamour, Dorothy, 149
Lampedusa, Giuseppe Tomaso di, 324
Lamport, Felicia, 124; "Ode to a Grecian Urn," 124
Lanciani, Rodolfo, 148
Landmark Society, The, 139n, 289, 394
Lange, Dorothea, 421
Langguth, A. J, 303, 303n2; Saki: A Life of Hector Hugh Munro, with Six Stories Never Before Collected, 303, 303n2
Lardner, Dionysius, 366
Larson, Harlan Ray (Lanny), 59, 207, 216, 231
Larson, Peter: Brownstone, 399n2; Richard Rodgers Production Award, The, 399n2
Lasdun, James, 56, 56n3; "Spiced and Curious," 56n3
Latham, Agnes: "The Savage Eye," 37, 37n3
Lavin, Irving, 81, 163, 226, 367
Lavin, Marilyn, 163, 186, 226
Lawlor, Charles B., 442; "The Sidewalks of New York," 441–442, 442n1
Lawrence, D. H., 415
Lawrence, Frances ("The Biograph Girl"), 358–359, 360
Lawrence, Russ, 262n2
Lea, Sydney, 368n, 377, 378, 426; The

Burdens of Formality: Essays on the Poetry of Anthony Hecht, 368n, 426, 426n
Leader, Zachary: *The Life of Kingsley Amis,* 302n
Legman, G.: *The Limerick: 1700 Examples, with Notes, Variants and Index,* 71n
Lehmann, Phyllis Williams, 194, 194n3
Lehmann-Haupt, Christopher: *New York Times* review of Brad Leithauser's novel, *Equal Distance,* 406n
Leighton, Frederic, First Baron, 309
Leithauser, Brad, 340–341, 376, 389, 389n, 400, 400n1, 406; *Equal Distance,* 400, 406n1; *Hundreds of Fireflies,* 340–341, 341n1, 400, 400n1
Leithauser, Bryan, 341, 406, 428–429
Leithauser, Mark, 341, 406, 428–429
Lemaire, Jean, 381; *Les Illustrations de Gaule et singularitez de Troye,* 381, 381n
Leo XIII, Pope, 383; *Rerum Novarum,* 383
Levine, Philip, 257n1, 285; National Book Critics' Circle Award, 257n1; *Ashes,* 257n1
Levit, Hershel, 194, 194n2; *Views of Rome: Then and Now,* 194, 194n2
Liberace, 444
Library of Congress (LOC), 70, 280, 281, 282, 323, 333, 334, 334n1, 335, 341, 353, 353n3, 354, 356, 367, 367n, 368, 384, 387–388, 388n; AH's annual report to, 368–370, 368n
Librex-Guggenheim Eugenio Montale Award for Poetry, 282, 384, 386n2, 387, 389
Lincoln, Abraham, 321
Lincoln Center, NYC, 61
Linker, Wayne A., 392
Linklater, Wayne A., 392; *Centennial Directory of the American Academy in Rome, The,* 392n2
Literary Review, The, 56n3
Little Brown, 16
Littlewood, J. E.: *A Mathematician's Miscellany,* 268n2
Llosa, Mario Vargas, 416; "In Nicaragua," 416n1
Locke-Ober Restaurant, Boston, MA, 118
Logan, William, 286; *Reputations of the Tongue,* 286n3; "When Beauty Shows No Mercy," 286n3
Lovelace, Richard, 326, 331; *The Poems of Richard Lovelace,* 326, 326n
Low Memorial Library, Columbia University, NYC, 352
Lowell House, Harvard University, MA, 118
Lowell, Robert, 76, 263, 285, 341, 353, 363, 364, 395
Lucas-Tooth, Laetitia, Lady. *See* Munro-Lucas-Tooth, Lady (Laetitia) Helen
Luther, Martin, 193n1
Lutyens, Sir Edwin, 454
Lynes, Mildred, 214, 216, 216n3
Lynes, Russell, 214, 216, 216n3, 345, 349, 404
Lyttelton, Margaret: *TLS* review of Frank Sear's *Roman Architecture,* 351, 351n2

MacArthur Fellowship, 341, 400
MacArthur Foundation, 339
MacDiarmid, Hugh, 32
MacDonald, Dale (WLM's second wife), 16, 17, 19, 29n, 37, 40, 43, 50, 50n2, n3, 57, 58, 59, 62, 63, 83, 120, 136, 140, 176, 180, 188, 190, 200, 201, 202, 206, 207, 392
MacDonald, Darius (WLM's second son by second marriage), 30
MacDonald, Dwight, 189n1
MacDonald, Ellen (WLM's daughter-in-law), 207, 287, 300, 331, 440
MacDonald, John (WLM's brother), 58
MacDonald, Nicholas (WLM's third son by second marriage), 30, 31n2, 37, 39, 57, 58, 132, 136, 158, 160, 176, 190, 195, 196, 200, 202, 206, 207, 210, 216, 227, 228, 256, 262, 265, 267, 275, 287, 297, 300, 310, 317, 334, 355, 363, 377, 405, 437, 444
MacDonald, Noel (WLM's first son by second marriage), 20, 29, 37, 39, 57, 58, 96, 120, 132, 136, 160, 190, 200, 201, 205, 206, 207, 210, 211, 262, 287, 300, 331, 363, 377, 405, 440
MacDonald, Susan Elrod (WLM's mother), 16
MacDonald, William Lloyd:
 ARTICLES AND ESSAYS BY: "Empire Imagery in Augustan Architecture," 346, 346n2, ; "Excavation, Restoration, and Italian Architecture of the 1930s," 269, 269n1, 321, 340, 340n1, 343; "The Small Baths at Hadrian's Villa," 158, 238, 254, 262, 267, 304;
 BOOKS BY: *The Architecture of the Roman Empire,* Vol. I (later subtitled *An Introducto-*

ry Study), 31–32, 39, 39*n1*, 63*n1*, 110, 267, 269, 281, 292, 321; *The Architecture of the Roman Empire*, Vol. II: *An Urban Appraisal* 63, 63*n1*, 64, 88, 88*n*,158, 243, 243*n1*, 281, 283, 298*n2*, 300, 317, 321, 325, 326, 332, 348, 351, 377, 406, 440, 440*n2*; *Columns in the Collection of the Cooper-Hewitt Musem*, 281, 325, 325*n*, 328*n3*; *Early Christian and Byzantine Architecture*, 31, 37*n1*, 298, 325; *Hadrian's Villa and Its Legacy* (with John Pinto), 377, 377*n5*; *Northampton, Massachusetts: Architecture and Buildings*, 53–54, 58*n1*, 136, 136*n*, 287, 292, 298, 326; *The Pantheon: Design, Meaning, and Progeny*, 54, 58*n1*, 122, 122*n2*, 136, 140, 140*n1*, 156*n1*, 157, 158, 171, 287, 291, 292, 298, 326, 339, 353*n2*; *Piranesi's Carceri: Sources of Invention*, 58*n1*, 223, 241, 298, 326; *A Selected Bibliography of Architecture in the Age of Justinian*, 325; Books co-edited by: *Princeton Encyclopedia of Classical Sites*, 298, 326; Lectures (genuine) by: Amy M. Sacker Memorial Lectures, 1982, 317: "Columns in the Collection of the Cooper-Hewitt Museum," 328; "Hadrian and Architecture," 291, 393*n2*; "Hadrian's Villa," 291; "On Understanding Hadrian's Villa," 291, 292, 303; "The Persistence of Classical Forms," 317; "The Persistence of Classicism," 291; "Piranesi's Carceri: Sources of Invention," 222, 223, 225, 229, 241, 241*n2*, 242, 255, 258, 265, 268, 298; "The Rational and Irrational in Piranesi: A Reappraisal," 291; "Renaissance and Baroque Transformations," 317; "A Revisionist View of Antiquity," 317; "Rome Unseen: Under the Seven Hills," 87; Lectures (Spoof) by: "Different-Shaped Crates," 42; "Great Hats I Have Worn," 66, 203; "'Little' Women," 42, 66, 205; Light Verse by: "A coming young pro from Alsace," 302; "Constantine's architect, Paul," 129; "Erat olim puella Romana," 154; "I've not heard a word from Ken Clark," 130; "A knight with an ebony pie-pan," 342; "Pompey's striker, polishing brass," 125; "A prize-winning rhymer named Hecht," 132; "Tsimmis, tsauris," 342; Light Verse Quoted by: "'Gainst the Hun and the Turk never once do we shirk," 195; "It was just a hardened old fossil –," 150 "There once was a young man from York," 155; "There once was a youth named Antinuous," 299; "There was a young lady named Colehill," 71, 155; "There was a young man, name of Rex," 129; "When Hadrian got the bad news," 299; Poems by: "Hadrian Orders the First Batavians to Swim the Danube," 218, 243

MacDonald, William Lloyd, Sr. (WLM's father), 16, 36, 230, 425*n*

McFeeley, William S., 321, 321*n*; *Grant: A Biography*, 321, 321*n*

MacKendrick, Paul, 54

Mackenzie, Sir Compton, 324

McKim, Charles F., 89, 386

Mackinnon, Lachlan, 286

McMichael, 387; "Hut Sut Song, The," 387

Macmillan Encyclopedia of Architects, The, 281, 298, 300, 312, 312*n1*, 344

McShane, Frank: *The Life of John O'Hara*, 303, 303*n1*

Maderno, Carlo, 319

Malamud, Bernard, 367

Malipiero, Gian Francesco, 280*n2*

Malraux, André, 191, 191*n*; *Anti-Memoirs*, 191, 191*n*

Manchester, William: *American Caesar, Douglas MacArthur 1880–1964*, 256, 256*n1*

Mandeville Press, The, 268*n1*

Manning, Cardinal, 391

Mansart, Francois, 344

Mansart, Jules Hardouin. *See* Hardouin-Mansart, Jules

Mansfield, Jayne, 339

Marchand, Leslie A.: *Lord Byron: Selected Letters and Journals*, 364, 364*n*

Maréchale de Luxembourg, La, 351

Mariani, Paul, 285

Marten, Sir Harry Neil, 351

Marvell, Andrew, 285, 328, 331; "Upon Appleton House," 328

Marx Brothers, The: *Animal Crackers*, 241*n1*

Marx, Groucho, 241*n1*, 377*n3*

Marx, Karl, 311

Mason, David, 56*n1*

Mason, George, 383; Virginia Declaration of Rights, 383

Massachusetts General Hospital, 312, 315, 320, 332, 334, 357

Massachusetts Institute of Technology (MIT), 53, 71, 133*n*, 177, 285, 298, 307*n2*; School

of Architecture, 119
Massachusetts Review, The, 243, 243*n*2
Masson, Georgina, 148, 148*n*; *Ancient Rome: From Romulus to Remus*, 148*n*
Matthews, "Moondoggie," 262*n*2
Matteson, Ira, 17
Maurus, Rabanus, 383
McKim, Charles Follen, 89, 89*n*2, 386
McClatchy, J. D., 30, 31*n*1, 50
McCloskey, William, 432
McCoubrey, Bettsy, 406
McCoubrey, John W., 406
McCue, Jim: *The Poems of T. S. Eliot: Volume 1: Collected and Uncollected Poems*," 463*n*3–464*n*
McMichael, Ted: "Hut Sut Song, The," 387, 387*n*1
Mead, William Rutherford, 89, 89*n*2, 386
Meier, Richard, 408
Melanchthon, Philip, 66
Melville, Herman, 285
Mencken, H. L., 111
Mendenhall, Thomas, 102, 102*n*1
Meredith, William, 76
Merejkowski, Dmitri, 264
Mérida, Extremadura, Spain, 116, 116*n*3
Merrill, James, 248, 341; "Samos," 341*n*3; "Scripts for the Pageant," 341*n*3; *The Changing Light at Sandover*, 341*n*3
Merritt, Howard, 75, 77, 80, 82, 83, 85
Merwin, W. S., 14, 285
Metropolitan Museum of Art, The, NYC, 123*n*, 344–345, 352, 423; *Constable's England*, 352, 352*n*2; *The Vatican Collections: The Papacy and Art*, 344
Metropolitan Opera House, The, NYC, 384
Michalik, Chester, 413, 421, 423; *Photographs*, 413, 413*n*, 421*n*
Michelangelo, 246, 264*n*, 386; *The Doni-Tondo*, 246*n*
Michigan University Press, 163
Microbe Hunters (Paul Henry de Kruif), 427
Middleton, Robin, 242
Middleton, Thomas, 451; *The Changeling*, 451
Miles Poetry Prize, 32
Miller, Archie, 83
Miller, Arthur, 399
Millon, Henry (Hank), 31, 200, 258, 319–321, 335, 339, 345, 349, 452
Millon, Judith (Judy), 321, 335, 339, 452

Milton, John, 69, 436, 441–442; "L'Allegro," 436, 436*n*, 441
Mitford, Nancy: *Noblesse Oblige: An Enquiry into the Identifiable Characteristics of the English Aristocracy*, 309, 309*n*2
Mizener, Arthur, 15, 15*n*1
Modern Language Association, The, 434
Monroe Community College, NY, 270
Montale, Eugenio, 386
More, Thomas, Sir, 139, 441
Morford, Mark, P. O., 31, 32*n*1
Morgan Library, NYC, 261, 404, 404*n*1, 451
Morgan, Henry (Dr I. J., The Mental Fox), 43, 43*n*2
Moss, Howard, 14, 257*n*1; *Notes From the Castle*, 257*n*1
Mount Holyoke College, MA, 62, 86, 281
Moynihan, Daniel Patrick, 428, 428*n*2
Moynihan, Patrick, 428*n*2
Moynihan, Patrick Henry, 428*n*2
Mozart, Wolfgang Amadeus, 94, 190, 259; String Quartet No. 15 in D. Minor, op. K421, 259*n*2
Muldoon, Paul, 285
Muni, Paul, 427, 427*n*1; *The Story of Louis Pasteur*, 427*n*1
Munro, Hector ("Saki"), 206*n*, 303
Munro-Lucas-Tooth, Lady (Laetitia) Helen, 365
Murdoch, Iris: *The Black Prince*, 423, 423*n*2
Murray, Sir James A. H., 380
Murray, K. M. Elisabeth, 380; *Caught in the Web of Words: James A. H. Murray and the Oxford English Dictionary*, 380, 380*n*1
Museum of Modern Art (MOMA), NYC, 257
Museu Nacional Militar, Lisbon, Portugal, 117, 117*n*3
Mussolini, Benito, 355
Myasthenia Gravis, 281, 312, 392, 418

Nash, Ogden: "Invocation," 443, 443*n*2
National Book Award, 211, 215*n*2, 306
National Book Critics' Circle Award, 257
National Endowment for the Arts, 333
National Endowment for the Humanities, 232; Fellowships, 143, 220, 223
National Gallery, The, London, 451; Sainsbury Wing (Robert Venturi and Denise Scott-Brown), 451
National Gallery, Washington, D.C., 143,

202, 304, 344, 420, 428, 428*n1*, 453*n2*
National Geographic Magazine, 418, 428
National Geographic Society, 359, 360, 369, 410
National Institute of Arts and Letters, 53, 85
National Museum of Western Art, Tokyo, 212
Neale, J. E.: *Elizabeth I and Her Parliaments*, 323, 323*n2*
Nemerov, Howard, 14, 453
Nero, Claudius Caesar Augustus Germanicus, 63
Neruda, Pablo, 32
Neuerburg, Norman, 388, 389
New Criterion, The, 56*n1*, 284
New England Enamel Company, The, 13
New England Review, The, 245*n1*
New England Review and Bread Loaf Quarterly, 285*n3*
New Republic, The, 55*n4*
New Statesman, The, 55
Newsweek, 89
Newton Arvin Prize in American Studies, 307
New Yorker, The, 15, 15*n2*, 55, 89*n1*, 273, 443*n2*
New York, 247*n*
New York Public Library, NYC, 416, 451
New York Review of Books, 99, 99*n3*, 234, 256*n3*, 319, 323, 452, 452*n2*
New York Times, 55*n5*, 56, 56*n1*, 57, 112, 124*nn1–2*, 157, 175*n*, 214, 214*n*, 216, 245, 248, 249*n*, 252, 285, 285*n1*, 286, 291, 303, 303*n1*, 307, 317, 325, 348, 348*n1*, 350, 392, 393*n1*, 406*n*, 418, 448; Book Review, 38, 56, 157, 157*n1*, 158, 252, 252*n*, 274, 290, 313, 317, 317*n*, 377; Magazine, 274*n3*, 416*n2*
New York University (NYU), NYC, 14, 53, 345; Institute of Fine Arts, 345
Nims, John Frederick, 226*n*
Nixon, Richard, 51, 60*n2*, 65*n1*, 127, 263
Nobel Committee of the Swedish Academy, 245*n3*
Northern Illinois University, Il, 361*n1*
Norton Anthology of English Literature, The, 464
Nunis, Richard A., 405

Oates, Joyce Carol, 337
Oberammergau, 61; Passion Play, 61
Oberlin College, OH, 257; Art Museum, 257

Observer, The (London), 45*n*
Offenbach, Jacques, 63; *La Grande Duchesse de Gerolstein*, 63
O'Gorman, Edward (Ned), 245, 245*n4*, 248–249, 249*n*, 251
O'Hara, John, 303
Oil crisis, Opec-sponsored, 60*n2*
Oliver Brothers Fine Art Restoration, Boston, MA, 224
Oliver, Richard, 293
Olivier, Laurence, 175*n*, 314
Orwell, George, 367; *1984*, 367
Owens, Jack, 387; "Hut Sut Song, The," 387, 387*n1*
Oxford Classical Dictionary, The, 35*n2*
Oxford Companion to Architecture, The, 144, 174, 192, 242, 243, 248, 262, 265, 269
Oxford English Dictionary, The, 221, 232, 234, 252, 315, 380
Oxford University, 268, 271
Oxford University Press (OUP), 53, 55, 56, 143, 174, 286, 390, 391

Paderewski, Ignacy Jan, 96*n3*
Palladio, Andrea, 291, 454
Pan American Airways, 16
Panini, Giovanni Paolo, 353; *Interior of Saint Peter's Rome*, 353, 353*n1*; *Interior of the Pantheon, Rome*, 353, 353*n2*
Panofsky, Dora, 135
Panofsky, Erwin, 169, 358; *Meaning in the Visual Arts*, 358, 358*n2*
Pantheon Books, 239
Pantheon, The (Rome), 122, 135, 135*n*, 140, 156, 164, 209, 240, 313, 318, 353, 375
Parish, P. J., 321, 321*n*; "The Career of an Enigma," 321, 321*n*
Parke-Bernet Gallery, NY, 222
Parker, H. M. D.: *History of the Roman World from A.D. 138 to 337, A*, 36*n1*
Pascal, Blaise, 264, 361, 377, 377*n6*
Pascal, Paul, 361*n1*
Patrologia Graeca, 437, 437*n*
Pausanias: *Description of Greece*, 431, 431*n1*
Pavlovskis, Zoja, 370; *Man in an Artificial Landscape*, 370
Peake, Mervyn, 225
Pearman, Jeannie, 235–236
Pearman, Richard S. L., 235–236
Pears, Peter, 19

Pearsall-Smith, Logan, 268
Pearson, Norman Holmes, 76
Peck, John, 216
Peggy Guggenheim Collection, The, Venice, 384
Pei, I. M., 69, 143, 202, 329; Wilson Commons Building, University of Rochester, Rochester, NY, 143, 143n1
Penguin Books, 54, 122, 216, 312, 419, 420, 423, 430
Penmaen Press, 55
Pentagon Papers, The, 60n2
Pepys, Samuel, 345
Perkins, G. Frances, 70
Peterson, Donald E., 271
Petersson, Robert T., 81, 83, 99, 141n1, 228, 244, 252, 292, 379, 455; *Art of Ecstasy, The*, 81, 99, 141, 292
Petersson, Suzanne, 81
Petronius (Gaius Petronius Arbiter), 63
Pevsner, Niklaus, Sir, 331
Philosophy Hall, Columbia University, NY, 352
Pinto, John, 377n5, 410, 443, 453; *The Trevi Fountain*, 443, 443n1
Piranesi, Giovanni Batista, 55, 194, 194n2, 221, 236, 238, 242, 261, 313, 318; *Vedute di Roma*, 194; *Views of Rome: Then and Now*, 194, 194n2
Plath, Sylvia, 416
Playboy, 90, 210, 305
Pliny the Elder, 173, 370
PLO (Palestinian Liberation Organization), 434n
Ploughshares, 55
PMLA (Journal of the Modern Language Association), 379
Poe, Edgar Allan; *The Cask of Amontillado*, 242; *The Pit and the Pendulum*, 242
Poetry, 55n3, 210, 225, 225n1, 226n, 227, 268n1, 272, 285, 343n2
Poetry International (London, 1967), 32, 32n3
Polledri, Paolo, 408–409
Polshek, James, 293, 293n
Pope, Alexander, 154n1, 395
Porter, Cole, 292; *Kiss Me, Kate*, 292
Portman, John Calvin., 141, 141n2
Post, Emily, 172, 172n2, 226n; *Etiquette: The Blue Book of Social Usage*, 172, 172n2, 173n
Post, Jonathan F. S., 50, 283, 430, 432; *The Selected Letters of Anthony Hecht*, 15n3, 31, 49n3, 51, 51n, 52, 52n1, 56, 284n3, 386n3
Post, Wiley, 139, 287
Pottle, Frederick A., 76
Powell, Anthony, 325, 387; *Venusberg*, 387, 387n2
Powell, Violet, 223n
Prairie Schooner, 33, 33n
Pratt, William, 285
Praz, Mario, 212, 212n2; *Mnemosene: The Parallel Between Literature and the Visual Arts*, 212, 212n2
Price, Reynolds, 159n1
Price, Roger, 431, 431n3; *The Great Roob Revolution*, 431, 431n3
Princeton Encyclopedia of Classical Sites, The, 54, 298, 326
Princeton University, NJ, 133, 163, 212, 249, 298, 326, 420, 424, 429; Institute for Advanced Studies, 163
Prior, Matthew, 442; "Democritus and Heraclitus," 442; *Poetical Works of Matthew Prior, with a Life by Rev. John Mitford, in Two Volumes, The*, 442, 442n3
Prior, Roger, 431
Pritchard, William, 392; "Pleasures of the Poison Pen," 392, 393n1
Pulitzer Prize, The, 32, 257, 364
Putnam, Samuel, 264, 264n; *The Portable Rabelais*, 264n1; *The Works of Aretino*, 264n2
Pynchon, Thomas, 195, 195n; *The Crying of Lot 49*, 195n

Queen's Gallery, The, London, 451

Rabelais, François, 264
Racine, Jean, 221, 272, 415
Radcliffe College, MA, 262
Rand, Calvin G., 349
Ransom, John Crowe, 13
Raphael (Raffaele Sanzio da Urbino), 345, 408
Rauch, John, 257n
Rauschenberg, Friedrich Wilhelm, 152n
Rauschenberg, Robert, 152, 152n
Reagan, Nancy, 340
Reagan, Ronald, 306n2, 340, 340n2, 340n2, 343, 343n1, 352, 401, 401n2

Reed, Henry Hope, 291, 386, 386n, 392; *Letarouilly on Renaissance Rome: The Student's Edition of Paul Letarouilly's Edifice de Rome moderne and Le Vatican et la Basilique de Saint-Pierre*, 385, 386, 386n; *Palladio's Architecture and Its Influence: A Photographic Guide*, 291, 291n; *The Golden City*, 392, 392n

Reinhardt, Max, 160

Renoir, Auguste, 212–213; *Parisian Women Dressed in Algerian Costume*, 212

Richardson, Lawrence, 451, 453; *A New Topographical Dictionary of Ancient Rome*, 453, 453n1; *Pompeii: An Architectural History*, 451, 451n

Ricks, Christopher, 56n2, 252n, 256, 463n3–464n; *Essays in Appreciation*, 464n; "Literature and the Matter of Fact," 464n; *The Poems of T. S. Eliot: Volume 1: Collected and Uncollected Poems*," 464n; "Poets Who Have Learned Their Trade," 56n2, 252, 252n, 256

Rilke, Rainer Maria, 14

Rimson, Goldie, 69

Rimson, Oscar, 69

Ripley, S. Dillon, 333

Ripperger, Helmut, 208n

Rivers, Joan, 379

Roberts, Isabel, 15, 161, 161n2, 240

Roberts, Laurance P., 15, 161, 161n2, 240, 248, 249, 404

Robert Sterling Clark Visiting Professor of Art (Clark Institute, Williamstown, MA), 281

Rochester Institute of Technology, Rochester, NY, 257

Rochester Memorial Art Gallery, Rochester, NY, 213

Rockefeller, Nelson, 220n2, 290, 292

Rockwell, Hays, The Right Reverend, 143, 143n3, 193n2, 215n4

Rockwell, Linda, 215n4

Rodgers, Richard: *A Connecticut Yankee* (Rodgers and Hart), 377n2; "Thou Swell," 377, 377n2

Rogers, Ernesto, 454

Rogers, Ginger, 425n

Rolfe, Frederick (Baron Corvo), 374, 381

Rome Prize, The (American Academy in Rome), 13, 14, 16, 43

Ronsard, Pierre de, 210

Roosevelt, Franklin D., 401

Rose, H. J.: *Oxford Classical Dictionary*, 35n2

Ross, Arthur, 386. *See also* Arthur Ross Foundation

Rossetti, Dante Gabriel: "The Blessed Damozel," 228n

Rostovtzeff, Michael, 148

Rostow, Walt, 220n2

Rothko, Mark, 418

Rowse, A. L., 452; *The Poet Auden: A Personal Memoir*, 452, 452n2

Rubens, Josh: *Brownstone*, 399n2; Richard Rodgers Production Award, The, 399n2

Rubens, Peter Paul, 168, 309

Rusk, Dean, 175

Ruskin, John, 135, 168–169, 171, 172, 173, 285

Russell, Bertrand, 169, 170

Russell, Jane, 337

Russell Loines Award, 32

Ruth B. Lilly Poetry Prize, 285

Rutland, Jennifer, 369

Ryan, Jack (unidentified contributor to *New York* magazine), 248n

Ryan, William G., 208n

Ryskamp, Charles, 404, 404n2

Sackville, Lady Victoria, 223n

Sackville-West, Vita, 223n

Safire, William, 274, 274n3; "On Language," 274n3

Sainsbury Wing, National Gallery, London. *See* National Gallery, London

Saint-Simon, Claude Henri de Rouvroy, comte de Saint-Simon, 110

Saki. *See* Munro, Hector

Salter, Mary Jo, 376, 389, 389n

Salzburg Seminar in American Studies, 159, 163

Samuelson, Paul, 220n2

San Francisco State University, CA, 307n1, 307n2

Santa Maria di Loreto, Rome, 103, 463

Sapor, King, 35–36

Sassetta, il (Stefano di Giovanni di Consolo), 345

Satkowski, Leon, 201, 239

Saturday Review, 294, 294n3

Satz, Barbara, 57–58, 58n1, 120, 122–123, 125, 133, 135–136, 138, 141, 142, 143, 160, 173, 174, 176, 177, 196, 198, 200,

210, 233, 242, 251, 252, 254, 261, 287, 292, 303
Schadt, Betsey Adams, 16
Schaffer, Ray, 219, 221, 223, 224; A La Veille Russie, NYC, 221
Schapiro, Meyer, 255, 258
Scheer-Schazler, Brigitte, 159*n1*
Schoonover, David, 341
Schumacher, Emily, 67, 68, 69
Schumacher, Patty, 393
Schumacher, Thomas L., 67, 68, 69, 299, 304, 393; *Il Danteum di Terragni (The Danteum)*, 299, 299*n*
Schuman, William, 416; *On Freedom's Ground*, 416, 416*n2*
Schwantner, Joseph, 340*n3*; *New Morning in the World*, 340*n3*
Schweitzer, Pierre-Paul, 220*n2*
Scollay Square, Boston, 231, 231*n2*
Scott, Clement, 387; "Oh Promise Me," 387, 387*n1*
Scott, W. B., 274; *Chicago Letter & Other Parodies*, 274, 274*n1*
Scott, Russell T., 334*n3*
Scott-Brown, Denise, 156, 257*n*, 406, 451; *Learning from Las Vegas*, 257*n*; *Learning from Levittown*, 257*n*
Scully, Vincent, 31, 245, 245*n2*; *Modern Architecture: The Architecture of Democracy*, 245, 245*n2*
Sear, Frank: *Roman Architecture*, 351*n2*
Searing, Helen, 298, 340*n1*; *In Search of Modern Architecture: A Tribute to Henry-Russell Hitchcock*, 321, 340*n1*, 343*n2*
Sears, Elizabeth, 32, 32*n2*; "The Art-Historical Work of Walter Cahn," 32*n2*
Segnatura Chapel, The Vatican, Rome, 408
Seneca, 63, 420
Serlio, Sebastiano: *Libro primo d'architettura*, 358, 358*n1*
Sewanee Review, The, 32
Sexton, Ann, 32
Shakespeare, William, 174*n1*, 196, 254, 285, 287, 293, 307, 314, 319, 347, 379, 381, 382, 390, 451, 463; *A Midsummer Night's Dream*, 268; *Hamlet*, 314, 464*n1*; *Henry V*, 390; *Julius Caesar*, 463; *Macbeth*, 314; *The Merchant of Venice*, 313, 319, 323, 335; *Othello*, 307, 397; *The Tempest*, 154*n1*, 307, 379; *Twelfth Night*, 174*n1*
Shapur, King. *See* Sapor, King

Shattuck, Roger: *The Forbidden Experiment: The Story of the Wild Boy of Aveyron*, 311, 311*n2*
Shaw, George Bernard, 384
Shaw, James Byam: *Old Master Drawings from Chatsworth: A Loan Exhibition from the Devonshire Collection*, 319, 319*n2*
Shaw, Robert, 254
Shelley, Percy Bysshe, 140
Sherman, General William Tecumseh, 287
Shorter Oxford English Dictionary, The, 165, 166, 366
Sills, Beverly, 133*n*
Simic, Charles, 285
Simon and Schuster, 249
Sissman, L. E., 341; "Canzone: Aubade," 341*n3*; *Dying: An Introduction*, 341*n3*
Sistine Chapel, The, Rome, 416
Sitwell Family, 324
Skelton, John, 369
Smit, Leo, 14
Smith College, MA, 20, 30, 32, 49, 50, 53, 55, 60, 61, 66, 83, 84, 86, 87, 94, 99*n2*, 102*n1*, 124, 126, 142*n*, 146*n1*, 194*n3*, 210, 212, 229, 255, 262, 265, 279, 280, 289, 289*n2*, 292, 297–298, 305, 306, 306*n1*, 306*n2*, 307, 307*n3*, 308, 325, 339, 344, 366, 391, 393, 395, 417; The Ada Comstock Program, 255, 255*n1*; Art Department, 227; College Planning and Resources Committee, 126; Dorius/Spofford Fund for the Study of Civil Liberties and Freedom of Expression, 307*n3*; Museum of Art, 406, 413, 413*n*
Smith, Constance, 18
Smith, Dave, 257, 257*n1*; *Goshawk, Antelope*, 257*n1*
Smith, Horace, 99
Smith, James, 98, 99*n1*; *Memoirs, Letters, and Comic Miscellanies of the Late James Smith, Esq.*, 99*n1*; "Pius Virgil," 99, 99*n1*; "Virgil, whose epic song enthralls," 98–99
Smith, Martin Cruz, 324; *Gorky Park*, 324
Smith, Milton (man shot while illegitimately trying to enter the Library of Congress), 387–388, 388*n*
Smith, Stan, 405
Smithsonian Institution, The, 281–282, 331, 332, 333, 393, 410; *Smithsonian* (magazine), 418, 428
Smoot, Reed, Senator, 443*n2*

Snodgrass, W. D., 56
Soane, Sir John, 451; London house of, 451
Socrates, 139, 327
Soleri, Paolo, 310; Arcosanti, 310, 310n2, 312
Sondheim, Stephen, 399
Sophocles, 53, 280, 283, 295, 328, 346; "Chorus from Oedipus at Colonos," 328n1; "Oedipus at Colonos," 53, 259, 327, 328n1, 390
Souter, A.: *Oxford Classical Dictionary*, 35n2
Spark, Muriel, 377; *The Only Problem*, 377n4
Specchi, Alessandro, 250, 252, 253, 260; *Templum Vaticanum*, 260
Spectator, The, 73, 365n–366n
Spencer, Harold: *Readings in Art History*, 298, 298n1
Spender, Stephen, 282, 384
Spengler, Oswald, 427; *Der Untergang des Abendlandes* (*The Decline of the West*), 427n2
Spofford, Edward, 306–307, 307n1
Sproull, Robert, 82, 83
St. Andrea at the Quirinal (Gian Lorenzo Bernini), 164
Stallworthy, Jill, 428
Stallworthy, Jon, 51, 51n, 428
Stanford University, CA, 307n1
Stanhope, Philip Dormer, 270n1
Stark, Freya, 280n2
Stark, Nancy L., 57, 75, 77, 82, 84, 86, 104
State University of Iowa, IA, 13
Statius, Publius Papinius, 370
Steffens, Henrik, 105
Steinberg, Leo, 402
Stein, Gertrude, 240
Stein, Roger B., 54
Stendhal (Marie-Henri Beyle), 324; *Journals*, 324; *Roman contes*, 324
Stevens, P. T., 53
Stevens, Wallace, 20; "Sunday Morning," 20
St. James' Church, NYC, 143
St. John Fisher's College, NY, 285
St. Mark's Basilica, Venice, 167, 168, 171, 172, 226n, 237, 240
St. Peter's Basilica, Rome, 135n, 164, 250, 260, 319, 353
Stinehour Press, 238
Stockman, David, 306, 306n2
Stoppard, Tom, 451; *Hapgood*, 451
Story of Alexander Graham Bell, The, 120
Story of Louis Pasteur, The, 427
Strachey, Lytton, 351n1, 391, 391n1; *Books and Characters: French & English*, 351n1; *Eminent Victorians: Cardinal Manning, Florence Nightingale, Dr. Arnold, General Gordon*, 391, 391n1
Strand, Mark, 14, 267
Summerson, Sir John: *The Classical Language of Architecture*, 329, 329n1
Sunday Times, The (London), 280n3, 419, 431
Sutherland, Sir James, 161; *The Oxford Book of Literary Anecdotes*, 161, 161n1
Swarthmore College, PA, 55
Syracuse University, NY, 171; College of Architecture, 171

Taft, William H., 289, 394
Taliesin (Frank Lloyd Wright), 310, 310n1, 312
Tate, Allen, 13, 14, 32, 76, 245, 245n4, 248, 248n, 249, 327, 327n2
Tate, Helen, 248, 248n, 249
Tate Wood, Nancy, 249
Taylor, Keene, 397
Taylor, L. R., 148
Taylor, Nancy, 397
Technology and Culture, 54n2, 171,n2
Teirstein, Andrew: *Papushko*, 399; Richard Rodgers Development Award, 399n2
Tennyson, Alfred Lord, 148, 273n1, 397; "The Brook," 273n1
Testa, Judith, 52, 361, 361n1; "Higgledy Piggledy / Emperor Hadrian," 361, 361n1
Thatcher, Margaret, 220n2, 365n
Thatcher, Marta K., 75, 89, 216, 220, 220n2, 226, 450
Thomas, D. M., 323; *The White Hotel*, 323, 324
Thomas, Dylan, 240
Three Mile Island, PA: nuclear accident at, 60n2
Thuna, Cynthia von. *See* Hadzi, Cynthia
Thurber, James: *New Yorker* cartoon for August 19th, 1939, 273n1
Tiepolo, Giovanni Battista, 372
Tillotson, Archbishop John, 380
Times Literary Supplement, The, (*TLS*), 37, 37n3, 55, 151, 151n2, 153, 156, 156n1, 157, 157n2, 158, 181, 209, 209n, 220, 221, 223, 223n, 231, 231n, 243, 258, 258n, 284, 284n2, 286, 286n4, 308, 321, 321n, 351, 379, 406, 407, 463

Times, The (London), 419, 420
Tinou. *See* Antinous
Tintoretto, 309
Tito, Josip Broz, 43
TLS. *See Times Literary Supplement, The*
Tolstoy, Leo, 360
Torme, Mel, 444
Toscanini, Arturo, 307
Toulmin, Stephen, 283
Towson State University, MD, 282
Trajan, 220, 267, 393, 462
Trajan's Column, Rome, 103, 461–463
Trajan's forum, Rome, 418
Treasure Houses of Britain: 500 Years of Private Patronage and Art Collecting, The, The National Gallery, Washington, D.C., 428, 428n1, 429
Tree, Iris, 18
Trevor-Roper, Sir Hugh, 365; "Blunt Censured, Nothing Gained," 365n–366n
Trilling, Lionel, 391
Trinity College, CT, 84, 85, 87
Trollope, Anthony, 324
Trottenberg, Arthur D., 16, 74, 91, 220, 252, 255, 293, 334
Trottenberg, Margaret ("Markie"), 91, 334
Tufts University, MA, 238, 254, 255, 256, 258, 263
Turbo, Quintus Marcius, 349, 431
Twain, Mark (Samuel L. Clemens), 66, 66n1, 402, 403, 454; "The Story of Grandfather's Old Ram," 402, 402n"; *Roughing It*, 402n
Twombly, Robert C., 220, 220n3; *Frank Lloyd Wright: An Interpretive Biography*, 220, 220n3

Unabomber, The (Ted Kaczinski), 434n
Ungaretti, Giuseppe, 32
University of California, Los Angeles, CA, 430
University of California, Santa Barbara, CA, 135
University of California, Berkeley, CA, 32, 53, 89, 91, 96, 132, 242, 254, 256, 265, 287, 292, 298, 309, 355
University of Chicago, IL, 354
University of Georgia Press, 248, 426
University of Maryland, MD, 91, 96, 100, 393
University of Massachusetts, MA, 200, 335, 346, 366
University of Michigan, MI, 434n
University of New Hampshire, NH, 16
University of Rochester, NY, 32, 49, 53, 62, 71, 75, 77, 86, 143, 285, 329n2, 335, 360, 415, 417; Art Department, 62, 86, 125, 126; Art Library, 213; Cutler Union, 225; Eastman Philharmonia Orchestra, 340
University of South Carolina at Chapel Hill, NC, 283
University of Texas at Austin, TX, 163, 283
University of the South, Sewanee, TN, 285
University of Virginia, VA, 299, 335–336, 342, 343, 393, 410; English Department, 342; School of Architecture, 393
Unterberg Poetry Center, The, New York, 364
Updike, John, 323

Valentine, Alan: *American Academy in Rome: 1894–1969, The*, 391n2
Valentine, Lucia, 391; *American Academy in Rome: 1894–1969, The*, 391n2
Valerian, Publius Licinius, 35, 36
Van Doren, John, 172, 173
Van Doren, Mira, 172
Van Duyn, Mona, 14, 50n4
Vasari, Giorgio, 201
Vatican Collections: The Papacy and Art, The, Metropolitan Museum of Art, New York, 344, 344n1, 348
Vatican Museums, Rome, 164
Vatican obelisk, 87
Vatican pine-cone, 135
Vatican, The, Rome, 61, 410, 453
Velázquez, Consuelo, 377; "Bésame Mucho," 376–377n1
Vendler, Helen, 452
Venturi, Robert, 15, 156, 256, 257n, 406, 451; *Complexity and Contradiction in Architecture*, 257n; *Learning from Las Vegas*, 257; *Learning from Levittown*, 257
Veronese, Paolo, 420; *The Last Supper*, 420; *Feast at The House of Levi, The*, 420
Victoria Advocate, The, 210n1
Vidal, Gore, 255, 280
Vietnam War, 60n2, 462
Vignola, Giacomo, 344
Viking Press, 148, 400, 420
Villino Bellacci. *See under* American Academy in Rome
Vintage Books, 323

Virgil (Publius Vergilius Maro), 146–147, 325
Vitruvius (Narcus Vitruvius Pollo), 328, 331, 375; *de Architectura* (translated by Sir Henry Wotton), 328n3, 329n2
Vizitelly, Frank Horace, 378
Voltaire (François-Marie Arouet), 154n1, 347
Vonnegut, Kurt: *Welcome to the Monkey House: Stories*, 89n3; "Welcome to the Monkey House," 89, 89n3
Voragine, Jacobus de, 208, 208n, 211; *The Golden Legend*, 208, 208n
Voyager II, 435
Voznesensky, Andrei, 32

Wain, John, 373, 373n, 374
Walcott, Derek, 341n2, 395
Wales, Carroll, 224
Walker & Co., 50
Walker, Donald, 220; *Frank Lloyd Wright: An Interpretive Biography*, 220
Wallace Stevens, 20; "Sunday Morning," 20
Ward-Perkins, John, 156nn1–2, 157, 158, 165, 165n, 169, 171, 351n2, 417; *Roman Architecture*, 165, 165n, 351n2; "Rome's Rotunda," 156
Warren, Robert Penn, 285
Washington Classical Society, 283, 393n2
Washington, George, 423
Washington Post, The, 388n, 399, 399n1; *Book World*, 330n
Washington Quarterly, The, 305n
Washington University, MO, 53, 101, 102, 102n3, 452n1
Watergate Scandal, 60n2; TV coverage of, 125
Watkins, David, 343n2
Watson, Peter, 419, 420; *The Caravaggio Conspiracy: How Five Art Dealers, Four Policemen, Three Picture Restorers, Two Auction Houses, and a Journalist Plotted to Recover Some of the World's Most Beautiful Stolen Paintings*, 419, 419n1
Waugh, Evelyn, 294, 309, 309n3, 324; "An Open Letter to the Hon[ble] Mrs. Peter Robb (Nancy Mitford) on a Very Serious Subject from Evelyn Waugh," 309, 309n3; *The Letters of Evelyn Waugh*, 294, 294n1
Waugh, Teresa, 294n2
Wayne, John, 373n, 429
Webber, Andrew Lloyd, 451; *Cats*, 451
Weber, Max, 383

Webster's Biographical Dictionary, 68, 68n3
Webster's New International Dictionary of the English Language, 130, 233, 233n4, 252, 366, 378
Webster's New World Dictionary of the American Language, 67, 67n2, 68, 69, 73, 122
Weese, Harry, 318
Weidenfeld & Nicholson, 308
Weinberg, Henry, 89
Weinberger, Caspar, 404
Weinstein, Allen, 255, 255n2, 304–305, 305n; *Perjury: The Hiss-Chambers Case*, 255, 255n2, 304
Weiss, Paul, 38
Wellington, Duke of, 321, 403
Wells College, NY, 16
Wesleyan University, CT, 99
Wheaton College, MA, 16, 282, 393
Wheelock, John Hall, 76
Whistler, James Abbott McNeill, 309
White, Patrick, 324
White, Robert, 249
White, Stanford, 89, 386
White, T. H., 192, 192n; *The Once and Future King*, 193n; *The Sword in the Stone* (Book 1 of *The Once and Future King*), 193n
Whitehall, Alice, 69n
Whitehall, Harold E., 69, 69n
Whitehall, Laura Robinson, 69
White House, The, Washington, D.C., 89, 257, 333, 334, 340, 340n2, 341
Whitman, Walt, 285
Who's Who in America, 91, 404, 404n1, 405
Whyte, William H., 404
Wiesner, Jerome B., 133n
Wilbur, Charlee, 18, 38, 45n, 159, 214, 216, 216n3, 266, 268–269
Wilbur, Richard, 14, 15, 18, 38, 45n, 76, 106, 140, 157, 157n3, 158, 159, 173, 174, 175n, 214, 216, 216n3, 217, 226, 226n, 227, 266, 267, 268, 269, 271, 272, 294, 366, 366n, 395, 415, 416; "Altitudes," 366, 366n; *New and Collected Poems*, 416n2; "On Freedom's Ground," 416, 416n2; *On Freedom's Ground*, 416; *Things of This World*, 366n
Wilkinson, C. H.: *The Poems of Richard Lovelace*, 326, 326n
William and Mary College, VA, 424
Williams College, MA, 275, 292, 309, 317
Williams, Miller: *A Roman Collection: Stories,*

Poems, and Other Good Pieces, 274n4
Williams, Norman, 400, 400n3; *The Unlovely Child*, 400n3
Williams, Tennessee: conversion to Roman Catholicism, 61, 61n1
Wills, Gary, 383; *Inventing America: Jefferson's Declaration of Independence*, 383, 383n2
Wilson, A. N., 386, 386n3; *Hilaire Belloc*, 386, 386n3
Wilson, Edmund, 391
Wilson, Woodrow, 306
Wilton-Ely, John, 261
Winckelmann, J. J., 135
Wind, Edgar, 87, 169, 442; *Pagan Mysteries in the Renaissance*, 87n, 442, 442n2
Winstanley, William, 382, 390; *Historical Rarities and Curious Observations Domestick & Foreign Containing Fifty Three Several Remarks ... with Thirty Seven More Several Histories, Very Pleasant and Delightful, Collected Out of Approval by William Winstanley*, 382, 390
Wittkower, Margot: *Born Under Saturn: The Character and Conduct of Artists: A Documented History from Antiquity to the French Revolution*, 420, 420n2
Wittkower, Rudolf, 284, 420; *Born Under Saturn: The Character and Conduct of Artists: A Documented History from Antiquity to the French Revolution*, 420, 420n2
Wodehouse, P. G., 312
Wolsey, Cardinal Thomas, 303n3
Woolf, Virginia, 324; *To the Lighthouse*, 324
Wordsworth, William, 285
World Literature Today, 285, 285n2
Wotton, Sir Henry, 329, 329n2; *The Elements of Architecture*, 329n2
Wren, Sir Christopher, 39, 454
Wright, Frank Lloyd, 139, 143, 204, 220, 310, 310n1, 370; Edward E. Boynton House, 139, 139n, 143, 204; Falling Water, 370; Taliesin West, 310, 312
Wright, James, 395
Wyatt, Sir Thomas, 285
Wyner, Nancy, 17
Wyner, Yehudi, 15, 17, 217

Yaddo Writers' Colony, Saratoga Springs, NY, 306
Yale Review, The, 452n1
Yale University, CT, 20, 30, 31, 32, 41, 53, 56, 75, 76, 124, 141, 145, 151n1, 155, 254, 282, 298, 306, 307n2, 331, 333, 341, 393, 400; Department of Art History, 20; Jonathan Edwards College, 333; Morse College, 149; School of Architecture, 124
Yale University Press, 37, 63n1, 243, 243n1, 267, 292, 339, 406, 409, 413, 427, 437, 440, 443
Yeats, William Butler, 280, 295, 367, 400
Yevtushenko, Yevgeny, 32
Young, Elizabeth, 45n
Young, Wayland, 45n
Yourçenar, Marguerite, 324, 345, 348

Zajac, Corda, 163, 227, 240, 252, 283, 440
Zajac, Jack, 15, 17, 88, 163, 227, 240, 252, 283, 440
Zeno, 354
Zonaras, Johannes, 35
Zosimus, 35, 36

Other Books from Waywiser

POETRY

Austin Allen, *Pleasures of the Game*
WITH A FOREWORD BY EAVAN BOLAND

Al Alvarez, *New & Selected Poems*
Chris Andrews, *Lime Green Chair*
WITH A FOREWORD BY MARK STRAND

George Bradley, *A Few of Her Secrets*
Geoffrey Brock, *Voices Bright Flags*
WITH A FOREWORD BY HEATHER MCHUGH

Robert Conquest, *Blokelore & Blokesongs*
Robert Conquest, *Penultimata*
Morri Creech, *Field Knowledge*
WITH A FOREWORD BY J. D. MCCLATCHY

Morri Creech, *The Sleep of Reason*
Peter Dale, *One Another*
Erica Dawson, *Big-Eyed Afraid*
WITH A FOREWORD BY MARY JO SALTER

B. H. Fairchild, *The Art of the Lathe*
WITH AN INTRODUCTION BY ANTHONY HECHT

David Ferry, *On This Side of the River: Selected Poems*
Daniel Groves & Greg Williamson, *Jiggery-Pokery Semicentennial*
WITH A FOREWORD BY WILLARD SPIEGELMAN

Jeffrey Harrison, *The Names of Things: New & Selected Poems*
Joseph Harrison, *Identity Theft*
Joseph Harrison, *Shakespeare's Horse*
Joseph Harrison, *Someone Else's Name*
WITH A FOREWORD BY ANTHONY HECHT

Joseph Harrison, ed., *The Hecht Prize Anthology, 2005–2009*
Anthony Hecht, *Collected Later Poems*
Anthony Hecht, *The Darkness and the Light*
Jaimee Hills, *How to Avoid Speaking*
WITH A FOREWORD BY ANTHONY THWAITE

Hilary S. Jacqmin, *Missing Persons*

Other Books from Waywiser

POETRY CONT'D

Carrie Jerrell, *After the Revival*
WITH A FOREWORD BY ALAN SHAPIRO

Stephen Kampa, *Articulate as Rain*

Stephen Kampa, *Bachelor Pad*

Rose Kelleher, *Bundle o' Tinder*
WITH A FOREWORD BY RICHARD WILBUR

Mark Kraushaar, *The Uncertainty Principle*
WITH A FOREWORD BY JAMES FENTON

Matthew Ladd, *The Book of Emblems*
WITH A FOREWORD BY ROSANNA WARREN

J. D. McClatchy, *Plundered Hearts: New and Selected Poems*

Dora Malech, *Shore Ordered Ocean*

Jérôme Luc Martin, *The Gardening Fires: Sonnets and Fragments*

Eric McHenry, *Odd Evening*

Eric McHenry, *Potscrubber Lullabies*

Eric McHenry and Nicholas Garland, *Mommy Daddy Evan Sage*

Timothy Murphy, *Very Far North*
WITH AN INTRODUCTION BY ANTHONY HECHT

Ian Parks, *Shell Island*

V. Penelope Pelizzon, *Whose Flesh is Flame, Whose Bone is Time*

Chris Preddle, *Cattle Console Him*

Shelley Puhak, *Guinevere in Baltimore*
WITH A FOREWORD BY CHARLES SIMIC

Christopher Ricks, ed., *Joining Music with Reason:
34 Poets, British and American, Oxford 2004–2009*

Daniel Rifenburgh, *Advent*
WITH AN INTRODUCTION BY RICHARD WILBUR

Mary Jo Salter, *It's Hard to Say: Selected Poems*

W. D. Snodgrass, *Not for Specialists: New & Selected Poems*

Mark Strand, *Almost Invisible*

Mark Strand, *Blizzard of One*

Other Books from Waywiser

POETRY CONT'D
Bradford Gray Telford, *Perfect Hurt*
Matthew Thorburn, *This Time Tomorrow*
Cody Walker, *Shuffle and Breakdown*
Cody Walker, *The Self-Styled No-Child*
Cody Walker, *The Trumpiad*
Deborah Warren, *The Size of Happiness*
Clive Watkins, *Already the Flames*
Clive Watkins, *Jigsaw*
Mike White, *Addendum to a Miracle*
WITH AN INTRODUCTION BY GJERTRUD SCHNACKENBERG
Richard Wilbur, *Anterooms*
Richard Wilbur, *Mayflies*
Richard Wilbur, *Collected Poems 1943–2004*
Norman Williams, *One Unblinking Eye*
Greg Williamson, *A Most Marvelous Piece of Luck*
Greg Williamson, *The Hole Story of Kirby the Sneak and Arlo the True*
Stephen Yenser, *Stone Fruit*

FICTION
Gregory Heath, *The Entire Animal*
Mary Elizabeth Pope, *Divining Venus*
K. M. Ross, *The Blinding Walk*
Gabriel Roth, *The Unknowns**
Matthew Yorke, *Chancing It*

ILLUSTRATED
Nicholas Garland, *I wish ...*
Eric McHenry and Nicholas Garland, *Mommy Daddy Evan Sage*
Greg Williamson, *The Hole Story of Kirby the Sneak and Arlo the True*

* Co-published with Picador

Other Books from Waywiser

Non-Fiction

Neil Berry, *Articles of Faith: The Story of British Intellectual Journalism*
Mark Ford, *A Driftwood Altar: Essays and Reviews*
Richard Wollheim, *Germs: A Memoir of Childhood*

Interviews

John Ashbery in Conversation with Mark Ford
Peter Dale in Conversation with Cynthia Haven
Thom Gunn in Conversation with James Campbell
Donald Hall in Conversation with Ian Hamilton
Michael Hamburger in Conversation with Peter Dale
Ian Hamilton in Conversation with Dan Jacobson
Seamus Heaney in Conversation with Karl Miller
Anthony Hecht in Conversation with Philip Hoy
Charles Simic in Conversation with Michael Hulse
W. D. Snodgrass in Conversation with Philip Hoy
Anthony Thwaite in Conversation with Peter Dale and Ian Hamilton
Richard Wilbur in Conversation with Peter Dale

Seven American Poets in Conversation: John Ashbery, Donald Hall, Anthony Hecht, Donald Justice, Charles Simic, W. D. Snodgrass, Richard Wilbur
WITH AN INTRODUCTION BY CHRISTOPHER RICKS

Three Poets in Conversation: Dick Davis, Rachel Hadas, Timothy Steele